Modernist Masterpieces

The Haubrich Collection at Museum Ludwig

edited by Julia Friedrich

Museum Ludwig
Verlag der Buchhandlung Walther König Köln

Contents

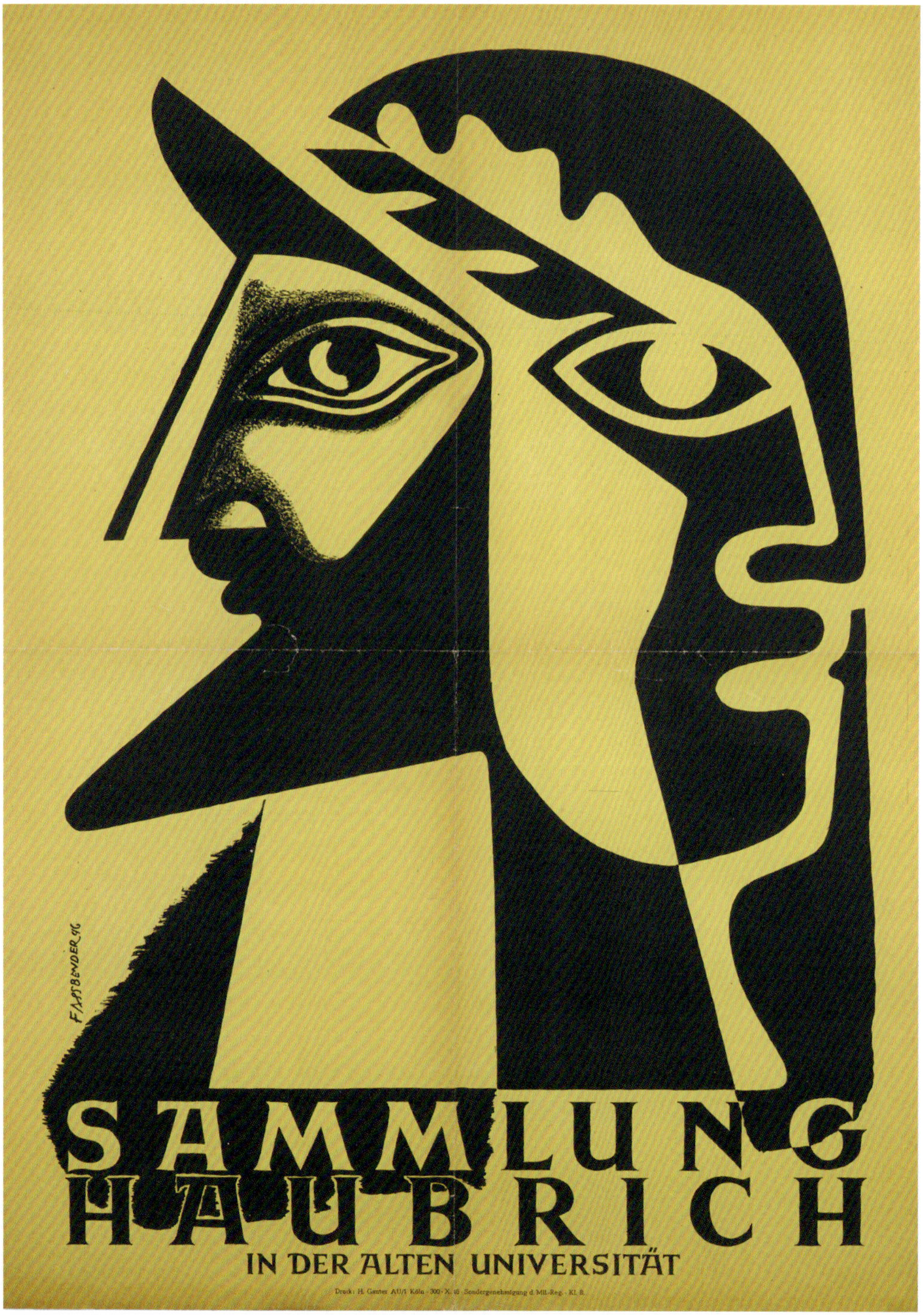

Poster for the first exhibition of the Haubrich Collection at the Alte Universität in Cologne, 1946. Designed by Joseph Fassbender.

Preface from the Director

Kasper König

Things have come full circle for me with the publication of this catalogue and the new presentation of the Haubrich Collection. When I assumed the directorship of Museum Ludwig in winter 2000, the 'mother' institution – the Wallraf-Richartz Museum – had just moved into her new home. I was therefore lucky enough to have the opportunity to reconfigure the collections of the expanded Museum Ludwig. A key aspect of this reconfiguration was the placement of the Haubrich Collection.

We did not receive all the works Haubrich had collected. A few pieces by artists born before 1870 remained in the Wallraf-Richartz Museum. Among these was James Ensor's **Enfant à la poupée**, a painting far ahead of its time, as was indeed the entire oeuvre of this visionary artist. But we nevertheless retained the vast majority of works in one of the most beautiful collections of classical Modernism in Europe. Our long-time curator and deputy director Evelyn Weiss had the idea of placing these works in the rooms of what used to be the Cologne Painting School. Stephan Diedrich decided to hang the paintings in the classic salon style, which resulted in a very fitting and effective presentation.

The historical significance of the collection is closely linked to the first time it was publicly displayed. The works were exhibited in 1946 in the partially destroyed Alte Universität, which until a year before had housed the Nazi administrative headquarters for the Cologne-Aachen area. The exhibition was hence a bold break with the past, both culturally and politically. This significance could have been commemorated by founding the Haubrich-Ludwig Museum, as the Haubrich Collection formed one of the cornerstones of Museum Ludwig, founded in 1976. Such a decision would have had a precedent; the Wallraf-Richartz Museum, too, unites the names of two significant patrons. Yet even today, the Haubrich Collection is only identified as such inside the museum – which is all the more reason for us to publish this catalogue and present the new configuration of the collection.

I am very grateful to Julia Friedrich for taking the initiative to survey the collection afresh. Part of this re-examination was the research into the provenances of works bought by (or with help from) Haubrich. We are particularly grateful to the Bureau for Provenance Investigation & Research in Berlin. The Bureau immediately recognized the importance of this project and provided significant financial support for its realization, thus allowing my colleague Dorothee Grafahrend-Gohmert to spend two years researching the works' provenances. Her findings are published in the appendix to this volume and will also be displayed on the labels throughout the permanent exhibition. Making these results public was a goal of the research process from the beginning.

Sincere thanks are also due to Michael Albers and the Rheinisches Bildarchiv team, who photographed all 250 pieces in the Haubrich Collection for this publication. The photographs reveal both the team's deft handling of the pieces and their painstaking care throughout the working process. Many thanks, too, to my colleagues at Museum Ludwig, including the restorers Kathrin Keßler, Petra Mandt and Astrid Schubert for examining the backs of the paintings for clues to their origins; to storage manager Axel Kuhn and the art-handling team for promptly transporting the works; to the coordinator Astrid Bardenheuer for managing the entire project; and to archivist Ulrich Tillmann for always having the required information at hand.

The lavish production of this catalogue was made possible by the Ernst von Siemens Kunststiftung, who gave their help promptly and most unbureaucratically. Last but not least, I would like to express my sincere thanks to the Friends of the Wallraf-Richartz Museum and Museum Ludwig. Without their early support, we could never have realized this book in this form.

Things have come full circle. My work here began with a new presentation of the collection, and my work ends with a new presentation. I am pleased to have this final opportunity to honour Josef Haubrich, his seminal bequest in 1946, and his wonderful collection.

Foreword from the Editor

Julia Friedrich

There couldn't have been a worse time to make this book. The Historical Archive of the City of Cologne collapsed on 3 March 2009. Among the many significant documents from the city's history destroyed during the disaster were the details of Josef Haubrich's bequest, the archives of the Kölnischer Kunstverein, the archives of several Cologne galleries as well as all acquisition records from the Wallraf-Richartz Museum and Museum Ludwig. Whether anything might be salvaged and in what state remains unclear as we go to press. It will take years if not decades to quantify this loss, much less to rectify it. Nevertheless, we decided to publish this book and to research the provenances of the works in the collection insofar as possible under the circumstances. In light of the situation, no one could have reproached us for choosing to further delay the already long-overdue research. Indeed, there were moments when Dorothee Grafahrend-Gohmert and I longed to do just that.

But how much longer could we have waited? It is unclear whether the archival materials will ever be accessible again. In the meantime, the few living people from that era are growing older; the history grows ever more distant with each passing year.

Together with director Kasper König and our colleagues at the museum, we therefore decided to produce this book despite these adversities. The information presented in these pages must nevertheless be understood as provisional.

Researching the provenances of the collection was long overdue, but this was not the only pressing reason for this publication. Since Peter Fuchs published his monograph in 1959 (a revised edition was published in 1971), there has not been a single book about the paintings and sculptures in the collection, except for an excellent catalogue devoted to the watercolours that form the heart of the collection, published by Alfred Fischer on the occasion of Haubrich's centenary in 1989.

It was high time to re-examine Haubrich as an individual, his bequest and the genesis of his collection. Accordingly, the book is divided into three parts: a biographical and historical section which places the collection and the bequest in context, an art-historical section with discussions of the most important works accompanied by first-class reproductions, and a provenance section in which all the works that Haubrich bought, helped to buy or bequeathed are assembled. This final section puts in print all the findings we have assembled thus far. After an extensive research process, Charlotte Neußer has collected her findings in an index that sheds light on the interrelationships connecting the collectors, galleries and institutions surrounding Haubrich. In many cases, gaps remain in the provenances of the works despite extensive research. In other cases, as with the works in the Multhaupt Collection, Grafahrend-Gohmert was able to establish that the works had not been lost due to political persecution. Many questions remain open and indeed, we hope that the publication of this book will help us answer some of them. In this context, I would like to take this opportunity to thank provenance researcher Roswitha Neu-Kock for her support of Grafahrend-Gohmert's work.

In August 2012, the Haubrich Collection will be presented anew. On display alongside the well-known works will be three canvases painted on both the front and the back. Two of these reverse paintings, Kirchner's **Fränzi in Meadows** and Jawlensky's **Variation**, have never before been displayed; Pechstein's **Portrait of the Artist's Wife** will be exhibited for the first time in forty years. In order to show both sides of the paintings, Berlin artist Eran Schaerf has chosen a method of presentation which allows the viewer to see the front and the back of the painting simultaneously by means of a mirror. We would like to thank him for his ingenious solution. We also owe thanks to master carpenter Armin Lüttgen and his colleagues Michael Bangert and Leif Lenzner for their highly professional implementation of the design.

Our cooperation with the students of the University of Cologne was a source of great pleasure. Isabel Brass, Ilona Ciesielski, Arnika Fürgut, Erec Gellautz, Lorena Jonas, Jessica Küsters, Maria Meyer, Agnieszka Smyrek and Lisa Weber examined works from the collection as part of the seminar 'Writing Essays – Researching Provenances'. We owe them our sincere thanks, as we do Professor Ursula Frohne, who made our co-operation possible. The results of our discussions have informed their critical pieces (for some students, the first time they will see their work in print). Their pieces are placed alongside essays by authors who have spent many years examining the works of these artists and aspects of classical Modernism. It was vital for me to mix both fresh and more experienced perspectives in order to keep alive this collection whose works are now so firmly established in the canon. The artworks should not be admired because of their monetary value but rather because even today they have something to say to us. That can well be something other than what they communicated to the artist, to Josef Haubrich as a collector, or to the city of Cologne as the recipient of his bequest. One might even find that the essays in this book contradict one another. What is important is that we are talking about these works again. This dialogue alone makes publishing this book worthwhile.

We would like to express our appreciation to:

Dr. Claudia Andratschke, Niedersächisches Landesmuseum Hannover; Archiv der Akademie der Künste, Berlin; Archiv Jüdisches Museum Berlin/Leo Baeck Institut; Dr. Andrea Bambi, Bayerische Staatsgemäldesammlungen München; Andreas Benedict, Lehmbruck Museum, Duisburg; Dr. Ursel Berger, Georg-Kolbe-Museum, Berlin; Heike Biedermann, Galerie Neue Meister Staatliche Kunstsammlungen Dresden; Dr. Marion Bornscheuer, Lehmbruck Museum, Duisburg; Dr. Karl-Heinz Cramer, Martinez; Dr. Götz Czymmek, Wallraf-Richartz-Museum & Fondation Corboud, Köln; Dr. Birgit Dalbajewa, Galerie Neue Meister Staatliche Kunstsammlungen Dresden; Renate Ebner, Nachlass Erich Heckel, Hemmenhofen; Jean Fabris, Association Maurice Utrillo,

Pierrefitte-sur-Seine; Marion Fey, Historisches Archiv der Stadt Köln; Stefan Frey, Zentrum Paul Klee, Bern; Galerie Vömel, Düsseldorf; Bettina Gembruch, Kunst- und Museumsbibliothek Köln; Hadwig Goetz, Kunstmuseum Stuttgart; Dr. Uwe Hartmann, Arbeitsstelle für Provenienzrecherche/-forschung am Institut für Museumsforschung der Staatlichen Museen zu Berlin – Stiftung Preußischer Kulturbesitz; Dr. Ute Haug, Hamburger Kunsthalle; Jürgen Hegemann, Deutsches Zollmuseum, Hamburg; Dr. Wolfgang Henze, Galerie Henze & Ketterer, Wichtrach; Dr. Günther Herzog, Zentralarchiv des internationalen Kunsthandels, Köln; Simone Heuken, Verband der Restauratoren e. V. Bonn; Georg Heusch, Hannes Maria Flach-Archiv, Köln; Margret Heuser, Galerie Margret Heuser, Düsseldorf; Dr. Meike Hoffmann, Forschungsstelle Entartete Kunst, Berlin; Katharina Höying; Dr. h.c. Andreas Hüneke, Forschungsstelle Entartete Kunst, Berlin; Carolin Jahn, Georg-Kolbe-Museum, Berlin; Angelica Jawlensky Bianconi, Alexej von Jawlensky-Archiv S.A., Locarno; Dr. Ralph Jentsch; Dr. Gesa Jeuthe; Dr. Birgit Jooss, Deutsches Kunstarchiv im Germanischen Nationalmuseum, Nürnberg; Alexandra Kaiser, The Archipenko Foundation, Bearsville, NY; Florian Karsch, Galerie Nierendorf, Berlin; Lisa Kern, Städtische Galerie im Lenbachhaus, München; Isgard Kracht; Hannah Krause, Kunsthalle Mannheim; Ursula Kube, Bundesamt für zentrale Dienste und offene Vermögensfragen, Berlin; Landesarchiv Berlin; Landesarchiv NRW, Düsseldorf; Alexander Lambertin, Foto Kino Video Erich Lambertin GmbH, Köln; Attila Lardori, Eidgenössische Zollverwaltung EZV, Bern; Dr. Hans-Jürgen Lechtreck, Museum Folkwang, Essen; Sabine Liebscher, Kulturhistorisches Museum Magdeburg; Heidi Meyer, Tigre/Buenos-Aires; Dietrich Maguhn, Nachlass Walter Dick, Köln; Nina Matuszewski, NS-Dokumentationszentrum, Köln; Dr. Roswitha Neu-Kock, Referat für übergreifende Museumsangelegenheiten/Provenienzforschung, Köln; Dr. Tanja Pirsig-Marshall, LWL Landesmuseum für Kunst und Kulturgeschichte, Münster; Pascal Räderscheidt, Gisèle Räderscheidt ART GmbH, Köln; Ev-Isabel Raue; Andreas Reidemeister; Christiane Remm; Dr. Silke Reuter, Museum für Kunst und Gewerbe Hamburg; Sylvia Rose, Geheimes Staatsarchiv Preußischer Kulturbesitz, Berlin; Lynette Roth, Busch-Reisinger Museum, Cambridge, Massachusetts; Maria José Salazar Herrería; Barbara Schäfer, Wallraf-Richartz-Museum & Fondation Corboud, Köln; Elisabeth Scheeben, Stadtarchiv Düsseldorf; Johannes Schmidt, Städtische Galerie Dresden – Kunstsammlung; Dr. Ingeborg Schnelling-Reinicke, Geheimes Staatsarchiv Preußischer Kulturbesitz, Berlin; Wolfgang Schöddert, Berlinische Galerie; Dr. Hans-Jürgen Schwalm, Museen der Stadt Recklinghausen; Dr. Ingrid-Leonie Severin, art service, Dargow; Prof. Dr. Rainer Stamm, Landesmuseum für Kunst und Kulturgeschichte, Oldenburg; Dr. Hanna Strzoda, Zentralarchiv Staatliche Museen zu Berlin – Stiftung Preußischer Kulturbesitz; Dr. Katja Terlau, Museum Kunstpalast, Düsseldorf; Dr. Christina Thomson, Zentralarchiv Staatliche Museen zu Berlin – Stiftung Preußischer Kulturbesitz; Esther Tisa-Francini, Museum Rietberg Zürich; Dr. Peter Trebau, Caracas; Dr. Vanessa Voigt; Rita Wagner, Kölnisches Stadtmuseum; Viktoria Wegelin, Köln; Margarete Wegner, Frankfurter Kunstkabinett Hanna Bekker vom Rath; Dr. Jürgen Weise, Stiftung Rheinisch-Westfälisches Wirtschaftsarchiv zu Köln; Dr. Daniela Wilmes, Institut für Kunstgeschichte und Archäologie der Universität Bonn. Dr. Petra Winter, Zentralarchiv, Staatliche Museen zu Berlin-Stiftung Preußischer Kulturbesitz.

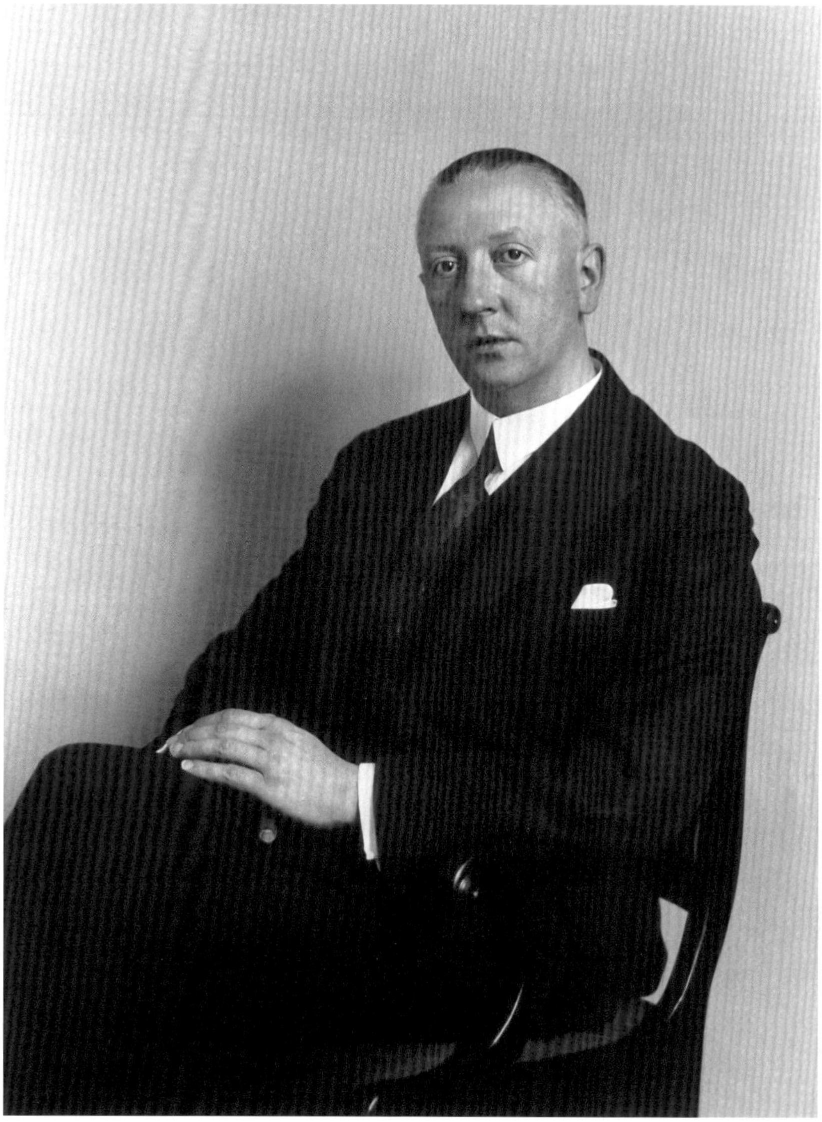

August Sander
Lawyer and Art Collector [Josef Haubrich]
from the project 'People of the Twentieth Century'
c. 1931, gelatin silver print, 26.9 x 19.9 cm

Julia Friedrich
Dorothee Grafahrend-Gohmert

Josef Haubrich. A Collector and his Collection

There was little to indicate that Josef Haubrich (1889–1961)[1] would become an important collector of modern art. In contrast to most art collectors, who came from upper-class families, he had a solid, middle-class background. His father, Wilhelm Nikolaus Haubrich, was director of the *Ortskrankenkasse für Fabriken* in Cologne, a public health insurance company. The family was interested in art, in keeping with its social station, and thus Haubrich became acquainted with various art collections during his travels. Beginning in 1907, he read law at the universities of Munich, Berlin and Bonn, finally receiving his doctorate for a dissertation on discounting outstanding accounts.[2] In 1915, he joined the chambers of Dr. Heinrich Bodenheim in Cologne, which flourished after the war, and he soon specialized in the lucrative field of commercial law.

Even with the epicurean lifestyle that Haubrich enjoyed, he had money enough for acquisitions, although his claim that there was no need to 'set an upper limit on my purchases' must be taken as an exaggeration.[3] For in the same breath he admitted that 'with my finances, I could no longer assemble a really first class collection of Old Masters'.[4] Yet the first artists whose works he purchased were old masters of German and Netherlandish art. Thus Haubrich's holdings contained three mid-fifteenth-century sculptures from a southern German Mount of Olives group, which now reside in Museum Schnütgen.

Compared to such treasures, contemporary art was to be had at a fraction of the price. 'He had a feeling for quality, so he soon realized that without powerful resources he would not get far with older art, and turned with great resolve to living artists', we read in an article from 1931.[5] Haubrich's friend Hans Schmitt-Rost put it less flatteringly: even in modern art he 'interested himself solely for artists who had more or less made it, who were acknowledged'.[6] That of course was the view expressed by one of the *Kölner Progressiven* (Cologne Progressives). For the traditional, culturally conservative circles in which Haubrich moved, if only because of his profession, even the realist painter Wilhelm

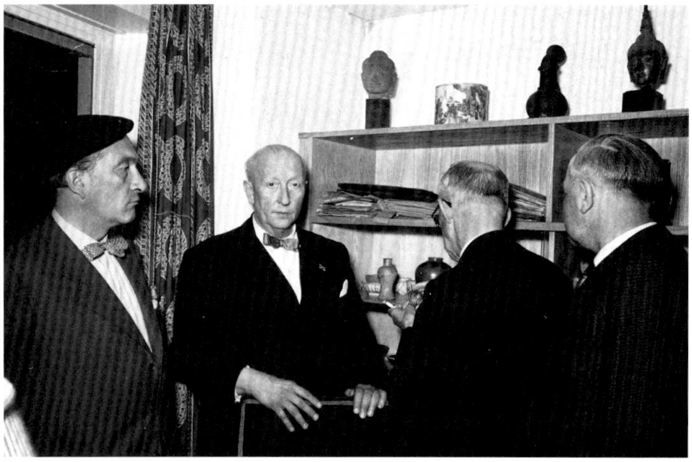

Haubrich in his home with Hans Schmitt-Rost *(left)* and Andreas Becker *(far right)*, standing in front of his collection of East Asian items, 1954.

Leibl was a red rag.[7] Thus the 1912 International Exhibition of the *Sonderbund westdeutscher Kunstfreunde und Künstler* in Cologne, which showed Vincent van Gogh, Paul Cézanne and already Pablo Picasso alongside the painters from the Brücke and Rhenish Expressionist groups, met with great distaste, not least from Kaiser Wilhelm. But others of course were fascinated, and for Haubrich it was 'a momentous revelation'.[8]

Four years later, in 1916, he visited a memorial exhibition for Franz Marc at Herwarth Walden's Galerie Der Sturm in Berlin; shortly thereafter he purchased his first modern artwork, a sculpture by Wilhelm Lehmbruck. And with his move in 1918 to the suburb of Marienburg in Cologne, the Haubrich Collection began to flourish in its new rooms, done in a colour scheme designed by Theodor Caspar Pilartz. He had still not fully arrived at what later was to be his main area, classical Modernism with an emphasis on Expressionism, for he still also collected East Asian art.[9]

Unlike other collectors, he did not hire advisers but gradually acquired his own deep knowledge of contemporary art, not least from the artists and gallerists with whom he was friends.

Haubrich's Art

Haubrich also wrote art critiques for a social-democratic newspaper, the *Rheinische Zeitung*, under the pseudonym of Dr. Ludwig Josef. An ongoing theme in his writing were the comparisons he made between the latest German art and that of France. In 1926 we read that the 'weak sculptures by Fritz Behn' – a state-subsidized artist with at that time Monarchist and later Nazi leanings – vanished next to the 'magnificent show' put on by Edgar Degas.[10] In 1927 he was delighted that Jankel Adler had 'freed himself of French influences'. He

Haubrich and guests at his 65th birthday, 1954.

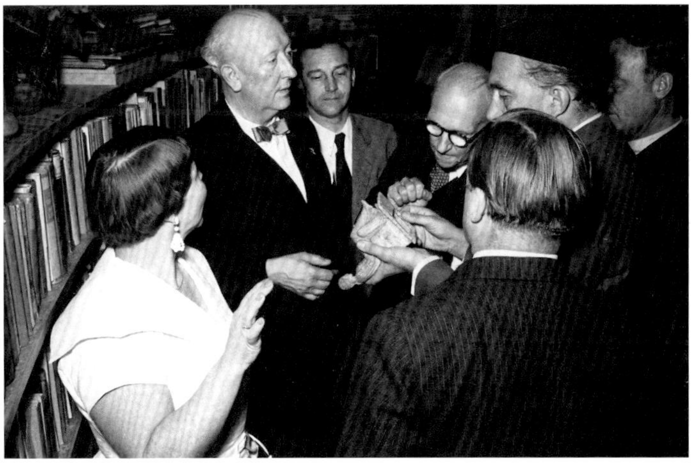

additionally thought it crucial to note that Adler was a Jew and that 'overall his work shows characteristics of his race, enriched by an Eastern influence', which he clearly meant as praise. 'Jankel Adler is one of the most unique and talented artists we have in Germany'.[11] In 1928 he cast judgement on Karl Hofer: 'His "Nightclub" is a poor piece that does not even begin to match his great inspiration, Seurat. Similarly with his "Prison Yard" it is best not to think of van Gogh'.[12] His concern was that German art should attain a formal quality on a par with the French, but without copying the latter. He was not interested in cutting off German art but on the contrary, in fostering European competition.

Haubrich not only wrote on the very latest works but, depending on what was being presented at that moment in Cologne, also on mediaeval or classicist works, as well as on local art politics. His articles are marked by a broad knowledge and the often harsh aesthetic judgements of the autodidact.

Wolfgang Braunfels established that initially there were three areas in the collection, although it was still unclear which was the most important: 'the works of a few lesser foreigners; works from his numerous artist friends in Cologne, whom he backed and supported; ... watercolours and oils by the greats of Germany, above all northern German Expressionists, accompanied by a small collection of sculptures'.[13] We may say in retrospect that the decision in favour of the third area, the (northern German) Expressionists, was reached in 1923, although Haubrich also gave ample consideration to the Anti-Expressionists, which is to say the representatives of Neue Sachlichkeit, and never completely forgot the Cologne artists.

Among his most impressive purchases between 1923 and 1933 are in particular the verist **Portrait of Doctor Koch** by Otto Dix (the very first modern painting to enter the collection), one of Dix's ruthless self-portraits (acquired 1932) along with a **Still Life** (1923) and the famous **Female Half-Length Nude with Hat** (1924) by Ernst Ludwig

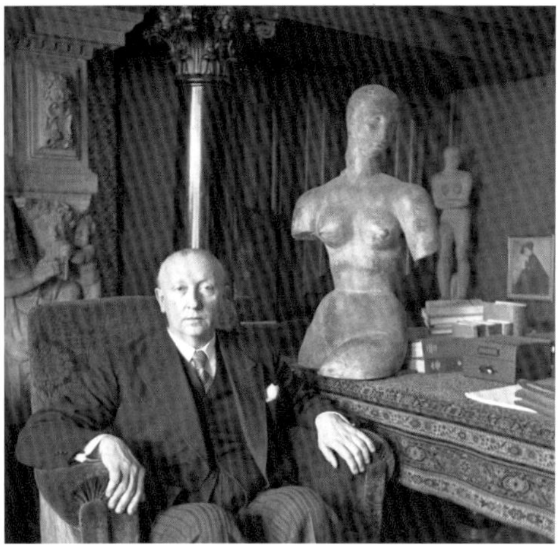

With Lehmbruck's *Torso of a Girl Turning* and *Woman Looking Back*, 1946.

Kirchner, which remains to this day a shining example of the collection. And Haubrich spent the enormous sum for that time (1923/24) of ten thousand gold marks – the equivalent of three or four villas –[14] on two paintings by the Belgian visionary James Ensor, which today are in the keeping of the Wallraf-Richartz Museum. Apart from these and the aforementioned Lehmbruck, the list contains equally important works by Marc Chagall, Max Ernst, Erich Heckel, Karl Hofer, Heinrich Hoerle, Moïse Kisling, Oskar Kokoschka, Carlo Mense, Paula Modersohn-Becker, Otto Mueller, Ernst Nolde, Georg Schrimpf, Paul Adolf Seehaus, Renée Sintenis and Maurice de Vlaminck. Watercolours formed the basic stock, paintings the substance, while sculptures by comparison were in the minority.

With this the foundations were laid. Haubrich chiefly bought German art, perhaps because it was the easiest to obtain. The collector quite deliberately declined, writes Braunfels, 'to integrate the great names of the Paris school, Picasso, Matisse, Braque or Rouault, into his collection'.[15] He was also reluctant to overstep the boundary into pure abstraction, and avoided works by members of the Constructivist or Blauer Reiter movements, as well as by proponents of Dada and the November Group.

He frequently purchased works from Galerie Nierendorf, which opened in 1920 in Cologne, and soon was friends with the gallerist Karl Nierendorf (1889–1947), along with the artists he represented: Peter Abelen, Michael Brunthaler, Heinrich May and others. He was quick to buy important works such as the **Portrait of Doctor Koch** by Otto Dix from Nierendorf. But he also remained faithful to his galleries in Düsseldorf and Berlin.

As is to be seen from Haubrich's records,[16] he bought very early from the Cologne industrialist Franz Nienhaus. Unfortunately we have been unable to draw any conclusions as to why Nienhaus parted with the works he owned between 1924 to 1927. It is unlikely that he dealt professionally in art, even if over a period of four years Haubrich bought three Neue Sachlichkeit paintings, two Expressionist paintings and two sculptures each

In front of Ensor's *Skeleton Looking at Chinoiseries*, 1946.

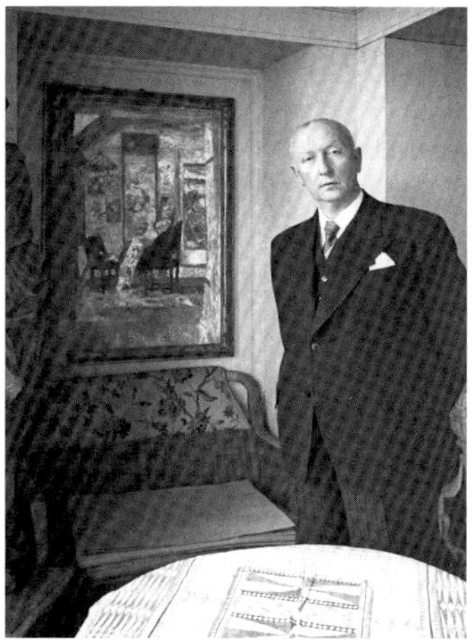

by Ernst Barlach and Wilhelm Lehmbruck. Presumably they were in personal contact. A further dealer from whom Haubrich purchased works during the Weimar Republic and the Nazi regime was Andreas Becker. Despite having completed his law exams, Becker decided to switch to art dealing and in 1924 took over the Cologne branch of the gallery run by the celebrated art dealer Alfred Flechtheim (1878–1937),[17] who championed and influenced the avant-garde as had scarcely another and played a decisive role in the Sonderbund Exhibition of 1912. Haubrich continued to buy works from Becker when the latter set himself up as an art dealer in his own right.

Becker had two strings to his exhibition bow: he presented not only contemporary art, but also art from East Asia at the suggestion of Haubrich's friend Nierendorf.[18] As already mentioned, Haubrich was also enthusiastic about East Asian art, which he frequently bought from Becker.[19] The latter's chief interest was the Cologne Progressives, and in 1931 he mounted a large exhibition for Otto Freundlich.[20] In 1932 Becker sold Haubrich **Carnival** by Heinrich Hoerle, one of the main representatives of the Progressives,[21] and Haubrich remained Becker's customer right until 1937, when the gallerist emigrated to France. On the latter's return, they re-established contact. Becker himself wrote: 'It is with gratitude that I remember all the friendly help that Josef Haubrich gave me through his advice and purchases, both at the time when I worked for Galerie Flechtheim and later in Galerie Dr. Becker und Newman'.[22]

The art dealer Aloys Faust was also from the circle of the Progressives. From 1932 he was involved in the journal *a bis z* edited by Hoerle and fellow artist Franz Seiwert. It seems that Faust worked in the first branch that Flechtheim established in Cologne, and he certainly worked later for Becker.[23] Shortly before Becker emigrated he set up his own art dealership in Cologne. But he had already worked independently from at least 1933, and had also sold works to Haubrich.

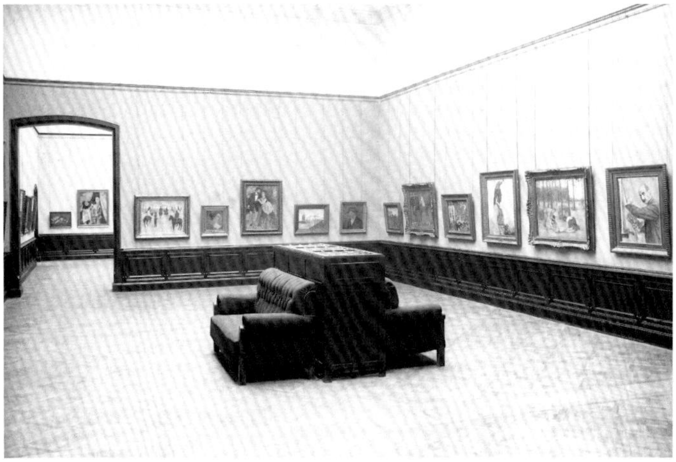

Modern section of the Wallraf-Richartz Museum with works by Liebermann that were later transferred to Haubrich's collection, 1920s.

Nazi Period

Opinions are divided when it comes to how Haubrich behaved during the National Socialist era. The question is not about his closeness to the regime, because apart from the *Nationalsozialistische Volkswohlfahrt* (the National Socialist People's Welfare Service, which annexed the workers' welfare agency, the *Arbeiterwohlfahrt*), the lawyer was not a member of any of the Nazi organisations – much to the detriment of his pocket. Rather, it is a matter of a very simple fact: the collector continued his previous activity 'with a strange lack of concern',[24] as if nothing had happened.

Neither the dismissal nor the denunciation and persecution of Jewish or progressive artists and professors, not even the exhibition 'Degenerate Art' or the act for the confiscation of 'degenerate art products' of 31 May 1938 seem to have distracted him in the least from his passion. In 1942, in an application to the Employment Bureau for a domestic help, he even ventured to mention his 'collection', adding that 'it is in the public interest to see to its upkeep. To this end please get a reference if required from the Wallraf-Richartz Museum in the Hanseatic City of Cologne'.[25]

Whilst his stance was held to his great credit directly after the war as showing a courageous and self-confident advocacy of unconventional and persecuted art, more recently it has been insinuated that he used this hour of need to make cheap purchases and colluded with the system's functionaries.

A classic example was Haubrich's relationship to Prof. Dr. Otto H. Förster (1894–1975), who had directed the Wallraf-Richartz Museum since 1933. After being compulsorily retired in 1946, Förster returned to his position in 1957. Haubrich kept in close contact with him and aided him in his business transactions in France until at least 1942.[26] Even Andreas Becker's recollections underline Haubrich's 'cooperation with

Modern section of the Wallraf-Richartz Museum in the 1920s.

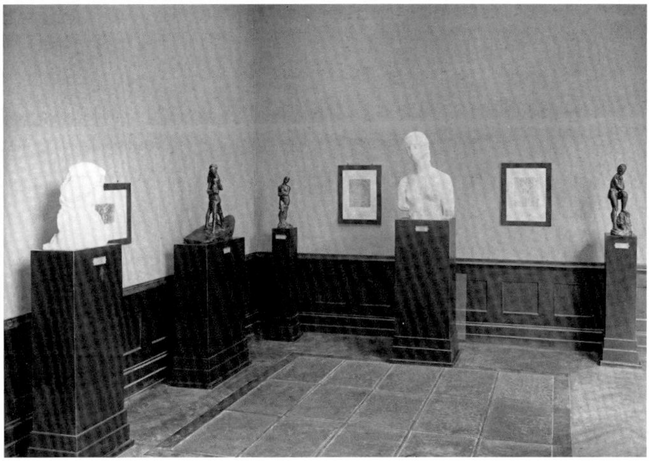

Professor Förster, who is to be thanked at this point for his help in rescuing modern artworks'.[27] But there can be no doubt of Förster's loyalty to the system. This is evident alone from the Teutophile titles of the exhibitions he organized: 'Deutsch heißt volkstümlich' ('Germany, Your Name is Tradition'), 1935; 'Neuerwerbungen deutscher Kunst 1933–37' ('New Acquisitions of German Art 1933-37'), 1937; and 'Große deutsche Zeichner von Runge bis Leibl' ('Great German Draughtsmen from Runge to Leibl'), 1939.

Katja Terlau sums it up: 'His term as museum director saw, for instance, the acquisition of the Carstanjen Collection, the re-arrangement of the museum, the first major Lochner exhibition, the "cleansing" of the holdings through the confiscation of so-called "degenerate" artworks, and the carefully directed expansion of the picture gallery.'[28] New works were added of Netherlandish, French and German provenance. But some did not remain for long: over 600 new acquisitions from German-occupied territories had to be returned after 1945 as war booty.[29] As for the Germans, the preference was for the nineteenth century, from Caspar David Friedrich to Lovis Corinth (although ironically the latter was represented in the 'Degenerate Art' exhibition).[30]

The persecution of Modernism meant that 'the one or the other work owned by German museums',[31] and not least the Wallraf-Richartz Museum, ended up in Haubrich's hands. For example, through the mediation of Aloys Faust, Förster sold a self-portrait by Max Liebermann to Haubrich as early as 1934, followed later by other paintings by the artist.[32] Haubrich, who was not particularly taken with Liebermann, left his purchases in the museum depot. Daniela Wilmes writes that the motive to sell Liebermann was anti-Semitic: 'Evidently museum director Förster was set on making the right impression in the year he joined the NSDAP. Haubrich proved unimpressed by this kind of populism, as shown by the purchase of the self-portrait. But it is hard to classify this as "rescuing" the artworks solely in the interest of the Wallraf-Richartz Museum.'[33]

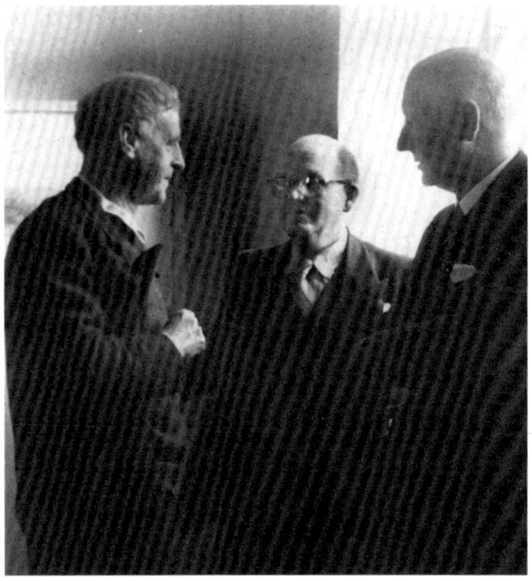 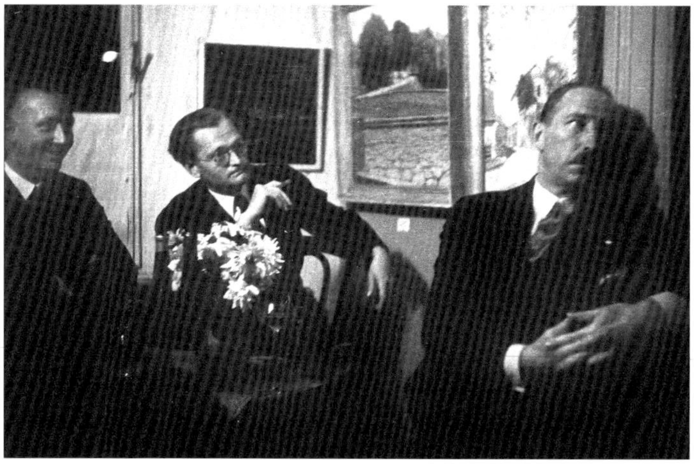

This 'populism' was to cost millions of people their lives, but Haubrich did not allow himself to be infected by it, and preferred to buy rather than risk the loss or destruction of a work that he did not otherwise care for strongly. Hans Schmitt-Rost recalled: 'On critical days some of what once was called Cologne society, including several pillars of its cultural life, did a fine job betraying Judaism and its importance. But not Josef Haubrich'.[34]

Alfred Flechtheim's gallery in Düsseldorf announced an exhibition of the Paul Multhaupt collection on 12 March 1933. The invitation bore a cross next to the name of the collector, who had committed suicide in January 1933.[35] Whether the exhibition ever actually took place is uncertain. What is certain is that Haubrich managed to purchase two paintings from the Multhaupt Collection – **Sabbath** by Marc Chagall, and **Young Woman and Men** by Emil Nolde – albeit not directly from Alfred Flechtheim, who fled to Paris a few months later. As Peter Springer writes, it must have been clear to Flechtheim that his hour had come when on 1 April, his birthday, an inflammatory article appeared in the National Socialist paper *Volksparole*, stating that '[t]he Flechtheim system ... must be wiped out'.[36] It had certainly been clear to him earlier too, because the same article pointed out that Alex Vömel, Flechtheim's buyer since 1923, had taken over the business already: 'Incidentally, Gallery Flechtheim has now disguised itself as Gallery Alexander Vömel'.[37] Vömel, who was not a Jew and who joined the NSDAP in 1937,[38] later continued to be referred to as a 'sidekick' of the 'Jewish high priest of art', Flechtheim.[39]

For a long time it was assumed that the exhibition of the Multhaupt Collection had been cancelled by the Gestapo. What in fact was affected was an auction of paintings by old and new masters from museums and private owners, which was to have been held in conjunction with the Gallery Hugo Helbing (Munich) and the Gallery Georg Paffrath (Düsseldorf) on almost the same date, on 11 March.[40]

left
Ewald Mataré, Karl Nierendorf and Haubrich, 1946.

centre
Haubrich with Andreas Becker *(centre)* and Consul Hans Carl Scheibler *(on the right)* at the Kunsthandlung Dr. Becker & Newman, 1933.

right
In conversation with Aloys Faust *(centre)* and Georg Meistermann *(on the right)*, 1950s.

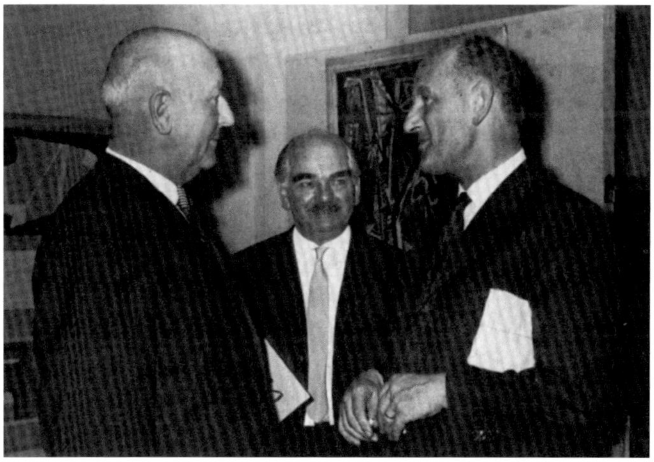

It was not until June 1933 that Haubrich received a letter from Vömel saying that he had spoken with Mrs. Multhaupt, who agreed to the sale of the Nolde painting, but since there were still unsettled matters regarding the inheritance, Haubrich should first keep the two paintings as a loan.[41] Haubrich gives the exact year and price of the purchase in his records,[42] so it seems matters were settled.

Haubrich bought works even more frequently from Vömel. In 1934 Vömel sold him Oskar Kokoschka's **Portrait of Tilla Durieux**, which had originally been owned by Flechtheim. Vömel, who had to pay off a mortgage Flechtheim had taken out with the city of Düsseldorf, along with his rent arrears, used these and other sales to cover the debts.[43] Apart from these works, Haubrich purchased several sculptures from him, including one by Gerhard Marcks and two early works by Arno Breker. He also remained a customer after 1945, when he purchased works by Rudolf Belling and Ewald Mataré.

Wilmes argues quite plausibly that Haubrich also managed to negotiate discounts for himself during the Nazi period, when prices for modern art started to fall, as for instance from Vömel. The author concludes that 'his chief interest lay in enlarging and physically preserving his collection'.[44] The latest studies have shown, however, that the prices for modern art as a whole remained stable during the Third Reich.[45] So perhaps the situation on the market studied by Wilmes was just a passing dip. Be that as it may, given the sums that Haubrich invested, it is not surprising that he kept an eye not only on the artistic but also on the financial value of his collection. Certainly he attempted with his limited budget to negotiate reasonable prices. But he did not speculate with art, nor did he pursue purely economic goals.

It should be remembered that Haubrich already had ambitions to become a public benefactor in 1923, long before he wrote his letter to the Employment Bureau in 1942 claiming there was a 'public interest' in his collection. Together with Karl Lange

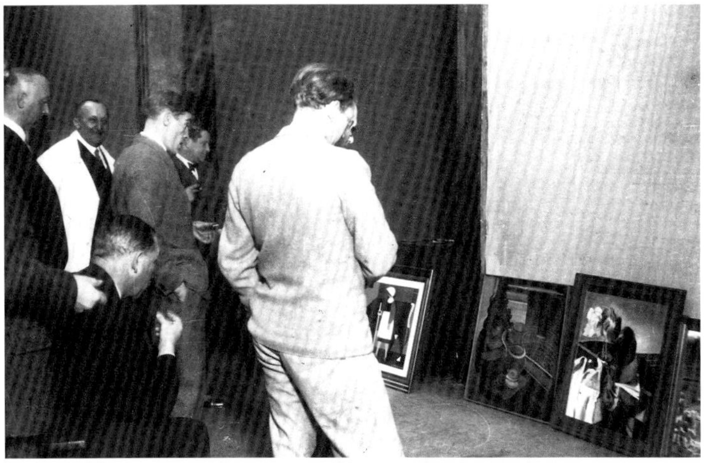

In the jury for the exhibition 'Kölner Künstler 1931' at the Kölnischer Kunstverein (KKV).
From the left: Haubrich, Walter Klug (director of the KKV), Consul Scheibler (chairman of the KKV, seated), Anton Räderscheidt, Ernst Bucher (director of the Wallraf-Richartz Museum) and Karl With (director of the Museum of Applied Arts).

of Krefeld and Herbert von Garvens-Garvensburg of Hanover, he offered the City of Cologne artworks as a gift. Dr. Hans F. Secker, head of the modern art section at the Wallraf-Richartz Museum, had prompted them to do so. But after negotiations lasting over a year, Lord Mayor Konrad Adenauer declined the offer because what they were offering, especially the Garvens's Collection, was too modern. The art world went up in arms at this decision.[46]

The heart of Garvens's Collection consisted of a complete set of etchings and a number of paintings by James Ensor, whom Garvens was regarded as having discovered in Germany, along with a cross-section of Modernists from Gustave Courbet and Henri Rousseau to Alexander Archipenko and Wassily Kandinsky. Likewise the Dadaists, with whom the collector was friends, must also have been represented.[47] At the same time the public administration in Cologne at the time, presumably on Adenauer's instructions, ensured that Otto Dix's painting *The Trench* 'was first equipped with a curtain to protect delicate souls, and then made to disappear once and for all from the municipal collection'.[48] Adenauer's predecessor Max Wallraf adopted a liberal stance and assured that a *Sonderbund* exhibition wasn't enough 'to make the pictures by the old masters of Cologne ... come tumbling from the walls'.[49]

In any case, contemporary art had a difficult position in official Cologne after 1914 and the death of Dr. Alfred Hagelstange, who as director of the Wallraf-Richartz Museum had also defended the Modernists when he met with the opposition of the municipal commission.[50] Nevertheless, or precisely because of that, Haubrich offered the museum a sculpture by Wilhelm Lehmbruck on loan in 1923.[51]

Quite early on, Haubrich became an active member of the Kölnischer Kunstverein, the city's arts society, and from 1932 he was a member of the board.[52] Up until his death he bought works at the Kunstverein's exhibitions and brokered other works through

From the left: Josef Jenniches (a staff member at the Kölnischer Kunstverein) with jury members Haubrich, With, Klug, and jury member Buchner on the far right, at the exhibition 'Kölner Künstler 1931' at the KKV.

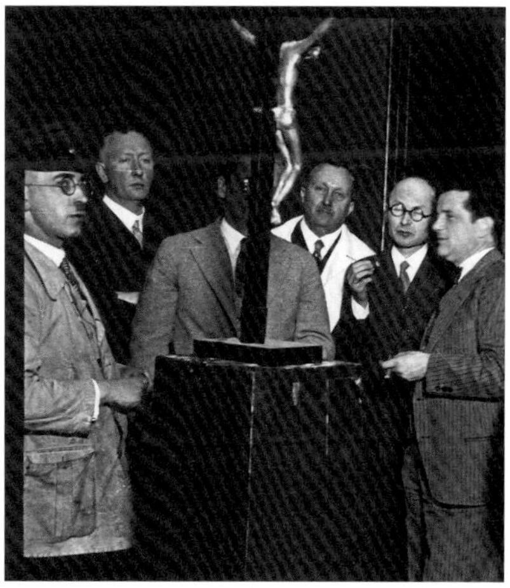

the society, including Maurice de Vlaminck's **Still Life with Flowers and Fruit**, Paul Adolf Seehaus's **Scottish Landscape with Lighthouse**, and Heinrich Hoerle's **Two Women**. Although he was barred in 1936 on account of his distance to the National Socialist regime, Haubrich remained in close contact with the society and purchased artworks via it. After the society was closed by the Allies, he moved for it to be reopened.[53]

'Degenerate Art'

The 'Degenerate Art' campaign in 1937 was in many respects a turning point. In a concerted action, every publicly owned work which the National Socialists viewed as 'degenerate' was impounded. Privately owned works were unaffected. The first wave of confiscations in July 1937 served above all to stock the vilifying exhibition 'Degenerate Art' in Munich. Over the following years the exhibition toured the whole of the German Reich.

The second wave in August attempted the blanket removal of Modernism from German museums. Ultimately the number of Modernist works that were confiscated from each museum depended on the size of their modern art holdings. In Cologne, where a somewhat conservative climate prevailed in the municipal administration and museum directorship following the era of Hagelstange, and Modernist acquisitions had been rather cautious, the campaign affected forty-five paintings, 143 watercolours, 295 prints and eight portfolios from the Wallraf-Richartz Museum.[54] Very similar figures were reported by the Staatsgalerie in Stuttgart: fifty-four paintings and sculptures, twenty-seven drawings and 328 prints.[55] Although directors such as Konrad von Lange (incumbent from 1901 to 1907) and Otto Fischer (1921 to 1927) in Stuttgart had fostered Modernism, they had met mostly with the indignation of the populace and had been rebuked by the local

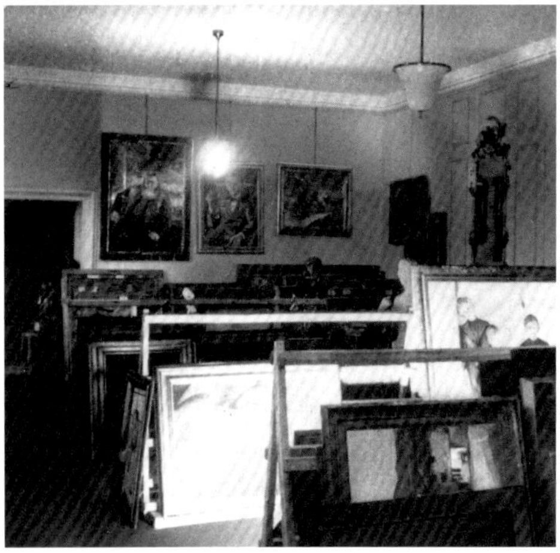

Dix's *Portrait of the Poet Theodor Däubler* and Grosz's *Doctor Eduard Plietzsch* on the wall of the depot at Schloss Schönhausen, c. 1941.

government. The term 'degenerate art' was not new; it had been used as early as 1924 in a row over Modernism in Stuttgart.[56]

In Hamburg, Alfred Lichtwark, director until 1914, had built up a modern art department 'resolutely and against great resistance at the time'.[57] His successor, Gustav Pauli, followed in his footsteps. The confiscations in Hamburg affected seventy-five paintings belonging to the Kunsthalle, sixty-four loans, and 1,200 works from the graphic cabinet. The Kunsthalle Mannheim saw the loss of all of 107 paintings, 'including major works by Ensor, Delaunay, Chagall, Beckmann, Grosz, and many others', fourteen sculptures, eighty-three watercolours, 119 drawings and 496 prints and portfolios.[58] The National Socialists had already organized an exhibition in that town in 1933 entitled 'Cultural Bolshevist Pictures'. Walter Passarge, the director in Mannheim from 1936 until his death in 1958, not only managed to buy prints by James Ensor and Edvard Munch in secret, he also hid all of the paintings by Max Liebermann and Oskar Kokoschka. Although he did not stand in the way of the confiscations, he did request the return of a number of the confiscated works through various applications to the *Reichskammer für bildende Künste* – and was partly successful.[59]

The Nationalgalerie in Berlin had demonstrated an exceptional openness towards Modernism. Ludwig Justi (1876–1957) built a *Museum der Gegenwart* there, the first museum in the world dedicated to contemporary art. After Justi was sacked in 1933, his successor, Eberhard Hanfstaengl, adopted a more moderate exhibition programme. In 1937 he, too, was dismissed. 'No other museum collection was as affected by the National Socialist iconoclasm against "degenerate art" as the modern section of the Nationalgalerie in Berlin', we read in a résumé. 'Almost the entire holdings of contemporary art were confiscated in 1937 and exhibited in large part at the denigratory exhibition "Degenerate Art" in Munich.'[60]

View of the exhibition 'Degenerate Art' in Munich in 1937, with Kirchner's *An Artists' Group* and *Five Women on the Street.*

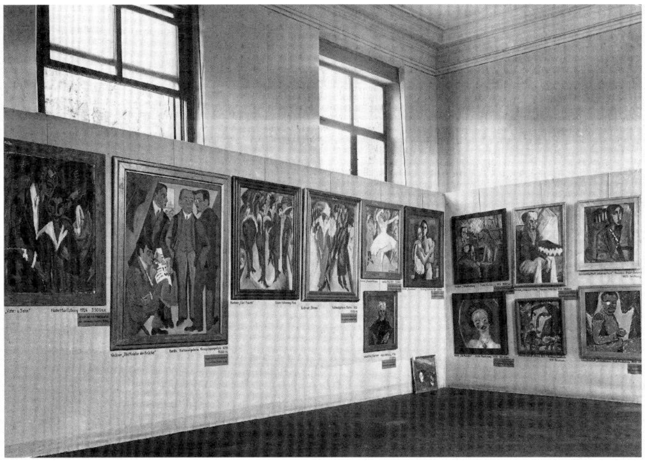

The works, which had been confiscated from all over Germany, were brought together, listed and placed in various categories. All pieces deemed 'internationally marketable' were taken to the depot at Schloss Schönhausen and gradually sold off.[61] Four art dealers – Bernhard Böhmer, Karl Buchholz, Hildebrand Gurlitt and Ferdinand Möller – were authorized to sell 'degenerate' artworks abroad. Although they were expressly forbidden from selling at home, none of the dealers adhered to this. Even in the 1940s, Haubrich bought a number of works from Gurlitt that had been confiscated as 'degenerate'.

All in all, five paintings confiscated from German museums landed in Haubrich's possession via Gurlitt: Otto Dix's **Portrait of the Poet Theodor Däubler** (formerly of the Nationalgalerie Berlin), Erich Heckel's **Canal** (Kunsthalle Bremen), Karl Hofer's **Masquerade** (Kunstsammlungen der Stadt Düsseldorf), Heinrich Campendonk's **Woman with Fishes** (Bayerische Staatsgemäldesammlungen Munich) and Georg Schrimpf's **Nude Girl in Front of a Mirror** (Kunsthalle Mannheim). It is not known how Haubrich came in contact with Gurlitt. Probably it was via Förster, who attended to business for the Wallraf-Richartz Museum in France, Belgium and Holland – countries in which Gurlitt was also active.[62] After 1945, Förster backed Gurlitt's nomination as director of the *Kunstverein für die Rheinlande und Westfalen* – the Düsseldorf art society – which suggests that they were well acquainted.[63]

Among the 'degenerate' artworks Haubrich acquired was the **Half-Length Portrait of Two Nude Women** by Otto Mueller. The fate of this work presented more twists than most: it was supposed to be sold in 1935, at auction number 188 at Max Perl's auction house, on behalf of its owners, the heirs to the Jewish art patron and notary Dr. Ismar Littmann. The auction however was hindered by the Gestapo, who confiscated a number of works, including Mueller's paintings. Hanfstaengl, at that time director of the Nationalgalerie in Berlin, was allowed to pick and choose; the rest were burnt.

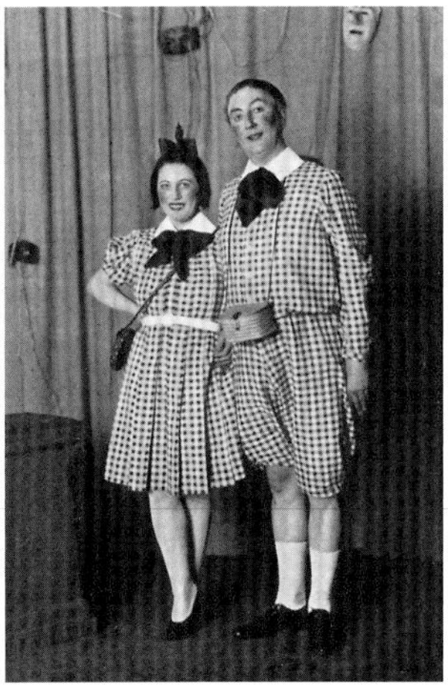

Haubrich with his wife Alice at a Carnival party.

Although the painting escaped the flames, no more than a year later it was confiscated yet again as 'degenerate'. The owner this time was the Nationalgalerie. And in this way it travelled via Schloss Schönhausen and Gurlitt to Haubrich. It was returned to the heirs of the Littmann family in 1999 and bought back on mutual consent by Museum Ludwig.[64]

Persecution

In 1939, the party court ruled that Haubrich's associate, Bodenheim, had to give up the law practice they shared.[65] The reason for this was that Haubrich's third wife, Alice Gottschalk, came from a Jewish family. This was also the reason why Haubrich had not been accepted into the National Socialist bar association and why he had been prevented from accepting any contracts from the courts and authorities.[66] With that the practice was split, and Haubrich moved his office to his home. His wife had already been stopped from practising her profession as a gynaecologist in 1938 as a result of the openly racist fourth decree of the Reich Citizenship Law. During these uncertain times Haubrich didn't buy a single artwork for a whole year.

Alice Haubrich brought a daughter Anneli to the marriage. In 1943 the Gestapo searched for the nineteen-year-old. She immediately fled to Vienna, where she entered into the service of a bribed SS man as a governess. Peter Fuchs tells the rest of the story: 'It cost Haubrich umpteen thousands of marks to maintain this hiding place. The suspicions of the authorities were allayed with the help of forged papers showing she was the victim of a bombing raid. Anneli Haubrich's efforts to find a way out of this fix succeeded when she discovered that her private studies were enough for her to work as a medical extern. But this led her to being enlisted as a nurse and finally she ended up

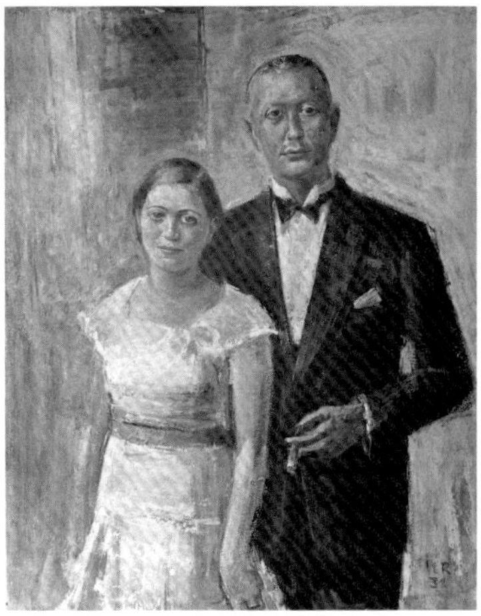

The Haubrichs, a portrait by Anton Räderscheidt, oil on canvas, 1931.

working once more for SS doctors. Towards the end of the war she found a way to escape to Denmark and finally returned to her step-father Haubrich after the liberation of Nazi Germany'.[67]

Haubrich's wife took poison and ended her life on 10 February 1944, the day on which the couple had been summonsed by the Gestapo in order to be expelled from their home. As Ruth 'Wiesel' Cramer, Haubrich's daughter from his first marriage, recalled, the aim in bombed-out Cologne was to 'move everybody living in mixed marriages ... to the old people's home in Cologne-Riehl. And everyone would have one room there. That was the death of Alice. She couldn't ask that of my father. ... She was the kind who either wanted to live well or not at all'.[68] In her farewell note, Alice Haubrich explained that she wanted to spare her husband and herself 'any more hardship and bitterness',[69] and asked him specially to see what had happened to Anneli, not knowing whether her daughter was still alive or not.

The question of why Haubrich did not also bring his wife to safety can perhaps be answered in that according to the Nazi racial laws, a marriage was only 'Jewish' when the husband was a Jew.[70] Jewish women, according to the letter of this law, could not be arraigned for *Blutschande* (desecrating the blood). This meant that some couples (such as Gertrud and Karl Jaspers) felt reasonably safe. But the authorities interpreted the law with increasing severity, so that towards the end of the regime Jewish wives in such marriages were also targeted by the bailiffs.

During house searches, the Gestapo also noted the presence of non-conformist art. In this case the police found fault with the painting **Masquerade** by Karl Hofer, which the collector had purchased from the segregated holdings of the Mannheimer Kunsthalle. 'With great presence of mind [he said] the signature CH was that of a Frenchman named Charles Hofer, and as it happened an easy line was being taken with

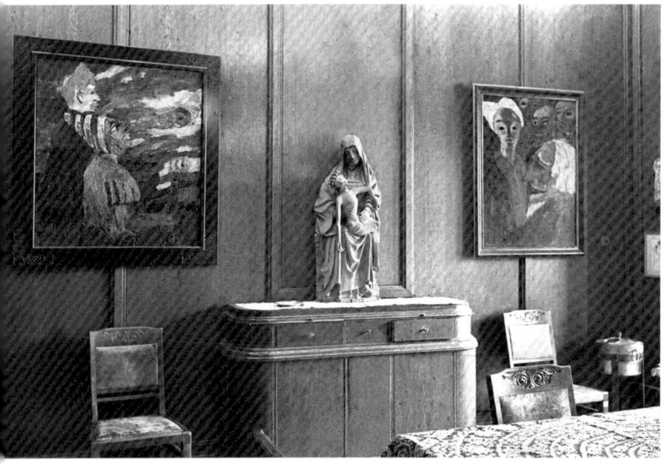 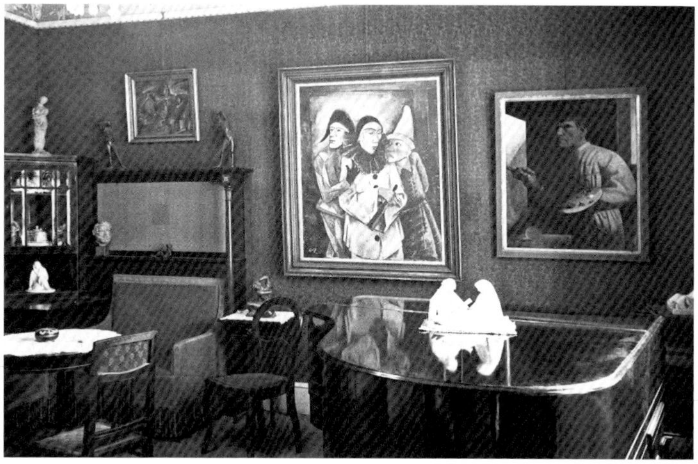

the French at that time out of political expediency'.[71] He hid other works in various locations, including in the castle belonging to the Count of Spee in Untermaubach.[72]

In this way Haubrich actually enlarged his collection during the Nazi era, apart from the hiatus already mentioned in 1939. Of particular note are the three Emil Noldes he acquired – **Young Woman and Men, After Sunset** and **Red and Yellow Roses** – which brought his collection of one of his most favourite artists to a very high level. Other acquisitions apart from the Noldes and the aforementioned works by Hofer, Liebermann and Mueller also demonstrated his foresight, including works by Jankel Adler, Max Beckmann, Heinrich Campendonk, Marc Chagall, Erich Heckel, Moïse Kisling, Oskar Kokoschka, Georg Schrimpf, Paul Adolf Seehaus and Renée Sintenis.

In short, we can say that Haubrich continued to expand his collection during the 1930s and 1940s, chiefly purchasing works by artists who were already represented. 'The foundations of his spiritual empire were laid, the programme marked out', as Braunfels observes. 'The standard they set was to become the benchmark for all later acquisitions. Only very strong works could contend with these Noldes and Kirchners'. The main emphasis remained watercolours. Right from the start Haubrich was clear in his mind 'that many of these artists had done their best work in watercolours'.[73]

Donation

Shortly before the liberation, a United States arts officer appeared at the Haubrich-Wegelin home, 'had the paintings and sculptures shown to him, requested a list and placed the house under special protection'.[74] Apart from a series of drawings by Paul Klee, which had been transferred to London and confiscated there as enemy assets,[75]

The collection at the Haubrich-Wegelin house, Lindenallee 5, 1945/46.

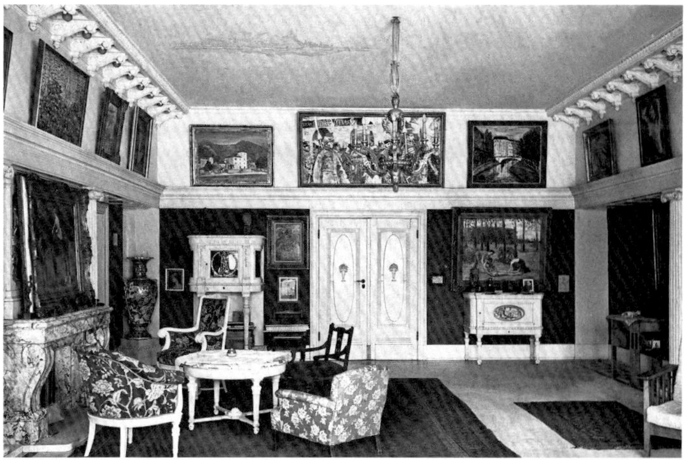

the collection remained complete. But after the withdrawal of the Americans, the British arrived and seized Haubrich's house.

This seizure gave Haubrich the final incentive to realize a plan he had cherished since 1923: donating the collection to the City of Cologne. His art, as Haubrich explained, belonged 'for social reasons to the public. I feel a special duty to youth. I want to give our youngsters, who are unaccustomed to liberty, or are largely unaware of what liberty is, the opportunity to take a long, close look at all the things that were kept forcibly from them over these twelve years.'[76]

It stood to reason from this that the collection – not as a monument to the collector but to classical Modernism – could by all means be mixed with other holdings, and should also be systematically enlarged. 'This donation is not digging a first-class grave, as it were', for the artworks, as was stated at the opening of the collection. Rather, they have become 'parts of a living, constantly-growing organism'.[77] In order to promote this growth, Haubrich requested a regular sum from the city equal to the salary of a town councillor, which came to be known as the Haubrich Fund. Apart from this, he reserved the right to borrow works for his private rooms.

The city council accepted the donation with enormous gratitude and with the full agreement of all political parties, both conservative or communist, and stated that 'this donation enables the people of Cologne to access what was denigrated as "degenerate art" during the twelve years of fascist dictatorship in Germany'.[78] Haubrich had waited for the right moment. At that point in time every political and social group that genuinely wished to turn away from Nazism was still in agreement about progressive art and its value.

Before suitable rooms could be provided for the collection in the new building of the Wallraf-Richartz Museum, it was exhibited from October 1946 onwards in the Alte Universität. Afterwards it went on tour and appeared in varying constellations at home and

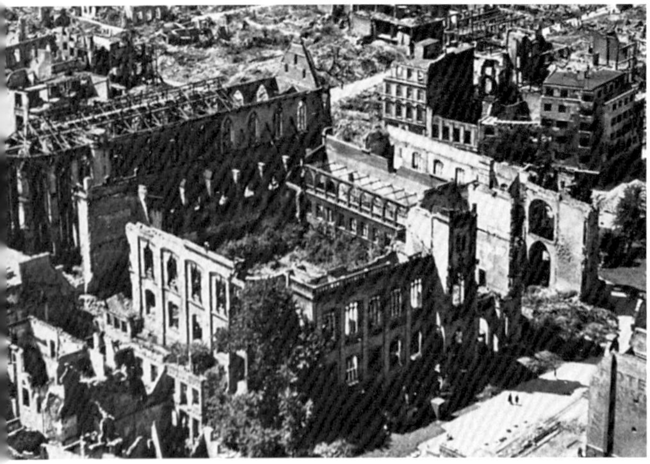

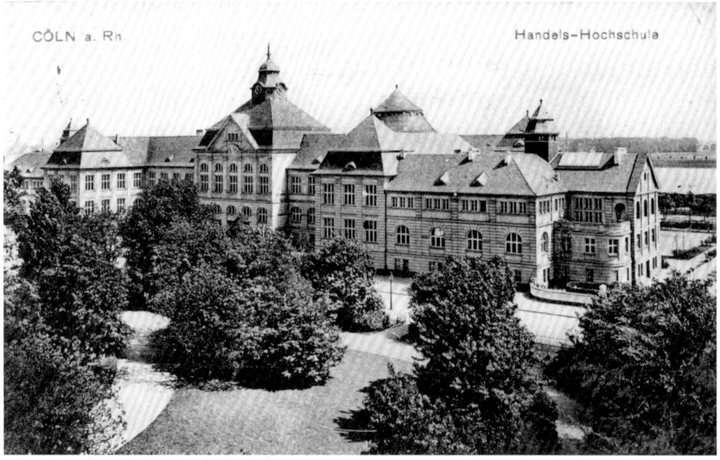

abroad under such titles as 'Sammlung Haubrich', 'Deutsche Malerei des 20. Jahrhunderts', 'Künder unseres Jahrhunderts', 'Peintres Expressionistes' or 'Expressionismo'. The venues were Coblenz, Brunswick, Wuppertal, Stuttgart, Mannheim, Hamburg, Oldenburg, Wiesbaden, Munich, Düsseldorf, Münster, Aachen, Munich again, Hagen, Dortmund, Wuppertal and Düsseldorf once more, Bonn, Recklinghausen, Amsterdam, Eindhoven, Brussels, Zurich, Bielefeld, Luxembourg, Trier, Leverkusen, Hamm, Turin, Liège, Basle, Berlin and Paris. It was hailed as 'the one and only major "collection of leading Expressionists" to have been saved and passed on', as 'a valid representation of Brücke Expressionism',[79] and said to 'document the spirit of cultural reconstruction in Cologne and in Germany'.[80] It asserts, as Siegfried Gohr wrote, 'a sense of purpose in life beyond mere survival'. Gohr tells us that Haubrich's employment of art as a 'democratic instrument' fascinated younger collectors such as Peter Ludwig. In his opinion, it may be assumed that Ludwig 'was not only impressed by the passion of an older man for Modernism, but also and above all by the possibility of employing art to public effect'.[81] After nine years, the Haubrich Collection returned to Cologne and made its entrance into the reopened Wallraf-Richartz Museum in its new home designed by Rudolf Schwarz. Cologne was now a centre of classical Modernism that was the envy of other large cities.

After the Donation

Although a unique collection had been created, as the exhibitions showed, it should not be forgotten that a large proportion of the works of classical Modernism that are now in the Haubrich Collection were first bought after 1946 in collaboration with Dr. Leopold Reidemeister (1900–1987). Until his move to Berlin in 1957, Reidemeister was the director

left
The Wallraf-Richartz Museum after its destruction, 1943.

centre
The Alte Universität, Cologne (1915).

right
Haubrich and Lord Mayor Hermann Pünder at the opening of the exhibition,1946.

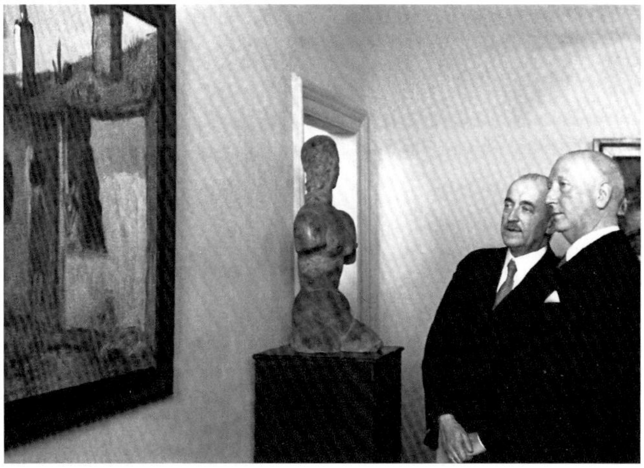

of the Wallraf-Richartz Museum and then (from 1954 on) of all the Cologne museums. Haubrich made his purchases in consultation with him, and in all likelihood many were made on Reidemeister's initiative.[82]

Many areas of classical Modernism came to be included during the post-war period that previously had not been of interest: Blauer Reiter (Alexej von Jawlensky), Bauhaus (Lyonel Feininger, Wassily Kandinsky) and Cubism (María Blanchard). But with a few exceptions, the Dada and Surrealist movements remained excluded. At the same time, works by a total of 110 contemporaries were bought which in many cases no longer have any real value for the museum. This means that although the collection was expanded, it lost its contour and came to resemble other museum holdings.

Ingrid Severin has shown that this process of mutual alignment was not without its problems: 'The controversial act of collecting contemporary art in the museum prior to 1933, which led to arguments and lively discussions, seems to have been settled in one fell swoop in 1945.' Short shrift was often given to the revolutionary paintings and artists, who were only re-discovered much later. This was the case not only in Cologne: the whole of Germany after 1945 was under the sway of 'the broadest conformity'. 'Preference was given to the Modernism that one had personally championed and witnessed.' A 'little appreciated Modernism' was to be rehabilitated, a former condition reinstated. 'This regressive, restorative approach to the reappropriation of cultural goods can be charted for over ten years in Cologne'.[83]

The concept of Modernism represented in this and other cities was therefore an abbreviated one and not always the subject of much reflection. Be that as it may, the enormous artistic importance from our present standpoint of (northern German) Expressionism remained the core of the collection. And a number of spectacular buys were to follow: **Five Women on the Street** (acquired 1947) and **An Artists' Group**

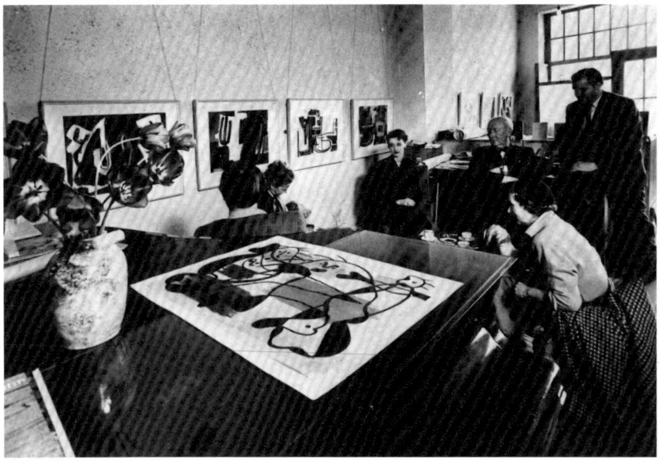

left
A meeting of the Friends of the Galerie der Spiegel, 1953.
From left: Hubert Berke, Eva Stünke, Dorothee Schwarz, Haubrich, Ms. Hossdorf, Hein Stünke.

right
The presentation of the Haubrich Collection in the new Wallraf-Richartz Museum building, 1958.

(1952) by Ernst Ludwig Kirchner, **Self-Portrait** (1948) by Paula Modersohn-Becker and the **Green Sofa** (1953) by Max Pechstein, which at that time was exhibited to show what is now seen as the back of the painting, **The Artist's Wife**.

Some of the works which were purchased up into the 1950s were also part of the 'Degenerate Art' campaign. In 1945, the art dealer Ferdinand Möller had a sizable number of the works which he had acquired on an exchange basis at Schloss Schönhausen, and which he still had for sale.[84] Although Haubrich had been in contact with Möller earlier and made him an offer for these artworks,[85] purchases of paintings from him for the Haubrich Collection are only first recorded in the post-war years. The works that came from the 'Degenerate Art' campaign and that were acquired through Möller's gallery are Kirchner's so-called **An Artists' Group** (formerly of the Nationalgalerie Berlin), **The Heathens** by Kokoschka (Stadtmuseum Dresden) and **Towers above the City** by Feininger (Staatliche Galerie Moritzburg, Halle).

Likewise a number of the pictures confiscated by the Nazis also went up for sale at auction rooms. In 1949, the Wallraf-Richartz Museum acquired the **Portrait of Doctor Eduard Plietzsch** by George Grosz at the Stuttgarter Kunstkabinett Roman Norbert Ketterer, which had received the work from Wilma Zelck and Albert Daberkow. At that same auction, Hans Melchers acquired the painting **Larkspur in the Window** by Karl Schmidt-Rottluff. In 1951 they sold it on to the Wallraf-Richartz Museum.

A total of twelve paintings from the 'Degenerate Art' campaign are in the collection. Similar numbers are to be found in other museums. One consequence that arose from the campaign was a system of mutual exchange, because after the Second World War, works that had been impounded from museums in 1937 often returned in roundabout ways to public collections. But only rarely was it possible for a museum to re-acquire a work that had been confiscated from its collection.

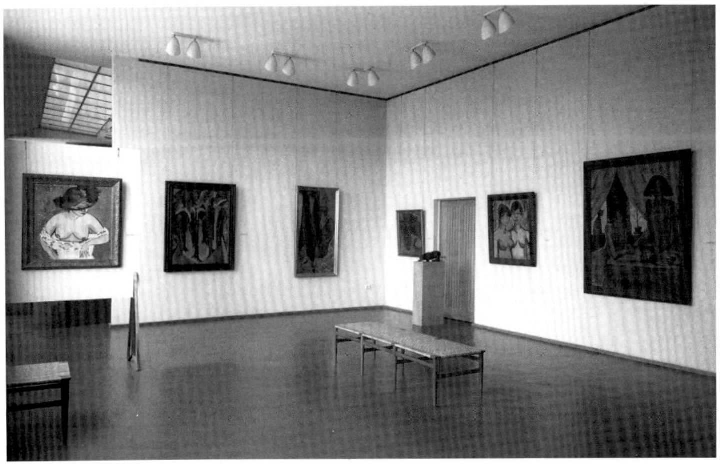

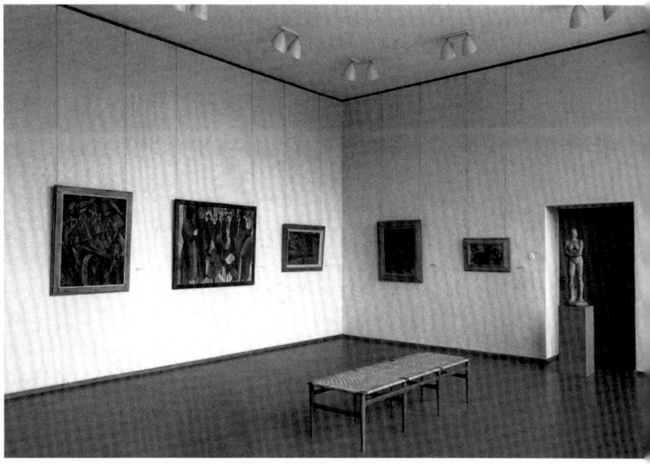

It is conspicuous that up until 1946, Haubrich purchased works almost exclusively in the Rhineland – even though as a good European he travelled a great deal and had, as already mentioned, assisted Förster in art purchases abroad. Only once he began to collaborate with museum director Reidemeister was the collection expanded by purchases from other regions, such as **Five Women on the Street** (from Galerie Franke in Munich) and Jawlensky's **Still Life with Vase and Jug** (from the Frankfurter Kunstkabinett run by Hanna Bekker vom Rath). The collection came to consist of works that Haubrich donated in 1946 and later to the museum, as well as of acquisitions purchased with the Haubrich Fund, not least from newly established galleries such as Änne Abels, Werner Rusche and Der Spiegel.

As a member of numerous juries and as deputy chairman of the Kölnischer Kunstverein, Haubrich continued to exert a major influence on artistic life in the city. His word had weight. He pushed through the purchase of Ernst Wilhelm Nay's **White Bull**, which the city council had been reluctant to buy.[86] He also accepted an offer from the Gerling Concern to donate two busts by Arno Breker to the collection. Reidemeister however declined the offer – for artistic and not political reasons.[87] Moreover, he received a number of works as presents from artists and bought others directly from them.[88]

In addition, Haubrich possessed several works that do not reside today in Museum Ludwig. He kept a few back for his private collection, and he had already parted with several before he made his donation.[89] With Haubrich's consent, a number of works were returned to him after the donation in 1946 because they were deemed unsuitable for a museum.[90] Moreover, some works were sold to raise funds for new purchases. Thus on 1 December 1946, the Kölnischer Kunstverein took on works from the collection for sale.[91]

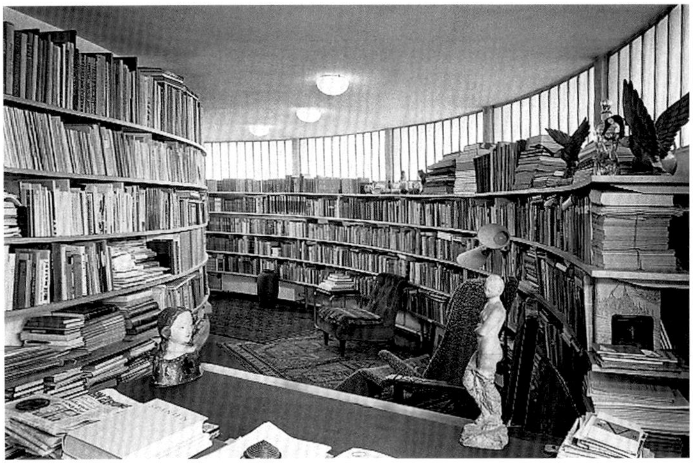

left
Haubrich's library in the rotunda, 1959.

right
Haubrich's house in Cologne-Müngersdorf with the 1951 rotunda designed by Wilhelm Riphahn, 1959.

Collectors in Comparison

Josef Haubrich was in two ways an extraordinary collector: he did not have unlimited means, and he did not want to keep the works for himself but saw himself right from the start as a benefactor. The first fact, his comparatively modest purse, probably went a long way to determining the structure of the collection and to making his main focus truly appealing to him, because he simply did not have the money for choice pieces from the Middle Ages and Renaissance, or such like. So the fact that his main focus came to be directed to Expressionist watercolours probably had *not only* artistic reasons.

Other collectors, such as the aforementioned Herbert von Garvens-Garvensburg, had far greater financial resources. Garvens, the son of a wealthy industrialist, proved himself all in all to be an open-minded, international and daring collector (he was early in collecting outsider art). After being turned down by Adenauer, he did not, as far as we know, make any further attempt to donate his collection, and after his death in 1957 it was scattered to the winds.[92]

Compared to Haubrich, the woman collector Ida Bienert showed a greater willingness to take risks. The daughter of a rich textile industrialist and wife of a Dresden manufacturer, she was introduced to modern art by the poet Theodor Däubler, whom she supported. 'The Bienert's home ... saw a steady coming and going of all the young, revolutionary and progressive spirits in the city's cultural circles'.[93] She began collecting around 1905, initially Cubism, later Bauhaus, and from 1925 she turned to the Constructivists. One of the main features of her collection of forty-six oil paintings, fifty-seven watercolours and gouaches were works by Paul Klee and Wassily Kandinsky. She lent a number of pieces to the Bayerische Staatsgemäldesammlungen, and dismantled her collection some time before her death in 1965.

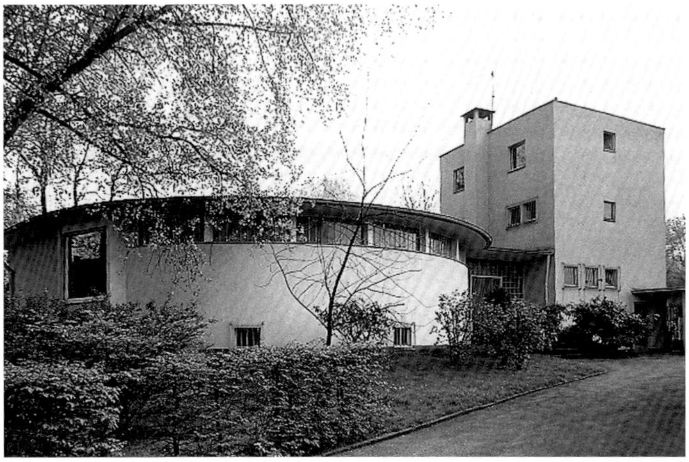

The example of the silk manufacturer Hermann Lange, one of the foremost private collectors of his day, demonstrates that it was possible to enthuse about modern art without being in any way 'revolutionary and progressive'. Lange rose to become a member of the board of the *Reichsverband der deutschen Industrie* (the German Chamber of Industry). Karoline Hille writes: 'It was one of the strange curiosities of modern art that while the cosmopolitan entrepreneur Lange was a "big shot" at the Ministry of Finance during Nazi rule, at the same time he openly surrounded himself with "degenerate" art in his villa, where he regularly held work meetings with the Nazi elite.'[94]

Unlike Bienert or Lange, Karl Ernst Osthaus, one of the best-known collectors of the last century, had decidedly social aims: 'The more people participate in art, the greater the social bond. And striving for this is a social act. Mediation becomes the responsibility of the museums.'[95] This is very much the way Haubrich expressed himself when he donated his collection. Originally, the Folkwang Museum, which was opened in 1902 by Osthaus, the scion of a family of bankers and industrial magnates, also contained exhibits from the natural sciences and applied arts. With time, the museum came to concentrate on the latest in art and assumed a pioneer role in this field. 'For Nolde, Kandinsky, Kokoschka, Marc and Kirchner, the Museum Folkwang became the first to acquire their works for its collection – just as previously it had done with van Gogh, Matisse and Hodler.'[96]

After 1933, Klaus Graf von Baudissin brought the Folkwang Museum in line with the NSDAP 'by at once arranging for recent art to be eliminated if it contradicted the spirit of National Socialist art policy'.[97] He took part in the first raids performed by the confiscation committee, as for example in the Wallraf-Richartz Museum. Even prior to 1937, Baudissin had not only re-hung the collection at the Folkwang Museum and put aside all of the examples of 'decadent art', but had also sold an unloved piece: Kandinsky's

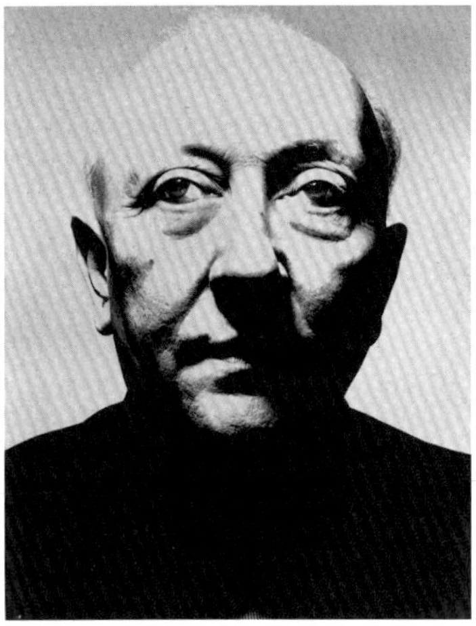

Portrait by Chargesheimer, 1956.

Improvisation 28 passed into the hands of the Guggenheim Museum in New York.[98] Apart from this, he rescinded the membership of the Jewish affiliates to the museum's support society.[99]

While all this was occurring in Germany, private collectors alone had the possibility of buying unwanted artworks. Bernhard and Margrit Sprengel, he a chocolate manufacturer, she a violinist, had scarcely been interested in the visual arts prior to the 'Degenerate Art' exhibition, but contrary to the intention of the organizers, they were all aflame after the exhibition. With the help of the gallerist Günther Franke, over the following years they purchased almost 600 German Expressionist works, a scarcely unbelievable number. But unlike Haubrich, they had at times to contend with real fears. Thus in reaction to the German invasion of Poland in 1939 they returned a sculpture to Franke by Ernst Barlach, who had been threatened by the Nazis even prior to 1933. Bernhard Sprengel wrote to Franke: 'Apart from which you will understand that I cannot decide at the moment to take the figure by Barlach. Is it enough when I say that the figure has given us so much pleasure we would be happy to have it once things have returned to normal?'[100]

The musician Willy Hahn, from 1923 onwards répétiteur and then conductor of various orchestras and freelance musician at the Berliner Rundfunk, was a collector who had even fewer resources than Haubrich. As his son Peter writes, he began buying 'works of what is now called "classical" Modernism early on, around 1920, often by chance and at what today were fantastically low prices; but later he lost most of the works, partly due to economic reasons, partly because he thought he had found, or genuinely had found something better, sometimes out of pure inquisitiveness or because he was taken in by a forgery. Appreciable war losses did the rest. He tried to make up for the gaps, in whatever circumstances he found himself. One of them was the bizarre NS campaign "Degenerate Art". Quite contrary to the wishes of its instigators, it presented an intrepid buyer like

With German President Theodor Heuss, 1959.

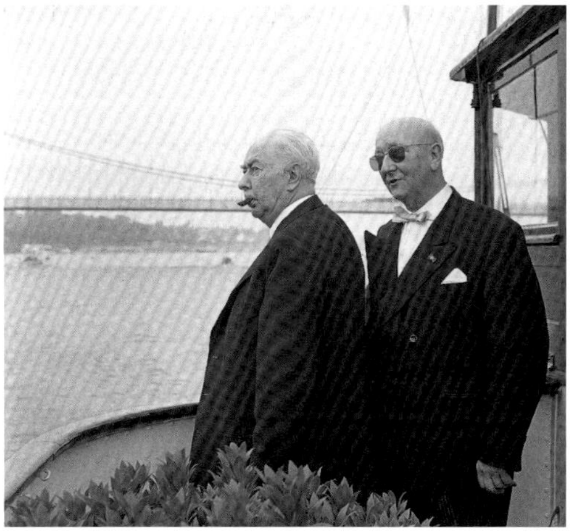

Hahn with the chance to buy works by decried artists, not infrequently of top quality, that previously had been publicly owned. Is one to blame him for profiting from an infamous deed? Or might the works otherwise have been destroyed, as really happened thousands of times over? It is impossible to decide with any complete certainty'.[101]

Everyone who bought modern art during the Nazi era – including Josef Haubrich – acted in a moral limbo. But it would have been more than questionable if one of these people enthralled by Modernism had denied their passion after 1933, or aligned his or her preferences with those of the new rulers. Haubrich did not allow himself be intimidated, despite the many rebuffs and threats, and ultimately he ensured that a city whose lords and masters had been dismissive of the new art in the 1920s nevertheless received an important collection of classical Modernism. All subsequent developments in the world of art in Cologne rest on these foundations.

1 Horst Keller, entry 'Haubrich, Josef', in *Neue Deutsche Biographie*, vol. 8, Berlin 1969, p. 73f. The authors wish to thank Erec Gellautz for his kind assistance during their research.
2 'Die Diskontierung von Buchforderungen'; see Peter Fuchs, 'Die Biographie', in Fuchs (ed.), *Josef Haubrich. Sammler und Stifter*, Cologne 1959, pp. 17–47, here p. 21.
3 Josef Haubrich, 'Schicksale meiner Sammlung', in Heinz Ladendorf and Horst Vey (eds.), *Mouseion. Studien aus Kunst und Geschichte für Otto H. Förster*, Cologne 1960, pp. 296–300, here p. 296.
4 Ibid.
5 Paul F. Schmidt, 'Gibt es noch Mäzene?', in *Die neue Linie*, 3/1931. Our thanks to Rainer Stamm for drawing our attention to this publication.
6 Hans Schmitt-Rost, *Josef Haubrich. Ein Freund.* Published by the Friends of the Wallraf-Richartz Museum, Cologne 1963, unpaginated.
7 Haubrich in his own words in *Köln, die Sonderbund-Ausstellung und der Expressionismus*, MS, 1950, Archiv Museum Ludwig, p. 2. Published under the title 'Umgang mit modernen Malern. Kultur, die nicht nur von Vergangenem zehrt', in: *Die Zeit*, 37 / 1950.
8 Haubrich 1950, unpaginated.
9 See Toni Feldenkirchen, 'Die Sammlung Haubrich', in: *Zeitschrift für Kunst*, 2 / 1947, cited here from Peter Fuchs (ed.), *Josef Haubrich. Sammler und Stifter*, Cologne, 1959, pp. 51–68, here p. 63; in addition Luise Straus-Ernst, 'Die Sammlung Haubrich in Köln', in *Kunstblatt*, 11/1927, pp. 25–34, here p. 34.
10 Dr. Ludwig Josef (Josef Haubrich), 'Bildende Kunst in Köln', in: *Rheinische Zeitung*, 15 December 1926. The name Behns has been given mistakenly as 'Fritz Berlin'.
11 Dr. Ludwig Josef (Josef Haubrich), 'Bildende Kunst in Köln', in: *Rheinische Zeitung*, 28 October 1927.
12 Dr. Ludwig Josef (Josef Haubrich), 'Bildende Kunst in Köln', in: *Rheinische Zeitung*, 6 February 1928.
13 Wolfgang Braunfels, 'Ein Sammler des deutschen Expressionismus. In Memoriam Josef Haubrich', in *Wallraf-Richartz-Jahrbuch*, 24 / 1962, pp. 375–380, here p. 376.
14 Fuchs, 'Die Biographie', op. cit., p. 27.
15 Braunfels, op. cit., p. 377.
16 Josef Haubrich created a filing card for every work he purchased prior to 1945. These list the main details, such as title, year of origin, dimensions and technique, together with the price, the previous owner and places where it had been exhibited or reproduced. Regrettably these cards vary in exactitude and are only partly preserved as copies. The originals cannot be consulted for the foreseeable future as a result of the disaster at the Historisches Archiv Köln.
17 Ottfried Dascher, 'Es ist etwas Wahnsinniges mit der Kunst', in *Alfred Flechtheim. Sammler, Kunsthändler, Verleger*, Wädenswil 2011, p. 163.
18 Toni Feldenkirchen, *Über den Kölnischen Kunstverein und anderes*, Cologne 1978, p. 178.
19 Historisches Archiv der Stadt Köln (HAStK), Best. 1639, Nr. 30, kindly placed at our disposal by Pascal Räderscheidt.
20 HAStK, Best. 1385, Nr. 1. statutory declaration by Johanna Freundlich neé. Kloss, kindly placed at our disposal by Wolfgang Schöddert.
21 Stadtmuseum Köln, estate of Schmitt-Rost, invitation card.
22 Andreas Becker, 'Mäzen der Moderne', in Peter Fuchs (ed.), *Josef Haubrich. Sammler und Stifter*, Cologne 1959, p. 57–68, here p. 62.
23 Feldenkirchen 1978, p. 177.
24 Schmitt-Rost, op. cit., unpaginated.
25 Letter from Josef Haubrich to the Arbeitsamt der Stadt Köln, 4 October 1942, HAStK, cited here from Daniela Wilmes, 'Privates Sammeln mit Kalkül. Aspekte der Sammeltätigkeit von Josef Haubrich im Nationalsozialismus', in Ute Haug und Maike Steinkamp (eds.), *Werke und Werte. Über das Handeln und Sammeln von Kunst im Nationalsozialismus*, Berlin 2010, p. 147–165, here p. 164.
26 Agnes von der Borch, 'Die nationalsozialitischen Aktionen "Entartete Kunst" in Köln und anderen Orten Deutschlands', in Gerhard Kolberg (ed.), *Die Expressionisten vom Aufbruch bis zur Verfemung*, Cologne 1996, pp. 292–301, here p. 299.
27 Becker, op. cit., p. 64.
28 Katja Terlau, 'Das Wallraf-Richartz-Museum und seine Ankaufspolitik 1933–1954. Vorläufiger Forschungsbericht', in *Wallraf-Richartz-Jahrbuch*, 2001,

pp. 277–292, here p. 281.

29 Ibid., p. 285. See also Beatrix Alexander, '"Verkaufslustige Neigung" – Gemäldeverkäufe aus dem Besitz der Stadt Köln', in *Jahrbuch des Kölnischen Geschichtsvereins*, 19 / 2009, pp. 101–122, here p. 110.

30 Terlau, op. cit., p. 283.

31 Haubrich 1960, p. 297.

32 Max Liebermann's works *Des Künstlers Tochter Käthe zu Pferde* (The Artist's Daughter Käthe on Horseback) of 1913 and *Der barmherzige Samariter* (The Good Samaritan) from 1911.

33 Wilmes, op. cit., p. 160.

34 Schmitt-Rost, op. cit., unpaginated.

35 'Paul Multhaupt 1884–1933', online with a reproduction of the card at http://www.raederscheidt.com/Paul_Multhaupt.html (last accessed on 14 April 2012). Multhaupt committed suicide on 19 January 1933 on account of his financial worries, so it may be assumed that the showing of the collection was intended as a sales exhibition.

36 Hendrik, 'Abgetakeltes Mäzenatentum. Wie Flechtheim und Kaesbach deutsche Kunst machten', *Volksparole*, 1 April 1933, cited here from Peter Springer, 'Alfred Flechtheim, Ein Kunsthändler neuen Typs', in Henrike Junge (ed.), *Avantgarde und Publikum. Zur Rezeption avantgardistischer Kunst in Deutschland 1905–1933* Cologne, Weimar, Vienna 1992, pp. 79–91, here p. 88f.

37 See Wilmes, op. cit., p. 164, as well as Dascher op. cit., p. 299.

38 Ralph Jentsch surmises that Vömel had already applied to join in 1933. See Ralph Jentsch, *Alfred Flechtheim und George Grosz, Zwei deutsche Schicksale*, Bonn 2008, p. 42.

39 *Westfälische Landeszeitung*, 4 December 1935.

40 Dascher, op. cit., p. 296.

41 HAStK Köln, Best. 1396 Nr. 30, kindly placed at our disposal by Pascal Räderscheidt.

42 Picture files for Emil Nolde, *Junge Frau und Männer* (1919), and Marc Chagall, *Sabbath* (1910), Archiv Museum Ludwig.

43 This work is part of an extensive restitution claim by Flechtheim's heirs for the loss of a private collection under persecution. Extensive research is currently being undertaken by Dr. Roswitha Neu-Kock to clarify the circumstances.

44 Wilmes, op. cit., p. 164.

45 See Gesa Jeuthe: *Kunstwerte im Wandel. Die Preisentwicklung der deutschen Moderne im nationalen und internationalen Kunstmarkt 1925 bis 1955*, Berlin 2011, p. 321.

46 Katrin Vester, 'Herbert von Garvens-Garvensburg, Sammler, Galerist und Förderer der Modernen Kunst in Hannover', in Henrike Junge (ed.), *Avantgarde und Publikum. Zur Rezeption avantgardistischer Kunst in Deutschland 1905–1933*, Cologne, Weimar, Vienna 1992, pp. 95–102, here p. 99.

47 See also Ingrid Severin, 'Bausteine für die Museen nach 1945. Die Sammlungen Haubrich – Sprengel – Reemtsma', in Ekkehard Mai und Peter Paret with assistance from Ingrid Severin (eds.), *Sammler, Stifter und Museen. Kunstförderung in Deutschland im 19. und 20. Jahrhundert*, Cologne, Weimar, Vienna 1993, pp. 265–329, here p. 271.

48 Straus-Ernst, op. cit., p. 25. See Gabriele Werner, 'Otto Dix – der Krieg', in Jörg Duppler and Georg P. Groß (eds.), *Kriegsende 1918. Ereignis, Wirkung, Nachwirkung*, Munich 1999, pp. 299–314, here p. 310.

49 Fuchs, 'Die Biographie', op. cit., p. 22.

50 Ibid., p. 24.

51 Wilmes, op. cit., p. 150

52 Ute Haug, *Der Kölnische Kunstverein. Struktur und Entwicklung einer Kunstinstitution in der kulturpolitischen Landschaft des 'Dritten Reichs'*, Aachen 1998, p. 29. Online publication, http://sylvester.bth.rwth.aachen.de/dissertationen/2002/072/index.htm (last accessed on 14 April 2012). Haubrich himself says he was already active on the board of the Kölnischer Kunstverein in 1923. See Johann Jakob Hässlin, *Kunstliebendes Köln. Dokumente und Berichte aus hundertfünfzig Jahren*, Munich 1957, p. 204.

53 Ibid.; Feldenkirchen 1978, p. 53.

54 Terlau, op. cit., p. 284. A list of the confiscated works may be found in Siegfried Gohr (ed.), *Museum Ludwig Köln. Gemälde, Skulpturen, Environments vom Expressionismus bis zur Gegenwart. Bestandskatalog*, vol. 2, Munich 1986, p. 290f.

55 Ina Conzen, Vera Klawitz (eds.), *Staatsgalerie Stuttgart. Die Sammlung. Meisterwerke vom 14. bis zum 21. Jahrhundert*, Munich 2008, p. 14.

56 Ibid., p. 13.
57 Hubertus Gaßner and Uwe M. Schneede (eds.), *Die Sammlungen der Hamburger Kunsthalle. vol. IV, Die Gemälde der klassischen Moderne*, Hamburg 2010, p. 7.
58 Ulrike Lorenz (ed.), *Kunsthalle Mannheim. Vergangenheit, Gegenwart, Zukunft*, Mannheim 2010, p. 28.
59 Kunsthalle Mannheim (ed.), *Entartete Kunst. Beschlagnahmeaktionen in der Städtischen Kunsthalle Mannheim*, Heidelberg 1983, p. 39.
60 Klaus-Peter Schuster, 'Die Geburt der Nation aus dem Geist der Kunst', in Schuster (ed.), *Die Neue Nationalgalerie*, Cologne, Berlin 2003, pp. 7–39, here p. 29.
61 Of approx. 20,000 confiscated works, roughly fifty percent passed through the hands of art dealers, some 7,500 works were destroyed, 180 were returned to their owners, while 2,600 works, which must have still existed at the end of the war, have gone missing. See Hüneke, op. cit., p. 96.
62 As an art dealer, Hildebrand Gurlitt entertained good relationships abroad and was ensconced in the role of official buyer of artworks for the Führermuseum in Linz in 1942.
63 Stadtarchiv Düsseldorf, Kunstverein für die Rheinlande und Westfalen, Depositum 4-159.
64 Evelyn Weiss, 'Schicksal eines Bildes', in Kulturstiftung der Länder, Museum Ludwig (ed.), *Otto Mueller. Zwei weibliche Halbakte*, Cologne 2001, pp. 5–17.
65 Fuchs, 'Die Biographie', op. cit., p. 34.
66 NRW Hauptstaatsarchiv Düsseldorf NW 1948 Nr. 157. (Josef Haubrich, 'Anlage zum Fragebogen vom 2. Januar 1946', MS.)
67 Fuchs, 'Die Biographie', op. cit., p. 35.
68 Marie Hüllenkremer, 'Als ich zehn war, wurde unser Haus ganz auf Kunst umgestellt'. (Interview mit Ruth 'Wiesel' Cramer und Karl-Heinz Cramer), *Kölner Stadt-Anzeiger*, 30 May 1996.
69 Haubrich, 'Anlage', op. cit., unpaginated.
70 'A household is Jewish (para. 3 of the act) when a Jewish man is head of the household or belongs to the house', cited from 'Erste Verordnung zur Ausführung des Gesetzes zum Schutze des deutschen Blutes und der deutschen Ehre. Vom 14. November 1935', *Deutsches Reichsgesetzblatt*, 1935, pp. 1334–1336, here p. 1335.
71 Haubrich 1960, p. 297.
72 Fuchs, 'Die Biographie', op. cit., p. 35.
73 Braunfels, op. cit., p. 378. The entire Haubrich Graphic Collection has been published in Alfred M. Fischer (ed.), *Meisterblätter aus der Sammlung Haubrich. Josef Haubrich zum 100. Geburtstag* (exh. cat, Museum Ludwig), Cologne 1989.
74 Ibid., p. 39.
75 Of the 14 drawings, one (Cat. Rais. 1662) is now in the Museum of Modern Art, New York, and three (Cat. Rais. 308, 437, 3954) are in private collections. It is not certain in the other cases which drawings they were, only those mentioned have been identified to date.
76 Haubrich during the negotiations with the Stadtverordneten-Versammlung in Cologne, 6th session, 2 May 1946, cited in Severin op. cit., p. 272.
77 Leopold Reidemeister: 'Ansprache anläßlich der Eröffnung der Sammlung Haubrich.', in 'Leopold Reidemeister zum Gedenken'. *Brücke-Archiv*, 15/16/ 1988, pp. 50-53, here p. 51.
78 Fuchs, 'Die Biographie', op. cit., p. 43.
79 Ibid., p. 276 und 278.
80 Leopold Reidemeister, (foreword), in *Sammlung Haubrich* (exh. cat., Alte Universität), Cologne 1946, p. 3f., here p. 3.
81 Siegfried Gohr, 'Sammler sammeln – Ein Bericht', in Gohr (ed.), *Wahre Wunder. Sammler & Sammlungen im Rheinland* (exh. cat. Museum Ludwig), Cologne 2001, pp. 184–191, here p. 186.
82 Cf. Leopold Reidemeister, 'Wiederaufbau – Wiedergutmachung. Ein Bericht', in 'Leopold Reidemeister zum Gedenken', *Brücke-Archiv*, 15/16 1988, pp. 36-46, especially p. 38ff.
83 See Ingrid Severin, 'Tendenzen einer Erinnerungspolitik. Ankäufe und Ausstellungen der Museen nach 1945', in Dieter Breuer und Gertrude Cepl-Kaufmann (eds.), *Öffentlichkeit der Moderne. Die Moderne in der Öffentlichkeit. Das Rheinland 1945–60*, Essen, 2000, pp. 475–505, here p. 479f.
84 The Act for the Sequestration of Products of Degenerate Art *(Gesetz über Einziehung von Erzeugnissen entarteter Kunst)* was never repealed after the war, neither by the Allied Control Council, nor later by the Federal Republic. One may thus conclude that confisca-

tion was within the law so long as the artworks were in the possession of state museums. Thus the acquisitions of 'degenerate' art made by the four art dealers were legally valid and trade with 'degenerate' art continued, as in Möller's case, after 1945. See Carl-Heinz Heuer, *Die eigentumsrechtliche Problematik der 'entarteten' Kunst*, information brochure, *Forschungsstelle 'Entartete Kunst'*, Berlin and Hamburg, undated.

85 Berlinische Galerie. Galerie Ferdinand Möller. Microfilm (BG.GFM-MF)-5314,353.

86 Archiv Museum Ludwig, picture file ML 76/ 2954.

87 Archiv Museum Ludwig, picture files ML 76/SK0092 and ML 76/SK0091 (latter handed over in 1957 to the Stadtmuseum KSM 1982/571).

88 In this way works by Jankel Adler, Buja Bingemer, Marc Chagall, Otto Dix, Ludwig Gies, Johannes Greferath, Erich Heckel, Peter Herkenrath, Heinrich August Hußmann, Dietmar Lemcke, Gerhard Marcks, Henry Moore, Theodor Caspar Pilartz, Richard Seewald, Guido Strazza and Hans Werdehausen entered the collection.

89 Cf. Haubrich's index card on ML 76/2759, Emil Nolde, *Rote und gelbe Rosen*. Haubrich acquired this work in exchange for Max Liebermann's *Tiergartenallee*.

90 Archiv Museum Ludwig, Akte Haubrich.

91 Geheimes Staatsarchiv Preußischer Kulturbesitz (GStA-PK), Nachlass Reidemeister, Anhang Severin Nr. 2.

92 Vester, op. cit., p. 100.

93 Henrike Junge, 'Vom Neuen begeistert – die Sammlerin Ida Bienert', in Junge (ed.), *Avantgarde und Publikum. Zur Rezeption avantgardistischer Kunst in Deutschland 1905–1933*, Cologne, Weimar, Vienna 1992, pp. 29–37, here p. 29.

94 Karoline Hille, '"Und vielleicht wird mich Europa lieben und mit ihm mein Russland". Der Grenzgänger Marc Chagall', in Ada Raev and Isabel Wünsche (eds.), *Kursschwankungen. Russische Kunst im Wertesystem der europäischen Moderne*, Berlin 2007, pp. 112–119, here p. 116.

95 Karl Ernst Osthaus, 'Über die Aufgabe der Museen', in Wilhelm R. Valentiner (ed.), *Umgestaltung der Museen im Sinne der neuen Zeit*, Berlin 1919, p. 83, cited here from Monika Lahme-Schlenger, 'Karl Ernst Osthaus und die Folkwang-Idee', in Henrike Junge (ed.), *Avantgarde und Publikum. Zur Rezeption avantgardistischer Kunst in Deutschland 1905–1933*, Cologne, Weimar, Vienna 1992, pp. 225–233, here p. 229.

96 Rainer Stamm, 'Karl Ernst Osthaus, Eine Sammlungsgeschichte der Moderne', in Museum Folkwang Essen (ed.), *'Das Schönste Museum der Welt' – Museum Folkwang bis 1933*, Essen/Göttingen 2010, pp. 155–167, here p. 165.

97 Conzen, Klawitz, op. cit., p. 14. See. Mario-Andreas von Lüttichau, 'Der Verlust der Moderne', in Museum Folkwang Essen (ed.), *'Das Schönste Museum der Welt' – Museum Folkwang bis 1933*, Essen/Göttingen 2010, pp. 201–212, here p. 209.

98 Lüttichau, op. cit., p. 206ff.

99 See Georg W. Klötzsch, *Phoenix Folkwang. Die Meisterwerke*, Cologne 2002, p. 38f.

100 Letter from Bernhard Sprengel to Günther Franke, 2 September 1939, cited in Vanessa-Maria Voigt, 'Der Handel mit der Moderne "im Hinterstübchen". Günther Franke als Kunsthändler des Sammlerpaares Margrit und Bernhard Sprengel', in Ute Haug and Maike Steinkamp (eds.), *Werke und Werte. Über das Handeln und Sammeln von Kunst im Nationalsozialismus*, Berlin 2010, pp. 128–146, here p. 135.

101 Peter Hahn, 'Der sammelnde Musiker. Zur Biografie von Willy Hahn', in Peter Hahn, Birgit Dalbajewa and Agnes Matthias (eds.), *Kokoschka als Zeichner. Die Sammlung Willy Hahn* (exh. cat., Kupferstich-Kabinett Dresden, Museum der Moderne Salzburg), 2011/2012; Ostfildern 2011, pp. 11–21. The Haubrich Collection includes the work *Dreamers* by Emil Nolde, which Haubrich had purchased from Willy Hahn in 1924.

Masterpieces of the Haubrich Collection

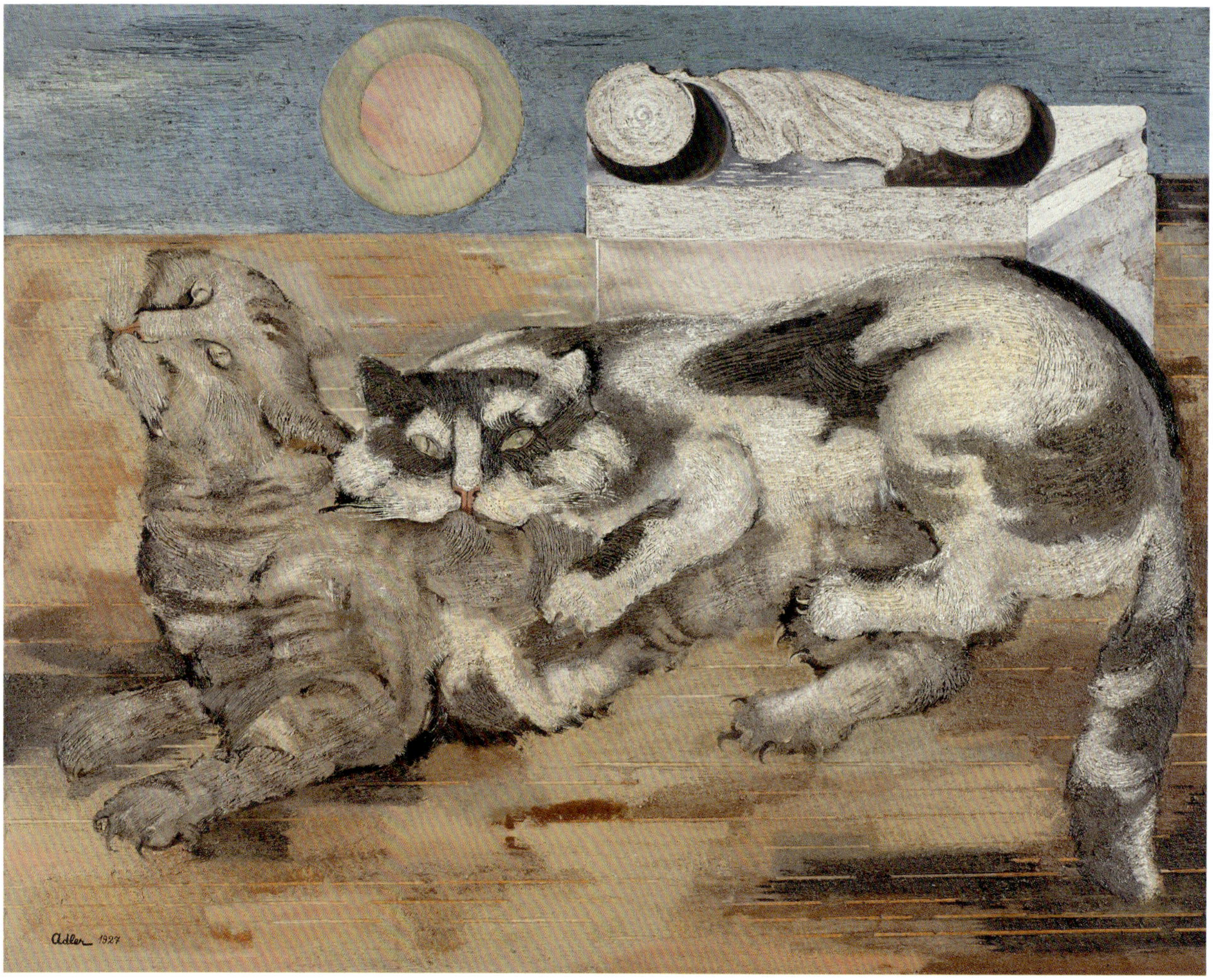

Cats
1927
Oil, chalk, sand on canvas
100.5 x 120.5 cm

Jankel Adler

Cats, 1927

Cats can be found everywhere in Jankel Adler's paintings from the 1920s. But in this picture they are not merely an attribute, an accoutrement or background figure. They are at the centre of the work which, despite the familiarity of the subject, seems strange. Two monumental beasts, more tigers than pussycats, are bristling with defiance against their elevation to symbolic realms. They will not force themselves into a pose, are not part of a historical tale, but are enough in themselves. Adler liberates the cats from kitsch, from the ornamental function they had been allotted in art history, and depicts them in their unrestrained animal brutishness. We are witness to an act of sexual conquest. With one bound, the tom seems to pounce on the female; he has her firmly in his teeth and is looking out of the picture with the resolute gaze of a conqueror.

The actual arrangement of the figures suggests gendered assignations. The tom is embedded in a somewhat classicist fragment of architecture (male), the she-cat in the earth (feminine). Both of them melt in colour and form into their respective backgrounds – even to the extent that Adler has mixed sand into the paint and given the picture a rough, but even, fresco-esque texture. Like other artists of the avant-garde, such as Willi Baumeister, he experimented with new materials without quite leaving the field of classical painting. He never departed for instance from figuration, even if the abstraction that can be seen in the landscape at the back is a profession of faith in anti-illusionist modernism. His paintings in the 1920s and 30s evince both: a feeling for tradition and a radical urge to modernize.

One year after they were done, the **Cats** were exhibited at the Deutsche Kunst Düsseldorf competition and awarded the gold medal. Adler, rooted in Düsseldorf's avant-garde art scene, was one of the celebrated artists of his day. The writer Else Lasker-Schüler wrote: 'Through the timeless jewel of this sublime art / Jankel Adler becomes the Hebrew Rembrandt'.[1]

But the political turn in 1933 meant that the Polish Jew – and later his family – lost their means of support in Germany. Urged to flee by his farsighted friends, his trail can be followed through France, Italy, Poland, Russia and the Balkans. While the work he left behind in Germany fell victim to the cultural vandalism of the regime, his art met with new recognition abroad. His works were shown in cities including New York, Warsaw, Paris and London. Stranded in England, Adler died unexpectedly in 1949. Germany remained for him a trauma; he never returned.

Lisa Weber

1 Quoted in Anna Klapheck, *Jankel Adler*, Recklinghausen 1966, p. 24.

Ernst Barlach

Singing Man, 1928

'Even the most serious of people feel at times that everything is but a game ...: joy that is the reason, joy that is the purpose of all being.'[1] By the middle of the 1920s, Ernst Barlach had found an unusually light, liberated tone. Up until then the sculptor, who was born in 1870 in Wedel near Hamburg, had been plunged time and again into prolonged crises by personal losses and his search for an artistic identity. But now Barlach was at the height of his career. After being accepted to the Prussian Academy of the Arts in 1919, he was soon to be honoured with large solo exhibitions in the Weimar Republic. His expressive wooden figures imbued with mental woes and vitality not only enthralled the experts; the State and the Church commissioned him with memorials in which he tackled the horrors of the First World War with great sensitivity.

In parallel with these commissions, Barlach developed in the seclusion of his studio in Güstrow a series of small sculptures, which included the **Singing Man**. This carefree work shows a seated man who is clutching one knee as he leans back and relaxes. His eyes closed and with a melody on his lips, he seems to be listening with pleasure to his tune. The motif had accompanied Barlach ever since his trip to Russia in 1906, which he went on following his studies in Hamburg, Dresden, Paris and Berlin. His encounters there with peasants, beggars and market women, which he captured in numerous sketches, would leave their mark on Barlach's oeuvre. From then on, he modelled the 'suffering, simple, wistful folk who, with yearnings beyond their means, are given to drink, song and music', and with whom he shared 'brotherly feelings'.[2] For all his fidelity to the human form, he preferred a clear, reduced line. Moreover, the diagonals and open axes give the **Singing Man** a sense of tension and simultaneously harmony. With this piece Barlach also explored the medium of bronze, which he had rarely used until then, and which he thought would enable him to capture 'the fleeting emotion in all its freshness'.[3]

Although Barlach was lauded as the re-discoverer of German Gothicism, he was already being vilified in nationalist circles. His opponents were to have their way during the Third Reich: over 400 of his works were lost from museums during the 'Degenerate Art' action in 1937, monuments were even destroyed, and the sculptor was banned from exhibiting. When Barlach died in 1938 at the age of 68 in Rostock, the artistic freedom for which he had fought so valiantly was long since unwelcome in Germany.

Isgard Kracht

1 Ernst Barlach to Karl Barlach, 19 April 1925, quoted in Friedrich Dross (ed.), *Ernst Barlach. Die Briefe II. 1925-1938.* Munich 1969, p. 21.
2 Ernst Barlach to Karl Barlach, 6 October 1920, quoted in Friedrich Dross (ed.), *Ernst Barlach. Die Briefe I. 1888-1924.* Munich 1968, p. 594.
3 Ernst Barlach to Alfred Flechtheim, 14 October 1930, quoted in Dross 1969, p. 232.

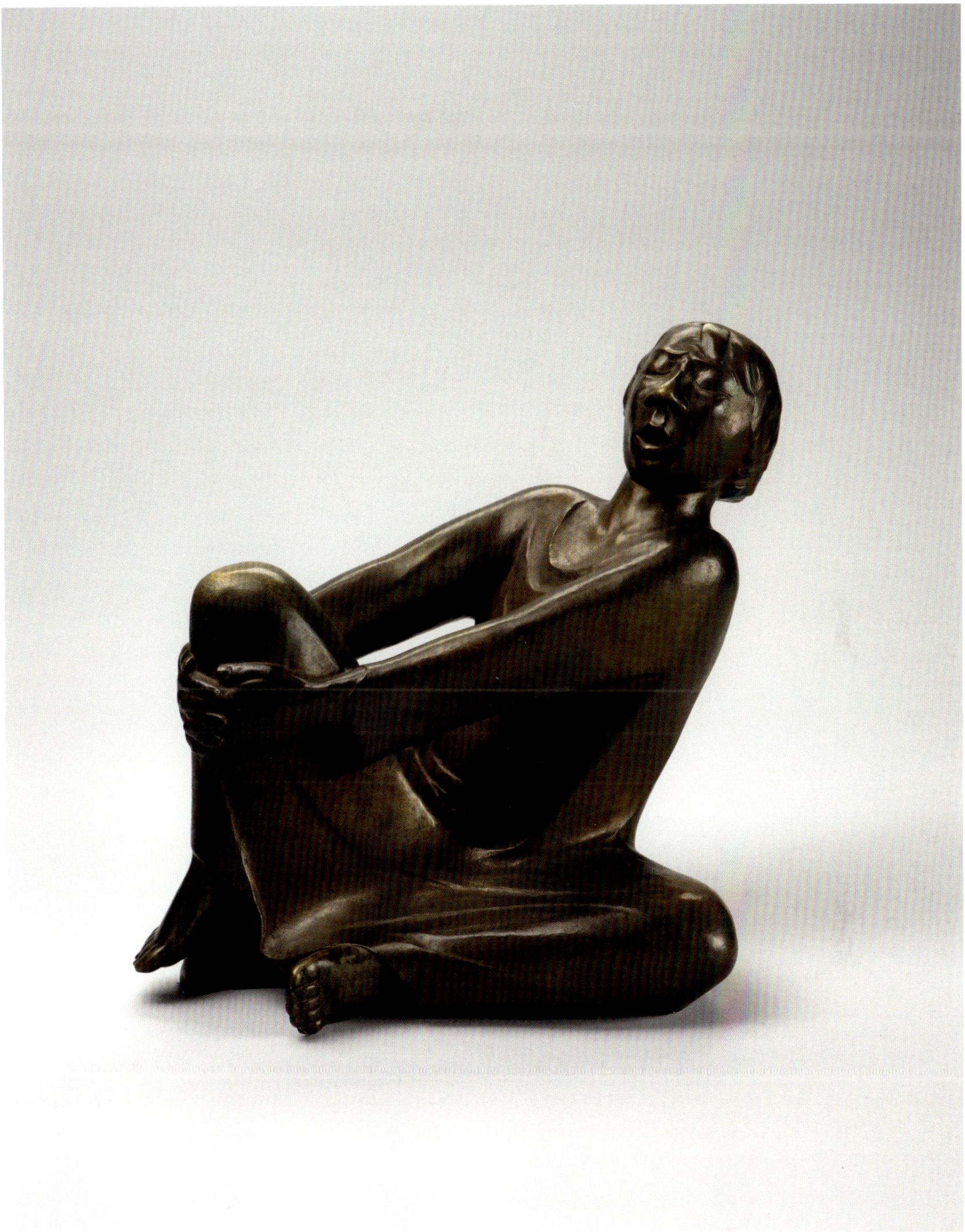

Singing Man
1928
Bronze
H.: 49 cm

Willi Baumeister

Standing Figure with Blue Patch, 1933

In 1928 Willi Baumeister became professor of typography at the Städelschule in Frankfurt am Main. In 1933 he created **Standing Figure with Blue Patch**, a painting that can be assigned to his series of *Line Pictures*. In this series he elevated the outline to a compositional theme in its own right while simultaneously moving on from geometric, Surrealist and Constructivist forms and approaching the surface in a more organic and flowing manner.

Baumeister almost always thought his formal concepts through in series of this kind. He would experiment with them till the point of exhaustion, always taking up one mode of design and one theme at a time. Thus, other variations on the Standing Figure can be found among his *Line Pictures*. Each individual work seems to be but one possibility among many, as is true of **Standing Figure with Blue Patch**.

The silhouette of the standing figure is gently embedded here in a rough, wall-like texture. Pushed into the background by the patch of blue are linear structures that seem to have been shaped according to the soft, almost blurred outline of the figure, albeit without providing any spatial coordinates. The impression arises of a temporal staggering in the motion that is articulated across the surface. Black lines running horizontally across the picture recall archaic blocks of texts.

Baumeister achieved the coarse quality of the picture surface by mixing sand into the matte brown paint. The contour of the figure is deeply incised into this masonry. Shaping the shadow of a line into a figure is an archaic idea. Baumeister had occupied himself since 1928 at the latest with prehistoric art, in particular with the formal language of cave paintings.

One of the first official acts performed by the National Socialist regime was to divest Baumeister of his professorship, and shortly thereafter he was branded a 'degenerate'. This caesura in his private and professional life, which forced him to take completely new stock of where he stood, did not affect his work, as can be seen from the date on the present piece. Officially a worker in a paint and dye factory, he continued his research and his art and completed the series of *Line Paintings* without any noticeable break. In 1945 he received a professorship in Stuttgart and became a formative figure in the German art world. The subject of the archaic and the unconscious that is so apparent in his *Line Paintings* was also explored in his book *Das Unbekannte in der Kunst* – one of the most-discussed books by an artist in the post-war era.

Lorena Jonas

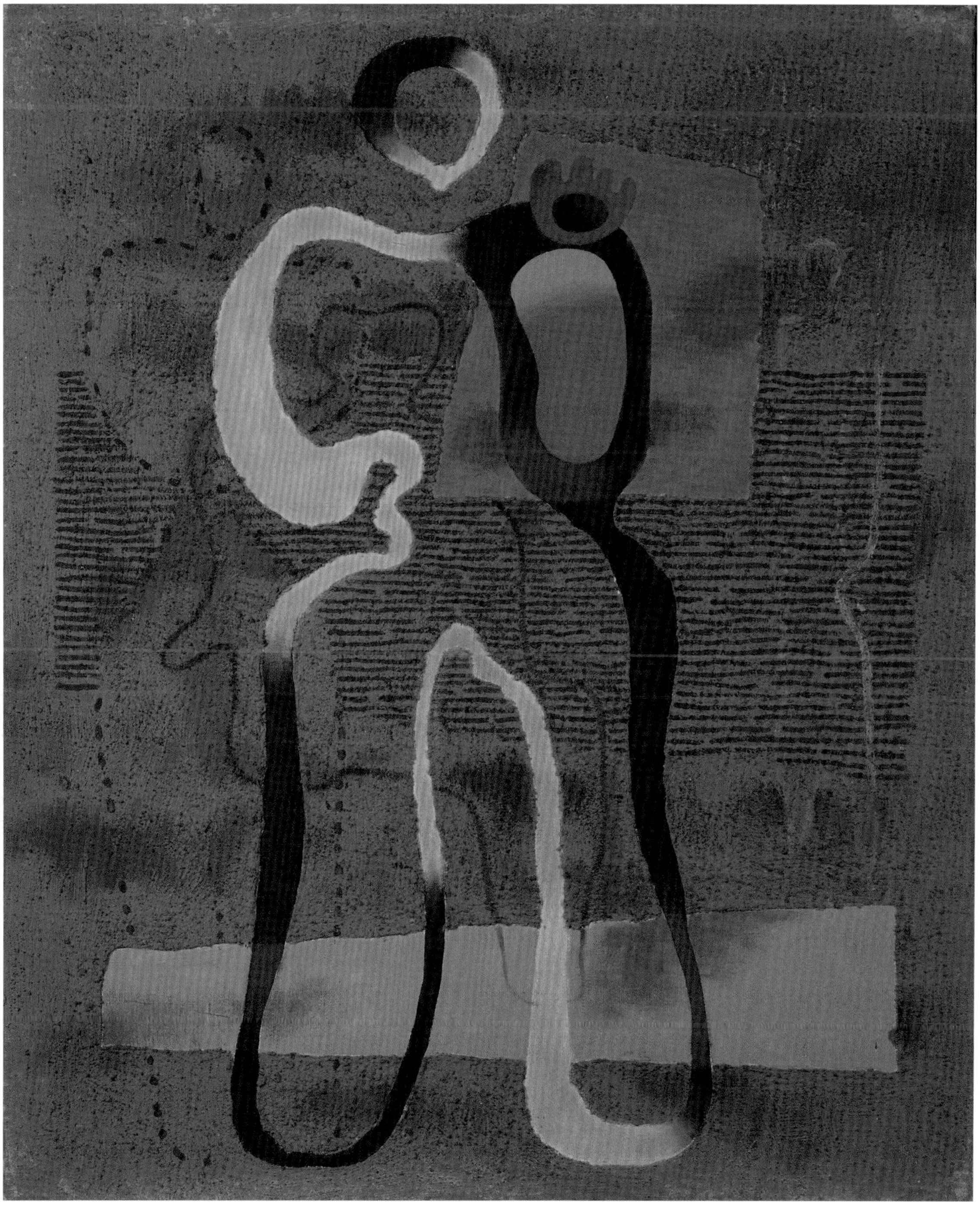

Standing Figure with Blue Patch
1933
Oil, sand on canvas
82 x 65.5 cm

Max Beckmann

Three Women in Profile, 1942

An avid theatregoer and lover of nightlife, Max Beckmann frequently depicted cabaret, circus and vaudeville performers. Painted in exile in Amsterdam, this canvas was also referred to by the artist in his diary as *Dressing Room* and later in the scholarship as *Three Dancers*.

Three female figures, each with a distinctive profile and hairstyle, stand closely staggered in space as if waiting attentively offstage for their debut. The white-powdered hair of the foremost figure is coiffed high in a Rococo style. Her wide neckband and left arm, raised holding a fan, frame her thickly painted, almost fully bared breasts. Painted over other details in the foreground, white brushstrokes fill a black outline to suggest a hoop skirt. In contrast to the complexion of the first figure and the bright blonde curls of the last are the dark, classical features of the woman at centre. To the left, half hidden behind the fan, is the grey face of a man in a black suit, perhaps a fellow performer. A pink circle and diagonal lines from lower left to middle right – a balustrade or the edge of a stage – further compress the space.

Beckmann's supporter and fellow émigré Stephan Lackner famously dubbed the artist's work his 'Theatre of the World', calling Beckmann a 'dramatist among painters'.[1] The year he painted **Three Women in Profile**, Beckmann also completed his fourth major triptych, entitled *Actors*, and a large canvas featuring a dancer and magician following a visit to Amsterdam's Carré Theatre.[2] By 1942, Beckmann had been in exile in the Netherlands for five years. Theatre was not only a pleasurable distraction or painterly subject, but also a direct metaphor for life in wartime. According to Beckmann: 'If one regarded all this – the whole war, or even all of life as only a scene in the eternal theatre, then many things would be easier to handle.'[3] Tired of the lousy, uncreative efforts of the 'unknown stage directors' orchestrating wailing sirens or bombing campaigns, Beckmann designed his own 'stage sets', scenes of life and entertainment to counter the oppressive monotony of war.[4]

Despite many hardships, Beckmann was extremely prolific in exile and was able to sell his work abroad thanks to an array of supporters. In 1924, Josef Haubrich disparagingly described Beckmann's painting – then strongly inflected by the artist's experience of the First World War – as 'bleak and despairing'. Not twenty years later, Haubrich acquired **Three Women in Profile**. Perhaps he still felt, as he had unwillingly admitted earlier, that the artist's work represented a 'true picture of our time'.[5]

Lynette Roth

1 Stephan Lackner, 'Das Welttheater des Malers Max Beckmann' (1938, first published 1939), in: *Ich erinnere mich ganz gut an Max Beckmann*, Mainz 1967, p. 63.

2 Erhard Göpel and Barbara Göpel, *Max Beckmann. Kataloge der Gemälde*, Bern 1976, nos. 591 and 604. Max Beckmann, *Tagebücher 1940– 1950*, Munich 1955, pp. 21, 22.

3 Max Beckmann, 12 September 1940, *Tagebücher 1940– 1950*, Munich 1955, p. 11.

4 Max Beckmann in a letter to Stephan Lackner, 20 November 1939, in: Klaus Gallwitz, Uwe M. Schneede and Stephan von Wiese (eds.), *Max Beckmann. Briefe. Band III: 1937-1950*, Munich 1996, p. 65.

5 Peter Fuchs, *Josef Haubrich. Sammler und Stifter moderner Kunst*, Kölner Biographien, herausgegeben vom Nachrichtenamt der Stadt Köln, 1979, p. 30.

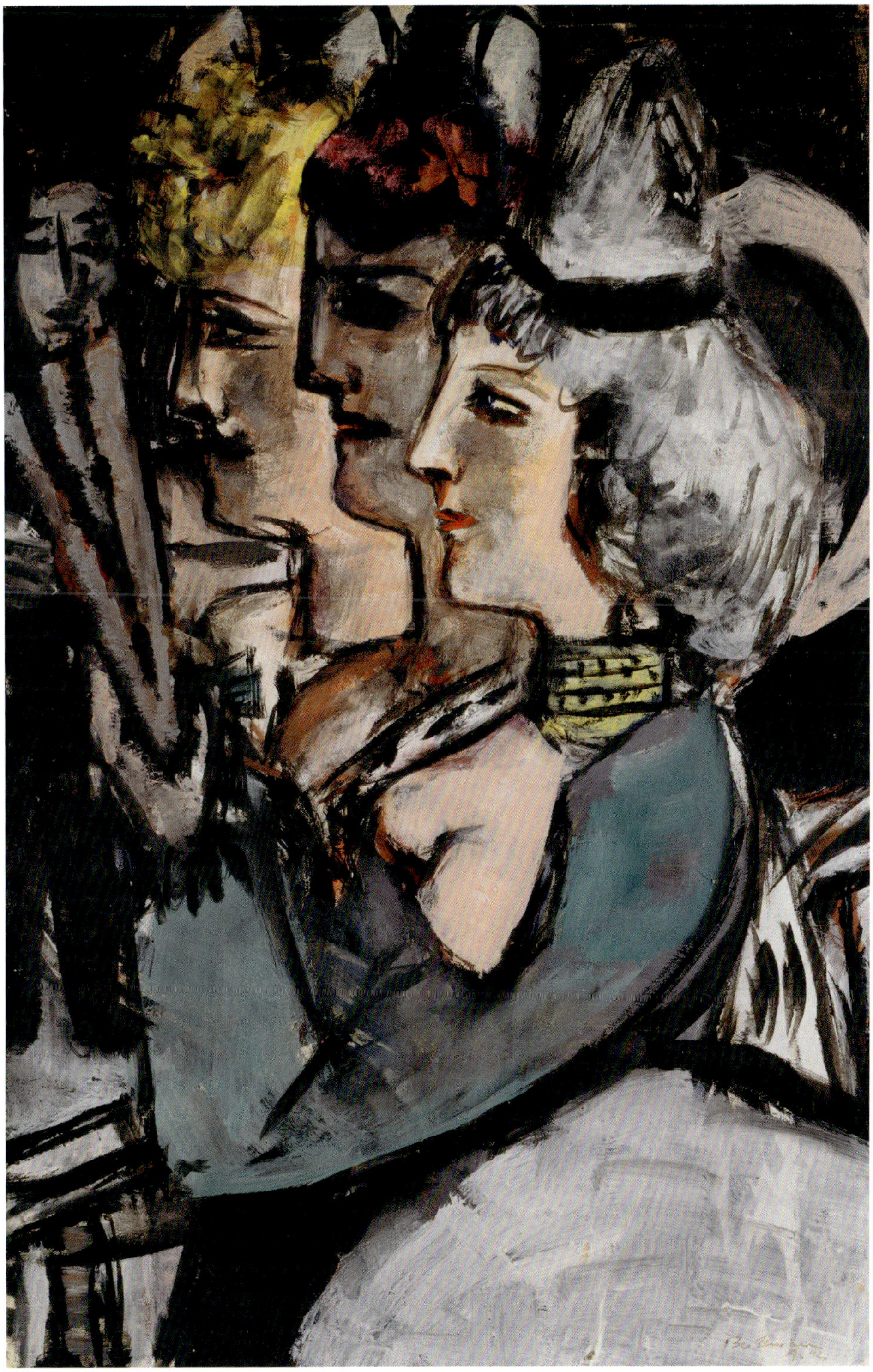

Three Women in Profile
1942
Oil on canvas
85 x 55 cm

Max Beckmann

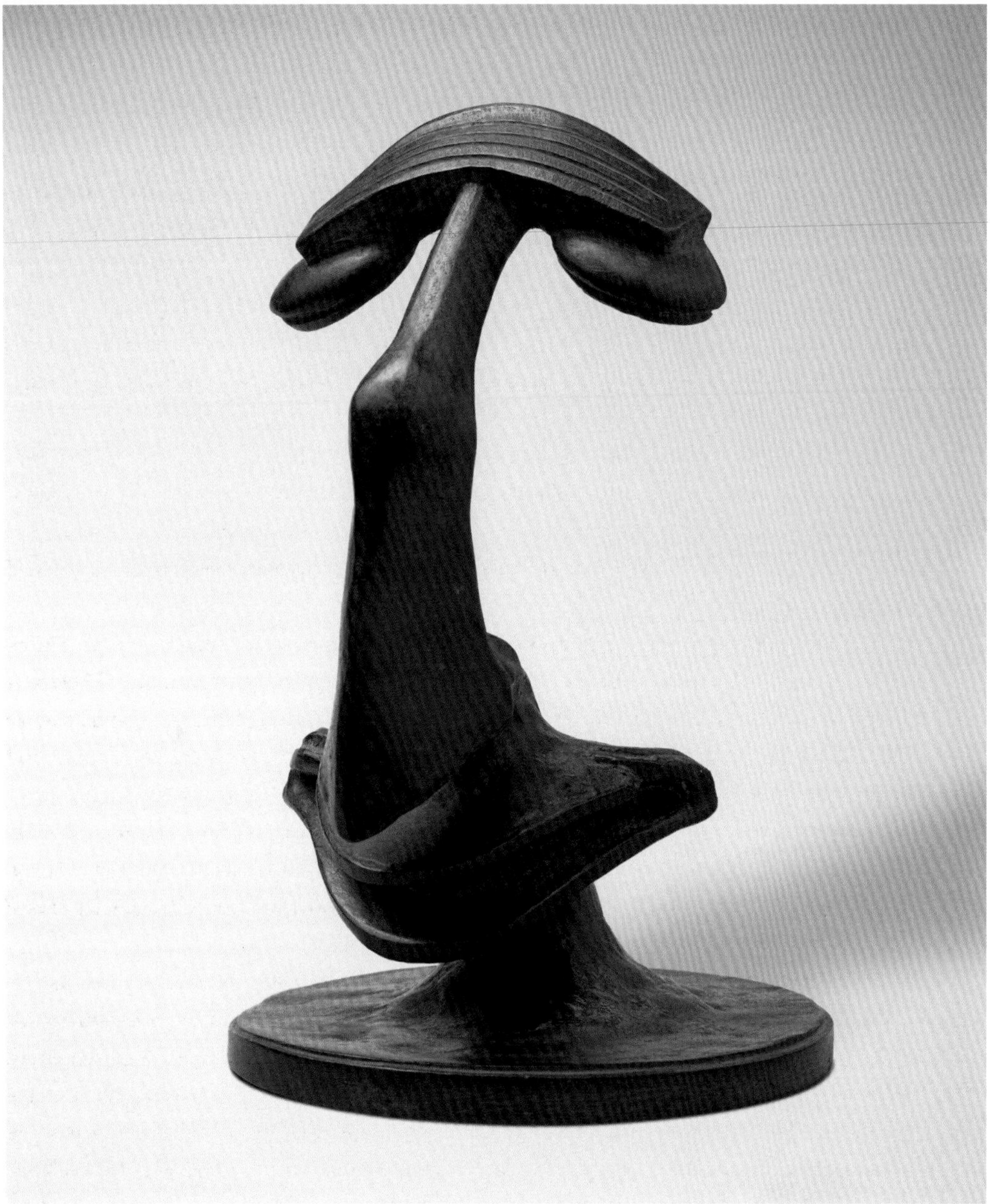

Portrait of Alfred Flechtheim
1927
Bronze
H.:18.7 cm

Rudolf Belling

Portrait of Alfred Flechtheim, 1927

As he explained in a letter to his friend and sponsor Alfred Flechtheim, Rudolf Belling saw the air surrounding a sculpture as no less a part of it than the mass he shaped: 'For me sculpture is first of all about our ideas of space. ... Which is why I model air just as I model solid material, and arrive at the point where the breaches, formerly known as "dead form", have the same value as their perimeter, which is to say the worked material ...'[1] His portrait of the famous art dealer is an impressive example of this forward-looking concept of sculpture.

Based on a wire maquette, the sculpture consists of a few facial elements that the artist has arranged around a hollow space. Like a caricaturist, he captures the salient features of Flechtheim's appearance in a succinct, reduced manner. Mass and space are interdependent, for only together do they result in the sculptural **Potrait of Alfred Flechtheim**.

However rigorously Belling employs his concept of space, our inevitably historical standpoint notices something else at first: Belling has used the centuries-old stereotype of the Jew with his large hooked nose, heavy eyelids and rubbery lips. The Jewish dealer uses his large nose to scent out shady deals, his hooded eyes suggest cunning and the protruding bottom lip hints at a bestial streak. This was how the anti-Semites in Germany pictured the Jewish foe. Flechtheim was to experience the anti-Semitic madness at first hand. His appearance was genuinely close to the stereotype and dealing in modern art was a thorn in the Nazis' side. Flechtheim was forced to close his gallery and to leave Germany. He died in 1937 in British exile.

But scarcely a person in 1927 could have imagined the disastrous turn history would take, and such anti-Semitic caricature could still retain something of its innocence as long as the murder that it was later supposed to justify could not yet be anticipated. Flechtheim had never made a secret of his Jewish origins and evidently treated the exaggerated portrait with a mixture of humour and self-irony. Belling, who himself was to be denounced as 'degenerate', and who emigrated to Istanbul, wrote in 1964 to the Wallraf-Richartz Museum: 'In his enthusiasm for the work, Flechtheim personally handed a number of copies of it to people in his immediate surroundings ...'[2]

Jessica Küsters

1 Rudolf Belling, letter to Alfred Flechtheim, *Das Kunstblatt*, 1920, p. 347.
2 Rudolf Belling, letter to the Wallraf-Richartz Museum, Cologne, dated 14 April 1964, archive at the Museum Ludwig.

María Blanchard

Red Still Life with Lamp, 1916-18

This Cubist painting by the Spanish painter María Blanchard has a very special story. It was found after her death in her studio, and initially the art dealer Daniel-Henry Kahnweiler took it to be a work by Juan Gris. With that it was handed over to the Museum of Modern Art in Madrid. But later Kahnweiler corrected his error. Blanchard had lived since 1916 in Paris and for a while shared a studio with Gris. According to the French art historian Emmanuel Bénézit, they even worked at times on the same canvases,[1] which strongly suggests a mutual influence.

Like Gris, Blanchard subscribed to synthetic Cubism, in which various picture levels and simplified geometric forms were broken, then juxtaposed as if in a collage so as to form a new whole. The works dispensed with both a central perspective as well as an illusionist depiction of the visual elements. Blanchard's objects seem two-dimensional, like abstract patches of colour without contour lines. The fine lines in the floor section are reminiscent of the joints between floorboards, even though they are not parallel and change colour as soon as they cross the border to the next area of colour. As a result, the whole spatial configuration seems unstable, and the small table and the black lamp give the impression that they are tipping over. Indeed, the lamp actually appears to be floating above the table. The square patch of white light that it casts has its compositional counterparts in the open page of the book and the small object resting beside it.

Like Gris, Blanchard also demonstrates thoroughness in her composition; the arrangement of the objects here recalls his work *Broc et verre (Jug and Glass)* from 1916.[2] But unlike in Gris's work, a tonality can be discerned here that, as Blanchard said herself, is more emotional: 'I am grateful to him for a great deal, but I think I have added a kind of sensuality to his severity.'[3] In particular this still life is dominated by the warm reddish hue of the title. Like the light of the lamp, it conveys energy and warmth. Blanchard's Cubist phase ended around 1920. Like many European artists, she returned after the end of the First World War to figuration, dedicating herself to sensitive depictions of mothers with children and child scenes.

Geraldine Spiekermann

1 Liliane Caffin Madaule, *Catalogue raisonné des œuvres de María Blanchard*, London 1992, 3 vols., vol. I, p. 160.
2 María José Salazar, *María Blanchard. Catálogo razonado, Pintura 1889–1932. Catalogue raisonné*, Madrid 2004, p. 128.
3 Caffin Madaule, op.cit., vol. III, p. 50. See also Caffin Madaule, vol. I, p. 13 and vol. III, p. 52.

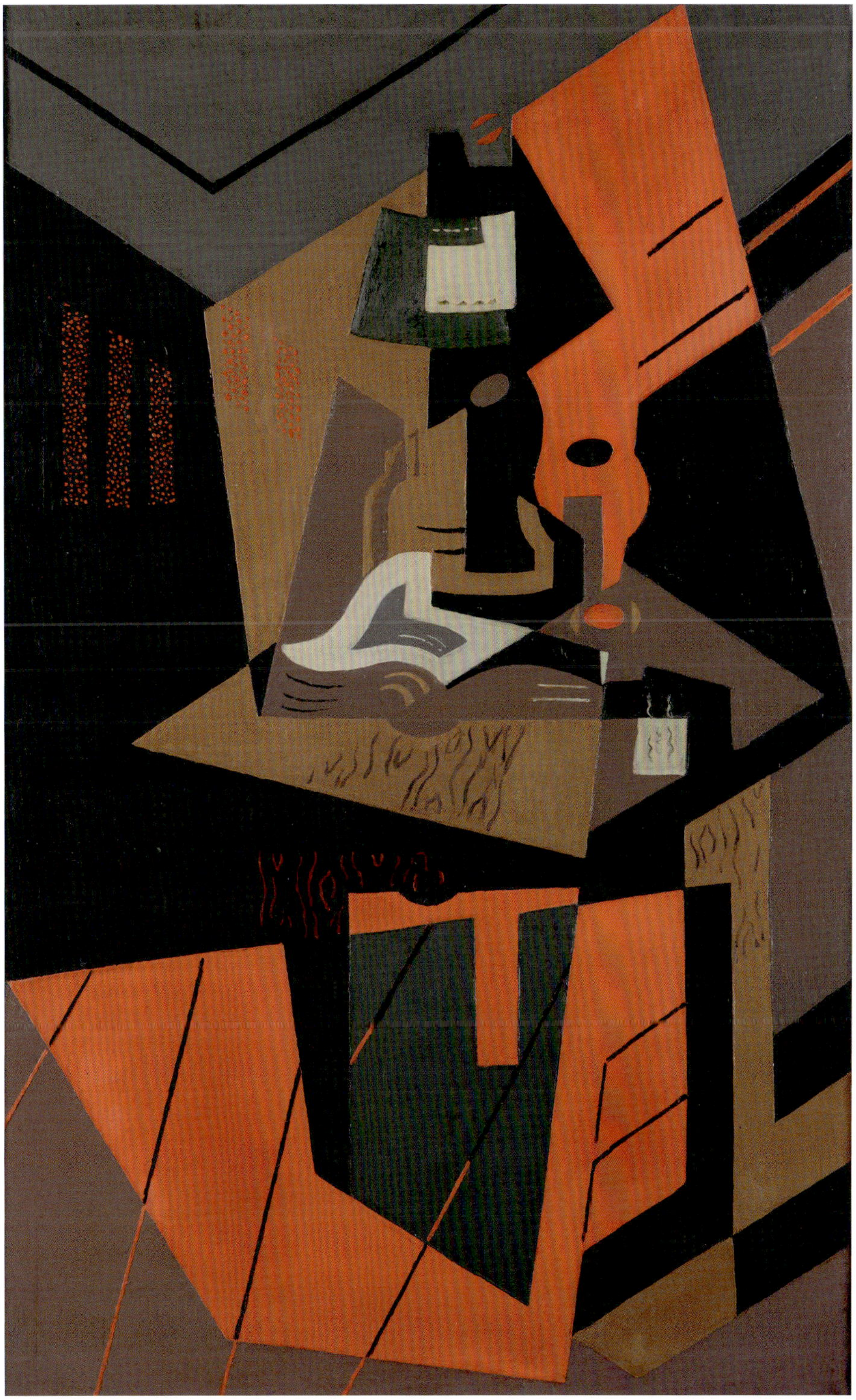

Red Still Life with Lamp
1916–18
Oil on canvas
118.5 x 74.5 cm

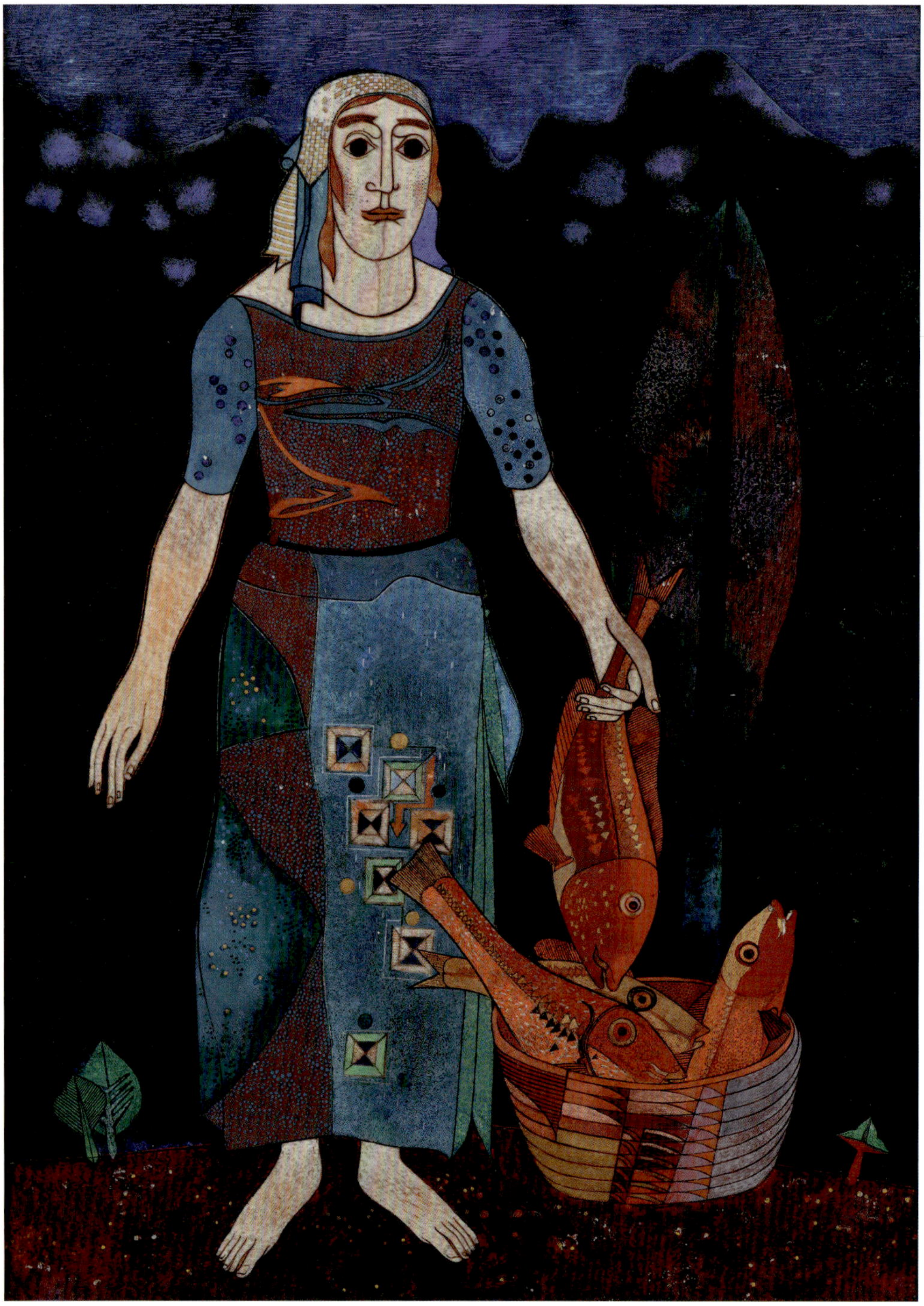

Woman with Fishes
1929
Oil on glass
67 x 48 cm

Heinrich Campendonk

Woman with Fishes, 1929

This reverse glass painting keeps the promise that is given in its title, **Woman with Fishes**: what we see is a woman with fishes. Both the choice of a simple motif as well as the technique that has been used testify to Heinrich Campendonk's closeness to the Blauer Reiter group and their enthusiasm for naïve art. Elisabeth Erdmann-Macke, August Macke's wife, remembered the 1910s in the Alpine foothills of upper Bavaria, the home of reverse glass painting: 'On our visits to the Marcs in Sindelsdorf ... we would all sit at the round table in the evening and paint glass pictures, Franz and Maria, August and I, and sometimes we were joined by Helmuth Macke and Campendonk, who were living in Sindelsdorf at that time. ... Sadly these pictures were destroyed during the war.'[1]

The artists turned to the folksy tradition of reverse glass painting in their search for means that lay outside the normal academic forms of expression, for a pristine, simple, even supernatural approach. Thanks to the luminosity of the glass, the paintings have a mystic aura. Incidentally, they are created by a quite different method to that used for canvas paintings, because they are painted front to back. The first layer of paint that is applied becomes for the viewer the top coat. The luminosity of the glass is then heightened by scratching away the paint. Campendonk kept returning to and experimenting with this technique for over forty years and created more than fifty such paintings. One was already displayed at the first exhibition of the Blauer Reiter in 1911 in Munich.

People and animals are central motifs in Campendonk's work, with individual motifs recurring like personal ciphers. The dark, fairy-tale setting and the seemingly naïve planar construction of **Woman with Fishes** try neither to explain what is depicted, nor to aestheticize it. The concern rather is with capturing an experience that is as immediate as possible, and with the vision of art as a creative act. Apart from the conscious choice of simple motifs and their rigorous artistic reduction, we encounter here Campendonk's investigation into planar fragmentation – as can be seen for instance in the linear elements in the woman's face – and into composition using patches of colour. In contrast with Cubist fragmentation, he did not abandon naturalism for the sake of a temporo-spatial approach, but instead in favour of a psychic, emotional form of depiction.

Jasmina Merz

1 Quoted in Klaus Lankheit: *Hinterglasmalerei im XX. Jahrhundert* (exh. cat., Gutenberg Museum Mainz), 1962, unpaginated.

Marc Chagall

Portrait of the Sister, 1909
Sabbath, 1910
Yellow House, 1924

Josef Haubrich acquired **Yellow House** for his collection straight off the easel, with the paint still wet.[1] As one of the organizers of the first major Chagall exhibition at the Kölnischer Kunstverein, he visited the artist in his Paris atelier in 1924 and went on to befriend him.

At that point in time, Marc Chagall had long been treated as a 'Modern Classic'.[2] His early success was thanks in large part to the Berlin gallery owner and publisher Herwarth Walden, who presented works by the artist from his gallery Der Sturm at the 1913 Autumn Salon in Germany. Chagall's intense, brilliant display of colours and his childlike, fantasy-based visual language thrilled viewers. Within a year, Walden mounted the first solo exhibition of the artist's works, presenting 38 oil paintings and 120 graphic works. Private collectors were Chagall's most enthusiastic supporters. Over the course of the 1920s, almost all of his early works, around 200 pieces in all, entered private collections. Haubrich, too, prized Chagall. **Yellow House** was the first of nine paintings and watercolours by Chagall that he acquired.

The dominant motif in this small-scale painting is a tall tree, which irresistibly draws the viewer's gaze to its shimmering, colourful crown. The dense tapestry of colours daubed and plastered in layers across the canvas, placed against the background of the saturated blue sky and the barely shadowed clouds, appears ready to spring off the canvas – or, indeed, out of the frame itself. Behind the lively nature scene, Chagall's modest family home in Belarusian Vitebsk glows in vivid colours. His mother, who ran a small grocery shop from their home, steps out of the dark interior into the doorway. But her apathetic expression, combined with the blank stare of the windows, turns the summery atmosphere of this scene into a melancholy recollection.

Memories of his childhood days were an inexhaustible source of inspiration for Chagall. The depiction of buildings and streets, inhabitants and scenes of village life in his hometown recur throughout the artist's oeuvre. Woven together with imaginative elements from Russian folk tales tinged with Hassidic Jewish influences, these places became a metaphoric visual language that has fascinated its beholders ever since.

A part of this fascination is quite possibly the fact that these are pictures of memories – that is, the world they depict had already vanished. Chagall left Russia in 1910 to study French art. He moved into a studio in Paris, but his rudimentary accommodations, the language barrier and his lack of artistic success conspired to nurture a great longing for his native idyll.

The City of Lights nevertheless played an important role in his artistic development. The ubiquity of art and the freedom of life in Paris made an intensive period of creativity possible. His painting **Sabbath**, one of his first works after his arrival in Paris, reveals the imaginative fertility of his surroundings. The subject of the painting, by contrast, expresses his deep connection to his roots. The picture shows a family on the Jewish day of rest, which begins Friday evening with the lighting of the two Sabbath candles. The clock strikes ten, the meal has been cleared away, all male members of the family are slouched in their chairs, the mother stands in the doorway, at once expectant and thoughtful, and a small boy – quite possibly Chagall's tuberculosis-ridden brother – is already in bed. We are witnesses to a family gathering with a dreamy, otherworldly air thanks to the eccentric shape of the room and the way in which the painting opens both out to the viewer as well as to its own inner space. Chagall's trick is to present this dreamy family memory in the style of Vincent van Gogh's well-known *Le café de nuit (The Night Café*, 1888). But whereas in van Gogh's painting the lonely drunks have gathered bleakly and by chance, the religious family ritual unites the figures in Chagall's depiction. Notwithstanding this, the family members are equally isolated from one another.

From the beginning, his family was the subject of Chagall's work. He took regular breaks from his two-year course of study at the Elizaveta Zvantseva School of Painting and Drawing in St Petersburg to return to his hometown of Vitebsk and devote himself to portraying his family members. The **Portrait of the Sister**[3] defies expectations to depict thirteen-year-old Mania, one of his eight younger siblings, as a mature woman. She has already thrown off her childhood poses: lost in thought, she turns her gaze away from her book into the distance. The soft blurring of the contours and the close proximity from which the portrait has been painted turn the piece into a tender, intimate depiction of the artist's sister. The tightly cropped composition gives the impression of a close-up. Photography, whose techniques Chagall knew well (he had, after all, worked for a time as a retoucher), may have inspired this composition. In contrast to **Yellow House** and **Sabbath**, both painted from memory, this painting, executed in muted, reduced colours, owes much to naturalism. The decorative elements, such as the lush blossoms in the girl's hair, the ornaments adorning her skirt and the flat background, play against one another rhythmically. These elements were modelled after the works of Henri Matisse, which Chagall much admired when they were exhibited in St Petersburg. The radical perspective makes the spatial configuration of the painting difficult to decipher, and one can only speculate that Mania has seated herself before a window.

Haubrich himself dubbed the portrait *Sister in the Garden*. He acquired it in 1933, the same year in which he bought the painting **Sabbath**. Alongside euphoria, the artist also experienced rejection in Germany. Negative feelings towards Chagall increased and became mixed with anti-Semitic undertones, quickly leading to a defamation of the artist's work. Four of his pieces were exhibited in the 1937 'Degenerate Art' exhibition. In 1941, he fled from the Germans, leaving France for the United States.

Ilona Ciesielski

1 Josef Haubrich: 'Schicksale meiner Sammlung', in: Heinz Ladendorf (ed.), *Mouseion. Studien aus Kunst und Geschichte für Otto H. Förster*, Cologne 1960, pp. 296–300, here p. 296.

2 Karoline Hille: '"Und vielleicht wird mich Europa lieben und mit ihm ganz Russland." Der Grenzgänger Marc Chagall', in: Ada Raev and Isabel Wünsche (eds.), *Kursschwankungen. Russische Kunst im Wertesystem der europäischen Moderne*, Berlin 2007, p. 112.

3 Thus titled in 1961 by Franz Meyer, Marc Chagall's son-in-law.

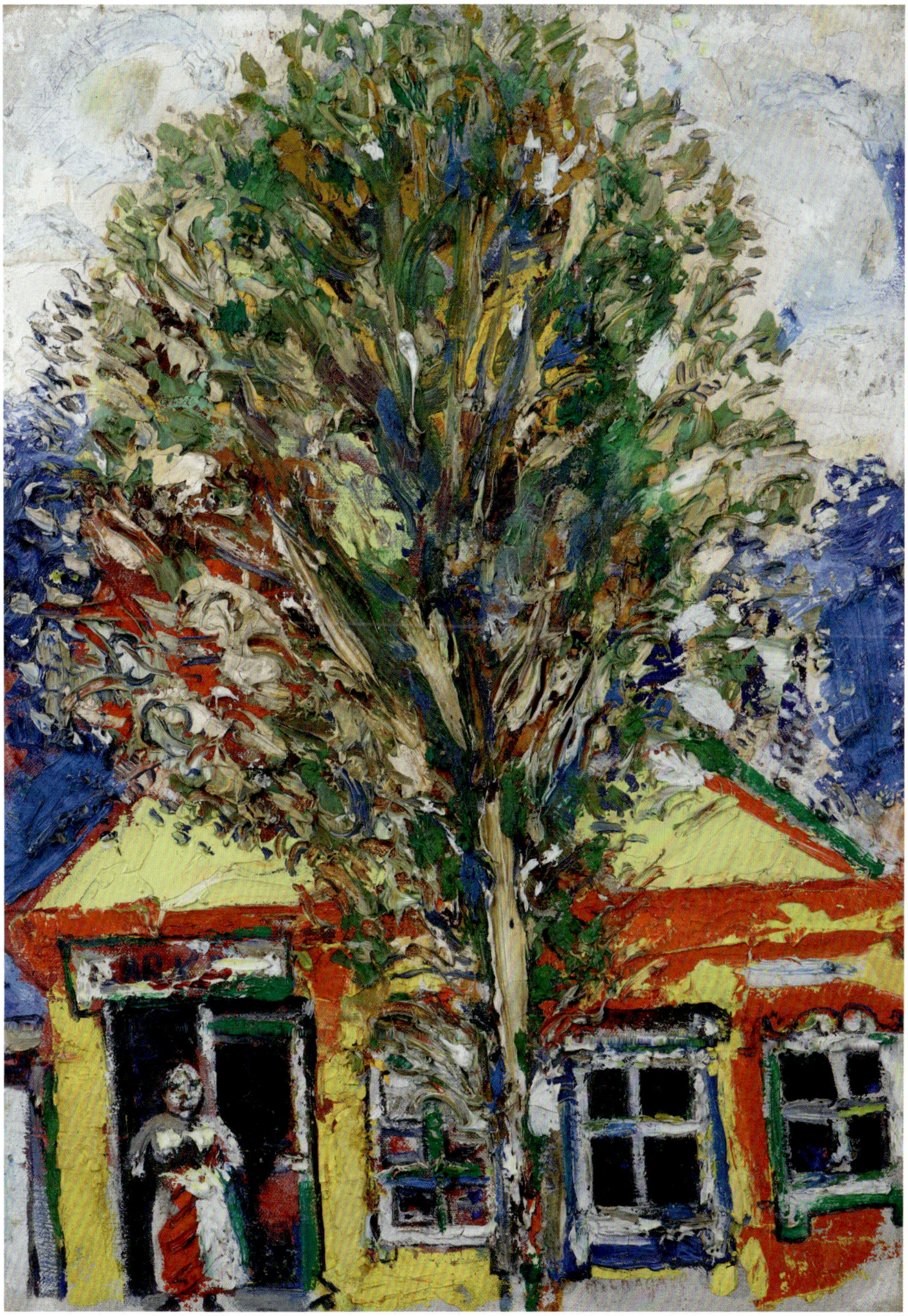

Yellow House
1924
Oil on canvas
54.7 x 37.8 cm

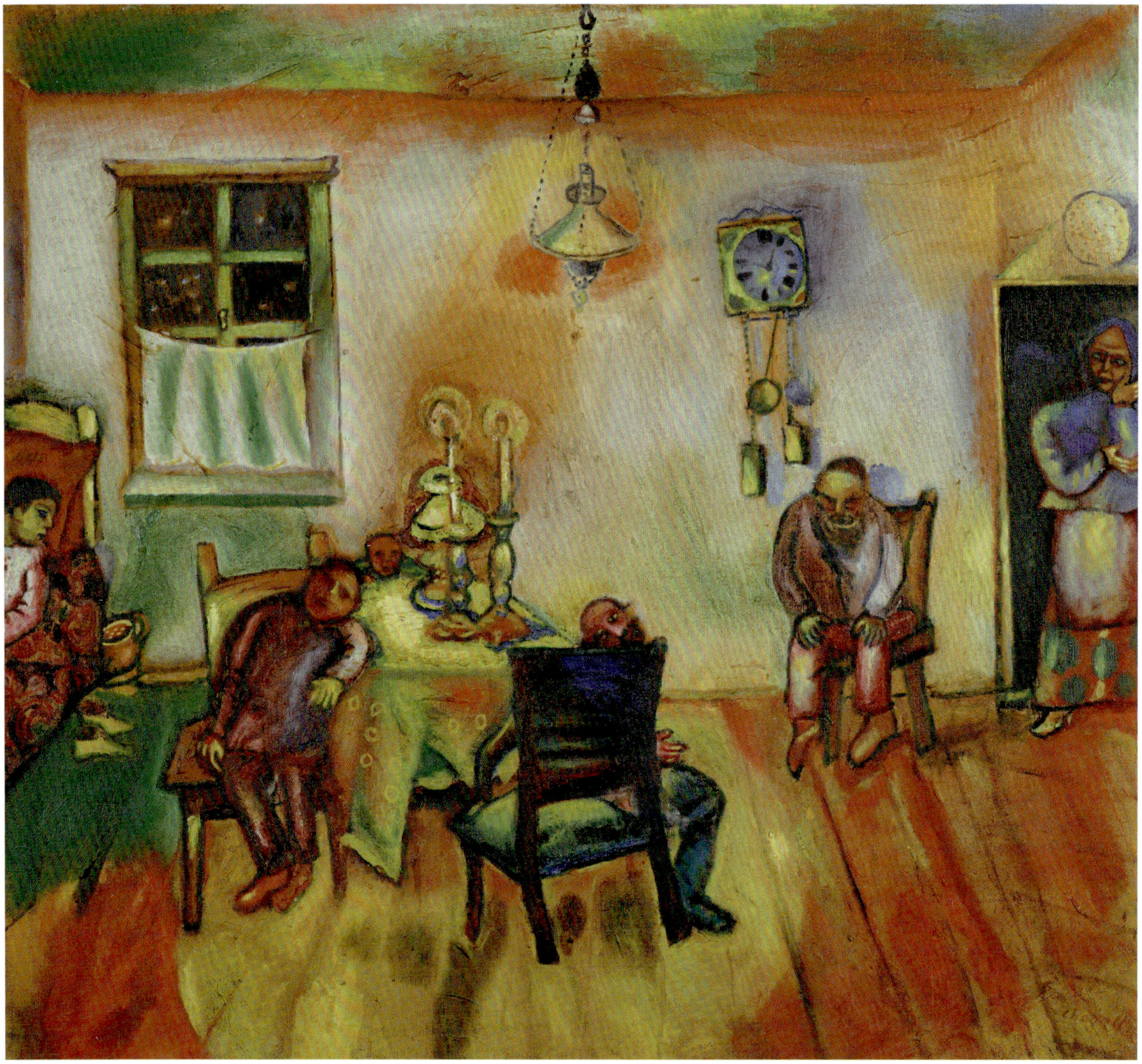

Sabbath
1910
Oil on canvas
90.5 x 94.5 cm

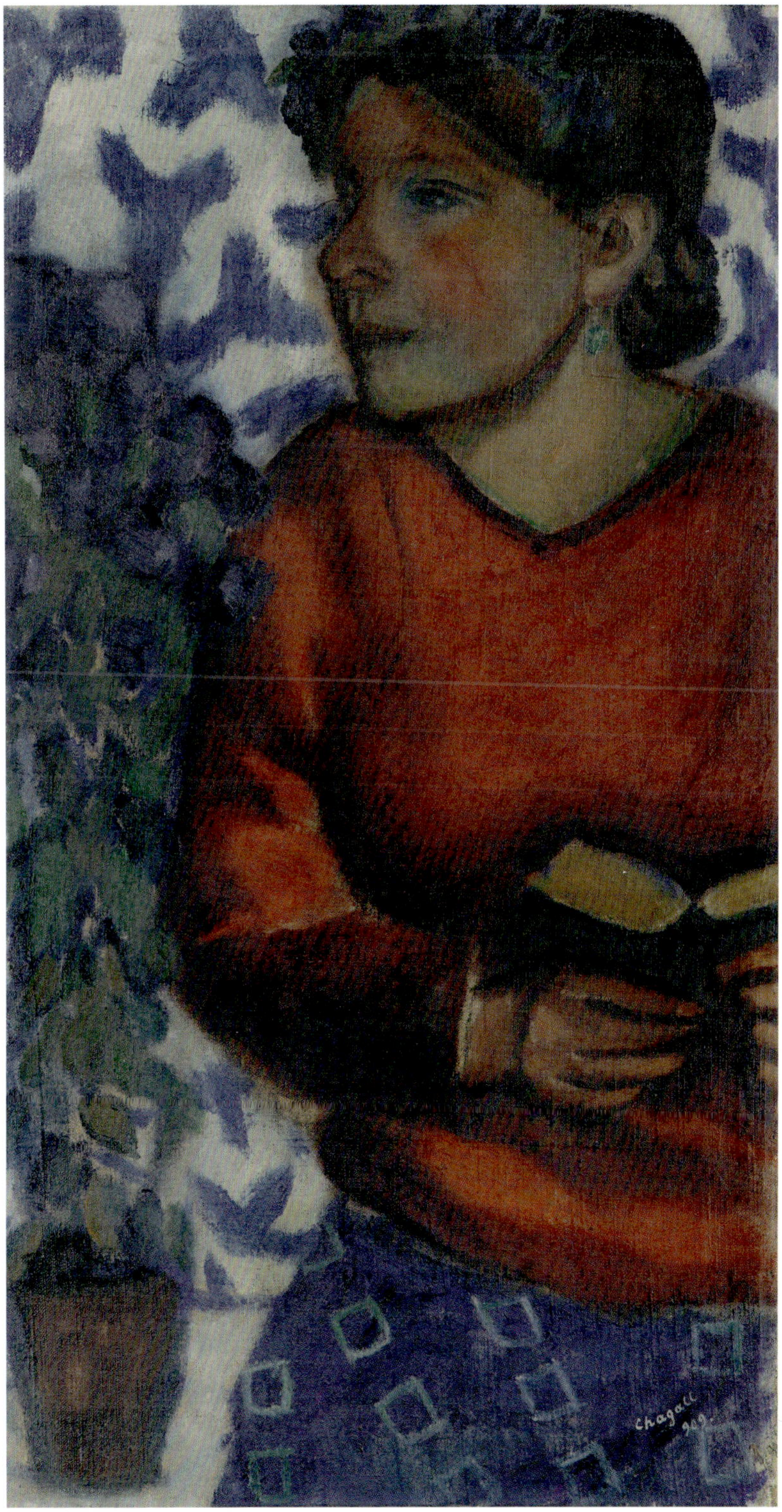

Portrait of the Sister
1909
Oil on canvas
92.5 x 48 cm

Otto Dix

Portrait of Doctor Hans Koch, 1921
Portrait of the Poet Theodor Däubler, 1927
Self-Portrait, 1931

Otto Dix was one of the greatest portrait painters of the twentieth century. His portrait-painting technique is fascinating not only because of its mimetic representation, but also because it creates a tension between the real model and the artistic image. Dix explains: 'The first impression one has of a person is the right one. When I have finished a painting, I can perhaps modify this impression and say: Well, he's not quite such a beast as he seemed.'[1] This first impression, which Dix might form based only on a person's external appearance, enabled him to create outstanding portraits, in which we believe we can see the inner essence of the person portrayed.

His portrait of the Düsseldorf urologist Hans Koch illustrates the fact that the painter's understanding of his model is nevertheless deeply subjective: the doctor is shown surrounded by menacing-looking medical apparatus, almost like a torturer. In his battered physicality, he himself looks like a victim of the possibilities of modern medicine. His eyes behind his pince-nez are at a strange angle, a crimson gash glows on his cheek, a scar runs across his receding chin. With his taste for unsparing exaggeration, Dix was one of the founders of the verist wing of the Neue Sachlichkeit. He uses more than just form to heighten expression. 'Everyone has his own particular colour that affects the entire picture.'[2] In the **Portrait of Doctor Hans Koch**, a pale, repulsive eggshell tone defines the entire interior. The colour is evident in the doctor's coat and again in the wall tiles – but also in the reflection of the steel instruments and the syringe, whose lustre Dix accentuated with an application of aluminium foil. The red-brown tones reference Dr. Koch's medical specialty: as a urologist, he dealt with the unappetizing innards of his patients.

A trained decorative painter and a student at the Dresden Academy, Dix, at the time he met Koch in the Rhineland, had as yet attained little success besides a *succès de scandale* at the First International Dada Fair (1920) in Berlin. Koch was not only a urologist, but also a writer and an ambitious collector who ran a gallery together with his wife, Martha. He became Dix's first major sponsor, buying two paintings and commissioning a portrait. A momentous encounter came about during the portrait sessions. To the backdrop of the popular dance 'Shimmy Jazz' playing on the gramophone and under the influence of copious amounts of alcohol, Dix and Koch's wife Martha became intimate.

After the completion of the portrait, she returned to Dresden with Dix. Koch reacted with aplomb. He divorced Martha and married her sister. Dix became his brother-in-law, and the two remained close friends. Koch sold the portrait to Josef Haubrich through the Nierendorf Gallery in 1923 – it was the first oil painting in Haubrich's collection.

In subsequent years, Dix began his ascent as an in-demand portraitist. He emerged unscathed from two court cases where he was accused of defamatory depictions, but was forced to withdraw his painting *The Trenches* (1920–23) from the Wallraf-Richartz Museum because the mayor Konrad Adenauer was displeased by its dramatic depiction of wartime atrocities. In 1926, Dix was awarded a professorship at the Dresden Academy. There he met the Expressionist poet Theodor Däubler and sketched him using charcoal during a joint studio visit. In the resulting portrait, Däubler's face and hands are captured with the greatest precision in the translucent glazed painting style commonly associated with the Old Masters. The finely drawn hair playing around the smoothly modelled volumes of the face evidences Dix's enthusiasm for Renaissance portraiture. His masterful adaptation of Renaissance techniques is a veritable emulation. A child of his time, Dix's choices nevertheless set his work apart from that of his role models: the colossal poet lounges casually on a wooden chair. The materiality of his suit has been painted summarily. The antique-looking pillars in the background seem like stage decoration. This impressive architectural ensemble is part of the Academy of Fine Arts on Brühl's Terrace in Dresden. The choice of 'Florence on the Elbe' as backdrop and the naturalistic portrayal of the poet have more in common with the neoclassical wing of the Neue Sachlichkeit movement than with the verist incisiveness of the physician's portrait. But this portrait, too, is not without irony. It is no coincidence that Dix places the melancholy writer in front of the Mount Olympus of poets, to which he never would have gained access.

In the **Self-Portrait**, the artist reflects on his own role. He sets himself in a studio with a painter's smock, painter's stick and palette. He stands squeezed between the window and the canvas, which is placed before him, still blank. If everyone has their own special colour, then the artist's colour is a non-colour. The entire picture has been done in grey; it remains as neutral as the artist, who reproduces the world he perceives. He has placed a crystal ball off to the side beside his painting tools. It is like a tiny world which gathers the light of the larger one, the world that the artist no longer needs to observe. His expression is dark, his eyes are shadowed. They are not the mirror of the soul, but instead block off the view of the artist-subject, who here functions merely as a medium.

Whether the artist was reflecting the political situation of his time – in 1930, the Nazi party was already part of the Thuringian government and paintings by Dix were confiscated – or whether his picture is to be read as a visionary foreshadowing of the Nazi era is another question.[3] At first glance it shows only an individual who is well-aware of his own role and of his own limits, an individual who sets the same standards for his self-portrait as he does for his portraits of others, be they the urologist or the poet.

In 1933, the artist, now branded a 'degenerate', lost his professorship and found refuge, together with his family, at Lake Constance in the castle of his brother-in-law Hans Koch. In the post-war years, despite the new abstract art doctrines, Otto Dix gained renewed appreciation – albeit less for his later Expressionist work than as a proponent of the verist wing of Neue Sachlichkeit in the 1920s.

Erec Gellautz

1 Quoted in Adam C. Oellers, *Ikonographische Untersuchungen zur Bildnismalerei der Neuen Sachlichkeit*, Mayen 1983, p. 53.
2 Quoted in Kerstin Stremmel/Uta Grosenick (eds.), *Realismus*, Cologne 2004, p. 44.
3 Cf. Olaf Peters, *Neue Sachlichkeit und Nationalsozialismus. Affirmation und Kritik 1931–1947*, Berlin 1998, p. 75f., and Dietrich Schubert, *Otto Dix in Selbstzeugnissen und Bilddokumenten*, Reinbek 1980, p. 105.

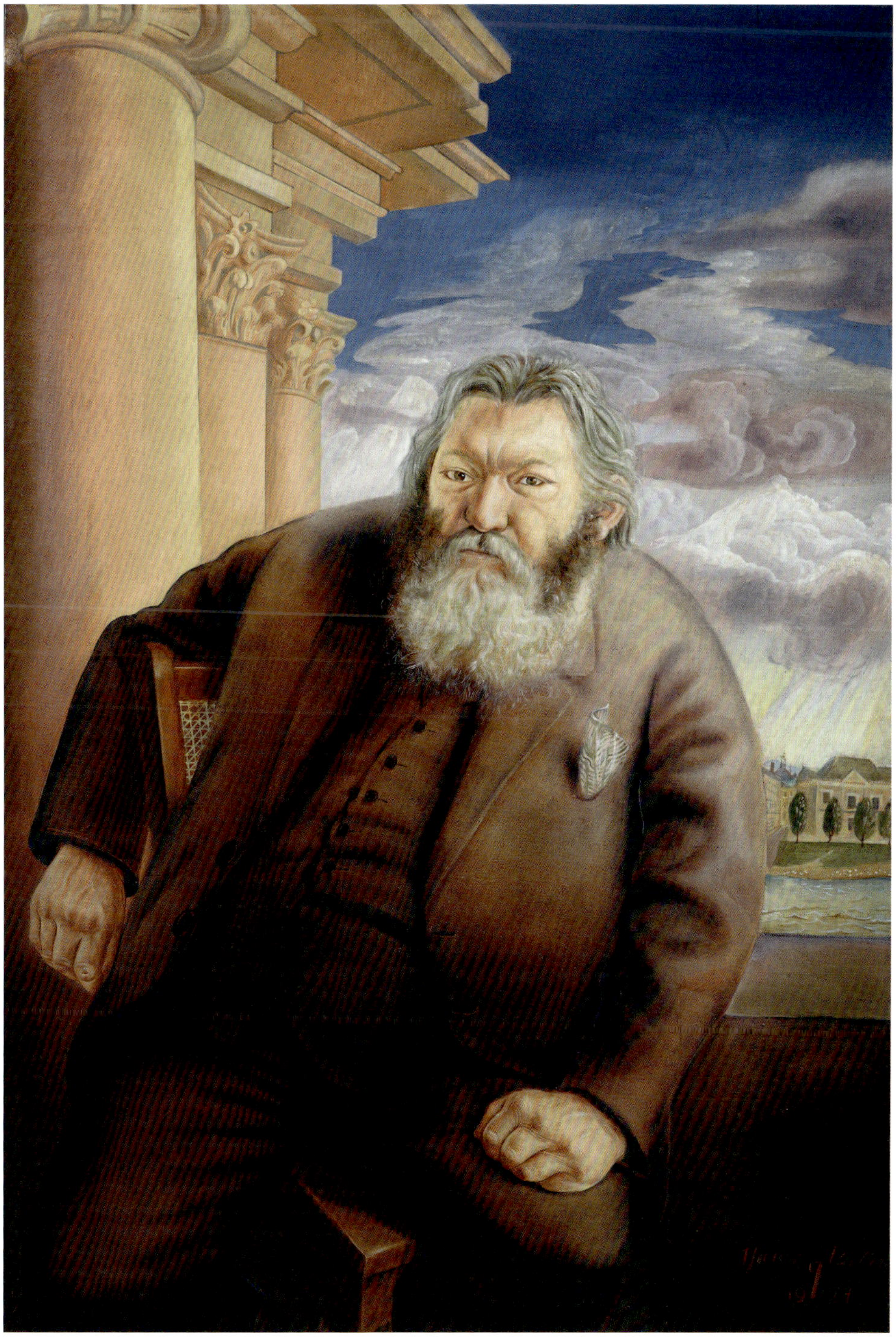

Portrait of the Poet Theodor Däubler
1927
Tempera on plywood
150 x 100 cm

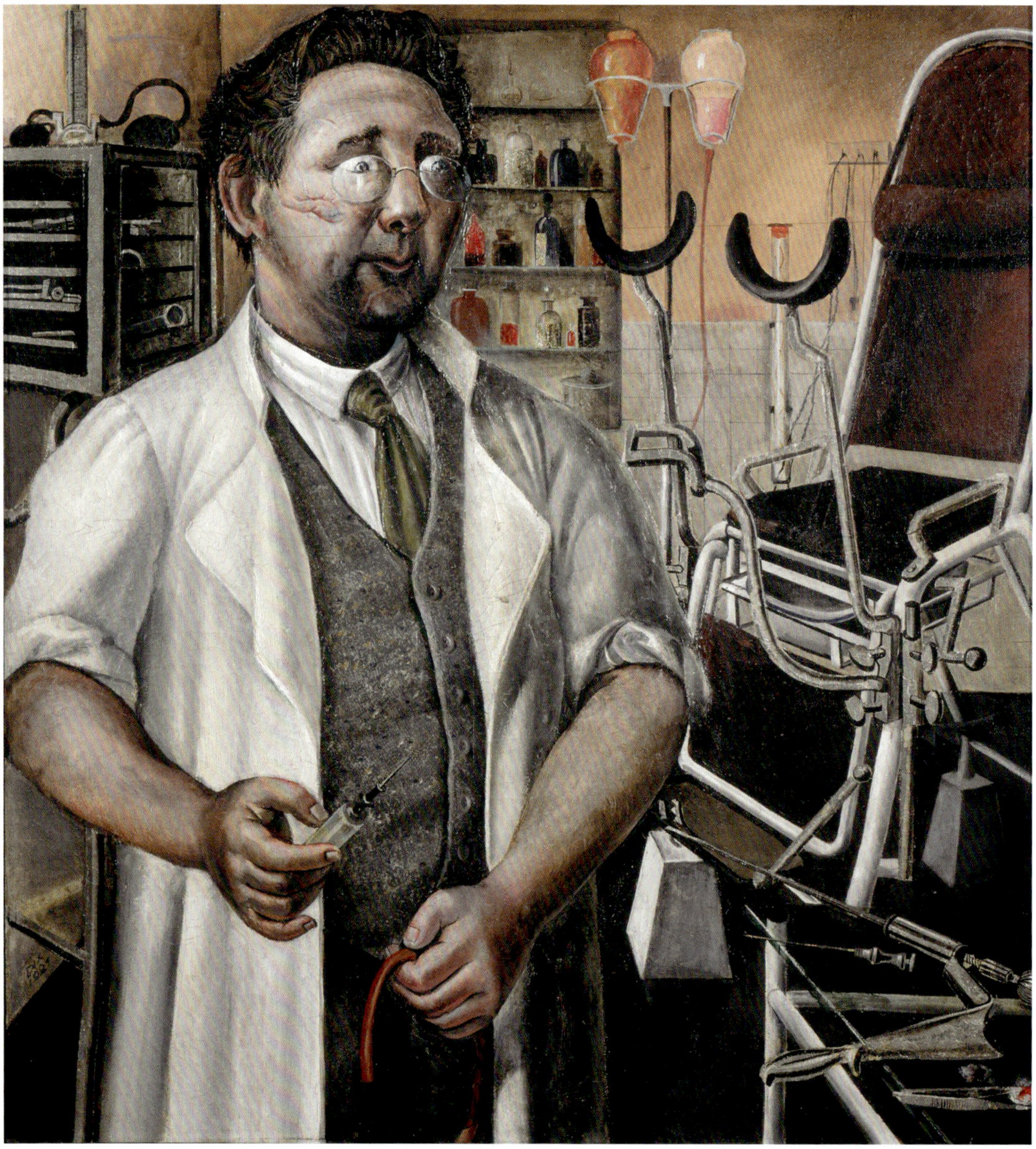

Portrait of Doctor Hans Koch
1921
Oil on canvas
100.5 x 90 cm

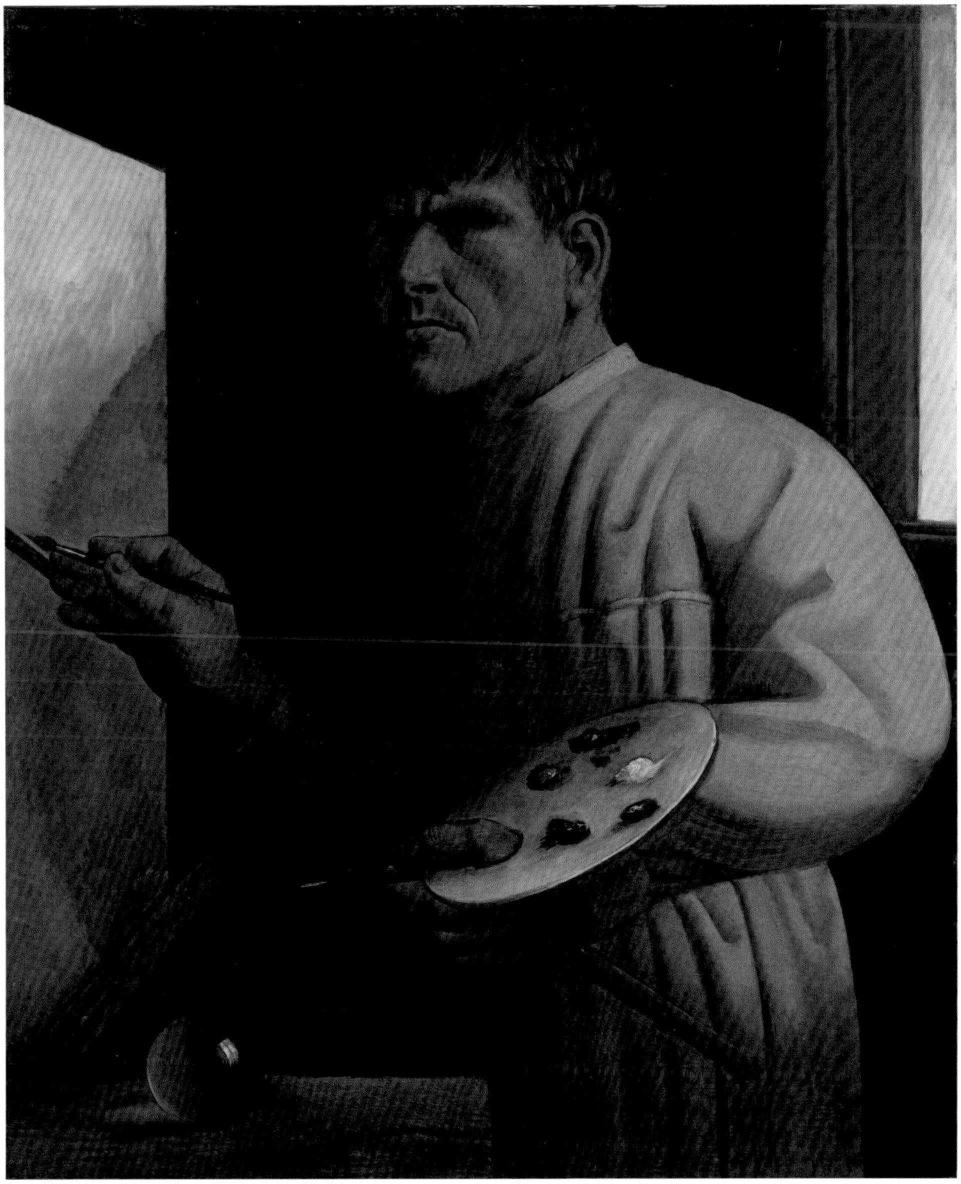

Self-Portrait
1931
Oil, tempera on wood
100 x 80 cm

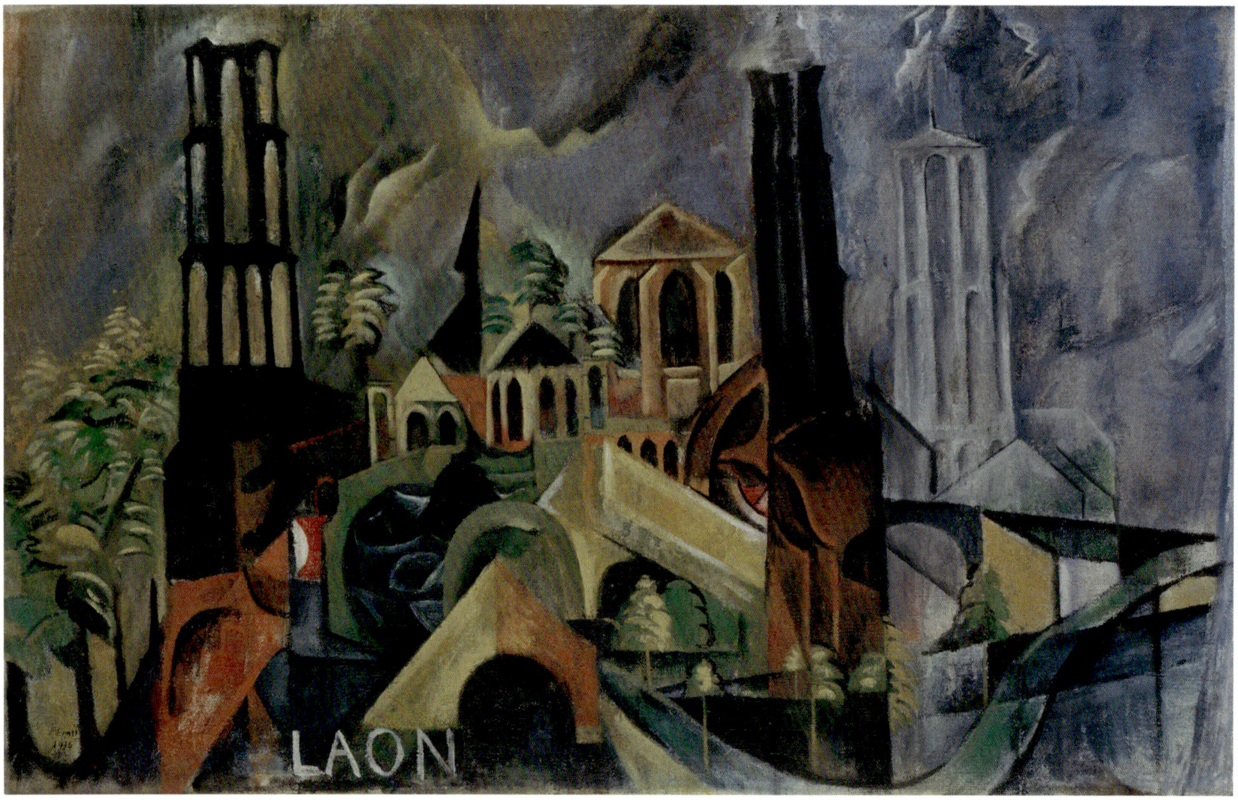

Laon
1916
Oil on canvas
65.5 x 100.5 cm

Max Ernst

Laon, 1916

In 1913, several years before Max Ernst's great career as Dada artist and Surrealist began, he was friends with August Macke and the Rhenish Expressionists and mixed with artist circles. During this period he familiarized himself through his art history studies with a large number of styles and also explored them on a practical level, trying them out and altering them, but without actually copying. It was here that he took his first steps as an artist. Through Macke he became acquainted with, among others, Robert Delaunay, who exhibited his paintings of Laon Cathedral in 1913 at the Gereonsclub in Cologne. From 1914 to 1918 Ernst was active as a war artist. In 1915 he was sent to the north of France, to that very town of Laon with its Gothic cathedral and many spires that had so impressed Delaunay that, after completing his military service, he returned there in 1912 in order to paint it.

Delaunay's paintings invite us to linger. They are friendly; peace reigns. When Max Ernst reached Laon, the First World War was raging. His painting shows the city in flames, the cathedral already half-destroyed and yellow venomous smoke licking up over it. A spire in deathly ash grey seems but a memory of its erstwhile beauty. Delaunay's influence, as well as that of the Cubists, is clearly recognizable.

Although Laon was extensively damaged by the war, the cathedral was in fact spared. Ernst, who in the previous two years had seen a great deal of suffering, has presumably worked his immediate war experiences out of his system here. The destruction he shows of the city and the cathedral might well point to the destruction of his own worldview and his values. From his imagined vantage point he looks out over the cathedral, which he extended out lengthways as in a cityscape. The horizontal format (on the reverse is an oil sketch of the same motif in vertical format) with the large lettering 'LAON' on the lower margin make the picture look almost like a postcard. Yet this is not a pretty memento, but rather a picture of horrifying beauty. In fiery red, blazing yellow and icy blue, it evokes the memory of the city dominated by its imposing cathedral. For Ernst it is now indelibly linked with his wartime experiences. The Cubist grammar of forms is simply predestined for capturing the shattering of the world, the dissolution of the intact form.

Maria Meyer

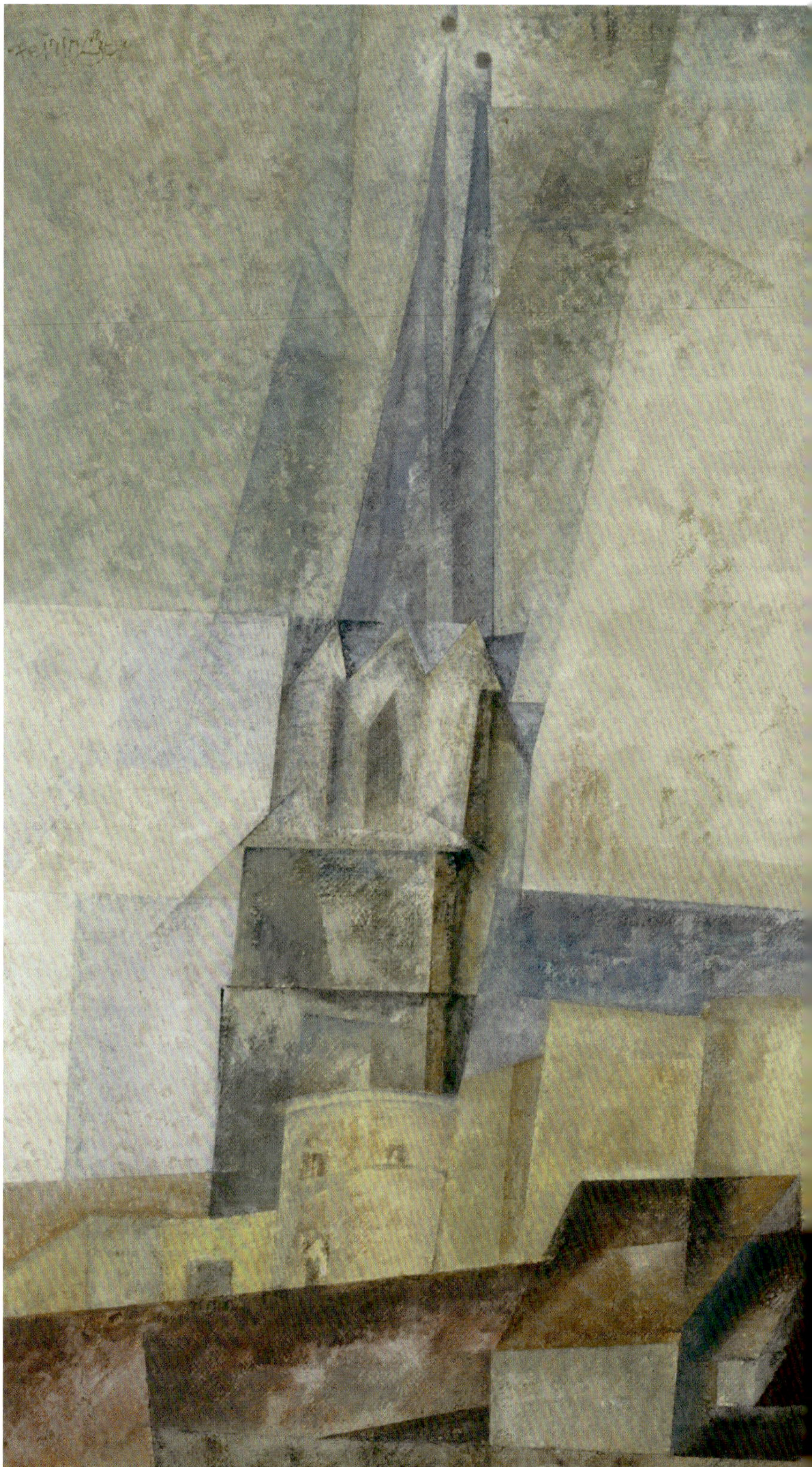

Towers above the City (Halle)
1931
Oil on canvas
88.3 x 124 cm

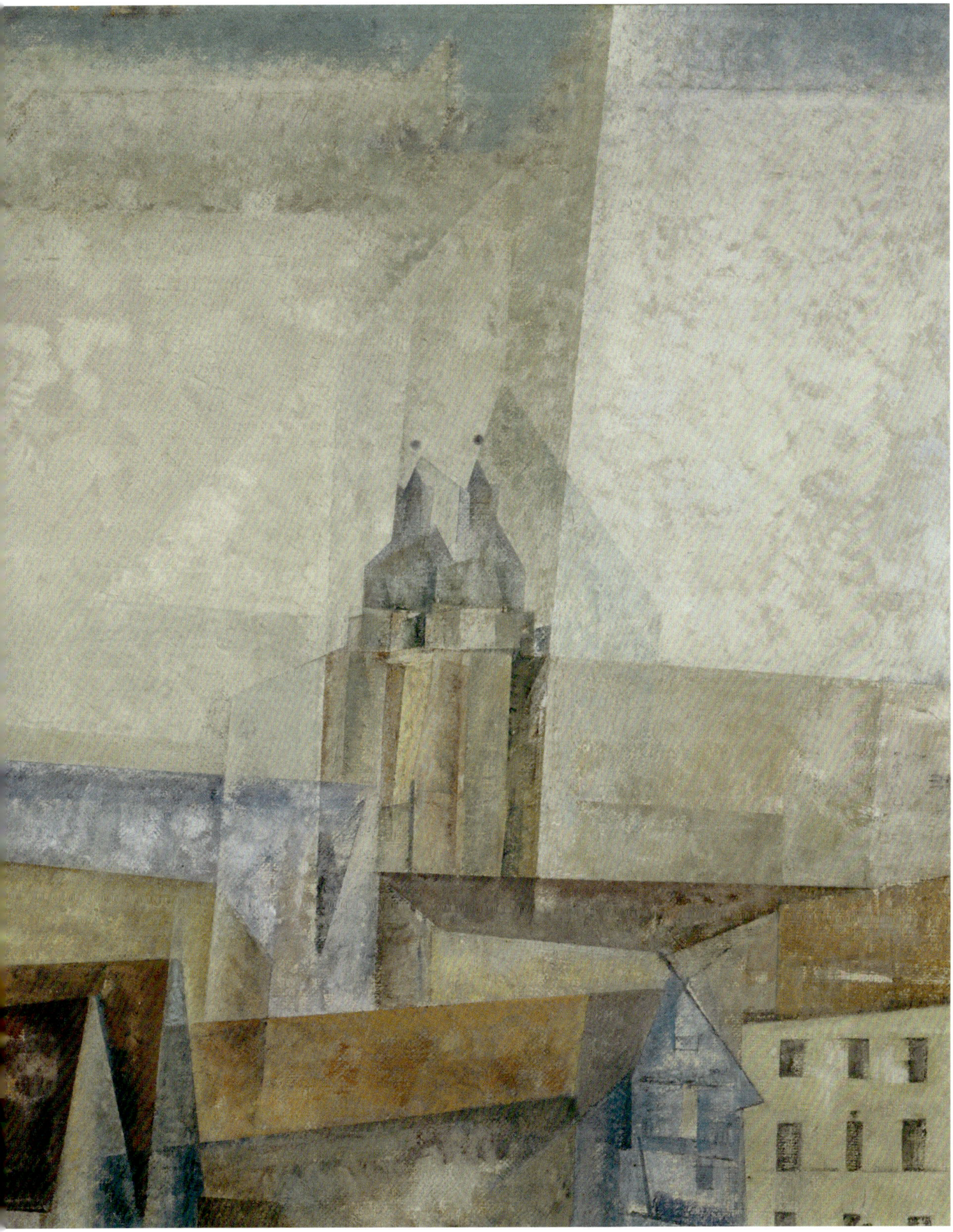

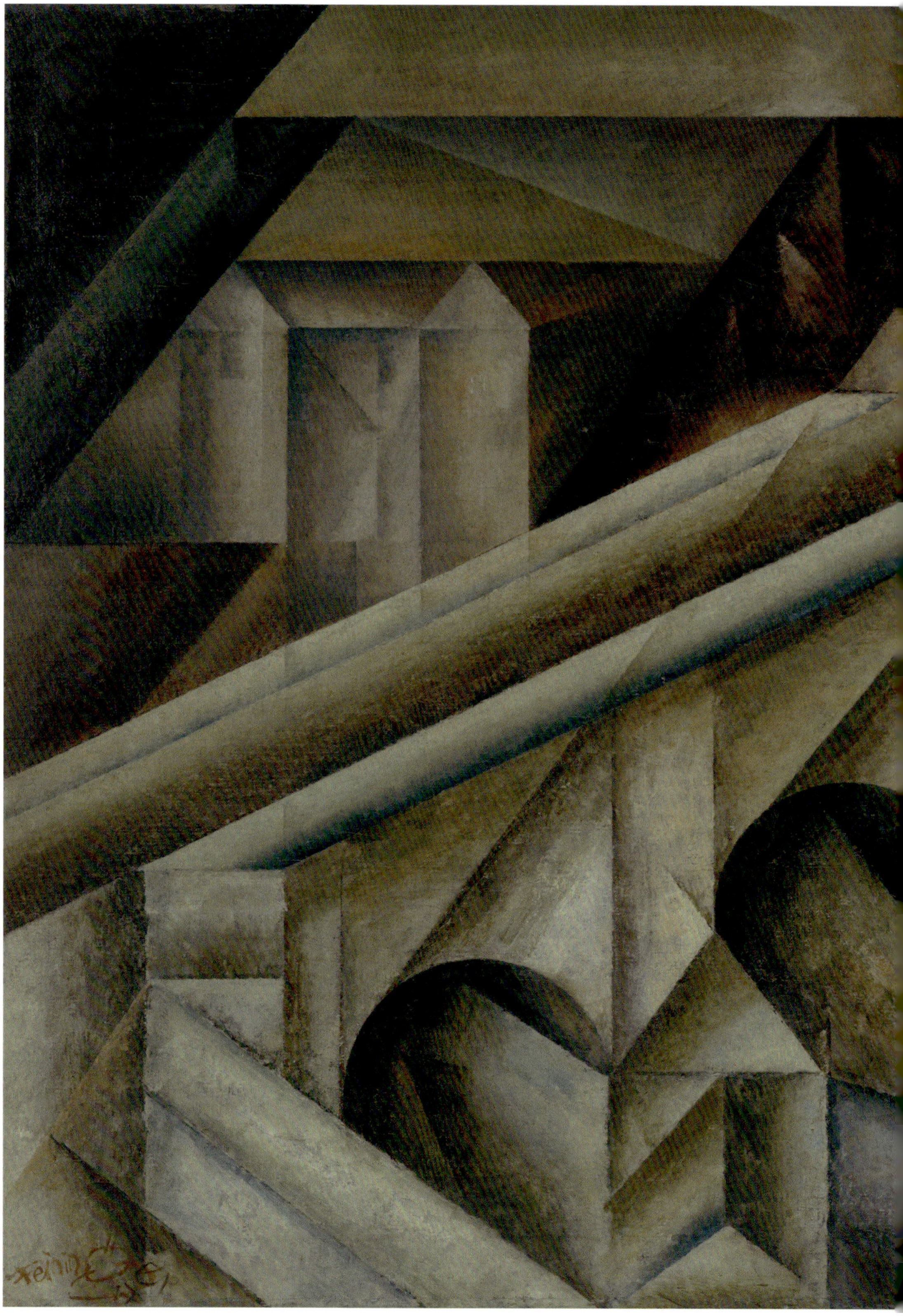

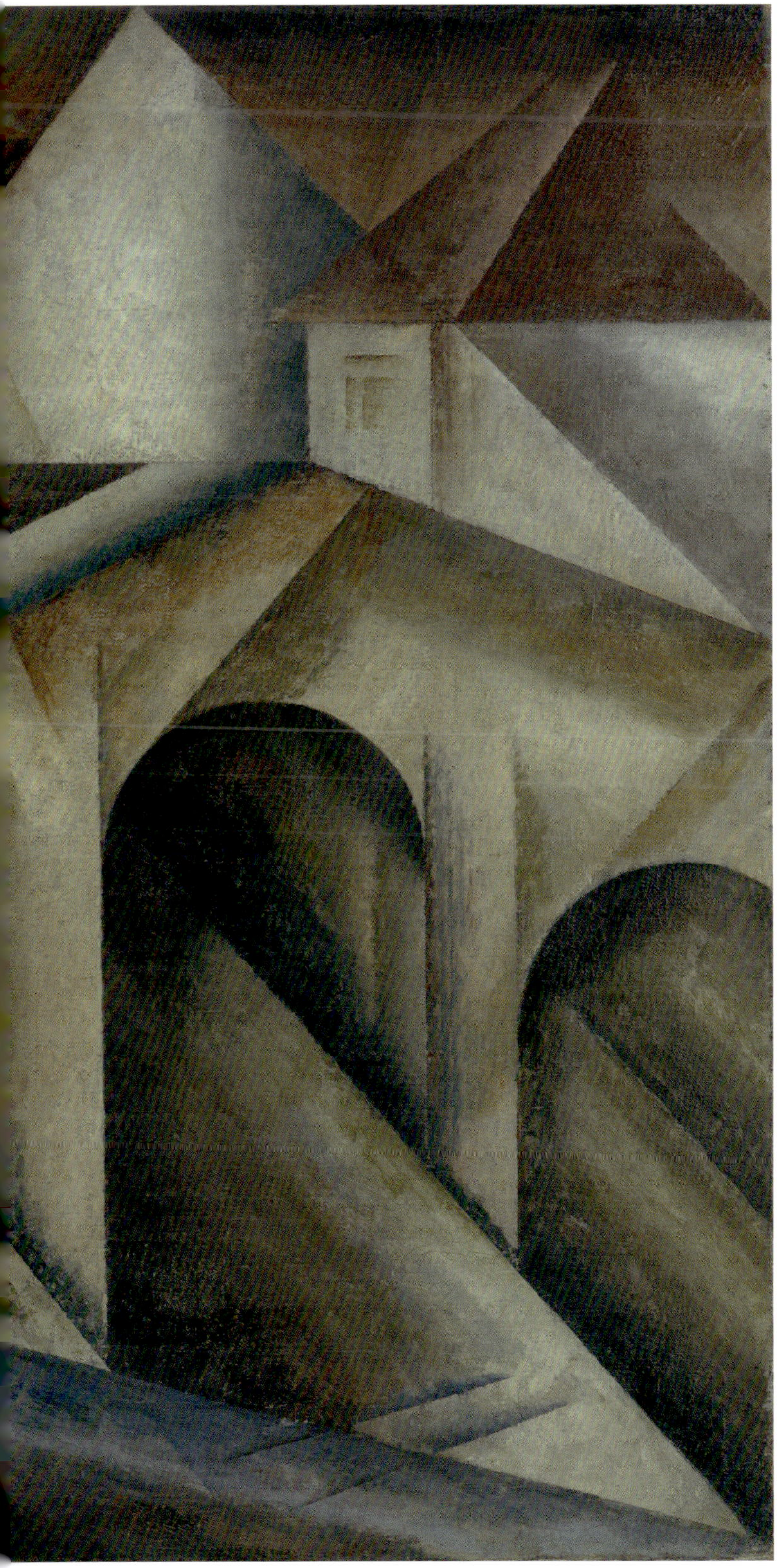

Bridge III
1917
Oil on canvas
80.5 x 100 cm

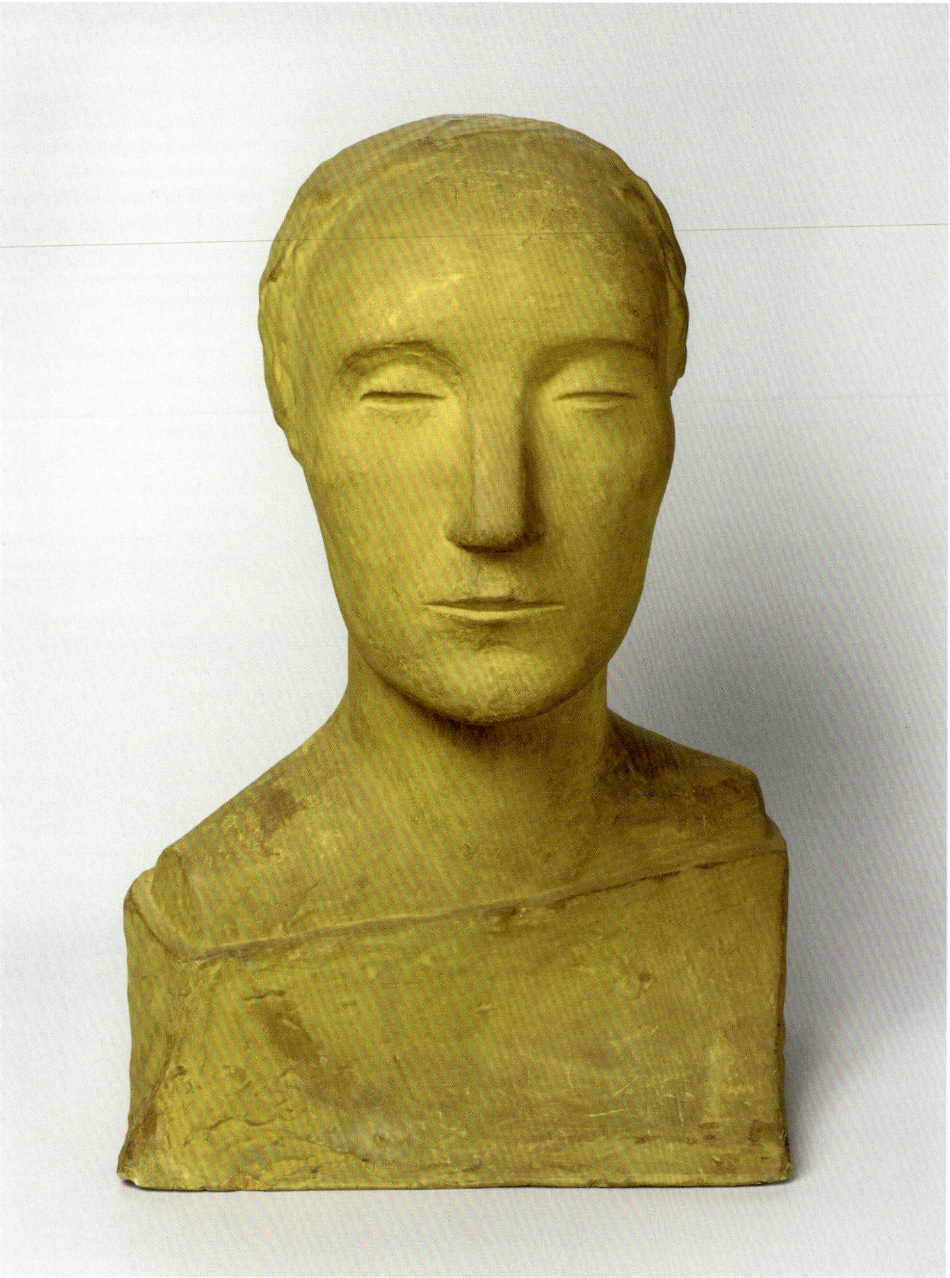

Bust of a Woman
1910
Plaster, painted yellow
H.: 52 cm

Otto Freundlich

Bust of a Woman, 1910

Otto Freundlich didn't begin his artistic career until the age of 27. But a central theme of his oeuvre as a whole can already be found in his first group of works, a series of plaster masks: the search for possibilities of abstracting a human head. The painter-sculptor wrote to a friend: 'I have found that my works leave quite an impression, and the silence of academic sculptors also says something. I see my path quite clearly, not in terms of what I want but what I must do: nothing programmatic.'[1]

And indeed, there was to be nothing programmatic about the course Freundlich would take. Although he worked in Montmartre and associated with the avant-garde artists there, finding a studio at the artists' house Bateau-Lavoir where Picasso also worked, he still managed to create one of the most unique and inventive oeuvres of his generation.

This 1910 bust was the artist's first fully sculptural work. It shows many deviations from the traditional bust: while its profile with a receding hairline is reminiscent of Renaissance depictions, Freundlich applied the rudimentary facial contours of his masks to the subject's face. The base is slightly twisted, diagonally reflecting the shoulder. By way of a slight counter motion, the neck turns the head back towards an *en face* position. Freundlich painted both head and base in a monochromatic yellow, thus taking a step toward the autonomy of colour. **Bust of a Woman** is not an individual likeness, but rather stands for a prototype of the new kind of human being.

Freundlich's search for new forms of expression was linked to an earnest interest in social reform: in the spirit of a socialist utopia of fraternal social solidarity, ethics and aesthetics would be interconnected. Key for Freundlich was 'the responsibility of *each* individual for the fate of all of humanity'.[2]

Freundlich's own utopian hopes were destined to be dashed: the Nazis pictured his monumental bust *The New Man* on the cover of the catalogue for the propaganda exhibition 'Degenerate Art'. As a Jew, Otto Freundlich was deported in 1943 and murdered at the Majdanek concentration camp. Many of his works disappeared or were destroyed.

Freundlich's significance as a pioneer of abstract art was only appreciated later. His visionary idea of a 'Paris-Moscow Street of Sculpture' has been partially realized since the early 1970s as a pacifist European project in his memory.

Erec Gellautz

1 Letter from Otto Freundlich to Herwarth Walden from early 1907, in: Verein August-Macke-Haus and Joachim Heusinger von Waldegg (eds.), *Otto Freundlich und die rheinische Kunstszene*, Bonn 2007, p. 115.

2 Otto Freundlich, 'Der bildhafte Raum (Auszug)', 1931, printed in: *Otto Freundlich, Schriften*, Uli Bohnen (ed.), Cologne 1982, p. 281 (italics in original).

George Grosz

Young Spanish Girl, 1927
Portrait of Doctor Eduard Plietzsch, 1928

By the mid-1920s, George Grosz had tired of political life in Berlin: he no longer saw himself in the role of the constant revolutionary. All the same, the critical view he took of the so-called pillars of society – the military, the church and representatives of the German educated elite – remained unchanged.
His travels to France and his stays in Paris during 1924 and 1925 reaffirmed his intention not to just spend several months each year in France, but 'to stay in France for a few years'.[1] Financially speaking, despite success and recognition in Berlin and abroad, he was still reliant on sales and thus on his art dealer Alfred Flechtheim, who maintained galleries in Düsseldorf and Berlin.

In early April 1927, Grosz travelled with his family to Pointe Rouge near Marseille. He wanted to spend the next few months until October on the French Riviera. From there, he wrote on 27 May to his brother-in-law Otto Schmalhausen in Berlin: 'My plan (with Flechtheim's speculation, of course) is to paint a series of "sellable" landscapes here: that is, without the element of scandal. If I can sell these, in the winter I can return to my favourite large-format paintings like *Eclipse of the Sun* or *Pillars of Society*.'[2]

In Pointe Rouge, Grosz painted studies of nature in oil on cardboard: 'Using nature, one has to simplify and "build" the image correctly. I do not want to paint "mimetically", but to compose by borrowing from nature's model. My interest is not in the "mood" or the "atmosphere", but in a special pictorial space, architectural structure, sculpture, etc.'[3] On 18 July, he moved with his family to Cassis-sur-Mer. There, he lived in a small tower high on a hill with a view over the vineyards and olive trees. There were hardly any amenities in this dwelling where he lived with his family and worked until mid-October, no electrical lighting, no running water. 'I don't want to return to Berlin', Grosz wrote to his brother-in-law.[4] He reported extensively about his work and his approach to painting, and that he had become obsessed with drawing and painting.

Far from the hectic life of the city, Grosz was able to live out for a short time in Cassis the fantasy of an ideal painter's life, also executing there the painting **Young Spanish Girl**. All the necessities of life could be obtained from his surroundings: wine, fruit, fish, etc. The gaze from his elevated location onto the fields and the sea inspired a constant stream of new motifs at various times of the day. Only a few portraits were created during this period: three of young women and a portrait of the artist's wife. **Young Spanish Girl** presumably shows a child who had been spending time with her parents in Cassis and who sat for the painter. The result is an impressive image of a delicate young girl, who appears serious and introverted, but is far removed from being one of the 'thin big-city girls' that the portrait is often interpreted as representing.

The following year, Grosz painted the **Portrait of Doctor Eduard Plietzsch**, a likeness of the famous art historian (1886–1961), who was a friend of the artist. Besides his political paintings, Grosz preferred painting portraits, executing more than thirty in the Neue Sachlichkeit style by 1928, several in a large format. Except for the *Boxing Champion Max Schmeling*, which Flechtheim had arranged, Grosz painted mostly friends, including the writers Max Herrmann-Neiße and Walter Mehring, as well as his wife, Eva, and her sister Lotte, his mother, and himself. The portraits were probably all painted in his studio at Nassauische Strasse 4 in Berlin-Wilmersdorf, which had a large westward-facing window providing light. One of the props Grosz liked to use in his portraits was the large armchair in the studio, in which he sat his models, first seen in the portrait of Hermann-Neiße from 1925. Grosz posed Plietzsch in such a way that the light from the studio window falls on the right side of his model. The image is painted in a fluid fashion; the subject is elegantly dressed, and his physiognomy evinces an arrogant scepticism and slight irony, characterizing Plietzsch just as his contemporaries described him.

The portrait was purchased in 1929 by the patronage society of the Staatliche Gemäldegalerie Dresden for that museum, where it was confiscated in 1937 as part of the 'Degenerate Art' action. An anonymous photograph exists of the depot of 'degenerate art' located in the attic of Schloss Schönhausen. The picture, which must have been taken around 1941, shows the painting hanging on the wall next to the *Portrait of the Poet Theodor Däubler* by Otto Dix, which had been confiscated from the Nationalgalerie in Berlin (see p. 24). Both paintings had been designated for destruction or sale abroad. The fact that today, despite these barbaric intentions, both are again available to the public at Museum Ludwig is thanks to a lucky happenstance of history.

Ralph Jentsch

1 Letter from George Grosz to Otto Schmalhausen, Pointe Rouge, 17 July 1927, in: *George Grosz: Briefe 1913–1959*, Herbert Knust (ed.), Reinbek 1979, p. 105.
2 Ibid., p. 101.
3 Ibid.
4 Ibid., p. 113.

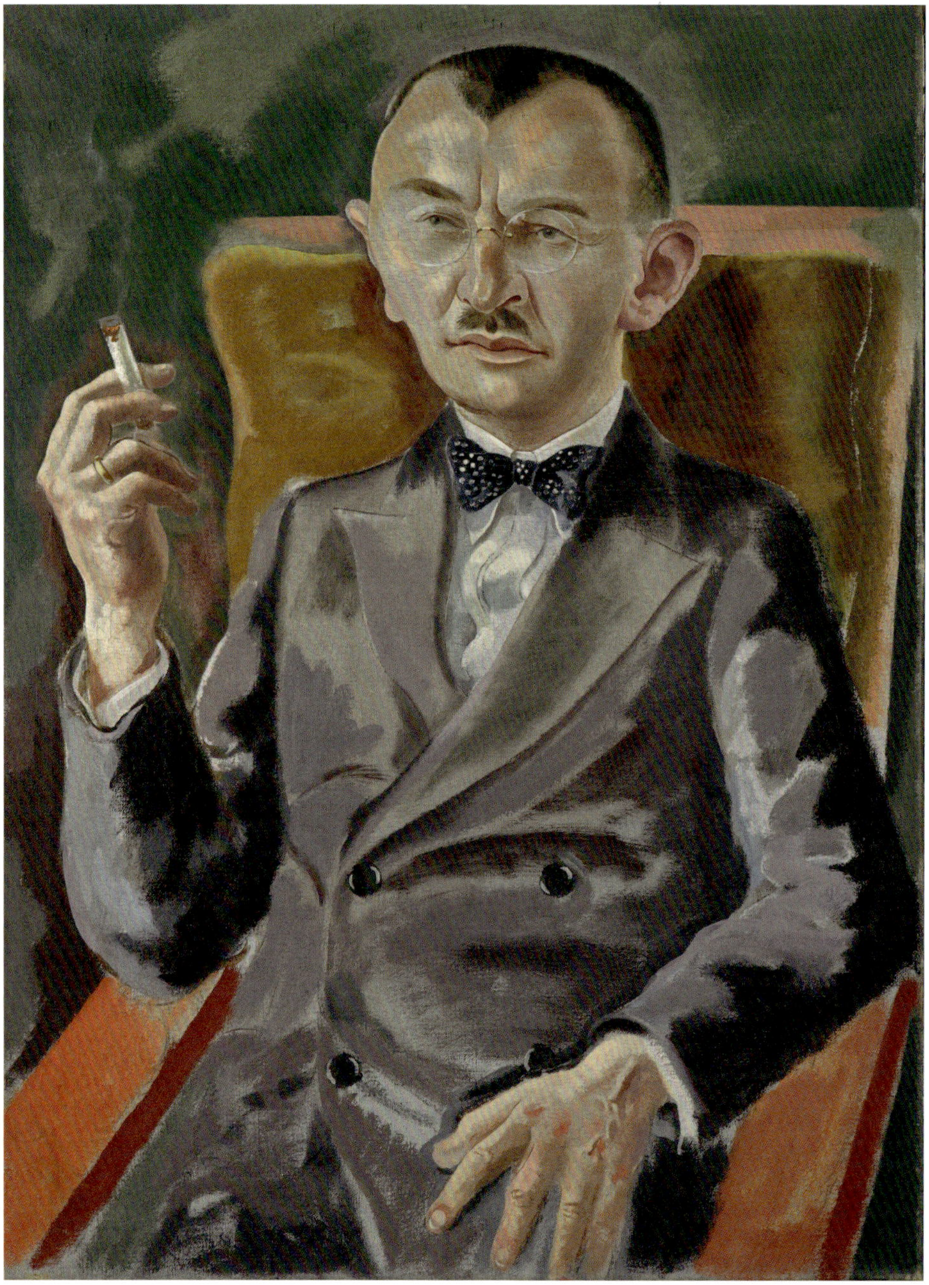

Portrait of Doctor Eduard Plietzsch

1928

Oil on canvas

110 x 79.5 cm

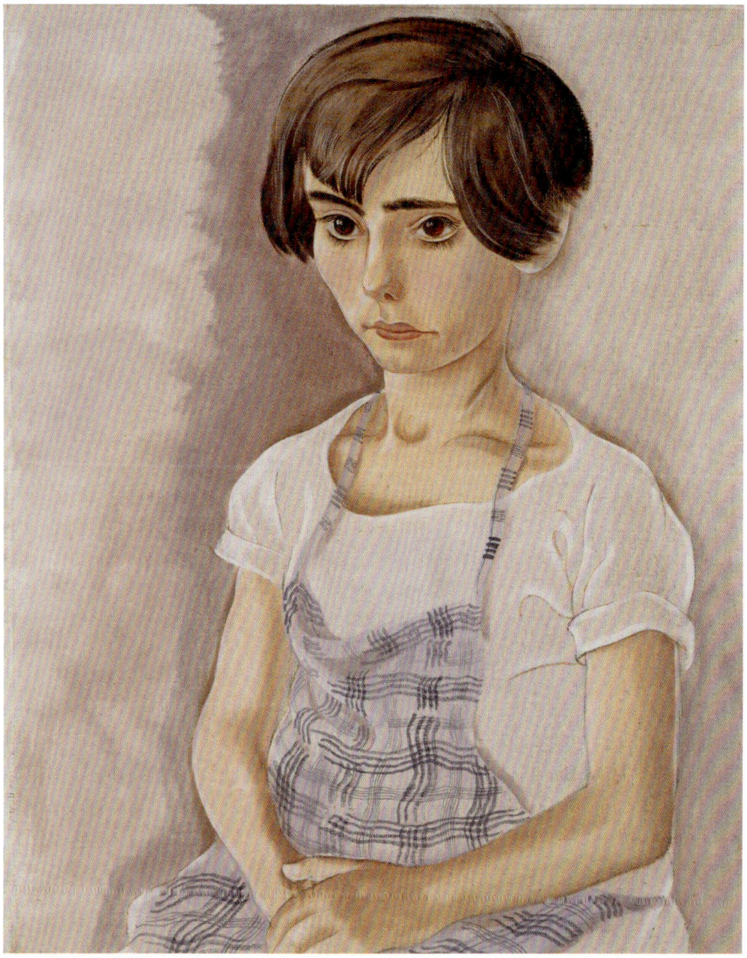

Young Spanish Girl
1927
Oil on canvas
65.5 x 50.8 cm

Erich Heckel

Beach, 1912
Canal, 1912
Forest Scene, 1913
The Bedini-Tafanis, 1928
Portrait of James Ensor, 1930

Within just a few years, several architecture students in Dresden, all of them barely over twenty, developed a style of painting that would decisively affect twentieth-century art. Their art aimed to be 'immediate and authentic', as stated in the 'programme' of Die Brücke, the artists' group they founded in 1905. The programme was in fact hardly a programme at all: the students indeed had no idea where their path would lead. What was clear was that they no longer wanted anything to do with academic painting using plaster casts as models, or based on professional models in artificial poses. They painted themselves and their girlfriends in their studios or outdoors enjoying everyday activities, swimming, playing or in conversation.

Their aim was to capture the characteristic nature of movements and quickly record them on the canvas. Accordingly, while working at the Moritzburg Lakes near Dresden from 1909 onward, Erich Heckel and Ernst Ludwig Kirchner in particular developed a loose style of painting using liquid paints, through which the canvas and the primer would shine. Anatomic precision and an accurate rendering of specific colouring were less important than the mood and harmony of the whole. Each Brücke artist sought out a seaside refuge in the summer months. Max Pechstein discovered Nidden on the Curonian Spit (today known as Nida and part of present-day Lithuania). Shortly thereafter, Kirchner chose the Baltic Sea island of Fehmarn. Initially, Heckel went to Dangast in the Jade Bight on Germany's North Sea coast with Karl Schmidt-Rottluff, but from 1912 he began his search anew. He first spent time on the Baltic Sea island of Hiddensee so that he could visit Kirchner on Fehmarn afterwards.

His painting **Beach** was created on the northeast coast of Hiddensee, before the cliffs, just a fifteen-minute walk from his summer residence at Hiddensoe's Restaurant and Boarding House in the village of Grieben. The yellow sandy beach curves around the dark-blue water, beside which the yellow becomes a more powerful red-orange. In the background on the left, a cliff overgrown with verdant foliage acts as a counterweight to the dark blue. At the edge of the cliff on the right, the darker yellow deepens into a red that also appears on the five figures in the foreground. The figures are suggested with just a few brushstrokes, some of which extend beyond the edges of their bodies; these have been left uncorrected, for the sake of immediacy. They produce a diagonal movement that starts from the figure in a dynamic sitting position on the left and proceeds out to the right foreground of the picture. The weaker movement of the two people on the beach in the background, who are walking towards the right, takes on added weight due to the fact that the figures are depicted in black, which colour can be interpreted neither as clothing nor shadow, but rather arises logically from the composition of the picture as a whole. Despite the spontaneity of execution, the colour accents have nevertheless been placed very consciously and deliberately.

Heckel preserved this loose 'Moritzburg' style of painting over many years during his summer sojourns, even though his and Kirchner's use of forms and colours otherwise changed significantly and became more individualized after the two artists moved to Berlin in 1911. In Heckel's Berlin paintings, almost all the colours have been mixed with black. The black lines of the drawings give the paintings a framework, but one that contains a certain disquiet and sense of oppression, due to the predominantly sharp angles of the forms. The painting **Canal** is one of his typical city subjects from this period. The Landwehr canal near the Hallesches Gate in Berlin is flanked by building façades to the left (the dome of the Church of the Holy Cross appears to rise above the gables of the brick buildings in the foreground) and bordered by a tree-lined pathway to the right. The scaffolding in front of the houses echoes the dark branches of the bare trees. These brown-black zones intrude from the right and left like wedges into the painting, which is otherwise dominated by the grey-white tones seen in the cloudy sky, the stuccoed buildings in the background, the bridge and the reflections in the water. The narrow green pathways on both banks of the canal fail to brighten the painting's autumnal mood.

Alongside his depictions of real subjects, from 1912 on Heckel increasingly began to create symbol-laden compositions inspired by books, visits to the cinema or his own imagination. Notably, he mostly chose titles that didn't reveal this quality of his paintings. Thus his famous painting of a scene from Fyodor Dostoevsky's novel *The Idiot* bears the innocuous title *Two Men at the Table*. **Forest Scene** (1913) also displays traits placing it in the same body of work. In 1913, the Hamburg collector Gustav Schiefler invited Heckel to come to Mellingstedt, a town north of Hamburg on the River Alster. This was before the artist discovered Osterholz on the Flensburg Fjord, which was to become his destination in future summers. The painting may have been executed in the forest near Mellingstedt, but the composition strongly suggests it was a work of imagination. The plants follow an ornamental order. A slender tree trunk topped by two curved branches separates off the right third of the painting and creates two distinct pictorial spaces. A man stands in the narrower space, his gaze directed at a woman lying in the broader space. He opens his hand in her direction, making clear he wants to introduce himself, and a flower grows upward near his pubic area. The woman has closed her eyes in apparent indifference, but reveals herself in her full beauty; her warm yellow colour decoratively distinguishes her from the red of the forest floor, while the man contains only a pale reflection of her beauty, and his red-brown skin colour almost disappears into his surroundings. The large heart-shaped leaf in the foreground is framed in another heart formed by its curved stem and the plants in the middle that are bowing towards it.

A painting by Otto Mueller (an artist who joined the Brücke group in Berlin and was much admired by the movement's other members) shows *Adam and Eve* in two halves of a painting divided by an ornamental tree. Stylistic considerations suggest that, despite previous claims to the contrary, this painting may have been executed as early as 1913. The similarity to Heckel's painting supports this theory. It is entirely possible that the two painters were inspired by one another.

During the First World War, Heckel served in a first aid station in Flanders that was at first under the command of a friend, the art historian Walter Kaesbach. Kaesbach was a member of the Berlin literary circle centred around the poet Stefan George, and brought a number of other young painters to his station, as well as the writer Ernst Morwitz, one of George's most trusted confidants; after Kaesbach was transferred, Heckel was responsible for the station. During quiet periods when the medical orderlies had less to do, they organized evening readings or painted. Heckel was primarily stationed in and around Ostend, and he visited local artists, including the sculptor George Minne in Laethem-Saint-Martin and the painter James Ensor in Ostend. He was mainly interested in the latter's landscapes and still lifes, and sought to bring many of these paintings to the attention of Kaesbach and other collectors. Heckel's burgeoning interest in classical styles was fed by his contact with members of George's circle, which expanded in Berlin after the war, and he gradually suppressed the stylistic elements of Expressionism.

In 1924 Heckel painted a portrait of Ensor, working for the first time from memory. The painting was destroyed along with Heckel's Berlin studio during the Second World War. It showed Ensor in a monumental half-length pose wearing an open coat, holding an umbrella cane diagonally across his body, standing with a determined gaze in a street in Ostend beside a display window containing his works. The second **Ensor Portrait**, from 1930, has the same location as its background. Here, the half-length portrait takes up only the lower half of the canvas; the Belgian painter wears a quizzical, questioning expression, and he pulls a cloak over his shoulder as if to ward off a chill. A new element in the painting is a sailor looking at the window display. The deep blue of his uniform and the red pompom on his hat bring fresh energy to the painting, while the viewer's gaze is lost at the end of the street in the ambiguity of the light-blue sky.

Mountain landscapes and city scenes were key themes for Heckel from the 1920s onwards, representing his travels through Germany, France, Switzerland, the Netherlands, England and Scandinavia. But now, the paintings were chiefly done later in his studio. Often there are accompanying watercolours which were deliberately composed as paintings, whose compositions were retained or only slightly modified. The narrow vertical painting **The Bedini-Tafanis** was for example first prepared as a watercolour, entitled *Departing Artistes*. There, the composition ended below the knee of the boy, and the curtain has been drawn more tightly, so that the second artist almost disappears into its dark folds. In the painting, both artists are represented in full length, with the boy thanking the audience in front of the curtain, which is decorated with an elaborate pattern.

The Bedini-Tafanis were a family of artistes who successfully toured throughout Europe in the 1920s and 30s. Heckel painted *The Bedini Troupe* again in 1931, with four individuals performing before a painted backdrop depicting an Italian landscape. It is uncertain whether the painting, which too was lost when Heckel's Berlin studio was destroyed in 1944, was based on more recent contact with the troupe. Most likely that was not the case, as two of the artists appear to be the same age as they were in the 1928 painting. The world of the circus and of wandering performers occupied Heckel well into his old age. *The Young Rider*, painted in 1955, is the last of his paintings to deal with this theme. Shortly thereafter, human figures disappeared almost completely from Heckel's paintings, appearing only as decorative figures, until the painter put down his brush completely in 1964.

Andreas Hüneke

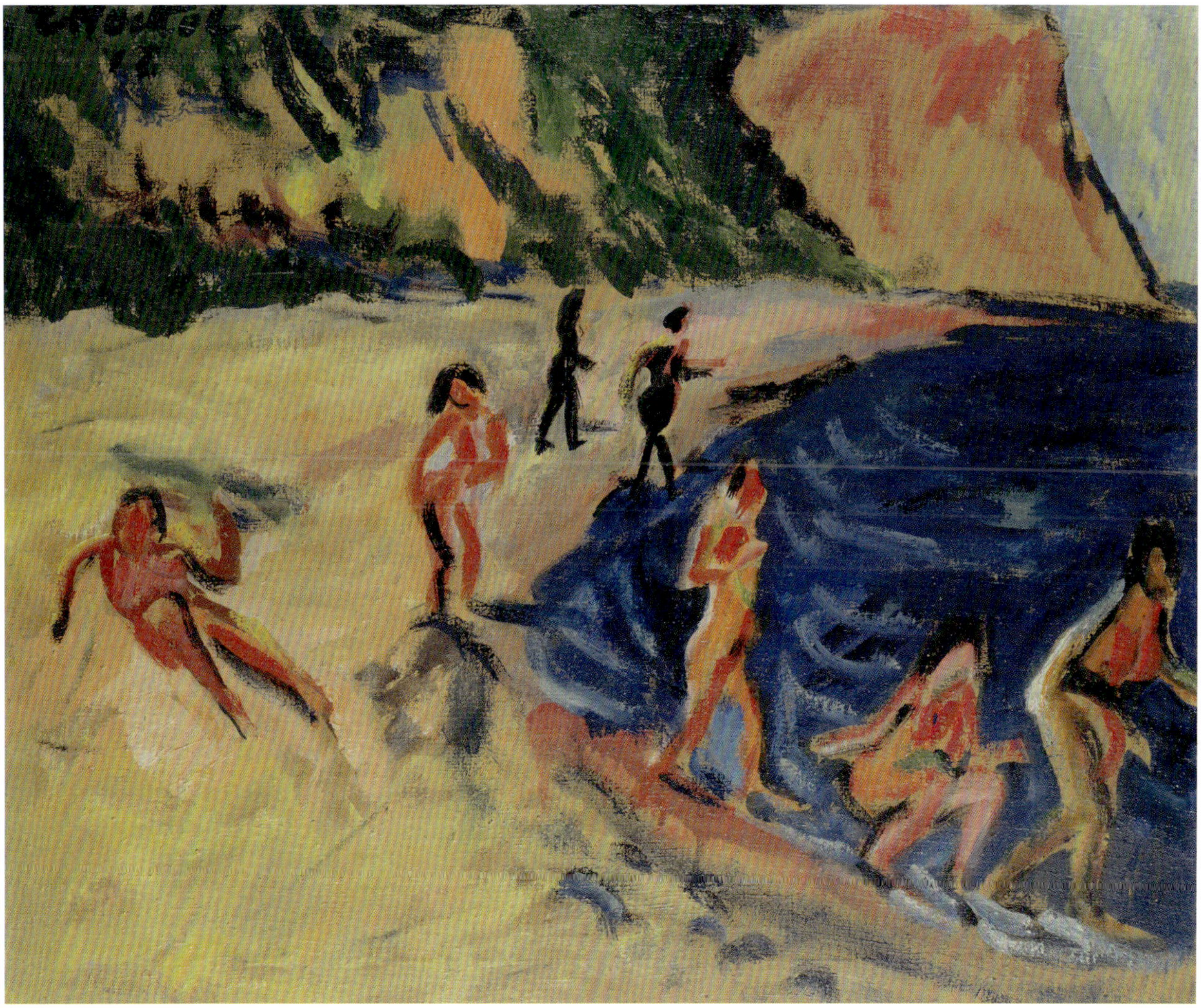

Beach
1912
Oil on canvas
70.5 x 81 cm

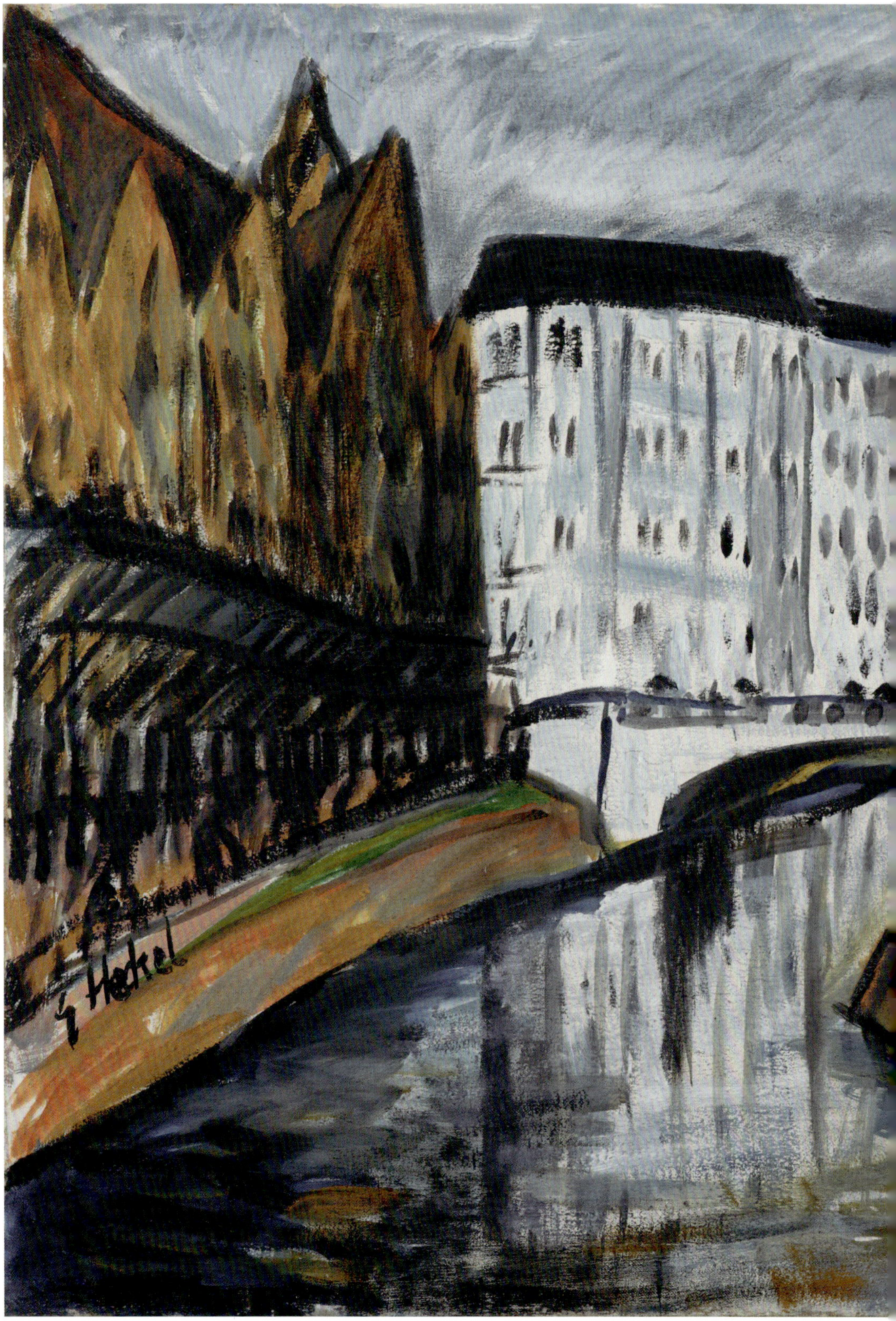

Canal
1912
Oil on canvas
83 x 100 cm

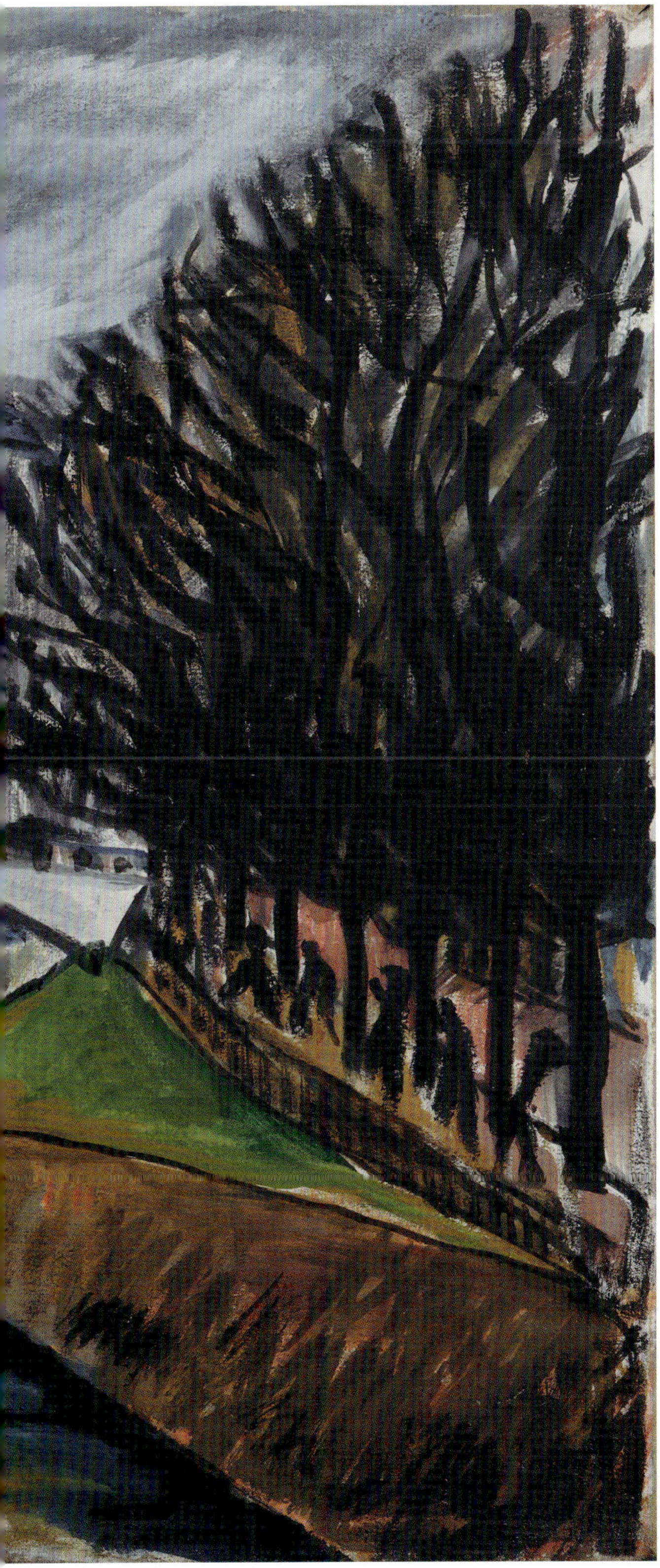

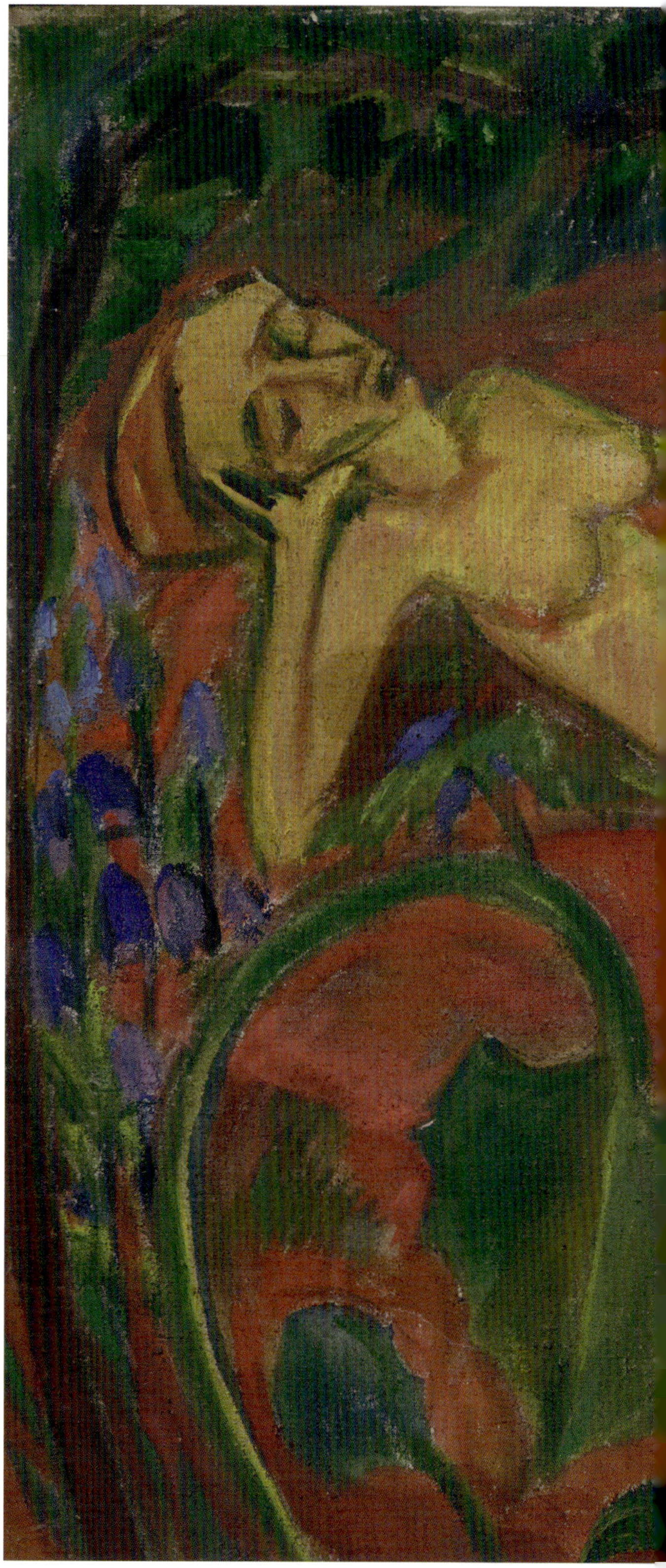

Forest Scene
1913
Oil on canvas
70 x 80.8 cm

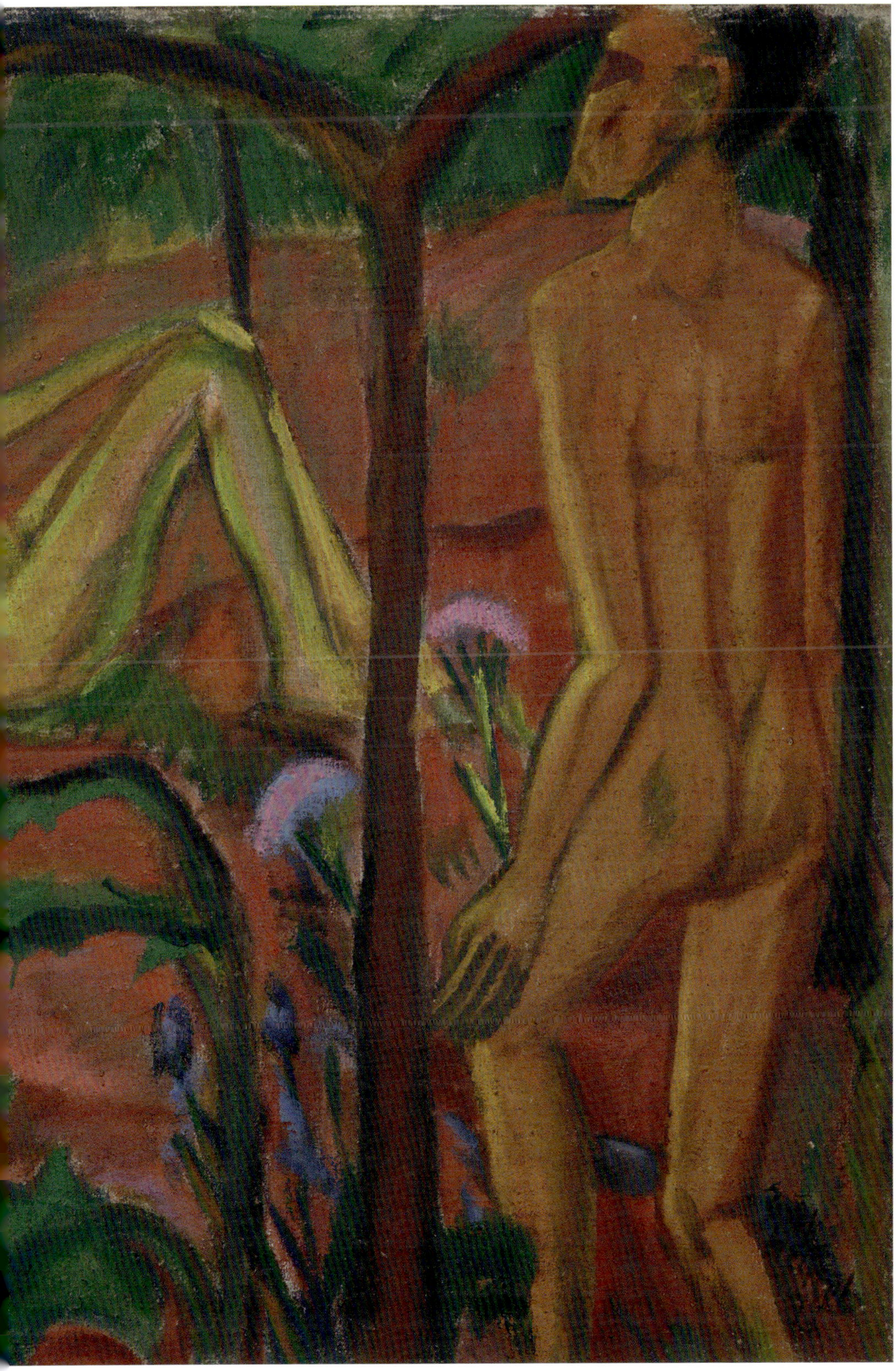

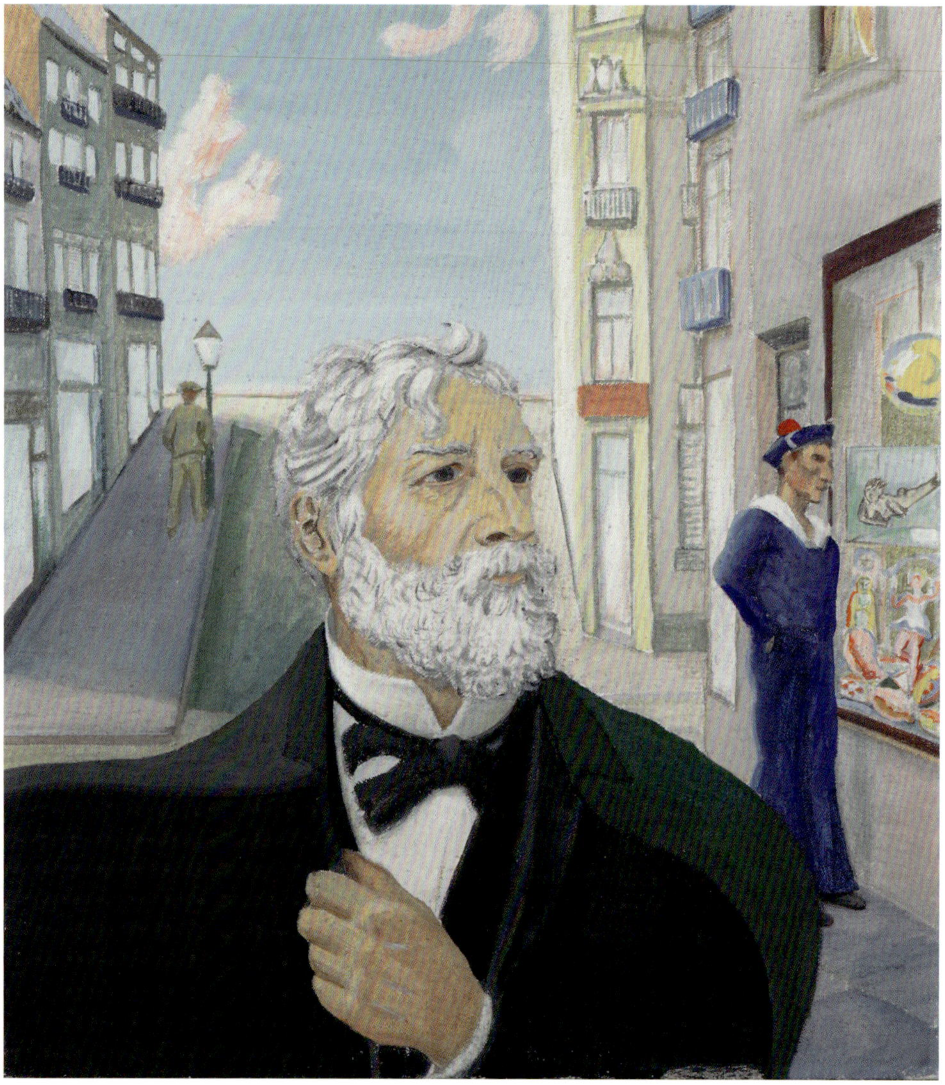

Portrait of James Ensor
1930
Oil on canvas
80 x 70 cm

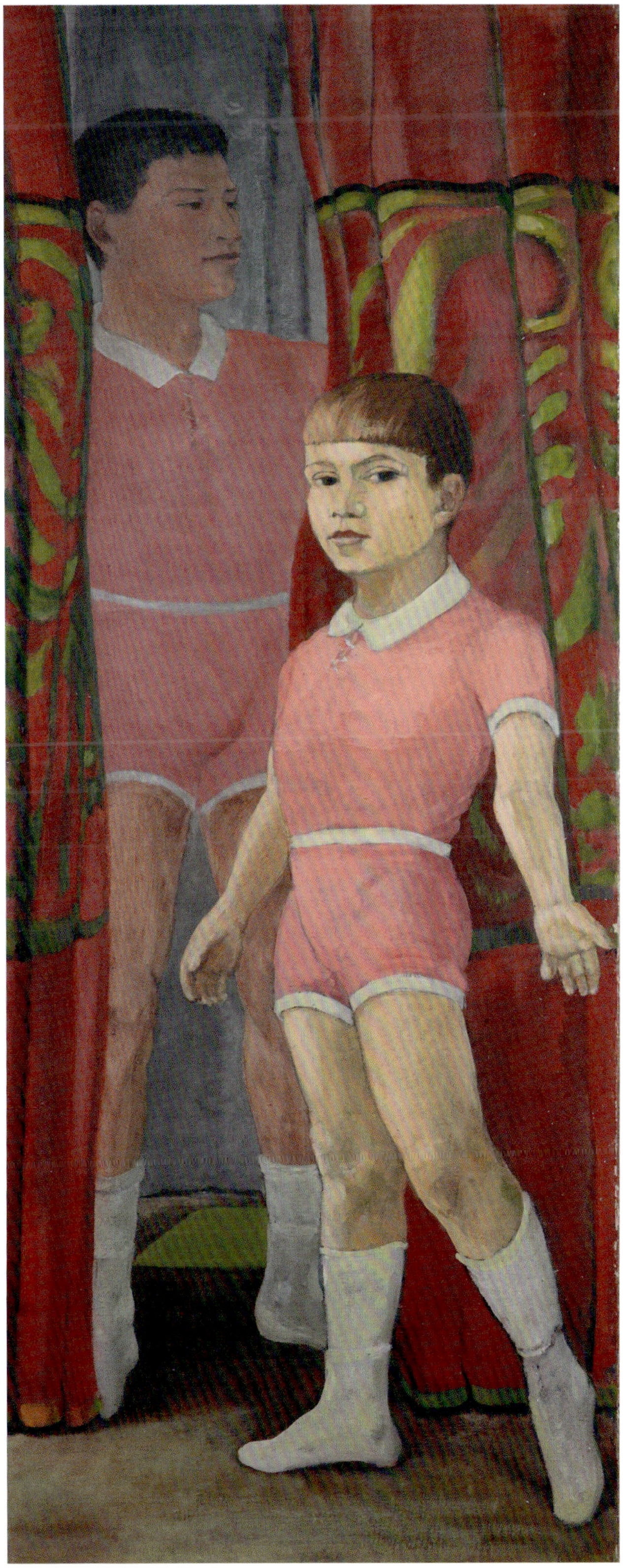

The Bedini-Tafanis
1928
Oil on canvas on wood
165.7 x 65.5 cm

Heinrich Hoerle

Carnival, 1929
Two Women, 1930

In **Carnival**, also known as **Masks**, five figures crowd a horizontal space. A painted framing edge divides the scene into two uneven parts. To the darkened left, the muscular arm of a masked figure in black and grey grabs the mouth of a reveller in a pointy orange hat, his right arm raised rigidly in a Nazi salute. The violent action skews the mask and with it the fixed expression of surprise, revealing the beige skin of an ear and cheek below. At the centre stands a stoic female figure, chest half-bared in a costume reminiscent of classical columns. Peeking over her shoulder is a witness to the scene with features similar to the artist's own. To the far right another masked figure salutes in tandem with the first. Politically positioned on the radical left, Heinrich Hoerle and his contemporaries, commonly known as the Cologne Progressives, also hosted popular carnival celebrations. While Hoerle's title references the beloved Rhenish tradition, the festivities serve here as a metaphor for the lurking threat of fascism.

Critics often remarked on frequent shifts in Hoerle's artistic style, his penchant for experimentation. Exemplary of his painting style in the late 1920s, **Carnival** combines flat, planar surfaces with shaded, volumetric forms. Painted the following year, **Two Women** shares a similar treatment of figures in space. Meticulously painted on the pressboard surface are two female nudes: one facing the viewer, the other seen only from behind. Despite perky rounded breasts, belly or buttocks, the figures appear tightly built – stiff and unmoving – into the compositional structure. The foremost figure holds her left arm perpendicular to her body, bending it at the elbow to grasp the crown of her red-haired head with her left hand. Parallel to her left, her right arm extends out in front of her body. A light green cloth is draped stiffly across – or perhaps more precisely, moulded around – her forearm. The index finger of her right hand points directly upwards from the knuckle at an impossible angle in direct alignment with the vertical axis formed by the backbone of her blonde counterpart.

In 1930, art critic Ernst Kallai saw Hoerle, and his close contemporaries Franz Wilhelm Seiwert and Jankel Adler, as developing a new architectonic form in painting by 'building' forms and colours into the structure of the picture plane.[1] In **Carnival** and **Two Women** Hoerle's interest in a rigorous linear composition dominates the organic, sensual quality of the figures. Human flesh and textiles resemble architectural elements.

In **Two Women**, the blonde figure faces away from the viewer in the direction of an expanse of green with sections of bright blue both above and below. A single tree dots the landscape and, in spite of the dark shadow it casts, appears flat, as if propped up within the space. Hoerle complicates a simple dichotomy of interior and exterior space with the addition of a spatially inexplicable and atmospheric sky at centre, typical of his more fantastical visions, referred to at the time as 'surrealist'.[2] One reviewer described Hoerle as knowing 'all manner of paint application … that is, paint application not just in planes, but also, for example, in wide dashes, in curls and in dots'.[3] Hoerle's varied brushstroke can perhaps best be seen where skin meets the thickly painted background to the left. As was his custom, Hoerle signed both paintings with only a small lower-case 'h'. In the upper left-hand corner of **Two Women**, this initial is encircled by a matted down section of the otherwise stippled structure – an impression akin to a stamp made by pressing a round object into the still-wet paint.

More than a collector of modern art, in the 1920s Josef Haubrich penned reviews under the pseudonym 'Dr Ludwig Josef'. Writing in 1927 in the Rheinische Zeitung, Haubrich praised Hoerle for his painterly virtuosity while at the same time criticizing how much the artist's work, mostly still lifes, owed to that of Pablo Picasso and Georges Braque.[4] By 1929 Haubrich had been following Hoerle's stylistic shifts for ten years. The purchase of **Carnival** from the Cologne gallery Dr. Becker & Alfred Newman the year of its making signalled acceptance of Hoerle's most recent work. In 1931, likely on commission, the artist completed both a pencil sketch and an oil drawing of Haubrich, both now also in the collection of Museum Ludwig. The collector purchased the painting **Two Women** in 1932 on the occasion of a major solo exhibition at the Kölnischer Kunstverein, which marked the high point of Hoerle's artistic career.

Lynette Roth

1 Ernst Kallai: „Freude am Bauen auch in der Malerei“, *Neue Frankfurter Zeitung*, July 1930, p. 179.
2 L. St. E. [Luise Straus-Ernst], 'Kölner Kunst 1928', in: *Das Kunstblatt*, September 1928, p. 288.
3 Dr Karl Pichl, 'Kölnischer Kunstverein', circa 1932. Clipping in Hoerle estate, private collection.
4 Dr Ludwig Josef, 'Bildende Kunst in Köln, 1. Kölnischer Kunstverein', in: *Rheinische Zeitung*, no. 201, Cologne 1927.

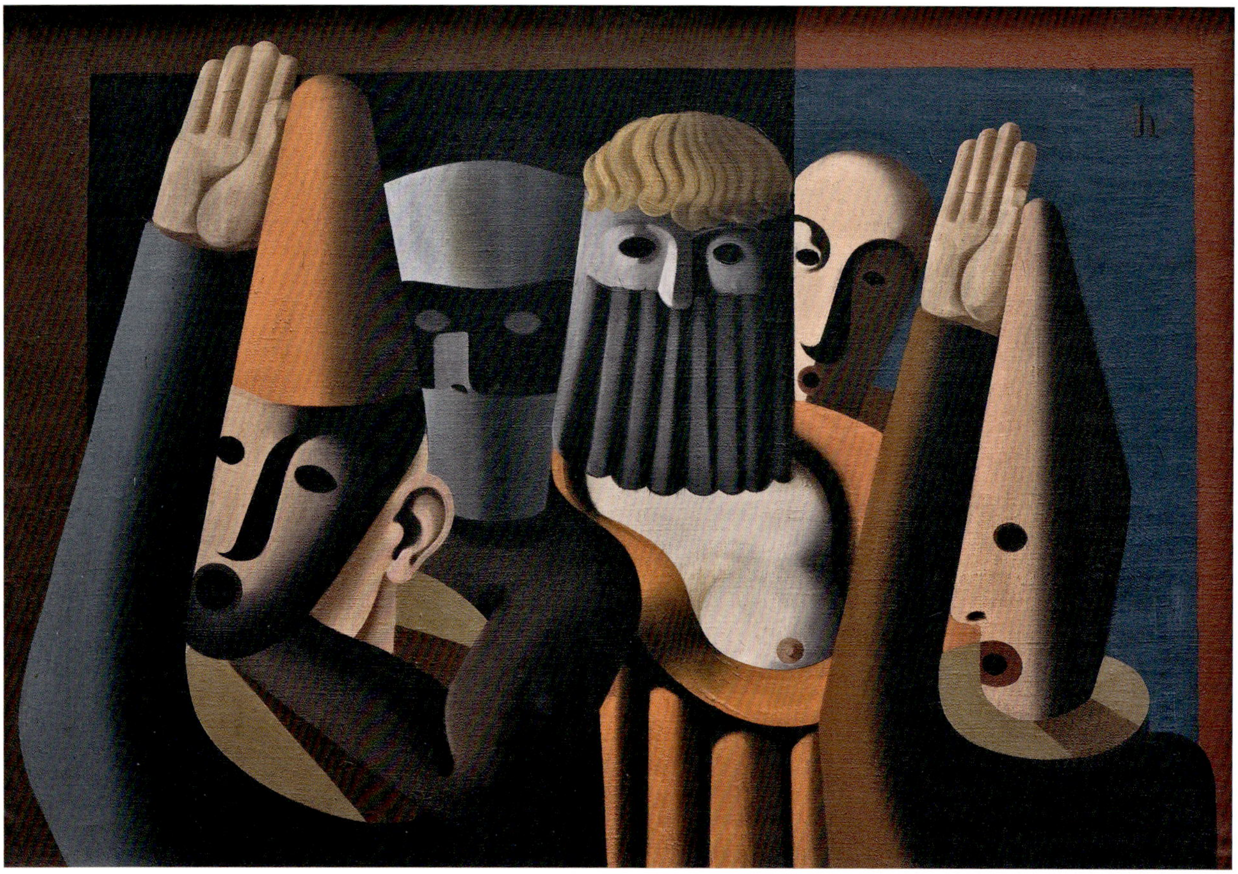

Carnival
1929
Oil on canvas
68.5 x 95.5 cm

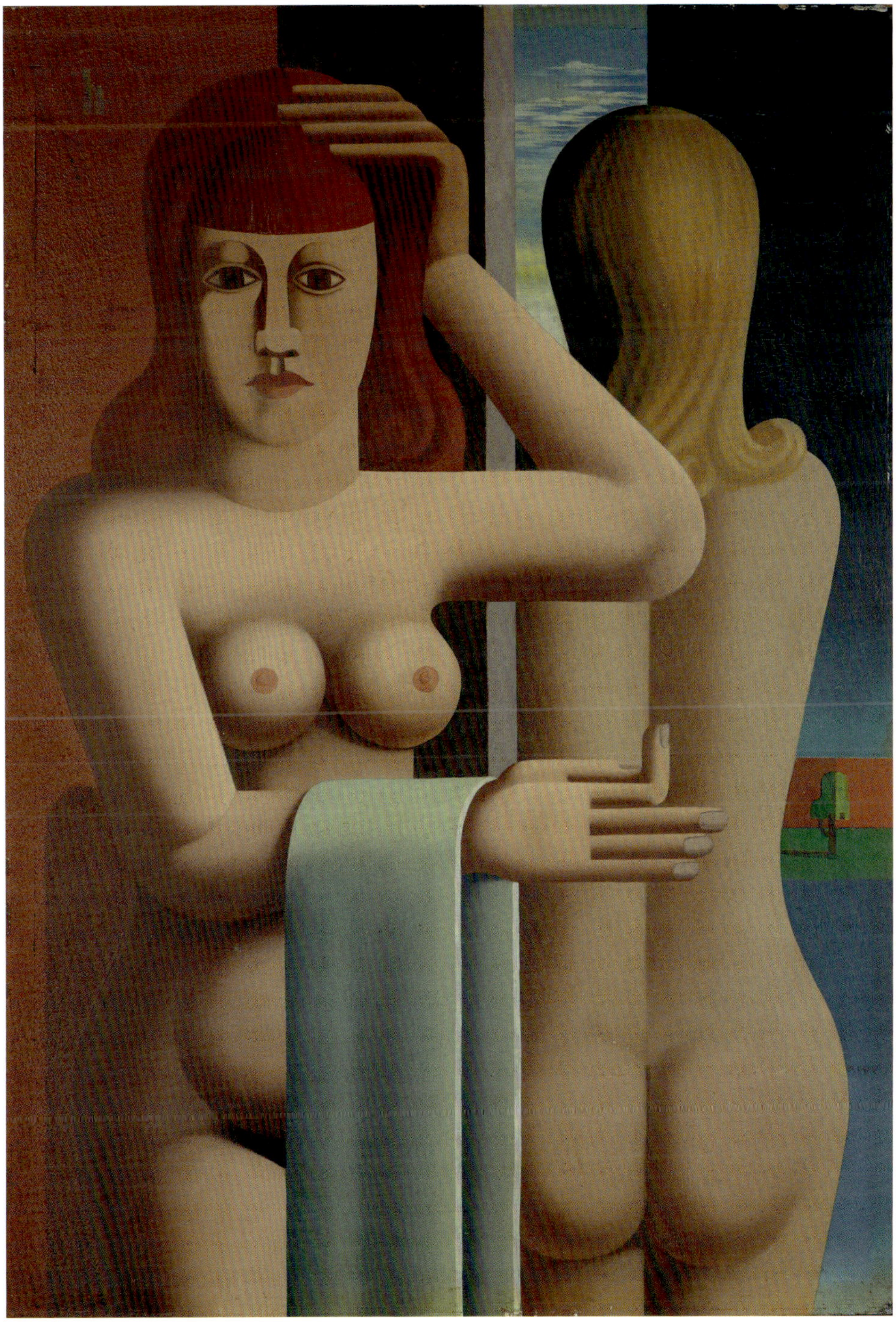

Two Women
1930
Oil on plywood
108 x 73 cm

Karl Hofer

Masquerade, 1922

Throughout his career as an artist, Karl Hofer occupied himself with masked figures and clowns from the world of the circus and vaudeville. This was not simply an expression of his love of masked balls. Using these figures, he could also convey his opinions on social and political events.

The title of Hofer's painting from 1922 points to a **Masquerade** in two senses: on the one hand, the painted and costumed clowns slip into their particular roles so that their merry japes and slapstick allow the audience to forget its fears and woes during the troubled times of the Weimar Republic – at least for the length of the performance. But at the same time the artist unmasks the clowns because their body language tells of loneliness and isolation. Standing very close to the Pierrot is a little clown dressed in brown, whose childish, inquiring gaze is full of pity as he looks at the melancholy figure in white. With his costume, his folded arms and closed eyes, Pierrot seems unapproachable. Similarly, the Harlequin standing to the left in his bright motley and tricorne is unable despite his protective gesture to give any consolation. His gloved and somewhat uncanny-looking hand alone signals the impossibility of his endeavour. Sulky and resigned, he averts his gaze and looks out of the picture space.

The social and financial problems around 1922 not only affected the circus artistes, but all of those not lucky enough to be among the winners of the post-war era. While the imagery adopted by Otto Dix, George Grosz and John Heartfield spoke a clear and drastic pictorial language, Hofer takes a subtler approach in his art. From 1933 onward, however, he was openly critical of National Socialism, which soon led to him being relieved of his state positions. And his art, now stamped 'degenerate', was removed from the German museums.

Hofer's figures may be read in this context as metaphors for the alienated person who must either first find himself outside of middle-class society, or hide his true self behind a mask. With Harlequin and the clown as his go-betweens, Hofer divulges his personal reaction to economic and social discrepancies and their impact on society. By depicting himself in this work (the harlequin has his features) and in other paintings, he indicates that he identifies with his cast of characters and also endeavours in his role as visual artist to enlighten and warn viewers.

Katharina Henkel

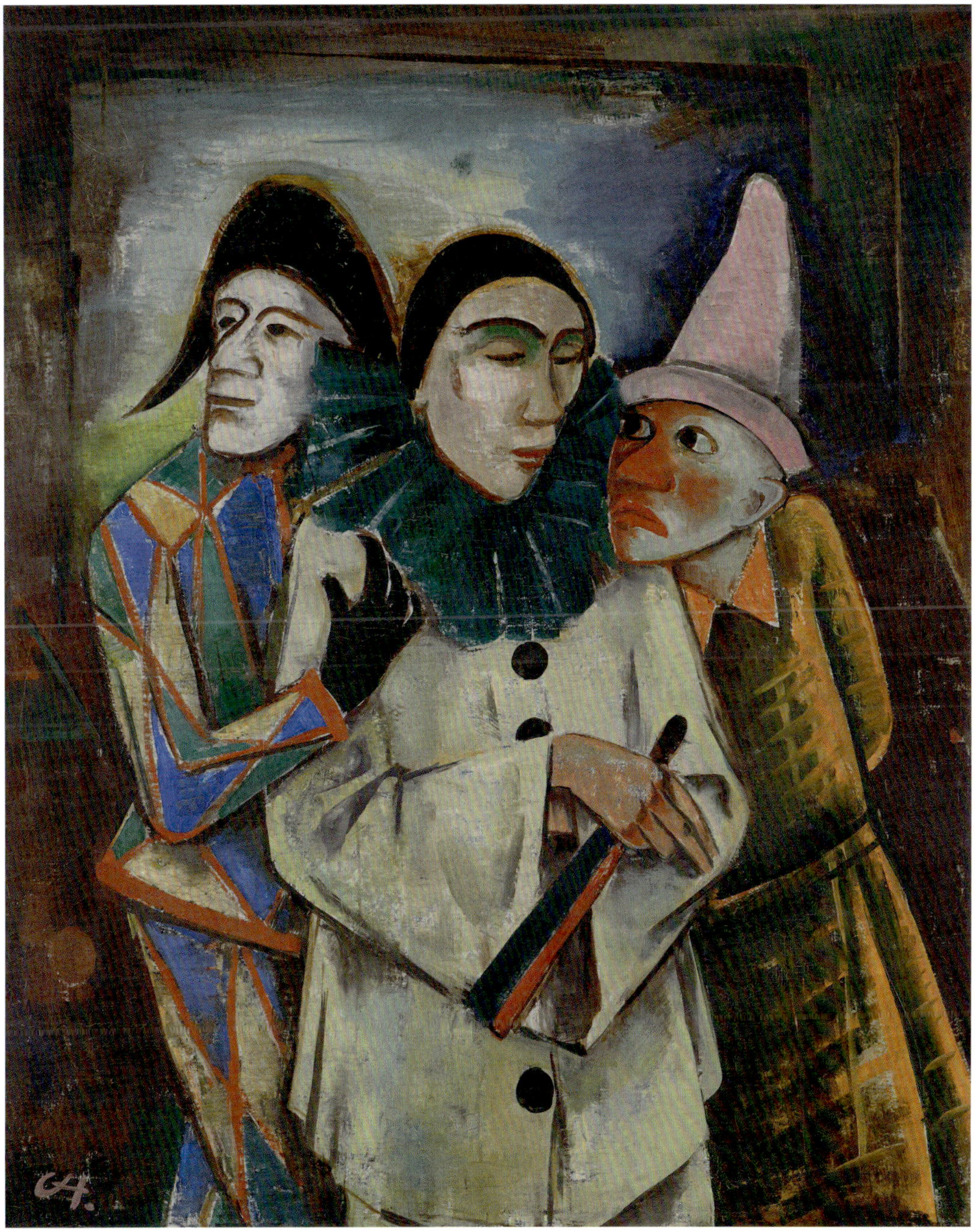

Masquerade
1922
Oil on canvas
129 x 103 cm

Alexej von Jawlensky

Still Life with Vase and Jug, 1909
Head of a Woman with Flowers in Her Hair, 1911
Variation, 1916
Variation, c. 1916
Head of a Woman, c. 1917
Constructivist Head, 1930

They say that behind every successful man is a woman. In the case of Alexej von Jawlensky, many women stood by him: Marianne von Werefkin was one. When she met Jawlensky, she was already a well-known painter; he was twenty-seven and had just abandoned his military career to become an artist. Immediately, she fell under his spell and put aside her own artistic work for ten years to support him with all her strength.

At the Werefkin family estate, Jawlensky also met Helene Nesnakomoff, who was fourteen years old at the time. The three of them moved to Munich in 1896 and lived in a spacious double apartment, which Werefkin paid for and Nesnakomoff looked after as Werefkin's personal servant. Werefkin's salon became a gathering place for Munich's bohemian community.

In 1903 and 1905, Jawlensky and Werefkin travelled to Paris. They saw the Fauves and Jawlensky met Henri Matisse. The French artist's work would have a lasting influence on Jawlensky, as can still be seen clearly in the 1909 painting **Still Life with Vase and Jug**. What is also plainly recognizable is the impression made during a joint visit to Murnau in 1908 with their artist friends Wassily Kandinsky and Gabriele Münter. Together, they worked to liberate colour from objects and to express a subjective feeling: 'In this still life, I conducted an intensive search, not for the material object, but rather I wanted to express in colours and shapes what vibrates within me.'[1]

This is an attitude that would shape the New Artists' Association of Munich, which Jawlensky founded with his friends in 1909. Even in the portraits he painted shortly thereafter, Jawlensky sought to express his inner self rather than to capture the essential nature or even the outward appearance of the sitter. In **Head of a Woman with Flowers in Her Hair**, a very typical picture for the period around 1911, the viewer's attention is immediately drawn to the magically wide-open eyes. It seems as if Jawlensky has strictly separated the colours in the painting from each other, arranging them in circles around the eyes: the yellow of the face, the brown of the hair, the red of the scarf, the blue of the background and the dress. Each area is separated from the next by black lines – Jawlensky adopted this so-called cloisonnist style from Paul Gauguin and developed it further. He isolates the black lines more and more, by not filling out the areas of colour to their edges.

Not only can the French influence be seen in this painting; Jawlensky's Russian origins are also in evidence. The frontal view of the face, the strong focus on the eyes, and the simple circular structure are reminiscent of the style of Russian icons. These early faces already display a search for spiritual expression – a search that would occupy Jawlensky particularly in the 1920s and 30s.

But before that, the First World War broke out and Russian artists had to leave Germany. Jawlensky moved with Werefkin to Saint-Prex, Switzerland. With them was Werefkin's former servant, the previously mentioned Helene Nesnakomoff, who had a twelve-year-old son with Jawlensky.

While in exile in Switzerland, Jawlensky produced his first series: the view from his window out onto a tree-lined street, which he would vary over a hundred times between 1914 and 1921. These 'Variations on a Scenic Theme'[2] focus primarily on the effect of the colours and their function in conveying a certain mood. The approach, which involved making incremental changes within very strict formal limits, resembles a scientific research project.

The **Variations** provide an insight into his interest in such a scientific approach. There is a painting on both the front and back sides of the canvas. On the front side, a black border surrounding the image indicates that the picture is completed. In both cases, a yellowish ground coat shines through the colours. This yellow – and not a black line – is what simultaneously separates and connects the colours. While the yellow dominates the mood of the picture on the reverse, where it is supported by a broad yellow stripe, it is applied more sparingly in the front image. The composition on the reverse gives the impression of a warm late summer's day; the front image evokes a cool day. Looking back, the artist explained that the atmosphere in the two pictures did not only arise from his observations of nature, but also reflected his own mood. 'I started painting something in order to express with colours what nature whispered to me', he recalled. 'In the course of hard work and with great excitement, I gradually found the right colours and shapes to express what my spiritual self demanded. Every day I painted these colourful variations, always inspired by the particular natural atmosphere in combination with my own spirit.'[3] If one considers the whole series, which has a monumental aspect despite the small format of the pictures,[4] the role of natural observation appears to become less and less significant over time. In later years, the painter's focus would indeed shift entirely to the representation of inner, mystical – and therefore abstract – subject matter.

Nevertheless, Jawlensky never entirely abandoned objective references. With the 1917 work **Head of a Woman**, he returned to the human face as subject. This head is not, however, an example of one of the many mystical or 'Christ' heads that he painted between 1916 and 1918, which are characterized by wide-open eyes and distorted features. Instead, the small painting more closely resembles the landscape variations. The placement of the colours in the face strikingly resembles the arrangement of colours in the **Variations**. Perhaps the reason that this connection is so clear is precisely because the sitters' eyes are closed. The viewer can get lost in the face, letting his or her gaze wander along the green line of the nose, rest on the brown patches on the cheeks, and absorb the sunny glow of the eyes. The warm orange-yellow of the background envelops the image in warmth. The face is full, round and almost classically beautiful. Not particularly stylised, distorted or disturbing, it is an unusually peaceful face and therefore unique for this period in Jawlensky's work.

Shortly before, in 1916, another woman had entered Jawlensky's life. The young German painter Emmy Scheyer saw one of his paintings in Lausanne and decided – in an almost eerie parallel with Marianne Werefkin – to give up her own painting career. She was so touched by his art and the 'blossoming and singing of his colours with their eternally beautiful and lively language',[5] that she decided she would rather dedicate herself to the promotion of his work. Despite all her enthusiasm, she always kept her feet on the ground. Without intending to, she became an art dealer, and that enthusiasm lent her credibility, something that artists such as Lyonel Feininger, Kandinsky and Paul Klee would come to appreciate. She represented those artists, together with Jawlensky, under the catchy name 'The Blue Four'. She arranged exhibitions in influential galleries, and also showed the artists' works in the United States from 1923 onwards, when she emigrated to California. It was there, in 1935, that the young John Cage acquired his first Jawlensky. He wrote a letter in German to the Russian artist, who was now living in the German city of Wiesbaden: '... have bought one of your paintings. Now it is in me. I write music. You are my teacher.'[6]

But let us return for a moment to Switzerland. Here, the Jawlensky-Nesnakomoff-Werefkin home situation was apparently becoming unbearable, and in 1921 they went their separate ways. Werefkin moved to Ascona in Switzerland, while Jawlensky went with Nesnakomoff and their son Andreas to Wiesbaden, where Scheyer organized a successful exhibition for the artist. In 1927 the first indications of arthritis appeared. The condition would become an increasing problem for Jawlensky in the coming years.

In the 1920s, Jawlensky increasingly focussed in his work on colour variations of an abstract head motif. The shapes became rudimentary, the parts of the face formulaic and constructivist, reduced to simple lines. The small panels radiate a sense of extreme concentration. The artist created hundreds of such works in his final years. And even if the facial features, such as those in the 1930 work **Constructivist Head**, can be traced back to a single individual – in this case Scheyer, whom Jawlensky had already depicted in a highly abstract pencil sketch in 1921 and who is recognizable by the black curls hanging down on either side of the cheeks[7] — nothing was further from his mind than creating a portrait. Just as in the variations on the same landscape, the same features are varied in the 'head' pictures. Jawlensky himself admitted that his emphasis had largely shifted to the spiritual: 'In Wiesbaden, for a few years, I painted only my large abstract heads. I was so focused on these works and wanted to achieve their perfect spiritual subject matter.'[8] Elsewhere, he wrote: 'For a period of some years, I painted these variations, and then I felt it was necessary to find a form for the face, because I had realized that the greatest art can only be created with religious sentiment. And I could only capture that in the human face. I understood that the artist must express the divine within him in his art, through colour and form. Therefore, the artwork is a visible God, and art is a "longing for God".'[9]

Jawlensky was not alone in making this connection between spirituality and avant-garde painting. Religion was an almost ubiquitous influence in Russian avant-garde painting in particular. But not all the artists who used religious imagery were religious themselves. Jawlensky, however, drew from a spirituality that became stronger and stronger in his final years, possibly because of his personal situation and the illness that gradually crippled him. In the last three years of his life, from 1938 to 1941, he was bed-ridden and depended on help from others. Nesnakomoff opened a beauty salon to make ends meet, and Jawlensky dictated his letters and memoirs to a young painter, Lisa Kümmel.

Julia Friedrich

1 Quoted by Helmut Friedel, Annegret Hoberg (eds.): *Der Blaue Reiter*, Munich, Berlin, London, New York 2004, unpaginated, Plate 86.
2 Jawlensky in his memoirs, quoted in: Tayfun Belgin (ed.), *Alexej von Jawlensky. Reisen, Freunde, Wandlungen* (exh. cat., Museum am Ostwall), Heidelberg 1998, p. 116.
3 Ibid.
4 Katharina Schmidt: 'Das Prinzip der offenen Serie. Zu Jawlenskys Werk von 1914 bis 1937', in: Armin Zweite (ed.): *Alexej Jawlensky 1864–1941* (exh. cat. Lenbachhaus, Munich; Staatliche Kunsthalle Baden-Baden) Munich 1983, pp. 87–105, here p. 95.
5 Scheyer in a letter to Jawlensky dated 8 January 1941, quoted by Isabel Wünsche (ed.), *Galka E. Scheyer und die Blaue Vier. Briefwechsel 1924–1945*, Wabern / Bern 2006, p. 2.
6 Wünsche, ibid., p. 317.
7 Drawing reproduced in Wünsche, ibid., p. 27.
8 Jawlensky in his memoirs, quoted by Belgin, op.cit., p. 118.
9 Letter to Willibrord Verkade, 1938, quoted by Friedel/Hoberg, op.cit., unpaginated, Plate 87.

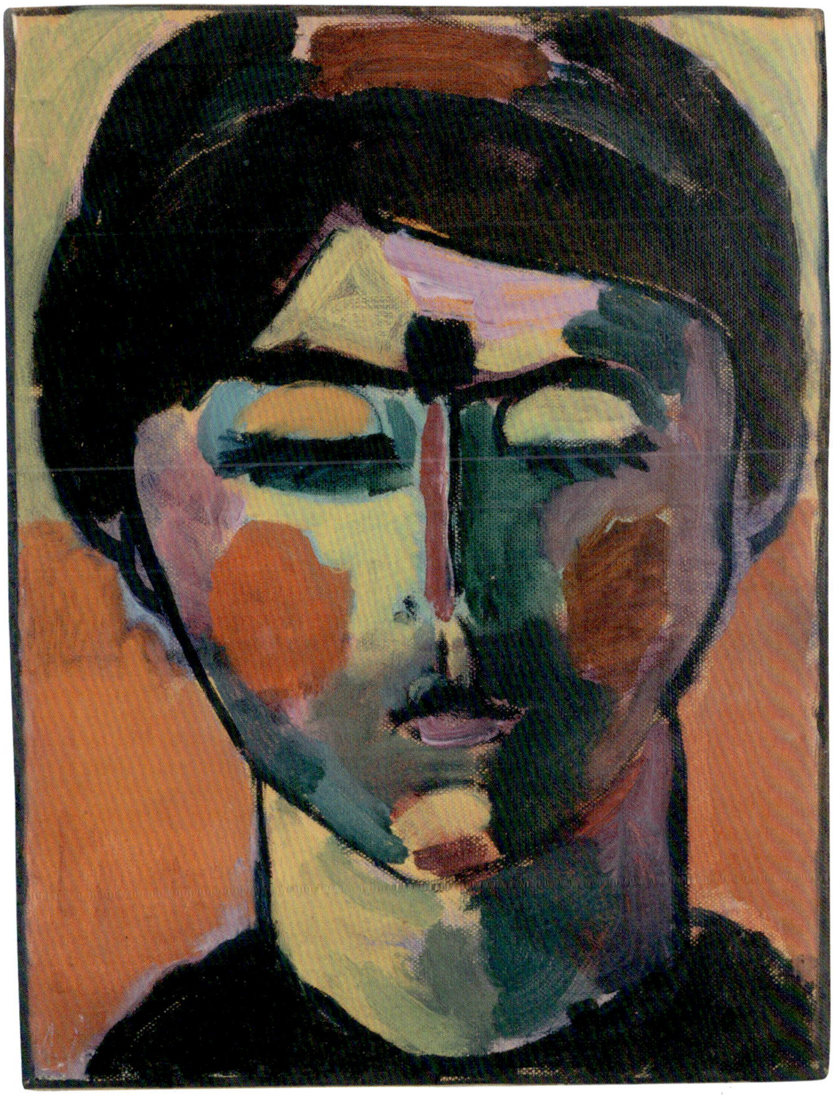

Head of a Woman
C. 1917
Oil on canvas board
36.2 x 27.2 cm

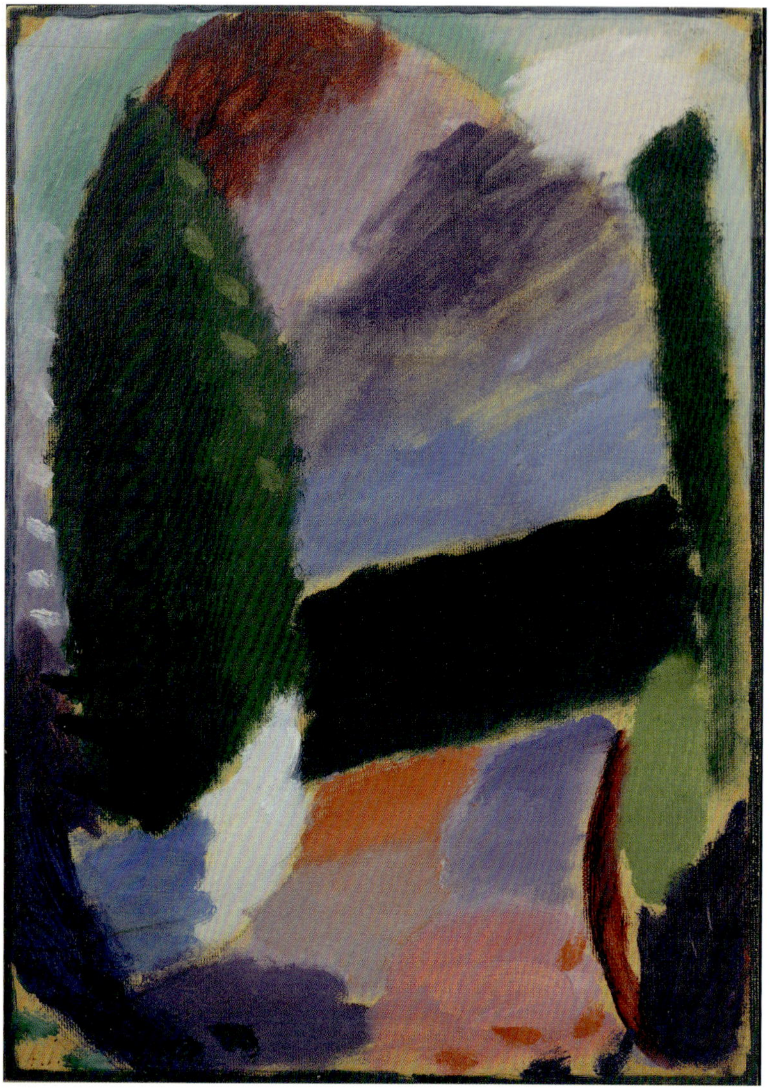

Recto:
Variation
1916
Oil on canvas board
37.8 x 26.2 cm

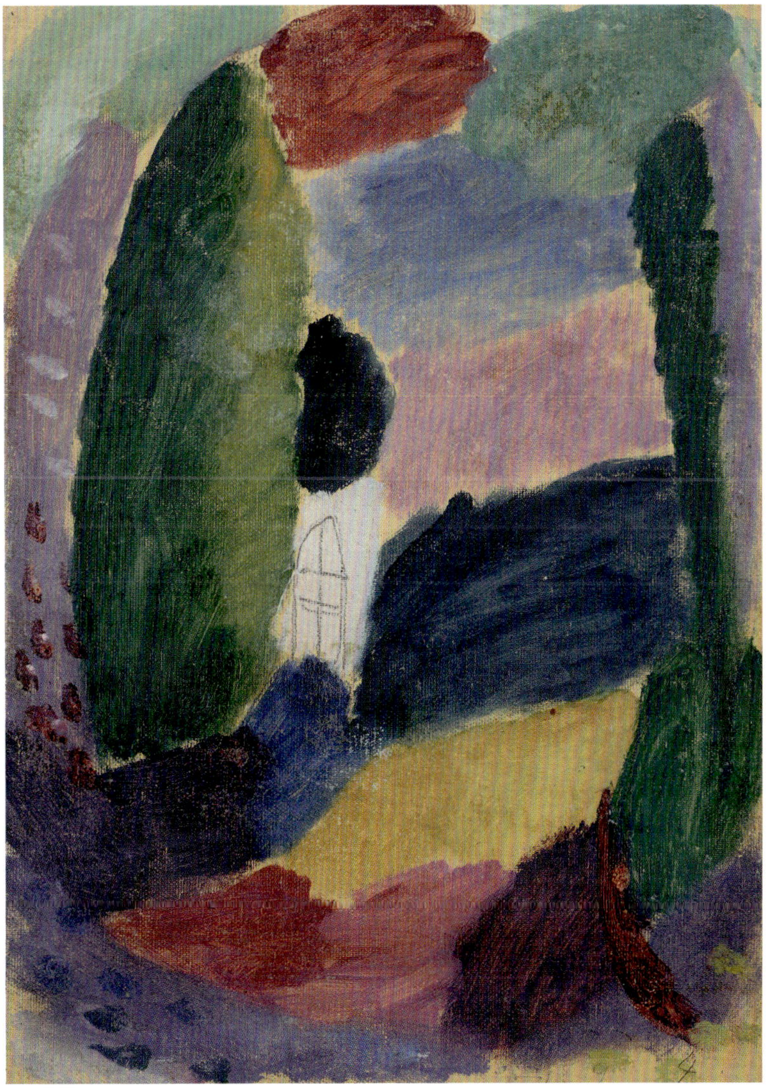

Verso:
Variation
C. 1916
Oil, graphite on canvas board
37.8 x 26.2 cm

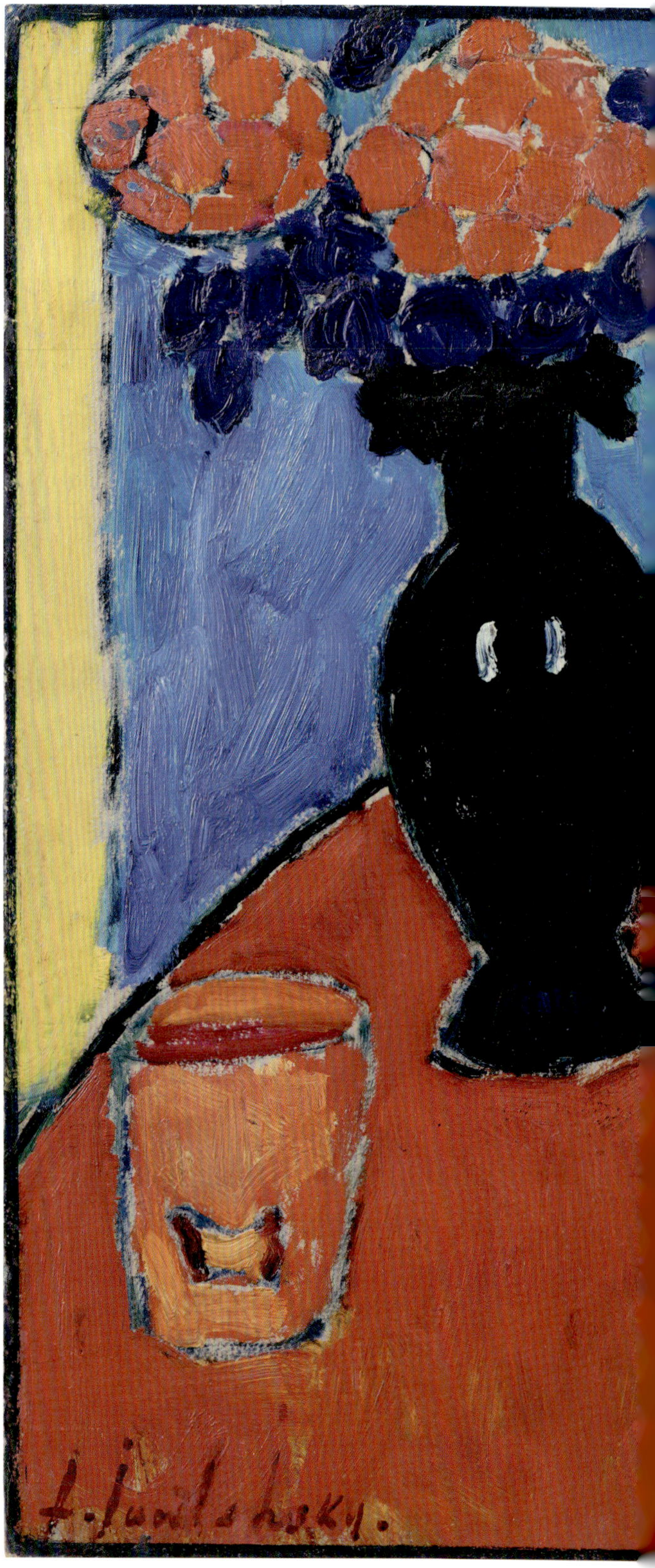

Still Life with Vase and Jug
1909
Oil, graphite on cardboard
43.5 x 49.5 cm

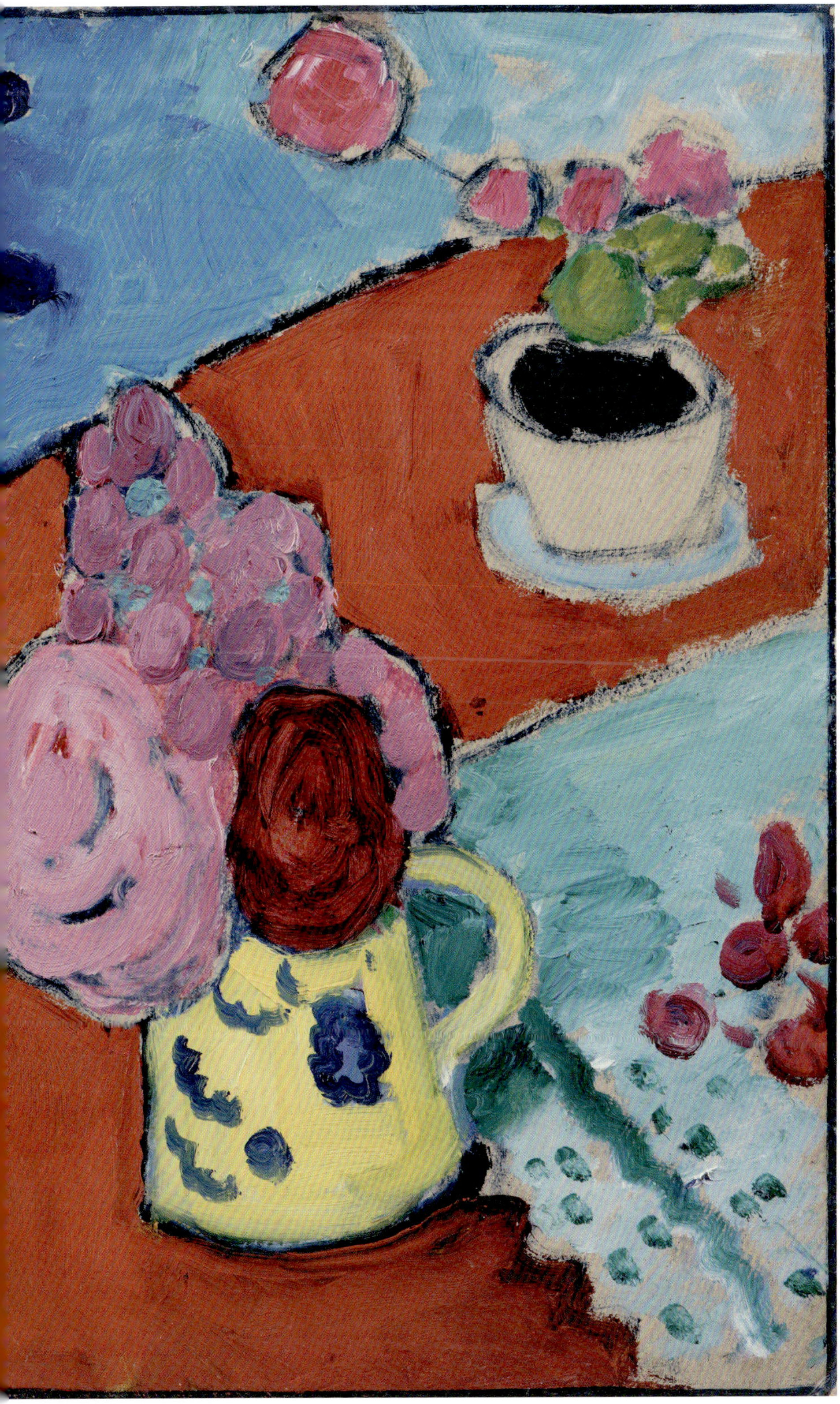

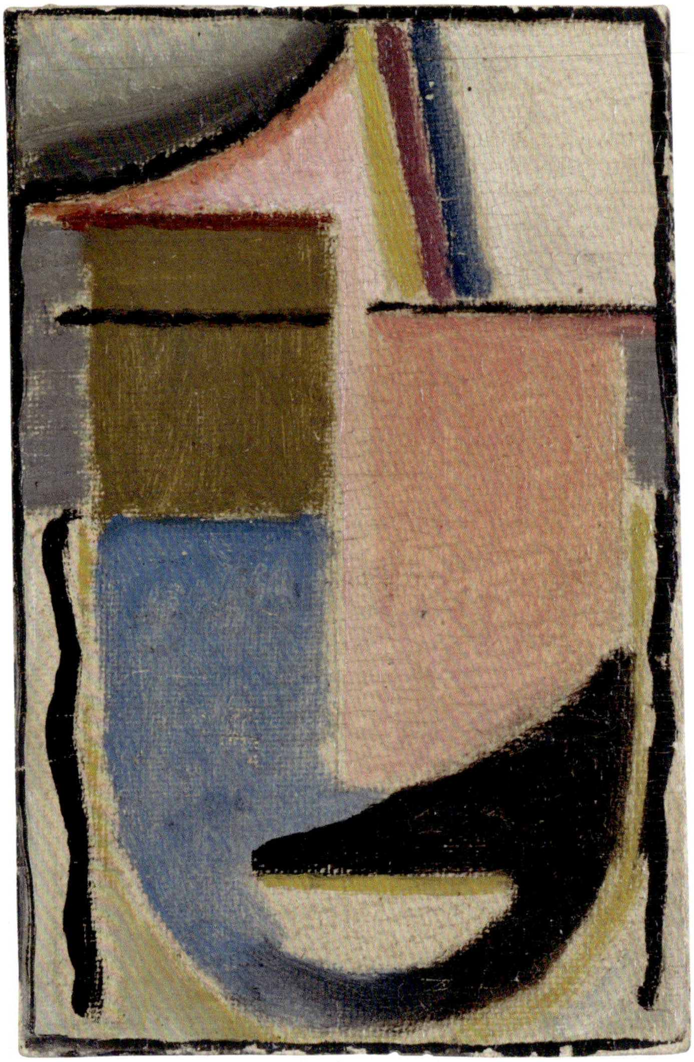

Constructivist Head
1930
Oil on cardboard
20.5 x 13 cm

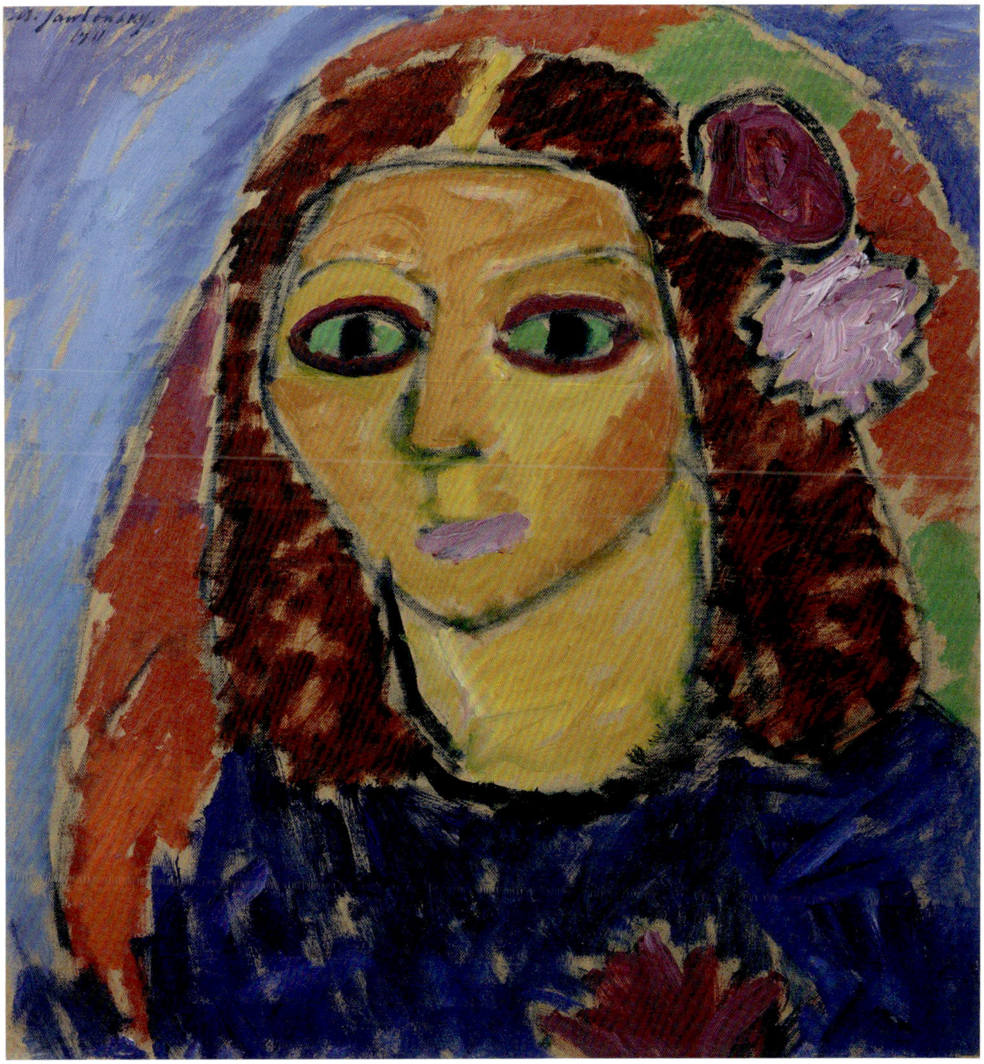

Head of a Woman with Flowers in Her Hair
1911
Oil on cardboard
53.8 x 49.6 cm

Wassily Kandinsky

Sharp-Calm Pink, 1924

This picture was painted in Weimar after Wassily Kandinsky had already been working at the Bauhaus for two years. He returned to Germany from Moscow in 1921, after the end of the First World War and the 1918 Russian Revolution. During the Bauhaus period, he began systematizing his vocabulary of geometric shapes: lines, rectangles, triangles and circles, whereby he particularly treasured the circle as a 'link to the cosmic'.

In **Sharp-Calm Pink**, these elements are presented in several variations. The pink element that gives the work its title crosses the vertically arrayed image from the upper left to the lower right. Adjacent to it on the right, there is a pedestal with a black and white chequerboard pattern that is stretched to form a narrow vertical rectangle. Because of the deep brown, almost black background, the dominant visual impression is rather dark, but there are a plethora of dark colourful elements in the painting, for example the small triangular shapes balancing on the chequerboard, some of them playfully tilted, and the colourful semicircles on the margins of the ochre-coloured trapezoid at the rear right. At the bottom of the painting, on the left, three larger triangles in blue, red and purple are arranged in front of and behind a zone of horizontal lines that are reminiscent of landscape elements, for example mountains around a lake.

The dark yellow circle with three lines emerging from it placed at the upper edge of the image, shining down on all the elements of the picture like a sun, also evokes a landscape. To complete the complexity of the shapes, the sharp end of the pink points to a colourful pattern of diagonally arranged small rectangles that are surrounded by a red semi-circle: an element of the decisive contact and central concentration of forms that is especially emphasized in a pencil sketch made in preparation for this painting. Unlike the geometric conception of the Constructivists, there is always a symbolic level in Kandinsky's 'absolute' painting – that is, the kind of painting that follows its own rules – with the geometric shapes acting like bodies in space. Emotion and drama dominate the image in a way unlike the work of any other abstract painter of the period.

The Bauhaus remained in Weimar until December 1924, when it was forced to move to Dessau by pressure from the National Socialists. As of 1925, Kandinsky's works begin to reveal a transformed formal vocabulary in which he increasingly included elements of technology and physics, for example beams of light – not as an allusion to applied art, but to illustrate the abstract forces in nature, an intention that he described in the 1930s with the term 'Concrete Art'.

Annegret Hoberg

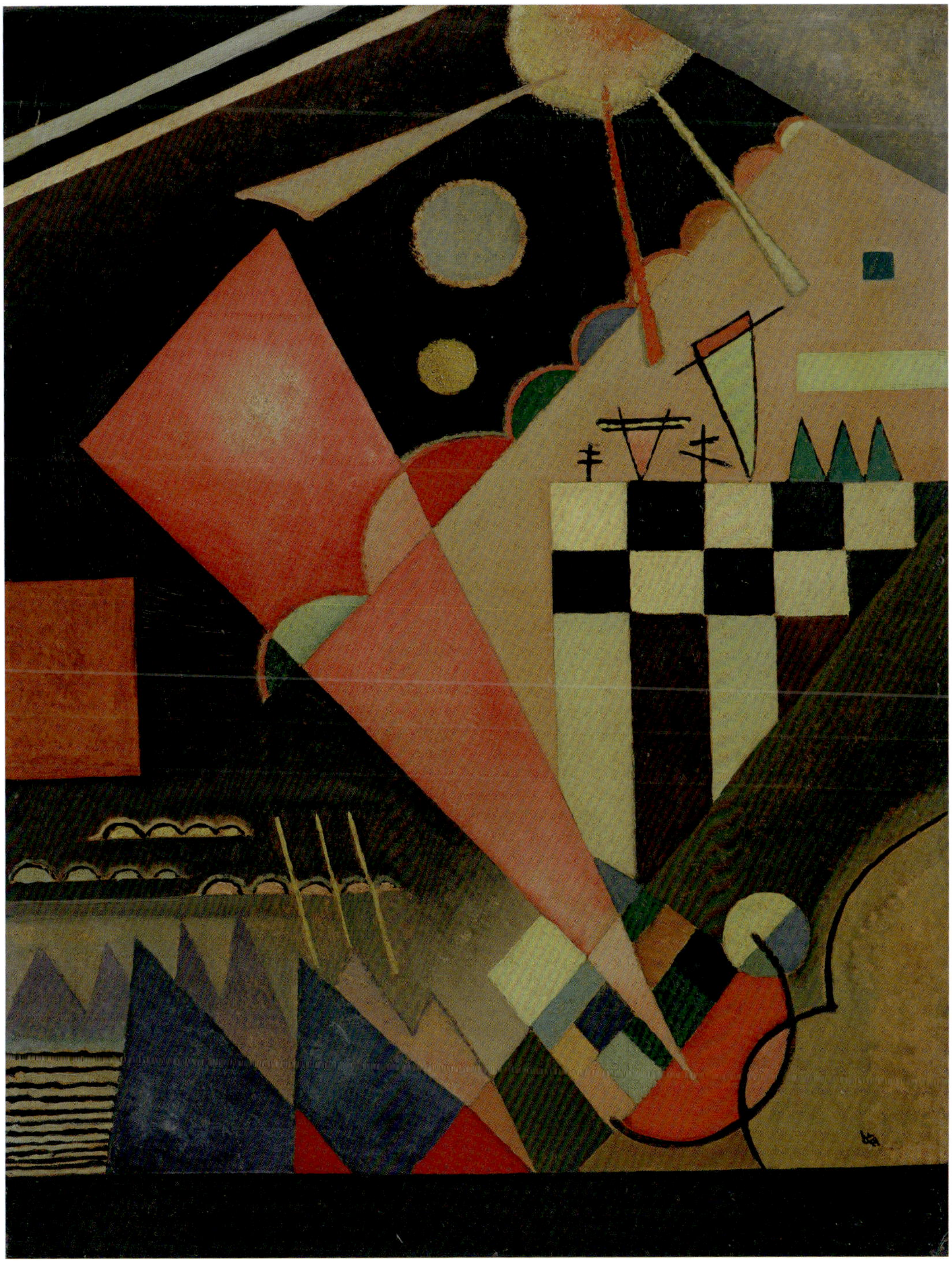

Sharp-Calm Pink
1924
Oil on cardboard
63.6 x 48.2 cm

Ernst Ludwig Kirchner

Female Half-Length Nude with Hat, 1911
Fränzi in Meadows, 1910
Still Life with Tulips, Exotica and Hands, 1912
Five Women on the Street, 1913
Forest in Winter, 1925/26
An Artists' Group, 1925-26

The wooden acrobat bends over backwards and balances a heavy vase on his belly, as if he wanted to impress the ghosts that hover in the air beside him. The red ghost holds up his hand in warning. Delicate women's hands lay a border of blue, green and black stripes on the table, as if they wanted to cast a protective spell – against the spirits, against the acrobat bending over backwards and against a casket in the shape of a house. This demarcation line separates two realities of different scale from one another: on one side are the hands and the tulips, whose dimensions correspond to those of the table, while on the other side are monumental miniatures.

A still life is generally regarded as a collection of inanimate objects. In his eerie painting **Still Life with Tulips, Exotica and Hands**, which is executed mainly in heavy, warm colours, Ernst Ludwig Kirchner has not kept to that convention. Instead, everything here is alive. Two tulips try to stretch their heads as far as possible out of the vase. They seem to be chattering with the owner of the hands, and, with this attempt at contact, the person, albeit unseen, becomes part of the picture.

Several photographs of Kirchner's studio in Dresden have survived. They show furniture that the artist has carved himself, a tree stump used as a stool, exotic containers, and erotic paintings on the walls and curtains. At the end of his architectural studies, Kirchner made the decision to become an artist. In 1906, together with Fritz Bleyl, Erich Heckel and Karl Schmidt-Rottluff, he founded the artists' collective Die Brücke, which additional artists would join in the following years. Their lifestyle and manner of working did not correspond to the conventions of the time. The artists took turns drawing each other with their girlfriends and models in fifteen-minute sittings, calling the results 'quarter-hour nudes'. During excursions to the Moritzburg Lakes, north of Dresden, they devoted themselves to the motif of the naked human in nature. Kirchner also found an important inspiration for his work in African wood sculptures from the Museum of

Ethnology. In 1911, he moved to Berlin. The famous painting **Female Half-Length Nude with Hat** was however created during his Dresden period.

As is characteristic for his pictures of this phase, the surface and material qualities reflect the speed and spontaneity of the painting process. In addition to the swiftly drawn lines and the fact that the glaze has run, the paint on the canvas is raw and rough. A preliminary sketch in orange-red shines through the later overpainting. Flowing veils of cerulean blue create a dynamic yet monochrome background. Kirchner has quickly painted the flowery cloth on the canvas, but for the pasty flesh tones of the upper body he has placed a number of minimally varying reddish-yellow tones over each other until the skin resembles ivory or porcelain. The blue plays into these tones and produces shadows that seem to have a greenish shimmer in places. Blue-black contours lend clarity to the forms – two jagged lines and two arcs for the armpits and breasts, two broad strokes for shoulder and hat, and a few lines for the face, neck and fingers. The mouth and the nipples entice the viewer with their bright red. The young woman's pose reflects a combination of cheekiness and seduction, but it is not clear how her movement will continue. Will she raise or lower her arms? Or to put it another way: Is the hat going on or coming off?

The reverse of the picture conceals a surprise. Here, the pure colours of the summer permeate both nature and people. Red, orange and even green venture into the ochre-coloured face of a girl. She is dressed in colours that look like they came from a child's paintbox. Her arms, delineated in pink and blue, frame a bright yellow-green bathing suit, over which dangle two dark strands of hair, shimmering in red. The arms, folded behind the back, remind the viewer of a jumping jack, but the hints of feminine breasts call the subject's childlike status into question. Just as he did in over a hundred other cases, Kirchner rejected this picture. He stretched the canvas and mounted it in reverse, with the result that **Fränzi in Meadows**, as the work is known, is hidden behind the female half-length nude. The picture shows Fränzi, the famous child model of the Brücke artists, who is clothed in this picture, together with three naked adults and was probably created on a summer's day in Moritzburg. It is interesting to compare this picture with Max Pechstein's *The Black-Yellow Bathing Suit*, since it seems likely that both painters set up their easels side by side.[1] In Pechstein's work, Fränzi, who is wearing a black- and yellow-striped bathing suit, appears as an incidental figure in a tall and deep landscape. In the background, the members of a nudist group wade through deep grass.

Kirchner adds urgency to the scene. In his picture, three nude figures dance in a frivolous conga line. The ambiguous actions of the characters take place directly behind the girl's head. The space and distance between her face and the naked bodies, whose colour corresponds to that of the face, become lost in the flatness of the green background – the meadow looks like it has been raised up into a vertical position. Despite this connection, Kirchner does not allow the child to observe the events behind her back. He confronts her with an elevated observer – in other words, the adult – although she does not seem to be seeking direct eye contact. Despite the explicit nature of the image, the world of the child meets that of the adults without distress or harm.

With their feathered hats and collars, the figures in **Five Women on the Street** look like birds. The elongated black figures shimmer in blue, green and purple tones, their pointy shoes reminiscent of claws. The women's faces remain impersonal. With their black-rimmed hollow eye sockets and their pink complexions, overlaid by a greenish grey, they have a morbid air. In this, the first of a total of eleven so-called 'Street Scenes' he created between 1913 and 1915, Kirchner has chosen as his motif 'curb swallows' or 'courtesans', as Berlin's street prostitutes were called at the time. The prostitutes were prohibited by law from approaching potential clients directly, and so they had to behave discreetly on the street, while their conspicuous clothing acted as a badge of their profession.[2] During Kirchner's wanderings through Berlin's streets, he made a large number of swift, frantic drawings in sketchbooks, which served as a basis for his studio works.

The **Five Women on the Street** stand together as a group, and yet they remain isolated. The electric light from the shop window on the right falls yellow-green on the kerb. The left figure is the only one who is looking furtively at the dark car at the roadside. Her four colleagues, on the other hand, stare to the right, whereby, starting with the large figure at the front and moving rightwards, each of the women is bending over slightly more, as if the women were subtly heading toward the window display. In theory it should only be possible to represent the shop window – which both separates the coveted goods inside from the prostitutes outside, but also puts them on the same level – using a distorted perspective. But Kirchner found a surprising solution that allows him to insert the vertical dividing line between the two worlds as a harsh fact within the picture. The front-most central figure looks like she had been cut off, as if her body were growing behind an invisible border or as if she were pressed against a pane of glass that runs down the middle of the sidewalk. This functions as a symbol of the impossibility of contact and of unattainable desire.

With the outbreak of the First World War, Kirchner experienced a serious life crisis. He suffered a breakdown right at the beginning of his military training and was released from service to enter a sanatorium. His poor health prompted his friends to persuade him to go to Davos in Switzerland for a rest cure. In 1918 he rented a farmhouse there, where he settled permanently. Just as earlier in Dresden and Berlin, he found the subject matter for his paintings, graphic works and sculptures in his immediate surroundings. In this case, he was inspired by the mountains and the life of the mountain farmers and their animals. During the second half of his time in Davos, from 1927 onward, his work changed, and he began to combine different stylistic devices in his images. The defamation of his person and his work by the Nazi regime in Germany, the fear of impending war and his health problems are all seen as motives for Kirchner's suicide in 1938.

In the foreground of the picture **Forest in Winter**, a path gets lost behind a snowbank after a few steps. To the right in the background, the hill slopes downward.

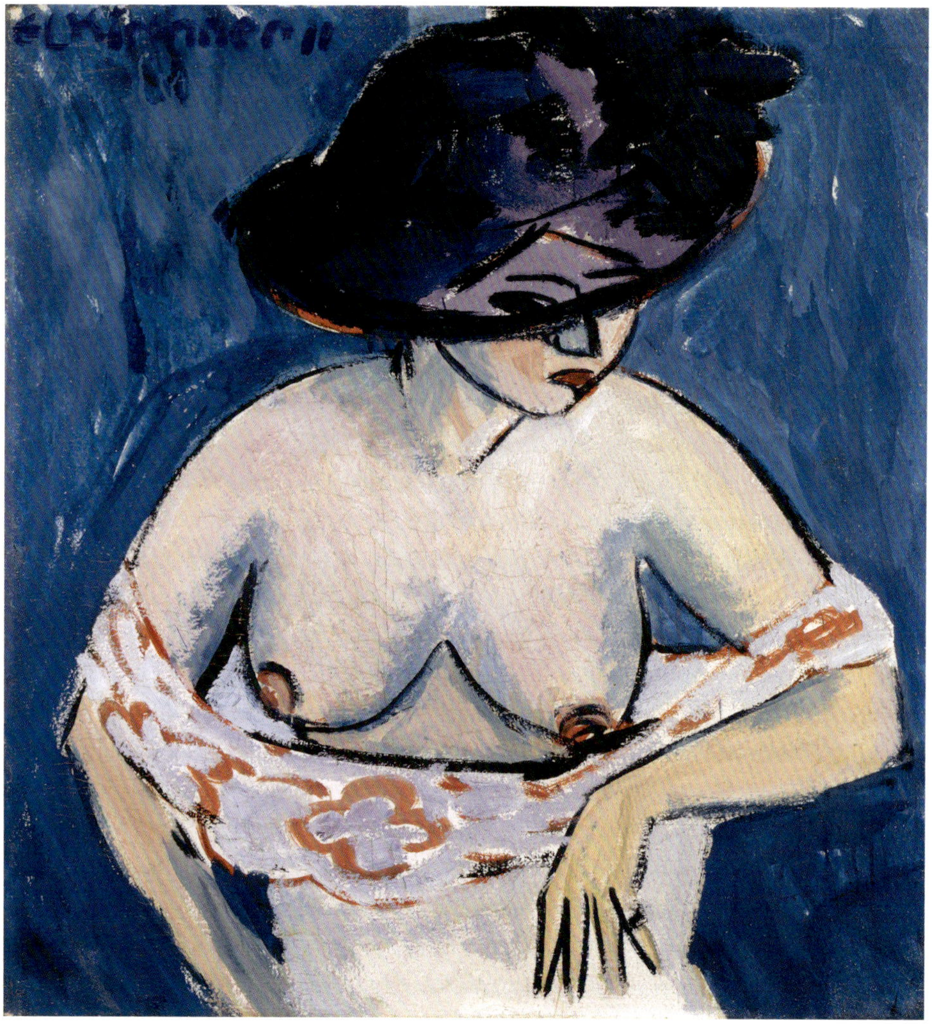

Recto:
Female Half-Length Nude with Hat
1911
Oil on canvas
76 x 70 cm

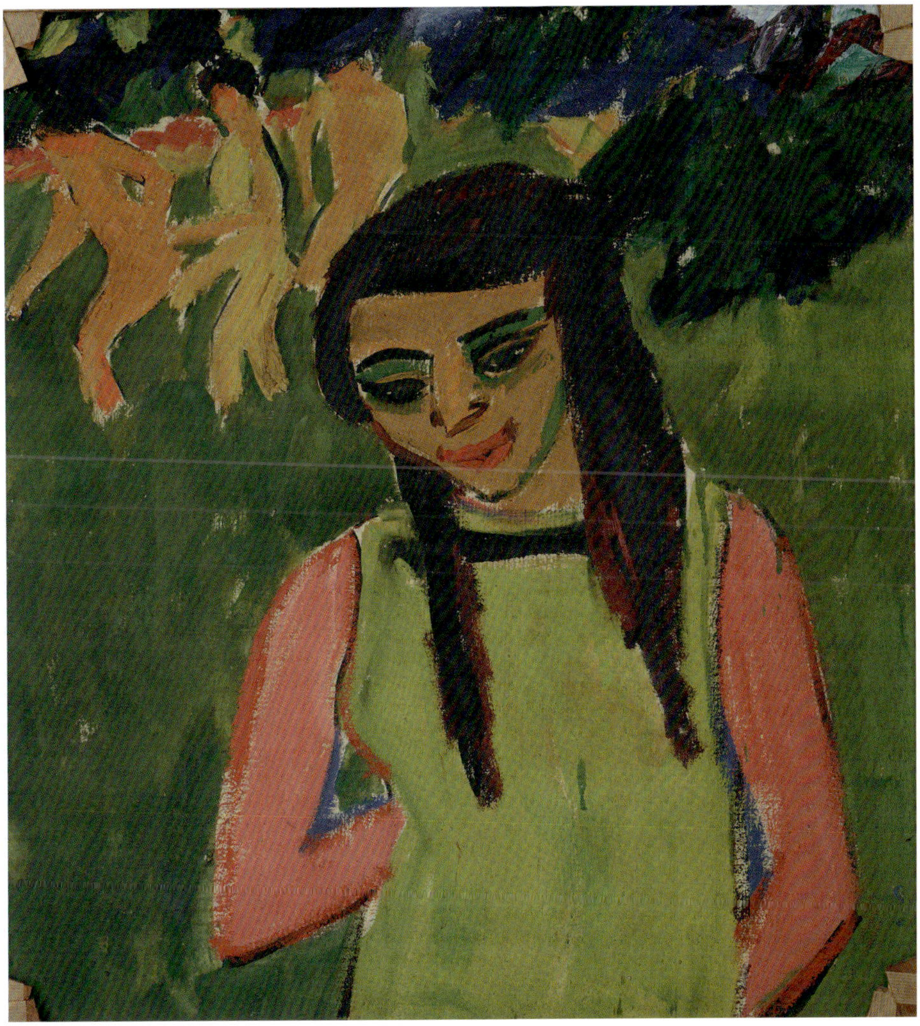

Verso:
Fränzi in Meadows
1910
Oil on canvas
76 x 70 cm

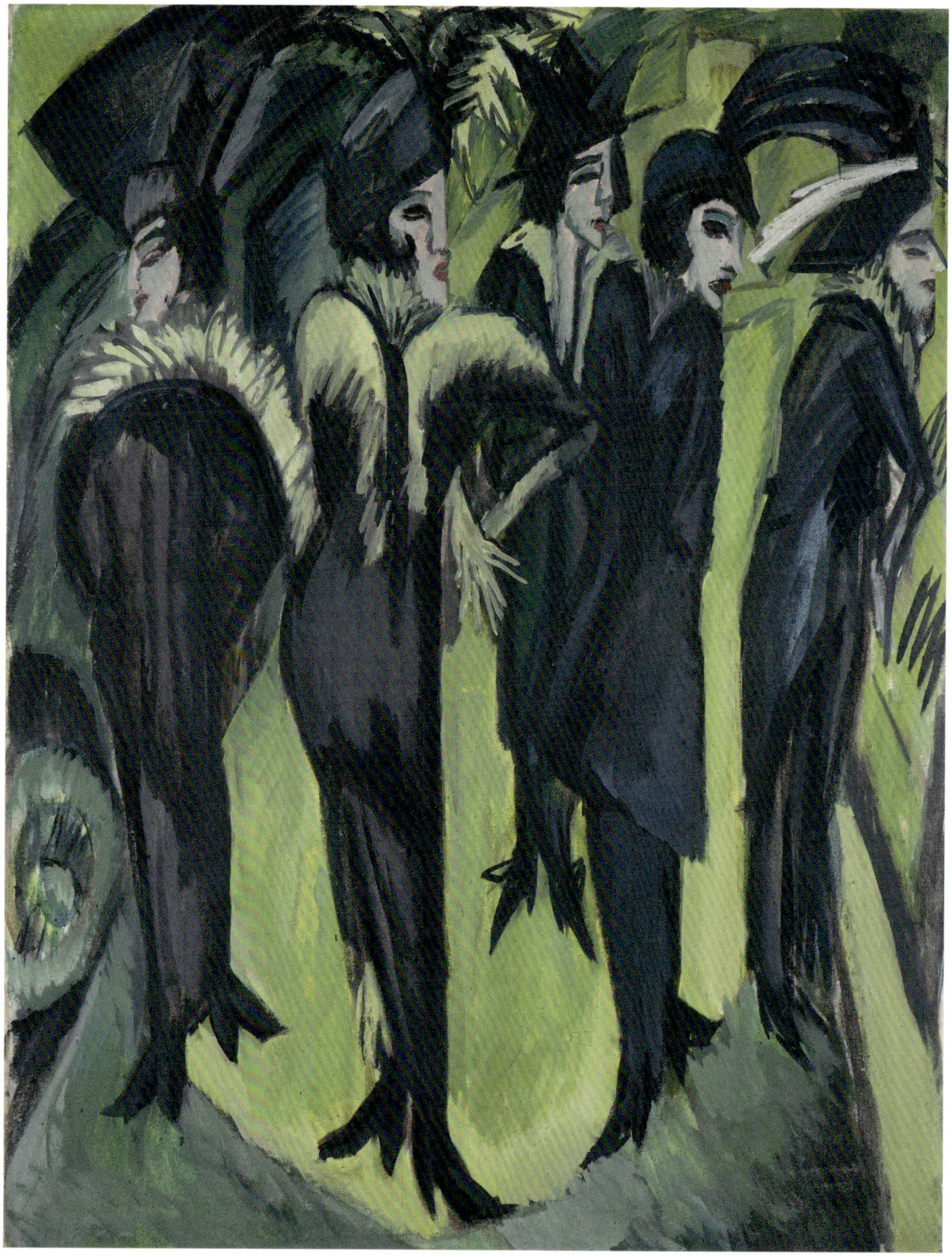

Five Women on the Street
1913
Oil on canvas
120 x 90 cm

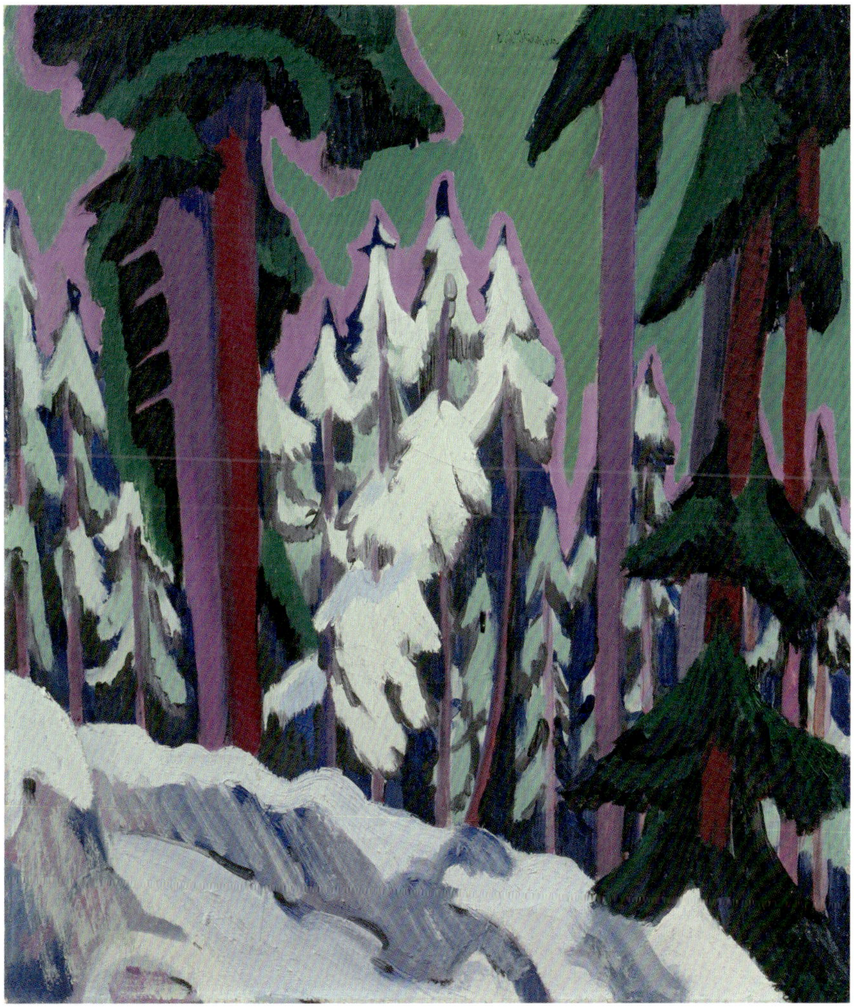

Forest in Winter
1925/26
Oil on canvas
95.5 x 80.5 cm

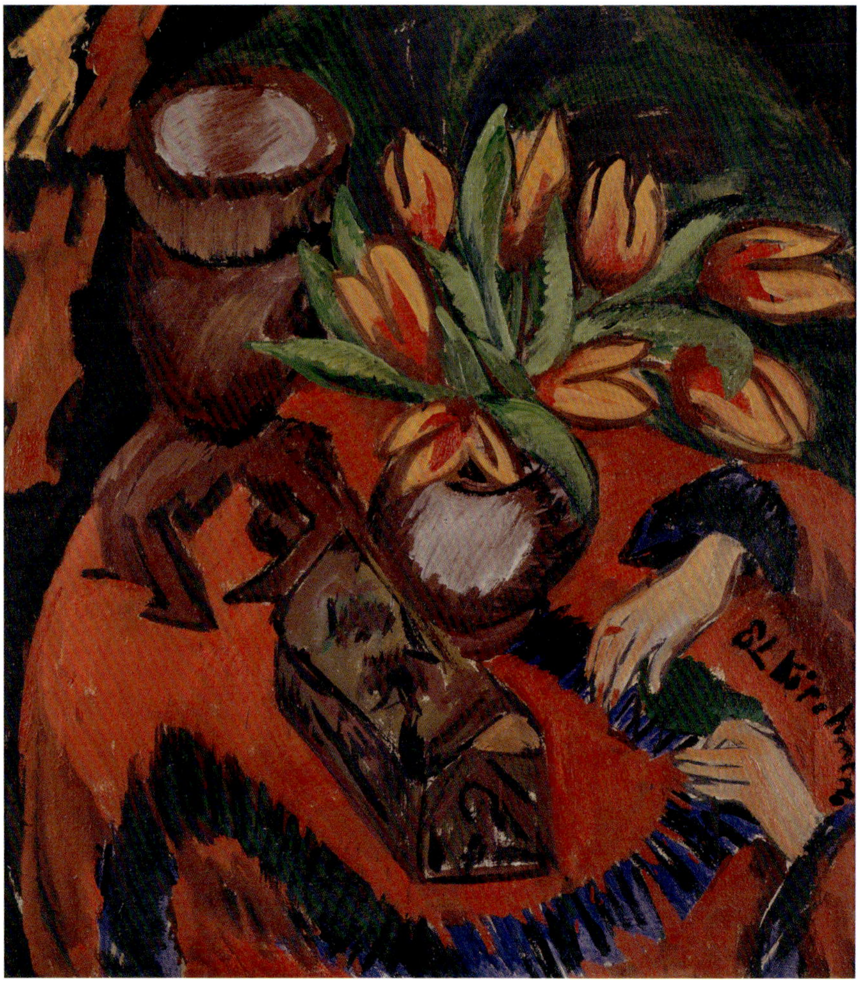

Still Life with Tulips, Exotica and Hands
1912
Oil on canvas
78.5 x 68.5 cm

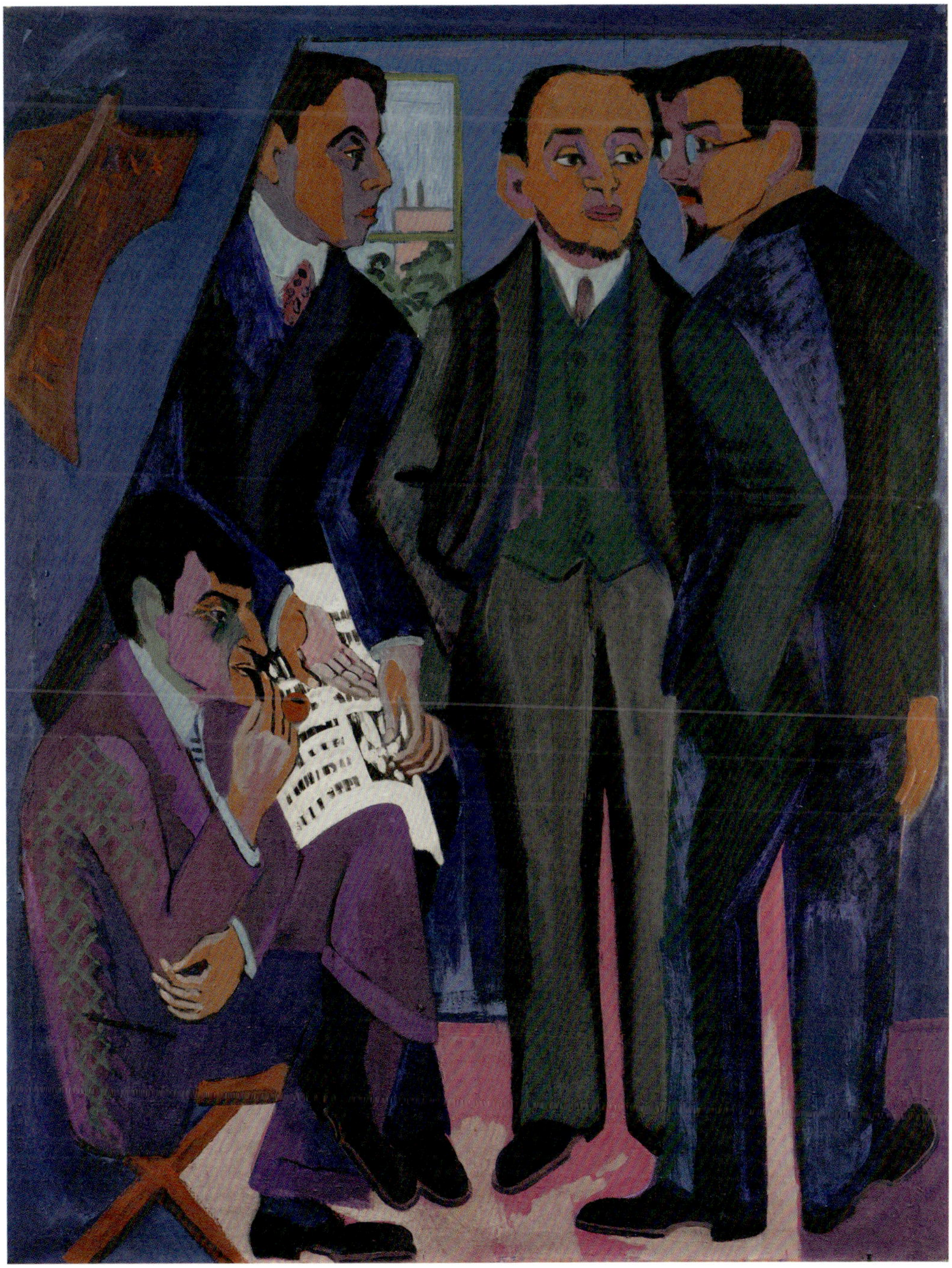

An Artists' Group
1925/26
Oil on canvas
168 x 126 cm

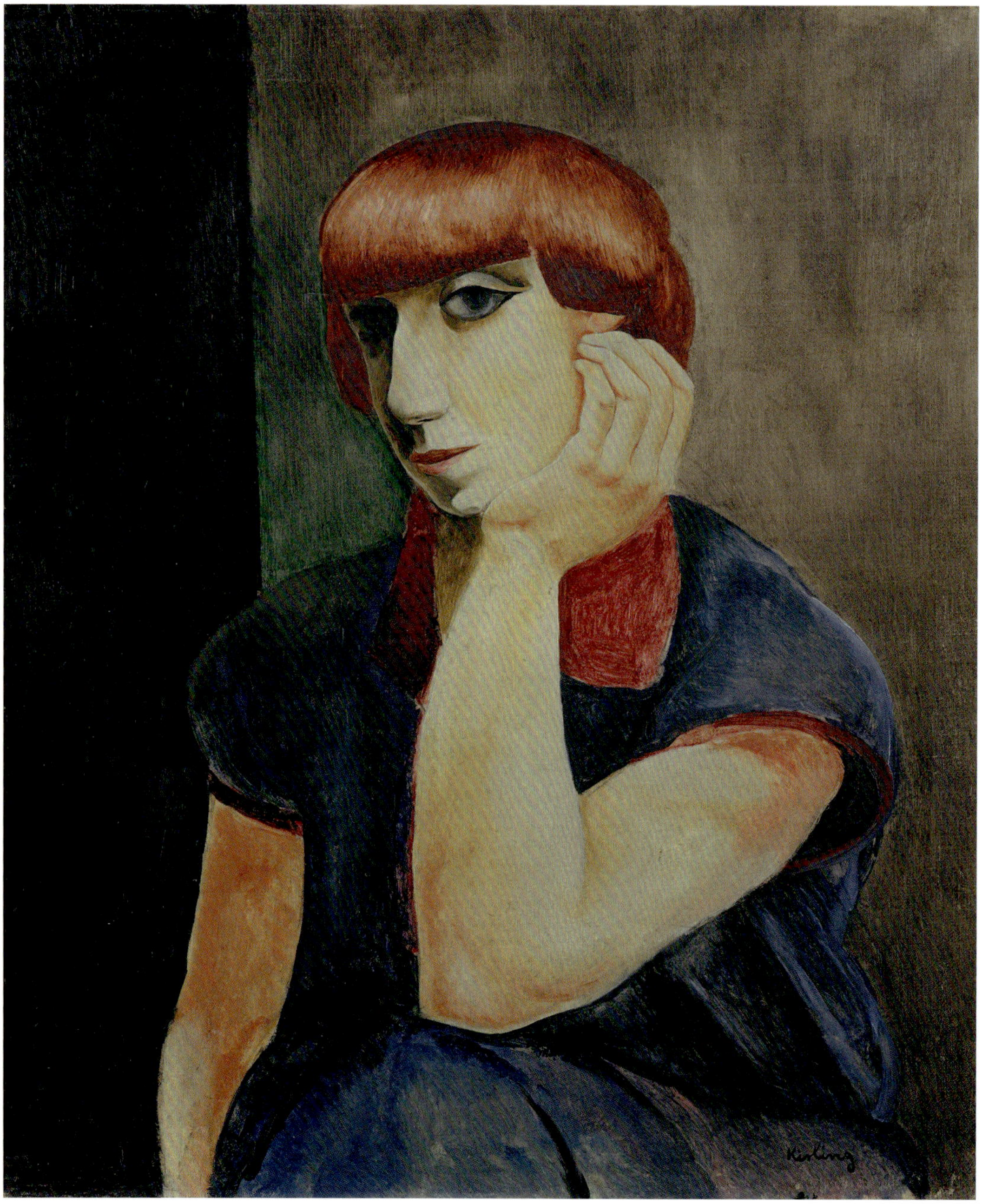

Portrait of Renée Kisling
1921
Oil on canvas
65 x 53.5 cm

Moïse Kisling

Portrait of Renée Kisling, 1921

'She had the loyalty, courage, high spirits and tough débrouillardise, and she put her hand to anything.'[1] If we believe the descriptions of her contemporary, Renée Gros must have been a 'force of nature'[2] of unbridled vitality. The young Moïse Kisling met the unusual model in Montparnasse, the notorious Paris neighbourhood where the intellectual and artistic greats of the day assembled. They married in 1917. Countless stories circulate about the dazzling couple and their remarkable public presence.

In this portrait of his wife, however, Moïse Kisling provides an image that differs fundamentally from these anecdotes. She rests like a timeless statue, lost in thought. Her large, turbid eyes look towards nothingness, like a visionary; her powerful arm is raised in a melancholic gesture. While her body threatens to be devoured by a deep darkness on the left, most of the figure is immersed in a gentle, warm light. The clear, and yet restrained formal language is contradicted by the painterly patches of colour. The rather objective appearance of the portrait seems to anticipate Jean Cocteau's call for a *retour à l'ordre*.[3] It thus startles the beholder with its simple directness. On closer inspection, nonetheless, the initially sober likeness proves to be quite emotional and profound.

Indeed, the success of the painter, who had immigrated to the centre of the art world from Krakow in 1910, was based on his numerous women's portraits and nudes. At first, these portraits featured the beautiful women of Montparnasse, such as the famous muse Kiki, but soon the affluent women of society also came to sit for Kisling: the critics turned this into a reproach. His discoverer and one-time advocate Adolphe Basler even turned away from the all-too-flattering portraitist for this reason.

All the same, portraits of women form the core of his art. In their composition, they approach the 'Neue Sachlichkeit' of his German contemporaries. Here, too, the likeness of an individual personality gives way to the stylised portrait of a particular type: the independent modern woman of the period.

Ilona Ciesielski

1 Sybille Bedford, *Jigsaw: An Unsentimental Education*, London 1989, p. 154.
2 Ibid., p. 153.
3 In his essay *Le Rappel à l'ordre* (1926), Jean Cocteau called for a return to figuration.

Oskar Kokoschka

Portrait of Tilla Durieux, 1910
The Heathens, 1918
Dresden, Neustadt III, 1921

After studying at the University of Applied Arts in Vienna, Oskar Kokoschka worked from March 1910 onward for the Expressionist journal *Der Sturm* in Berlin. By the end of May he was already preparing his first exhibition for the salon run by his art dealer, Paul Cassirer. Cassirer offered him a contract that, in Kokoschka's words, 'must be almost without comparison in the history of art: I didn't have to deliver any "goods" whatsoever, but the pictures I did give to him were not to be of a lesser standard than those he already knew from me'.[1]

That same year he painted this portrait of the celebrated actress Tilla Durieux. Cassirer commissioned the artist to paint his fiancée before marrying her on 24 June 1910, just three days after the opening of the exhibition. The delicate pastel shades of pink and pale blue in the background to the left become an earthy reddish brown in the right part of the painting. The pale dress, which is set off from the undefined space by dark contours, reveals light dashes of paint and highlights done in pure yellow. With its lean use of paint, which barely hides the texture of the canvas, the portrait comes across as light and immaterial. The whole of the paint seems to be in the process of dissolution. Durieux's portrait is strongly shaped by a swift, animated brush and nervous scratches around the eyes – Kokoschka positively tore at his model's skin.

Despite the prevailing levity, she has a challenging gaze, if not a gimlet eye, yet one that simultaneously puzzles. In a letter from 1909, the artist wrote to a girlfriend that he really wanted to 'do a nerve-frazzled portrait'.[2] Kokoschka never in fact finished his portrait of Tilla Durieux; he ended up fleeing from the charismatic actress's presence: 'Her art of seduction was too great, and I believe I never finished the portrait and left it and my paintbox at her place.'[3]

Beginning in 1912, Kokoschka lived for three years with Alma, the widow of the composer Gustav Mahler. After the unhappy demise of this relationship he volunteered for service in the First World War. He suffered major injuries, which he had treated in December 1916 in Dr. Teuscher's Sanatorium in Dresden-Loschwitz. In the summer of 1918 he ordered a life-size doll from Hermine Moos's workshop – one that should at all costs look like his former lover. That same year he also set to work on his large figural composition **The Heathens**.

Two naked figures lying in an intimate embrace, their heads tilted towards one another, fill the whole breadth of the painting and the rich green background. The man's face has the features of Walter Hasenclever, an author and friend of Kokoschka's.[4] The woman has crossed her legs and is leaning on the chest of the man, who has propped himself up on one arm. He lovingly clasps her left hand in his own, while gently stroking her right arm with his right hand. The gentleness of their gestures and their gazes is in fascinating contrast to the choppy manner in which the paint has been applied. Kokoschka mixed the paint directly on the canvas and then applied it in thick clumps with brush and spatula to produce large patches of colour. Striking is the blue in the woman's face and the way her foot and lower leg melt into the subtropical green of the ground – an unmistakable indication that she is bound to the soil.

This seemingly idyllic scene may recall paradise, but the reverse side of the work bears a direct reference to Wilhelm Heinse's utopian novel *Ardinghello und die glückseligen Inseln* (1787): 'Ardinghello: It is true that a rose exudes several scents when it wilts on its stem.'[5] Heinse openly professed in his novel an unrestrained devotion to the fleeting sensual pleasures of love, nature and art. Nor should one overlook the title Kokoschka gave the work: according to the Christian tradition, 'pagans' are unable to enter paradise, because they are too attached to earthly concerns. This is conveyed in Kokoschka's work by the colour of the lower leg and the intimacy evoked. Entry into paradise is ruled out once and for all for this heathen couple, just as it was for Kokoschka and his lost love, whom he hoped to somehow replace with a life-size doll.

He completed the painting in April 1919 – the same month in which, after an eight-month wait, he at last received the doll. It has been conjectured that the blue of the woman's face indicates inanimateness and thus that the doll was his model.[6]

Kokoschka was at a loss for words in trying to express his disappointment on receiving the doll. In vain he sought to recognize his former lover in this 'botched mixture of cloth and wood wool'.[7] During a night of champagne with friends, the doll was destroyed in the Großer Garten in Dresden and left to be removed at dawn by the refuse collectors.[8] Prior to this, in October 1919, he had signed a contract to teach at the State Academy of Fine Arts in Dresden. He found a large studio in a princely location on the first floor of the Academy on Brühl's Terrace. From the window he began in 1919 to paint the banks facing him across the river (Neustädter Ufer) in a number of sequences.

In the version **Dresden, Neustadt III**, our view of the River Elbe is restricted by the Augustus Bridge on the left, and by the neorenaissance building housing the Treasury on the right. Rising up above the block-like row of houses, the tall tower of the Dreikönigskirche supplies a vertical accent. A firm path made with reddish sand between the broad waters of the Elbe and the lush green meadow on the bank emphasizes on the other hand the horizontal direction. The landscape is chiefly characterized by the luminosity of the coloured surfaces, while the restless areas of paint in the sky and the reflections in the water animate the otherwise vacant riverscape.

Kokoschka did a total of twelve landscapes during his Dresden years, ten of them variations of the view from his studio window: 'From the tallest buildings or hills, *on the top*, right up above', as Kokoschka described his favourite view onto cities.[9] The Dresden views show this use of an elevated vantage point, which the painter was to return to in all of his later city portraits. During this troubled period in Dresden, which included his desperate attempt to overcome a failed romance by means of a fetish doll, the year 1921 marked the beginning of a highly creative phase and, with it, his transition from Expressionist portraitist to a painter of cityscapes.

Geraldine Spiekermann

1 Oskar Kokoschka, *Das bin ich*, Munich 1970, p. 160f.
2 Olda Kokoschka and Heinz Spielmann (eds.), *Oskar Kokoschka. Briefe*, 4 vols., Düsseldorf 1984–1988, vol. I (Briefe 1905–1919), p. 10.
3 Oskar Kokoschka, *Mein Leben*, Munich 1971, p. 116.
4 Johanna Winkler and Katharina Erling (eds.), *Oskar Kokoschka. Die Gemälde 1906–1926*, Salzburg 1995, p. 81.
5 Ibid.
6 Ibid.
7 Kokoschka 1971, p. 191f. See also *Kokoschka und Dresden* (exh. cat., Staatliche Kunstsammlungen Dresden Gemäldegalerie Neue Meister, Österreichische Galerie Belvedere), Vienna/Leipzig 1996, p. 15f.
8 Ibid.
9 Quoted in Heinz Spielmann, 'Kokoschkas Bilder der europäischen Städte', in: Gabriele Koller and Oswald Oberhuber (eds.), *Oskar Kokoschka. Städteportraits* (exh. cat., Österreichisches Museum für angewandte Kunst), Vienna 1986, p. 36.

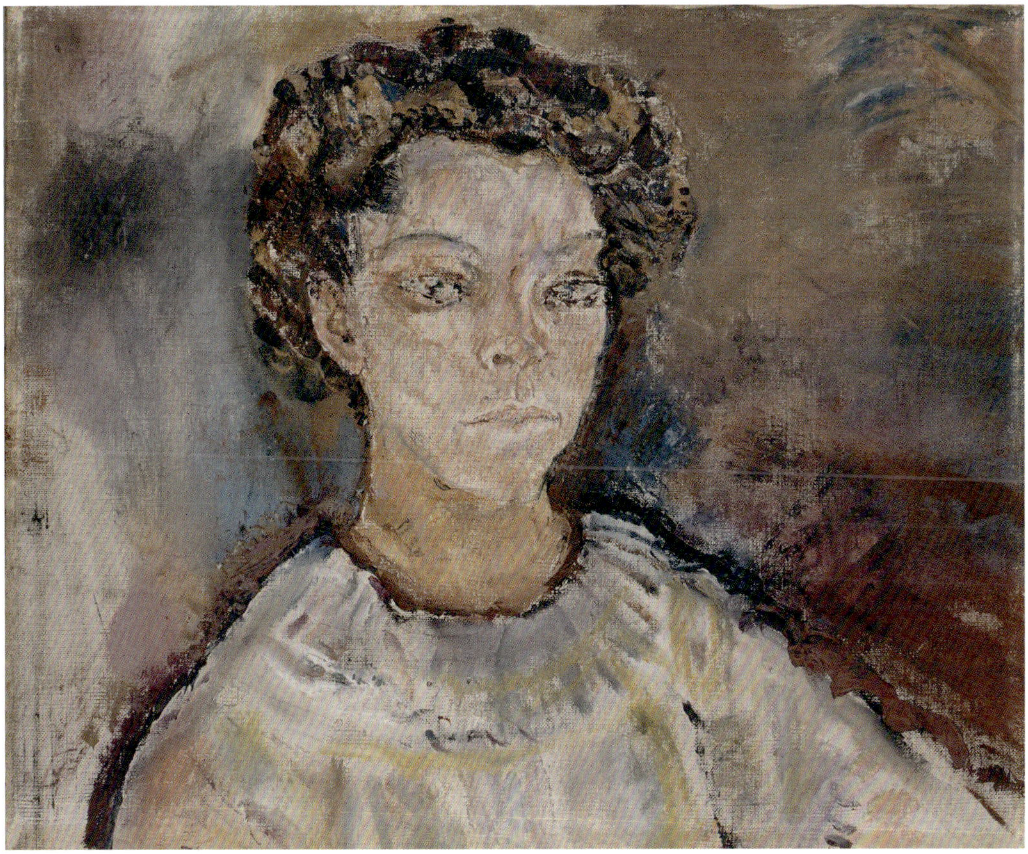

Portrait of Tilla Durieux
1910
Oil on canvas
56 x 65 cm

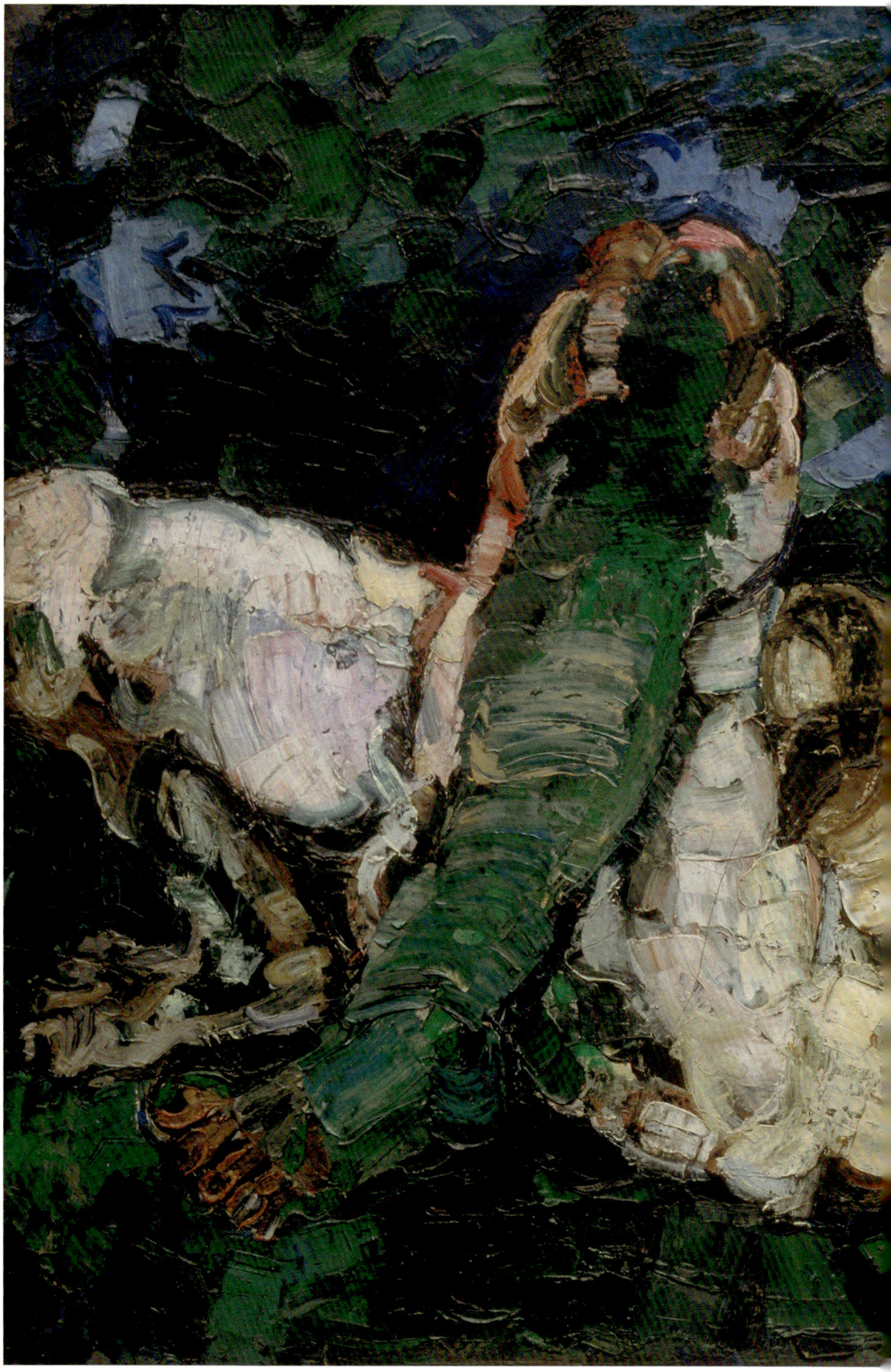

The Heathens
1918
Oil on canvas
75.5 x 126 cm

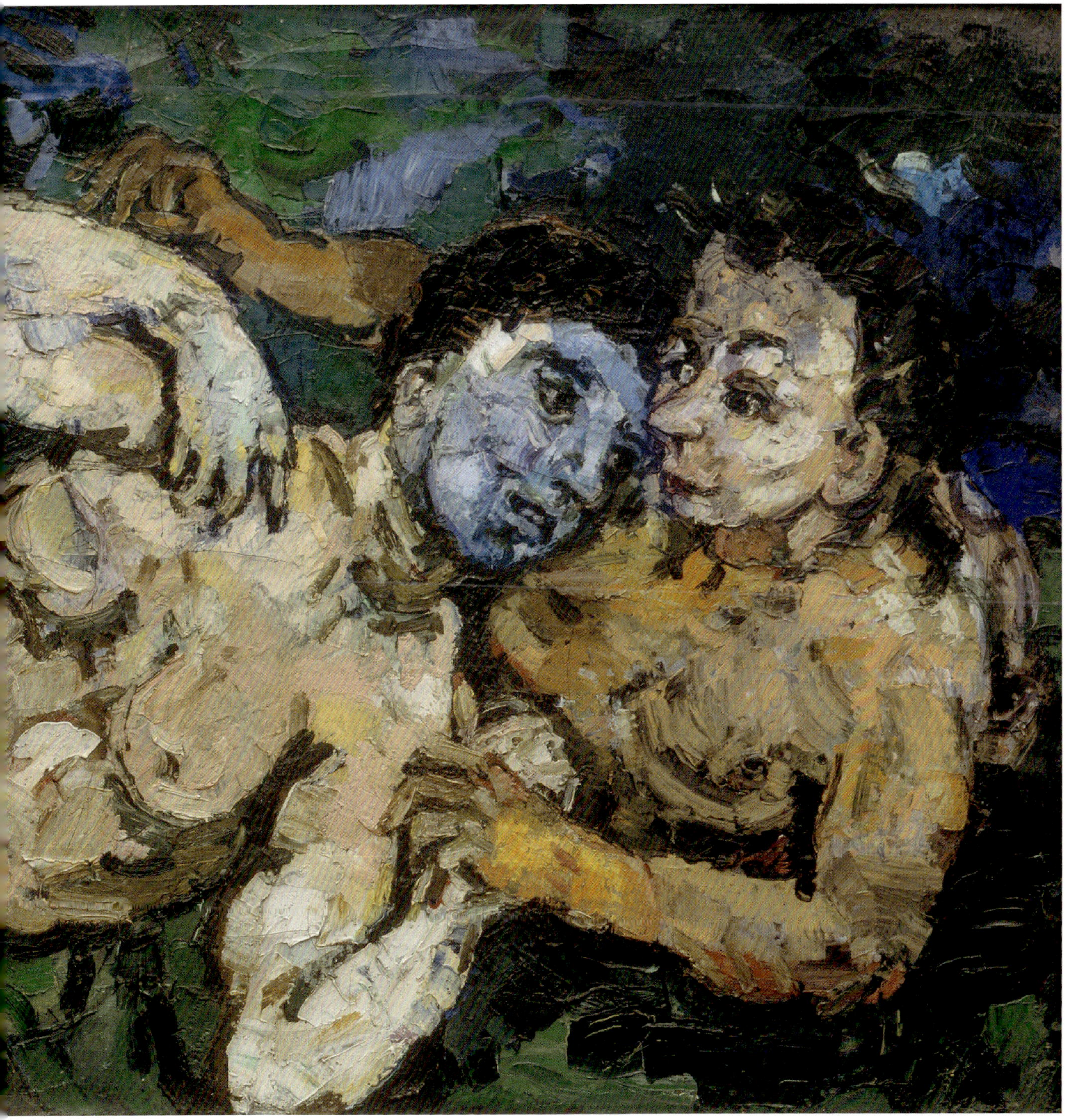

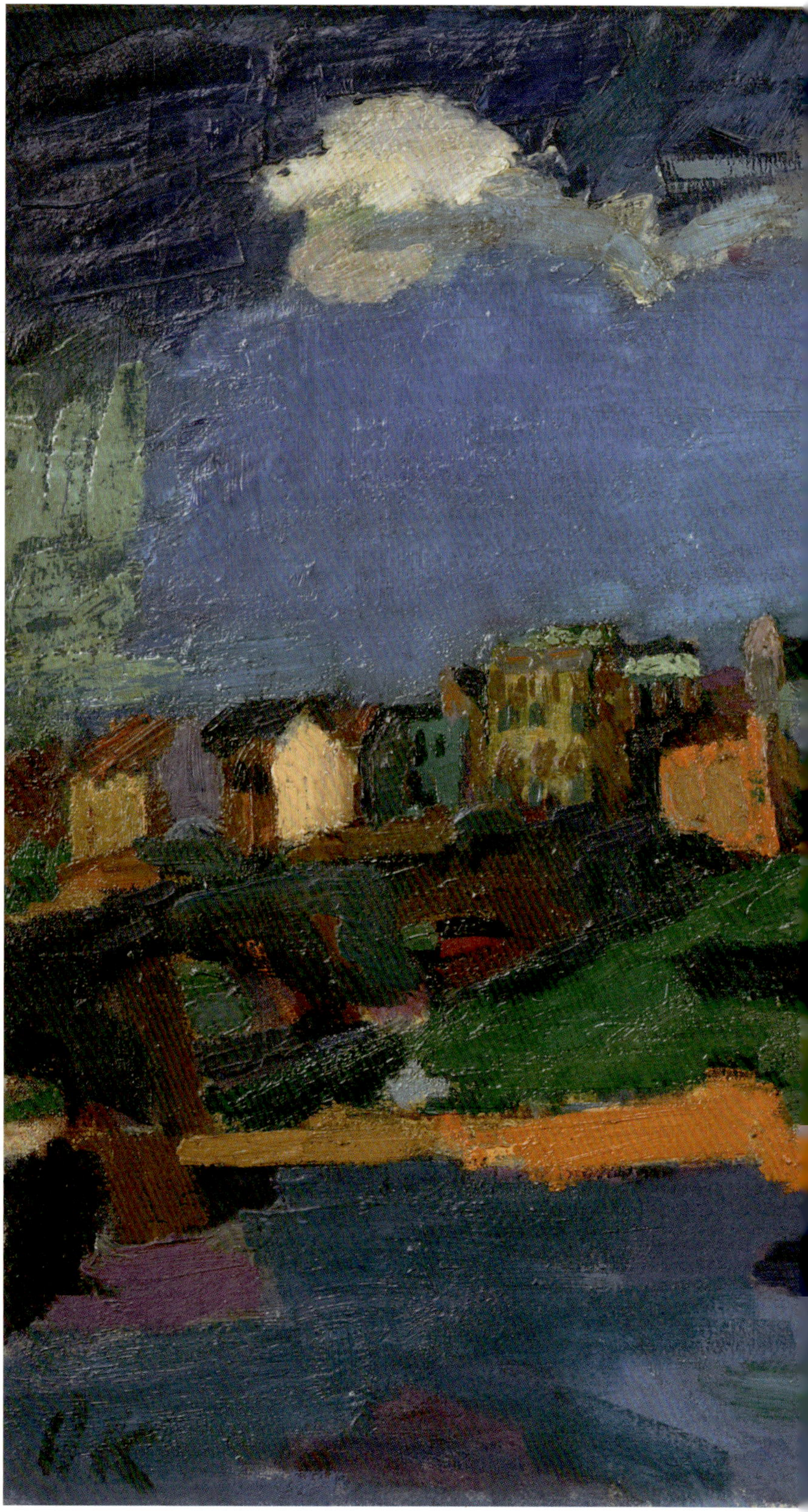

Dresden, Neustadt III
1921
Oil on canvas
70 x 99 cm

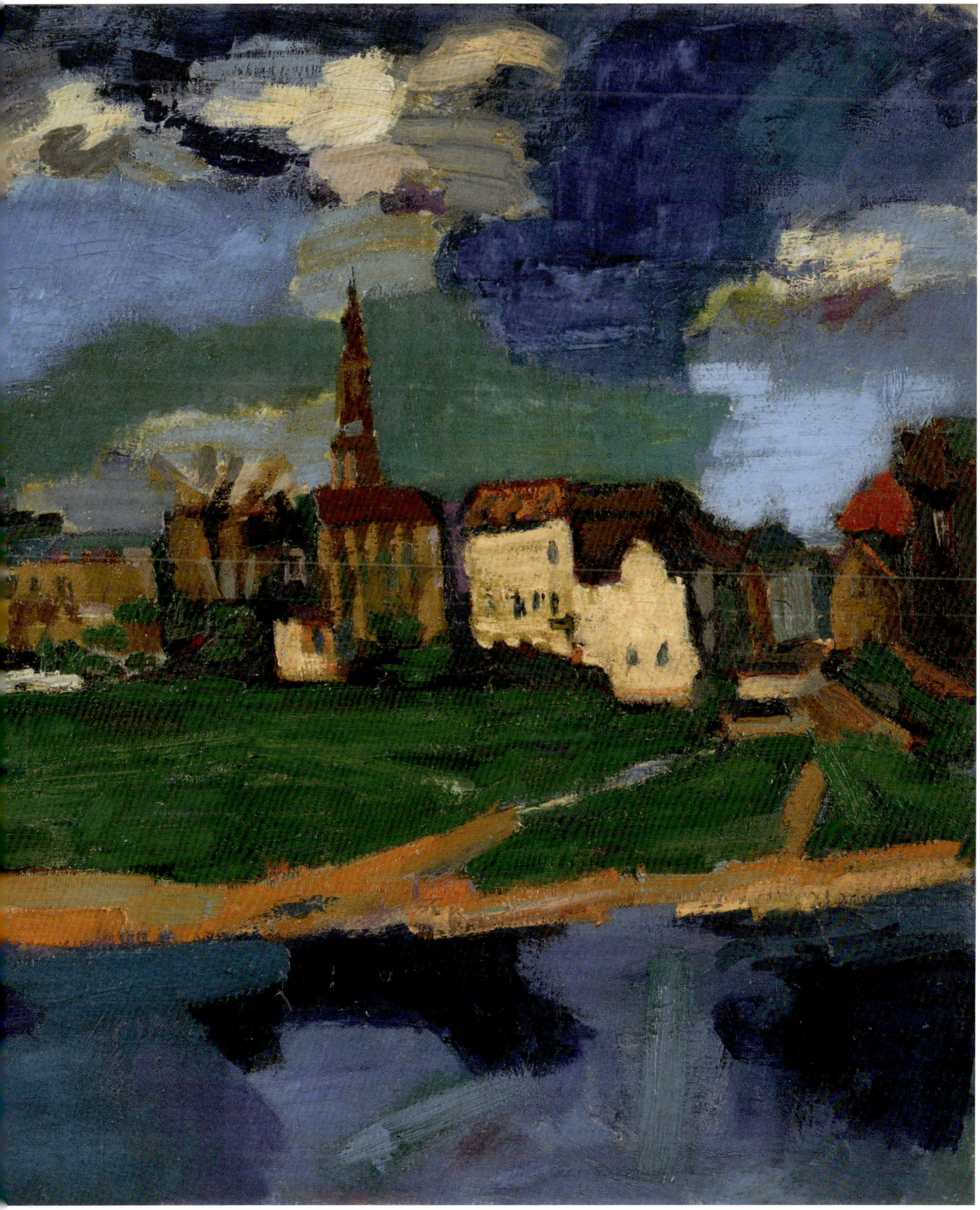

Wilhelm Lehmbruck

Bust of Mrs. L., 1910
Woman with Head Bowed, 1911
Torso of a Girl Turning, 1913/14
Woman Looking Back, 1914
Head of a Youth, 1914

This work is complete in its incompleteness; in other words, it remains forever incomplete even in its finished state. Wilhelm Lehmbruck intended the bust of his wife, Anna, as a fragment. The torso seems broken off, one arm somewhat longer than the other. Both arm stumps are much too short to actually do anything, but long enough to suggest motion in the upper body and head, which are inclined slightly to the side. To keep the body from losing its balance, Lehmbruck had to extend the second arm somewhat. But it, too, hovers close to the ground, only increasingly the impression of *non-finito*, of modelling not entirely completed. While the torso requires a flat surface on which to stand, the arm stump is also treated on the underside. A brutality is alluded to that contrasts with the finely elaborated rest of the sculpture, with the perfect female upper body and the calmly contemplative, peaceful face.

When Lehmbruck began working on the **Bust of Mrs. L.**, he had already engaged intensely with the work of Auguste Rodin on several trips to Paris. Rodin's introduction of the fragment and the *non-finito* flow into Lehmbruck's works, as can be seen, yet are combine with the simplified form and modern smoothness of Aristide Maillol's female figures. Lehmbruck's surfaces differ from those of Maillol, however. This is due to the modelling of the surfaces, and to the material used. In 1910, Lehmbruck began casting his figures in cement-bound artificial stone. This technique, borrowed from building construction, is less expensive than bronze casting and yet weather resistant. For Lehmbruck, cast stone was more than just a cheap alternative. He used its qualities in a targeted fashion and experimented with this synthetic material, which is not only variable in terms of hardness, but in colour as well.[1] For example, there are other casts of the **Bust of Mrs. L.** in shades of grey, different from the very dark tone of the bust in the collection at Museum Ludwig. The colour of the material, either a cool blue-grey or a warmer black-grey, lends the figure a more or less artificial, more or less stony appearance.

Experimentation with the found form dominated Lehmbruck's work from 1910 on, when he moved from Düsseldorf to Paris. Here, directly after the move, the expressionistically stretched figure of the *Kneeling Woman (Große Kniende)* was created, larger than life-sized. The fragile tectonics, the almost architectural structure of the figure, which has been called 'gothic', and the Expressionist formal impulse are barely visible in the sectional piece the **Woman with Head Bowed.** As if wanting to examine the distant head more closely, Lehmbruck cut it off boldly at breast height and had it cast in different versions. The head is now at the same time an autonomous sculpture and *pars pro toto*, a part containing the whole.[2] It can be regarded at eye level, even if this only brings it closer to us in spatial terms, altering nothing of the ideational distance that the bowed head expresses.[3] On the contrary, this distance – a distance of the artist to his own work as well – is amplified still further by the cut through the nipples. Still today, this seems radical and strange. Its cold-bloodedness stands in harsh contrast to the expression of the face, lost in contemplation. The sculptor here proves to be a calculating craftsman, who despite all the interiority and unworldliness of the figure casts a technical, critical gaze on his own work, as if seeking to dissect it. The cut through the broadest part of the upper body allows for the most stability. At the same time, it is the most sensitive part of a woman's body. Stability and fragility are spliced together. While it can be said of quite a few works that they have lost their explosive impact over the decades, this is most certainly not the case for this sculpture.

Head of a Youth also shows how intensely Lehmbruck engaged with the form of the bust. Directly subsequent to the epochal sculpture *Ascending Youth (Emporsteigender Jüngling*, 1913/14), it, too, forms an autonomous partial piece of the attenuated figure, which ascends while looking down towards the ground. The cut here is placed just under the shoulders, creating a pedestal-like basis for the head, which is stretched forward. Balanced and symmetrical, the shoulders and the chest form a gentle, wave-like foundation for the head, which is modelled to appear extremely mobile. Here, not only the brow but the entire face is furrowed in thought. In contrast to the smooth, passive heads of the female figures, an agitation can be found within the **Head of a Youth** that the figure as a whole, frozen in its grounded stride, does not possess, either in terms of movement or modelling. While **Woman with Head Bowed** shows an extremely peaceful face, the **Head of a Youth** is captured in a restive state. The contemplative gentleness of the female figures is contrasted with the brooding tension of this male figure.

Torso of a Girl Turning is also a fragment. To be more precise, it is actually the fragment of a fragment. The expanded version of **Torso of a Girl** remains a torso, but has longer legs. The leg stretched towards the front is completed up to knee level, so that the figure steps forward while turning. In **Torso of a Girl**, the movement of the stride is limited to the motion of the torso, so that it can barely be registered. Lehmbruck is able to make the movement palpable from the middle of the body, without arms and legs, as if the impulse did not come from the limbs but from an inner centre. This centre is located at the cut of the abdomen that separates the movement of upper and lower body. But Lehmbruck also sought to formulate the act of looking back, as expressed in the figure as a whole. The head, turning to the side, is closely bound to the upper body. The hair, which emphasizes the bridge of the neck to the head, appears, like the entire head, to be under a veil, making the face into an additional rounded form that fits harmoniously into the voluminous curves of the torso. Lehmbruck achieves a classically balanced, virtuoso formulation of the figure looking back.

Another formulation of the subject of the figure looking back can be found in a small statue made that same year. Here, head and body are strictly distinguished from one another. The body moves, while the head turns unnaturally to the left, so far that the face is not even visible in profile. From the front we look, very strangely, onto the rear of the head, which has only been roughly worked. The statue thus provokes two radically separate views, from the front of the block-like body and from the side of the unusually expressive face. This female head is not introverted or bowed down, but looks off into the distance, reacting to a particular event. The head, in contrast to **Torso of a Girl**, is seen here as a fragment, an autonomous part of an entire figure. Alongside ideas from Cubism,

Lehmbruck's studies of sectional elements seem to be reflected in the **Woman Looking Back**, in which the contrast between head and body is taken to extremes. So much so that the somewhat crude-looking work has very little in common with the highly elegant, larger than life statues. The greatest difference is not their proportions or the way the works are modelled, but their motif. This **Woman Looking Back** is not just an abstract formal study, nor is it any longer just the expression of a philosophical idea: it is anecdotal. It recalls the biblical tale of Susanna, who is observed by old men as she is bathing. Or, alternatively, looking at the stony appearance of the head, it is Lot's wife, who, although forbidden to do so, turns back to look at Sodom, and is petrified to a pillar of salt. The **Woman Looking Back** tells of nakedness and shame, flight and guilt. She is of our world, a world that would be shattered later that same year.

Lehmbruck, as a German national, was forced to flee Paris overnight in 1914. Back in Berlin, he reacted swiftly to the new reality. His sculptures *Wounded (Stürmender/Getroffener)*, *Dead Soldier (Gefallener)*, and *Fallen Man (Gestürzter)* were executed the next year. In 1919, tortured by depression, he took his life in Zurich.

Julia Friedrich

1 Katharina Barbara Lepper, 'Anmerkungen zur Bedeutung von Material, Fassung und Form in Wilhelm Lehmbrucks Werk am Beispiel der *Büste der Knienden* und des *Kopfes des emporsteigenden Jünglings*', in: Eva Mongi-Vollmer (ed.), *Wilhelm Lehmbruck: Büsten*, Frankfurt/M. 2007, p. 45ff.

2 Eva Mongi-Vollmer, 'Pars pro Toto: die Teilstücke', in: ibid., pp. 22-39, here p. 22.

3 Cf. Katharina Barbara Lepper, 'Das plastische Werk', in: Christoph Brockhaus (ed.), *Wilhelm Lehmbruck: 1881–1919*, Cologne 2005, pp. 22-33, here p. 25.

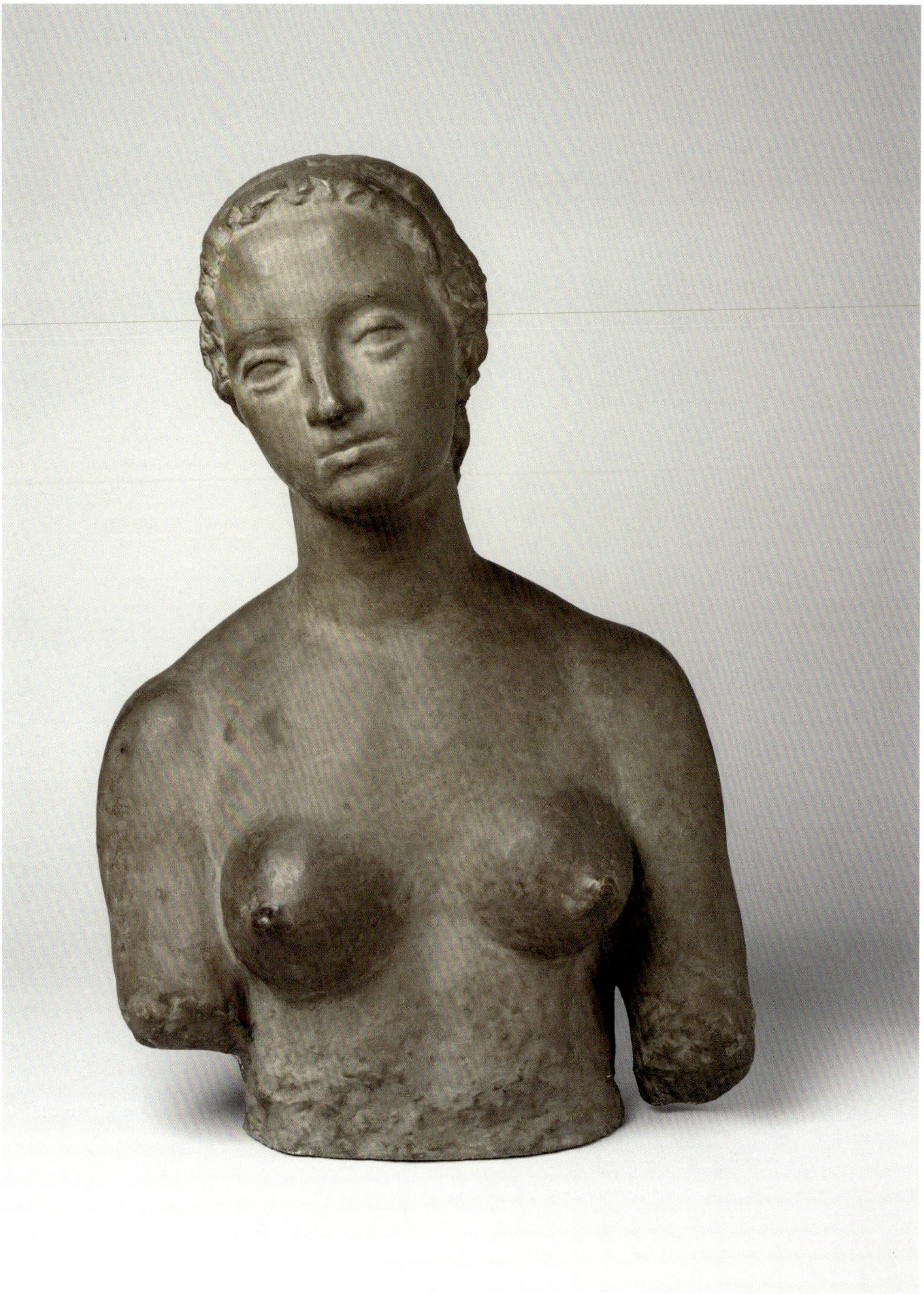

Bust of Mrs. L.
1910
Cast stone
H.: 80 cm

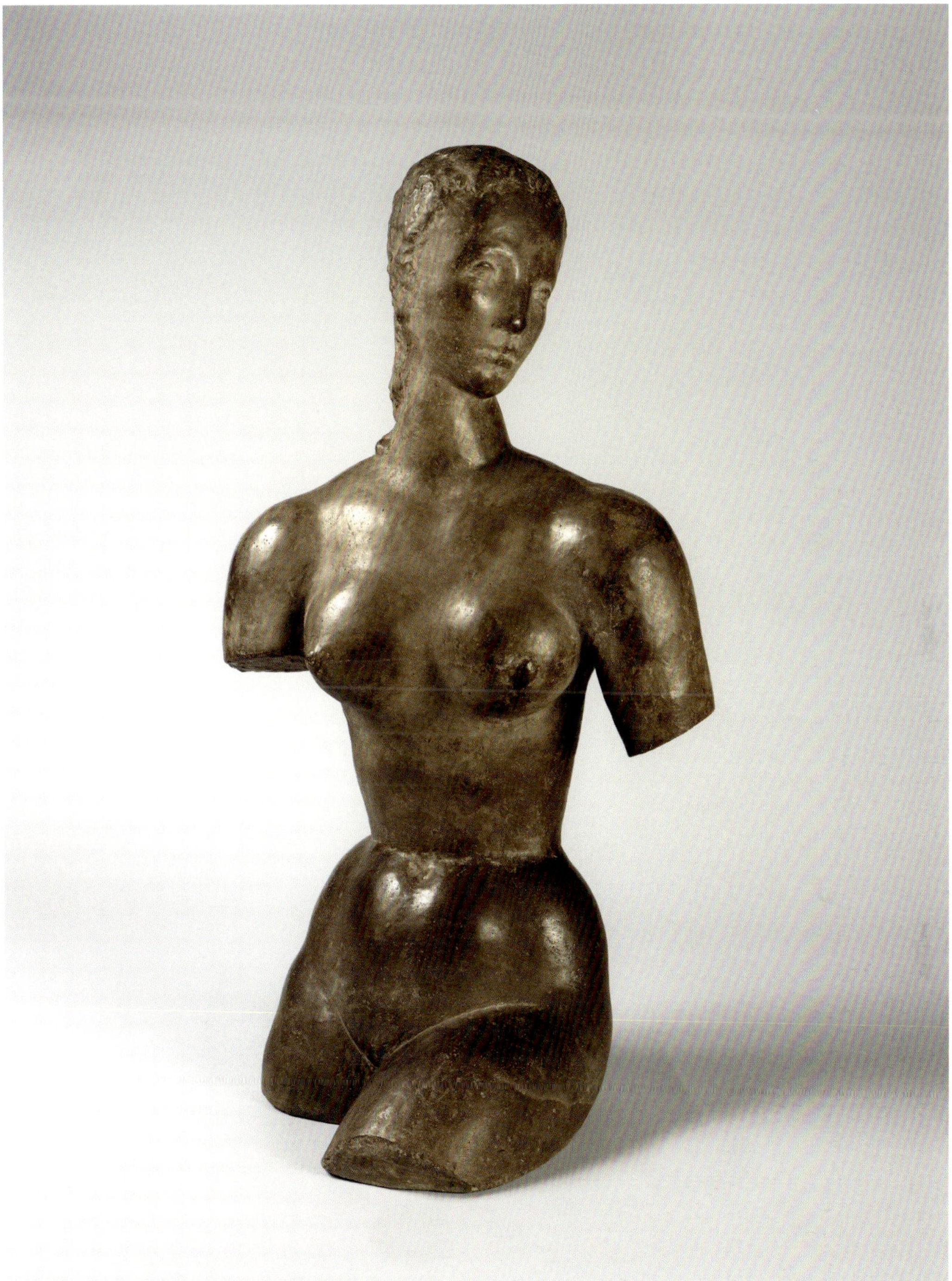

Torso of a Girl Turning
1913/14
Cast stone
H.: 95 cm

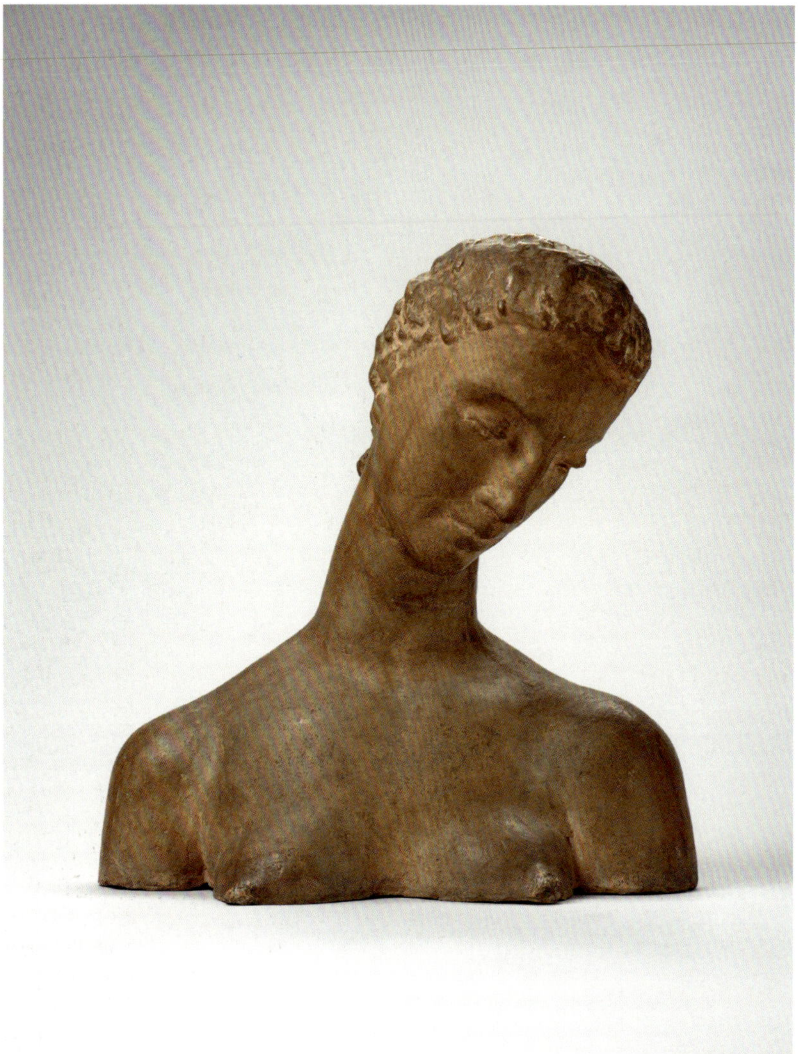

Woman with Head Bowed
1911
Terracotta
H.: 48.5 cm

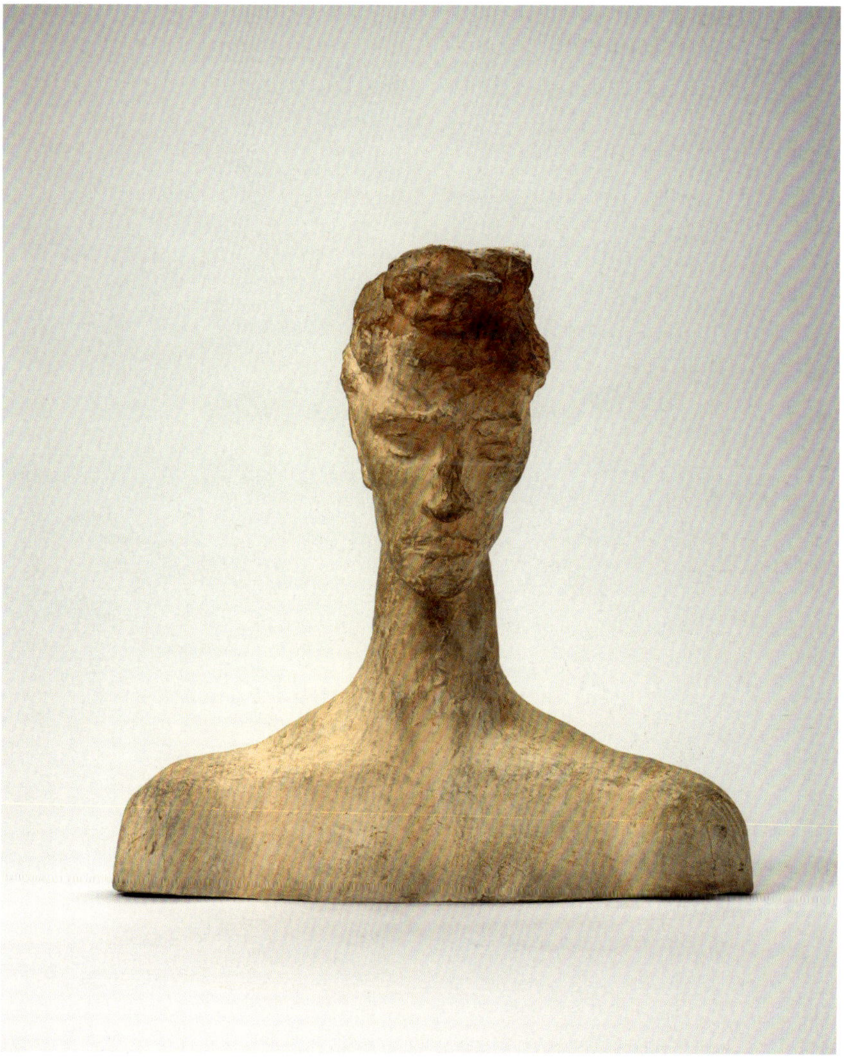

Head of a Youth
1914
Terracotta
H.: 46 cm

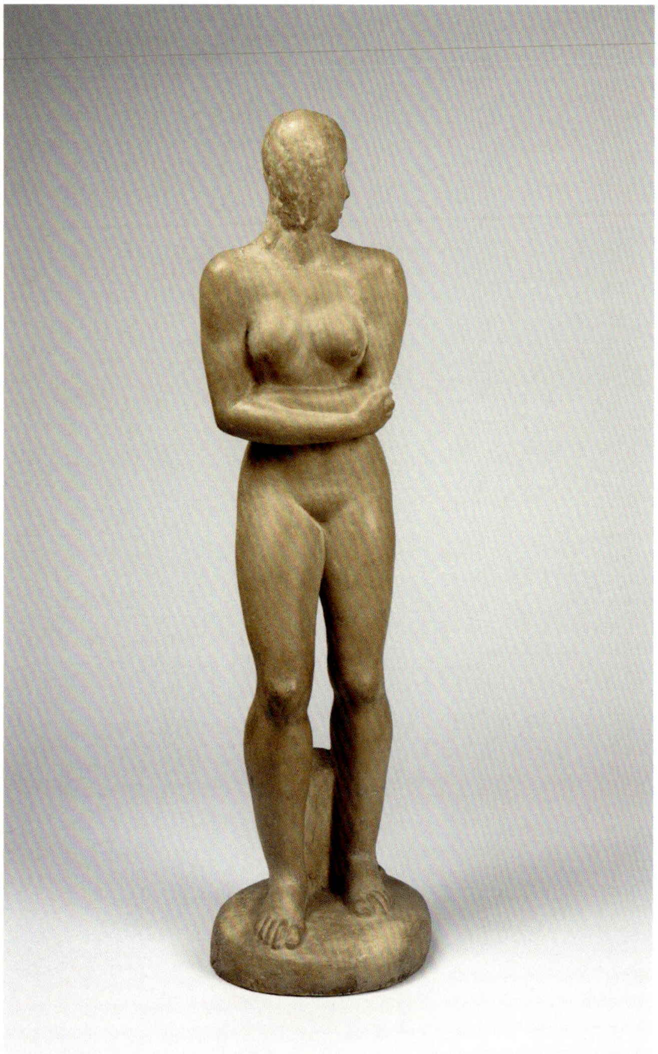

Woman Looking Back
1914
Cast stone
H.: 92 cm

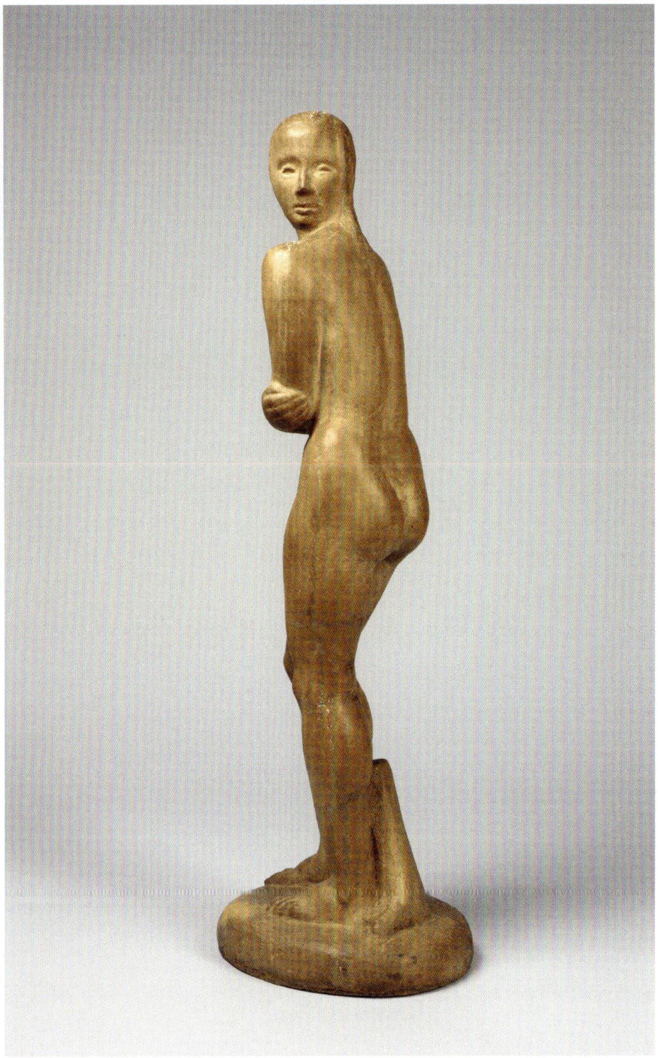

August Macke

Lady in a Green Jacket, 1913
Farewell, 1914

As if glowing from inside, **Lady in a Green Jacket** stands apart from the other paintings placed around it in the museum. Light was a central subject for Macke, as were motion, fugacity, the mood of a scene, and interior, psychological states. He was interested in the 'composition of the vital', which could not be captured by mere 'imitation', but could only be achieved by creating a 'tension' between the painted colours and shapes.[1] At age twenty, Macke studied the urban moments captured by the paintings of the French Impressionists. Three years later, inspired by Henri Matisse, he increased the luminosity of his colours, unnatural in their appearance and applied over large surfaces. In April 1913, the painter was thrilled by Robert Delaunay's crystalline-seeming paintings, which 'are capable of filling one with a veritably celestial joy in the sun and in life'.[2]

In **Lady in a Green Jacket**, broad expanses of the painting are dominated by the yellow that glows forth amidst the five figures depicted, a woman standing alone and two couples. The clear blue of the lake causes the yellow of a wall parapet and the opposite shoreline to shine. It spreads across the painting as a whole, from the orange, rusty red ground across the brighter buildings to the lemon yellow in the leaves of the trees, and conversely the blue is echoed by the bright sky and in several items of clothing. The dark accents of the two male silhouettes, the tree trunks and the woman's skirt in the foreground cut through the yellow and increase its luminosity to a glimmer. None of the motifs are given a uniform hue; the colours glow forth, linger, and lead the eye inexorably onward.

The most isolated elements here are the green jacket and the glowing red hat worn by the woman standing alone. Here, the colours seem the calmest, and the shapes also isolate themselves vis-à-vis the vibrant rhythms. The woman stands still in the midst of it all, turning slightly to the left. The couple towards which her gaze wanders looks to the right, whereas the second man repeats the outlines of the first and the woman with him looks downward. The directions in which the strollers are looking guide the gaze of the beholder. Most movements lead toward the right: the direction in which the couples are facing and the curve of the lake. Only the woman in the green jacket turns hesitatingly towards the left; her movement is anticipated by the tree on the right. Several central figures claim our attention: the woman at the foreground and the people in the side parts of the painting. The bright, oscillating clothing worn by the two women in the background dissolves the chain of figures and directs our gaze deeper into the space. The painting, which is only 44 by 43.5 cm, thus gains in terms of spatial breadth, making the colours step forward in a quite unperspectival fashion, almost like stained glass, creating their own spatiality.[3]

Macke called this routing and reordering of our vision 'rhythm'.[4] Each of his paintings has its own 'colourful, formal tension', whose 'vitality' is shaped by the artist from his own 'sensitivity'.[5] We only become truly cognizant of the loose links and the sunny brightness of this painting by way of the contrasts of the individual elements and the darkness. While the woman in the green jacket also partakes of the rhythm of strolling and the holiday excursion of the city dwellers, she stands apart, isolated.

The lake depicted is Lake Thun in Switzerland, where Macke moved in the fall of 1913, and where he stayed a good half-year. During this period, he painted his most famous works, filled with a luminous harmony, but also animated with contrasts and breaks. It was only the 'tension', the 'simultaneously different', that according to Macke generates the 'simultaneously vital'.[6]

'Shapes are powerful expressions of a powerful life', Macke wrote in the *Almanach Der Blaue Reiter*: 'Whenever they (the joys, the sufferings of man) are not behind them, where shapes are empty, without cause, then there is no art.'[7] In an especially arresting, profoundly touching way, this is true of the large painting that, according to his wife, was the last work completed before his enlistment for the First World War (in early August 1914). Later, it was given various titles: **Farewell / Street with Passersby at Twilight / Mobilization**. The rhythm of the colours and shapes is completely different from that in Macke's other works. A sallow, colourless light from the background emphasizes the black of the rigid silhouettes. The red is a rusty brown, the yellow muted, green and blue disappear into black. On the left, two women are standing together, the older one holding a strikingly white piece of paper. On the right, two men seen from the back bend beyond the edge of the image, their heads invisible. The black, silent silhouettes are reminiscent of Edvard Munch's *Death Room*.[8] A dog sniffs over to a small child who seems to want to run towards the beholder. Perhaps the most compelling figure is the rigid girl with the empty oval face, which draws our gaze towards the middle of the painting, yet remains inscrutable. And yet we have a sense here that we can grasp something we cannot see.

Erich Franz

1 August Macke, 'Antwort auf die Rundfrage der Zeitschrift (über das "Neue Programm")', in: *Kunst und Künstler*, 1914, quoted in Gustav Vriesen, *August Macke*, Stuttgart 1957, p. 262.
2 Letter from August Macke to Bernhard Koehler, 17 March 1913, in: Werner Frese and Ernst-Gerhard Güse (eds.), *August Macke: Briefe an Elisabeth und die Freunde*, Munich 1987, p. 298. On Macke's reaction to French Modernism, see Ursula Heiderich's essays in: *August Macke und die frühe Moderne in Europa* (exh. cat. Westfälisches Landesmuseum für Kunst und Kulturgeschichte Münster, Kunstmuseum Bonn), Ostfildern-Ruit 2001.
3 Ursula Heiderich, *August Macke: Gemälde. Werkverzeichnis*, Ostfildern 2008, p. 94 f.
4 Letter to Bernhard Koehler dated 30 March 1913, in: Frese/Güse. op.cit., p. 302.
5 Cf. 'Notizen August Mackes über Kunst', in: Heiderich, op.cit., p. 255.
6 Ibid.
7 August Macke, 'Die Masken', in: *Almanach Der Blaue Reiter*, Munich 1912, quoted in Vriesen, op.cit., p. 283.
8 On Macke's references to Edvard Munch, see Heiderich, op.cit., pp. 276-279.

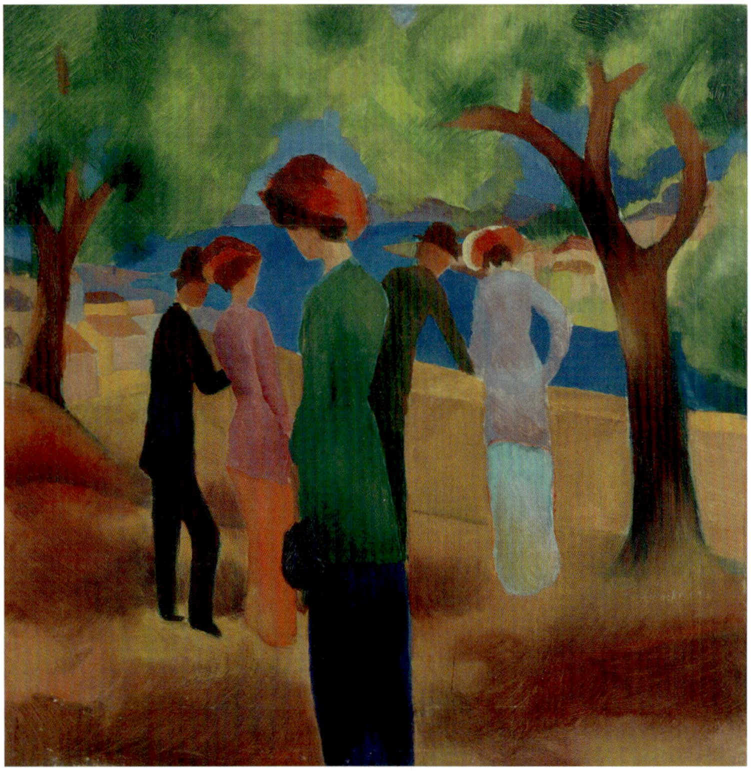

Lady in a Green Jacket
1913
Oil on canvas
44 x 43.5 cm

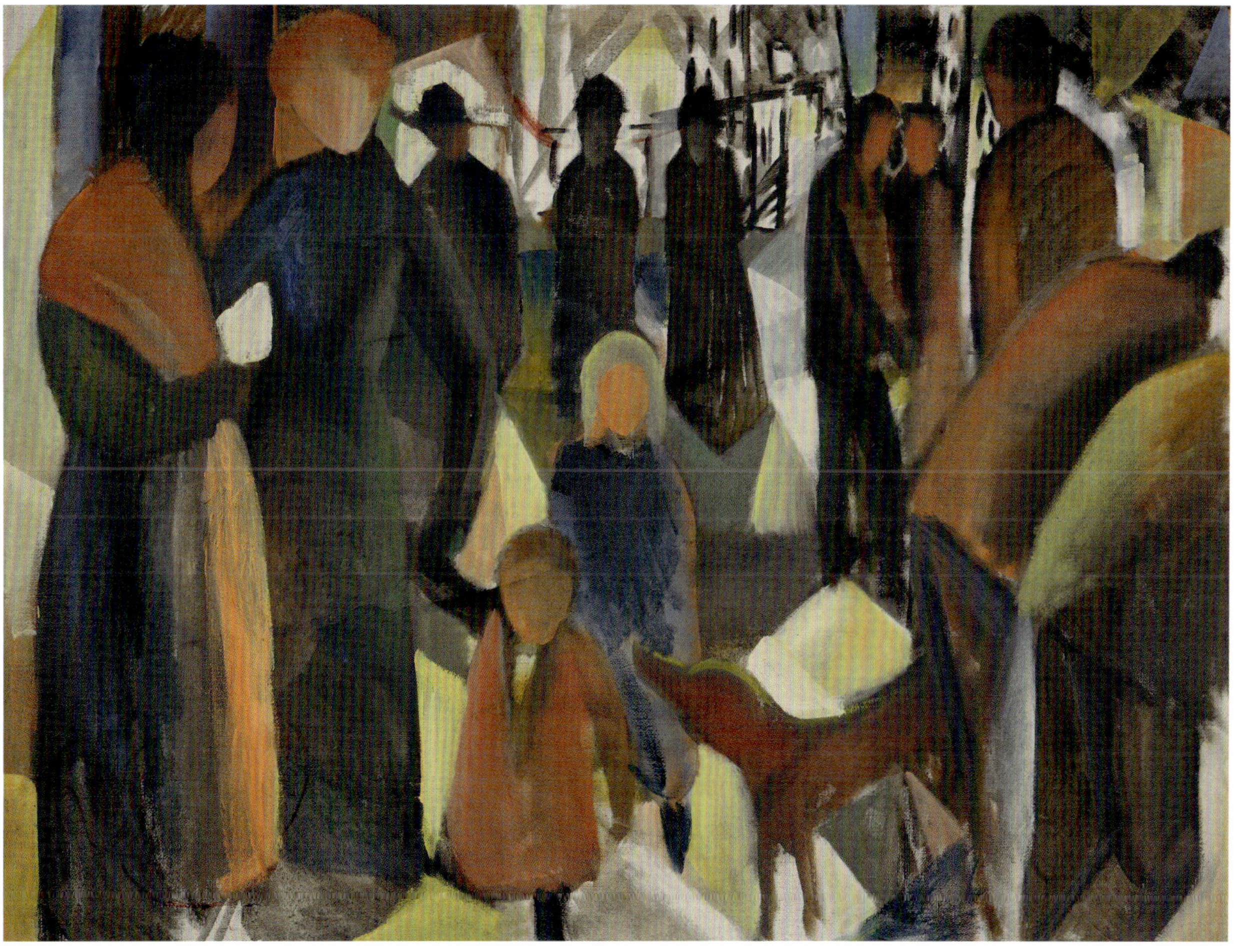

Farewell
1914
Oil on canvas
101 x 130.5 cm

Aristide Maillol

Standing Bather, 1900
Leda, c. 1902
Seated Girl, before 1907

Artworks are often based on mythological tales. But sometimes the artist concentrates so much on a single aspect that the story becomes scarcely recognizable. This is the case with Aristide Maillol's small statuette **Leda**. The erotic motif of Leda and the swan has often been treated in art. According to the myth, Leda was desired by Zeus, who seduced her in the form of a swan and made her pregnant. But Maillol dispenses completely with the depiction of the swan and thus with any clear-cut narrative. Central to this work is a meditation on the female figure: a seated nude, her upper body leaning gently forward and her head lowered, Leda has raised one hand in defence, the sole reference to the myth. While her hand points in one direction, her eyes look in the other, making it impossible to grasp the figure from any one angle. The decision to compose the work in this way lends visibility to her movement, which comes across however as reserved and introspective, as if contained and restricted by an invisible cube.

Maillol's sculptural language is devoted to achieving a balance in the distribution of volumes and masses. He avoided sweeping movements when devising his works, whose main focus is always a clear vertical line. As a great admirer of antique art, he distinguished between a 'resting architecture' and an 'architecture of movement', two aspects that he attempted to unite in his sculptures, which, like buildings, were pieced together step by step from component parts.[1] His nudes are engrossed solely in themselves; they seem self-contained and possessing an inner repose, nested as they are in a rectangle, triangle or lozenge.[2]

The figure **Seated Girl** underlines this introversion: unlike **Leda**, she is leaning gently backwards, with one hand placed on her thigh, the other resting on the chair, and one leg stretched out in front. As she looks out into empty space, her pose conveys relaxation and the absence of any outside distractions. What is so fascinating about Maillol's work is the way he combines the contradictory modes of calm and movement within one sculpture. This can also be observed in another of Maillol's statuettes from the Haubrich Collection: his **Bather**, a standing nude who has assumed a simple and natural pose on her weight-bearing and free legs, giving the impression that she is about to take a short step forward while nevertheless remaining pillar-like in space. Her right arm seems to reflect this movement and is pointing in the direction of her gaze.

Initially Maillol studied painting before taking up sculpture. In 1895 he came in contact with the Nabis. The influence of this group of artists can already be observed in his first sculptural works, which were wood reliefs. Shortly thereafter, he began to model sculptures. His breakthrough came with the first exhibition of his works in 1902, mounted by the art dealer and publisher Ambroise Vollard, who gathered around him artists like Pablo Picasso, Henri Matisse, Paul Cézanne and many others at the beginning of the twentieth century.

Maillol created **Leda** and the **Bather** around 1900 as small works in clay, which Vollard then sold as bronzes. The category of the statuette is virtually predestined for the art market because it presupposes the art lover and collector. However, Maillol, with his notion of antique sculpture, did not personally regard the bronze cast as the finished work, but rather the plaster model. He preferred a colourless surface and later insisted that every new sculpture that was exhibited should first be shown in the form of the plaster model.[3]

Pierre-Auguste Renoir, who also was part of Vollard's circle, did three paintings in 1907 entitled *Étude d'une statuette de Maillol*, which are studies of the **Seated Girl**. A figure by Maillol also appears in two other Renoirs, one of them his portrait of Ambroise Vollard, in which the subject is shown holding Maillol's *Kneeling Girl*.[4] This *Kneeling Girl* was a prototype for *The Mediterranean*, one of Maillol's most renowned sculptures.

The innovative quality in his work, which otherwise has such a classical feel, is especially apparent when compared with the sculptures of Rodin, whose style came to dominate the latter half of the nineteenth century. Maillol created firm bodies and avoided dissolving form in a painterly way. With his ideal of making figures that resemble 'perfect architecture'[5] he attempted to resist any personal characteristics or individual features. Unlike Rodin, Maillol shunned sweeping gestures and strong facial expressions, for in his opinion the whole was more important than the details: 'What is interesting is not the imitation of nature, but rather the artist's vision.'[6]

Anna Brohm

1 Henry Frère, *Gespräche mit Maillol*, translated from the French by Hans Voss, Frankfurt/M. 1961, p. 49.
2 Hans Joachim Albrecht, 'Körpersprache und plastische Kunst', in: Christoph Brockhaus (ed.), *Lehmbruck, Rodin und Maillol*, Duisburg 2005, pp. 14-26, here p.18.
3 *Étude d'une statuette de Maillol*, c. 1907, oil on canvas.
4 *Ambroise Vollard*, 1908, oil on canvas, Courtauld Institute of Art Gallery, London.
5 Frère, op.cit., p. 141.
6 Ibid., p. 118.

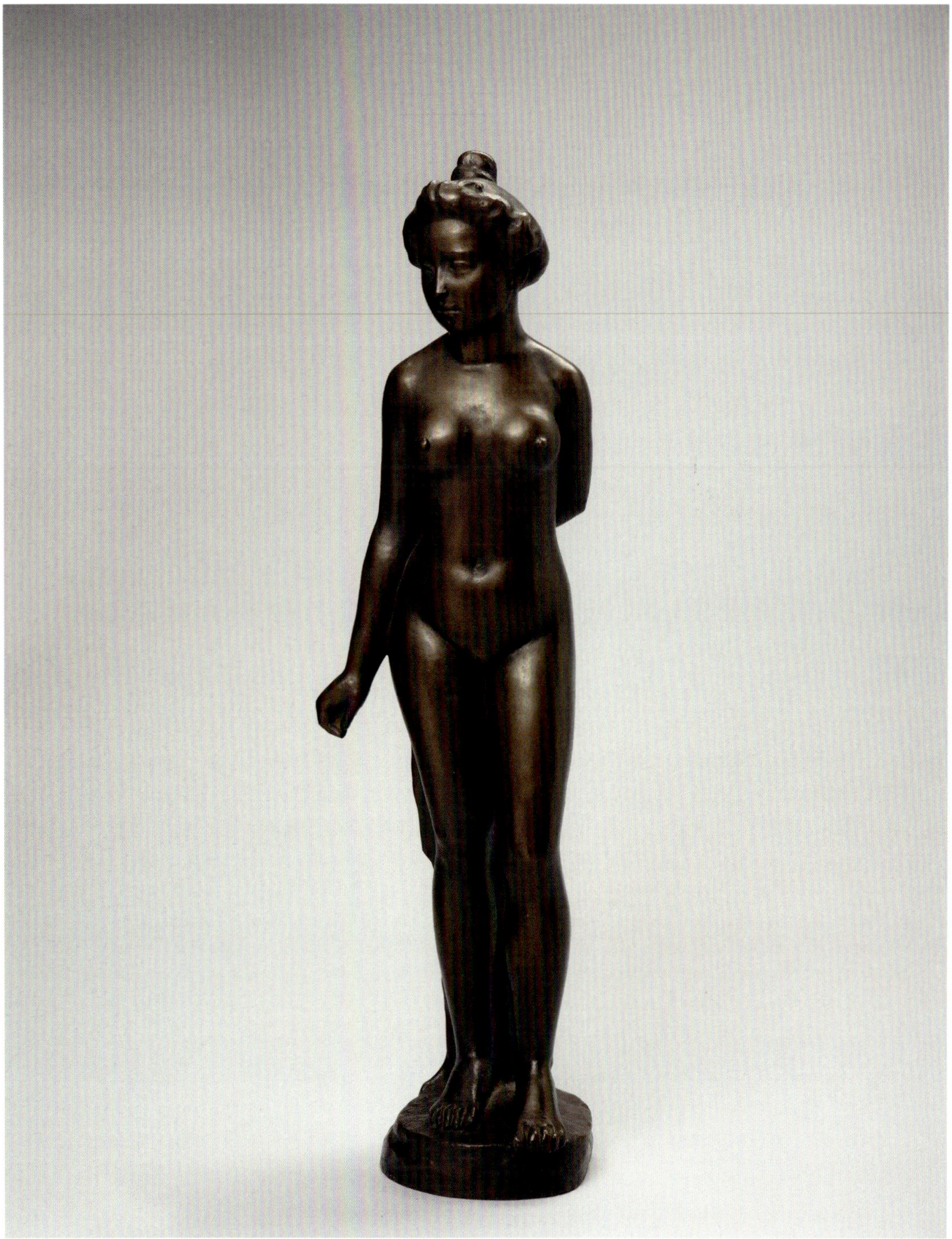

Standing Bather
1900
Bronze
H.: 66 cm

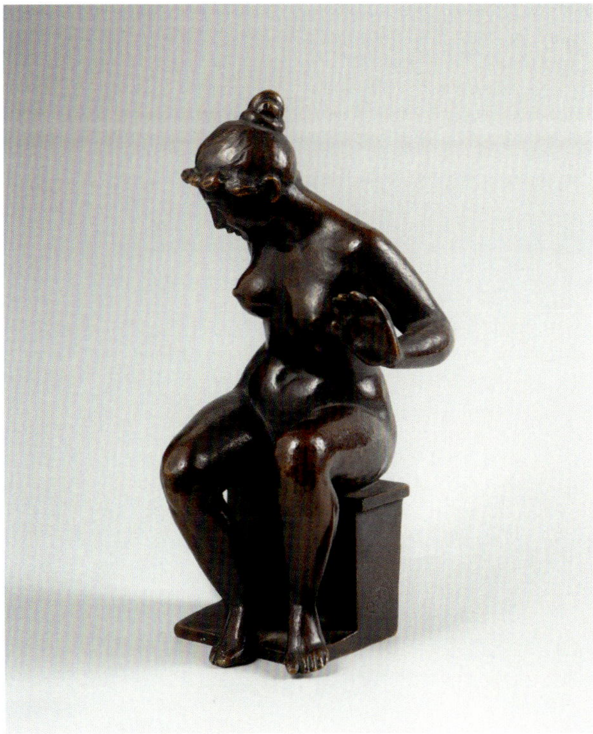

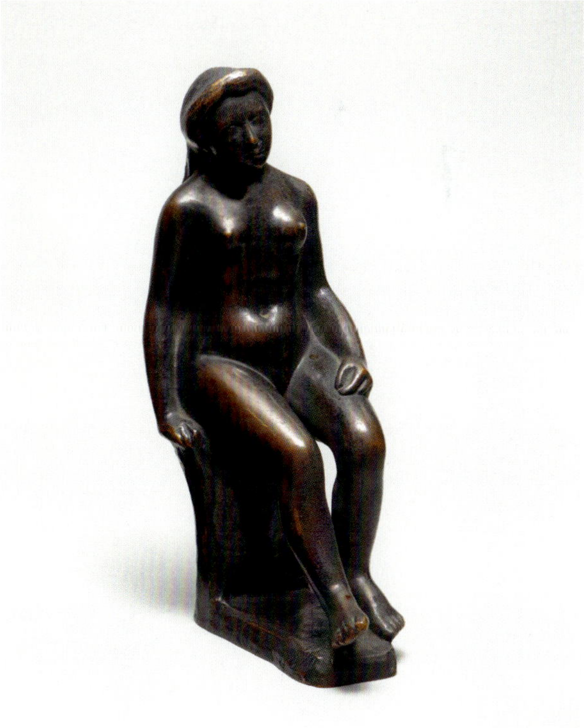

Leda
C. 1902
Bronze
H.: 28.5 cm

Seated Girl
Before 1907
Bronze
H.: 23 cm

Ewald Mataré

Hen, 1924
Sleeping Cat, 1929
Female Torso, 1932
Symbol of a Horse, 1941/42

Ewald Mataré trained as a painter at the Berlin Academy and came almost by chance to sculpture, which was to dominate his subsequent work. While staying on the North Sea island of Spiekeroog in the summer of 1922, he failed to find any pieces of driftwood he could use for a woodcut, so he did his first carving instead. He chiselled his figures directly into the block of wood in *taille directe* style, as the Expressionists did. But unlike them, he disguised any traces of the work process by polishing the surface of the carving.

The smooth surface tempts us to touch the work, and for Mataré this act of ' grasping' – in both senses of the word – is a fundamental part of every sculpture. In addition, polishing allowed him to accentuate the natural grain of the wood, as is shown quite magnificently in **Female Torso**. With its concentric circles, the grain emphasizes the figure's strongly feminine curves and thus heightens its sensuous charms. This **Torso** is part of a sequence of nudes from the 1930s that awaken associations with archaic fertility idols. It has, however, a unique place in this sequence due to its block-like form and the concentration on the trunk. Mataré was inspired to take up this motif by naked bathers on the island of Hiddensee.[1] The particular value he attached to this work is clear from the fact that, subsequent to the wooden model, he created a much larger version of the sculpture in black diabase in 1933.

From the outset Mataré concentrated not only on human depictions but also animals, which contributed strongly to his early popularity. Surprisingly, he restricted himself to very familiar animals, mostly domestic varieties. The 'Mataré cow' became an established concept. But he also took horses, cats and chickens as his models. Working from nature was especially important to him because he wanted to make a complete break with the handed-down traditions of figuration. His nature studies enabled him to identify the natural dispositions of the various species of animal, and to convey them through his sculptures. The cat, for instance, combines two aspects: on the one hand the prowling wild cat, on the other the cuddly nature of the domestic pet. Mataré picked out both aspects in his various works, with **Sleeping Cat** being more the portrait of a pet. Once again, the warm polished wood invites us to run our fingers softly over the curled-up creature.

The tactile aspect of Mataré's sculpture came to its peak in objects presented in a reclining rather than upright pose. This group includes his **Symbol of a Horse**, which as a result of its small size and shape nestles snugly in a person's two hands. Due to his choice of material, palm wood, the sides with their lengthwise stripes are not completely smooth but have a fine fluting. As in his other works, he brings out here the structure and quality of the material and uses it as a means of aesthetic expression.

When Mataré felt that a sculpture was successful, he had it cast in bronze. That he was prompted to do this by the material, and not simply as a means of reproduction, is evident inasmuch as many of his bronzes were cast only once. **Hen**, done from a version in amaranth wood, was cast both in brass as well as bronze – in each case only one time. Although, with its dark patina, the metal resembles the original polished wood in hardness and smoothness, and in the way it hides the traces of carving, it amplifies the effect created by the silhouette because it does not have the distinctive grain of the wood.

After Mataré's work was denounced by the National Socialists, he became one of the leading post-war figures in the Rhenish art scene. He was rehabilitated when he was once again given a position as professor at the Düsseldorf Academy of Art, where Joseph Beuys was one of his students. His fame was not only based on motifs of his own free choice, such as those described, but also on his commissions for churches, among them the doors at the south entrance to Cologne Cathedral.

Isabel Brass

1 Sabine Maja Schilling, *Ewald Mataré. Das plastische Werk. Werkverzeichnis*, Cologne 1994, p. 169.

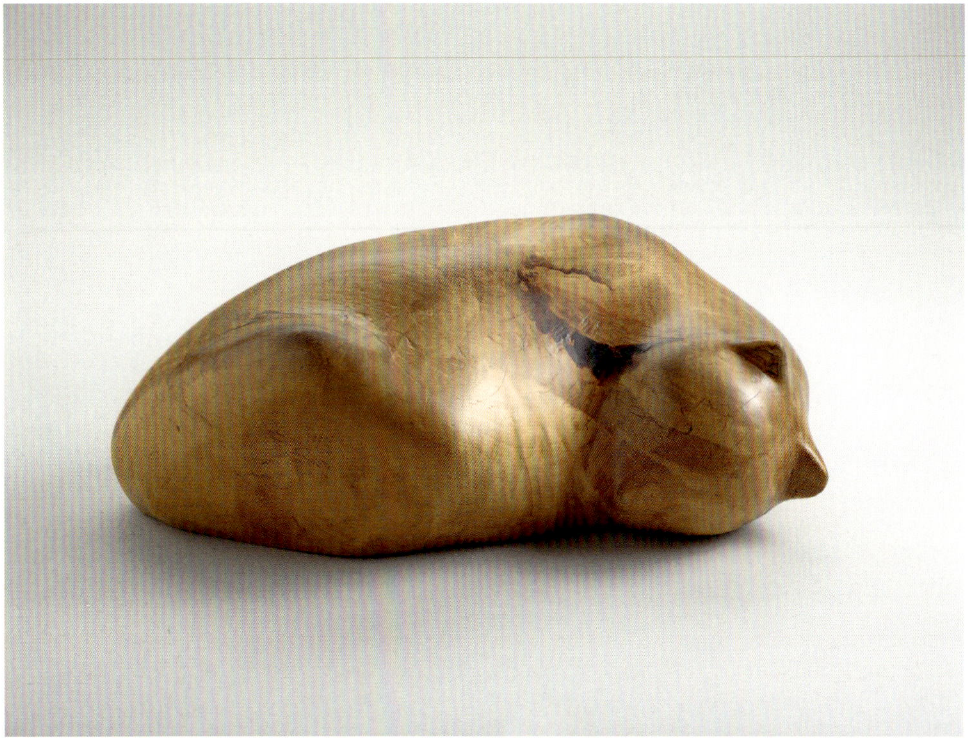

Sleeping Cat
1929
Poplar wood
H.: 16 cm

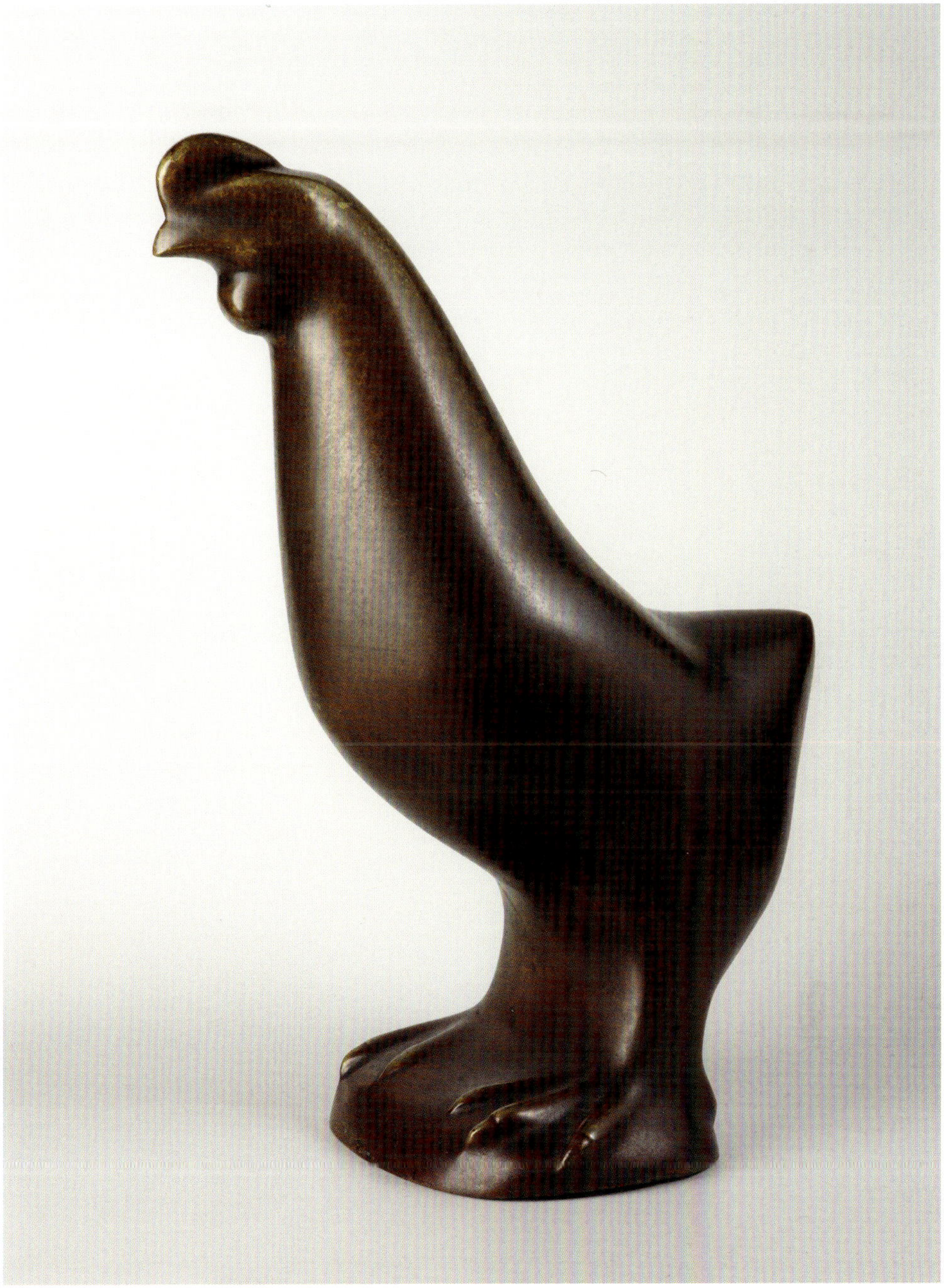

Hen
1924
Bronze
H.: 49 cm

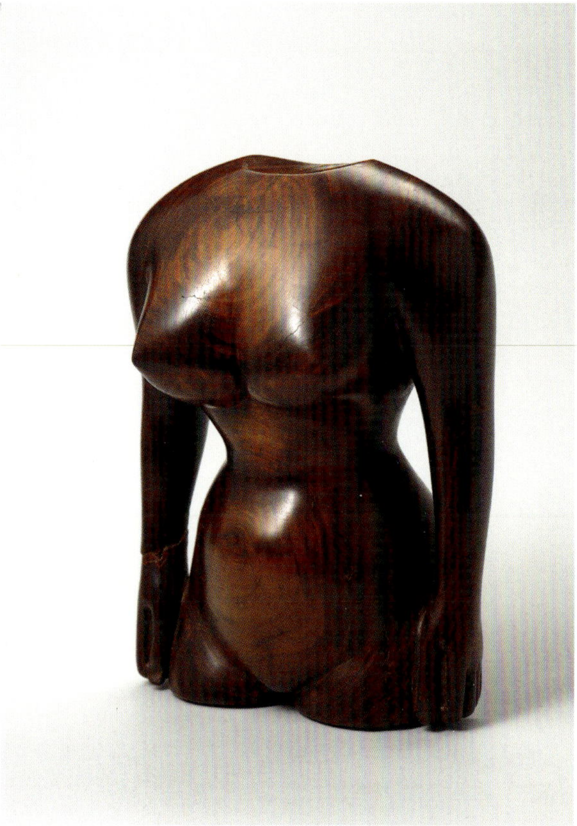

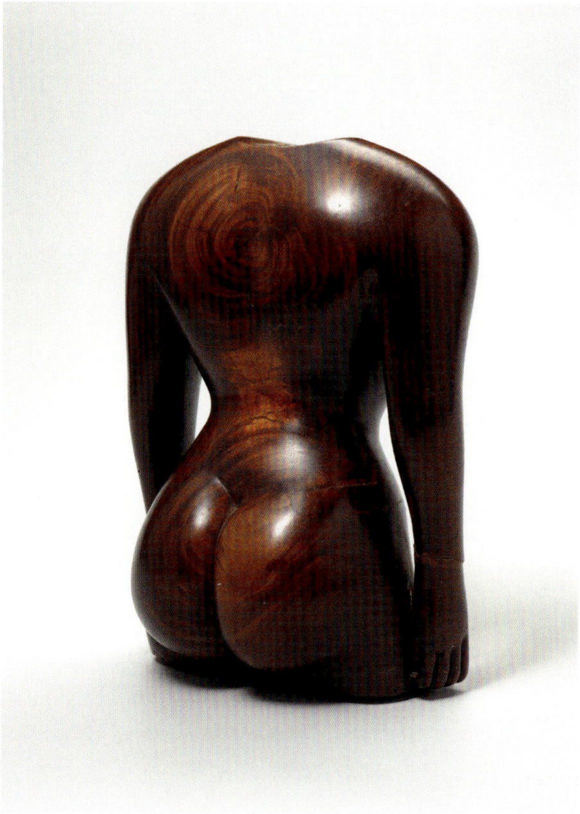

Female Torso
1932
Teak
H.: 20 cm

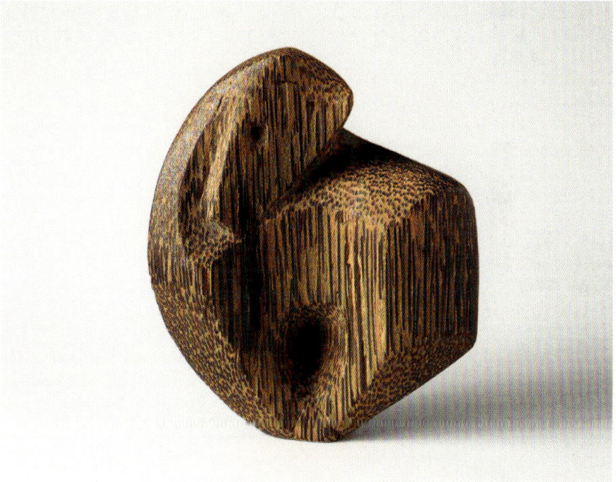

Symbol of a Horse
1941/42
Palm wood
H.: 14.5 cm, B: 12 cm

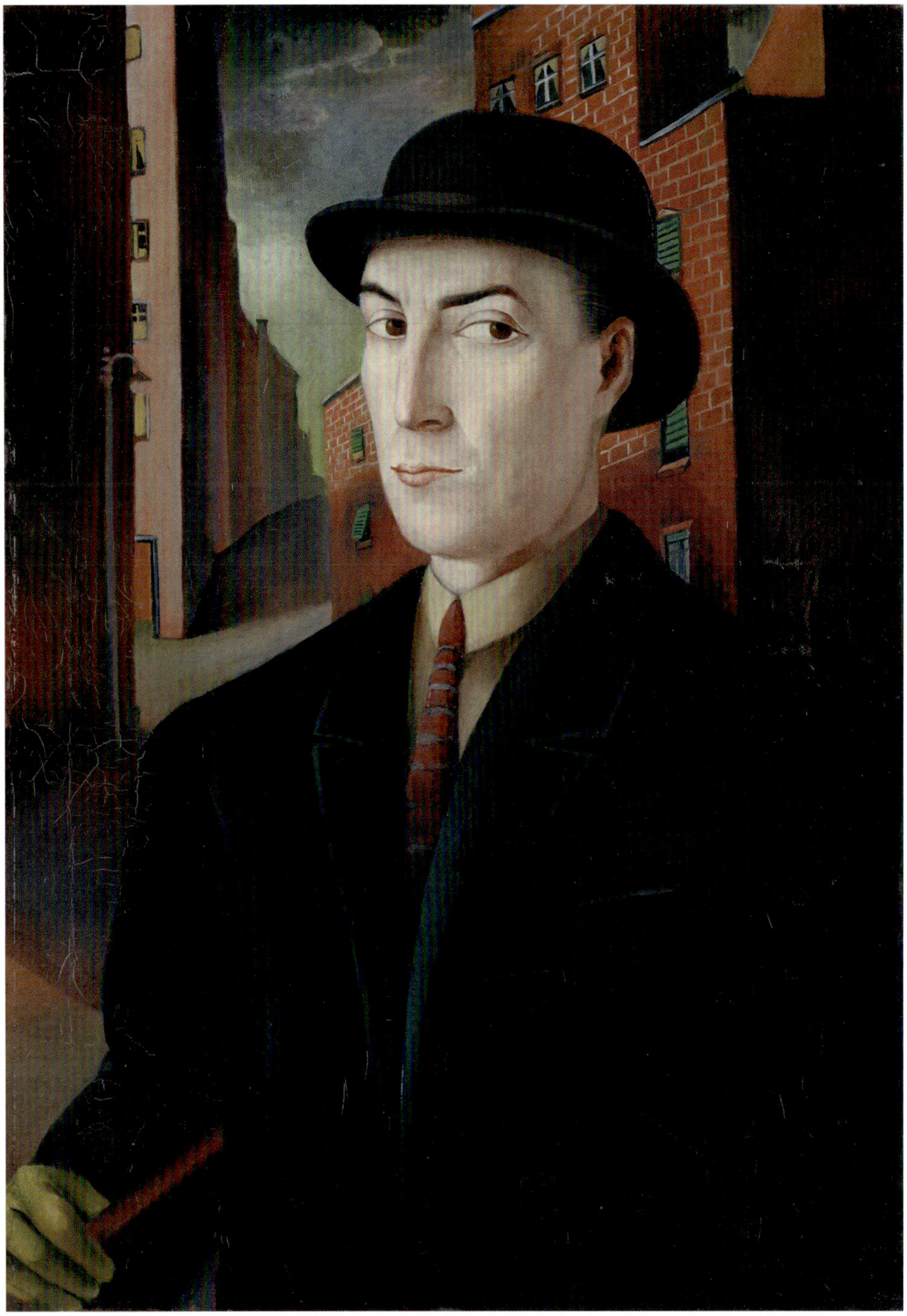

Portrait of H. M. Davringhausen
1922
Oil on canvas
86.5 x 59.5 cm

Carlo Mense

Portrait of H. M. Davringhausen, 1922

While in Munich, Carlo Mense created this portrait of the painter Heinrich Maria Davringhausen, a friend who had similarly done a portrait of him some years before. The shattering of form by the pre-war avant-gardes was frequently countered by artists in the 1920s by the kind of figuration vaunted by the Neue Sachlichkeit movement, which drew on the traditions of the Old Masters. But while others painted the harsh realities of contemporary life amidst massive inflation and unemployment, Mense did a large number of almost otherworldly, idyllically religious country scenes. Consequently, the present painting forms quite an exception in his oeuvre.

It shows the painter in his hat and dark coat as a half-length portrait in front of a deserted suburban streetscape. His penetrating gaze and raised eyebrows reveal scepticism, and even a slight haughtiness. His elegant appearance and dandyish mien contrast with the faceless, anonymous tenement buildings in the background. In much the same way that this mask-like, coolly modelled physiognomy has been reduced to a few striking features – the prominent nose, a small, closed, thin-lipped mouth and wide-open, almond-shaped eyes – the depiction of the façade is also highly schematic.

The scene is illumined by a pallid, storm-tossed sky which divides the painting with its strong contrasts into luridly lit sections and powerful shadows. As a result of the slight slant of the façades on both sides, the red brick house at the back appears to be toppling over, giving the painting an unstable, menacing cast. The compacted spatial construction with its distorted perspectives, the off-key proportions, the high-set horizon and the motif of emptiness all display strong echoes of the Italian *pittura metafisica*, whose protagonists Mense not only knew through their journal *Valori Plastici*, but had also exhibited with in 1922 in Milan. As in many paintings indebted to this style, the isolated figure has not been incorporated into his surroundings, giving the impression that flat pieces of stage scenery have been pushed together, or that the over-large figure has been depicted in front of a section of a painting. Not a soul is to be seen, not only on the street but also at the undersized windows. The strongly shadowed row of houses disappearing into the distance has been reduced to mere patches of colour and is without any openings. This solitary person and his urban surroundings are mutual strangers, however close they are in space – within a melancholy cityscape in which the pattern on the man's tie resembles the brickwork of the facades that are both home and prison to him.

Andreas Prinzing

Paula Modersohn-Becker

Worpswede Landscape, c. 1903
The Blind Little Sister, c. 1903
Self-Portrait in Front of Blue Background, 1906

The three paintings by Paula Modersohn-Becker in the Haubrich Collection reflect almost the entire oeuvre of the artist, who died at a young age. **Worpswede Landscape** demonstrates the artist's fascination with the light and landscape of Worpswede, an artists' colony near Bremen in northern Germany. The double portrait of two sisters who seem connected to each other embodies Modersohn-Becker's lifelong exploration of figurative painting and her search for what she described as the 'great simplicity of form', while the work **Self-Portrait in Front of Blue Background** is an example of the mature work of her Paris years.

After she had seen the works of Worpswede-based artists including Hans am Ende, Fritz Mackensen, Otto Modersohn, Fritz Overbeck and Heinrich Vogeler in the Bremen Kunsthalle, Paula Becker, as she was then called, went to Worpswede for the first time in the summer of 1897, where she got to know the painters of the artists' colony. Fascinated by the region's untouched moors, its light and the low horizon, she decided to become a painter herself. Becker had earlier begun her artistic training at the drawing and painting school of the Association of Berlin Female Artists and Friends of Art, and now she continued her studies under Mackensen. Her teacher focussed on showing her how to draw using models, but Becker also produced landscape studies: 'I ... walked to the moors, past lonely farmsteads surrounded by pine trees, through the unbelievably green meadows along the Hamme, through heathland covered with red heather, past slender nodding birches',[1] the artist wrote in a letter to her parents describing her first stay in the unique landscape.

Becker's further development as an artist was influenced by dividing her time between Worpswede and Paris. In the French capital, a centre for the arts, she continued her training at the Académie Colarossi and Académie Julian, private art schools. In Worpswede, she met the German poet Rainer Maria Rilke in 1900 and they remained friends for the rest of their lives. The following year she married Otto Modersohn, whose income meant that her basic needs were met. Between her stays in Paris in the years 1900, 1903, 1905 and finally in 1906/07, she kept returning to the rural seclusion of the artists' colony.

It was in the poorhouse that Modersohn-Becker found most of the subjects depicted in the figurative paintings she made in Worpswede. She considered the poorhouse children – as well as an old woman she often used as a subject who was nicknamed 'Dreebeen' ('Three-Legs') because of her wooden walking stick – to be the village's most interesting 'individuals'. 'I want to draw groups of children at the poorhouse',[2] she wrote in February 1903 in Paris, as she planned her future compositions. Indeed, her strikingly unsentimental portraits of children became the most important subject of her paintings during that period.

Hence it is no coincidence that one of the Worpswede child portraits, **The Blind Little Sister**, was the first of the artist's works to become part of the Haubrich Collection. As the critic Luise Straus-Ernst noted in 1927, the composition is a good example of the 'severe, unemotional language'[3] of the painter, who eschewed any hint of sentimentality.

A typical feature of her paintings is the way the subjects are constrained within the pictorial space. The artist often intertwined her figures with elements of the landscape to emphasize how they are embedded in the natural setting. In this case, it is the arm placed around the blind girl's shoulder, with which her sister is guiding her, which is justified both in terms of the composition and the motif and contributes to the haunting effect of the painting. Paula Modersohn-Becker 'hates to be conventional', wrote Otto Modersohn in 1903, expressing both his admiration and sense of alienation from the pictures that his wife created that year. She preferred to depict everything as 'angular, ugly, bizarre, wooden',[4] rather than having her pictures seem pleasing to the eye.

While **Worpswede Landscape** and **The Blind Little Sister** were both created during the artist's time in Worpswede, the small and self-confident **Self-Portrait in Front of Blue Background** was painted in 1906 during Modersohn-Becker's last – and longest – residence in Paris. The painter regards the viewer with a quizzical look, yet also appears poised and self-contained. The space in the painting is taken up almost entirely by the portrait itself. The concentration on the face, which seems lifeless and almost mask-like, is intensified by the contrast between the warm, thickly applied skin tones and the cool grey-blue of the monochrome background.

This example of her new approach to portrait painting, which concentrates on the essentials and in particular frees the picture from any narrative trappings, shows Modersohn-Becker at the peak of her creativity. Pictures like these far outstrip those of her role models from the Worpswede period. They show the artist's intensive examination of the mummy portraits of late antiquity, which she studied at the Louvre, as well as her knowledge of the new ideas of French Modernism, which she absorbed in Paris with equal enthusiasm.

The influence of the Egyptian mummy pictures is revealed both through the artist's letters and diaries as well as by the recollections of Heinrich Vogeler, who followed Modersohn-Becker's artistic development after her arrival in Worpswede with friendly interest. 'For a while Paula loved to construct these narrow portraits within the limits of the frame. At times the pictures, with the lively expression of the eyes, are reminiscent of the work of Greek artists, and of those narrow wooden boards, decorated with portraits, that were buried with the mummified dead in their tombs in ancient Egypt. We recognize the impasto painting technique of these Greek painters in Paula Modersohn-Becker's pictures; she uses it in an effort to convey the lively emotion of the tone, without having to give up anything of the simplicity and clarity of the form and the colour.'[5]

While the mummy portraits were commissioned in the prime of the subject's life in order to grant the sitter immortality, Modersohn-Becker transcends her mirror-image self-portrait in a disconnected state of suspension between life and death. The painters of late antiquity preserved the vitality of their subjects, up to and including the reflected light in the pupils. The eyes in Modersohn-Becker's self-portrait, however, seem strangely wooden and abstract. In contrast to most other self-portraits from the period around 1900, which show artists in their studios, palette in hand, or as bohemians with cigarettes, Paula Modersohn-Becker's portraits with their monochrome backgrounds stand out because of their rejection of every genre touch and their total lack of emotion. They resist all narrative elements and insist instead on the pure power of painting.

Rainer Stamm

1 Paula Becker to her parents, letter of July 1897, quoted in: Günter Busch and Liselotte von Reinken (eds.), *Paula Modersohn-Becker. The Letters and Journals*, translated by Arthur S. Wensinger and Carole Clew Hoey, Evanston, IL 1990, p. 78.

2 Ibid., p. 300 (diary entry from 25 February 1903).

3 Luise Straus-Ernst, 'Die Sammlung Haubrich in Köln', in: *Das Kunstblatt*, 1 / 1927, pp. 25–34, here p. 32.

4 From Otto Modersohn's diary, 26 September 1903; quoted in Busch / Reinken, op.cit., p. 324.

5 Heinrich Vogeler, 'Paula Modersohn-Becker. Zum Gedächtnis einer Frühverstorbenen', *Das Wort*, 11 / 1938, pp. 115–128, here p. 121; cf. Rainer Stamm (ed.): *Paula Modersohn-Becker und die ägyptischen Mumienportraits* (exh. cat., Kunstsammlungen Böttcherstraße, Bremen, and Museum Ludwig, Cologne) Munich 2007.

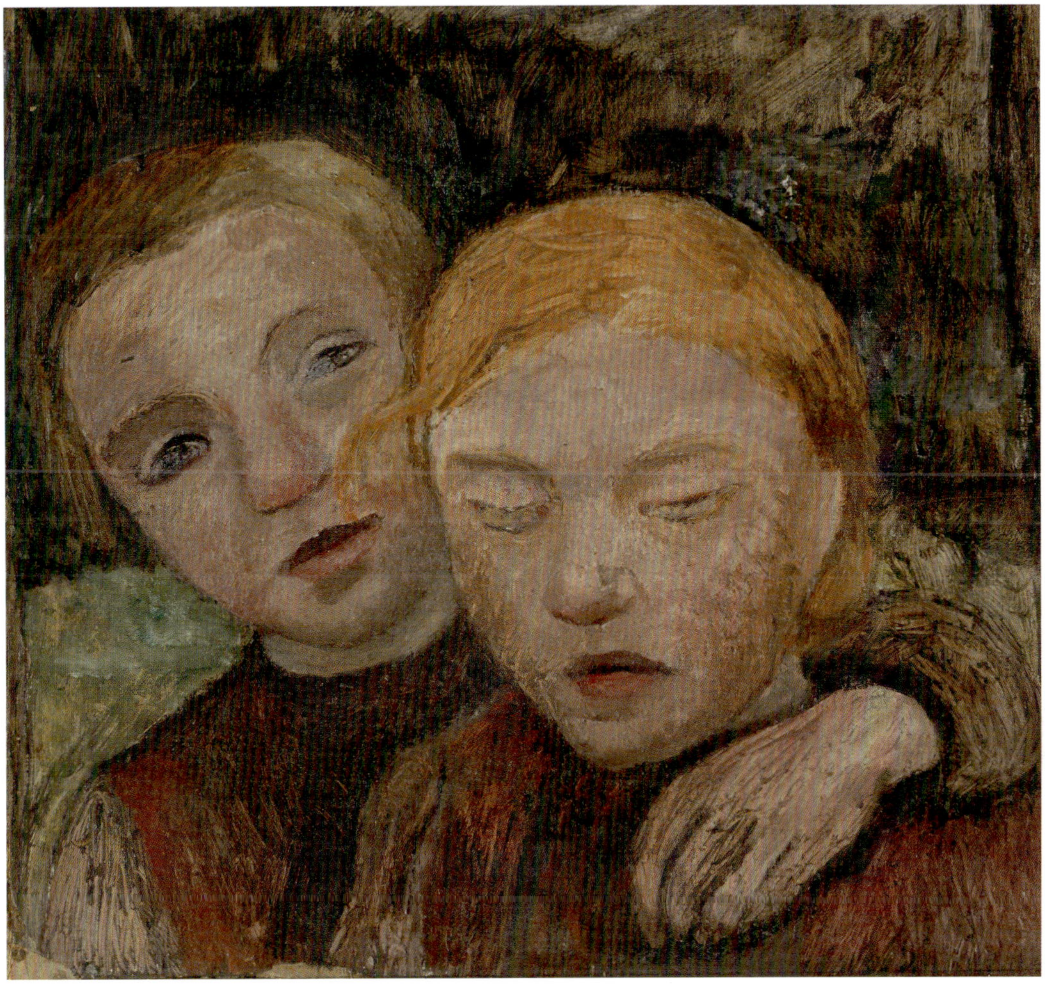

The Blind Little Sister
C. 1903
Oil on cardboard
32.2 x 33.5 cm

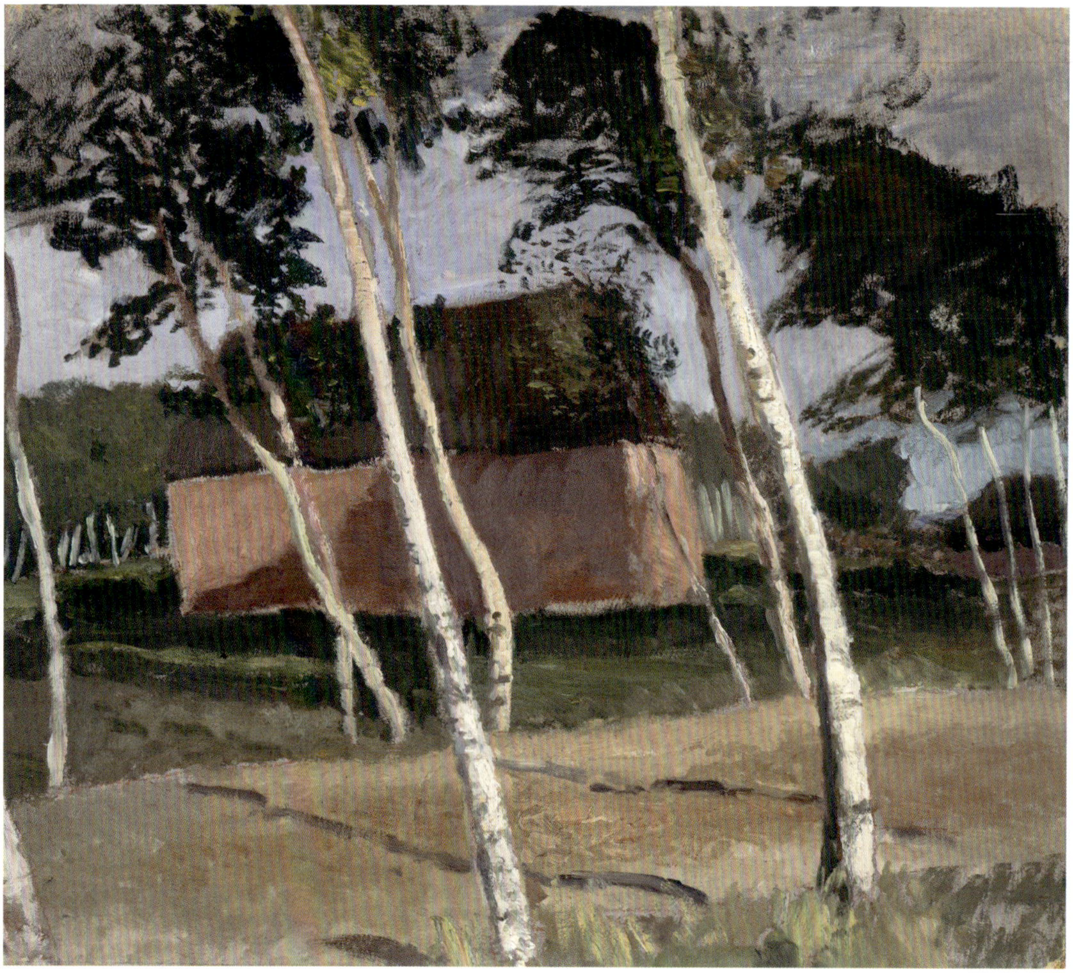

Worpswede Landscape
C. 1903
Oil on fibreboard
61.5 x 67.8 cm

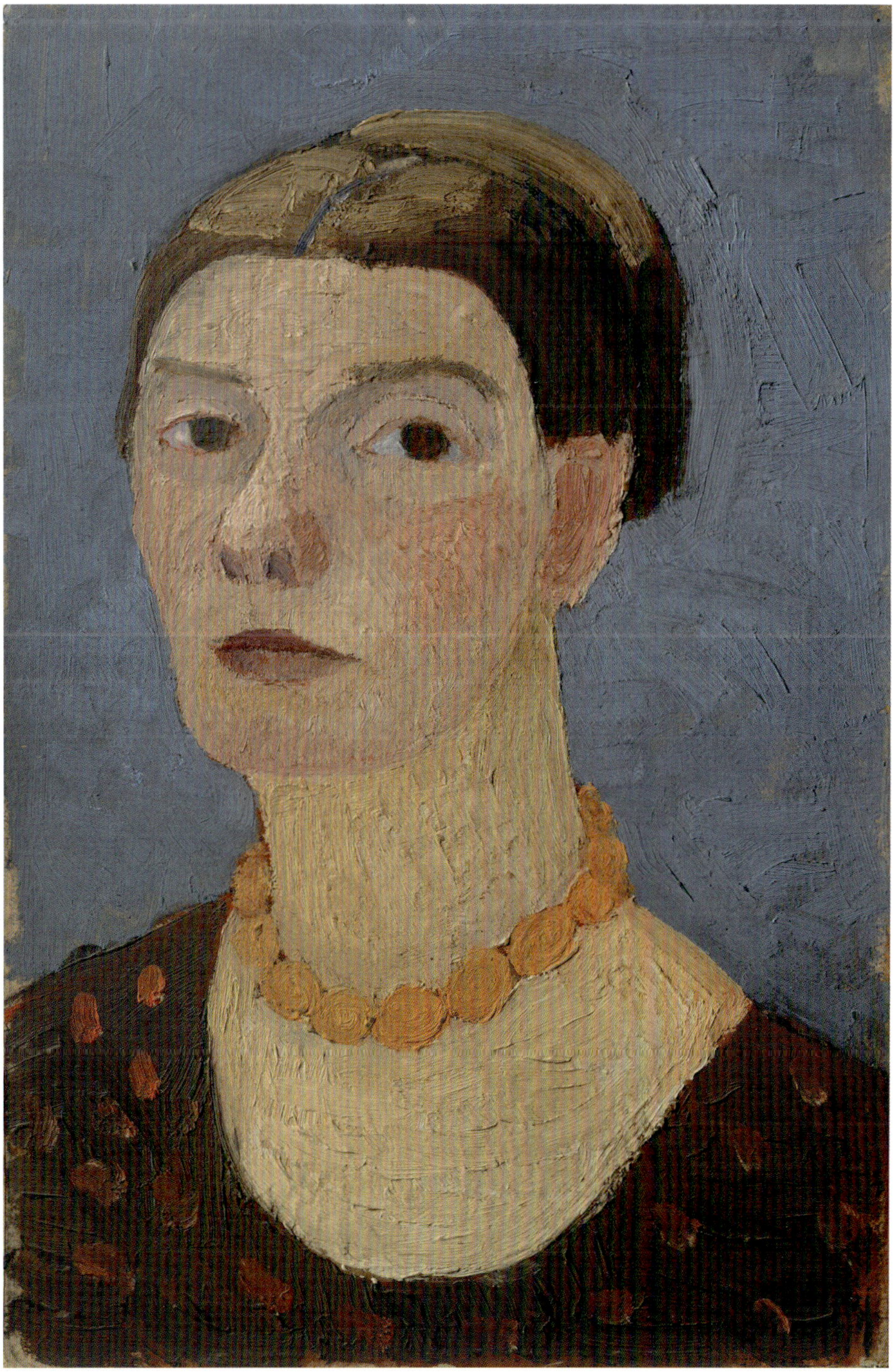

Self-Portrait in Front of Blue Background
1906
Oil on cardboard
45.7 x 29.7 cm

Otto Mueller

Half-Length Portrait of Two Nude Women, c. 1919
Gypsy Hut with Goat, c. 1925
Two Gypsy Women with a Cat, 1926/27

After Otto Mueller's death in 1930, the art critic Paul Westheim described the artist as a 'mixture of Hellenic and Gypsy blood'.[1] Even during his lifetime, Mueller reacted to all the rumours about his origins with a kind of amused silence and declined to comment on any speculation about his supposed origins. Today, however, researchers are certain that Mueller was in no way descended from the Sinti or the Roma.[2] He must have taken pleasure in being confronted with so much innuendo during his lifetime. After all, Mueller felt attracted to the unconventional Sinti and Roma lifestyle. His fascination was so great that, in his final years, his art focussed almost exclusively on these ethnic groups. In addition to his numerous paintings of bathing women, he was also famous for his *Gypsy Portfolio*, published in 1926–27.

Mueller had been living in Breslau (of which he was not particularly fond) for four years, had left behind his past as a member of the Brücke artistic group, and had devoted himself entirely to teaching at the local arts academy when he encountered the wandering Roma for the first time in 1924. He travelled to the cities of Split and Ragusa (today Dubrovnik) in what is now Croatia with his wife, Elsbeth Lübke, and his long-time companion Maschka Meyerhofer. Excited and inspired by a way of life that was foreign to him, he subsequently visited southeast Europe every year. While there, he often encountered Roma who had settled down in small villages. The painting **Gypsy Hut with Goat** uses warm, earthy colours to depict the perfectly idyllic village he visited in 1925. In the picture, two Roma children and a goat seek shelter from the hot midday sun in the shade of a small mud shack.

Two Gypsy Women with a Cat from the following year is a work full of erotic tension. It shows a domestic scene with two partially nude women sitting at a rudimentary dining table. They seem to consider their nakedness to be normal; they gaze at the viewer with self-assurance. Numerous symbols of femininity adorn the interior: there are two vessels (symbolizing the receptive female body) on the table, a plant (a symbol of fertility) on the windowsill, and a somewhat crudely painted grey cat in the window. In art history, cats frequently accompany female nudes as a symbol of dissolute love, infidelity and unpredictability – one need only recall the black cat in Édouard Manet's *Olympia*

(1863). In Mueller's representation, however, the cat sits in the window like a shadow. Like all the other elements in the picture, the cat relates to the women by means of its colour and pattern. The cat and the polka-dot vessel are grouped with the woman in the grey dress, while the plants with their soil and the small bowl are linked to the woman wearing a reddish-brown shirt over her brown skin. The composition of the room turns out to be a telling detail. The curtain, also a relic of traditional representations of nudes, does more than provide a formal parallel to the two female figures. If one considers the position of the vertical window jamb, one might speculate that it is an unconscious reference to the absence of the masculine in the painting. In any case, the domestic scene, which at first glance appears to depict the life of the Roma, reveals itself to be the artist's construction, rooted in art history.

At the turn of the century, Erich Heckel, Ernst Ludwig Kirchner and Max Pechstein led the Brücke artists in breaking with academic ideas of painting and seeking to paint the female body naturally. A genuinely liberated nudity became one of the key criteria for 'authenticity'. During visits to the country, such as those undertaken by Brücke artists to Moritzburg in 1909–10, the naked body was linked to nature. For Mueller, who only joined the group in 1910, the female nude in nature was a central theme. Nude figures painted in a simplistic manner in a setting of wild, untouched nature became his trademark. The nude and nature merge in his idyllic scenes. He heightened the authentic feel of his paintings by using rough-textured canvases and dry distempers.

The 1919 double portrait **Half-Length Portrait of Two Nude Women** is an advanced, monumental version of nudes in nature. In this painting, the women are pushed up so close to the picture plane that the green merely couches them decoratively. Though the features of Mueller's lover Maschka Meyerhofer can, as usual, be found here, no one would think to interpret these figures as representing modern women from a big European city. Mueller's women, with their pointed chins, full lips and slit-like eyes, represent the exact opposite: pristine and strange nature. They look out of the painting provocatively, with something unpredictable in their gaze.

When Mueller actually met members of the Roma in the 1920s, his ideas about their unspoiled authentic nature were confirmed. Impoverished and marginalized due to their background, the Roma lived at the fringes of society. While the broad public saw the Roma as thieves and wild animals that needed to be tamed, Mueller transfigured the reality into an idyll. With hardly a change to the physiognomy of his subjects, the women in his paintings of the 1910s came to represent what a contemporary called the 'Slavic type'.[3] But now they truly do represent an alien world, and thereby become the perfect projection surface for Mueller's idea of femininity as the authentic, wild and other.

Mueller's interest in the Roma, whom the Nazis considered 'non-Aryan', as well as his simplistic, Expressionist style, eventually led to the seizure of his artworks. He did not live to see the inclusion of his paintings, among them **Half-Length Portrait of Two Nude Women**, in the notorious 1937 exhibition 'Degenerate Art'. Once Nazi propaganda had subsided after 1945, Mueller's romanticized depictions once again found a receptive audience – perhaps not coincidentally in a society that would not confront the persecution of the Sinti and the Roma for many years to come.

Agnieszka Smyrek

1 Paul Westheim in a letter to Elfriede Müller dated 27 September 1930. Quoted in *Otto Mueller. Malerei, Zeichnungen und Druckgraphik* (exh. cat., Städtisches Kunstmuseum Mülheim an der Ruhr 1974), p. 12.

2 Ulrike Lorenz, 'Otto Müller, Expressionist, Träumer, Außenseiter', in: Kunstforum Ostdeutsche Galerie Regensburg (ed.), *Otto Mueller – Verlorenes Paradies, Werke aus der Sammlung Karsch* (exh. cat., Kunstforum Ostdeutsche Galerie), Regensburg 2006, p. 16.

3 Mario-Andreas von Lüttichau, *Otto Mueller. Ein Romantiker unter den Expressionisten*, Cologne 1993, p. 70f.

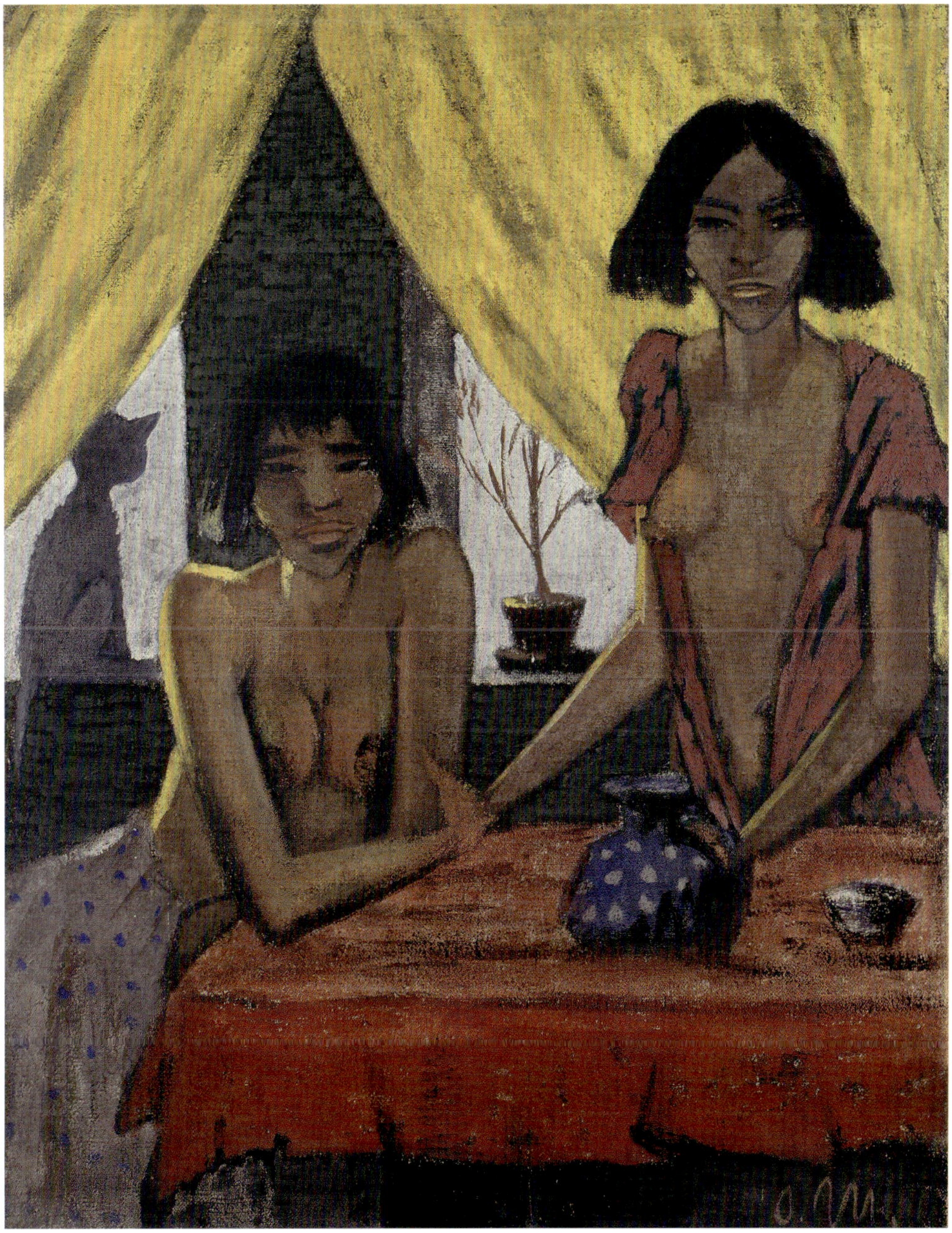

Two Gypsy Women with a Cat
1926/27
Distemper on canvas
144.5 x 109.5 cm

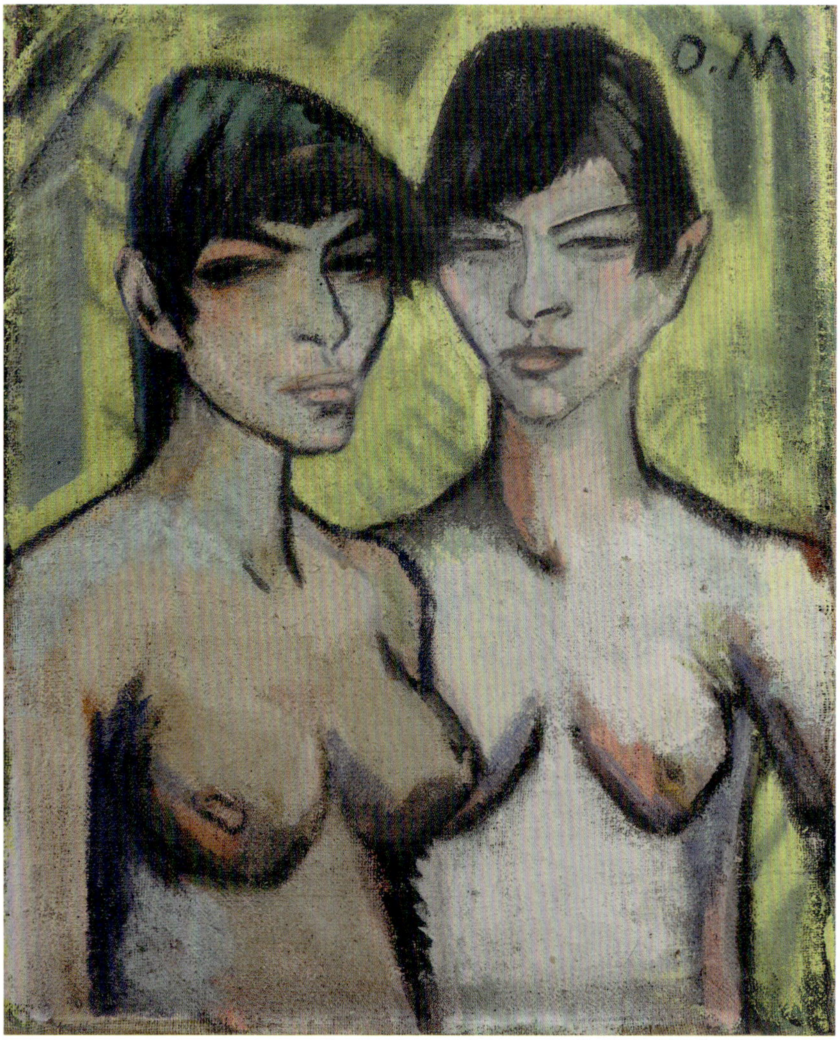

Half-Length Portrait of Two Nude Women
C. 1919
Distemper on burlap
87.4 x 70.6 cm

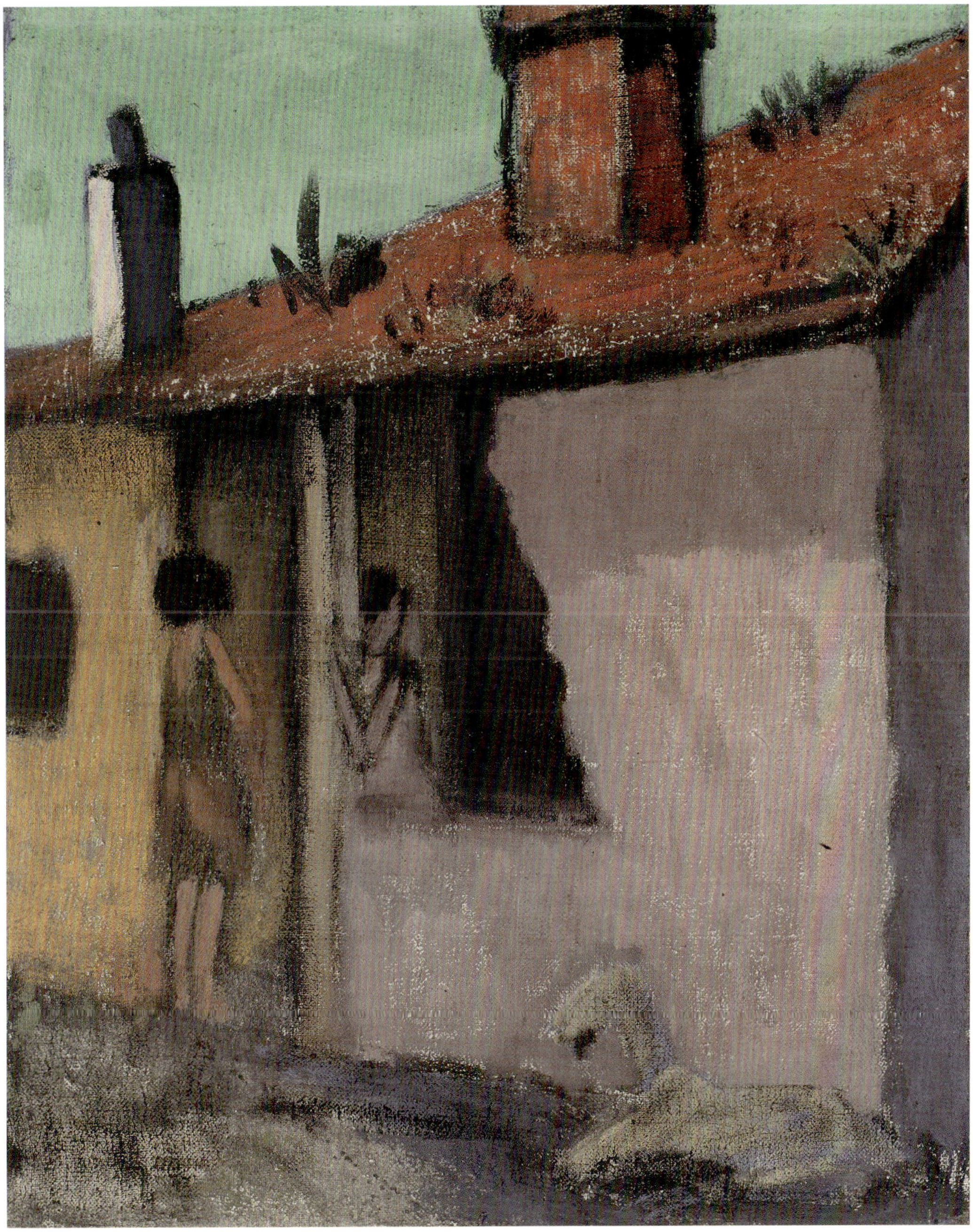

Gypsy Hut with Goat
C. 1925
Distemper on canvas
115.5 x 90 cm

Emil Nolde

Family (Bonnichsen), c. 1915
After Sunset, 1915
Dreamers, 1916
Young Woman and Men, 1919
Flower Garden, 1925

Emil Nolde was seventy-four years old and living a secluded life in the North Frisian town of Seebüll when he once again found himself in a situation that gave him serious concerns about the future of his artistic oeuvre. The plight of the artist, who had long been branded 'degenerate' by the Nazi regime, became critical in 1941. Over a thousand of his works that had hitherto been owned by museums had already been seized and subsequently 'valuated' (in other words, sold off) or destroyed as part of the Nazis' 'Degenerate Art' campaign. But now, the president of the Reich Chamber of Fine Arts demanded that Nolde present his most recent, privately held works for review. The artist, fearing that they, too, would be confiscated, planned an ambitious rescue operation. Rolled-up paintings were hidden with friends and family, or secretly taken over the Danish border by bicycle.

His younger sister Cathrina Bonnichsen, who was living in Stemmild in Denmark, helped Nolde to save his works from the Nazi authorities by taking several oil paintings and drawings into her protection. She, too, had posed for her brother on several occasions, many years previously. The painting **Family (Bonnichsen)** shows Cathrina Bonnichsen together with her husband, Lorenz, and their son Emil.

During this period, Nolde painted several portraits of his relatives, who still practised the agricultural way of life that he himself had long ago left behind as a young man. Back then, he had lived on his family farm on the German-Danish border near Tondern, he still bore the surname Hansen, and he had decided – against his father's will – to pursue a career as a painter. Shortly after completing an apprenticeship as a furniture designer and wood carver in the nearby town of Flensburg, he moved to Switzerland in 1892, where he worked as a drawing teacher for five years at the Museum for Industries and Trade in St. Gallen. There he created his first oil paintings, after which he spent time studying at private painting schools in Munich, with Adolf Hölzel in Dachau and at the Académie Julian art school in Paris. In a decision that seems highly appropriate, given Nolde's focus on his home region, he chose to rename himself after his place of birth. And hence the farmer's son Emil Hansen became the painter Emil Nolde.

At the time when he painted the portrait of his sister's family, Nolde was already a well-travelled man who sought artistic inspiration both in the pulsating city life of Berlin as well as in his home region, whose stark, lonely and expansive marshlands he experienced as a place of creative production. He was also still processing his experiences from the Medical-Demographic German-New Guinea Expedition which he joined in October 1913 at the invitation of the Prussian Imperial Colonial Office. The South Seas journey lasted nearly a year, taking Nolde and his wife, Ada, from Moscow and Tokyo to New Guinea. On his return to the Baltic Sea island of Alsen, he sought for months to reproduce the fascination of his foreign experiences and to depict the contrasts – but also the similarities – between the local and the exotic. Whether full-bearded Russians, dark-skinned natives or even his own family depicted as red-cheeked northerners, during those weeks Nolde created more and more paintings of groups of people following the same strict classificatory approach and also using identical compositions.

The unique natural drama of the South Seas stayed in the painter's memory, 'unforgotten ... like a wonderfully delightful distant place'.[1] Thus in his atelier he not only painted the glowing sunsets, impressive stormy skies and saturated greens of the landscape behind the Frisian dykes, but he also drew on his memories of the exotic colours of the tropics. Hence the painting **After Sunset** might depict a certain twilight in the South Seas that the artist experienced as a particularly 'marvellous orgy of colours' but which only lasted 'for a very few minutes; then it was dark'.[2] In the picture, approaching dark clouds cover the last rays of sunshine on the distant horizon, and the sky above the choppy sea is depicted in a shimmering green tinged with blue. It is a dramatic, atmospheric picture, based on Nolde's subjective perceptions and his constant attempt to capture what he called the 'primeval and essential'.[3] His aim was not to simply reproduce nature but to capture its imaginary forces in colour and form, using these elements to compose mystical landscapes of the soul.

In doing so, the artist can be placed in a Romantic tradition, as can be seen particularly clearly in his painting **Dreamers**. It shows two hikers who look longingly towards the sky, their figures illuminated in the violet light of the moon. The fairy-tale-like and exaggerated depiction of both figures is inspired by the mythical creatures and clairvoyants that Nolde had long used as a source for his grotesque and visionary figures. They express his deep artistic need to make his spiritual experience of nature tangible on the canvas. Yet the colour palette he used also corresponds to the theme of ecstatic natural experience, with the tumultuous and excessively heightened intensity of the hues expressing externally the moment of inner communion.

Nolde first developed the potential of colour as an artistic and independent means of expression primarily in his famous floral and garden paintings. These pictures were either executed in his studio or painted in the open air in the garden that Nolde had planted himself. **Flower Garden** is one of the floral impressions that the enthusiastic flower aficionado frequently captured after moving into the Utenwarf farmhouse at Ruttebüller Lake. The bright crimson poppies and the billowing foxgloves unfold an individual pictorial rhythm on the canvas that almost liberates them from their surroundings. Just a year later, the work was exhibited in Tokyo, demonstrating the high regard in which the painter was also held abroad.

As he neared his sixtieth birthday, Nolde was one of the most prominent contemporary artists in the Weimar Republic. Art critics celebrated him as an important representative of German Expressionism. He self-confidently viewed himself as a creator of 'northern, strong, acerbic, internal art'.[4] The painter cultivated his artistic independence out of personal conviction, and this autonomy also influenced his public persona. For example, he distanced himself from the Brücke group of artists in 1907, after just one year. Nolde precipitated a scandal when the jury of the Berlin Secession rejected his work two years later. In a strongly worded public critique, he attacked the president, Max Liebermann. Nevertheless, he only accepted his expulsion from the Secession with great reluctance.

Nolde's energetic, opinionated personality made waves. His works were also hotly debated, in particular his religious paintings. While the floral and landscape scenes met with acclaim, the depictions of religious figures with their coarse, broad brushstrokes, garish colours and mask-like faces met with a confused reception. Religious paintings are nonetheless an important component of Nolde's body of work. Nowadays, art historians assign more of his works to this category than Nolde himself did. For example, the picture **Young Woman and Men** is regarded as relating to the Biblical motif of Susanna bathing, which has often been depicted by artists. The picture shows several old men crowding around a woman, whom they regard with curious or even lustful gazes. But Nolde leaves open the question of whether she is the seduced or the seductress. Instead, transcending all religious statements, he confronts the viewer with the seemingly unfathomable feminine mystique.

Nolde's grotesque figures and his powerful, often bawdy, use of colour and line came under increasing attack during the Nazi era and were ultimately denounced as 'degenerate'. The infamous 'Degenerate Art' exhibition of 1937 severely criticized the artist and his works. It hit him particularly hard, not only because there had been a fierce debate during the early years of the regime about whether Expressionism could serve as the official art of Germany, but also because Nolde's position as one of its leading representatives was controversial. In 1934, Nolde himself had joined the National Socialist Working Group of Northern Schleswig, which would become absorbed into the Nazi party's Northern Schleswig chapter just a few months later. But not even being a member of the party was enough to protect the artist from the 'Degenerate Art' campaign, which brutally put an end to the controversy surrounding him. No other artist had as many of his works seized from German museums as did Nolde. Moreover, in 1941 he was prohibited from painting, 'due to insufficient trustworthiness'.[5]

Nolde, who as an artist had always emphasized his ties to his homeland, fought for the return of his paintings with an aggressively nationalistic stance. Up until the very end, he still hoped to be rehabilitated, but the restrictions on him remained in place until the downfall of the Third Reich. The new post-war German republic, however, immediately honoured his work and the Expressionist movement as a whole. Thus the elderly Emil Nolde was able to exceed his former successes both in Germany and internationally, and would soon go on to enjoy a reputation as a West German cultural icon.

Isgard Kracht

1 Emil Nolde, *Welt und Heimat. Die Südseereise 1913-1918*, written in 1936, Cologne 1965, p. 146.
2 Ibid.
3 Emil Nolde, *Jahre der Kämpfe*, Berlin 1934, p. 177.
4 Nolde 1965, p. 116.
5 Adolf Ziegler, president of the Reich Chamber of Fine Arts, to Emil Nolde, 23 August 1941, quoted in Thomas Knubben, *'Mein Leid, meine Qual, meine Verachtung'. Emil Nolde im Dritten Reich*, in: Tilman Osterwold and Thomas Knubben (eds.), *Emil Nolde. Ungemalte Bilder. Aquarelle 1938 bis 1945 aus der Sammlung der Nolde-Stiftung Seebüll*, Ostfildern-Ruit 2000, p. 146

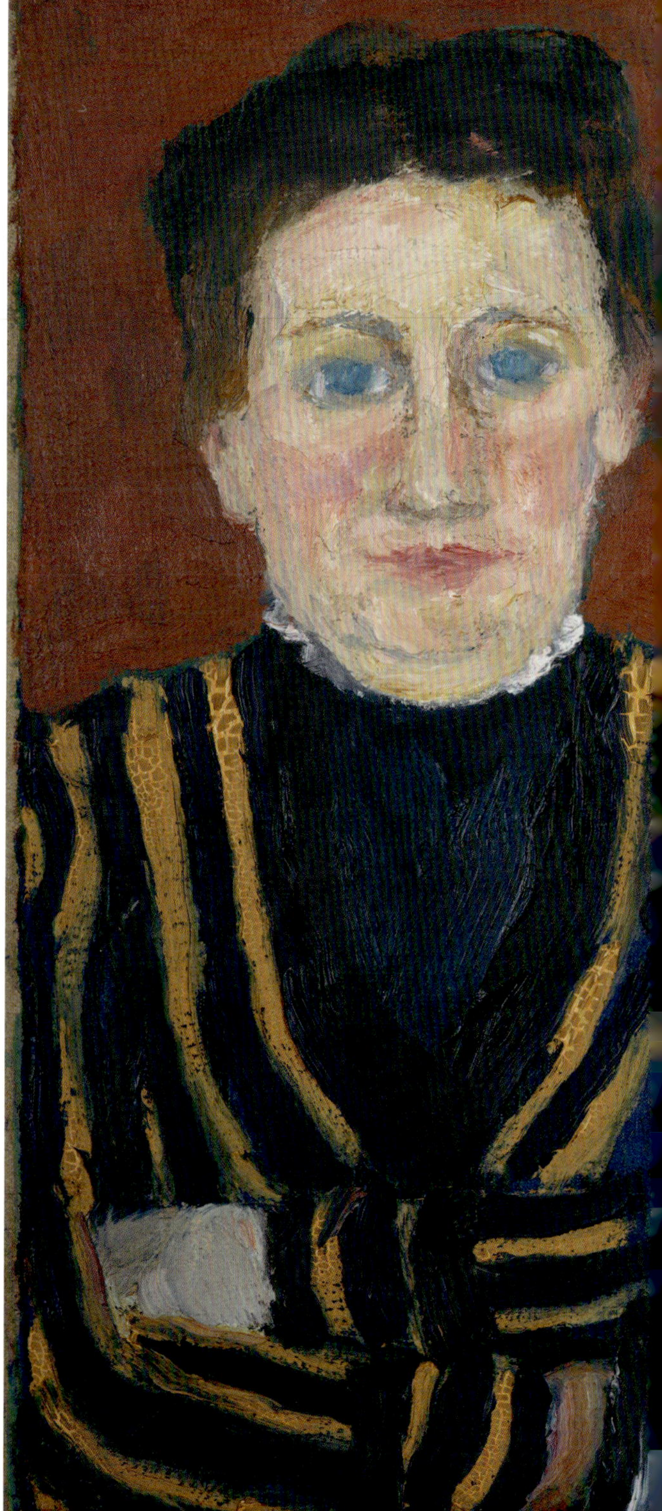

Family (Bonnichsen)
C. 1915
Oil on canvas
73.3 x 89 cm

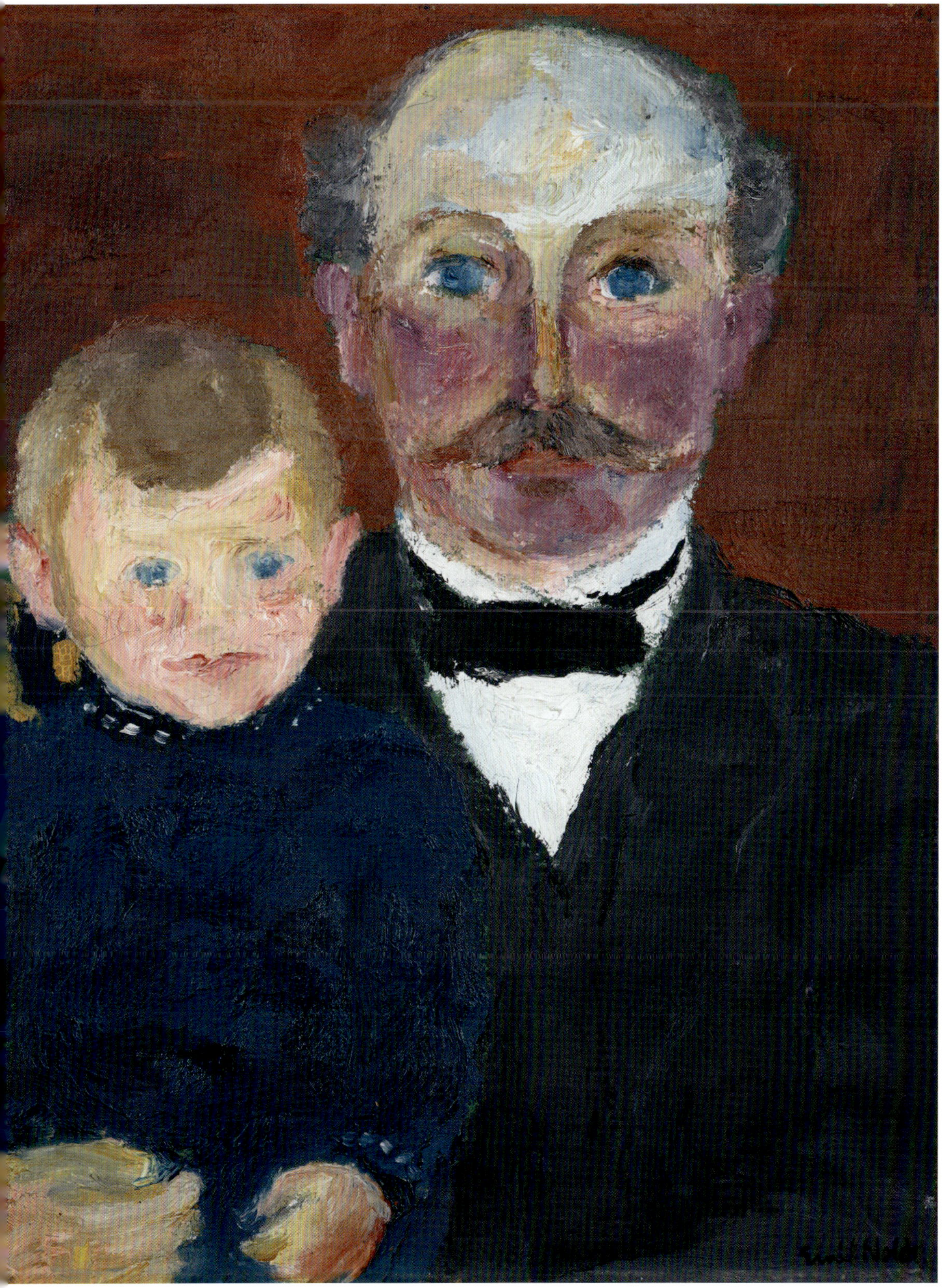

Emil Nolde

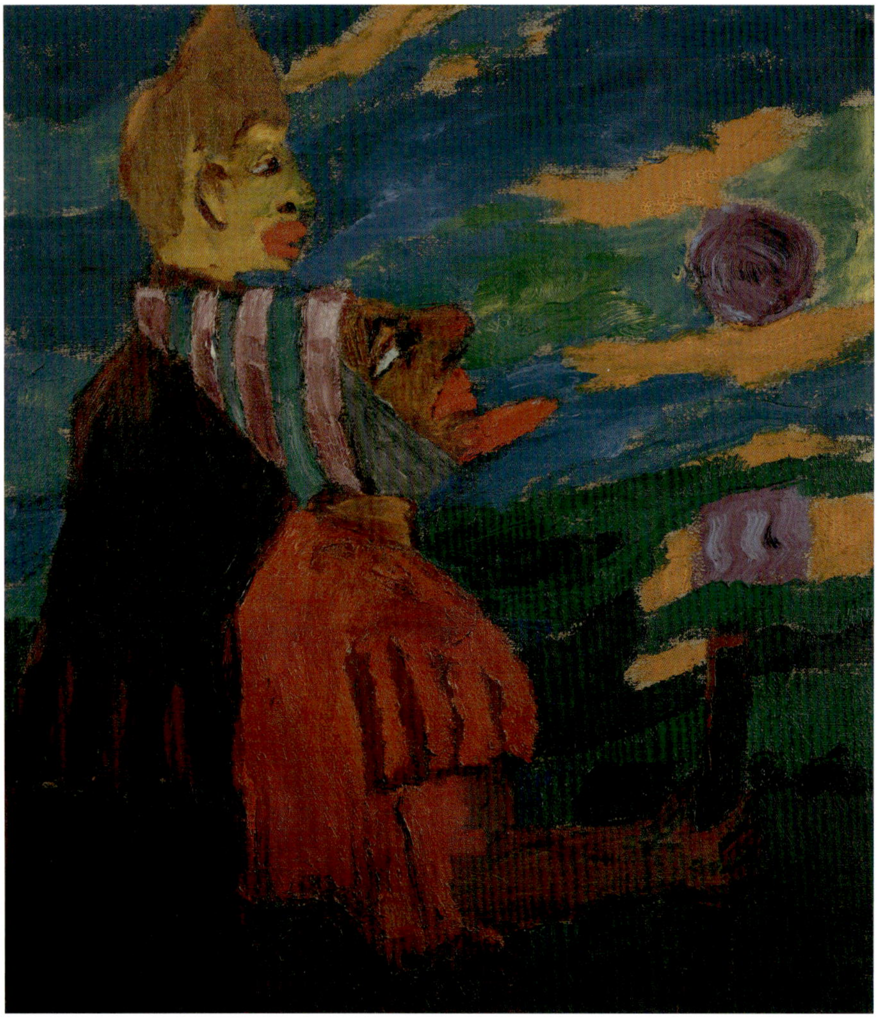

Dreamers
1916
Oil on canvas
100.7 x 86.4 cm

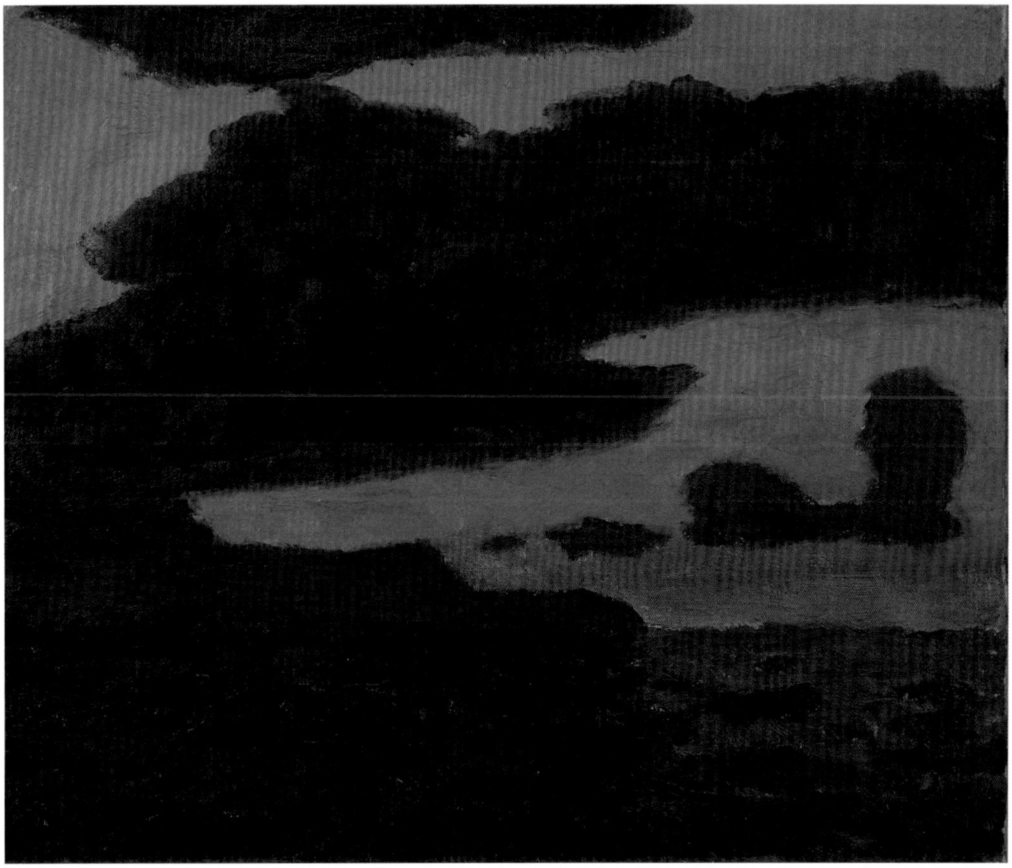

After Sunset
1915
Oil on canvas
86.7 x 100.5 cm

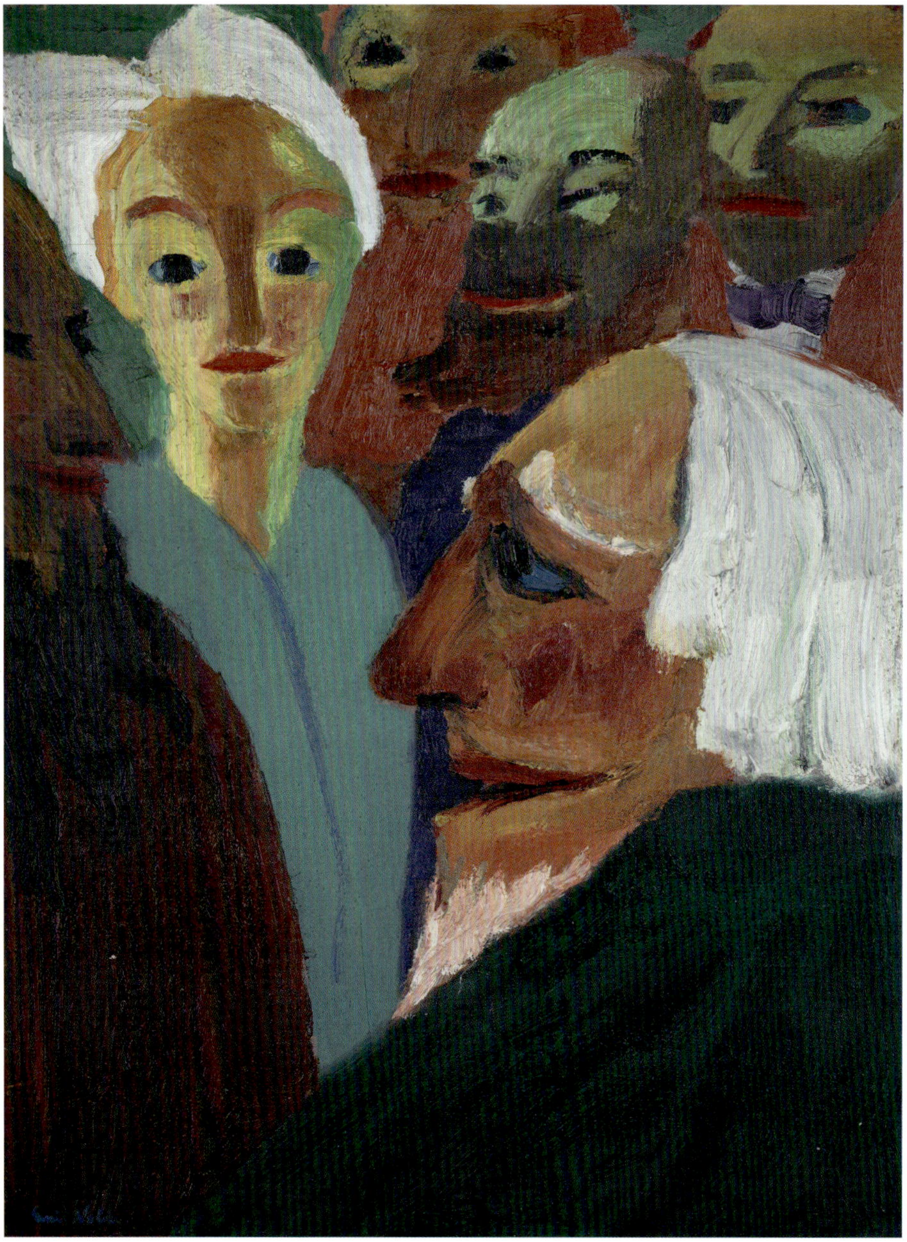

Young Woman and Men
1919
Oil on plywood
101 x 73 cm

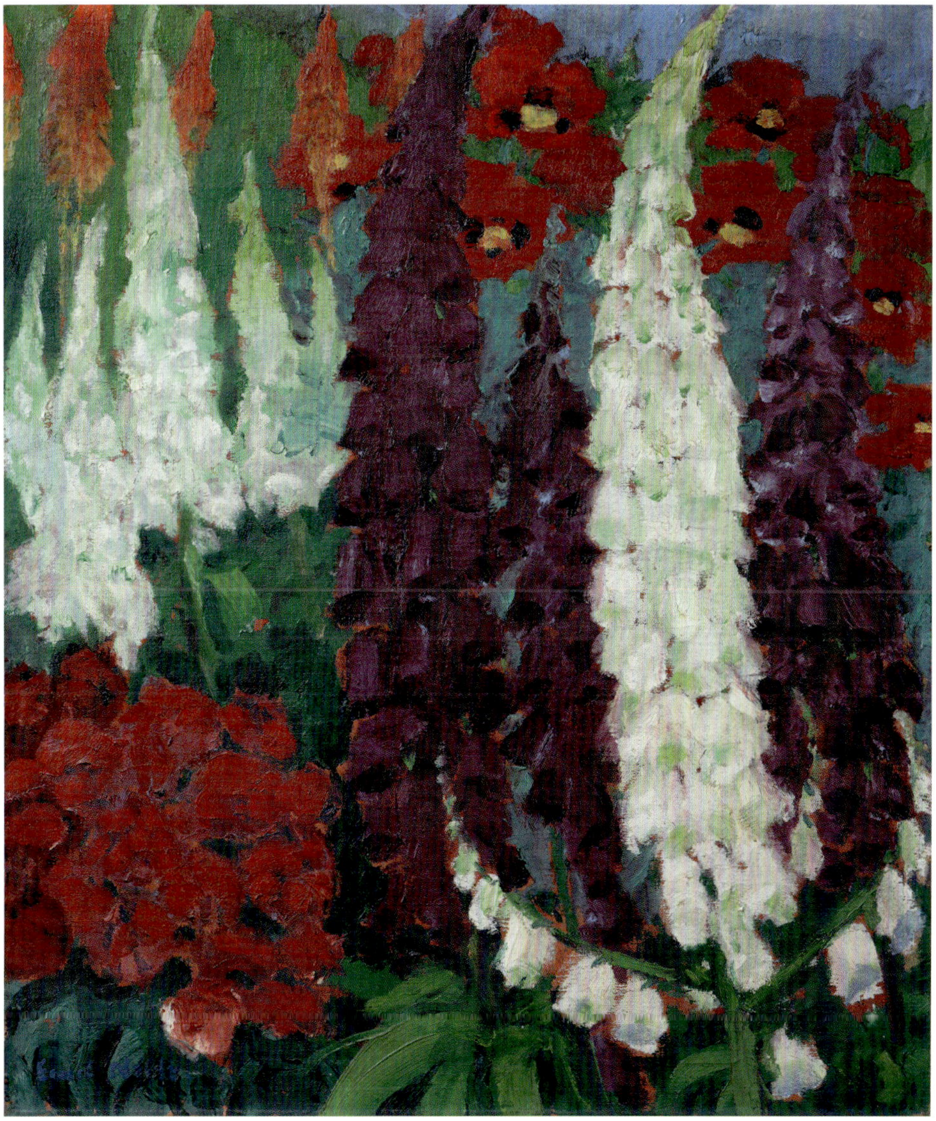

Flower Garden

1925

Oil on canvas

89.5 x 73.5 cm

Max Pechstein

The Green Sofa, 1910
Portrait of the Artist's Wife, 1910

How old is the girl in this painting? And what was Max Pechstein's motivation in painting her? This kind of question would have met with little interest in 1953, when **The Green Sofa** was acquired for the Haubrich Collection. During the post-war years, Expressionism was valued for the freedom with which its proponents selected their style and subject. To examine an Expressionist painting for the realities lurking behind it would have at best seemed naïve, at worst suspicious: naïve, because this approach would fail to acknowledge the autonomy of art; suspicious, because it would ignore the artistic value of a painting and instead question the moral integrity of the painter, who had himself become a victim. The Nazi propaganda exhibition 'Degenerate Art', which included paintings by Pechstein, was held in 1937, the same year the artist was excluded from the Prussian Academy of Arts. He was only rehabilitated in 1951, when named an honorary senator at the Berlin University of the Arts, in West Berlin.

On first glance, what we see in the painting offers no reason to pose any further questions: a girl dozing on a sofa. She is wearing a striped bathing suit, her face and arms red from the sun, her chin resting in one hand. She seems comfortable, an impression underscored by the sleeping cat. In terms of style, the paintings made by the Brücke artists in 1909 and 1910 are considered a breakthrough. During this period, Pechstein, Erich Heckel and Ernst Ludwig Kirchner developed a new technique of oil painting that enabled the expressive gestural mode that became known as the 'Brücke style'. In Pechstein's painting, the splotches and impasto layers of paint and quickly sketched black outlining attest to this. In thematic terms as well, **The Green Sofa** belongs to a group of paintings that is celebrated by art history as a break with the classical nude, the traditional poses being replaced by a naturalness and freshness.

By now we know who is depicted in this painting, and this knowledge makes it impossible to view the painting in simply formalist terms. The person portrayed is Fränzi Fehrmann, a working-class girl born on 11 October 1900 in Dresden.[1] She was not even nine years of age when she first accompanied the Brücke painters on swimming excursions to the Moritzburg Lakes. The painting **Green Sofa** shows her dressed, but in other paintings by Pechstein, for example *Sitting Girl*, she is nude, just as in numerous other paintings, drawings, lithographs and woodcuts by Kirchner and Heckel.

We have written testimony about Fränzi Fehrmann from several of the artists from the circle. Kirchner wrote in his diary: 'We had in Dresden a young girl as a model, twelve years of age. She came to us often, and when Heckel was there he drew along with us. Years past, and suddenly the young girl appeared again at sixteen. Heckel, as a horny Saxon, jumped her and screwed her thoroughly.'[2]

Kirchner also notes that Heckel caught agonorrhoea from her. He seemed to think – or preferred to imagine – that the girl was older than she was. Pechstein reports that several paintings were confiscated by the police in 1910 as part of a vice investigation, which was however closed soon thereafter.

Did a vice crime take place? Or wis it what we would today call abuse? As far as Pechstein is concerned, he seemed less attracted to Fränzi than to the sixteen-year-old Charlotte Kaprolat, whose portrait can be seen on the reverse, and whom he married in 1911, when she was eighteen. She also sat for numerous nudes that Pechstein painted in the years 1909/10 for the posters of the Berlin Secession. Like Fränzi Fehrmann, Charlotte Kaprolat also came from a humble background, and worked as a model to earn money for her family.

How does this knowledge change our perception of the pictures of Fränzi Fehrmann? They appear against a different horizon of interpretation. The quoted entry from Kirchner's diary cannot definitively answer the question of whether assault took place. That the paintings emerged in an atmosphere that was felt by the artists to be sexually charged is undeniable. And yet those who see the young female nudes of the Brücke as counter images to bourgeois salon painting and as a break with tradition should ask themselves whether they would send their own daughter as a model on such bathing expeditions. And we should keep in mind that the answer given to such a request by a bourgeois family around 1910 would have been a resolute 'no!'. There is no chance that children from the middle classes would have been subjected to a comparable situation. The supposed achievement of the nude painting of this girl is based on a power differential that relies on old hierarchies: on the one hand, male, bourgeois, adult artists, on the other, young girls from the working class. Fränzi Fehrmann was used to stage a freedom that was denied to her. The paintings thus cease to be symbols of freedom. Those seeking to document the liberation of art must look to other paintings by the Brücke artists.

Julia Voss

1 See Norbert Nobi (ed.), *Der Blick auf Fränzi und Marcella: Zwei Modelle der Brücke-Künstler Heckel, Kirchner und Pechstein*, (exh. cat., Sprengel Museum Hanover, Stiftung Moritzburg), Hanover 2010.

2 Quoted in Aya Soika, *Max Pechstein: Das Werkverzeichnis der Ölgemälde*, (Munich, 2011), p. 55.

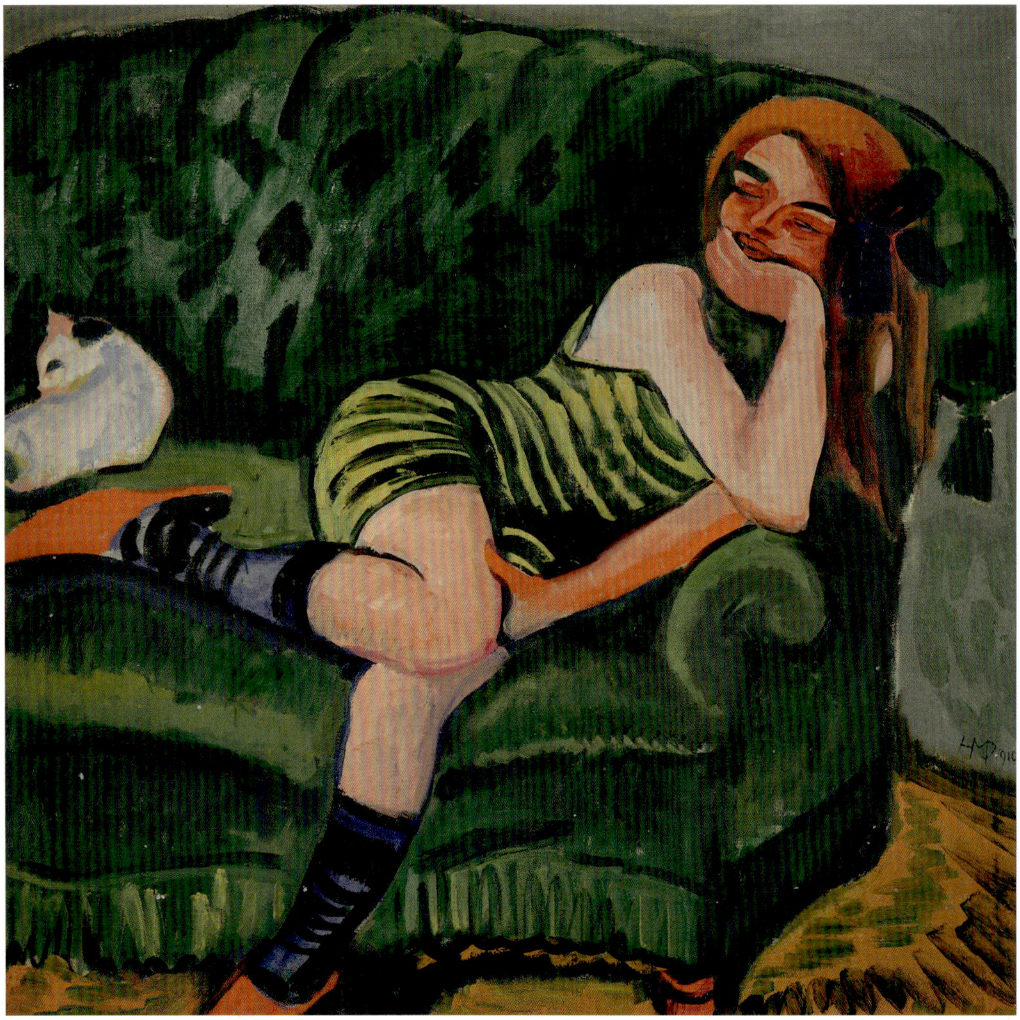

The Green Sofa
1910
Oil on canvas
100.5 x 101 cm

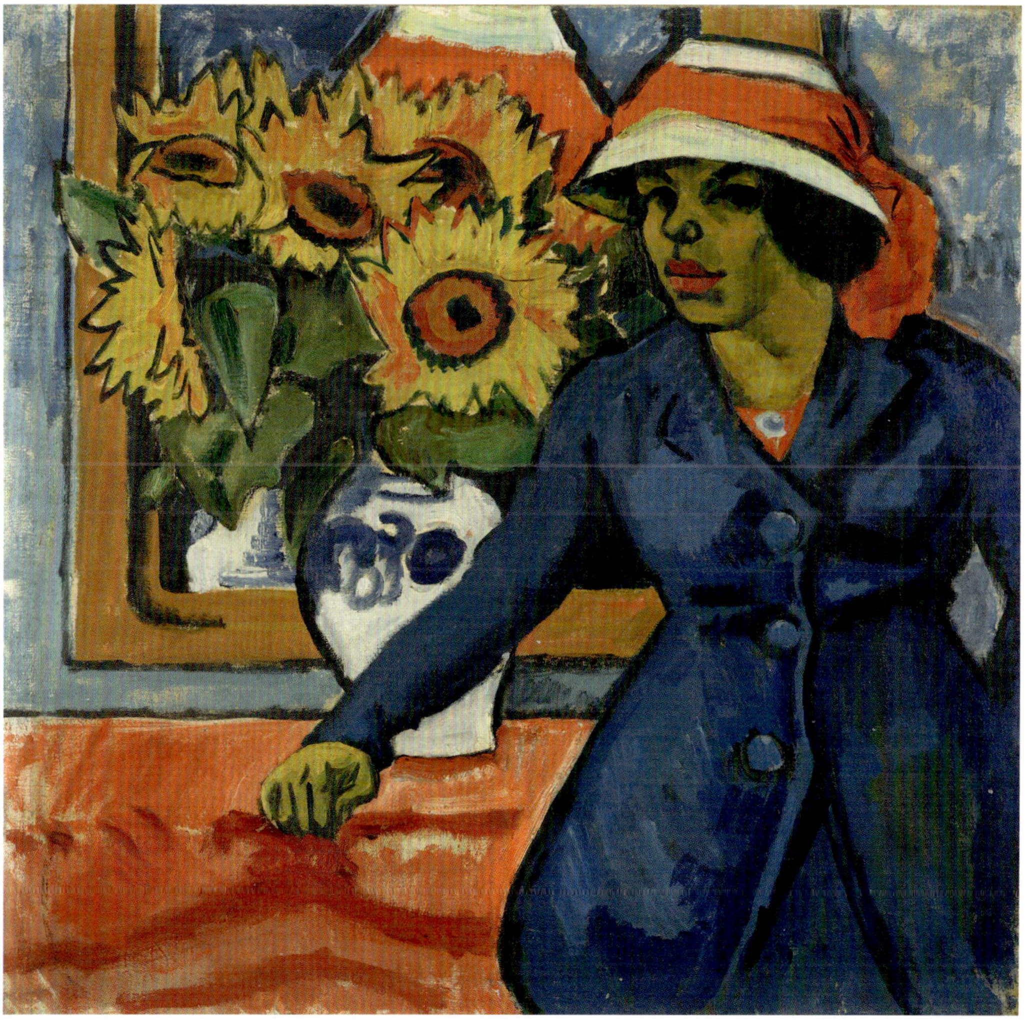

Portrait of the Artist's Wife
C. 1910
Oil on canvas
101 x 100.5 cm

Karl Schmidt-Rottluff

Still Life with Negro Sculpture, 1913
Larkspur in the Window, 1922

Still Life with Negro Sculpture is one of Karl Schmidt-Rottluff's first works to feature artefacts from non-European cultures. While the other painters of Die Brücke had already begun in 1909 to devote themselves to non-European art, which they studied above all at the Ethnographical Museum in Dresden, Schmidt-Rottluff took longer to develop the necessary taste. But after moving in autumn 1911 to Berlin, the influence of indigenous art began to emerge in his style. This may well be linked with the large quantity of African art, mainly originating from the German colonies, that resided in the Ethnological Museum in Berlin.[1] The artist's extensive collection, set up around 1913, contained not only articles of everyday use, such as combs and containers, as well as a remarkable range of natural finds such as shells and stones, but also artworks imported from Africa and Oceania by the colonial rulers.

Schmidt-Rottluff's activities as a collector were not principally concerned with studying the origin or significance of the items, but rather with their formal design. Like many Modernist artists, he recognized a style in them that corresponded with his own artistic intentions: a breaking away from linear patterns of perception, which were regarded as clichéd and obsolete. Just how far the non-European works were linked for him with the forms developed by Cubism, which had begun to enter his work in 1910, is clear from a letter to Lyonel Feininger in 1912: 'I believe Cubism is neither German nor French. Rather it is a manifestation of form that may be found everywhere in art. I shall bring a Balinese pipe with me to Berlin – it is the greatest and most mysteriously articulated Cubist idea of form that I know.'[2] On top of this interest in form came the magic charge in the objects, which were mostly of a ritual nature. And in addition to the magic came that enchantment which things often have when they are poorly understood. They stood for a departure from the neat and tidy paths of European civilization, which were regarded as obsessive.

And with that, the small articles in the still life received a further frisson. The artist's eye inspects them closely from above, so as to capture their expressive power with a few powerful strokes. The use of the complementary colours blue and orange, which dominate this simple but effective composition, gives the arrangement a special charge. At the same time, the work explores the form of the clay pipe heads from West Africa (present-day Cameroon, which at that time was a German colony). One pipe head is shown head-on, and the other from the side. Schmidt-Rottluff later came to incorporate the concave form at the back of the pipe head repeatedly in his own wooden carvings and woodcuts. With their two readily visible openings, the objects – which were referred to in those days as 'negro sculptures', as in the title – are identifiable as pipe heads. The mask in the background remains, however, schematic.

The nonchalant arrangement of the objects together with the small bowl on the table allows us to surmise that the objects belonged to the artist. They appear repeatedly in his works, and in 1913 they must have been among the first examples of non-European art to enter his collection.[3]

The still life **Larkspur in the Window**, done almost a decade later, seems to have been guided by quite different interests. Not only are the objects with their weighty sig-nificance missing, but also the strong graphic accents. This still life demonstrates a more painterly approach.

The plants and flowers that appear repeatedly in the artist's work reflect his strong feelings for nature and its enormous importance for his oeuvre. Schmidt-Rottluff has combined the bouquet by the window, which is to say a still life, with the suggestion of a landscape. The stasis of the still life is counteracted by the fleeting view of a woman leaning on a railing. Both are framed by the window jambs on the left and the tree on the right. The indeterminate spatiality of the early still life has given way to a rather conventional perspective onto the outside world. Also evident is a new approach to the colour surfaces. While the artist sought the greatest possible simplicity in the earlier painting, such that every object, every surface is delineated by thick black lines, the colours have now become autonomous. They extend into one another, while the expressive line dwindles into single, decorative-looking strokes. The paint, so the suggestion, is granted a life of its own, much as in a watercolour whose genesis the artist is unable to control into every last detail. In this way Schmidt-Rottluff achieves a vitality that draws on his early quasi-Cubistic work using new painterly means.

Jessica Küsters

1 Cf. Janina Dahlmanns, 'Die Stilleben Karl Schmidt-Rottluffs – Aus der Kunst- und Wunderkammer des Malers', in: Magdalena M. Moeller (ed.), *Karl-Schmidt-Rottluff. Formen und Farbe*, Munich 2007, pp. 39–47, here p. 45.

2 Letter to Lyonel Feininger, undated, probably December 1912, quoted in Andreas Gabelmann, 'Wege ins Neue: Schmidt-Rottluff und seine Auseinandersetzung mit Futurismus, Kubismus und Primitivismus', in: Magdalena M. Möller and Tayfun Belgin (eds.), *Karl Schmidt-Rottluff. Ein Maler des 20. Jahrhunderts. Gemälde, Aquarelle und Zeichnungen von 1905 bis 1972* (exh. cat., Museum am Ostwall, Dortmund; Brücke-Museum Berlin; Kunsthalle Kiel; Museum der Bildenden Künste, Leipzig), Munich 2001, pp. 212–228, here p. 216.

3 Ibid., p. 46f.

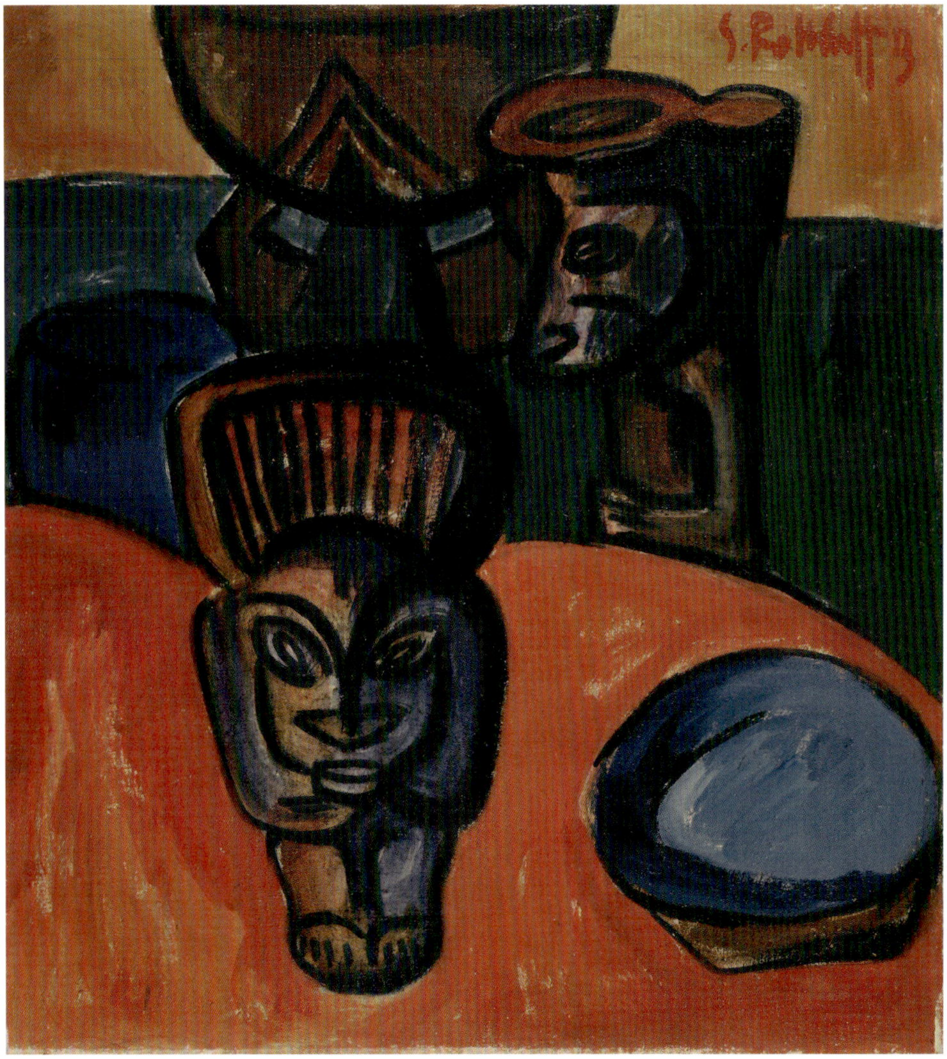

Still Life with
Negro Sculpture
1913
Oil on canvas
73 x 68.5 cm

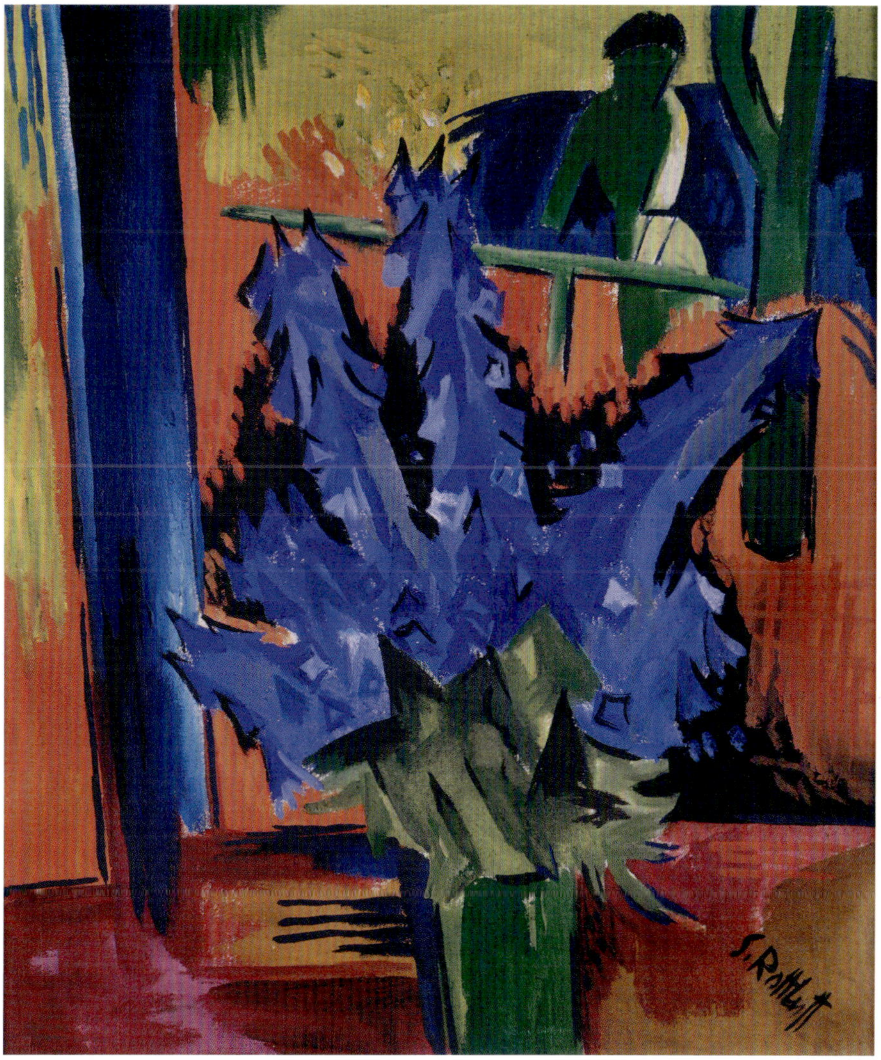

Larkspur in the Window
1922
Oil on canvas
91 x 76 cm

Georg Schrimpf

At the Window, 1923
Swineherd, 1923
Nude Girl in Front of a Mirror, 1926

When the legendary Neue Sachlichkeit exhibition opened in Mannheim in 1925, Georg Schrimpf, who was represented with twelve works, was one of the most important participants. Born in Munich in 1889, the painter achieved recognition in the avant-garde art scene early on. After a short stint in the military, Schrimpf was already exhibiting his paintings at the renowned Berlin gallery Der Sturm in 1915, while the prominent German art dealer Hans Goltz showed his works in Munich in 1921. At that time, the Bavarian city was a hub for the latest Italian painting. Viewing works by Carlo Carrà and Giorgio de Chirico helped Schrimpf advance his own ideas for a post-Expressionist painting style.

Schrimpf had been involved in the short-lived Munich Soviet Republic of 1919, which attempted to establish a socialist state in Bavaria, and was arrested after the movement was quashed. Nevertheless, as early as the 1920s, Schrimpf was regarded as a representative of the 'right wing' of Neue Sachlichkeit. This clearly was based less on political classification than an aesthetic position, notwithstanding the fact that prominent representatives of this right wing – Alexander Kanoldt, Franz Lenk and Schrimpf himself – were able to take on professorships in painting after the Nazis took power in 1933, and were not condemned by the regime at an early stage, in contrast to those representing the movement's so-called verist wing, such as Otto Dix, George Grosz and Georg Scholz.

The Mannheim museum director Gustav Friedrich Hartlaub was the one who originally divided the movement into two wings: 'Our exhibit is characterized by the – in itself purely external – feature of the objectivity with which the artists express themselves. In the process, two groups can easily be identified. One of them – one might almost speak of a "left wing" – rips the objective elements out of the world of real facts and expels the result at its own speed and temperature. The other tends to seek eternally valid subject matter in order to express timeless laws of existence within the field of art. One group has been called the "verists", while one could almost call the other "classicists", but both descriptions are only half true and describe the range of works only imprecisely ...'[1]

Schrimpf's artistic development emerged out of early Cubism. His paintings are characterized by a fixed composition, reduced and clear volumes, and Cubist simplification. His use of colour, however, has more in common with the Blauer Reiter group, setting clear highlights and making use of primary colours such as yellow and blue whose intensity disrupts the colour scheme. Schrimpf's figurative pictures, which he began to develop during the First World War, represent a synthesis of Jugendstil, Expressionism and Henri Rousseau's naive monumentality. The individual, harmoniously embedded in nature while simultaneously neutralized by it, appears as the main focus of the image. Moreover, religious allusions are not entirely absent in the works.

The three paintings in the Haubrich Collection date from the first half of the 1920s, the period during which Schrimpf gained widespread recognition and was soon regarded as one of the most important representatives of Neue Sachlichkeit painting. **Swineherd** belongs to the group of human and animal compositions that show individuals resting in gently undulating landscapes, surrounded by the animals in their charge. The figure depicted defines the foreground, dominating it with his monumentality, while the animals, relegated to tightly confined space, mark the visual depth of field of the middle distance, before the gaze is allowed to expand within the distant landscape. Contemporary critics recognized an important characteristic of the paintings, namely the contrast between the massive, heavy bodies and the meticulous reproduction of details such as the grass. Curt Gravenkamp found this 'proximity of the humans unsettling'.[2] Indeed, its effect is odd: the apparent idyll is disrupted on a content level through the depicted state of melancholy absorption as well as on a formal level through the montage-style constructivist aspect.

In **Nude Girl in Front of a Mirror** from 1926, this aspect of construction plays out consciously in the stark contrast between the interior and the nude. The tilted mirror, seen from behind, appears to cut into the soft body of the woman, whose arms are folded defencelessly behind her head. In addition, the figure is caught between the two vertical lines formed by the mirror's stand and the chair-back to the rear. Here, the apparent realism of Neue Sachlichkeit shows itself to be informed by abstraction and constructivism, with a decisively well-considered composition serving as a sign of modernity.

At the Window depicts one of Schrimpf's best-known motifs: a woman, seen from behind in an interior, looking out at an idealized landscape with apparent longing or melancholy. The inner life of the bourgeois subject is transferred onto the formal structure of the tightly composed picture, which shows nothing more than a bare room, a basic stool, a plain barefoot woman, and a simple window sloping to the left. In his use of this motif, Schrimpf is deliberately placing himself within an established artistic tradition. The figure seen from behind in an interior looking out a window can be found from the late Middle Ages on, particularly in the works of seventeenth-century Dutch painters. Caspar David Friedrich's 1818 *Woman at the Window*, Moritz von Schwind's 1858 *Early Morning* or Fritz von Uhde's 1891 *At the Window* represent the motif's high points in German painting of the nineteenth century.[3] The use of such motifs played a not insignificant role in Schrimpf's becoming one of the leading representatives of the so-called New German Romantic painting from the late 1920s onwards.[4] This term was used by art critics and exhibition organizers in a response both to the transformation of Neue Sachlichkeit into a formally less radical objectivity as well as to the prevailing atmosphere, which was becoming increasingly poisoned by nationalism.

When the Nazis took power, modern art increasingly became a target. The Nazis' supporters' pent-up hatred of Modernism was vented in the form of so-called shame exhibitions, as well as in dismissals and other administrative measures. The legitimisation strategy couched within the label of New German Romanticism was, in the case of Schrimpf, quite successful. The painter was appointed to a position at the State Academy of Arts Education in Berlin's Schöneberg district, where he taught from October 1933 onwards. But his avant-garde past would catch up with him. He was represented in the infamous 1937 'Degenerate Art' exhibition in Munich with a piece from 1915. However, something happened that was both unusual and significant: Rudolf Hess, Hitler's deputy and a collector of Schrimpf's 1930s landscapes, had the incriminating work removed from the hate-mongering exhibition. Schrimpf, who had conformed to the prevailing taste with his art even though he himself did not hold Nazi sympathies, enjoyed for a moment protection from the highest places. The fact that he still lost his professorship, and yet was honoured with a commemorative exhibition and a monograph in 1940 after his early death in 1938, reveals the inconsistencies of the Nazis' art policy.[5]

Olaf Peters

1 Gustav Friedrich Hartlaub, 'Zum Geleit', in: *Neue Sachlichkeit. Deutsche Malerei seit dem Expressionismus* (exh. cat., Städtische Kunsthalle Mannheim), Mannheim 1925, unpaginated.

2 Cf. Curt Gravenkamp, 'Die deutsche Neuromantik in der Malerei der Gegenwart', in: *Die Kunst für alle*, 1931/32, p. 196.

3 Cf. J. A. Schmoll, known as Eisenwerth, 'Fensterbilder. Motivketten in der europäischen Malerei', in: Ludwig Grote (ed.), *Beiträge zur Motivkunde des 19. Jahrhunderts*, Munich 1970, pp. 13-165.

4 Cf. James A. van Dyke, '"Neue Deutsche Romantik" zwischen Modernität, Kulturkritik und Kulturpolitik 1929-1937', in: Dieter Schwarz (ed.), *Adolf Dietrich und die Neue Sachlichkeit in Deutschland* (exh. cat., Kunstmuseum Winterthur and Landesmuseum Oldenburg), 1994/95, pp. 137-165.

5 Cf. Erich Müller-Kamp (ed.): *Georg Schrimpf*. Introduction by Matthias Pförtner, Berlin 1940 (*Die Kunstbücher des Volkes*, 4).

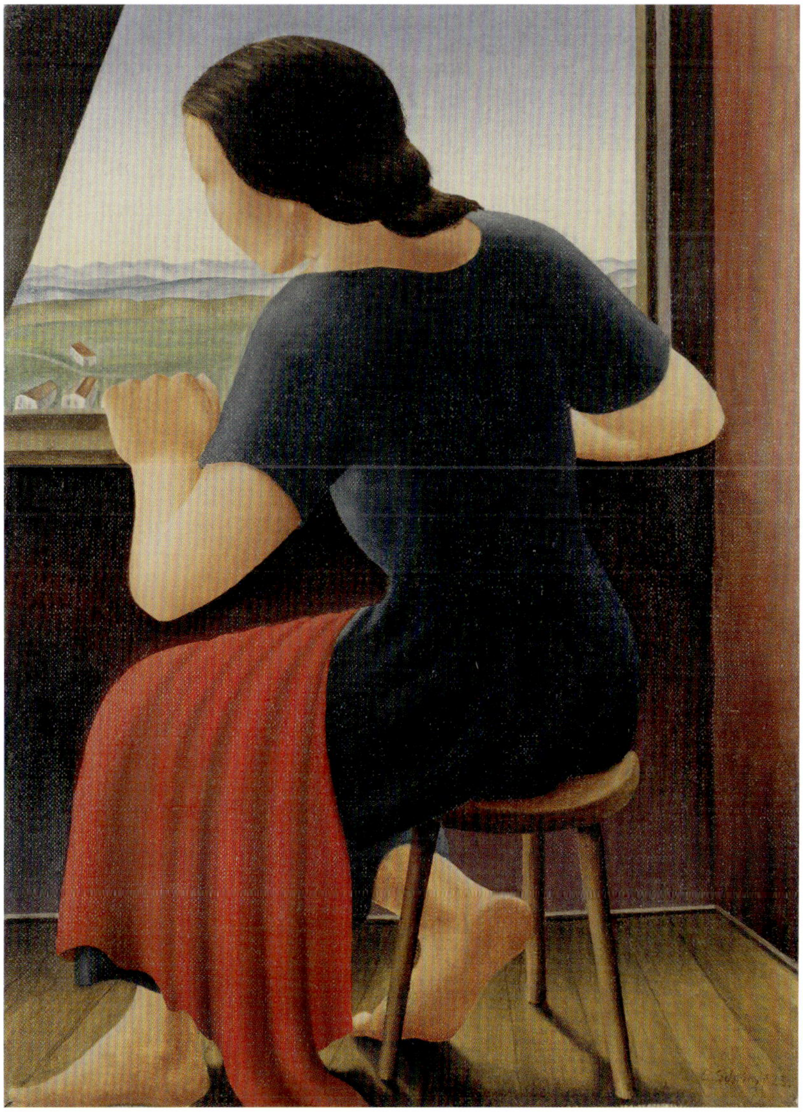

At the Window
1923
Oil on canvas
52.5 x 37.5 cm

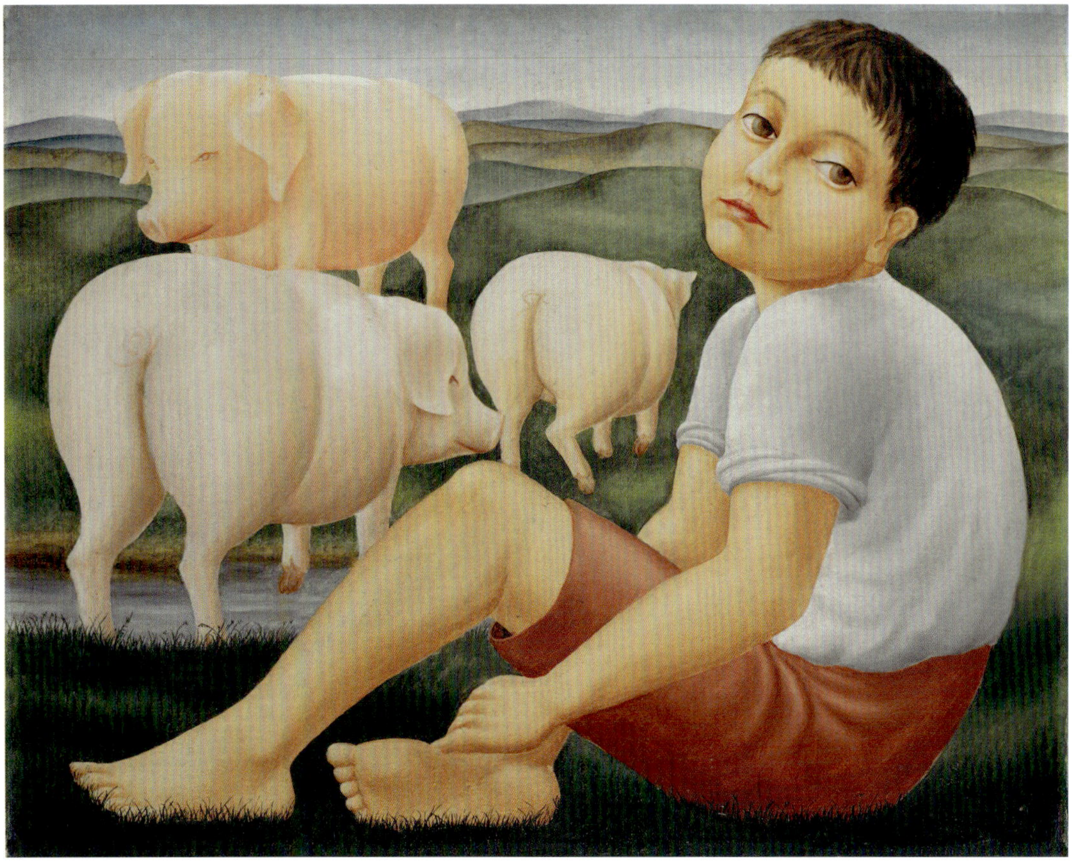

Swineherd
1923
Oil on canvas
49.5 x 60 cm

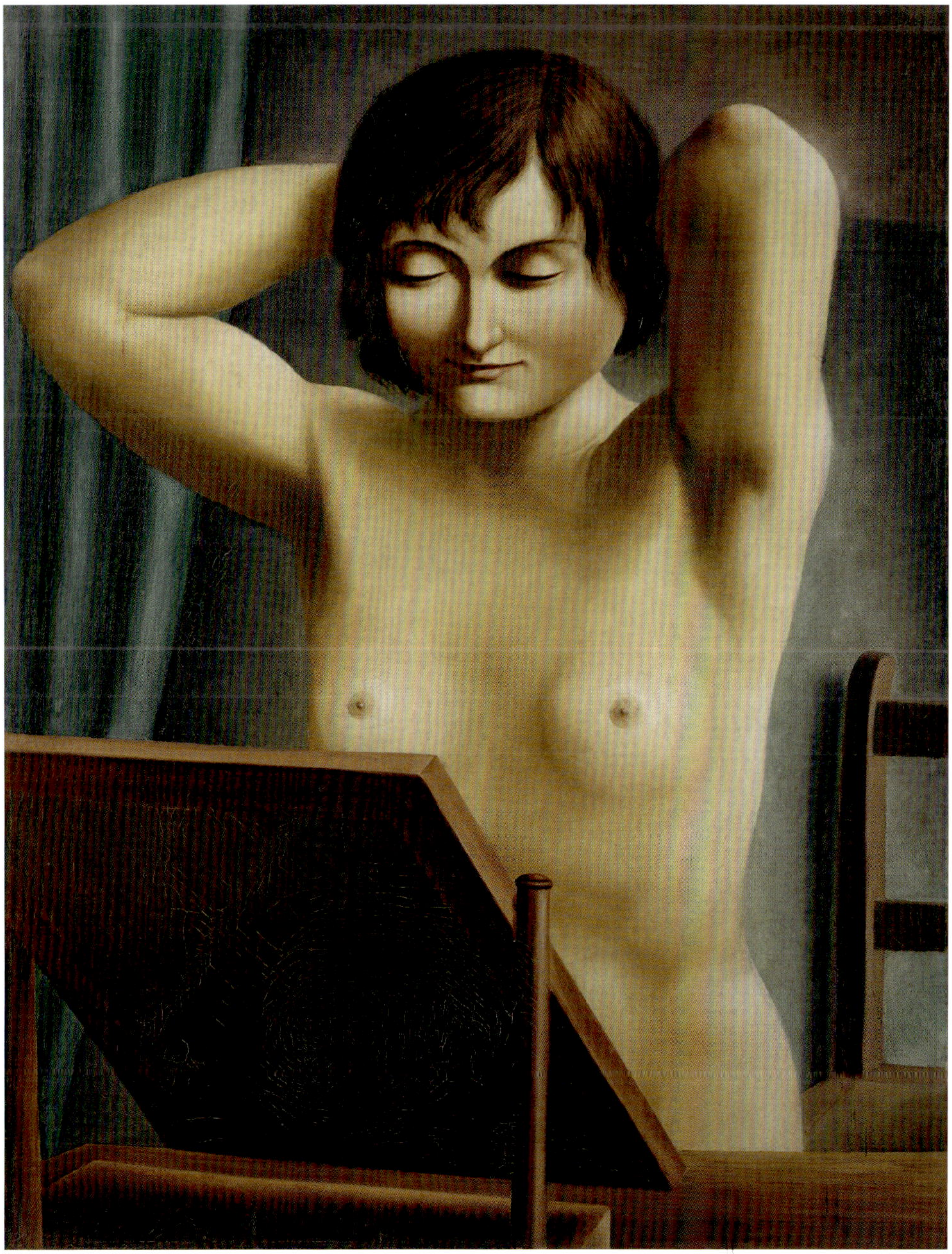

Nude Girl in Front of a Mirror
1926
Oil on canvas
70.5 x 53 cm

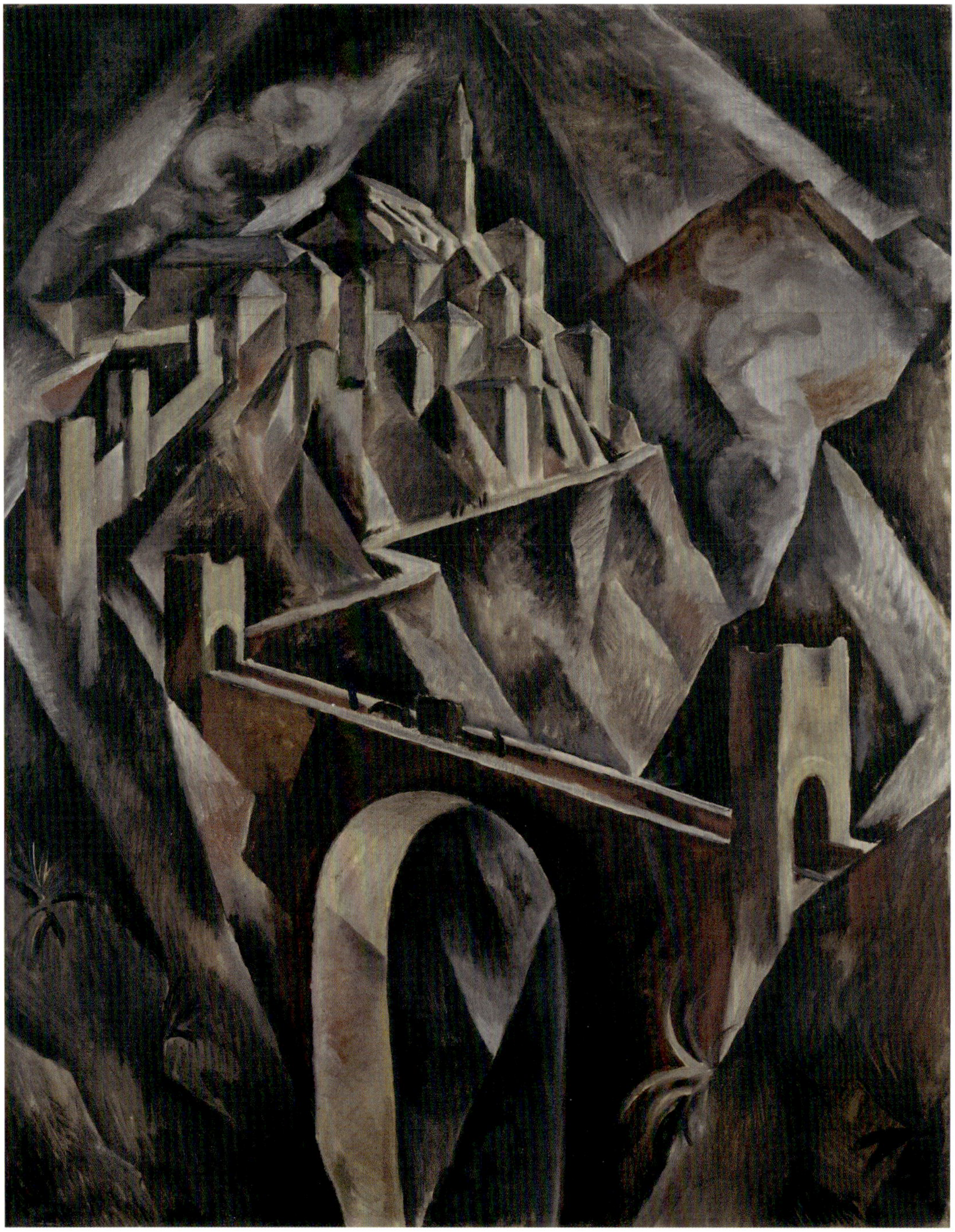

Alpine Town
1915
Oil on canvas
100 x 77 cm

Paul Adolf Seehaus

Alpine Town, 1915

In his **Alpine Town**, Paul Adolf Seehaus has conjured up a land of shadows. Cubist buildings thrust their way into a monochrome rockscape. As a bed-ridden child, the artist had already dreamt of the rugged countryside of Scandinavia. This passion was to remain with him for the rest of his life. Just turned twenty, he travelled to Ireland, Scotland and Scandinavia and discovered there landscapes of bleak majesty that seemed to correspond far more to the worlds in his own mind than the shallow meadows of the Rhineland. Coasts and mountains run like a purple thread through his oeuvre.

Seehaus was fascinated by the possibilities of creating new forms – colour was always secondary for him.[1] Fascinated as he was by landscapes, he saw himself as part of a tradition hailing from Caspar David Friedrich. 'A landscape painter must love countries the way he loves women; he must keep them in his heart and not merely in his eye',[2] as he wrote. At the same time, he had no interest in depicting people, because 'sculptors, like painters, convey the inordinate expressiveness of human and animal limbs, but landscapes are the sole province of the painter'.[3]

And the landscape is the chief protagonist in **Alpine Town**. Mountains frozen into crystalline structures form the backdrop to a journey into a dark and harsh world. A few houses tower up, lost and windowless, towards the heavens. Forms that look as if they are being viewed in stroboscopic light create a clear Cubist arrangement. Seehaus dispenses however with a strict, schematic standardization of the structures. He has taken pains to capture the essence of the objects as closely as possible – as can be seen from the figures of the bridge and the houses, which have been worked in a striking and realistic manner. Colour, for its part, disappears into the background, released from its descriptive tasks.

Already in his schooldays Seehaus made first contacts with German Expressionists. He revealed himself to be highly gifted. Soon he had caught the attention of August Macke, who took him on as a master student for free.[4] After his school finals, Seehaus began to study art history at the University of Bonn. More so even than Macke, he fell under the influence of Robert Delaunay and Paul Cézanne. Soon he exhibited with the Rhenish Expressionists and participated in exhibitions by the Neue Secession and Junges Rheinland. Paul Adolf Seehaus died of pneumonia in 1919, just a few years after his inspiration, Macke. He was twenty-seven, and at the height of his career.

Lisa Weber

1 Cf. Paul Adolf Seehaus, *Briefe und Aufzeichnungen*, Bonn 1930, p. 18.
2 Paul Adolf Seehaus, 'Der Landschaftsmaler' (Fragment), in: *Das Kunstblatt*, 4 / 1920, p. 29.
3 Ibid.
4 Seehaus 1930, p. 11.

Richard Seewald

Cat with Salamander, 1933

Richard Seewald's early paintings were influenced by the Expressionism of the Brücke group. In terms of style he felt indebted to the 'order of the absolute', while playing nevertheless – as so clearly in **Cat with Salamander** – with motifs taken from Surrealism.[1]

The painting **Cat with Salamander** goes back to an experience that Seewald, a keen observer, described in vivid tones: 'Then out of the undergrowth of stalks came a black cat, an enormous tom without a single fair-coloured hair. And there sideways in his mouth was a greenish-blue emerald lizard. At that moment, he saw me and froze, just as I did. Eye to eye, we stood there for a while, he directing his amber eyes at me without blinking.'[2] These yellow eyes now fixate the beholder. The cat is creeping up to the lush plantain, head lowered, the hair of its neck bristling. Its outline lights up in an iridescent green before the oversized forest of leaves. An emerald green lizard hangs limply from its mouth, while a fire salamander flees into the foreground in panic. The exudations from its skin are as poisonous as the hemlock that is blossoming on the upper margin. A praying mantis, one of the emblems of the Surrealists, is sitting on a blade of grass above the cat. A predator like the cat, it, too, looks out at the viewer. Compared to the size of the cat, the luxuriant vegetation is almost a forest primeval. Seewald also suggests this when he observes that 'all cats in grass are tigers prowling through the jungle'.[3]

Looking at the year it was painted, the uncanny and threatening feeling in the painting may be interpreted as a comment on the new rulers after 1933. They placed Seewald, who had already vacated his professorship at the Kölner Werkschulen (a series of schools in Cologne offering training in the visual arts, architecture and design) and moved permanently in 1931 to Ticino, on the list of 'degenerate artists'. Three of his paintings in the Wallraf-Richartz Museum were confiscated. In 1939 Seewald took on Swiss citizenship. He was not only a painter, graphic artist and illustrator, but above all a writer. But even in this role he remained a deeply visual person: 'We think in pictures, or not at all.'[4]

Geraldine Spiekermann

1 *Richard Seewald. 85 Jahre. Bilder, Zeichnungen, Graphik, 1912–1973* (exh. cat., Galerie Wolfgang Ketterer) Munich 1973, unpaginated.
2 Quoted in: Karl Ruhrberg (ed), *Handbuch Museum Ludwig*, Cologne 1983, p. 720.
3 Ibid.
4 Richard Seewald. 85 Jahre, op.cit., unpaginated.

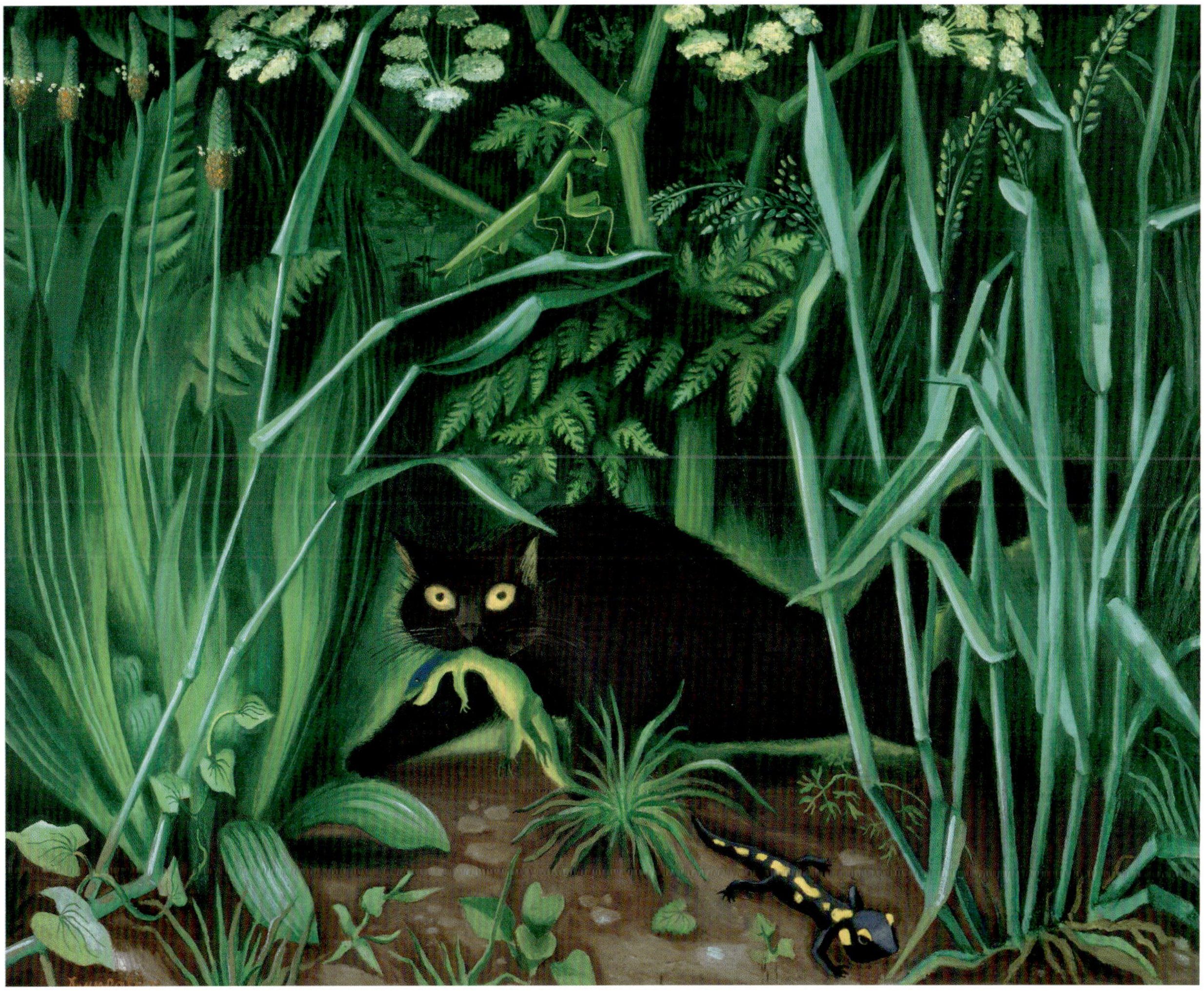

Cat with Salamander
1933
Oil on canvas
95 x 115 cm

Renée Sintenis

Small Daphne, 1918
Wary Deer, 1920
Donkey, 1923
Young Ox, 1929

In 1920s Berlin, Renée Sintenis, towering in stature at almost two metres, was considered 'the giantess with the menagerie of little animals'.[1] In 1907, she began to study drawing at Berlin's Museum of Decorative Arts. Her father soon tried to put an end to her pursuing a career in the arts, forcing her to take up training as a secretary instead. When she finally fled back to the art world, her relationship with him was destroyed forever.

At the outbreak of the First World War, Sintenis was living in a tiny, virtually unheated room when she first began to model animal figures. At the insistence of her teacher at the time and later husband, Emil Rudolf-Weiß, she submitted them to the Berlin Secession, where they were indeed presented in 1915. Before long, Rainer Maria Rilke became an enthusiast and a key advocate of her work, and the public was also soon charmed. By the early 1920s, Sintenis was one of the best-earning female artists of her day.[2] She herself, with her hair cropped short and preferring to wear a suit rather than a dress, became an emblem of the New Woman. During the Second World War, she lost her husband and many of her friends, and in a fire a large number of her works as well. All the same, she continued working on her menagerie, writing to a friend in 1940: 'You'll laugh about how I fuss over my animals, because your mind is so filled with worrying about people, but life is funny that way.'[3]

Her young animals run throughout the course of her work: they are creatures that exist only for themselves. The animal as 'moulded nature'[4] suspects nothing of the harshness of existence, especially in its youth: it breathes, eats and is alive. As if to prove this, Sintenis's **Wary Deer** stands insecurely on its long legs, bending one of its front legs to be able to turn its head to the rear. Its back is arched, every muscle tensed. It pauses a moment to evaluate the situation, its movements still timid and inexpert. The **Young Ox** also turns its head in the direction of its diagonally placed hind legs, almost losing its stability. It seems as if it still needs to become acquainted with its sinewy young body and its movements. The **Donkey**, in contrast, stands rigidly in a slightly bent resting position, its heavy, large head bent downward, ears pricked up. Sintenis knows her animals: she often spent the entire day at the Berlin Zoo. But she never used powerful stallions as models, concentrating instead on the awkward young animals. Her 'smiling sculptures' were top-sellers; they were used as desktop paperweights or miniature sculptures for the mantelpiece. In 1932, she created a sculpture of a young bear that is just learning to walk: this figure is still today awarded to the winners of the Golden Bear at the Berlinale film festival.

In contrast to Sintenis's menagerie, the figure of **Daphne** has something symbolic about it. Her story has been depicted by many painters and sculptors since antiquity. Fleeing from the love of the young god Apollo, Daphne asks her father, the river god Peneios, to take away her beauty. He transforms her into a laurel bush, which has since then been dedicated to Apollo. Unlike other artists, Sintenis casts her Daphne in a moment of motionlessness: with her legs firmly pressed together, Daphne stretches her thin body towards the sky. She tosses her arms awkwardly upward and her chest swells one last time; her face is directed towards the ground with the eyes closed, but her mouth is slightly open. On her head and her underarms, laurel leaves can be seen sprouting, and her bronze skin already has a hard and wooden glint like the bark of a tree. She is no longer fleeing; rather, she surrenders to her transformation with a deep breath.

Sintenis's small-format **Daphne**, enlarged greatly at the behest of the Lübecker Museen, was cast once more and gilded twelve years after its making. In the garden at Behnhaus, it is placed beneath a tree, so that her hands rise into its leafy canopy. Daphne's body is tall, slender and firm, and it is often said that Sintenis modelled the figure on herself. Others see Sintenis's **Daphne** as a 'work of maturity and awareness, which in addition marks a renunciation, a turning away from her own figure'.[5] While Sintenis had previously created several young women and torsos, this was to be her last female figure.

Arnika Fürgut

1 Silke Kettelhake, *Renée Sintenis: Berlin, Boheme und Ringelnatz*, Berlin 2010, p. 63. 2010, S. 63.
2 Ibid., p. 106.
3 Ibid., p. 337.
4 Hanna Kiel, *Renée Sintenis*, Berlin 1956, p. 62.
5 Ibid., p. 30.

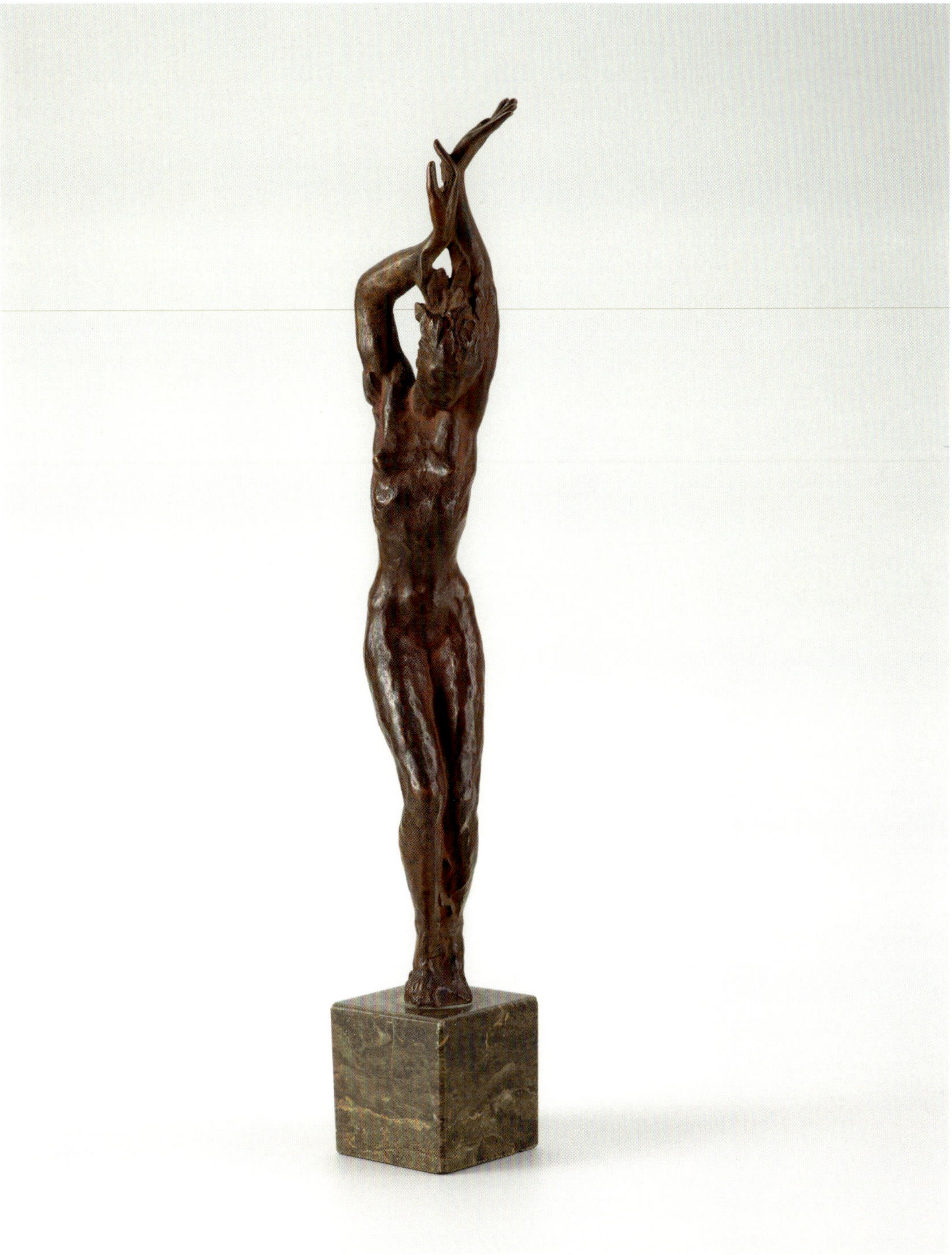

Small Daphne
1918
Bronze
H.: 29.5 cm

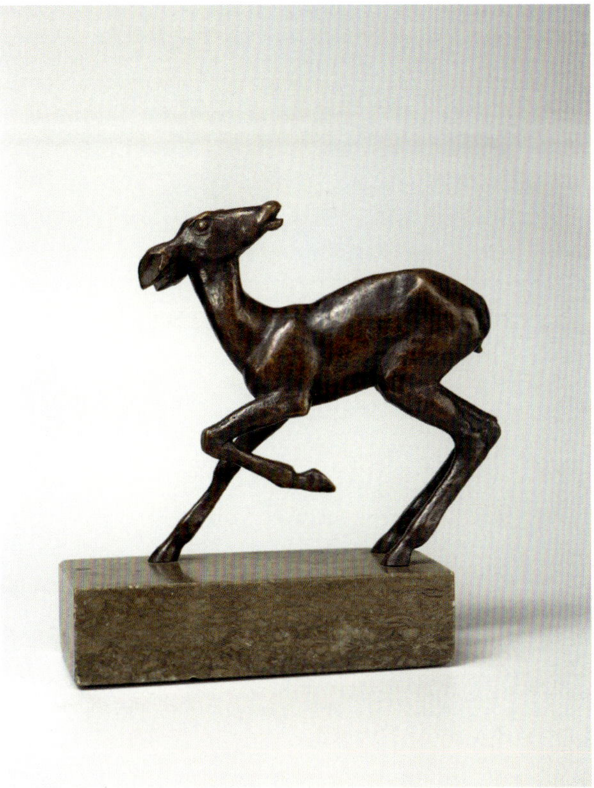

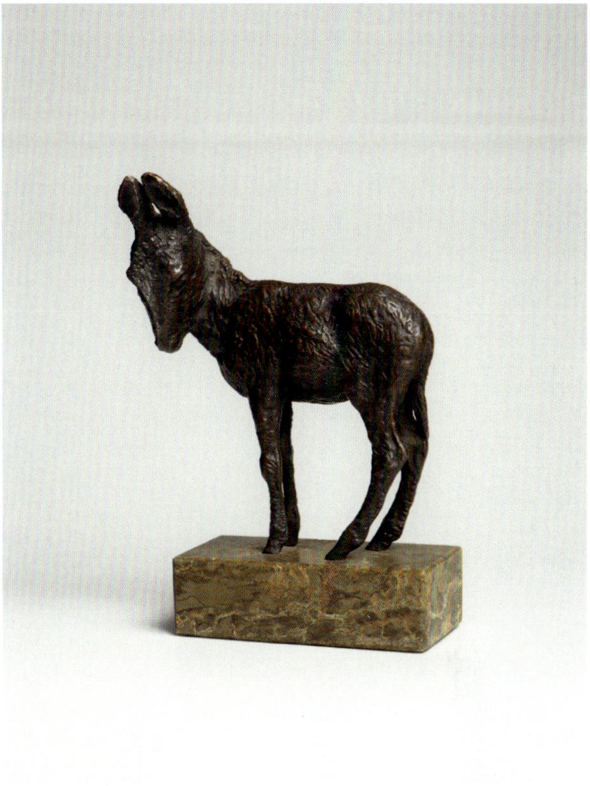

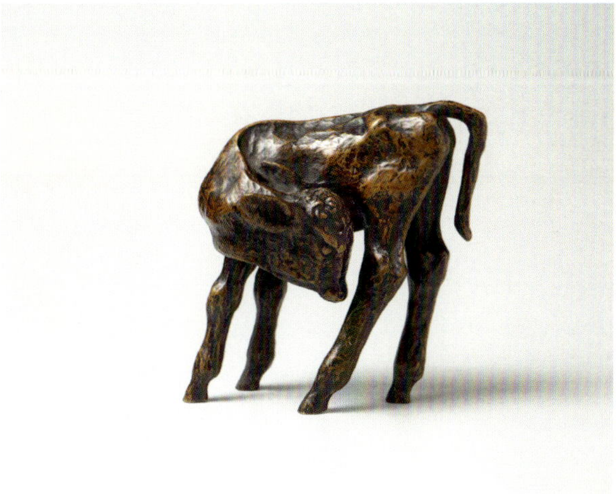

Wary Deer
1920
Bronze
H.: 12 cm

Donkey
1923
Bronze
H.: 13 cm

Young Ox
1929
Bronze
H.: 12.5 cm

List of Works
Brief Lexicon
Timeline

List of Works

Compiled by
Dorothee Grafahrend-Gohmert

Note:

WRM = Wallraf-Richartz Museum

ML = Museum Ludwig

Haubrich Fund = The municipal stipend dispensed to Haubrich to be used for purchasing modern art.

The original titles, if extant, are shown in parentheses.

Catalogue raisonné numbers, if extant, are provided with the name of the editor of the work in question.

With the founding of the Museum Ludwig in 1976 all works from the Wallraf-Richartz Museum by artists born after 1870 were inventoried within the holdings of the new museum.

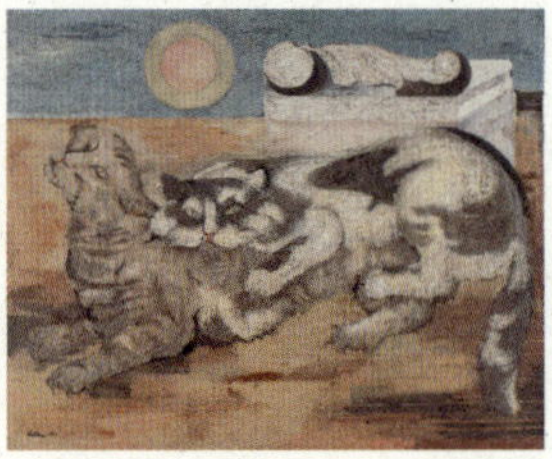

Adler, Jankel
1895 Tuszyn–1949 Aldbourne

Cats (Katzen)
1927
Oil, chalk, sand on canvas
100.5 x 120.5 cm
ML 76/2733

Purchased by Haubrich from the artist, 1933. Haubrich Donation, 1946.

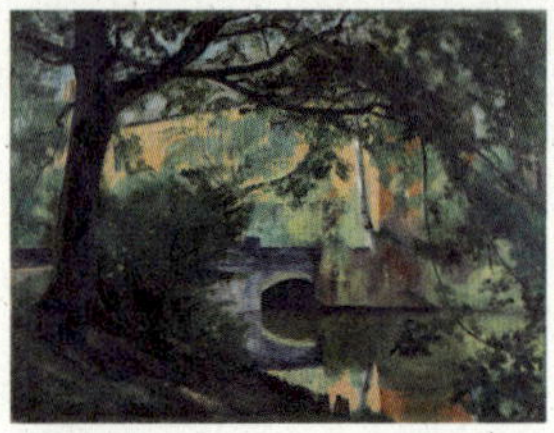

Ahlers-Hestermann, Friedrich
1883 Hamburg–1973 Berlin

Park, Schloss Flamersheim, near Euskirchen (Der Park von Schloß Flamersheim bei Euskirchen)
1935
Oil on canvas
60 x 75 cm
ML 76/2807

Donated by Haubrich, 1948. Previous ownership could not be established.

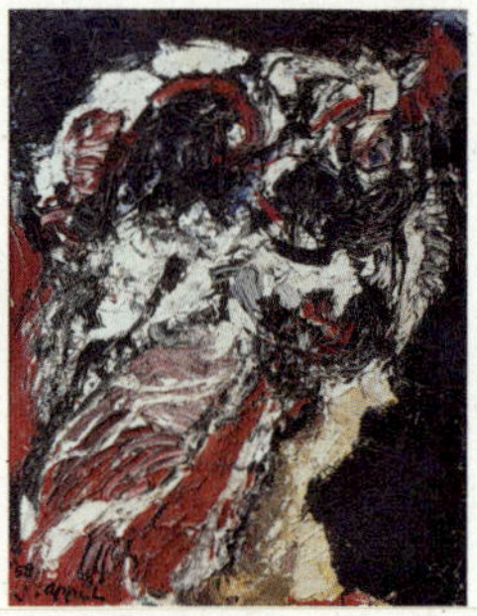

Appel, Karel
1921 Amsterdam–2006 Zürich

Personage (Personnage)
1958
Oil on canvas
116 x 89 cm
ML 76/3082

Kölnischer Kunstverein. Purchased by WRM with funding from the Haubrich Fund, 1959.

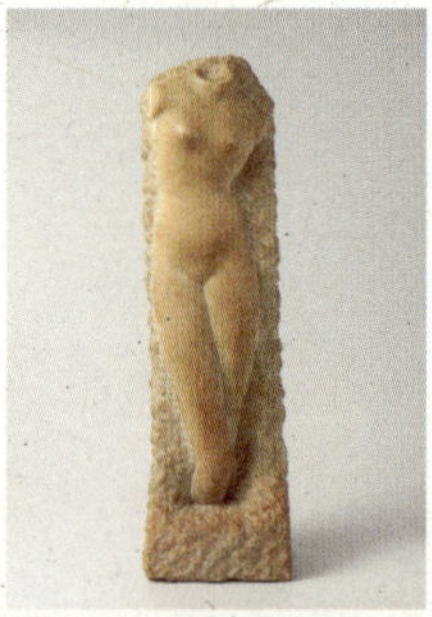

Archipenko, Alexander (Workshop)
1887 Kiev–1964 New York

Female Nude (Weiblicher Akt)
1922 or 1923–1948
Marble
H.: 51 cm
ML 76/SK 98

Galerie Alex Vömel, Düsseldorf. Purchased by WRM with funding from the Haubrich Fund, 1950. According to a letter from A. dated 8 April 1963, the marble statue was made by his assistant Carlo Pott in Berlin and not authorized by the artist. In 1964, WRM compensated with the purchase of A.'s bronze sculpture *Flat Torso (Flacher Torso)*, 1914 (ML 76/SK 241; ill. in Gohr 1986, p. 10).

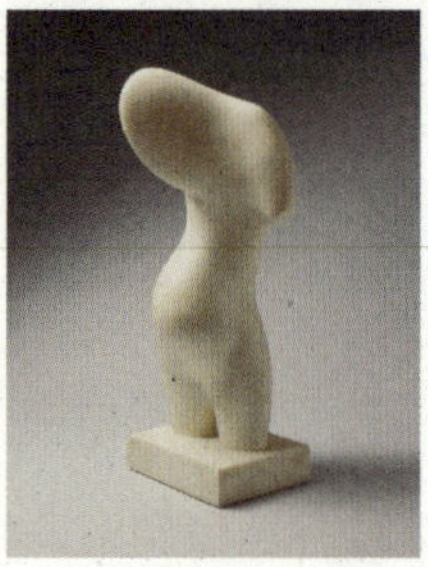

Arp, Jean
1886 Strasbourg–1966 Basel

Female Torso (Weiblicher Torso)
1953
Marble
H.: 88 cm
ML 76/SK 151
Jianou 121

Galerie Christoph Czwiklitzer, Cologne, by direct reception from the artist. Purchased by WRM in part with funding from the Haubrich Fund, 1956.

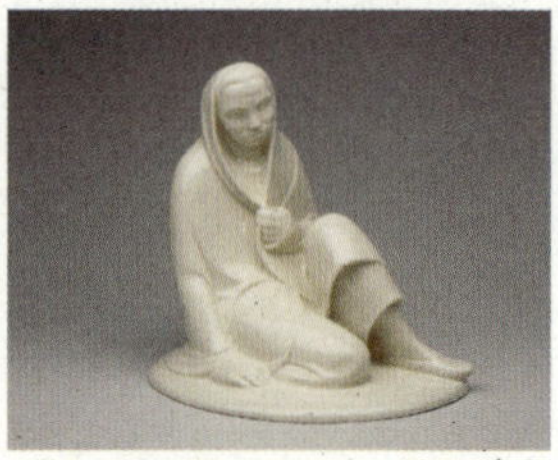

Barlach, Ernst
1870 Wedel–1938 Rostock

Seated Girl (Sitzendes Mädchen)
1908 plaster / 1909 porcelain
Porcelain, glazed
H.: 22.5 cm
ML 76/SK 78
Laur 129

Purchased by Haubrich from Franz Nienhaus, Cologne, 1926. Haubrich Donation, 1946.

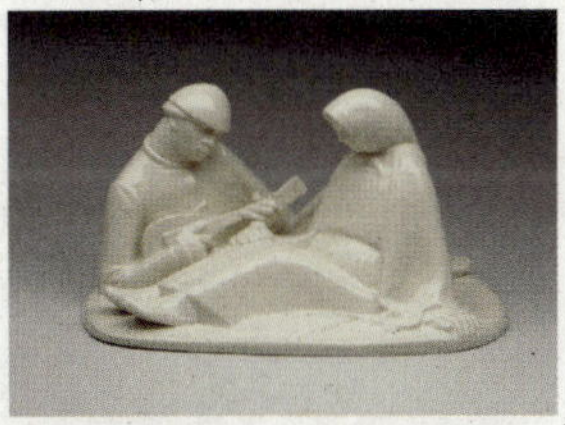

Russian Lovers
(Russisches Liebespaar)
C. 1908/09 plaster/
1909 porcelain
Porcelain, glazed
H.: 19 cm
ML 76/SK 77
Laur 135

Purchased by Haubrich from Franz Nienhaus, Cologne, 1926. Haubrich Donation, 1946.

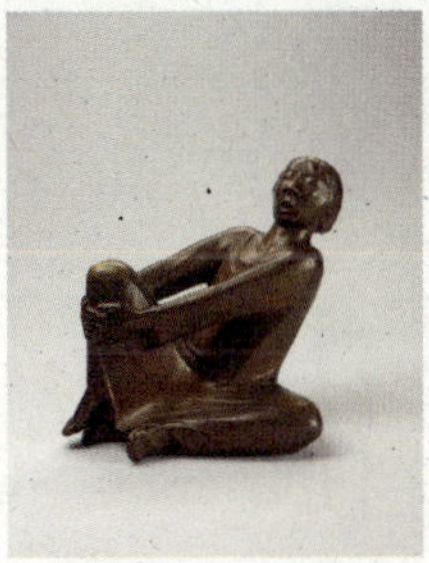

Singing Man
(Der singende Mann)
1928 plaster / 1930–1940 bronze
Bronze
H.: 49 cm
ML 76/SK 90
Laur 432

Farbenfabriken Bayer AG, Leverkusen. Given to Haubrich for the Haubrich Collection, 1950. It has been not been possible to determine the edition from which the ML cast originates.

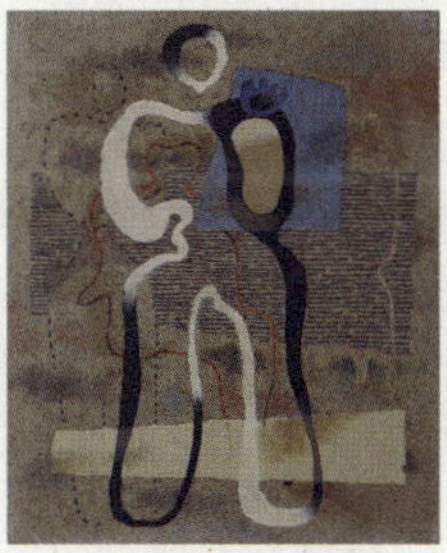

Baumeister, Willi

1889 Stuttgart–1955 Stuttgart

Standing Figure with Blue Patch
(Stehende Figur mit blauer Fläche)
1933
Oil, sand on canvas
82 x 65.5 cm
ML 76/2789
Beye/Baumeister 517

Purchased, together with a series of other works by B., by Carl Oskar Jatho with moneys from compensation for wartime damages, 1942. During the war, Jatho left the work in Stuttgart with the artist, who protected it from destruction. Purchased by Galerie Werner Rusche, Cologne, in preparation for an exhibition of B.'s work, 1947. Purchased by WRM with funding from the Haubrich Fund, 1949.

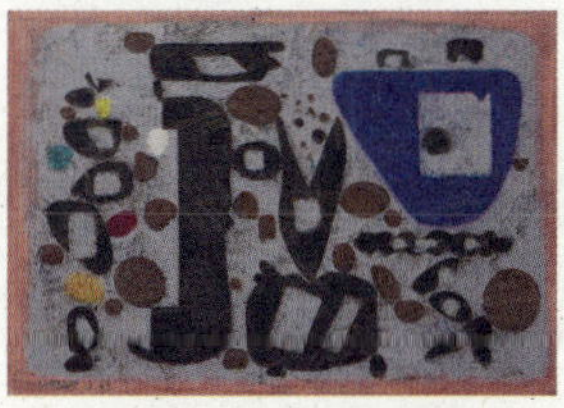

Stone Grind
(Steinschliff)
1947
Oil on canvas
46.5 x 65 cm
ML 76/2795
Beye/Baumeister 1538

Purchased by WRM from Galerie Ralfs in Braunschweig with funding from the Haubrich Fund, 1948.

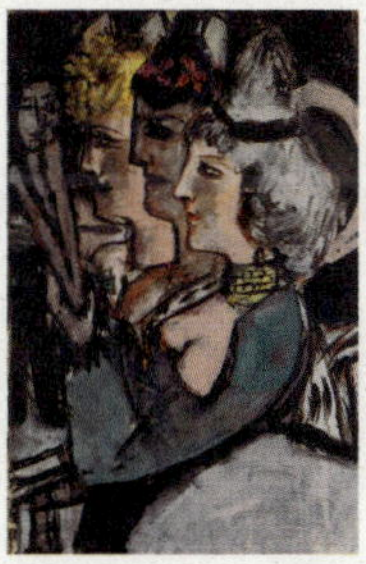

Beckmann, Max

1884 Leipzig–1950 New York

Three Women in Profile
(Drei Frauen im Profil)
1942
Oil on canvas
85 x 55 cm
ML 76/2734
Göpel 614

Purchased by Hans Peters, Cologne, from the artist's Amsterdam studio, 1942. Sold in the same year to Cologne sculptor Joseph Jaekel. Purchased from Jaekel by Haubrich under the title *Three Dancers*, 1943. Haubrich Donation, 1946.

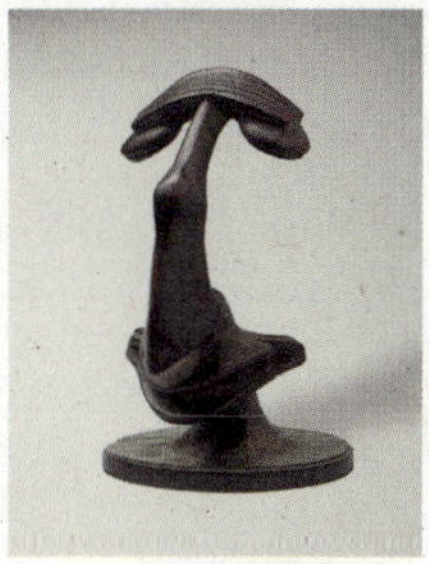

Belling, Rudolf

1886 Berlin–1972 Krailling

Portrait of Alfred Flechtheim
(Bildnis Alfred Flechtheim)
1927
Bronze
H.:18.7 cm
ML 76/SK 170
Nerdinger 58

Purchased by WRM from Galerie Alex Vömel, Düsseldorf, with funding from the Haubrich Fund, 1958. In the 1950s, the gallery sold editions of this work from various casts, and it has not been possible to determine the edition from which the ML cast originates.

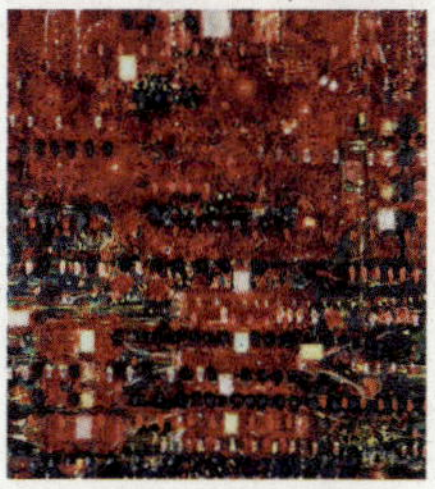

Bingemer, Buja

1927 Cologne–1989 Cologne

Choreography for a Summer Party (Choreographie zu einem Sommerfest)
C. 1958
Oil on canvas
90 x 80 cm
ML 76/3034

Purchased by WRM with funding from the Haubrich Fund, 1958.

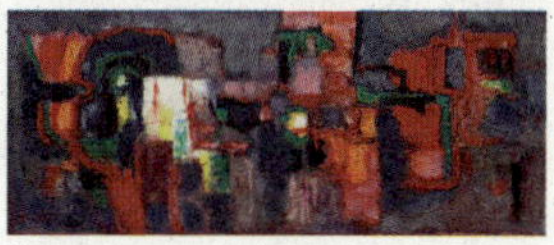

Birolli, Renato

1905 Verona–1959 Milan

Night (La notte)
1956
Oil on canvas
20 x 60 cm
ML 76/2987

Galleria il Milione, Milan. Purchased by WRM with funding from the Haubrich Fund, 1956.

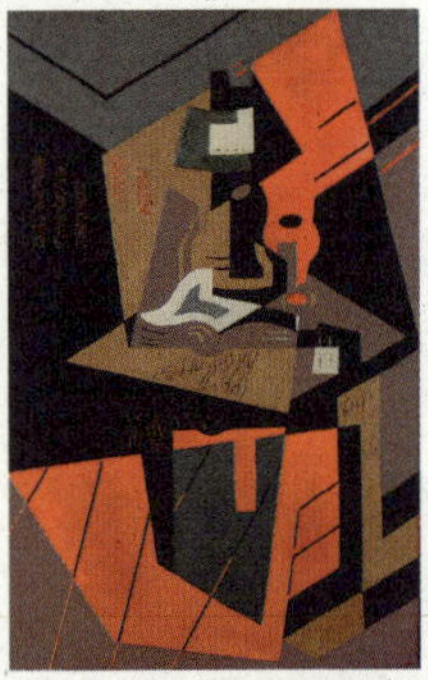

Blanchard, Maria
1881 Santander–1932 Paris

Red Still Life with Lamp
(Nature morte rouge à la lampe)
1916–18
Oil on canvas
118.5 x 74.5 cm
ML 76/3092
Salazar 50

From 1916 to 1918, Blanchard worked closely with Léonce Rosenberg, Paris, who tried to sell the painting at his gallery. After B.'s death, her sister Carmen G. Blanchard took possession of all works. In 1932, Daniel-Henry Kahnweiler certified the painting as a work by Juan Gris. It remained falsely attributed at Museo de Arte Moderno, Madrid. The mix-up was clarified in 1955, and WRM purchased the work in 1960 at Maratier Dr. Lange, Paris, with funding from the Haubrich Fund.

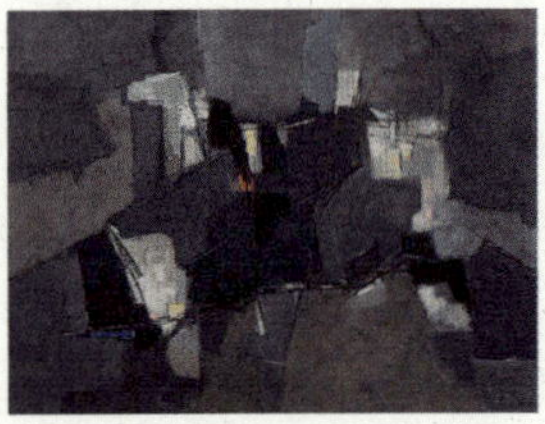

Bott, Francis
1904 Frankfurt am Main–1998 Lugano

Age of Frontier
(L'âge de la frontière)
1956
Oil on canvas
88.5 x 116 cm
ML 76/3040
Henze 391

Galerie d'Art Moderne, Basel. Purchased by WRM with funding from the Haubrich Fund, 1958.

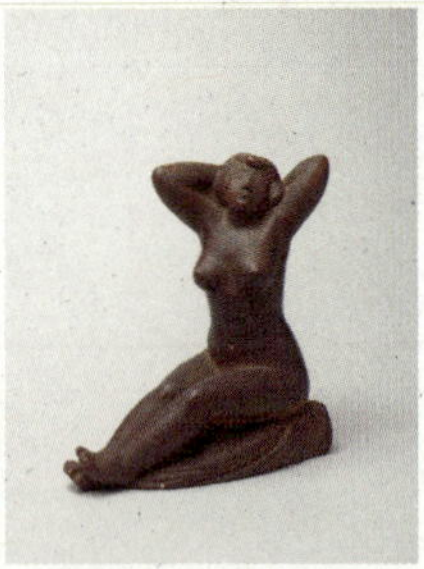

Breker, Arno
1900 Elberfeld–1991 Düsseldorf

Seated Girl (Sitzendes Mädchen)
1926
Plaster
H.: 20 cm
ML 76/SK 72

Purchased by Haubrich from Galerie Alex Vömel, Düsseldorf, 1942. Haubrich Donation, 1946.

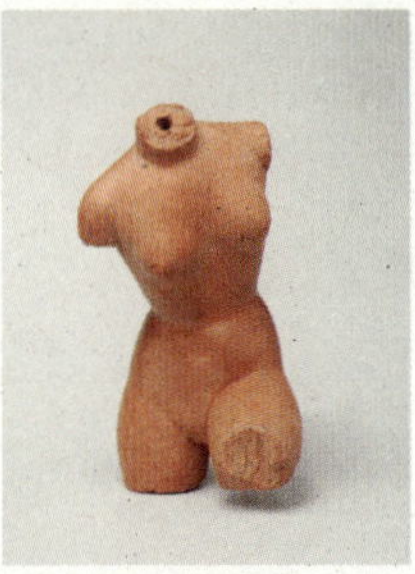

Torso of a Girl (Mädchentorso)
1927
Terracotta
H.: 25 cm
ML 76/SK 71

Purchased by Haubrich from Galerie Alex Vömel, Düsseldorf, 1942. Haubrich Donation, 1946.

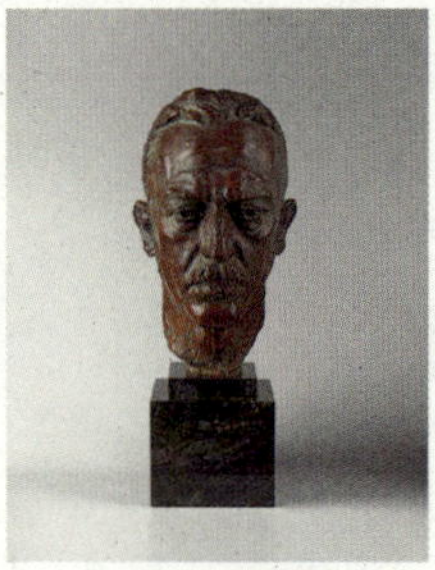

Head of Robert Gerling
(Kopf Robert Gerling)
1928
Bronze
H.: 42.5 cm
KSM 1982/571

Gift from the Gerling Konzern, Cologne, to Haubrich for the Haubrich Collection, 1951. Transferred to the Cologne City Museum, 1957.

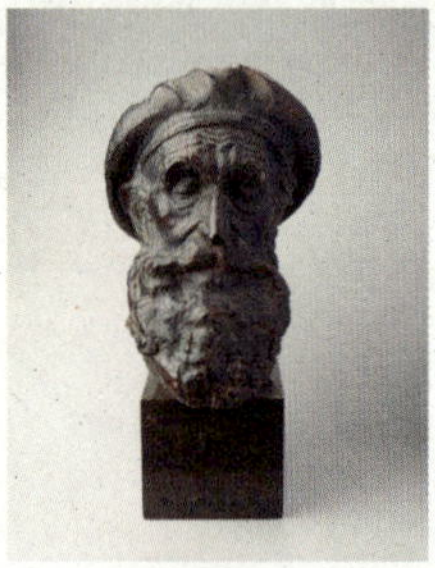

Aristide Maillol
1943
Bronze
H.: 45 cm
ML 76/SK 92

Gift from the Gerling Konzern, Cologne, to Haubrich for the Haubrich Collection, 1951.

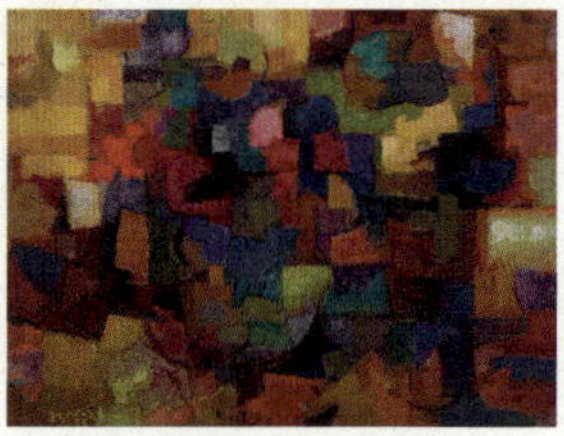

Brunori, Enzo
1924 Perugia–1993 Rome

Anemones
1956
Oil on canvas
63.5 x 82.5 cm
ML 76/2988

Galleria il Milione, Milan. Purchased by WRM with funding from the Haubrich Fund, 1956.

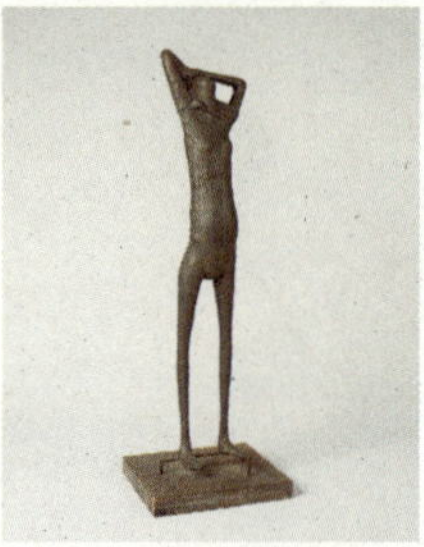

Butler, Reg
1913 Buntingford–1981 Berkhampstead

Girl
1953
Bronze
H.: 88 cm
ML 76/SK 150

Galerie Christoph Czwiklitzer, Cologne. Purchased by WRM with funding from the Haubrich Fund, 1956.

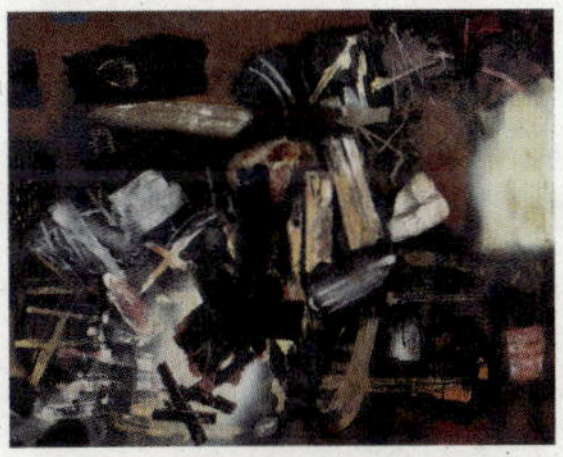

Cadoret, Michel
1912 Paris–1985 La Ferté-Alais

Souvenir
1958
Oil, chalk on canvas
102 x 127 cm
ML 76/3039

Kölnischer Kunstverein. Purchased by WRM with funding from the Haubrich Fund, 1958.

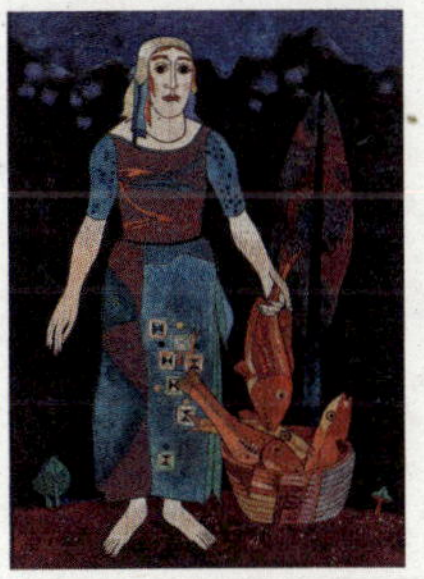

Campendonk, Heinrich
1889 Krefeld–1957 Amsterdam

Woman with Fishes
(Frau mit Fischen)
1929
Oil on glass, rear covered with light blue paper
67 x 48 cm
ML 76/2980

Acquired by Munich's Bavarian State Painting Collections at the art exhibition 'Düsseldorf-München', Düsseldorf, 1932. Confiscated as 'degenerate' in 1937. Entered the possession of Hildebrand Gurlitt, 1940, by way of an exchange. Sold by Gurlitt to Haubrich, 1943. Donated by Haubrich to the City of Cologne (not as part of the 1946 Haubrich Donation), 1952.

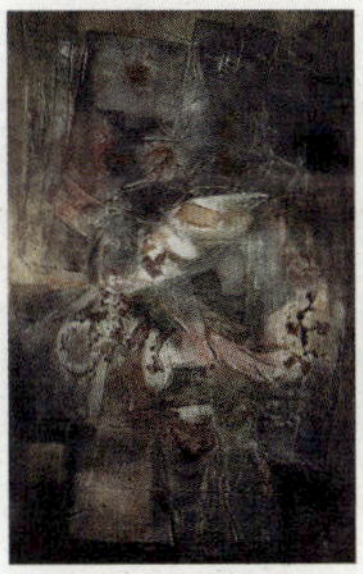

Canonico, Felice
1922 Messina–1997 Milan

Southern Climate
(Clima meridionale)
1959
Tempera, collage on canvas on plywood
120 x 75.5 cm
ML 76/3087

Galerie Änne Abels, Cologne. Purchased by WRM with funding from the Haubrich Fund, 1959.

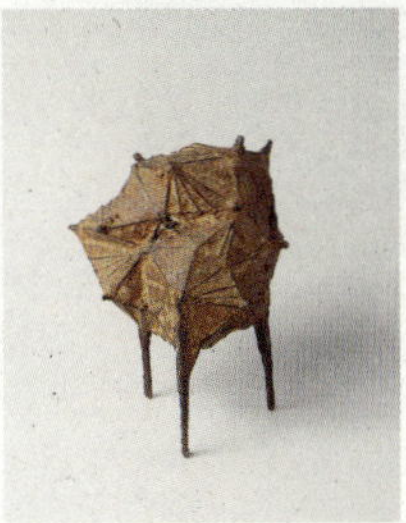

Chadwick, Lynn Russell
1914 London–2003 Stroud

Moon of Alabama
1957
Welded steel frame with filling of artificial stone
H.: 28.5 cm
ML 76/SK 215

Galerie Hella Nebelung, Düsseldorf. Purchased by WRM with funding from the Haubrich Fund, 1960.

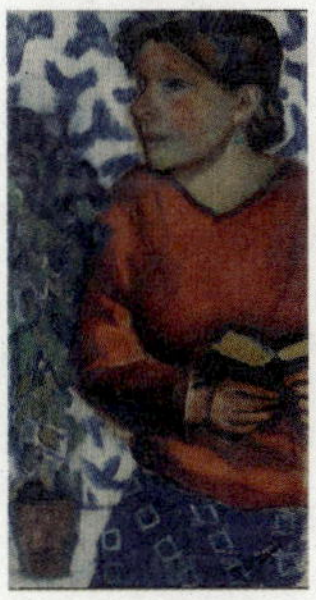

Chagall, Marc
1887 Vitebsk–
1985 Saint-Paul-de-Vence

Portrait of the Sister
1909
Oil on canvas
92.5 x 48 cm
ML 76/2736

In the possession of Münster publisher Johannes Bredt. Due to financial difficulties, placed for sale by Bredt with his friends the Nierendorf brothers in the late 1920s. Acquired by Haubrich from Karl Nierendorf in exchange for a landscape by Utrillo, 1931. Haubrich Donation, 1946.

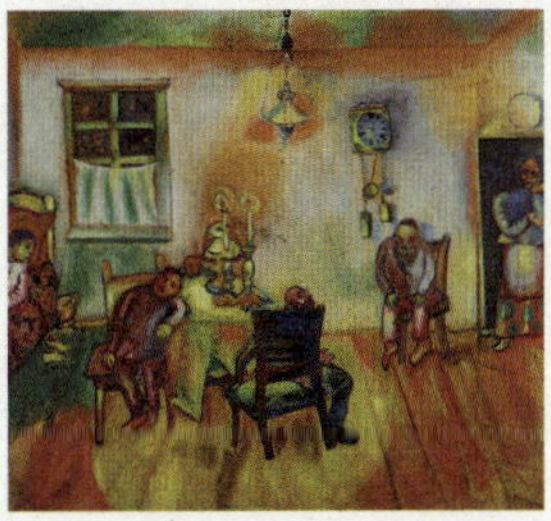

Sabbath
1910
Oil on canvas
90.5 x 94.5 cm
ML 76/2735

Purchased by Düsseldorf industrialist Paul Multhaupt from J. B. Neumann, Berlin. Multhaupt named as owner in the catalogue of the first "International Art Exhibition" in Düsseldorf, 1922. After his suicide on 19 January, 1933, the work was to be exhibited on 12 March, 1933, at Galerie Alfred Flechtheim, Düsseldorf. Purchased by Haubrich from Galerie Alex Vömel, Düsseldorf, several months later (for more on this, see Friedrich/Grafahrend-Gohmert, p. 20). Haubrich Donation, 1946.

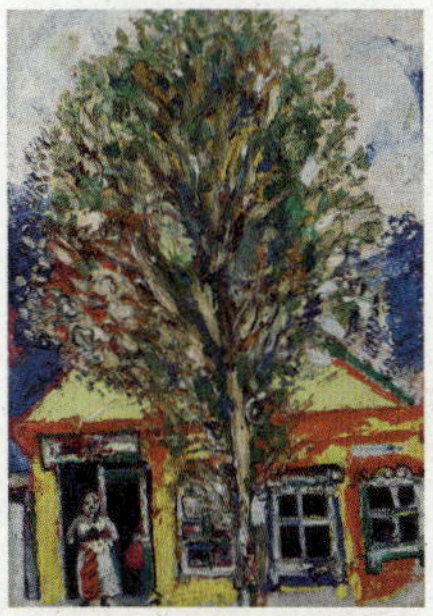

Yellow House
1924
Oil on canvas
54.7 x 37.8 cm
ML 76/2737

Purchased by Haubrich directly from the artist in preparation for a Chagall exhibition at the Kölnischer Kunstverein, 1925. Haubrich Donation, 1946.

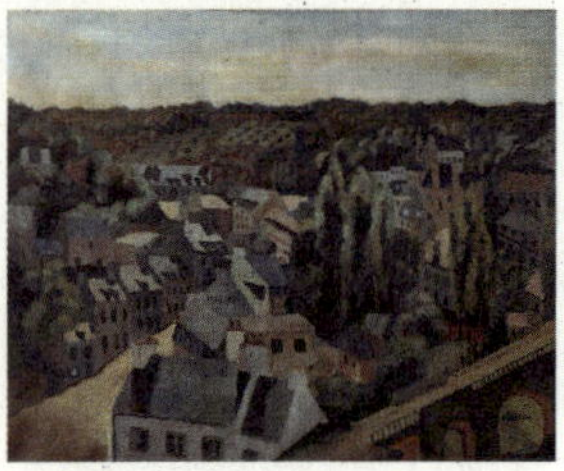

Clairin, Pierre Eugène
1897 Cambrai–
1980 Thorigné-en-Charnie

City View
C. 1926
Oil on canvas
60 x 73 cm
ML 76/2784

Purchased by Haubrich from Galerie Sigmund Salz, then located in Cologne, 1927. Mentioned by Luise Straus-Ernst in 'Die Sammlung Haubrich in Köln', *Das Kunstblatt* 11 (1927), p. 28. Haubrich Donation, 1946.

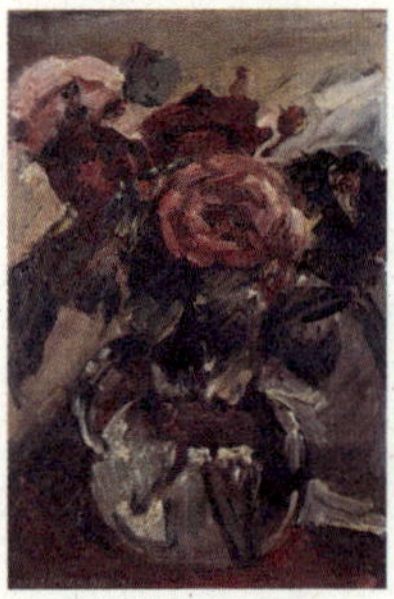

Corinth, Lovis
1858 Tapiau (today Gvardeysk)–1925 Zandvoort

Red Roses in a Glass Jug (Rote Rosen in einem Glaskrug)
1919
Oil on wood
54.5 x 36 cm
WRM 2785
Berend-Corinth/Hernad 761

Galerie Herbert Cramer, Frankfurt am Main. Kunsthaus Lempertz, Cologne. Haubrich Donation, 1946. Today WRM.

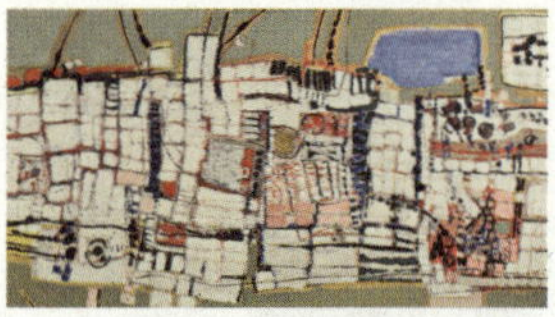

Corneille
1922 Liège–2010 Auvers-sur-Oise

The White City (La cité blanche)
1955
Oil on canvas
79 x 146 cm
ML 76/3085

Galerie Helios Art, Brussels. Purchased by WRM with funding from the Haubrich Fund, 1959.

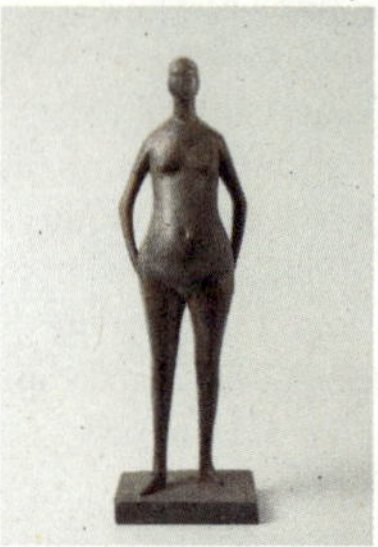

De Angelis, Giovanni
1938 Ischia, lives in Ischia

Pregnant Woman
1961
Stone cast
H.: 57.5 cm
ML 76/SK 202

Purchased by WRM directly from the artist with funding from the Haubrich Fund, 1961.

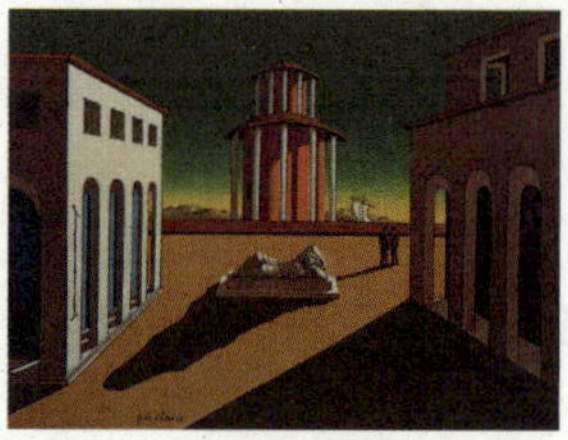

De Chirico, Giorgio
1888 Volos–1978 Rome

Piazza d'Italia
1956
Oil on canvas
55 x 70 cm
ML 76/2992

Galerie Christoph Czwiklitzer, Cologne. Purchased by WRM in part with funding from the Haubrich Fund, 1957.

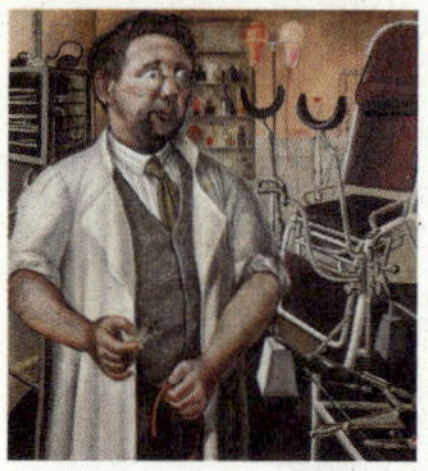

Dix, Otto
1891 Untermhaus (near Gera)–1969 Singen am Hohentwiel

Portrait of Doctor Hans Koch (Bildnis Doktor Hans Koch)
1921
Oil on canvas
100.5 x 90 cm
ML 76/2739
Löffler 1921/13

In the possession of the subject, Hans Koch, Düsseldorf, 1921. Sold by Koch via Galerie Nierendorf Köln – Neue Kunst to Haubrich, 1923. Haubrich Donation, 1946.

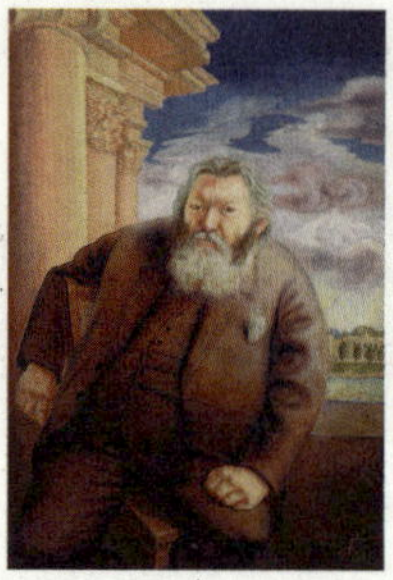

Portrait of the Poet Theodor Däubler (Bildnis des Dichters Theodor Däubler)

1927
Tempera on plywood
150 x 100 cm
ML 76/2738
Löffler 1927/9

Purchased for the new section of the Nationalgalerie in the Kronprinzenpalais, Berlin, 1928. Confiscated in 1937. Received on commission first by Wolfgang Gurlitt, Berlin, 1940, then by Bernhard Böhmer, Güstrow. Acquired by Hildebrand Gurlitt by way of exchange and sold to Haubrich, 1941. Haubrich Donation, 1946.

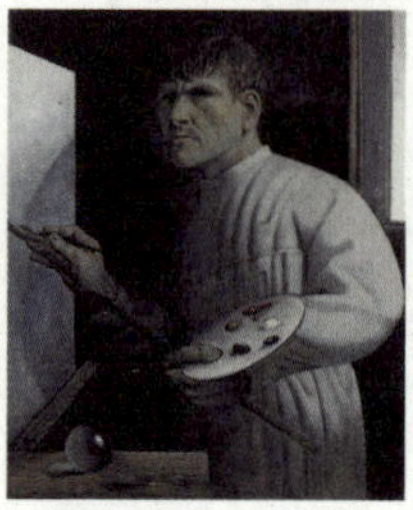

Self-portrait (Selbstbildnis)
1931
Oil, tempera on wood, doubled with canvas
100 x 80 cm
ML 76/2740
Löffler 1931/1

Submitted by the artist to the exhibition 'Rheingruppe',

Düsseldorf, and purchased there by Haubrich, 1932. Haubrich Donation, 1946.

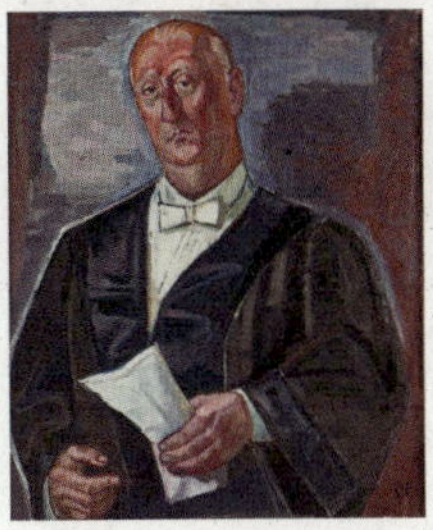

Portrait of Doctor Josef Haubrich (Bildnis Doktor Josef Haubrich)
1951
Oil on canvas
100 x 81 cm
ML 76/2869
Löffler 1951/6

Donated by Haubrich, 1951.

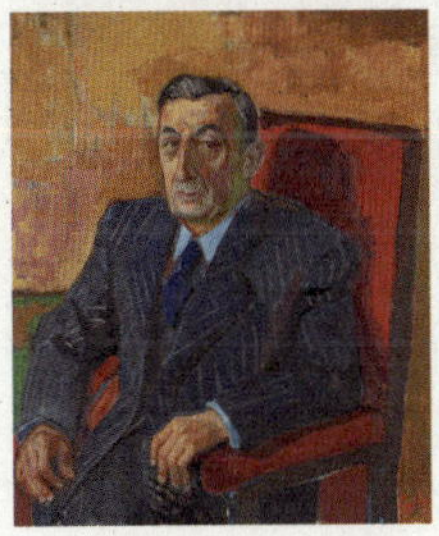

Portrait of Mayor Robert Görlinger (Bildnis Bürgermeister Robert Görlinger)
1951
Oil on canvas
100 x 81 cm
ML 76/2885
Löffler 1951/7

Commissioned by Haubrich, 1951, and donated to WRM that same year. On long-term loan to the Cologne City Museum.

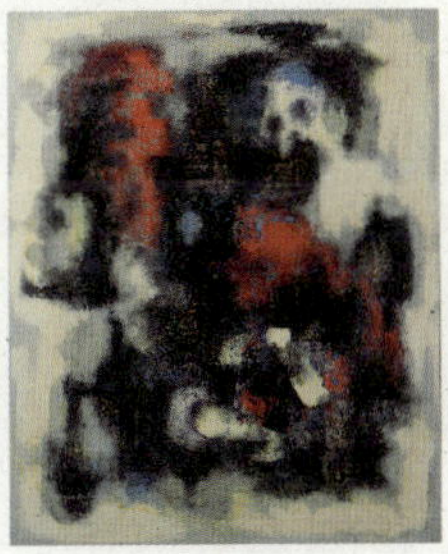

Dobashi, Jun-ichi

1910 Tokyo–1975 Tokyo

Fire Dance (La danse du feu)
1959
Oil on canvas
100 x 81 cm
ML 76/3090

Galerie Fricker, Paris. Purchased by WRM with funding from the Haubrich Fund, 1959.

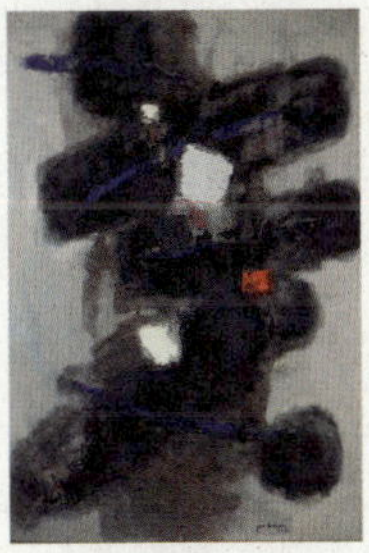

Red and Blue (Rouge et bleu)
1960
Oil on canvas
196 x 130 cm
ML 76/3126

Galerie Fricker, Paris. Purchased by WRM with funding from the Haubrich Fund, 1961.

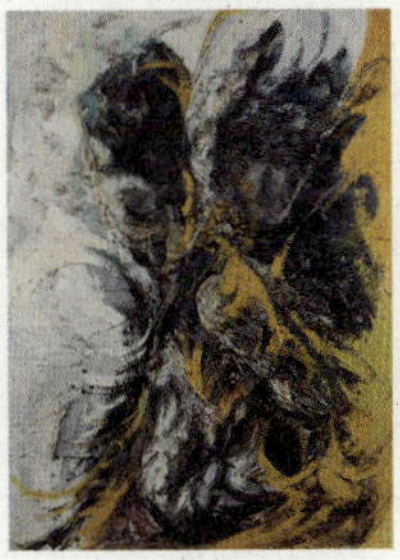

Dōmoto, Hisao

1928 Kyoto, lives in Kyoto

Painting No. 1
1958
Oil on canvas
162 x 114 cm
ML 76/3088

Galerie Rodolphe Stadler, Paris. Purchased by WRM with funding from the Haubrich Fund, 1960.

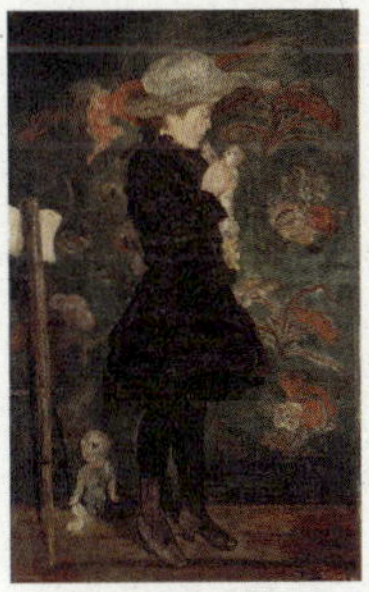

Ensor, James

1860 Ostend–1949 Ostend

Girl with Doll (Enfant à la poupée)
1884
Oil on canvas
149 x 91 cm
WRM 2742
Tricot 253

Acquired by Haubrich from Karl Nierendorf, Berlin, 1924. Nierendorf thought to have received the work from Joseph Burthoul, Brussels. Haubrich Donation, 1946. Today WRM.

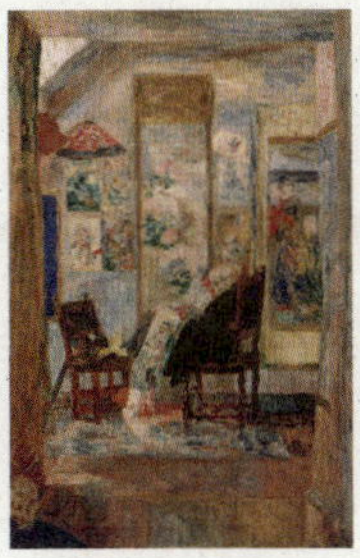

Skeleton Looking at Chinoiseries (Squelette regardant des chinoiseries)
1910
Oil on canvas
99.5 x 64.5 cm
WRM 2741

Acquired by Haubrich from Karl Nierendorf, Berlin, 1924. Nierendorf thought to have received the work from P. Desmedt, Brussels, about whom no further information has been found. Haubrich Donation, 1946. Today WRM.

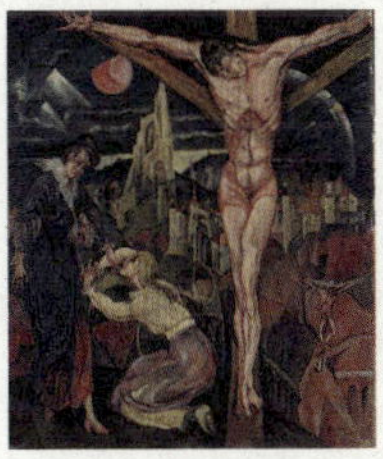

Ernst, Max

1891 Brühl–1976 Paris

Crucifixion (Kreuzigung)
1913
Oil on cardboard on plywood
50.5 x 43 cm
ML 76/2804
Spies 69

Purchased by WRM with funding from the Haubrich Fund, 1949. Previous ownership unknown.

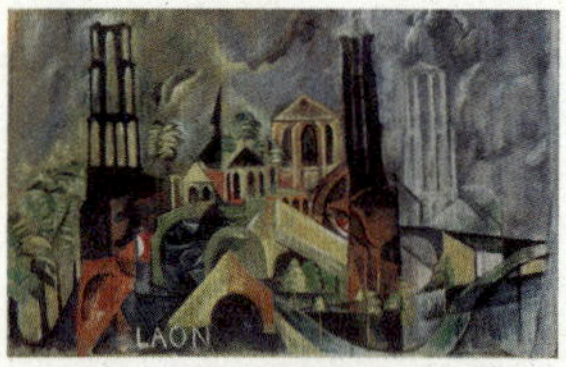

Laon
1916
Oil on canvas
65.5 x 100.5 cm
ML 76/2774
Spies 259

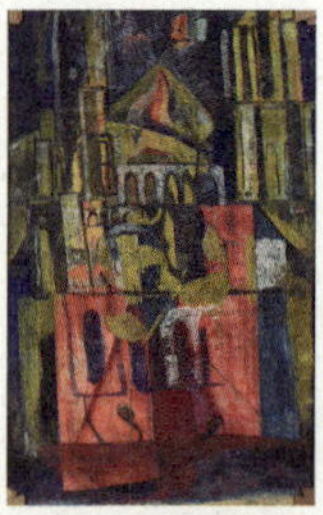

Verso:
Sketch, Façade, Cathedral of Laon (Skizze der Fassade der Kathedrale von Laon)
1916
Oil on canvas
100.5 x 65.5 cm
ML 76/2774
Spies 260

Purchased by Haubrich from E.'s friend Alfred Salmony, Cologne, 1931. Haubrich Donation, 1946.

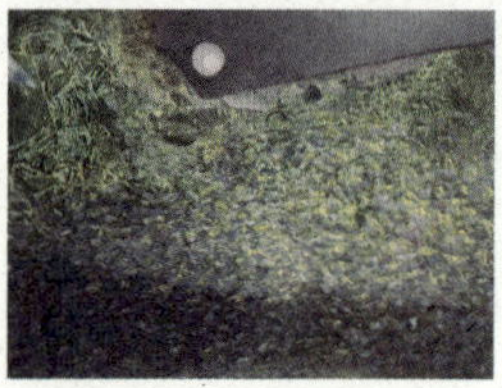

Song of the Cicadas to the Moon (Sauterelles à la lune)
1953
Oil on canvas
88.5 x 116 cm
ML 76/2900
Spies 3029

Michael Hertz, Bremen. Galerie der Spiegel, Cologne. Purchased by WRM with funding from the Haubrich Fund, 1953.

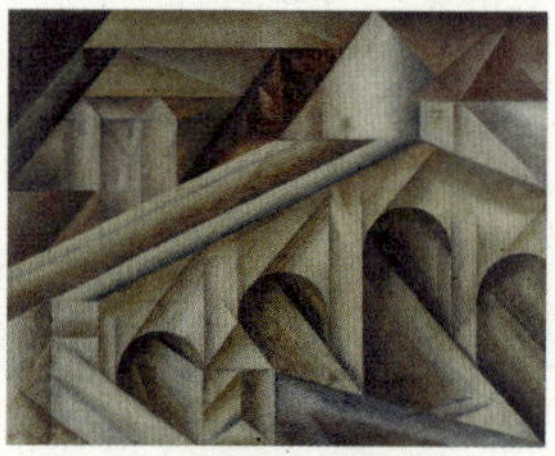

Feininger, Lyonel
1871 New York–1956 New York

Bridge III (Brücke III)
1917
Oil on canvas
80.5 x 100 cm
ML 76/2865
Hess 174

Owned by Walter Kaesbach prior to 1919, according to F.'s second wife, Julia. Labelled as a loan from Kaesbach at the Feininger exhibition at Berlin's Nationalgalerie in 1931. Purchased by WRM from Paula Hess and Kaesbach in Hemmenhofen with funding from the Haubrich Fund, 1950.

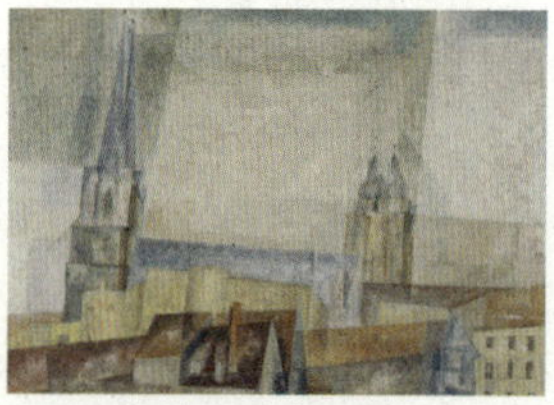

Towers above the City (Halle) (Türme über der Stadt [Halle])
1931
Oil on canvas
88.3 x 124 cm
ML 76/2889
Hess 341

Purchased on commission by the City of Halle for the Moritzburg City Museum, 1931. Confiscated in 1937. Exchanged by Ferdinand Möller, 1940. Purchased by WRM from Möller with funding from the Haubrich Fund, 1952.

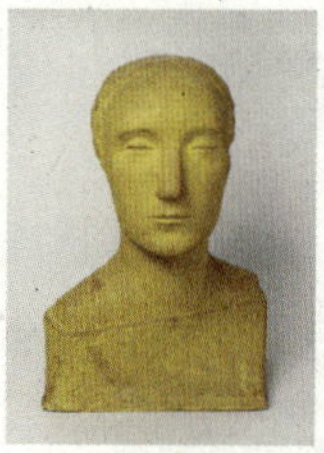

Freundlich, Otto
1878 Stolp (today Słupsk)–1943 Lublin-Majdanek Concentration Camp

Bust of a Woman (Frauenbüste)
1910
Plaster, painted yellow
H.: 52 cm
ML 76/SK 97

Other editions of the bust were sold at the Sonderbund exhibition, Cologne, 1912. This plaster version, however, could not be traced back to this point. Haubrich Donation, 1946.

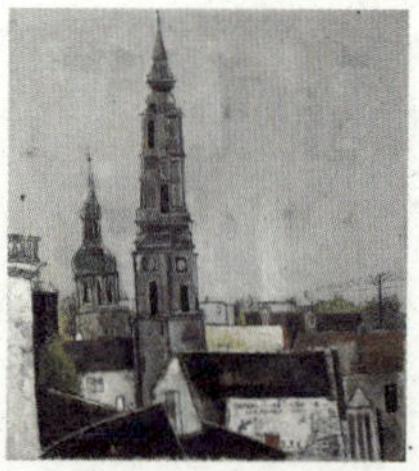

Fuhr, Xaver
1898 Neckarau–1973 Regensburg

City View (Stadtansicht)
C. 1928
Oil on canvas
82 x 71 cm
ML 76/2744
Zienicke 34

Purchased by Haubrich from Karl Nierendorf, Berlin, who received it directly from the artist, 1928. Haubrich Donation, 1946.

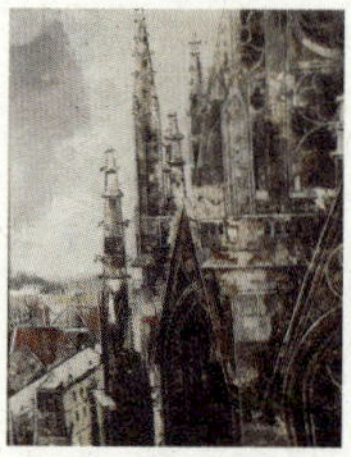

Gothic Cathedral (Gotische Kathedrale)
C. 1928
Oil on canvas
97.5 x 77 cm
ML 76/2745
Zienicke 35

Purchased by Haubrich from Karl Nierendorf, Berlin, who received it directly from the artist, 1931. Haubrich Donation, 1946.

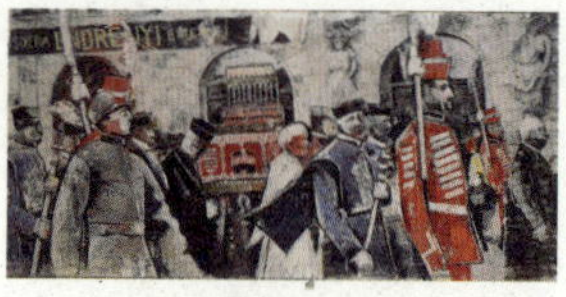

Procession of St. Stephen (Stefansprozession)
1929/30
Oil on canvas
100 x 200 cm
ML 76/2743
Zienicke 75

Purchased by Haubrich from Karl Nierendorf, Berlin, who received it directly from the artist, 1930. Haubrich Donation, 1946.

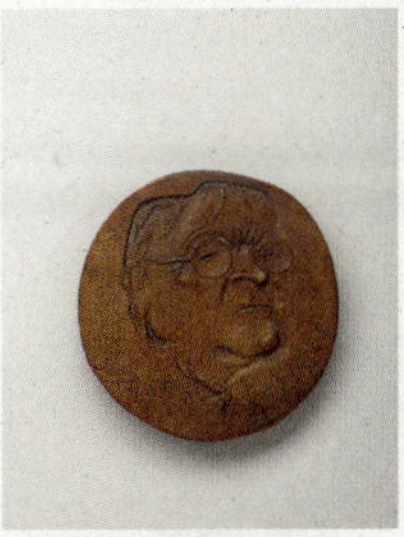

Gies, Ludwig
1887 Munich–1966 Cologne

Jan Thorn Prikker
C. 1928
Bronze
H.: 8.5 cm, W.: 8.0 cm
ML 76/SK 114
Ernsting 237

Purchased by WRM directly from the artist with funding from the Haubrich Fund, 1952.

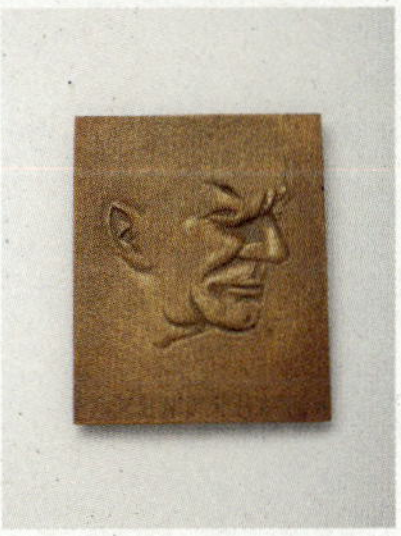

Edmund Körner
1928–30
Bronze
H.: 10.8 cm, W.: 8.4 cm
ML 76/SK 113
Ernsting 245

Purchased by WRM directly from the artist with funding from the Haubrich Fund, 1952.

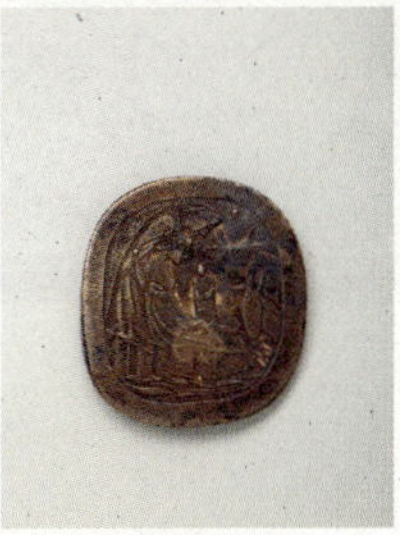

Holy Family (Heilige Familie)
1942
Silver
H.: 8.5 cm, W.: 7.5 cm
ML 76/SK 112
Ernsting 289

Purchased by WRM directly from the artist with funding from the Haubrich Fund, 1952.

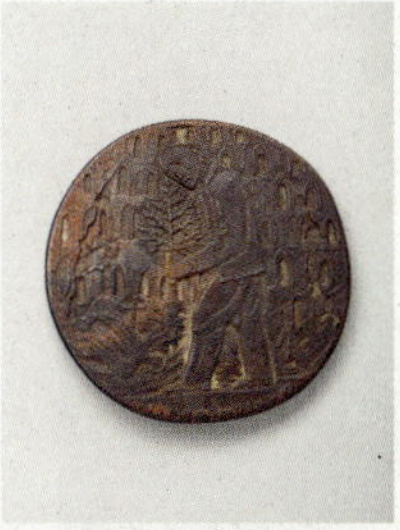

Christmas (Weihnacht)
1947
Bronze
H.: 12.2 cm, W.: 11.8 cm
ML 76/SK 111
Ernsting 320

Purchased by WRM directly from the artist with funding from the Haubrich Fund, 1952.

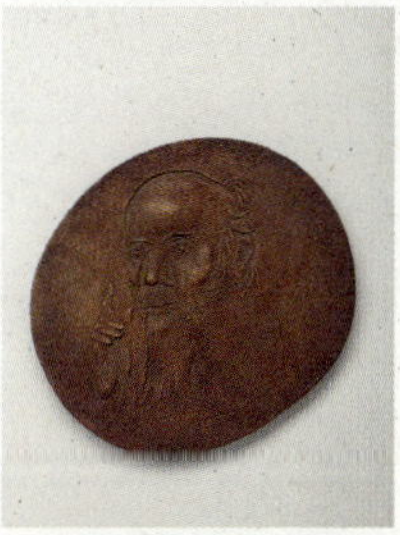

Dominikus Böhm
1950
Bronze
H.: 12.8 cm, W.: 13.8 cm
ML 76/SK 115
Ernsting 339

Purchased by WRM directly from the artist with funding from the Haubrich Fund, 1952.

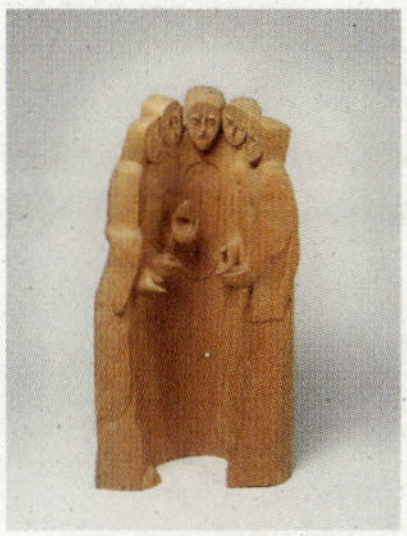

Council (Beratung)
1953
Oakwood
H.: 78 cm
ML 76/SK 143

Purchased by WRM with funding from the Haubrich Fund, 1955.

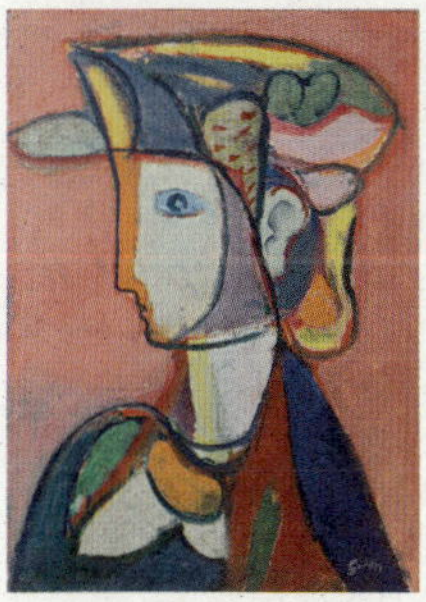

Gilles, Werner
1894 Rheydt–1961 Essen

Greek (Die Griechin)
1947
Oil on cardboard
51 x 36.4 cm
ML 76/2791
Schwengers G 218

Galerie Günther Franke, Munich. Purchased by WRM with funding from the Haubrich Fund, 1948.

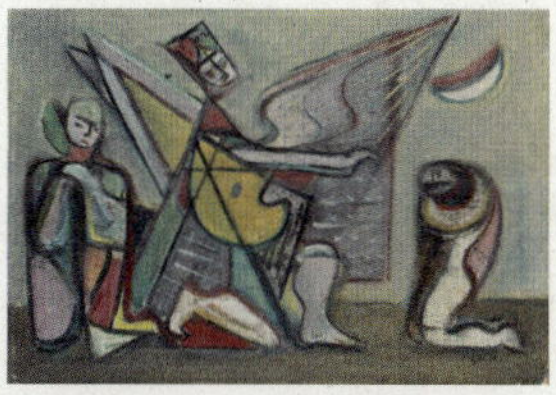

Annunciation (Verkündigung)
1948
Oil on canvas
45 x 65 cm
ML 76/2801

Kölnischer Kunstverein. Purchased by WRM with funding from the Haubrich Fund, 1948.

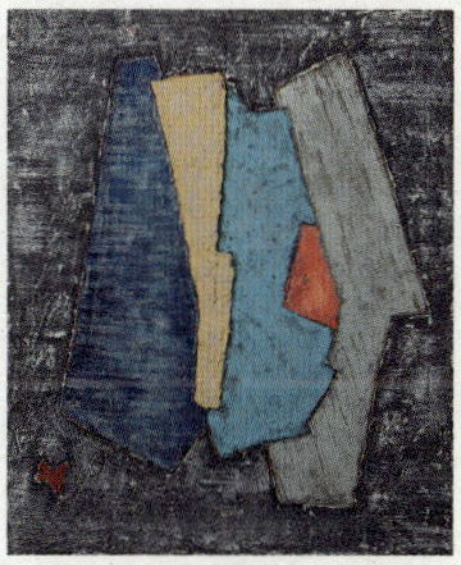

Graeff, Werner
1901 Wuppertal–
1978 Blacksburg, Virginia

Composition
1953
Oil on canvas
76.5 x 62.5 cm
ML 76/2953

Galerie Christoph Czwiklitzer, Cologne. Purchased by WRM with funding from the Haubrich Fund, 1954.

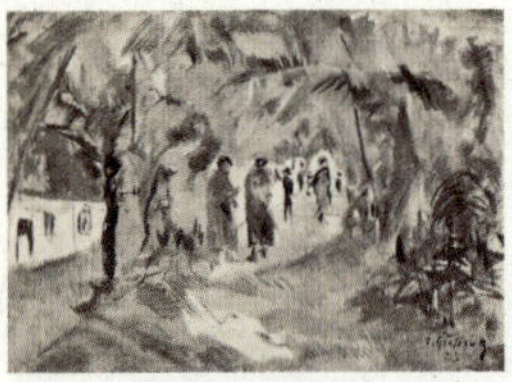

Greferath, Johannes
1872 Schelsen–1964 Cologne

Park in Sevilla
1923
Oil on canvas
46 x 64.5 cm
WRM 1222

Donated by Haubrich to WRM, 1923. Transferred to Schloss Gaibach during the war, 1943. Found to be missing at the time of its return to Cologne and considered lost.

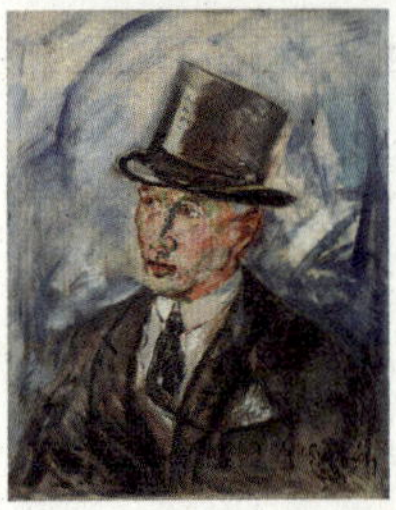

Portrait of Doctor Josef Haubrich (Bildnis Doktor Josef Haubrich)
1923
Oil on canvas
81 x 63 cm
ML 76/3111

Given to WRM in 1961 by the Haubrich family.

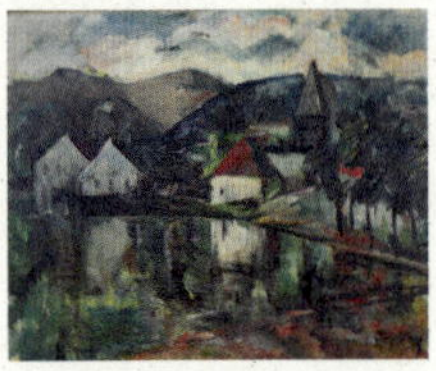

Landscape (Landschaft)
C. 1928
Oil on canvas
63 x 74 cm
ML 76/2808

Donated by Haubrich, 1948.

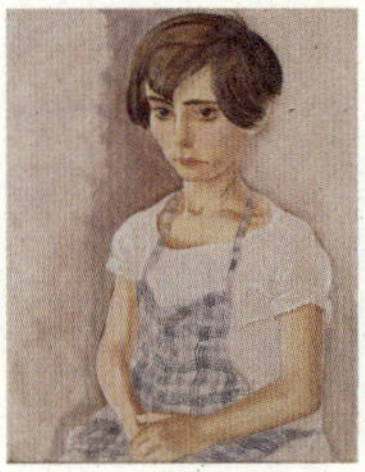

Grosz, George
1893 Berlin–1959 Berlin

Young Spanish Girl (Junge Spanierin)
1927
Oil on canvas
65.5 x 50.8 cm
ML 76/2856

Titled *Junge Spanierin* by G. and placed by the artist on commission with Alfred Flechtheim in 1927. Purchased by WRM with funding from the Haubrich Fund, 1950. According to G.'s estate, the artist was not paid for the work. The inventory book includes a later reference to intermediary owner Moritz Bing. Despite extensive research, it remains unknown how Bing got hold of the work or from whom WRM purchased it.

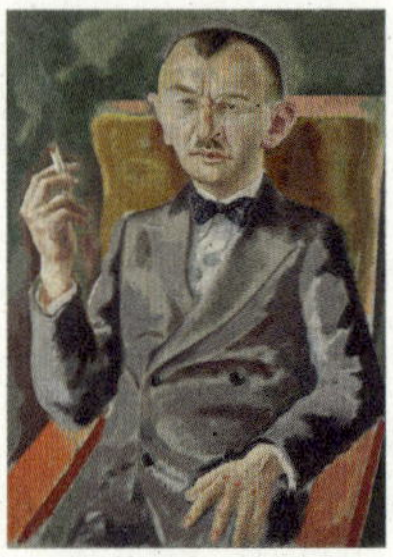

Portrait of Doctor Eduard Plietzsch (Bildnis Doktor Eduard Plietzsch)
1928
Oil on canvas
110 x 79.5 cm
ML 76/2814

Purchased for the Staatliche Gemäldegalerie Dresden by the museum's patronage society, 1929. Confiscated in 1937. Brought by Rolf Hetsch to Bernhard Böhmer in Güstrow, 1943/44. After Böhmer's suicide, inventoried with his estate on 3 May 1945. Submitted for auction on 11 April 1949 to Stuttgarter Kunstkabinett Roman Norbert Ketterer, Auction 5, Lot no. 1239, by estate administrator Wilma Zelck, Böhmer's sister-in-law. Purchased at auction by WRM with funding from the Haubrich Fund, 1949.

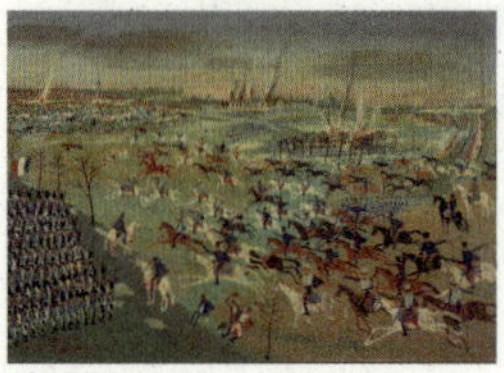

Guérin, Armand Marie
1913 France–1983 France

Battle of Waterloo
n. d.
Oil on fibreboard
78 x 106 cm
ML 76/3006

Galerie Hella Nebelung, Düsseldorf. Purchased by WRM with funding from the Haubrich Fund, 1957.

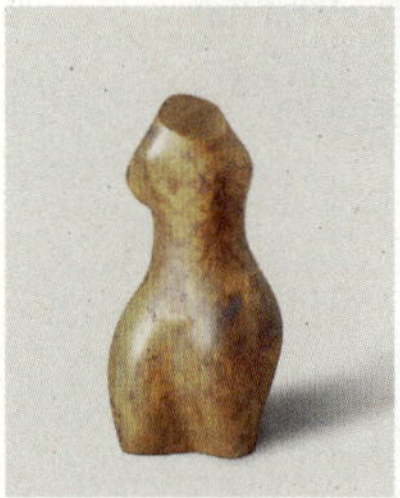

Hartung, Karl
1908 Hamburg–1967 Berlin

Female Torso (Weiblicher Torso)
C. 1939
Brass
H.: 24 cm
ML 76/SK 196

According to information provided by the artist, this cast was made after the Second World War and purchased by WRM with funding from the Haubrich Fund, 1961.

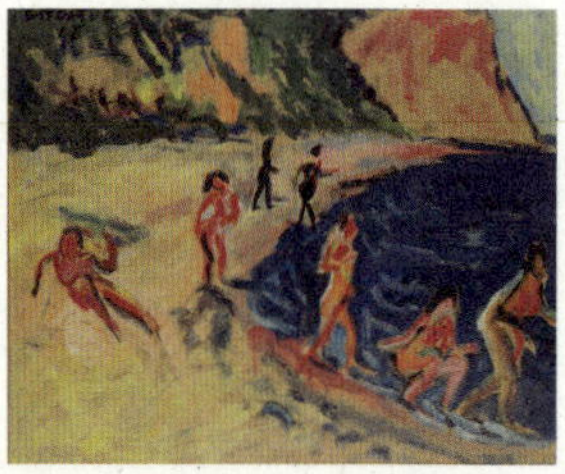

Heckel, Erich
1883 Döbeln–1970 Radolfzell

Beach (Strand)
1912
Oil on canvas
70.5 x 81 cm
ML 76/2748
Hüneke 1912/28

H. Richter, most likely the artist and filmmaker Hans Richter, received this work, titled *Strand* on verso by H., from Galerie Hans Goltz. Both Richter and H. exhibited with Goltz in 1916. It remains unknown how the work came to Cologne's Dom-Galerie. Purchased there by Haubrich, 1932. Haubrich Donation, 1946.

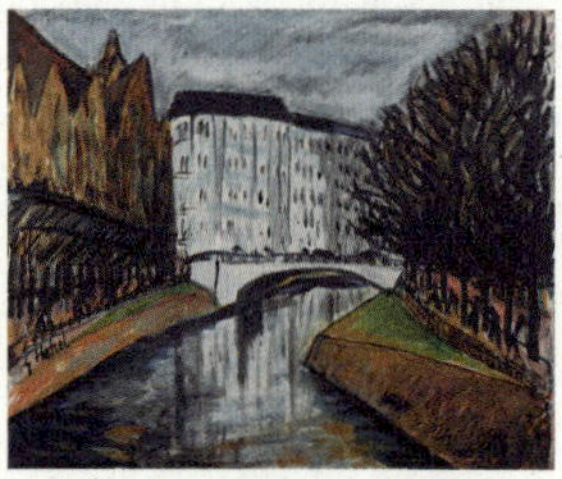

Canal (Kanal)
1912
Oil on canvas
83 x 100 cm
ML 76/2746
Hüneke 1912/62

Titled *Kanal* on verso by H. In the collection of the Kunsthalle Bremen since 1913. Confiscated as 'degenerate' in 1937. Entered the possession of Hildebrand Gurlitt, 1941, and sold to Haubrich, 1942. Haubrich Donation, 1946.

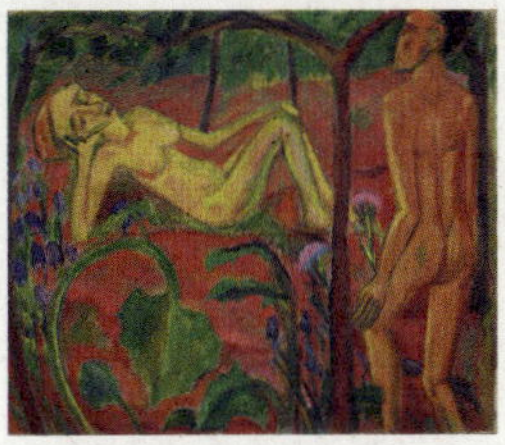

Forest Scene (Szene im Wald)
1913
Oil on canvas
70 x 80.8 cm
ML 76/2747
Hüneke 1913/36

Purchased by Haubrich from Franz Nienhaus, Cologne, 1925. Haubrich Donation, 1946.

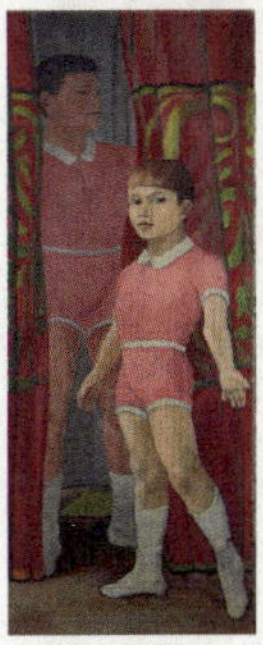

The Bedini-Tafanis
(Die Bedini-Tafani)
1928
Oil on canvas on wood
165.7 x 65.5 cm
ML 76/2787
Hüneke 1928/3

Titled on verso by the artist *Die Bedini Taffani* [sic] after the circus troupe. Lent to WRM by H. and purchased directly from him months later with funding from the city and the Haubrich Fund, 1948.

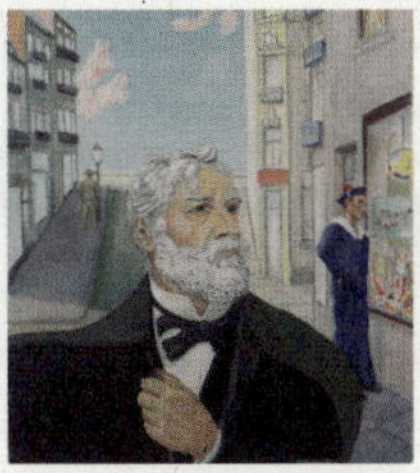

Portrait of James Ensor
(Bildnis James Ensor)
1930
Oil on canvas
80 x 70 cm
ML 76/2786
Hüneke 1930/2

Lent to WRM by H. and purchased directly from him months later with funding from the city and the Haubrich Fund, 1948.

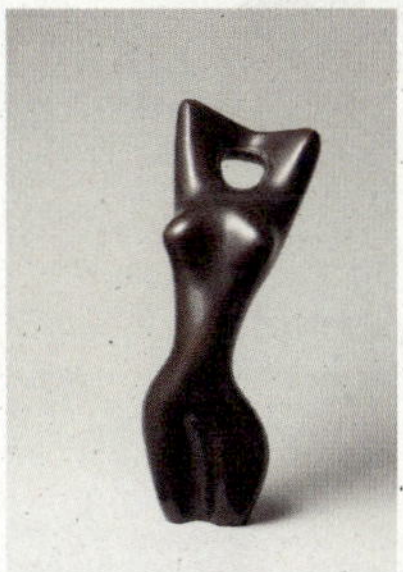

Heiliger, Bernhard

1915 Stettin (today Szczecin)–1995 Berlin

Figure with Arms Raised
(Figur mit erhobenen Armen)
1949
Bronze
H.: 26.5 cm
ML 76/SK 141
Salzmann/Romain 17

Galerie Christoph Czwiklitzer, Cologne. Purchased by WRM with funding from the Haubrich Fund, 1956.

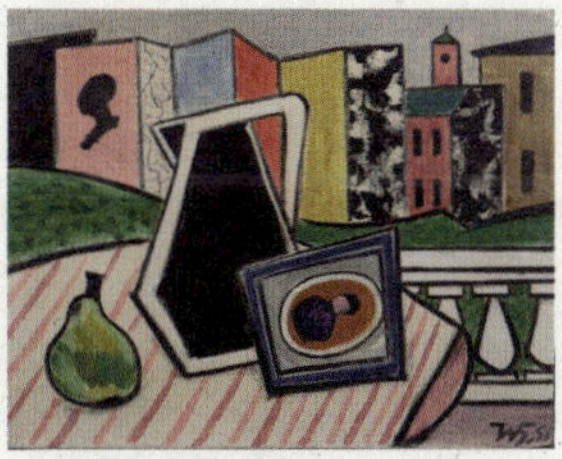

Heldt, Werner

1904 Berlin–1954 Sant'Angelo

Still Life on a Balcony
(Stilleben auf dem Balkon)
1951
Oil on canvas
57 x 71 cm
ML 76/3078
Schmied/Seel 703

Galerie Hella Nebelung, Düsseldorf. Purchased by WRM with funding from the Haubrich Fund, 1959.

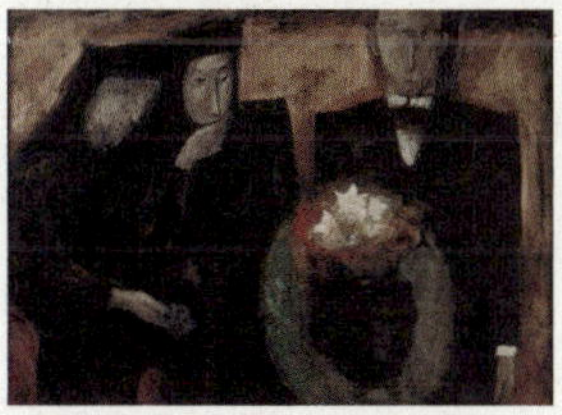

Herkenrath, Peter

1900 Cologne–1992 Mainz

Mourners (Trauergesellschaft)
C. 1946
Oil on canvas
100.5 x 146.5 cm
ML 76/2810

Purchased by WRM with funding from the Haubrich Fund, 1947.

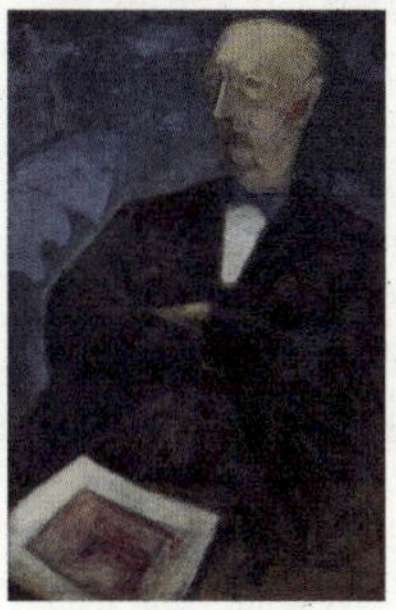

Portrait of Doctor Josef Haubrich
(Bildnis Doktor Josef Haubrich)
1949
Oil on canvas
109.5 x 70.5 cm
ML 76/2870

Donated by Haubrich, 1951.

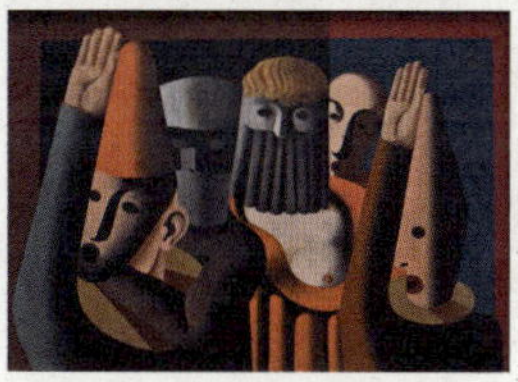

Hoerle, Heinrich

1895 Cologne–1936 Cologne

Carnival (Fastnacht)
1929
Oil on canvas
68.5 x 95.5 cm
ML 76/2776

Under the title *Maskenbild* (*Mask Painting*), purchased in 1929 by Haubrich from the Cologne Kunsthandlung Dr. Becker & Newman, who showed a Hoerle exhibtion from December to January. H. himself noted the title *Fastnacht* on a photograph of the painting. Haubrich Donation, 1946.

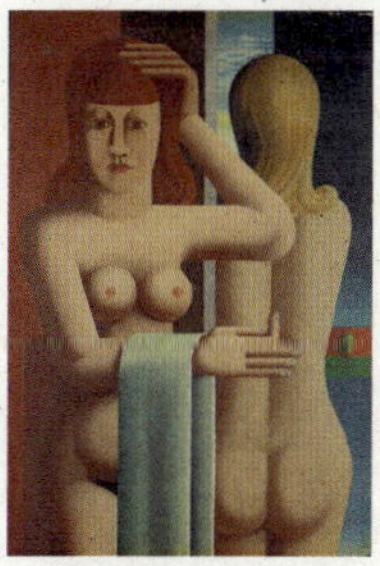

Two Women
(Zwei Frauen)
1930
Oil on plywood
108 x 73 cm
ML 76/2880

Titled *Zwei Frauen* on verso by H. Purchased by Haubrich at the artist's September exhibition at the Kölnischer Kunstverein, 1932. Haubrich Donation, 1946.

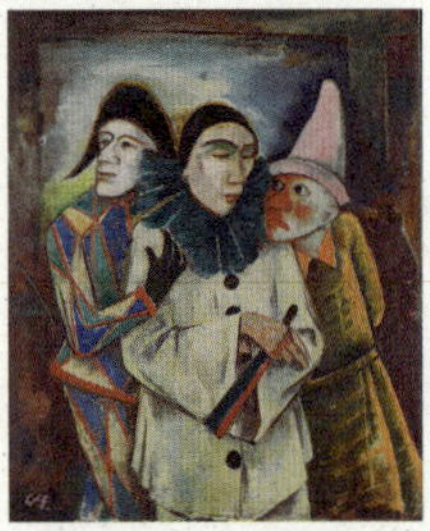

Hofer, Karl
1878 Karlsruhe–1955 Berlin

Masquerade
(Maskerade)
1922
Oil on canvas
129 x 103 cm
ML 76/2750
Eisenbeis/Wohlert 499

Titled *Maskerade* on verso by H. Purchased by City of Düsseldorf art collections at the city's 'International Art Exhibition' (Haus L. Tietz), 1922. Confiscated in 1937. Held on commission by Karl Buchholz, 1939. Entered possession of Hildebrand Gurlitt, 1940, and sold to Haubrich, 1942. Haubrich Donation, 1946.

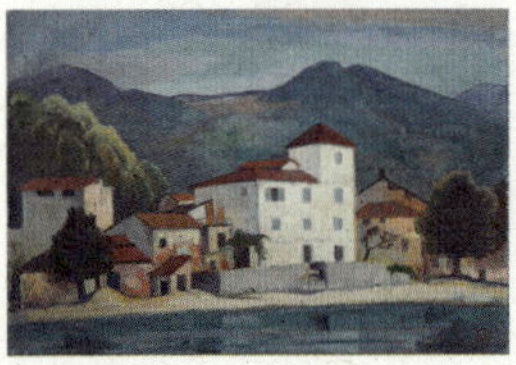

Large Ticino Landscape / Caslano
(Grosse Tessinlandschaft / Caslano)
1925
Oil on canvas
70.2 x 100 cm
ML 76/2749
Eisenbeis/Wohlert 664

Titled *Caslano* on verso. Purchased by Cologne businessman Berthold Levy from Galerie Alfred Flechtheim in Düsseldorf, 1928. Purchased by Haubrich from Kunsthaus Lempertz, 1931, where Levy had his extensive glass collection auctioned in the same year. Haubrich Donation, 1946.

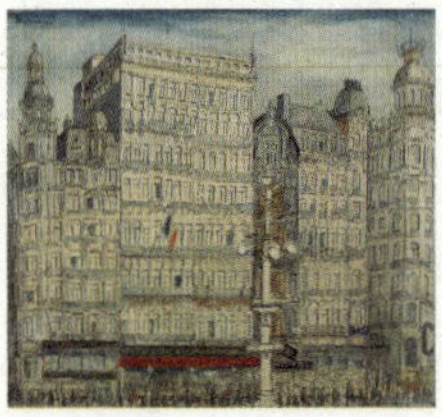

Hussmann, Heinrich August
1899 Stassfurt–1987 Cologne

Ostend (Ostende)
1934
Oil on canvas
48.5 x 52.5 cm
ML 76/3089

Purchased by WRM directly from the artist with funding from the Haubrich Fund, 1959.

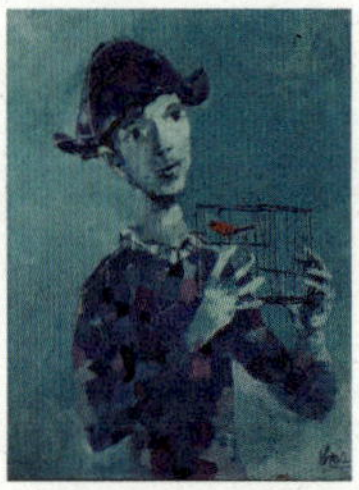

Ibarz, Miguel
1920 Mequinenza/Saragossa–1987 Barcelona

Harlequin with Birdcage
(Arlequín jaula)
Before 1961
Oil on canvas
81 x 60 cm
ML 76/3131

Kunstkabinett Hanna Bekker vom Rath, Frankfurt am Main. Purchased by WRM with funding from the Haubrich Fund, 1961.

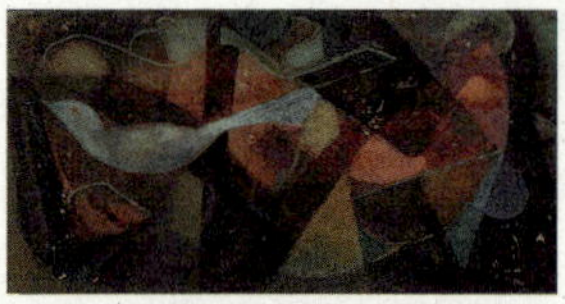

Imkamp, Wilhelm
1906 Münster–1990 Stuttgart

Nightingale (Nachtigall)
1948
Oil on cardboard
21 x 39 cm
ML 76/2867

Purchased by WRM with funding from the Haubrich Fund, 1950.

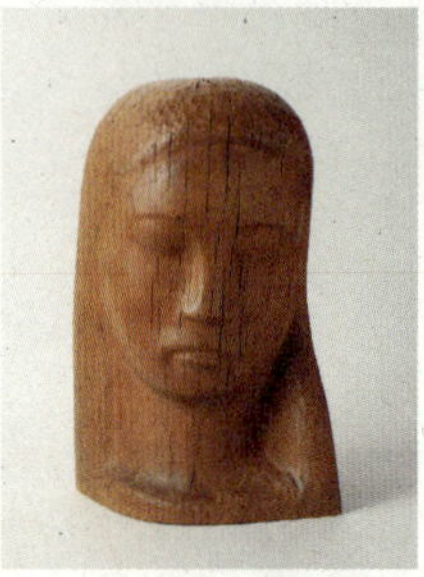

Jaekel, Joseph
1907 Wallmenroth–1985 Cologne

Head of a Girl (Mädchenkopf)
1948
Oakwood
H.: 39 cm
ML 76/SK 87

Donated by Haubrich, 1949.

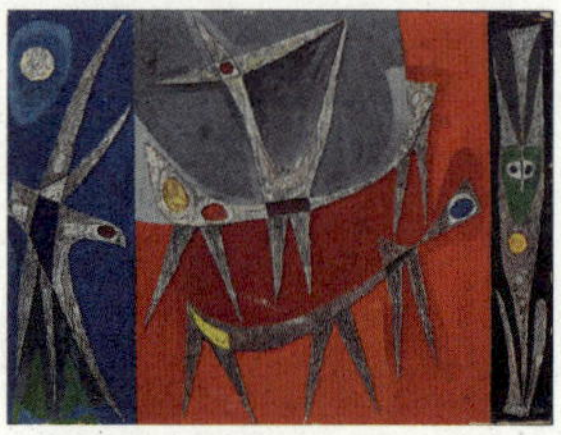

Jaenisch, Hans
1907 Eilenstedt–1989 Amrum

Signs of March (Märzbote)
1951
Oil on fibreboard
75 x 100 cm
ML 76/2966

Galerie Christoph Czwiklitzer, Cologne. Purchased by WRM with funding from the Haubrich Fund, 1955.

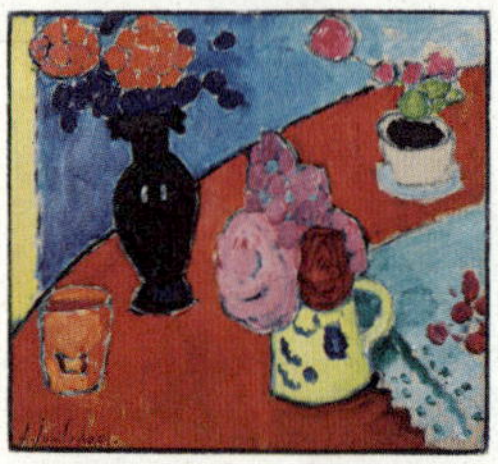

Jawlensky, Alexej von
1864 Torzhok–1941 Wiesbaden

Still Life with Vase and Jug
(Stilleben mit Vase und Krug)
1909
Oil, graphite on cardboard
43.5 x 49.5 cm
ML 76/2725
Jawlensky 299

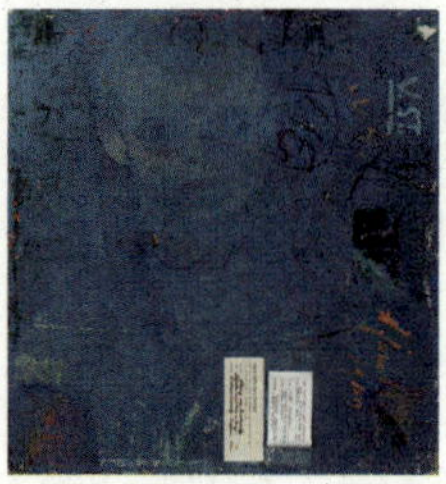

Verso:
Sketch of a woman's head, painted over (Skizze eines Frauenkopfes, übermalt)

1909
Oil on cardboard
49.5 x 43.5 cm
ML 76/2725
Jawlensky 299v

Received from the artist by his friend Hanna Bekker vom Rath, Frankfurt am Main, 1929. Purchased there by WRM with funding from the Haubrich Fund, 1947.

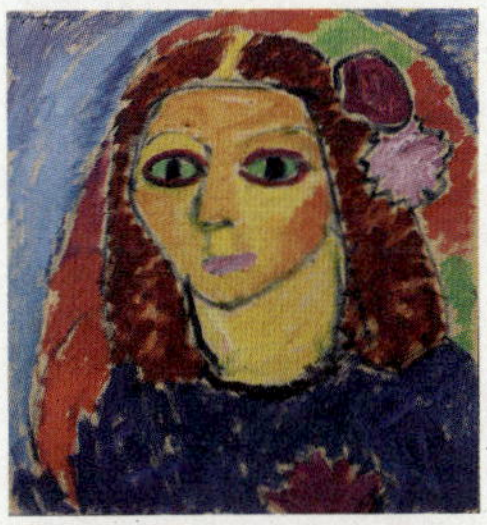

Head of a Woman with Flowers in Her Hair (Frauenkopf mit Blumen im Haar)
1911
Oil on cardboard
53.8 x 49.6 cm
ML 76/2864
Jawlensky 404

Purchased by WRM from Luise Braun, Kaiserslautern, with funding from the Haubrich Fund, 1951. Luise Braun is perhaps related by blood or marriage to another Jawlensky collector, Dr. Braun, to whom he dedicated the drawing *Reclining Nude* (*Liegender Akt*, 1913): 'Dear esteemed Doctor Braun, cordially remembered.' No additional information could be found about Dr. Braun or Luise Braun.

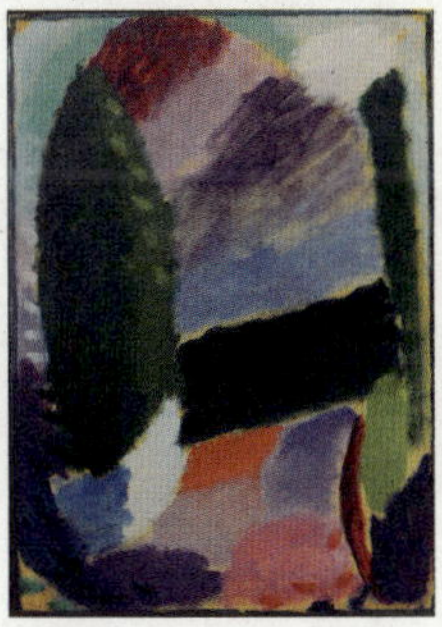

Variation
1916
Oil on canvas board
37.8 x 26.2 cm
ML 76/3024
Jawlensky 762

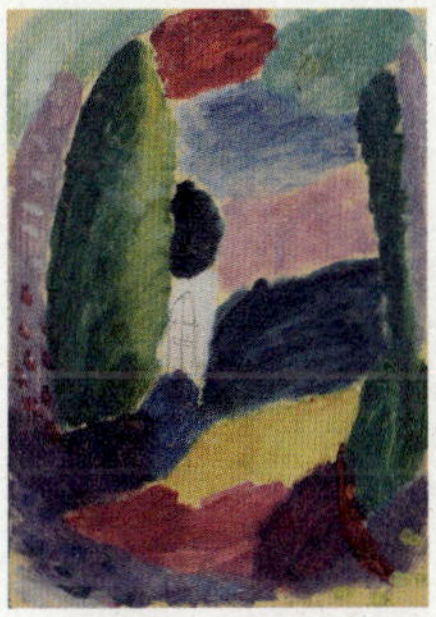

Verso:
Variation
C. 1916
Oil, graphite on canvas board
37.8 x 26.2 cm
ML 76/3024
Jawlensky 762v

Donated by Haubrich, 1958. The inventory book notes 'from old holdings of the Haubrich collection', indicating that Haubrich had owned the work for some time. It has not been possible to establish the work's provenance nor where Haubrich purchased it.

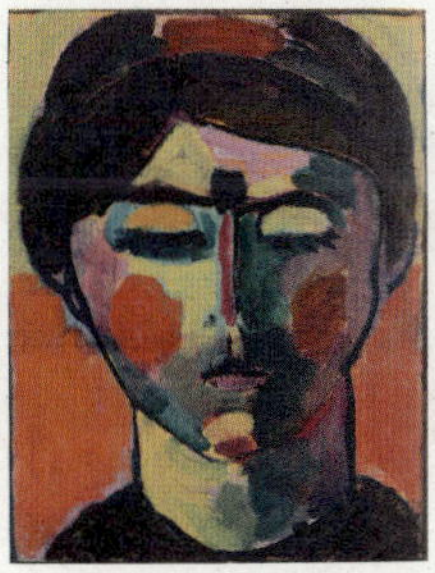

Head of a Woman (Frauenkopf)
C. 1917
Oil on canvas board
36.2 x 27.2 cm
ML 76/2960
Jawlensky 857

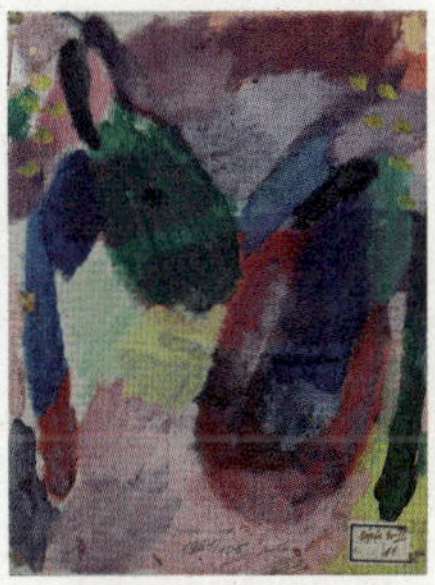

Verso:
Unfinished 'Variation'
C. 1916
Oil on canvas board
36.2 x 27.2 cm
ML 76/2960
Jawlensky 857v

Galerie Hella Nebelung, Düsseldorf. Purchased by WRM with funding from the Haubrich Fund, 1950.

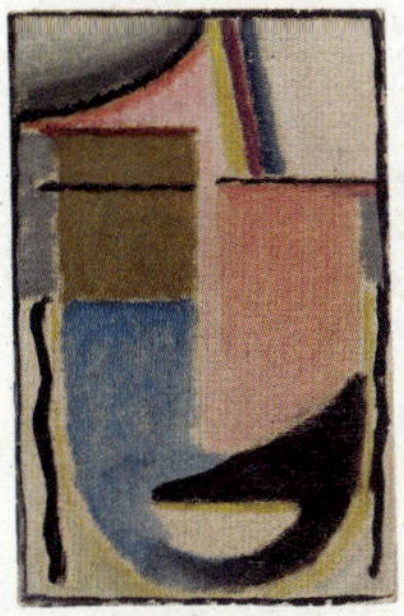

Constructivist Head (Konstruktiver Kopf)
1930
Oil on cardboard
20.5 x 13 cm
ML 76/3007
Jawlensky 1342

Galerie Christoph Czwiklitzer, Cologne. Purchased by WRM with funding from the Haubrich Fund, 1957.

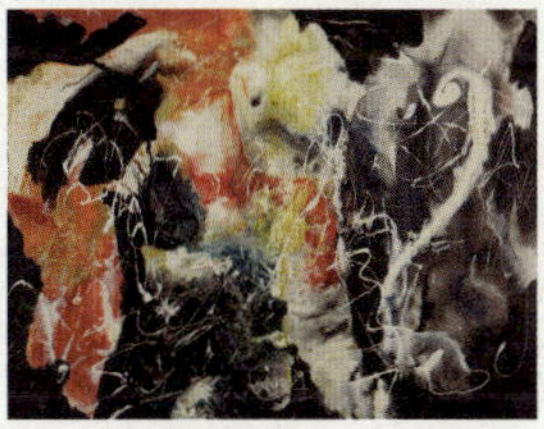

Jenkins, Paul
1923 Kansas City–2012 New York

Star Shepherd
1957
Oil on canvas
114 x 146 cm
ML 76/3010

Galerie Christoph Czwiklitzer, Cologne. Purchased by WRM with funding from the Haubrich Fund, 1957.

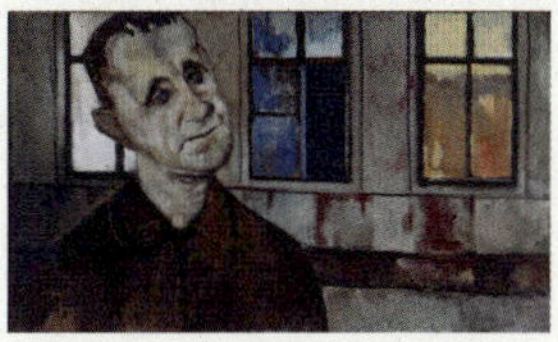

Kallmann, Hans Jürgen
1908 Wollstein–1991 Pullach

Portrait of Bert Brecht (Bildnis Bert Brecht)
1956
Oil on canvas
73 x 121 cm
ML 76/3013

Purchased by WRM directly from the artist with funding from the Haubrich Fund, 1957. On permanent loan to the Kallmann Museum, Ismaning.

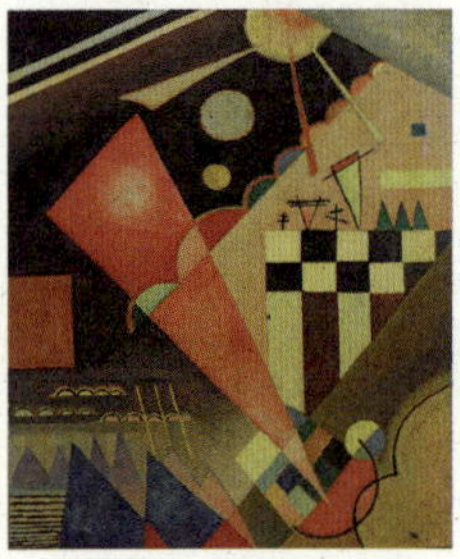

Kandinsky, Wassily
1866 Moscow–
1944 Neuilly-sur-Seine

Sharp-Calm Pink
(Das scharfruhige Rosa)
1924
Oil on cardboard
63.6 x 48.2 cm
ML 76/2881
Roethel/Benjamin 716

Included, under the title *Das scharfeckige Rosa* (*Sharp-Edged Pink*), in the catalogue of the exhibition held by Galerie Ernst Arnold, Dresden, for Kandinsky's sixtieth birthday, 1926. The owner was listed as Friedrich Bienert, who purchased it from the gallery at an earlier date. Sold by Bienert, through Galerie Werner Rusche, Cologne, to finance his move from Dresden to Munich, and purchased by WRM with funding from the Haubrich Fund, 1952.

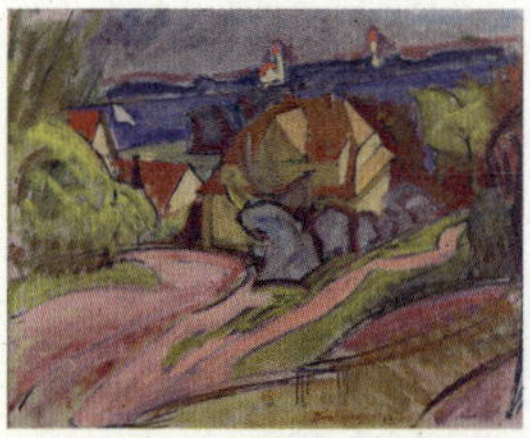

Kerschbaumer, Anton
1855 Rosenheim–1931 Berlin

View of Schwanenwerder
(Blick auf Schwanenwerder)
1922
Oil on canvas
73 x 92.5 cm
ML 76/2778
Wetzel-Kerschbaumer G 1922/1

Haubrich Donation, 1946. Previous ownership could not be determined.

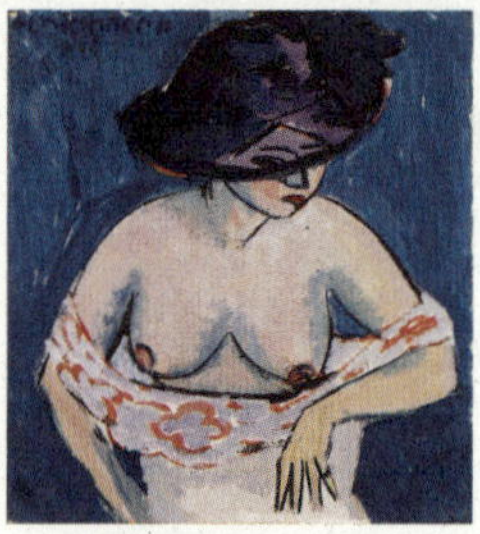

Kirchner, Ernst Ludwig
1880 Aschaffenburg–1938 Davos

Female Half-Length Nude with Hat (Weiblicher Halbakt mit Hut)
1911
Oil on canvas
76 x 70 cm
ML 76/2752
Gordon 180

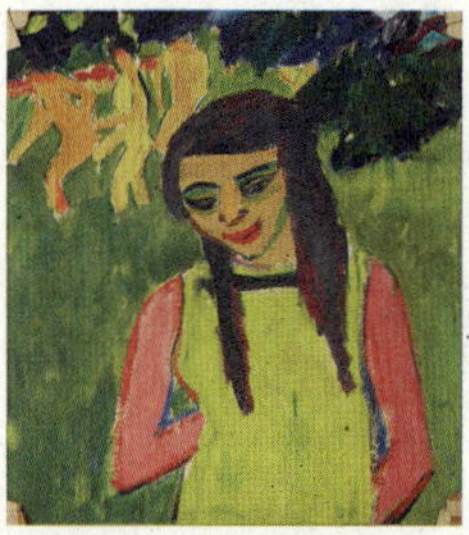

Verso: *Fränzi in Meadows (Fränzi in Wiesen)*
1910
Oil on canvas
76 x 70 cm
ML 76/2752
Gordon 180v

Thought to have belonged to Adolphe Basler from Paris, who sold it via Galerie Sigmund Salz, then still in Cologne. Listed as part of a private collection at the 'International Art Exhibition', Düsseldorf, 1922. It has not been possible to establish which one. Purchased, according to Haubrich's own records, in 1924. First mentioned by Luise Straus-Ernst, 'Die Sammlung Haubrich in Köln', *Das Kunstblatt* 11 (1927), p. 29. Haubrich Donation, 1946.

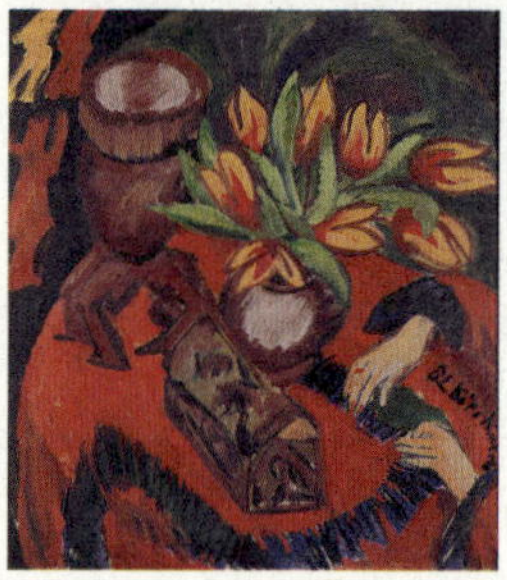

Still Life with Tulips, Exotica and Hands (Stilleben mit Tulpen, Exoten und Händen)
1912
Oil on canvas
78.5 x 68.5 cm
ML 76/2751
Gordon 234

In the property of J. B. Neumann. Upon Neumann's move to the U.S., he had the work sold by Karl Nierendorf, the business manager of his Berlin graphic arts dealership, to Haubrich, 1923. Haubrich Donation, 1946.

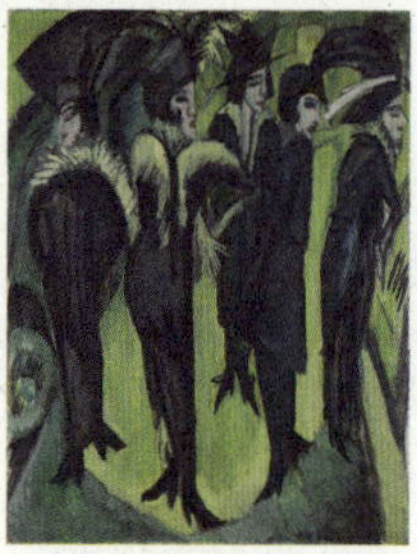

Five Women on the Street
(Fünf Frauen auf der Straße)
1913
Oil on canvas
120 x 90 cm
ML 76/2716
Gordon 362

Purchased for the Museum Folkwang, Essen, 1926. Confiscated as 'degenerate' in 1937. Through Ferdinand Möller, Berlin, entered the possession of Baron and Baroness Le Tanneux de St. Paul at Schloss Seeseiten near Seeshaupt on Lake Starnberg, 1940. Purchased by WRM through Galerie Günther Franke, Munich, with funding from the Haubrich Fund, 1947.

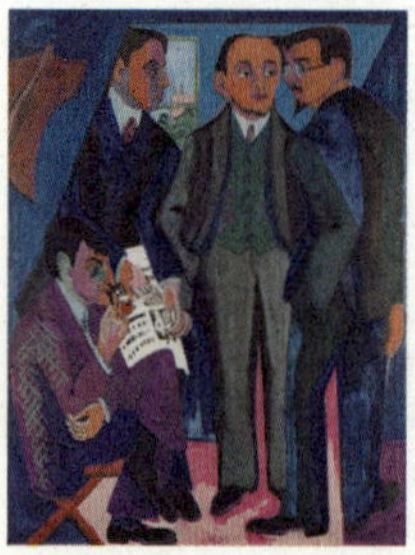

An Artists' Group (The Painters of the Brücke) (Eine Künstlergemeinschaft [Die Maler der Brücke])
1925-26
Oil on canvas
168 x 126 cm
ML 76/2863
Gordon 855

Purchased for the new section of Berlin's Nationalgalerie, the Kronprinzenpalais, at the exhibition of the Deutscher Künstlerbund in Hannover, 1928. Confiscated as 'degenerate' in 1937. Acquired by

Ferdinand Möller by exchange, 1940. Offered to the Nationalgalerie for reacquisition, but ultimately purchased by WRM in part with funding from the Haubrich Fund, 1952.

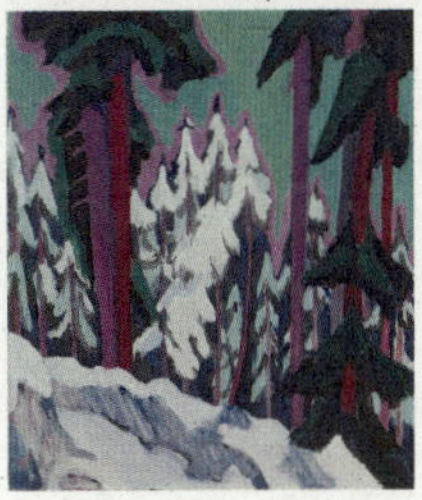

Forest in Winter (Wald im Winter)
1925/26
Oil on canvas
95.5 x 80.5 cm
ML 76/2897
Gordon 833

Acquired from the Kirchner estate in Biberach by Wilhelm Grosshennig, 1953. Purchased by WRM from Grosshennig's Düsseldorf gallery with funding from the Haubrich Fund, 1953.

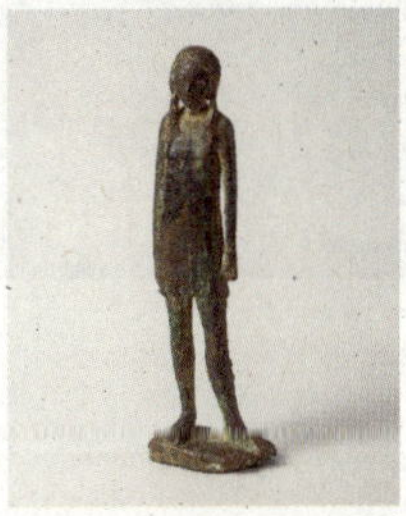

Kirchner, Heinrich
1924 Erlangen–
1984 Pavolding im Chiemgau

Standing Girl with Braids (Stehendes Mädchen mit Zöpfen)
1934
Bronze
H.: 25.5 cm
ML 76/SK 104

Purchased by WRM directly from the artist with funding from the Haubrich Fund, 1959.

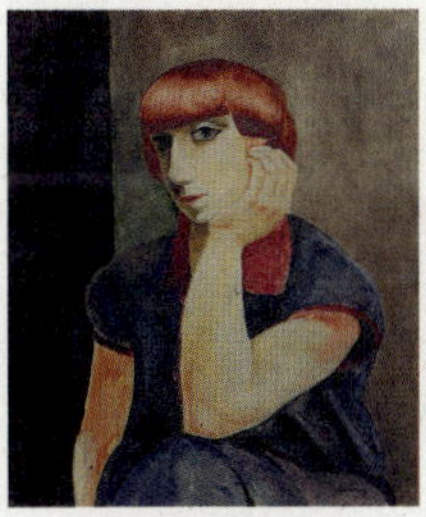

Kisling, Moïse
1891 Krakow–
1953 Sanary-sur-Mer

Portrait of Renée Kisling
1921
Oil on canvas
65 x 53.5 cm
ML 76/2782

Thought to have been purchased by Haubrich from Galerie Sigmund Salz in Cologne, 1925. First noted as present in the collection through a reference made by Luise Straus-Ernst in 'Die Sammlung Haubrich in Köln', *Das Kunstblatt* 11 (1927), p. 31. Haubrich Donation, 1946.

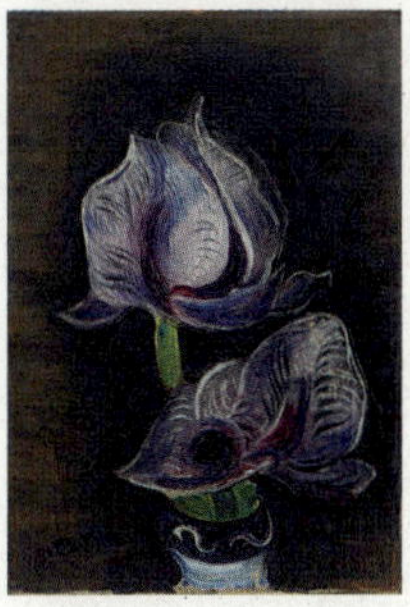

Irises
C. 1936/37
Oil on canvas
32.5 x 22 cm
ML 76/2783

Purchased by Haubrich from Galerie Dr. Andreas Becker, Cologne, 1937. Haubrich Donation, 1946.

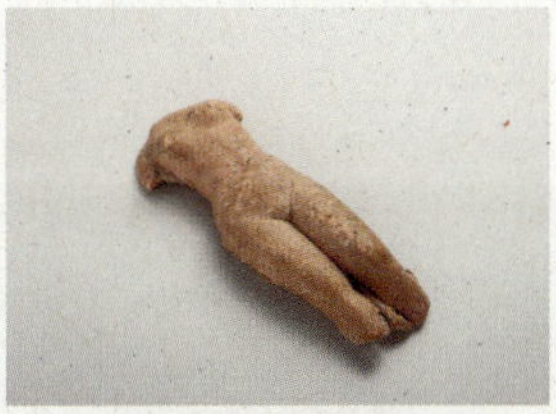

Kogan, Moissey
1879 Orhei–1943 Auschwitz Concentration Camp

Female Torso with Unmodelled Rear (Frauentorso ohne ausgeformte Rückseite)
C. 1922
Terracotta
H.: 20 cm
ML 76/SK 213
Henkel 146

Galerie Zak, Paris. Purchased by WRM with funding from the Haubrich Fund, 1960.

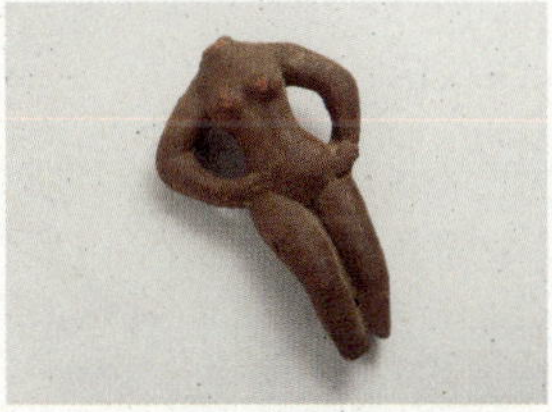

Female Torso with Arms Akimbo (Weiblicher Torso mit Händen an der Hüfte)
C. 1922
Terracotta
H.: 17.6 cm
ML 76/SK 214
Henkel 147

Galerie Zak, Paris. Purchased by WRM with funding from the Haubrich Fund, 1960.

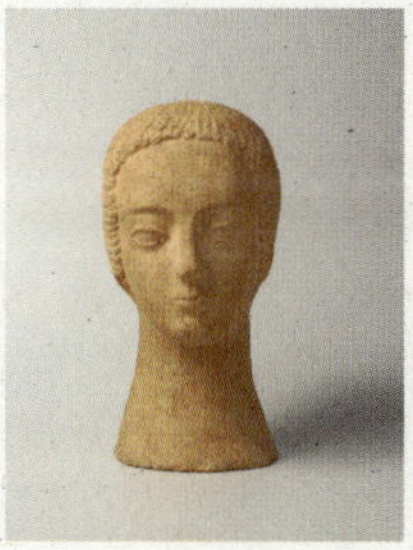

Head of a Girl I (Mädchenkopf I)
1925
Terracotta
H.: 30 cm
ML 76/SK 204
Henkel 111

Galerie Zak, Paris. Purchased by WRM with funding from the Haubrich Fund, 1960.

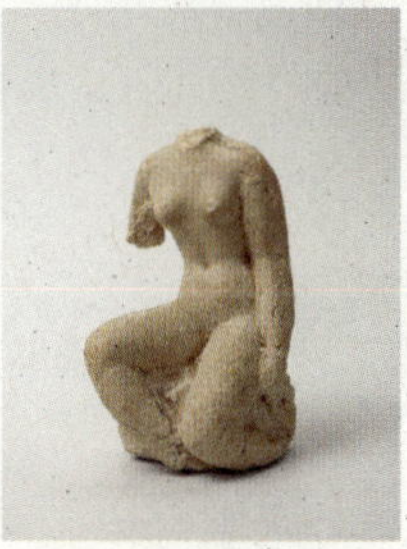

Seated Female Torso (Sitzender Frauentorso)
C. 1927
Terracotta
H.: 15 cm
ML 76/SK 209
Henkel 151

Galerie Zak, Paris. Purchased by WRM with funding from the Haubrich Fund, 1960.

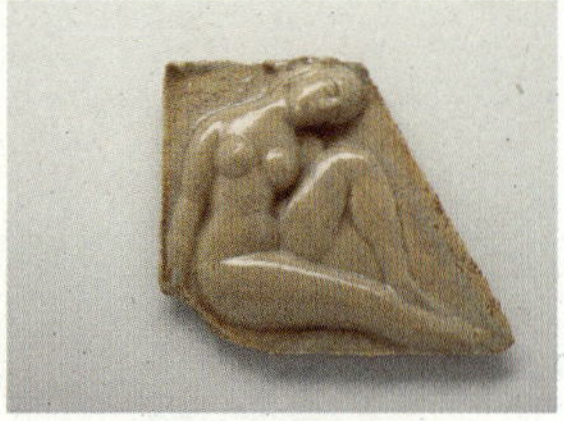

Seated Nude
(Sitzender Mädchenakt)
C. 1927
Ceramic, glazed
H.: 15 cm
ML 76/SK 210
Henkel 96

Galerie Zak, Paris. Purchased by WRM with funding from the Haubrich Fund, 1960.

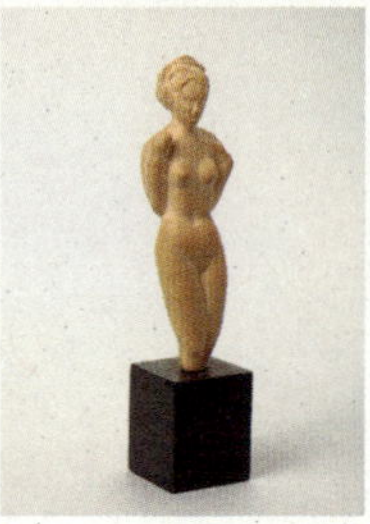

Standing Woman with Arms Bent (Stehende mit angewinkelten Armen)
C. 1933
Terracotta
H.: 13.5 cm
ML 76/SK 212
Henkel 170

Galerie Zak, Paris. Purchased by WRM with funding from the Haubrich Fund, 1960.

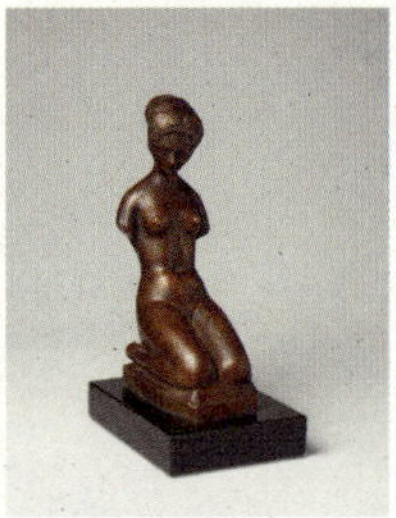

Kneeling Woman with Arms Raised and Braids
(Kniende mit erhobenen Armen und Zöpfen)
C. 1933
Bronze
H.: 14.5 cm
ML 76/SK 207
Henkel 169

Galerie Zak, Paris. Purchased by WRM with funding from the Haubrich Fund, 1960.

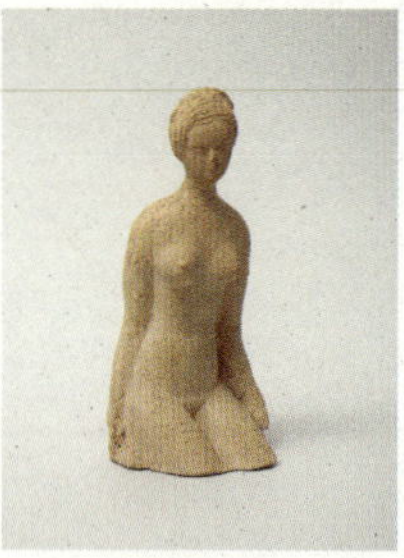

Seated Nude Bending Forward (Sitzender Frauenakt nach vorne geneigt)
1933
Terracotta
H.: 16.7 cm
ML 76/SK 211
Henkel 167

Galerie Zak, Paris. Purchased by WRM with funding from the Haubrich Fund, 1960.

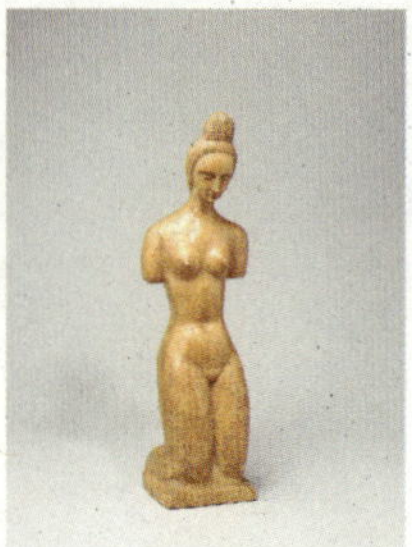

Kneeling Female Nude with Hair in a Bun (Kniender Frauenakt mit hochgestecktem Haarknoten)
C. 1933
Plaster
H.: 27.7 cm
ML 76/SK 206
Henkel 180

Galerie Zak, Paris. Purchased by WRM with funding from the Haubrich Fund, 1960.

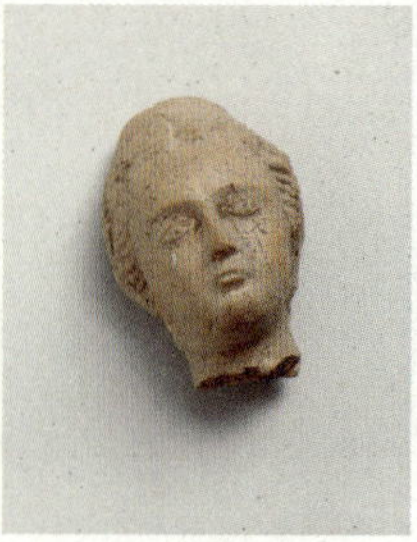

Head of a Woman II
(Frauenkopf II)
C. 1933
Terracotta
H.: 9 cm
ML 76/SK 205
Henkel 119

Galerie Zak, Paris. Purchased by WRM with funding from the Haubrich Fund, 1960.

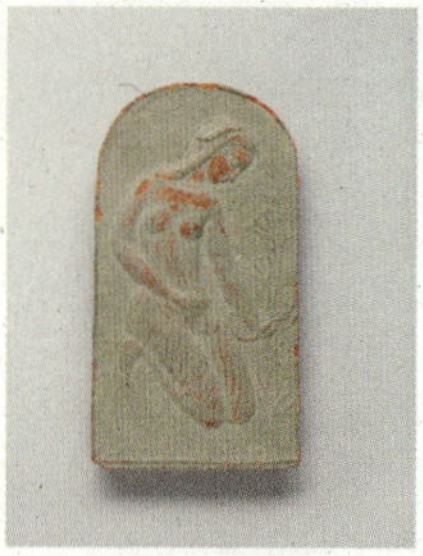

Kneeling Girl Next to a Plant
(Kniende neben einer Pflanze)
1935
Terracotta
H.: 14.3 cm
ML 76/SK 208
Henkel 106

Galerie Zak, Paris. Purchased by WRM with funding from the Haubrich Fund, 1960.

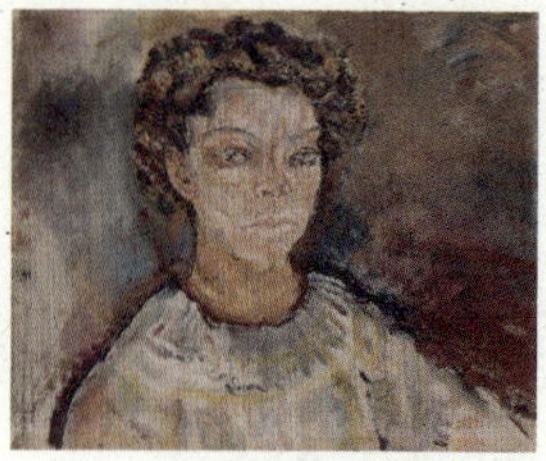

Kokoschka, Oskar
1886 Pöchlarn–1980 Montreux

Portrait of Tilla Durieux
(Bildnis Tilla Durieux)
1910
Oil on canvas
56 x 65 cm
ML 76/2753
Wingler 46

Noted as linked to Alfred Flechtheim first in 1918. Held by Hermann Lange, Krefeld, as of 1927. Exhibited with the notation 'Private collection, Alfred Flechtheim' in 1931. After Flechtheim's flight from Germany, sold to Haubrich in 1934 by Alex Vömel, who paid Flechtheim's debts with the sum obtained. Haubrich Donation, 1946. (Research by Roswitha Neu-Kock.)

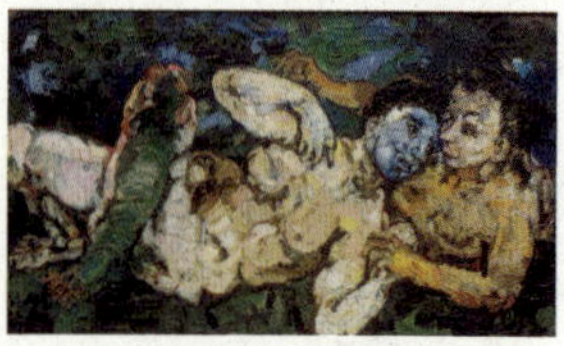

The Heathens (Die Heiden)
1918
Oil on canvas
75.5 x 126 cm
ML 76/2820
Wingler 124

Acquired by Stadtmuseum Dresden, 1920. Confiscated in 1937. Held by Galerie Ferdinand Möller, 1941. Purchased from Möller by WRM in part with funding from the Haubrich Fund, 1950.

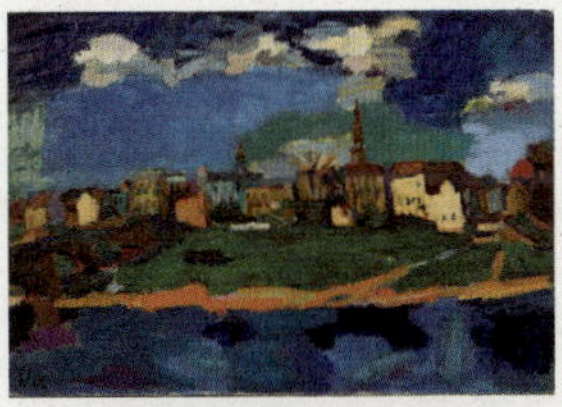

Dresden, Neustadt III
1921
Oil on canvas
70 x 99 cm
ML 76/2754
Wingler 136

Sold to Haubrich by Galerie Hermann Abels on behalf of an unknown Berlin collector, 1927. Haubrich Donation, 1946.

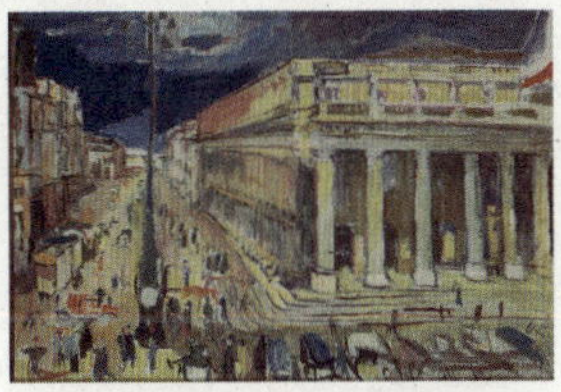

The Theatre in Bordeaux (Das Theater in Bordeaux)
1925
Oil on canvas
81 x 116.5 cm
ML 76/2840
Wingler 177

Also mistakenly labeled *Börse von Bordeaux* (*Bordeaux Stock Exchange*). Purchased by the Nationalgalerie Berlin from Galerie Paul Cassirer, Berlin, 1925. Confiscated in 1937. Acquired by Bernhard Böhmer for Galerie Fischer, Lucerne, 1941. Might have belonged to the collector Willy Hahn as of 1943, as noted in the 'degenerate art' databank. Purchased by WRM from Galerie Werner Rusche, in part with funding from the Haubrich Fund, 1950.

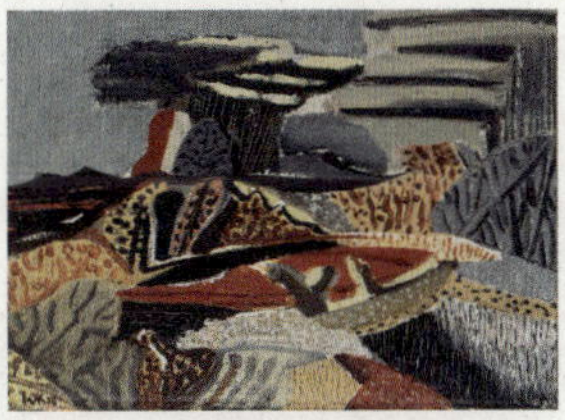

Kröhnke, Walter
1903 Hamburg–1944 Russia

Landscape (Landschaft)
1938
Oil on canvas
24.5 x 33 cm
ML 76/2951

Kröhnke Estate. Galerie Werner Rusche, Düsseldorf. Purchased by WRM with funding from the Haubrich Fund, 1953.

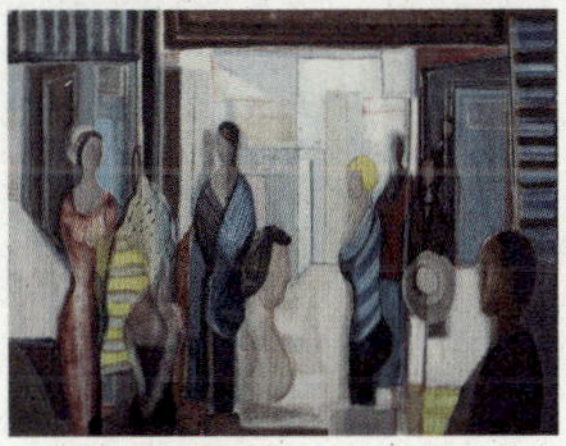

Kügler, Rudolf
1921 Berlin, lives in Berlin

Fashion Salon (Modesalon)
1950
Tempera on fibreboard
75 x 95 cm
ML 76/2858

Purchased by WRM at the exhibition 'Berliner Künstler heute' at Cologne University with funding from the Haubrich Fund, 1950.

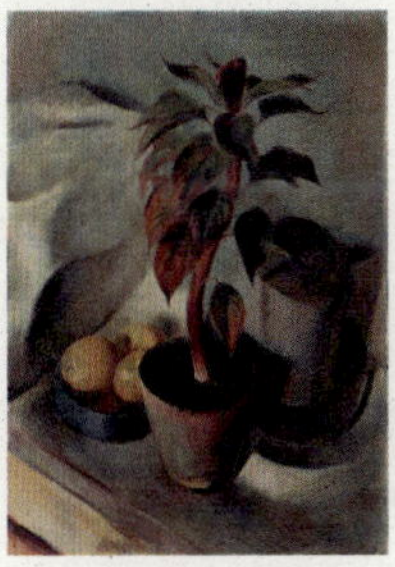

Lauterburg, Martin
1891 Neuengg–1960 Bern

Still Life with Plant (Stilleben mit Blattpflanze)
1917
Oil on canvas
77 x 53 cm
ML 76/2964

Hauswedell & Co., Hamburg. Purchased by WRM with funding from the Haubrich Fund, 1955.

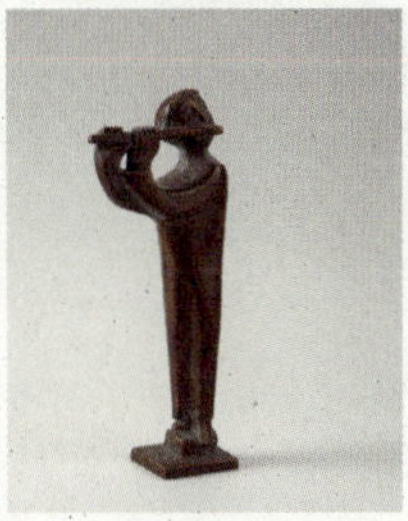

Lehmann, Kurt
1905 Koblenz–2000 Hannover

Flutist (Flötenspieler)
1950
Bronze, door handle
H.: 22 cm
ML 76/SK 127

Purchased by WRM with funding from the Haubrich Fund, 1955.

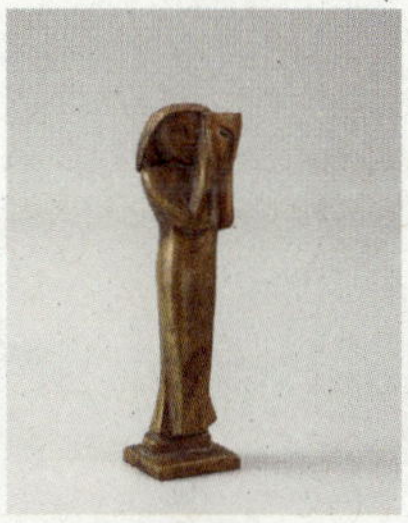

Woman with Mask (Frau mit Maske)
1950
Bronze, door handle
H.: 22 cm
ML 76/SK 128

Purchased by WRM with funding from the Haubrich Fund, 1955.

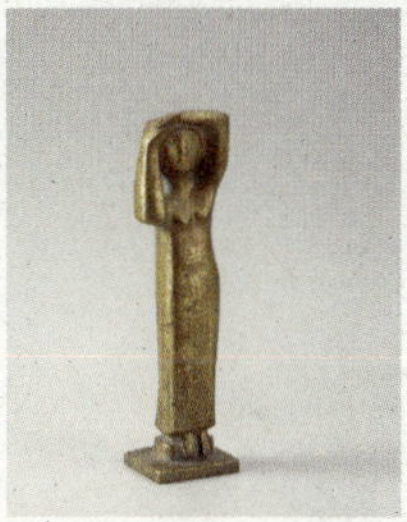

Woman Looking (Schauende)
1950
Bronze, door handle
H.: 22 cm
ML 76/SK 129

Purchased by WRM with funding from the Haubrich Fund, 1955.

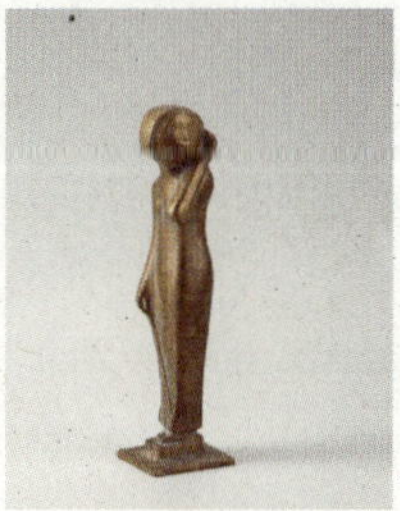

Woman Listening (Horchende)
1950
Bronze, door handle
H.: 22 cm
ML 76/SK 130

Purchased by WRM with funding from the Haubrich Fund, 1955.

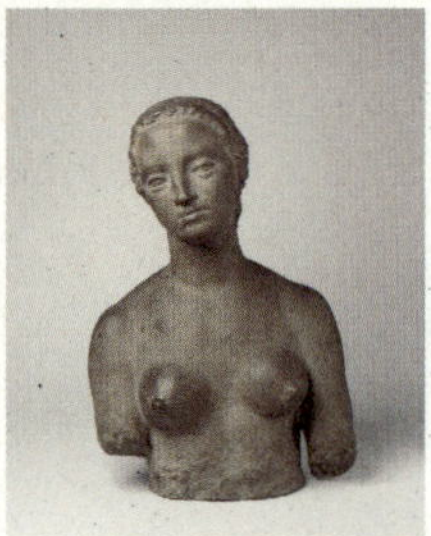

Lehmbruck, Wilhelm
1881 Duisburg–1919 Berlin

Bust of Mrs. L. (Büste Frau L.)
1910
Cast stone, tinted grey
H.: 80 cm
ML 76/SK 57
Schubert 50

Purchased by Haubrich from Galerie Hermann Abels, Cologne, 1927. Haubrich Donation, 1946.

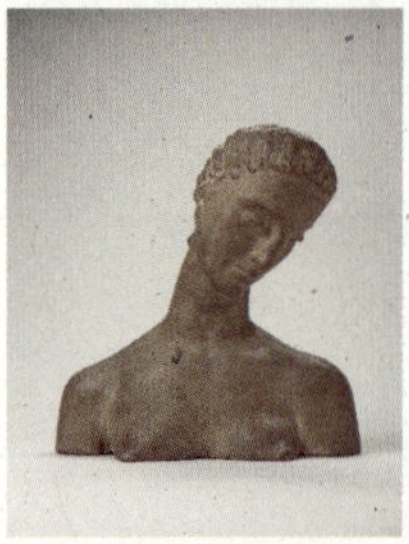

Woman with Head Bowed (Geneigter Frauenkopf)
1911
Terracotta
H.: 48.5 cm
ML 76/SK 99
Schubert 61

Purchased by WRM with funding from the Haubrich Fund, 1950. Part of the Strecker Collection, ML, since 1959.

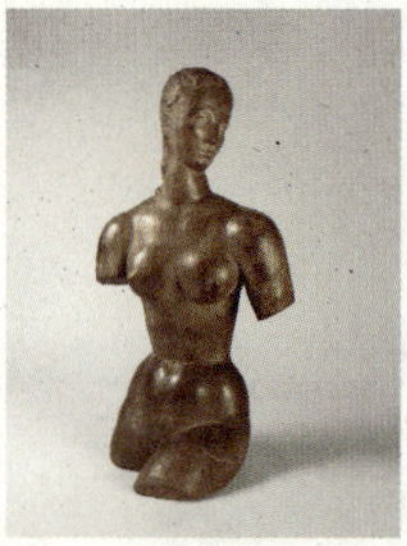

Torso of a Girl Turning (Mädchentorso, sich umwendend)
1913/14
Cast stone, tinted grey
H.: 95 cm
ML 76/SK 61
Schubert 75

Purchased by Haubrich from Galerie Hermann Abels, Cologne, 1927. Haubrich Donation, 1946.

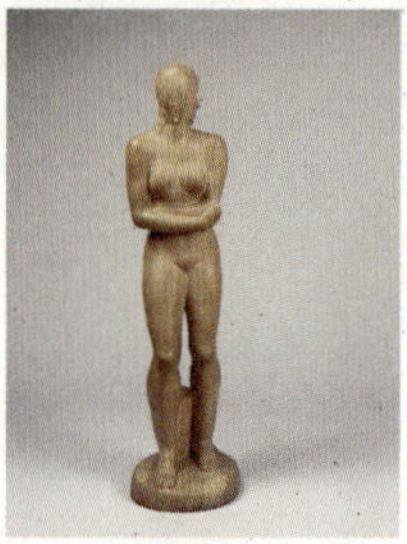

Woman Looking Back (Rückblickende)
1914
Cast stone, tinted yellowish
H.: 92 cm (with base)
ML 76/SK 122
Schubert 79

Purchased by Haubrich from Franz Nienhaus, Cologne, 1925. Haubrich Donation, 1946.

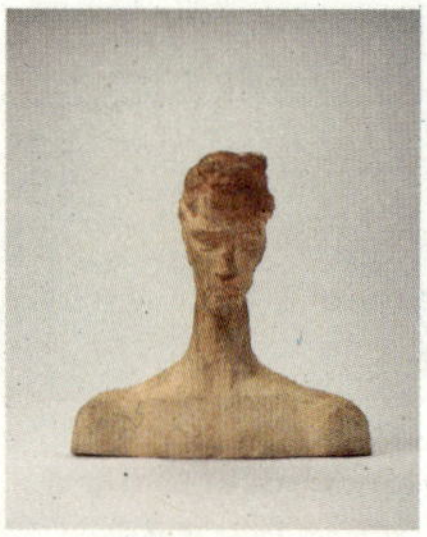

Head of a Youth (Jünglingskopf)
1914
Terracotta
H.: 46 cm
ML 76/SK 59
Schubert 69

Purchased by Haubrich from Franz Nienhaus, Cologne, 1925. Haubrich Donation, 1946.

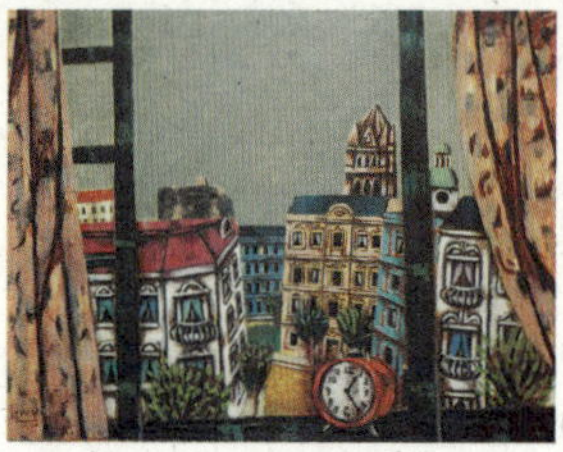

Lemcke, Dietmar
1930 Gołdap, lives in Berlin

City (Stadt)
1954
Oil on canvas
81 x 100 cm
ML 76/2974

Purchased by WRM directly from the artist with funding from the Haubrich Fund, 1955.

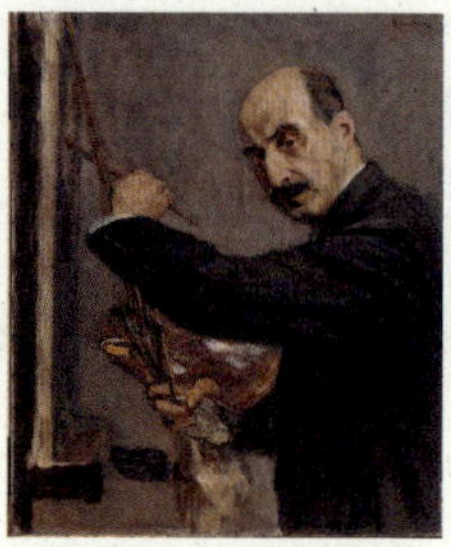

Liebermann, Max
1847 Berlin–1935 Berlin

Self-portrait (Selbstbildnis)
1908
Oil on canvas
87.5 x 71 cm
WRM 1186
Eberle 1908/6

Purchased by WRM in 1910, but sold to Haubrich via Aloys Faust in 1934. Haubrich Donation, 1946. Today WRM.

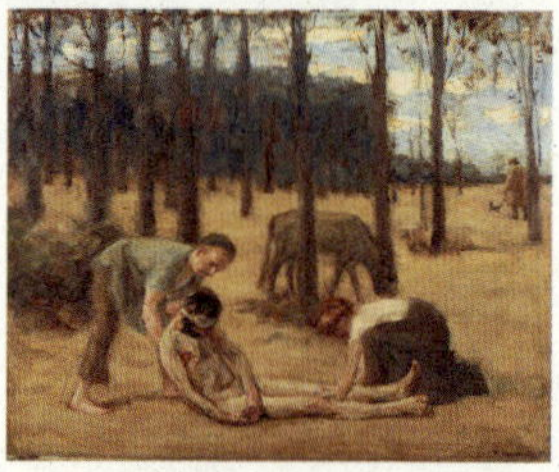

The Good Samaritan (Der barmherzige Samariter)
1911
Oil on canvas
93 x 112 cm
WRM 1187
Eberle 1911/1

Purchased by WRM from Paul Cassirer, Berlin, with funding from the Heidemann Fund in 1913. Offered to Haubrich for purchase, 1940, and received by him, together with L.'s *The Artist's Daughter Käthe on Horseback* (WRM 1183), in exchange for *Portrait of Emile de Girardin* (WRM 2645) by Louis-Alexandre Gosset de Guines (better known under the pseudonym André Gill). Haubrich Donation, 1946. Today WRM.

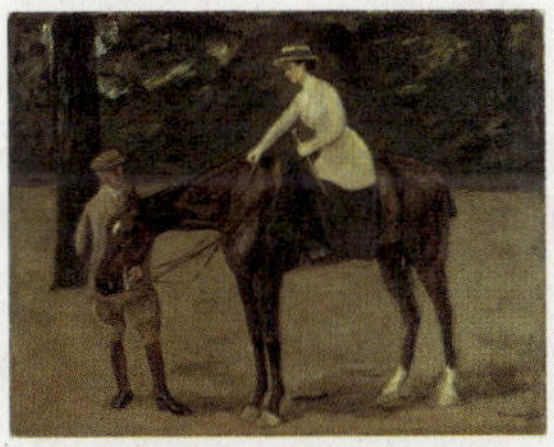

The Artist's Daughter Käthe on Horseback (Des Künstlers Tochter Käthe zu Pferde)
1913
Oil on canvas
80 x 100 cm
WRM 1183
Eberle 1913/9

Acquired by WRM as a gift from Richard von Schnitzler, 1913. Offered to Haubrich for purchase in 1940 and received by him, together with *The Good Samaritan* (WRM 1187) in exchange for *Portrait of Emile de Girardin* (WRM 2645) by Louis-Alexandre Gosset de Guines (better known under the pseudonym André Gill). Haubrich Donation, 1946. Today WRM.

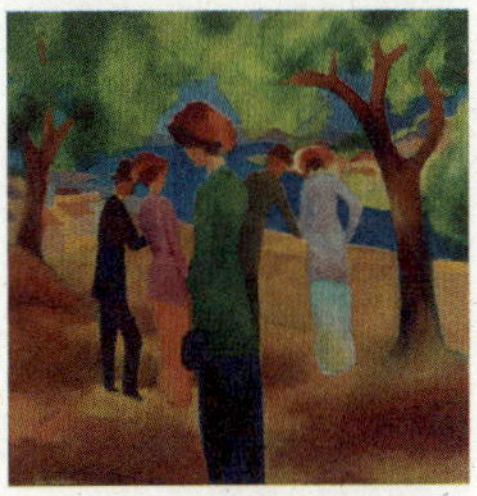

Macke, August

1887 Meschede–1914 Perthes-lès-Hurlus

Lady in a Green Jacket (Dame in grüner Jacke)
1913
Oil on canvas
44 x 43.5 cm
ML 76/2713
Heiderich 521

Purchased by WRM from the artist's son, Wolfgang Macke, Bonn, with funding from the Haubrich Fund, 1947.

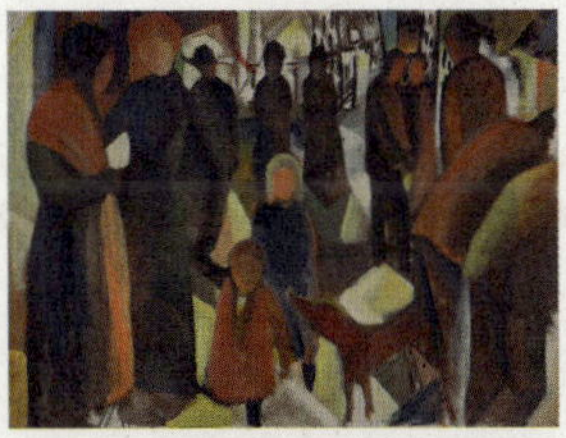

Farewell (Abschied)
1914
Oil on canvas
101 x 130.5 cm
ML 76/2714
Heiderich 590

Purchased by WRM from the artist's son, Wolfgang Macke, Bonn, with funding from the Haubrich Fund, 1947.

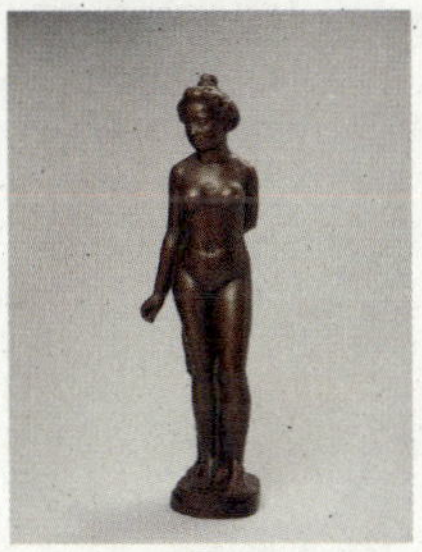

Maillol, Aristide

1861 Banyuls-sur-Mer–1944 Banyuls-sur-Mer

Standing Bather (Baigneuse debout)
1900
Bronze
H.: 66 cm
ML 76/SK 64

Purchased by Haubrich from Aloys Faust, Cologne, 1935. Previous ownership uncertain. Cast in such high numbers that it has not been possible to determine the edition from which the ML cast originates. Haubrich Donation, 1946.

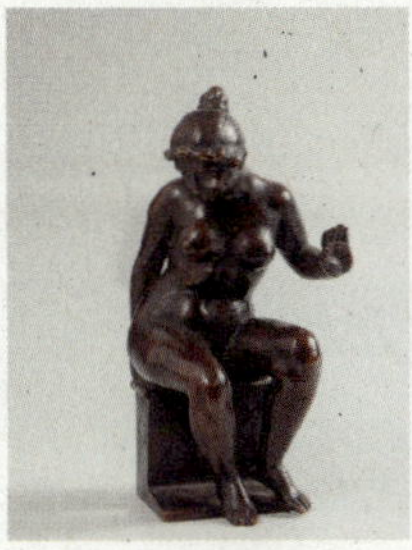

Leda
C. 1902
Bronze
H.: 28.5 cm
ML 76/SK 63

Purchased by Haubrich from Aloys Faust, Cologne, 1933. Previous ownership uncertain. Cast in such high numbers that it has not been possible to determine the edition from which the ML cast originates. Haubrich Donation, 1946.

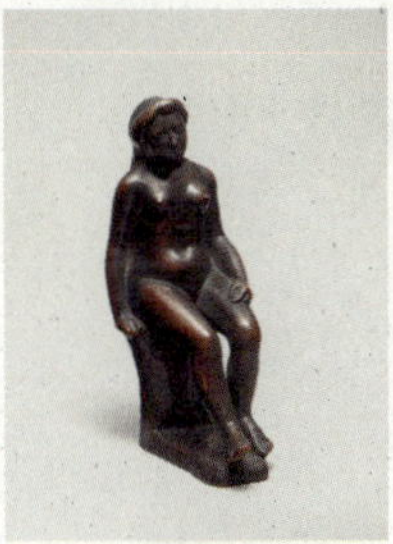

Seated Girl (Femme assise)
Before 1907
Bronze
H.: 23 cm
ML 76/SK 62

Purchased by Haubrich from Aloys Faust, Cologne, 1934. Previous ownership uncertain. Cast in such high numbers that it has not been possible to determine the edition from which the ML cast originates. Haubrich Donation, 1946.

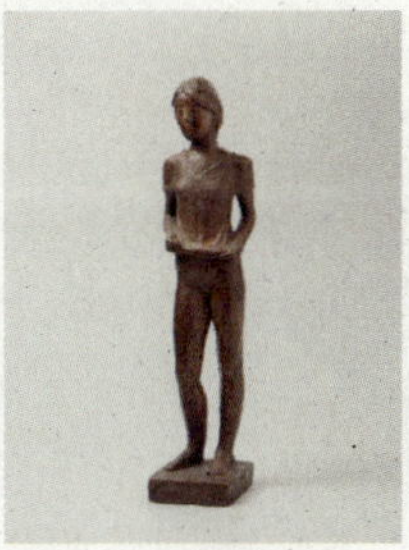

Marcks, Gerhard

1899 Berlin–1981 Burgbrohl

Brigitte, Standing, Wearing a Blouse (Stehende Brigitte im Hemd)
1930
Bronze
H.: 50 cm
ML 76/SK 65
Busch/Rudloff 215

Purchased by Haubrich from Galerie Alex Vömel, Düsseldorf, 1942. Haubrich Donation, 1946.

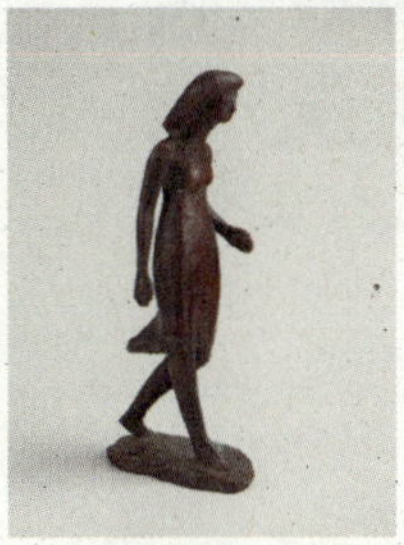

Secretary (Sekretärin)
1943
Bronze
H.: 25 cm
ML 76/SK 105
Busch/Rudloff 425

Galerie Rudolf Hoffmann, Hamburg. Hoffmann showed regular exhibitions of Marcks' work. Purchased by WRM with funding from the Haubrich Fund, 1952.

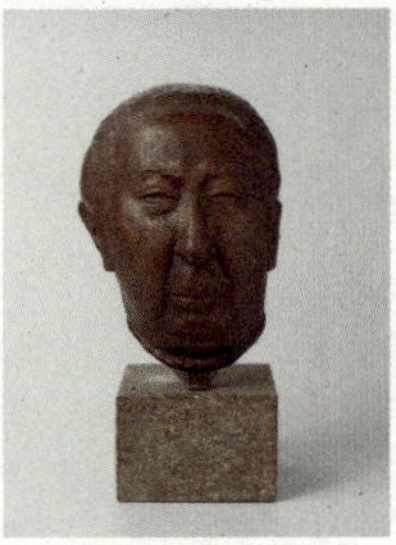

Theodor Heuss
1952
Bronze
H.: 31.5 cm
ML 76/SK 152
Busch/Rudloff 582

Purchased by WRM directly from the artist with funding from the Haubrich Fund, 1955.

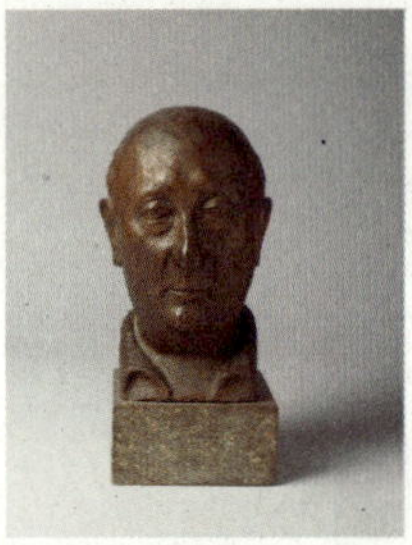

Josef Haubrich
1953
Bronze
H.: 34.5 cm
ML 76/SK 123
Busch/Rudloff 600

Purchased by WRM directly from the artist with funding from the Haubrich Fund, 1953.

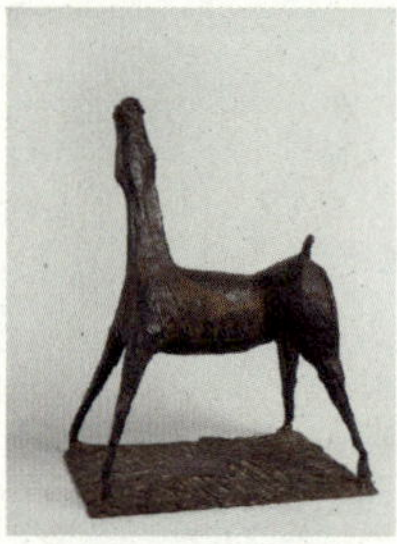

Marini, Marino

1901 Pistoia–1980 Viareggio

Little Horse (Il Cavallo)
1950
Bronze
H.: 52 cm
ML 76/SK 131
Carandente 336 b

Titled *Il Cavallo* by Marini. Galerie der Spiegel, Cologne. Purchased by WRM with funding from the Haubrich Fund, 1954.

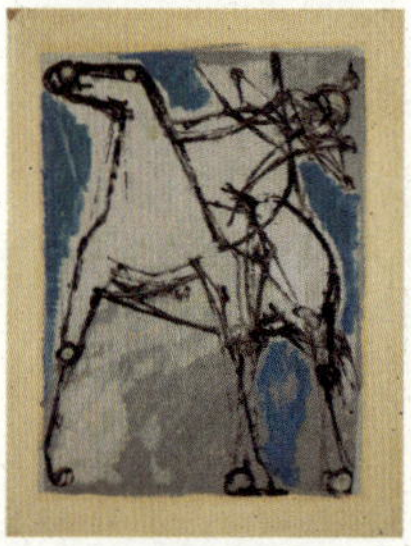

Rider (Il Cavaliere)
1952
Oil on cardboard on fibreboard
85.5 x 61.5 cm
ML 76/2975

Galerie der Spiegel, Cologne. Purchased by WRM with funding from the Haubrich Fund, 1956.

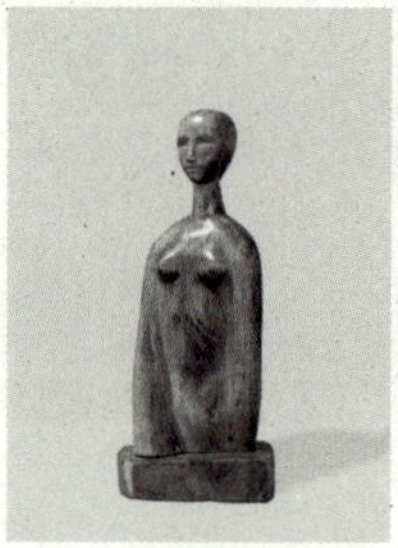

Mataré, Ewald

1887 Aachen–1965 Büderich

Torso of a Woman (Frauentorso)
1922
Poplar wood
H.: 25 cm
ML 76/SK 165
Schilling 4

Galerie Alex Vömel, Düsseldorf. M. was friends with Vömel. Purchased by WRM with funding from the Haubrich Fund, 1957. Missing since 1978.

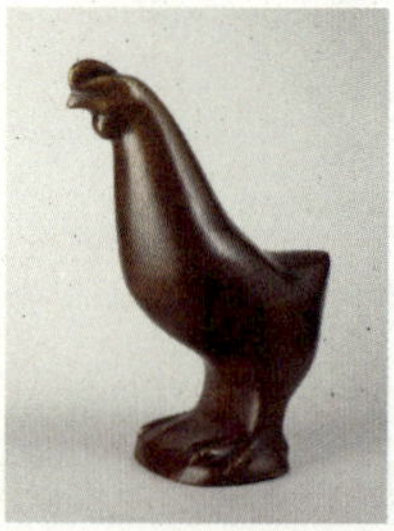

Hen (Huhn)
1924
Bronze
H.: 49 cm
ML 76/SK 80
Schilling 25b

Three casts were made of this sculpture. It is not known how the work entered the Haubrich Collection. Haubrich Donation, 1946.

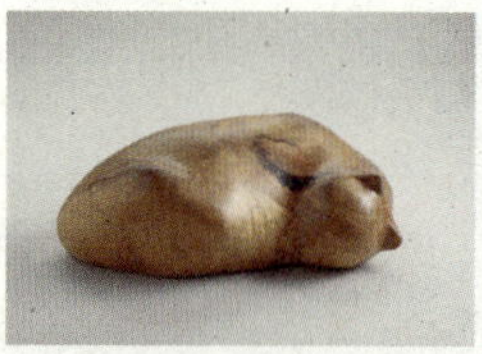

Sleeping Cat (Schlafende Katze)
1929
Poplar wood
H.: 16 cm
ML 76/SK 79
Schilling 57

Haubrich Donation, 1946. Previous ownership unknown.

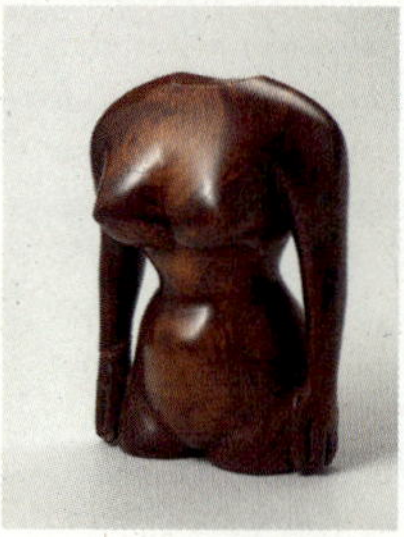

Female Torso (Weiblicher Torso)
1932
Teak
H.: 20 cm
ML 76/SK 144
Schilling 76

Galerie Hella Nebelung, Düsseldorf. Purchased with funding from the Haubrich Fund, 1955.

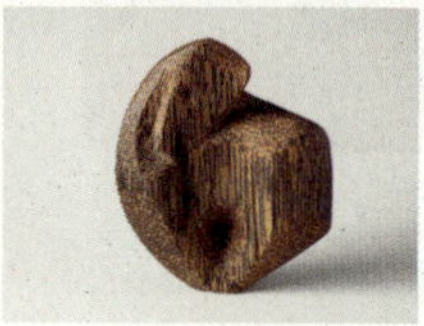

Symbol of a Horse (Tierzeichen Pferd)
1941/42
Palm wood
H.: 14.5 cm, W: 12 cm
ML 76/SK 164
Schilling 222

Galerie Alex Vömel, Düsseldorf. M. was friends with Vömel. Purchased by WRM with funding from the Haubrich Fund, 1957.

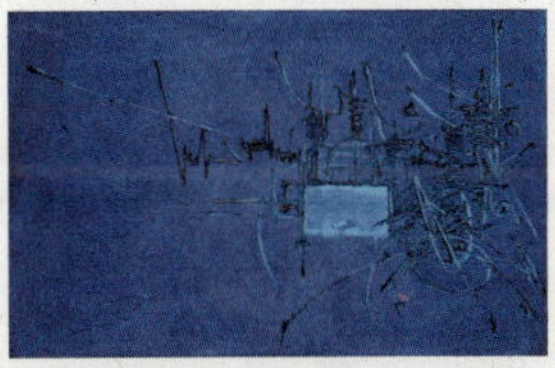

Mathieu, Georges
1921 Boulogne-sur-Mer –2012 Paris

Dāna
1958
Oil on canvas
65 x 100 cm
ML 76/3075

Kölnischer Kunstverein. Purchased by WRM with funding from the Haubrich Fund, 1959.

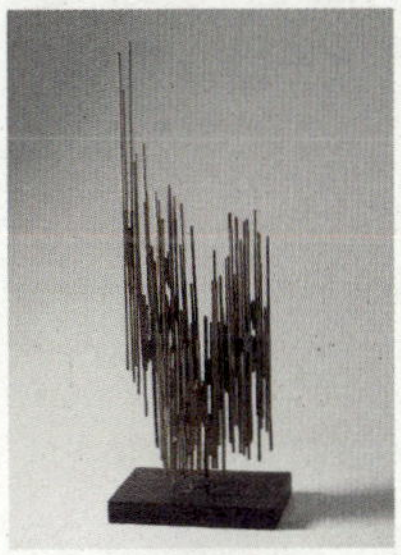

Matschinsky-Denninghoff, Brigitte and Martin
1923 Berlin–2011 Berlin
1921 Grötzingen, lives in Berlin

Shape in Tin (No. 34)
(Form in Zinn [Nr. 34])
1957
Tin, brass
H.: 49 cm
ML 76/SK 173
Költzsch/Schwarz 43

Galerie Otto und Etta Stangl, Munich. Purchased by WRM with funding from the Haubrich Fund, 1958.

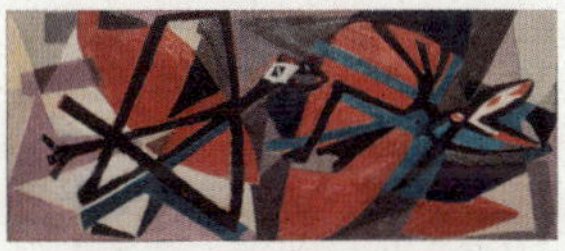

Meistermann, Georg
1911 Solingen–1990 Cologne

Birds (Vögel)
C. 1946
Oil on canvas
28.5 x 65 cm
ML 76/2802
Ruhrberg/Schäfke 109

Kölnischer Kunstverein. Purchased by WRM with funding from the Haubrich Fund, 1949.

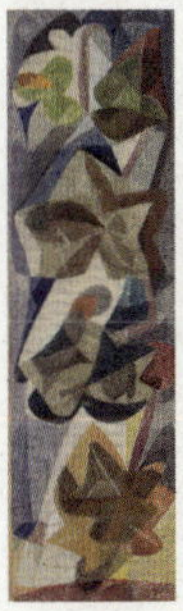

Ivy (Efeu)
1948
Oil on canvas
32 x 9 cm
ML 76/2813
Ruhrberg/Schäfke 146

Purchased by WRM with funding from the Haubrich Fund, 1949.

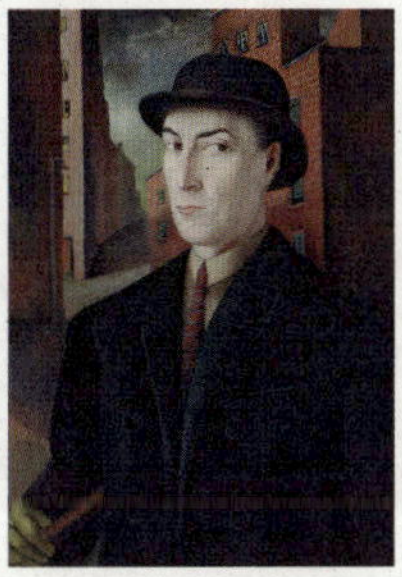

Mense, Carlo
1886 Rheine–1965 Bad Honnef

Portrait of H. M. Davringhausen
(Bildnis H. M. Davringhausen)
1922
Oil on canvas
86.5 x 59.5 cm
ML 76/2777

Purchased by Haubrich from Franz Nienhaus in Cologne, 1924. Haubrich Donation, 1946.

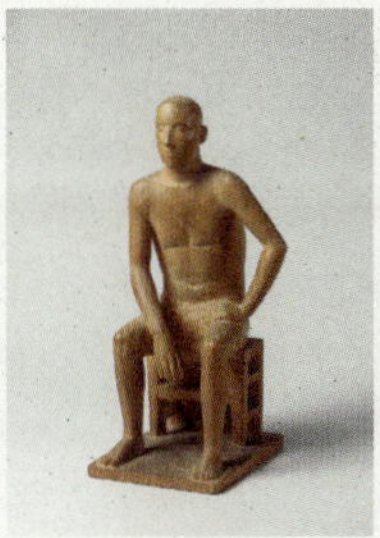

Mettel, Hans
1903 Salzwedel–1966 Falkenstein

Seated Man (Sitzender Mann)
1945/46
Pear wood
H.: 27 cm
ML 76/SK 74

Donated by Haubrich, 1947.

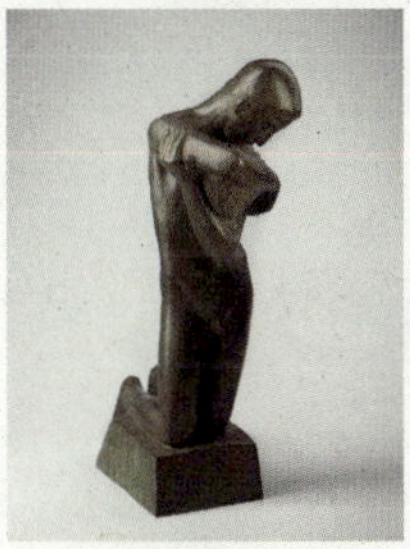

Minne, George
1866 Ghent–1940 Laethem-Saint-Martin

Kneeling Boy with Shell
(L'Agenouillé à la coquille)
1926
Bronze
H.: 69 cm
WRM SK 66

Purchased by Haubrich at the exhibition 'Belgian Art' in Budapest, 1927. Haubrich Donation, 1946. Today WRM.

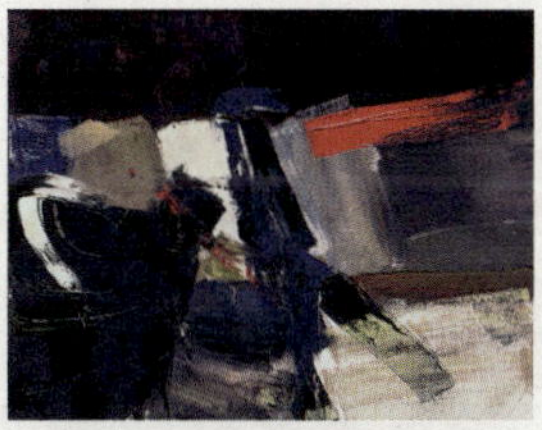

Miotte, Jean
1926 Paris, lives in New York

Deliverance (Délivrance)
1960
Oil on canvas
73 x 92 cm
ML 76/3112

Galerie Jacques Dubourg, Paris. Purchased by WRM with funding from the Haubrich Fund, 1961.

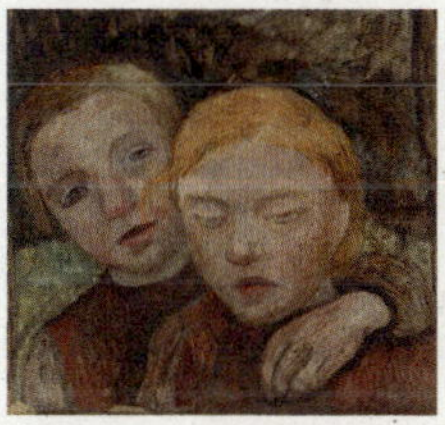

Modersohn-Becker, Paula
1876 Dresden–1907 Worpswede

The Blind Little Sister
(Das blinde Schwesterchen)
C. 1903
Oil on cardboard
32.2 x 33.5 cm
ML 76/2756
Busch/Werner 407

Purchased by Haubrich from Karl Nierendorf, Cologne, probably 1923. First mentioned as belonging to the collection in a 1927 article by Luise Straus-Ernst, 'Die Sammlung Haubrich in Köln', *Das Kunstblatt* 11 (1927), p. 33, ill. p. 25, but under the title *Knabenköpfe* (*Boys' Heads*). Haubrich Donation, 1946.

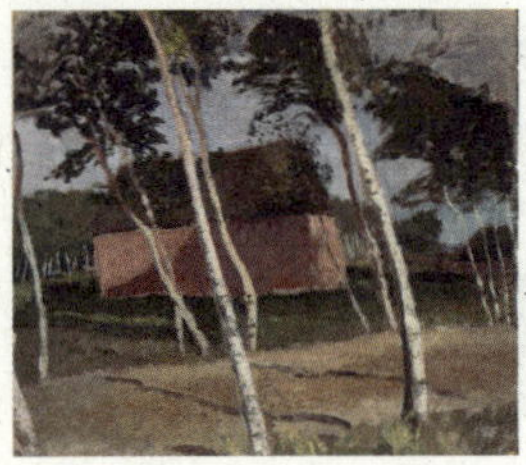

Worpswede Landscape (Worpsweder Landschaft)
C. 1903
Oil on fibreboard
61.5 x 67.8 cm
ML 76/2868
Busch/Werner 437

Given to Galerie Hermann Abels, Cologne, by Tille Modersohn, Bremen, the artist's daughter. Purchased by WRM with funding from the Haubrich Fund, 1951.

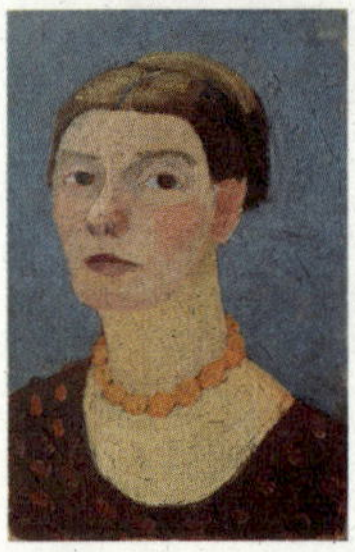

Self-Portrait in Front of Blue Background (Selbstbildnis vor blaugrauem Grund)
1906
Oil on cardboard
45.7 x 29.7 cm
ML 76/2730
Busch/Werner 626

Sold to WRM by Ernst König, the son-in-law of Leopold Graf Kalckreuth, Stuttgart, after the latter's death. Purchased by WRM with funding from the Haubrich Fund, 1948.

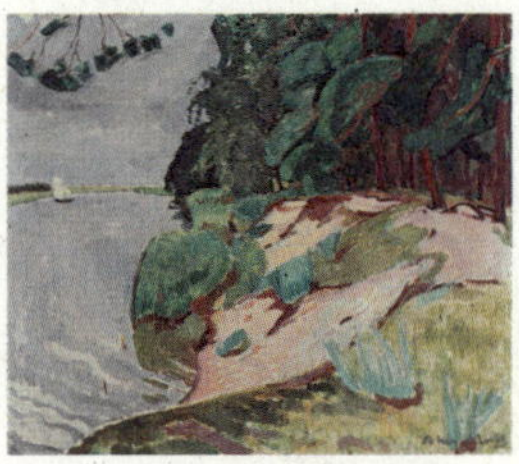

Moll, Oskar
1875 Brieg (today Brzeg)–1947 Berlin

Landscape on the Shores of Lake Grunewald (Landschaft am Grunewaldsee)
C. 1916
Oil on canvas
70 x 80 cm
ML 76/2775

Purchased by Haubrich from Franz Nienhaus, Cologne, 1927. Haubrich Donation, 1946.

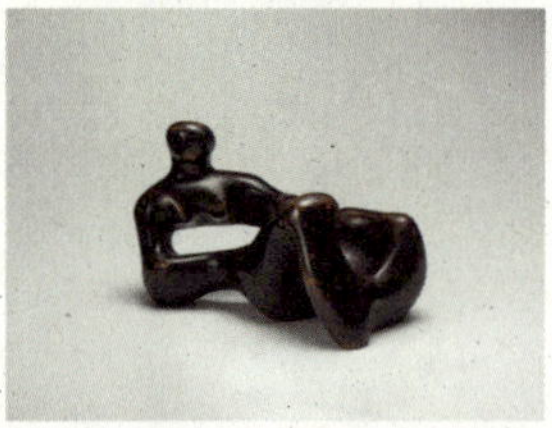

Moore, Henry
1898 Castleford–1986 Hadham

Reclining Figure
1938
Bronze
H.: 8.5 cm
ML 76/SK 88

British Military Government. Purchased by WRM with funding from the Haubrich Fund, 1949.

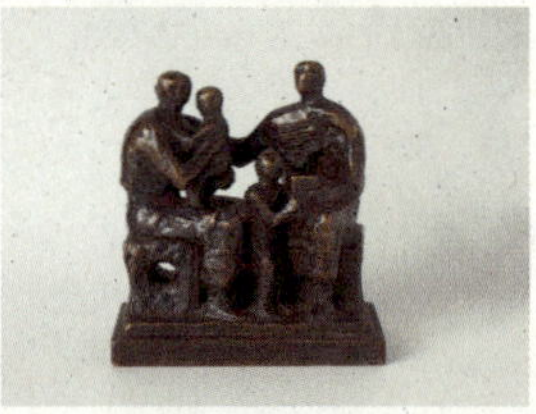

Family Group
1944
Bronze
H.: 15.5 cm
ML 76/SK 154

Galerie Christoph Czwiklitzer, Cologne. Purchased by WRM with funding from the Haubrich Fund, 1956.

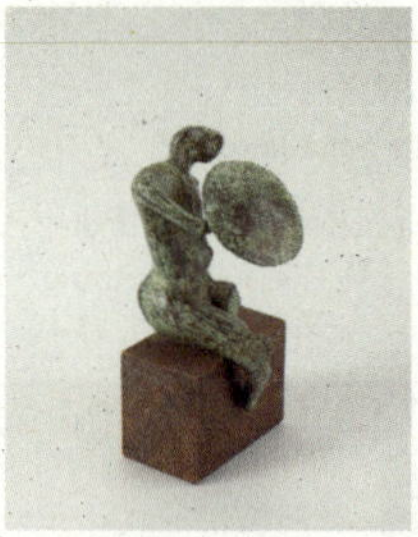

Warrior with Shield
1952/53
Bronze
H.: 18 cm
ML 76/SK 133

Purchased by WRM from the artist through the British Council (mistakenly called Royal Council in the inventory book) with funding from the Haubrich Fund, 1954.

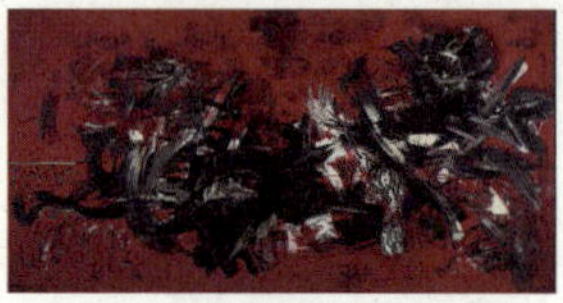

Moreni, Mattia
1920 Pavia–1999 Brisighella

Sterpaglia verso la spiaggia (Thicket on the Beach)
1956
Oil on canvas
120 x 230 cm
ML 76/3073

Galleria il Milione, Milan. Purchased by WRM with funding from the Haubrich Fund, 1959.

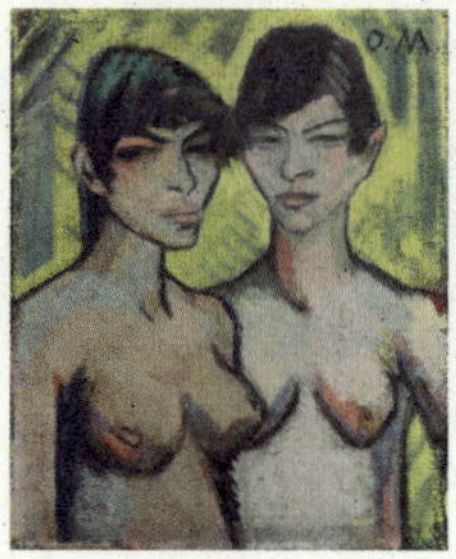

Mueller, Otto
1874 Liebau (today Lubawka)–1930 Breslau (today Wrocław)

Half-Length Portrait of Two Nude Women (Zwei weibliche Halbakte)
C. 1919
Distemper on burlap
87.4 x 70.6 cm
ML 76/2757
Lüttichau/Pirsig 193

Submitted to auction at Auktionhaus Max Perl, Berlin, by Hans Littmann, son of the collector Ismar Littmann, Breslau, on 28 February 1935. Confiscated by the Gestapo at Auction 188 (Lot 2552) and brought to the Nationalgalerie Berlin in 1936. Confiscated again in 1937 as 'degenerate'. Included in the auction of 'degenerate art' by Galerie Theodor Fischer in Lucerne on 30 June 1939, where it did not sell. Acquired by Hildebrand Gurlitt, 1940, and sold by him to Haubrich, 1942. Haubrich Donation, 1946. The painting was returned to the heirs of the Littmann family in 1999, and repurchased for ML with the help of Kulturstiftung der Länder, the Stiftung Kunst und Kultur Nordrhein-Westfalen, the City of Cologne and Monica and Jürgen Naumann in 2000.

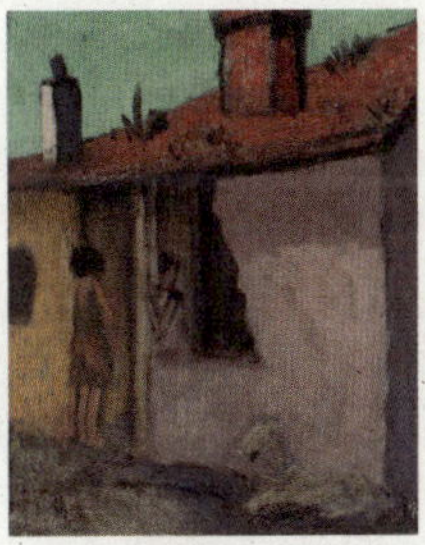

Gypsy Hut with Goat
(Zigeunerhütte mit Ziege)
C. 1925
Distemper on canvas
115.5 x 90 cm
ML 76/2758
Lüttichau/Pirsig 403

After M.'s death in 1930, purchased by Haubrich from Karl Nierendorf, Berlin, 1932. Title noted by Haubrich on an index card as *Zigeunerhütte mit Ziege*; on the painting's verso a title has been written in an unknown hand: *Hütte mit rotem Dach (Hut with Red Roof)*. Haubrich Donation, 1946.

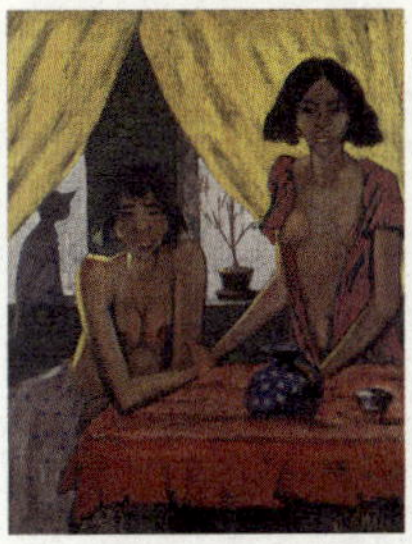

Two Gypsy Women with a Cat
(Zwei Zigeunerinnen mit Katze)
1926/27
Distemper on canvas
144.5 x 109.5 cm
ML 76/2872
Lüttichau/Pirsig 418

Taken by Maschka Mueller from M.'s estate. Sold to Galerie Wilhelm Grosshennig, Düsseldorf, at her death, 1952. Purchased by WRM, in part with funding from the Haubrich Fund, 1952.

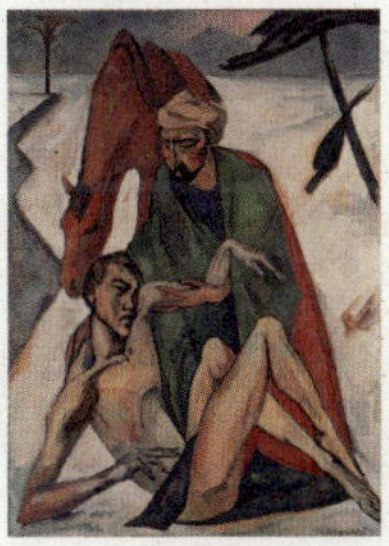

Nauen, Heinrich
1880 Krefeld–1940 Kalkar

The Good Samaritan
(Der barmherzige Samariter)
1914
Gouache on paper on canvas
170 x 120 cm
ML 76/2874
Drenker-Nagels/Malcomess 674

Acquired by the Society for the Promotion of Twentieth-Century German Art, 1919. Auctioned, together with the Society's holdings, in 1924 and purchased by Alfred Fischer (Essen). Given by Fischer to his friend Edmund Körner. Purchased by WRM from Körner's heirs with funding from the Haubrich Fund, 1952.

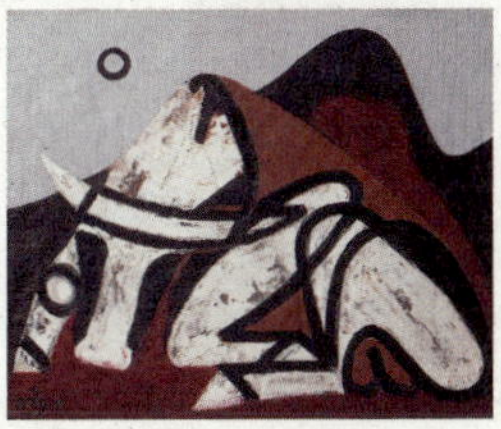

Nay, Ernst Wilhelm
1902 Berlin–1968 Cologne

White Bull (Weißer Stier)
1934
Oil on canvas
64 x 75 cm
ML 76/2954
Scheibler 148

Galerie der Spiegel, Cologne. N.'s work featured regularly in the gallery's exhibitions. Purchased by WRM with funding from the Haubrich Fund, 1955.

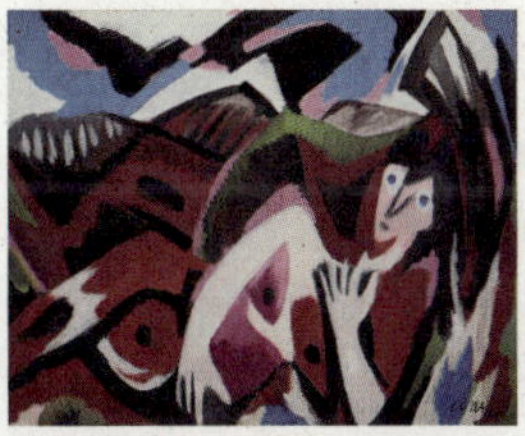

Woman in the Taunus Mountains
(Frau im Taunus)
1939
Oil on canvas
95.5 x 115.5 cm
ML 76/2962
Scheibler 255

Purchased from Alexandra Reitzenstein-Seel and Eberhard Seel, Berlin, with funding from the Haubrich Fund, 1955.

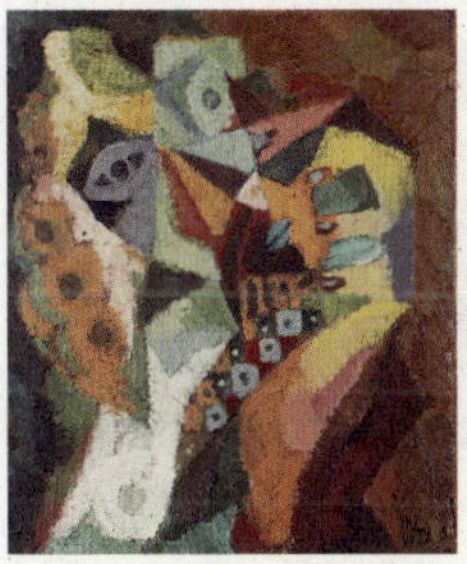

Head of a Girl (Mädchenkopf)
1947
Oil on canvas
68.5 x 56 cm
ML 76/2794
Scheibler 381

Galerie Werner Rusche, Cologne. Purchased by WRM with funding from the Haubrich Fund, 1948.

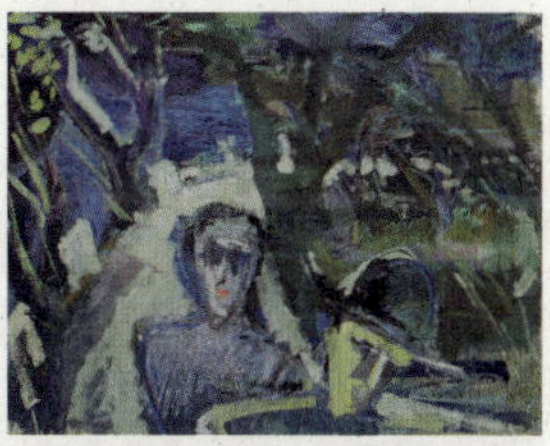

Nesch, Rolf
1893 Obereßlingen–1975 Oslo

Elbe Promenade in Hamburg
(Elbchaussee in Hamburg)
1931
Oil, chalk on canvas
80.5 x 100 cm
ML 76/2956

Consigned to Hildebrand Gurlitt by Robert Köhler, Hamburg, about whom no other information has been found. Sold to WRM by Gurlitt in his function as chairman of the Düsseldorf art society, the Kunstverein für die Rheinlande und Westfalen. Purchased with funding from the Haubrich Fund, 1954.

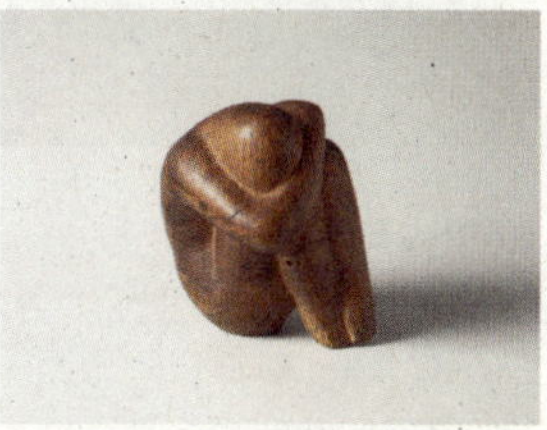

Nieder-Schabbehard, Jochen
1919 Cologne–2004 Cologne

Crouching Woman (Hockende)
Before 1950
Wood
H.: 10 cm
ML 76/SK 96

Donated by Haubrich, 1950.

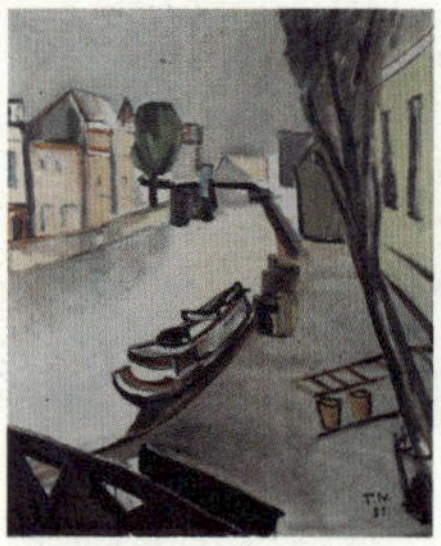

Niederreuther, Thomas
1909 Munich–1990 Munich

Small Town in Holland
(Kleine Stadt in Holland)
1951
Oil on canvas
100 x 80 cm
ML 76/2965

Galerie Christoph Czwiklitzer, Cologne. Purchased by WRM with funding from the Haubrich Fund, 1955.

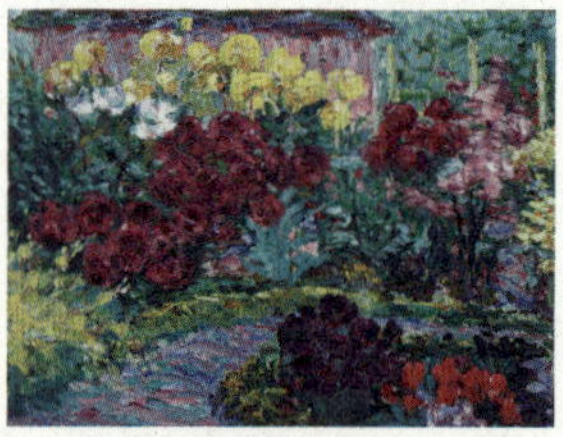

Nolde, Emil
1867 Nolde–1956 Seebüll

Red and Yellow Roses
(Rote und gelbe Rosen)
1907
Oil on canvas
64.5 x 83 cm
ML 76/2759
Urban 222

Titled *Rote und gelbe Rosen* by N. on verso. Exchanged by the daughter of Carl Steinbart, Irmgard Bender (Bonn), with Haubrich in 1943 for a work entitled *Tiergartenallee (Allée in the Tiergarten)* by Max Liebermann. Haubrich Donation, 1946.

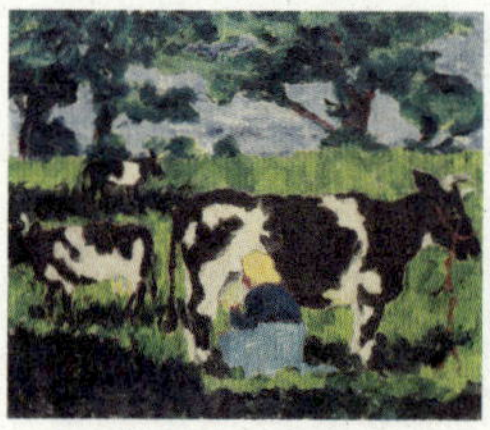

Black-and-White Cows
(Schwarzweiße Kühe)
1913
Oil on canvas
86 x 101 cm
ML 76/2762
Urban 576

Titled *Schwarzweiße Kühe* by N. on verso. Purchased by Haubrich from Hermann Burg, Cologne, 1923. Haubrich Donation, 1946.

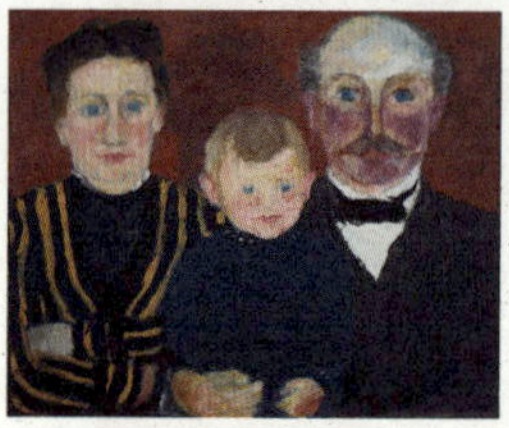

Family (Bonnichsen)
(Familie [Bonnichsen])
C. 1915
Oil on canvas
73.3 x 89 cm
ML 76/2728
Urban 677

Titled *Familie* by N. on verso. Heinrich Kirchhoff, Wiesbaden. Herbert Leyendecker, Wiesbaden. Purchased by WRM with funding from the Haubrich Fund, 1948.

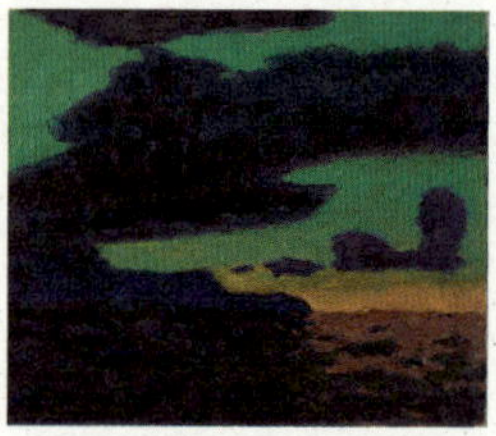

After Sunset
(Nach Sonnenuntergang)
1915
Oil on canvas
86.7 x 100.5 cm
ML 76/2764
Urban 650

Received by Hans Melchers from an unknown collector named Schwarz in Mannheim. Sold to Haubrich, 1944. Haubrich Donation, 1946.

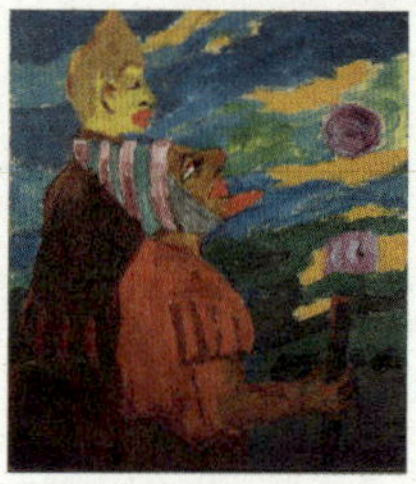

Dreamers (Schwärmer)
1916
Oil on canvas
100.7 x 86.4 cm
ML 76/2760
Urban 739

Sold by Hannover's Kestnergesellschaft to Karl Nierendorf, Cologne. Purchased by Willy Hahn, Cologne, who sold it to Haubrich in 1924. Haubrich Donation, 1946.

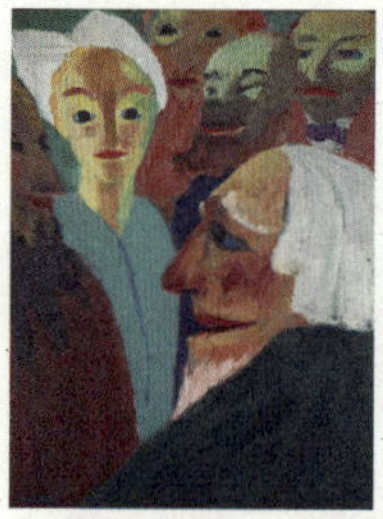

Young Woman and Men
(Junge Frau und Männer)
1919
Oil on plywood
101 x 73 cm
ML 76/2761
Urban 882

In the possession of Düsseldorf industrialist Paul Multhaupt. After his suicide on 19 January 1933, the work was to be shown at Galerie Alfred Flechtheim on 12 March 1933. Purchased by Haubrich several months later from Galerie Alex Vömel. Haubrich lists the title *Jesus unter den Schriftgelehrten (Jesus among the Doctors)*, which was kept in the literature, although N. had titled it on verso *Junge Frau und Männer*. Haubrich Donation, 1946.

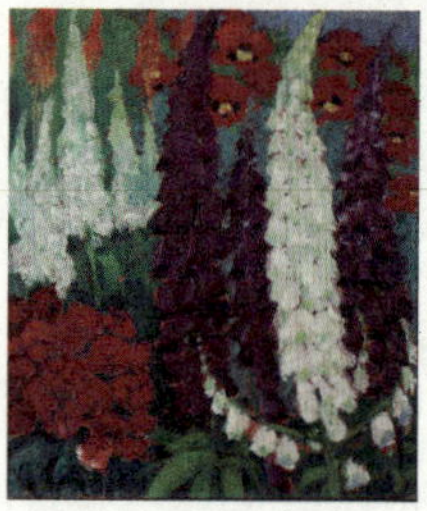

Flower Garden (V.) (Poppies and Foxgloves) (Blumengarten (V.) [Mohn und Fingerhüte])
1925
Oil on canvas
89.5 x 73.5 cm
ML 76/2763
Urban 999

Titled *Blumengarten (V.) (Flower Garden)* on verso. Sold by Karl Nierendorf, Berlin, supposedly acting on N.'s behalf, to Haubrich, 1927. Haubrich Donation, 1946.

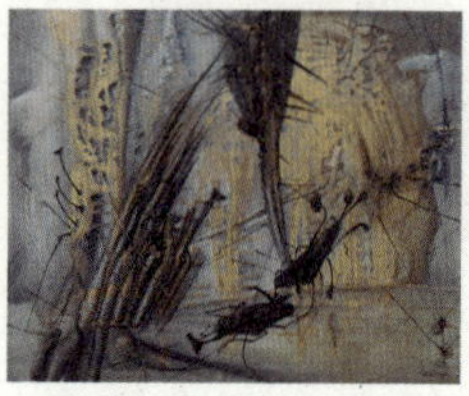

d'Orgeix, Christian
1927 Foix, lives in Alès

Scarabs
1956
Oil on canvas
54 x 65 cm
ML 76/3036

Galerie Hella Nebelung, Düsseldorf. Purchased by WRM with funding from the Haubrich Fund, 1958.

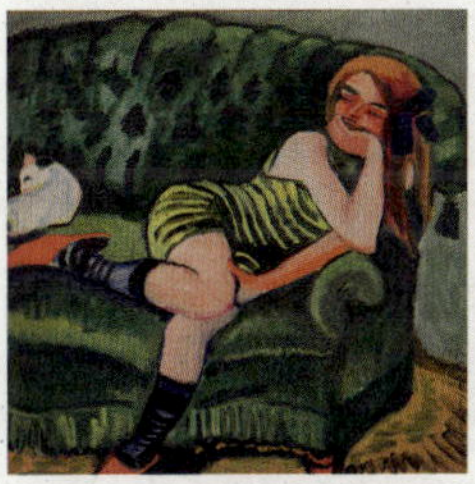

Pechstein, Max
1881 Zwickau–1955 Berlin

The Green Sofa (Das grüne Sofa)
1910
Oil on canvas
100.5 x 101 cm
ML 76/2891
Soika 1910/40

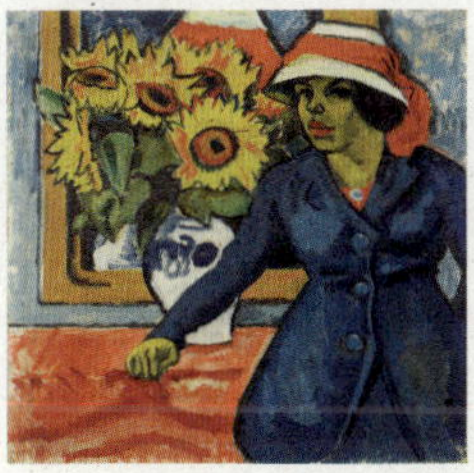

Verso:
Portrait of the Artist's Wife
(Die Frau des Künstlers)
C. 1910
Oil on canvas
101 x 100.5 cm
ML 76/2891
Soika 1910/68

Galerie Heinz J. Firle, Cologne. Galerie Änne Abels, Cologne. Purchased by WRM with funding from the Haubrich Fund, 1953.

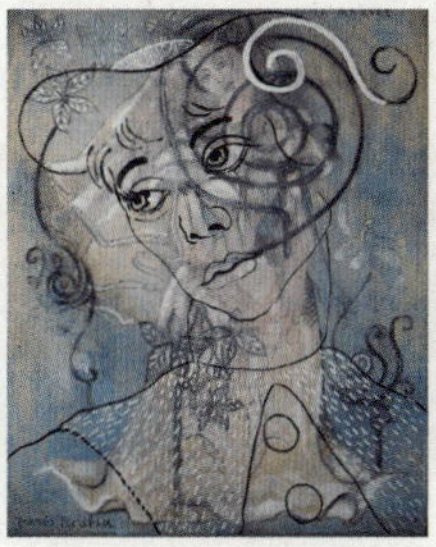

Picabia, Francis
1887 Paris–1953 Paris

The Bride (La mariée)
C. 1929
Graphite, ink, oil on wood
121.5 x 96.5 cm
ML 76/3101
Borràs 495

Galerie Léonce Rosenberg, Paris, was P.'s most important representative in the 1930s. The painting has not been proven part of Rosenberg's holdings, but there were sale attempts. Jacques Dubourg, Paris, also tried to sell the work. Purchased by WRM, most likely from Dubourg, with funding from the Haubrich Fund, 1960.

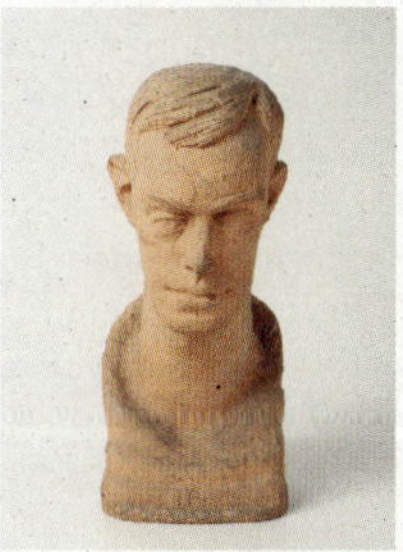

Pilartz, Theodor Caspar
1890 Cologne–1955 Cologne

Portrait of Walter Ruttmann
(Bildnis Walter Ruttmann)
Before 1918
Terracotta
H.: 44 cm
ML 76/SK 138

Kölnischer Kunstverein. Purchased by WRM with funding from the Haubrich Fund, 1956.

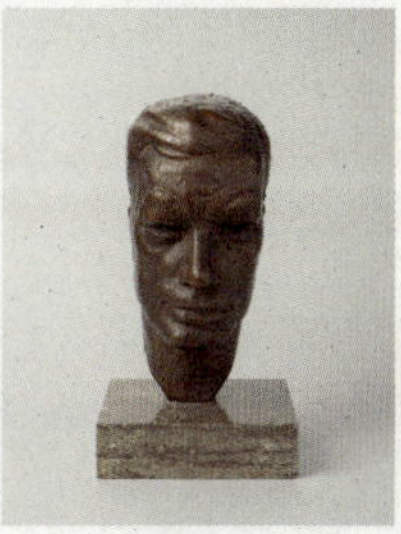

Bust of Vladimir Sokoloff
(Büste Wladimir Sokoloff)
Before 1928
Bronze
H.: 41 cm
ML 76/SK 86

Given to Haubrich by the artist in 1928. Haubrich Donation, 1946.

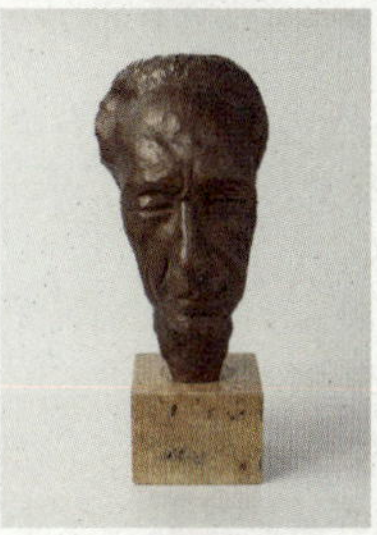

Bust of Dolbin (Büste Dolbin)
1935
Bronze
H.: 41 cm
ML 76/SK 73

A version in green stucco was given to Haubrich by the artist, 1930. Haubrich exchanged the plaster version for a bronze version, paying the difference, in 1935. Haubrich Donation, 1946.

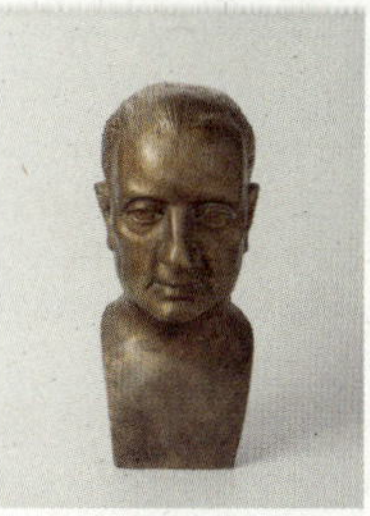

Bust of Doctor Haubrich
(Büste Doktor Haubrich)
C. 1948
Bronze
H.: 43 cm
ML 76/SK 166

Purchased by WRM directly from the artist with funding from the Haubrich Fund, 1957.

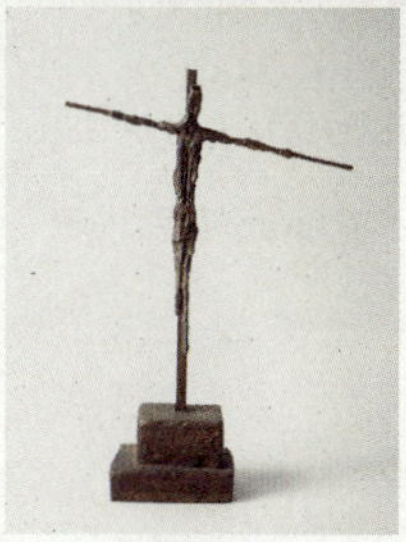

Richier, Germaine
1904 Grans–1959 Montpellier

Christ of Assy (Christ d'Assy)
1950
Bronze
H.: 48 cm
ML 76/SK 184

Galerie Christoph Czwiklitzer, Cologne. Purchased by WRM with funding from the Haubrich Fund, 1959.

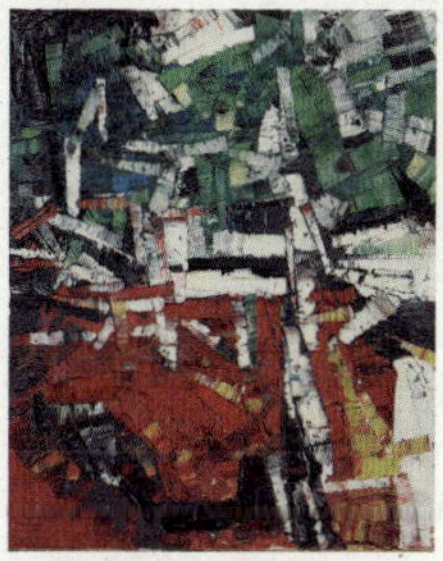

Riopelle, Jean-Paul
1923 Montreal–2002 Quebec City

Encounter (Rencontre)
1956
Oil on canvas
100 x 81 cm
ML 76/2998
Riopelle 1956.001H.1956

Galerie Jacques Dubourg, Paris. Purchased by WRM with funding from the Haubrich Fund, 1957.

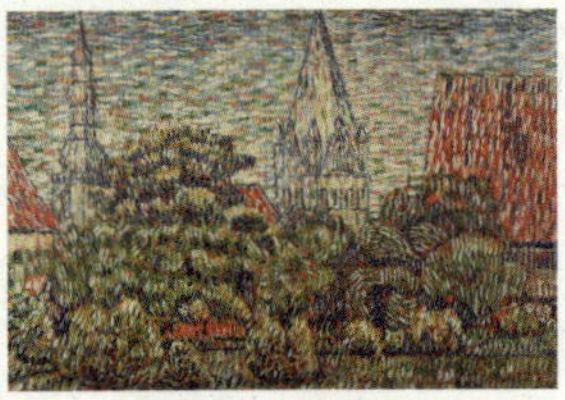

Rohlfs, Christian
1849 Groß Niendorf–1938 Hagen

Towers of Soest (Türme von Soest)
1906
Oil on cardboard
67.5 x 97.5 cm
WRM 2765
Vogt 394

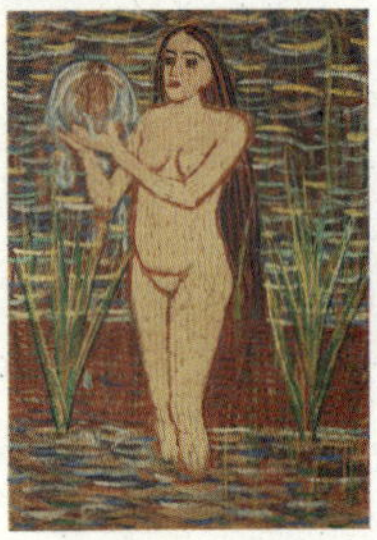

Verso:
Female Nude (Weiblicher Akt)
1905/06
Oil on cardboard
97.5 x 67.5 cm
WRM 2765

Purchased by Haubrich from Aloys Faust, 1934. Haubrich Donation, 1946. Today WRM.

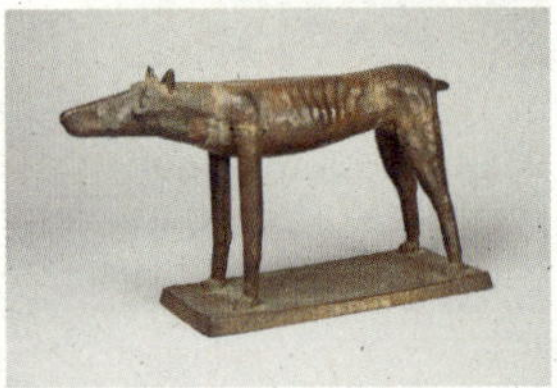

Rumpf, Franz
1930 Andernach–1963 Andernach

Dog (Hund)
1956
Brass
H.: 50 cm
ML 76/SK 174

Purchased by WRM directly from the artist with funding from the Haubrich Fund, 1958.

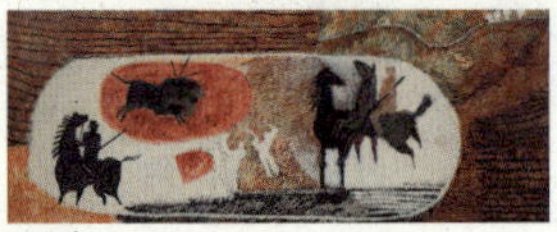

Schiller, Erhard Christian
1939 Danzig (today Gdańsk)–2008 Cologne

Bullfight (Stierkampf)
Before 1961
Oil on fibreboard
47 x 115 cm
ML 76/3125

Purchased by WRM with funding from the Haubrich Fund, 1961.

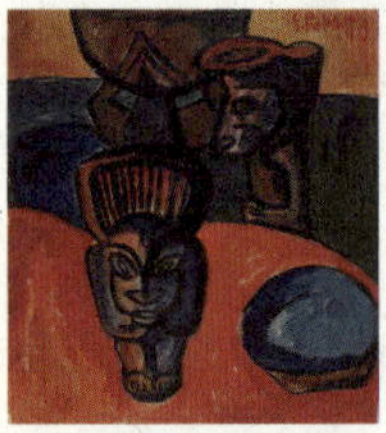

Schmidt-Rottluff, Karl
1884 Rottluff bei Chemnitz–1976 Berlin

Still Life with Negro Sculpture (Stilleben mit Negerplastik)
1913
Oil on canvas
73 x 68.5 cm
ML 76/2766

Documented as having been in Otto and Maschka Mueller's apartment in Berlin in 1914. When Mueller left Berlin in 1919, the work seems to have remained with Maschka. Purchased by Haubrich at Hugo Perls' Berlin auction house, most likely before his emigration to Paris in 1931. Haubrich Donation, 1946.

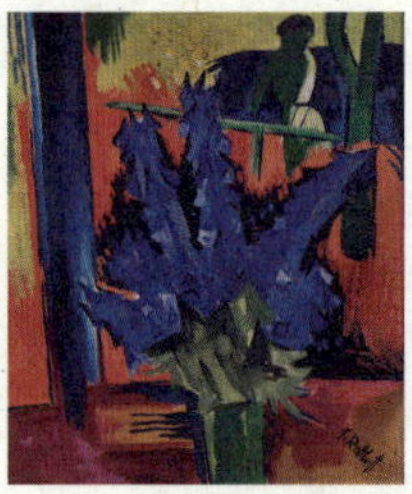

Larkspur in the Window (Rittersporn am Fenster)
1922
Oil on canvas
91 x 76 cm
ML 76/2873

Rittersporn was purchased by Kaiser-Friedrich Museum in Magdeburg from Goldschmidt & Wallerstein, 1922. Confiscated in 1937 and given first to Wolfgang Gurlitt in 1940 and, in the same year, on commission to Bernhard Böhmer. Returned upon request in 1943/44, then stored with Böhmer in Güstrow for protection from bombing. Considered as part of the Böhmer estate at his death on 3 May 1945 and auctioned by Wilma Zelck and Albert Daberkow on 11 April 1949 at Stuttgarter Kunstkabinett Roman Norbert Ketterer, Auction 5, Lot no. 1268. Purchased by WRM from Dr. Hans Melchers with funding from the Haubrich Fund, 1951. Mistakenly titled *Lupinien am Fenster (Lupins at the Window)* in the 1991 reconstruction of the 'Degenerate Art' exhibition, whereas the artist had titled the work on verso as *Rittersporn am Fenster.*

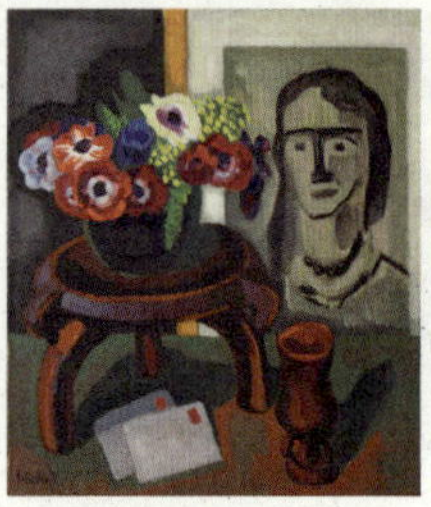

Regards to Nolde (Gruß an Nolde)
1936
Oil on canvas
89.5 x 76.5 cm
ML 76/2731

Sold at the exhibition '30 Deutsche Künstler' to an unknown person by Ferdinand Möller, Berlin, acting on the artist's behalf, 1936. Purchased by WRM as one of the first works acquired for the Haubrich Collection and funded by the Haubrich Fund, 1946. The sale was organized by Walter Buchler, Braunschweig, for an anonymous collector.

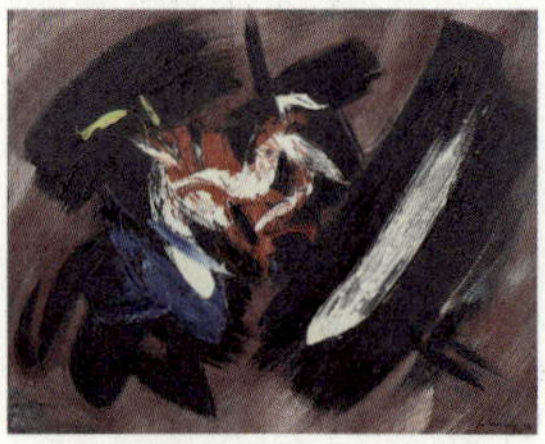

Schneider, Gérard Ernest
1898 Sainte-Croix–1986 Paris

Composition
1957
Oil on canvas
81 x 100 cm
ML 76/3009

Galerie der Spiegel, Cologne. Purchased by WRM with funding from the Haubrich Fund, 1957.

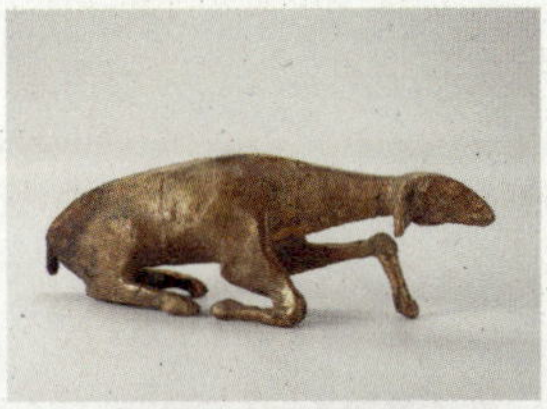

Schnitzler, Christa von
1922 Cologne–
2003 Frankfurt am Main

Sheep (Schaf)
1957
Bronze
H.: 13 cm
ML 76/SK 171

Kölnischer Kunstverein. Purchased by WRM with funding from the Haubrich Fund, 1958.

Scholz, Werner
1898 Berlin–
1982 Alpbach

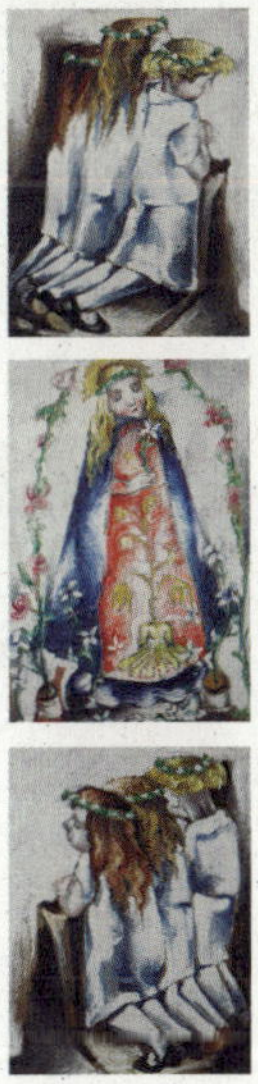

Tyrolean Madonna (Triptych) (Tiroler Madonna [Triptychon])
1933
Oil on cardboard
Central panel 119.3 x 78 cm, side panels 100 x 73 cm each
ML 76/2788

Purchased by Haubrich at a group exhibition at the Kölnischer Kunstverein, 1934. A triptych by the artist was acquired by WRM at the same exhibition and confiscated as 'degenerate' in 1937. Haubrich Donation, 1946.

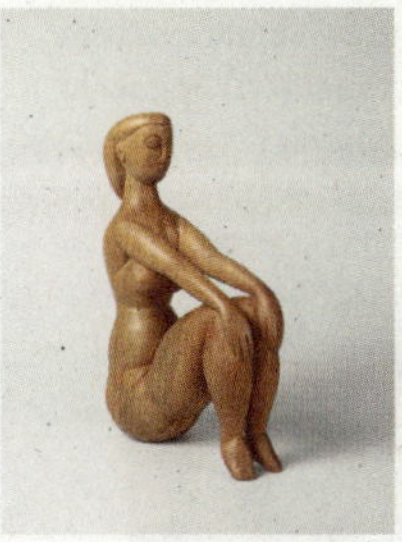

Schrieber, Ludwig Gabriel
1907 Burgwaldniel–
1975 Nesselwang

Squatting Woman (Hockende)
1948
Nutwood
H.: 22 cm
ML 76/SK 95

Donated by Haubrich, 1950.

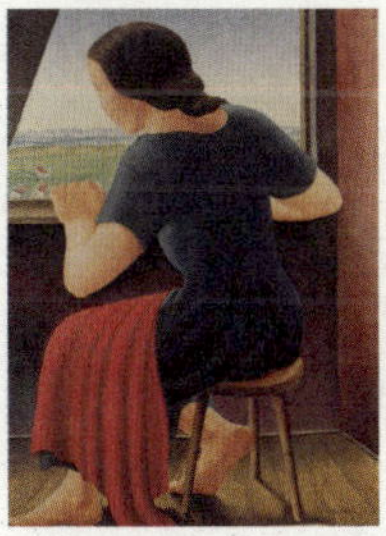

Schrimpf, Georg
1889 Munich–1938 Berlin

At the Window (Am Fenster)
1923
Oil on canvas
52.5 x 37.5 cm
ML 76/2780
Hofmann/Praeger 1923/7

Purchased by Haubrich from Franz Nienhaus, Cologne, 1926. Haubrich Donation, 1946. Discussed by Franz Roh in *Das Kunstblatt* 7 (1923), ill. p. 268, under the title *Am Fenster*. Also known as *Mädchen am Fenster (Girl at the Window)*.

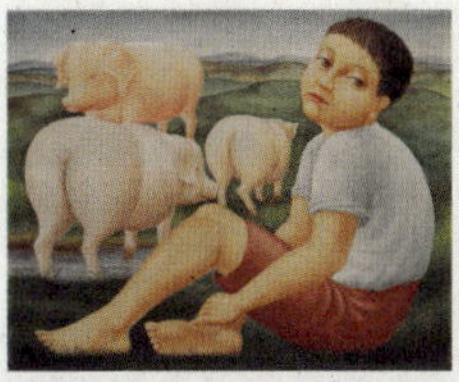

Swineherd (Schweinehirt)
1923
Oil on canvas
49.5 x 60 cm
ML 76/2779
Hofmann/Praeger 1923/17

Purchased by Haubrich from Franz Nienhaus, Cologne, 1926. Haubrich Donation, 1946.

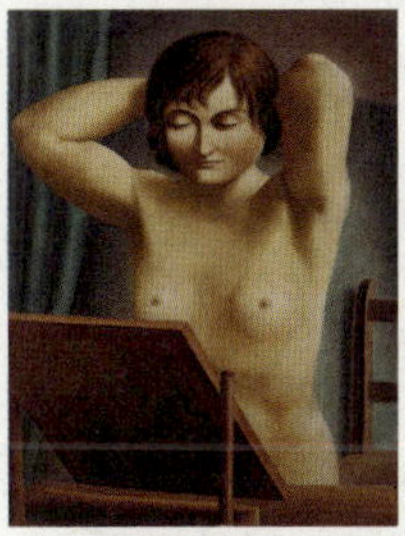

Nude Girl in Front of a Mirror (Mädchenakt vor dem Spiegel)
1926
Oil on canvas
70.5 x 53 cm
ML 76/2781
Hofmann/Praeger 1926/4

Purchased by Kunsthalle Mannheim from the artist in the fiscal year 1926/27. Confiscated in 1937. In 1940 it came into the possession of Hildebrand Gurlitt, Hamburg, who sold it to Haubrich in 1943. Haubrich Donation, 1946.

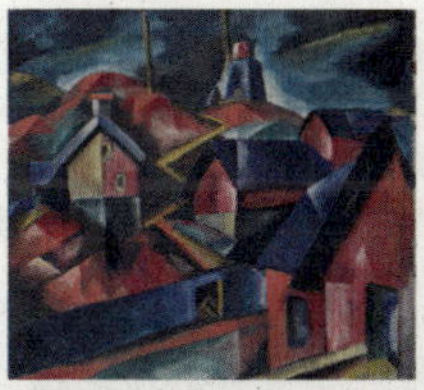

Seehaus, Paul Adolf
1891 Bonn–1919 Hamburg

Scottish Landscape with Lighthouse (Schottische Landschaft mit Leuchtturm)
C. 1914
Oil on canvas
45 x 49 cm
ML 76/2768

Purchased by Haubrich from Inge Peipers, Barmen (Wuppertal) via the Kölnischer Kunstverein, 1928. Haubrich Donation, 1946.

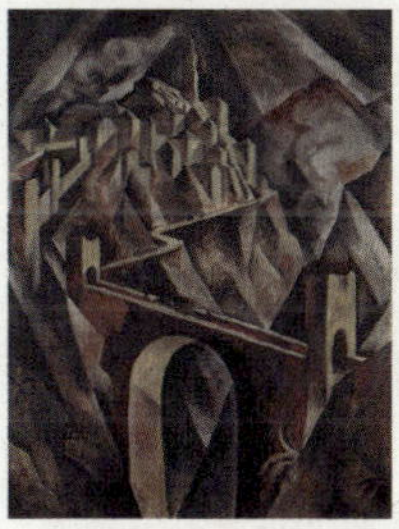

Alpine Town (Bergstadt)
1915
Oil on canvas
100 x 77 cm
ML 76/2767

Sold by the art collections of the City of Düsseldorf to Galerie Hermann Abels, 1936. Purchased that same year by Haubrich from Abels. Haubrich Donation, 1946.

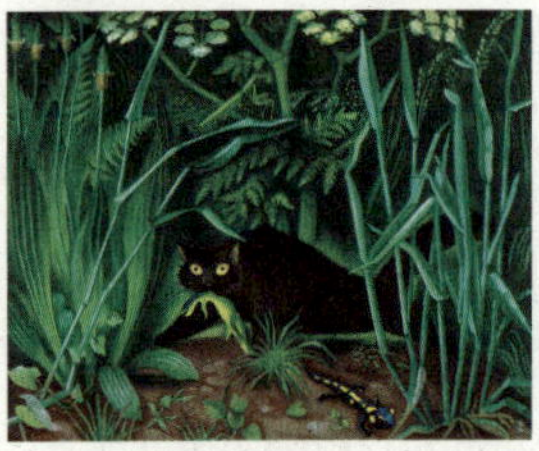

Seewald, Richard
1889 Arnswalde (today Choszczno)–1976 Munich

Cat with Salamander (Katze mit Salamander)
1933
Oil on canvas
95 x 115 cm
ML 76/2809

Given to Haubrich for the WRM Haubrich Collection by the artist during his visit to Cologne in 1949.

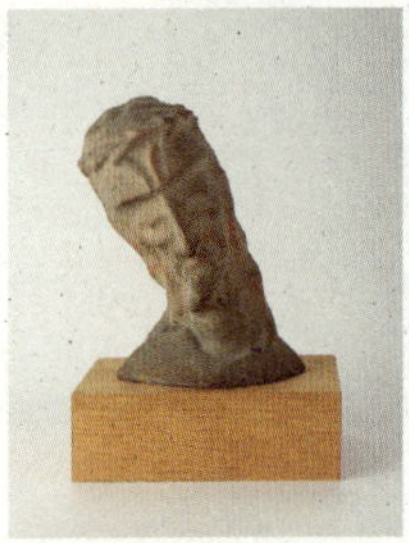

Seiwert, Franz Wilhelm
1894 Cologne–1933 Cologne

Christ's Head (Christuskopf)
1916/17
Terracotta
H.: 27 cm
ML 76/SK 185

Purchased by WRM from Else Geller-Zaertling, Neuss, with funding from the Haubrich Fund, 1959. According to her, the sculpture was already in her husband's possession at the time of her marriage in 1932.

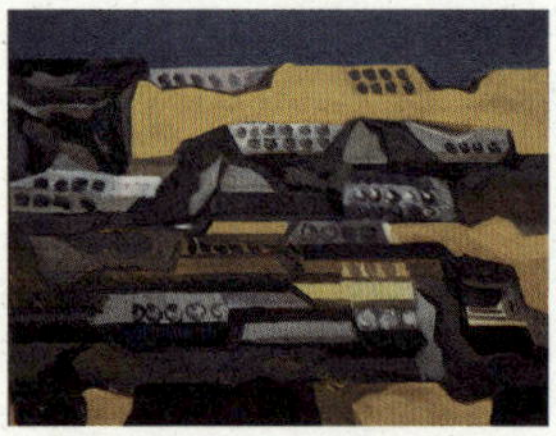

Senger, Joachim
1929 Berlin–1976 Munich

Terraced Landscape (Spain) (Terrassenlandschaft [Spanien])
1957
Oil on canvas
50 x 64 cm
ML 76/3091

Purchased by WRM with funding from the Haubrich Fund, 1959. Title written on the canvas frame by S.

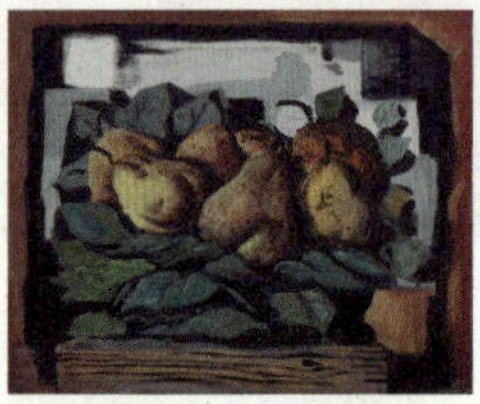

Serna, Ismaël Gonzalez de la
1887 Granada–1968 Paris

Still Life with Pears
C. 1927
Oil on cardboard
50 x 61 cm
ML 76/2769

Purchased by Haubrich at Galerie Zak, Paris, 1928. Haubrich Donation, 1946.

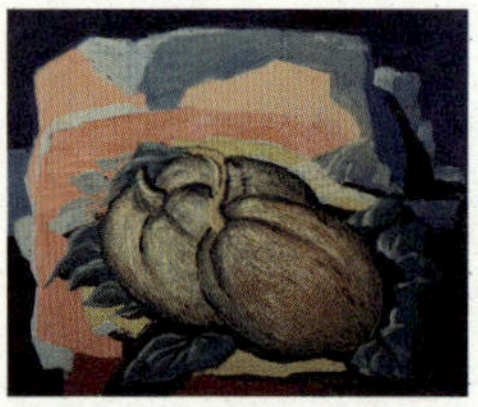

Still Life with Pumpkins
1927
Oil on cardboard
53.6 x 64.5 cm
ML 76/2770

Purchased by Haubrich from Erich Otto Jaffé, Cologne, in 1928. Haubrich Donation, 1946.

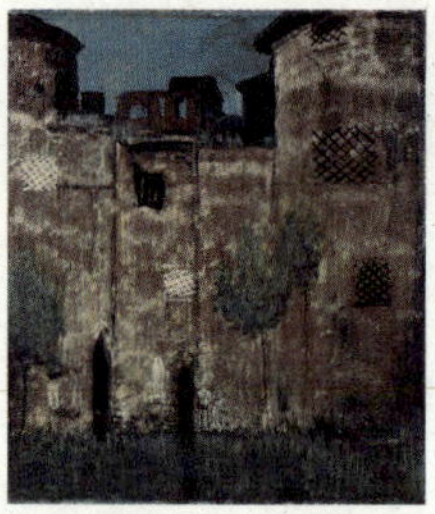

Spanish Castle
C. 1927/28
Oil on canvas
64.7 x 54 cm
ML 76/2771

Purchased by Haubrich at Galerie Alfred Flechtheim, Düsseldorf, 1928. Haubrich Donation, 1946.

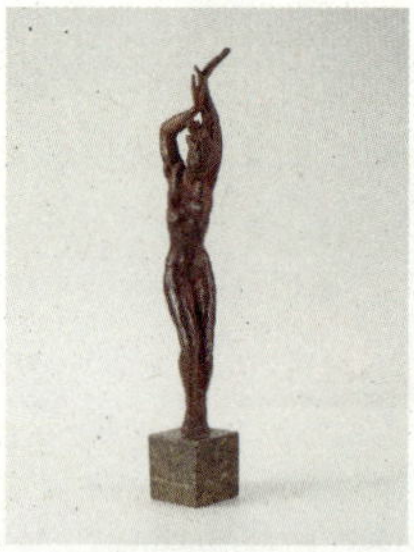

Sintenis, Renée
1888 Glatz (today Kłodzko)–1965 Berlin

Small Daphne (Kleine Daphne)
1918
Bronze
H.: 29.5 cm
ML 76/SK 67
Buhlmann 63

Acquired by Haubrich from Erich Otto Jaffé, Cologne, 1925. First mentioned as part of the collection in an article by Luise Straus-Ernst 'Die Sammlung Haubrich in Köln', *Das Kunstblatt* (1927), p. 33. Haubrich Donation, 1946.

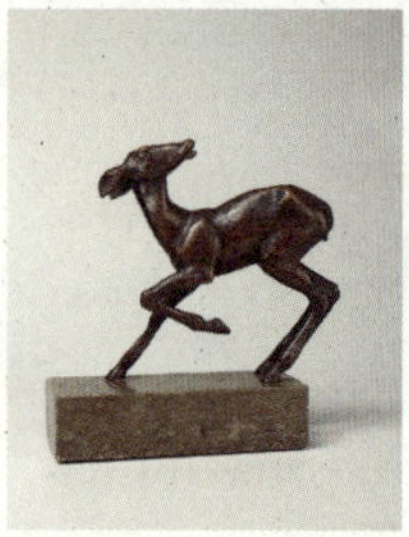

Wary Deer (Verhoffendes Reh)
1920
Bronze
H.: 12 cm
ML 76/SK 68
Buhlmann 184

In 1927, Haubrich acquired the small sculpture from Karl Nierendorf, Berlin. Previous ownership uncertain. Cast in such high numbers that it has not been possible to determine the edition from which the ML cast originates. Haubrich Donation, 1946.

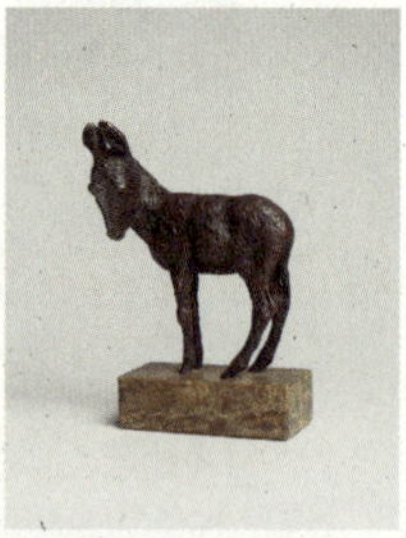

Donkey (Esel)
1923
Bronze
H.: 13 cm
ML 76/SK 69
Buhlmann 191

Purchased by Haubrich from Kunsthandlung Dr. Becker & Newman, Cologne, 1927. First mentioned as part of the Haubrich Collection by Luise Straus-Ernst, 'Die Sammlung Haubrich in Köln', *Das Kunstblatt* 11 (1927), p. 33. Haubrich Donation, 1946.

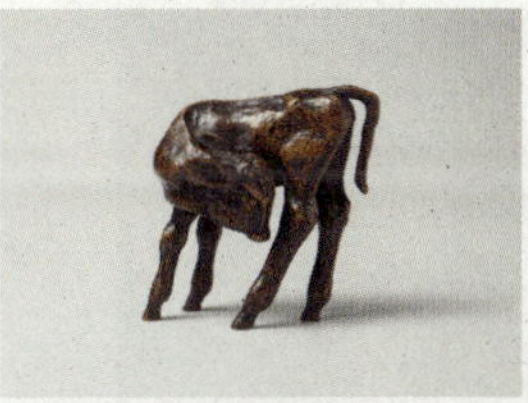

Young Ox (Junger Ochse)
1929
Bronze
H.: 12.5 cm
ML 76/SK 70
Buhlmann 200

Purchased by Haubrich from Aloys Faust, 1935. Previous ownership could not be established, for the sculpture was cast in high numbers and no conclusions could be drawn about the cast. Haubrich Donation, 1946.

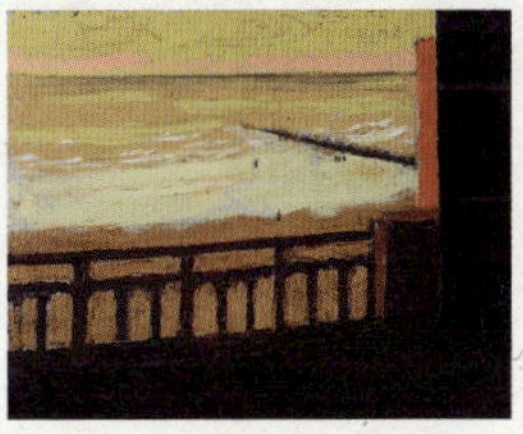

Slabbinck, Hendrik
1914 Bruges–1991 Antwerp

Terrace (Die Terrasse)
C. 1960
Oil on canvas
60 x 73 cm
ML 76/3113

Das Belgische Haus, Cologne. Purchased by WRM with funding from the Haubrich Fund, 1960.

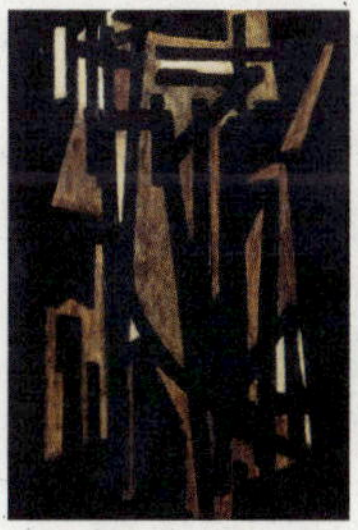

Soulages, Pierre
1919 Rodez, lives in Paris

Painting (Peinture)
1950
Oil on canvas
146.5 x 97 cm
ML 76/2971
Encrevé 47

Galerie Otto und Etta Stangl, Munich. Purchased by WRM with funding from the Haubrich Fund, 1955.

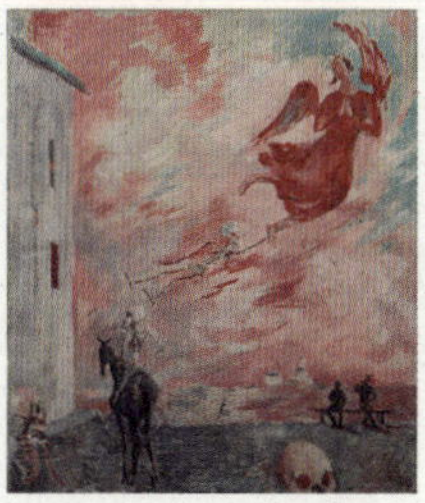

Sozonow, Vsevolod
1899 St. Petersburg–1966 London

Angel of Death (Engel des Todes)
Before 1948
Oil on canvas
61 x 50.5 cm
ML 76/2805

Purchased by WRM after the exhibition 'Christliche Kunst der Gegenwart' through the assistance of Michael Ross, London, with funding from the Haubrich Fund, 1948. Like the artist, the previous owner lived in London, but remains unknown.

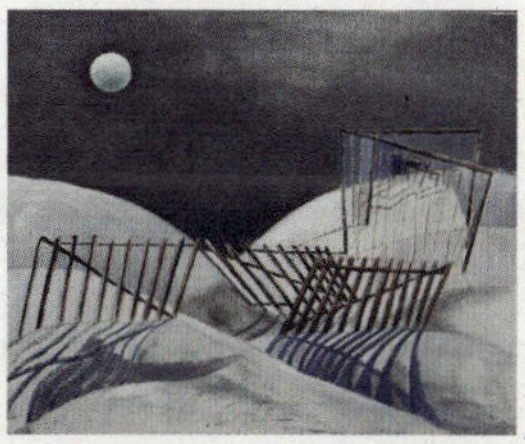

Steinforth, Peter
1923 Berlin–1981 Darmstadt

Snow Drifts (Schneeverwehungen)
1951
Oil on canvas
62 x 74 cm
ML 76/2878

Purchased by WRM directly from the artist with funding from the Haubrich Fund, 1952.

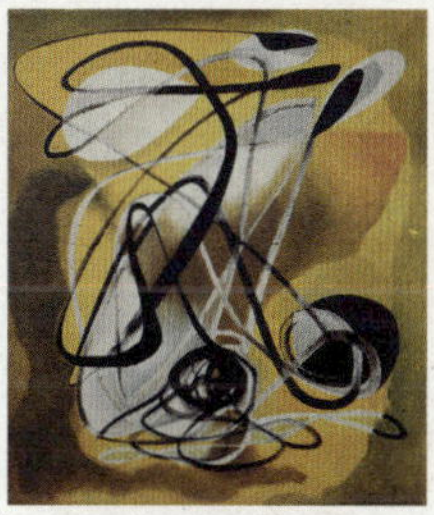

Confused Lines (Verirrte Linien)
1953
Oil on canvas
119.5 x 99 cm
ML 76/2948

Purchased by WRM directly from the artist with funding from the Haubrich Fund, 1954.

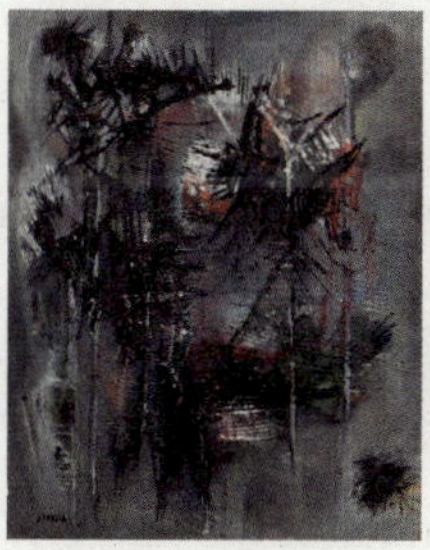

Strazza, Guido
1922 Santa Fiora, lives in Rome

Wounded Creature (La creatura ferita)
1957
Tempera, oil on fibreboard
70 x 55 cm
ML 76/3011

Purchased by WRM directly from the artist with funding from the Haubrich Fund, 1957.

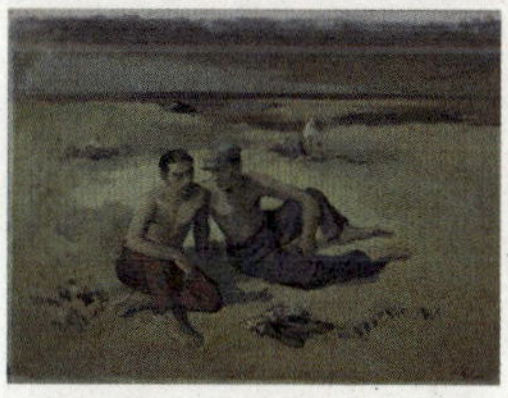

Strecker, Paul
1900 Mainz–1950 Berlin

Bathers on a Baltic Beach (Badende am Ostseestrand)
1934
Oil on canvas
50 x 65 cm
ML 76/2842

Purchased by Haubrich, 1935. Purchase documented by a receipt from Galerie Dr. Andreas Becker, Cologne. Haubrich Donation, 1946.

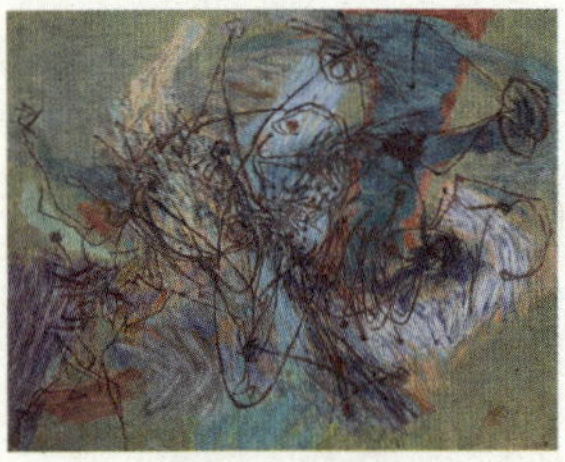

Trier, Hann
1915 Düsseldorf–
1999 Castiglione della Pescaia

Puya I
1954
Tempera on canvas
65.5 x 80 cm
ML 76/3084
Fehlemann/Gerlach-Laxner 110

Galerie der Spiegel, Cologne. Purchased by WRM with funding from the Haubrich Fund and in exchange for another work by the artist, 1959.

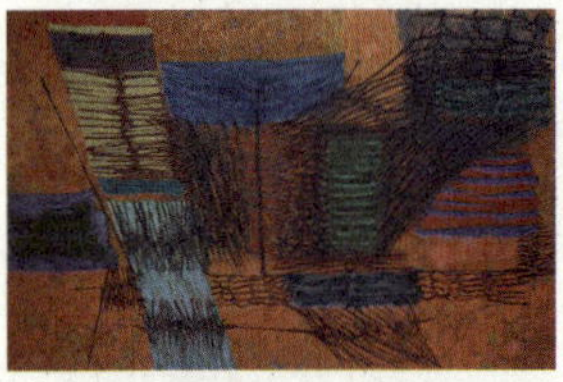

Separation (Trennung)
1956
Tempera on canvas
97.5 x 146.5 cm
ML 76/3030
Fehlemann/Gerlach-Laxner 163

Galerie der Spiegel, Cologne. Purchased by WRM with funding from the Haubrich Fund, 1958.

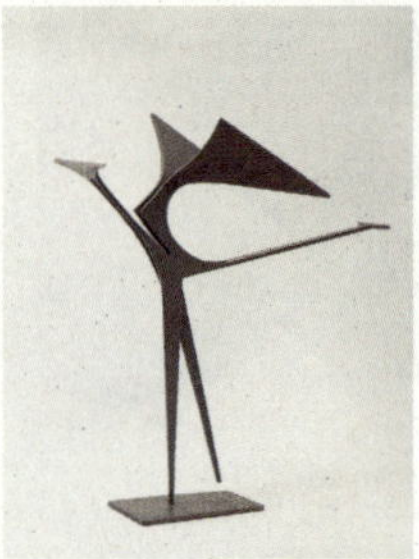

Uhlmann, Hans
1900 Berlin–1975 Berlin

Bird (Vogel)
1954
Steel
H.: 47.5 cm
ML 76/SK 126

Purchased by WRM directly from the artist with funding from the Haubrich Fund, 1955.

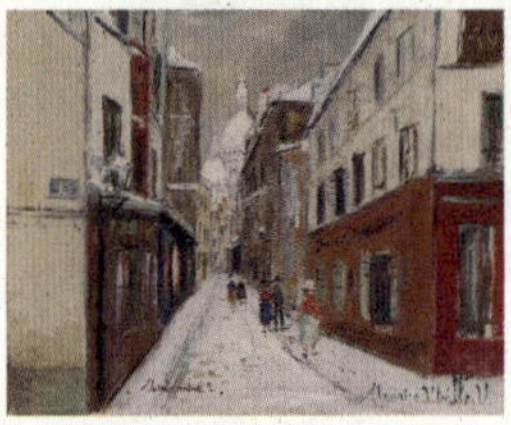

Utrillo, Maurice (attributed)
1883 Paris–1955 Dax

Montmartre with Sacre-Cœur
1942/43
Oil on canvas
37.5 x 46 cm
ML 76/2772

Purchased by Haubrich from the Kölnischer Kunstverein, 1944. Haubrich Donation, 1946. The Association Maurice Utrillo has recently cast doubt on the painting's authenticity, and the matter is currently under examination.

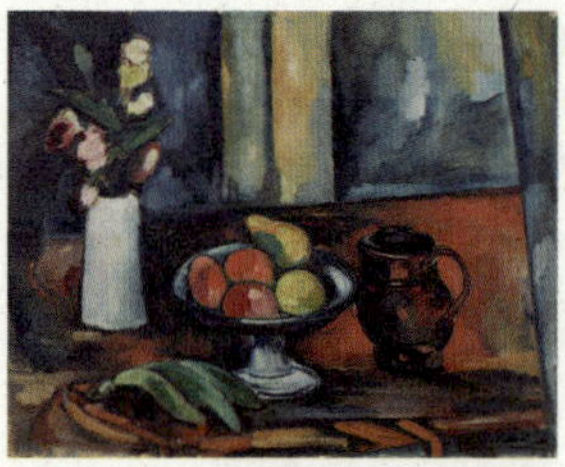

Vlaminck, Maurice de
1876 Paris–1958 Rueil-la-Gadelière

Still Life with Flowers and Fruit (Nature morte au bouquet et aux fruits)
1911
Oil on canvas
60 x 73 cm
ML 76/2773

Acquired by Haubrich from the Kölnischer Kunstverein in exchange for an unknown work, 1925. Haubrich Donation, 1946.

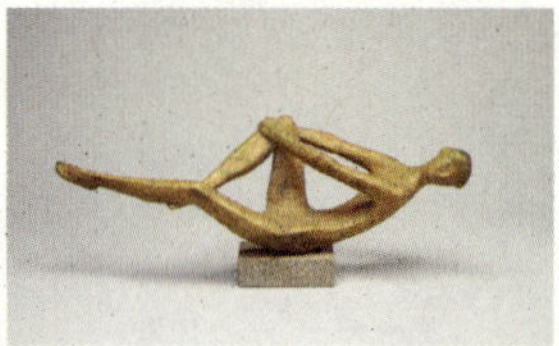

Volwahsen, Herbert
1906 Schellendorf–1988 Murnau am Staffelsee

Balance
1958
Bronze
H.: 29 cm
ML 76/SK 182

Purchased by WRM directly from the artist with funding from the Haubrich Fund, 1958.

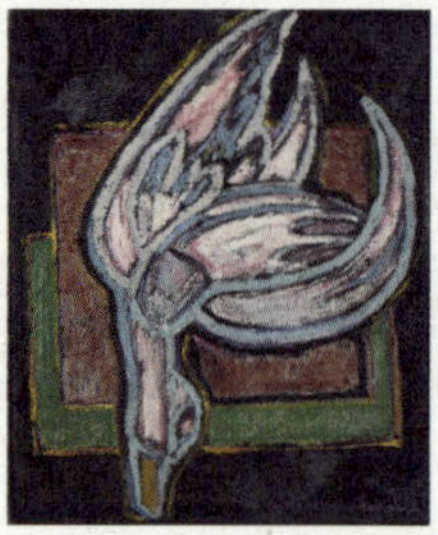

Vordemberge, Friedrich
1897 Osnabrück–1981 Cologne

Still Life with Wild Duck (Stilleben mit Wildente)
C. 1949
Wax crayon on canvas
99 x 78 cm
ML 76/2871

Donated by Haubrich, 1951

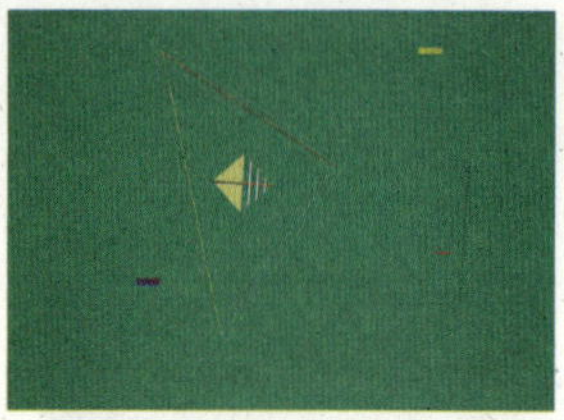

Vordemberge-Gildewart, Friedrich
1899 Osnabrück–1962 Ulm

Composition No. 122/1941
1941
Oil on canvas
60.5 x 80.5 cm
ML 76/2944
Helms/Valstar-Verhoff 122

Purchased by WRM with funding from the Haubrich Fund, 1953. Previous ownership could not be established. The previous owner mentioned in the museum files, Ferdinand Möller, merely borrowed the work for an exhibition at his Cologne gallery (September/ October 1954).

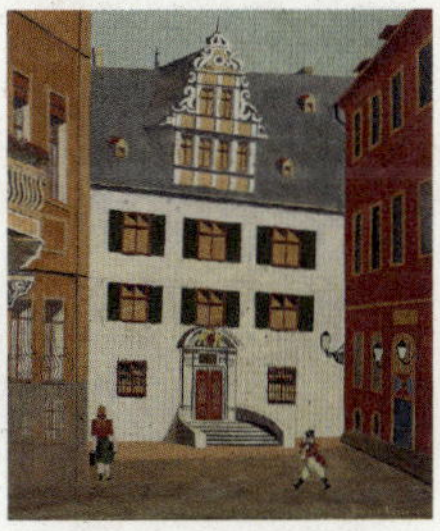

Weert, Jan van

**1871 's Hertogenbosch–
1955 Düsseldorf**

Group of Buildings (Häusergruppe)
C. 1950
Oil on fibreboard
54.5 x 45 cm
ML 76/2890

Galerie Alex Vömel, Düsseldorf. Purchased by WRM with funding from the Haubrich Fund, 1952.

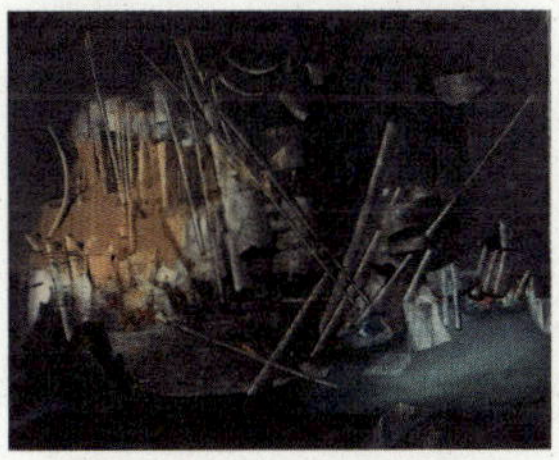

Weichberger, Philipp

1936 Bremen–1985 New York

Small Fire (Kleines Feuer)
Before 1958
Oil on canvas
80.5 x 100 cm
ML 76/3071

Galerie Hella Nebelung, Düsseldorf. Purchased by WRM with funding from the Haubrich Fund, 1959.

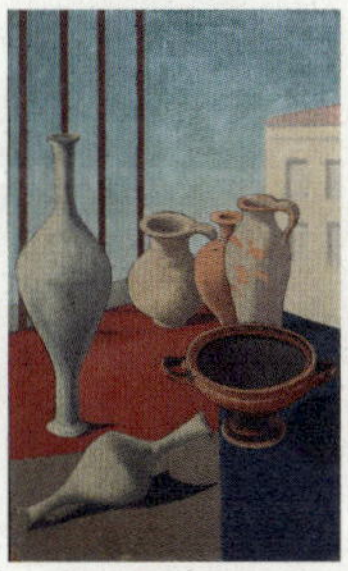

Werdehausen, Hans

1910 Bochum–1977 Höxter

*Jars in Sicily
(Krüge in Sizilien)*
1935/36
Oil on cardboard
59.5 x 35 cm
ML 76/3072

Purchased by WRM from the artist at his solo show in Recklinghausen, with funding from the Haubrich Fund, 1958.

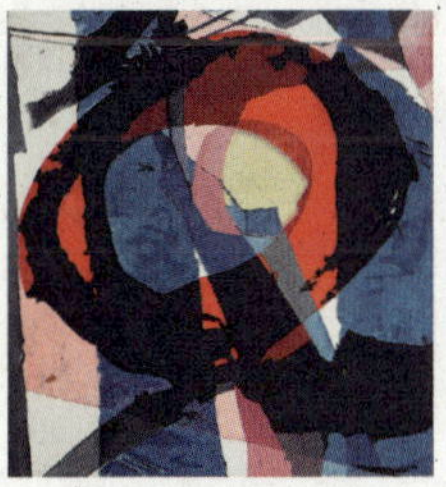

Discus (Diskus)
1955/56
Oil on canvas
100 x 90 cm
ML 76/3038

Purchased by WRM from the artist at his solo show in Recklinghausen, with funding from the Haubrich Fund, 1958.

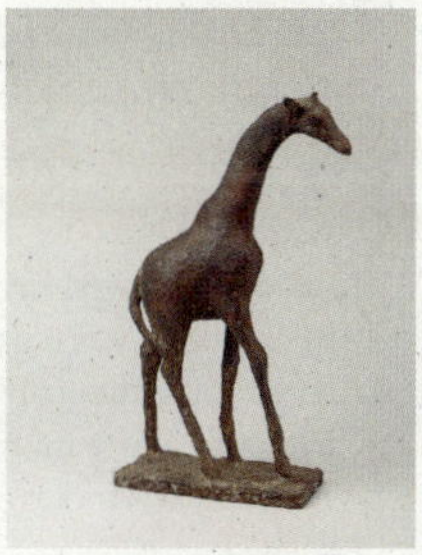

Wrampe, Fritz

1893 Munich–1934 Munich

*Walking Giraffe
(Giraffe, schreitend)*
1928
Bronze
H.: 37 cm
ML 76/SK 100

Purchased by WRM from W.'s estate administrator Heinrich Kirchner, Munich, with funding from the Haubrich Fund, 1951.

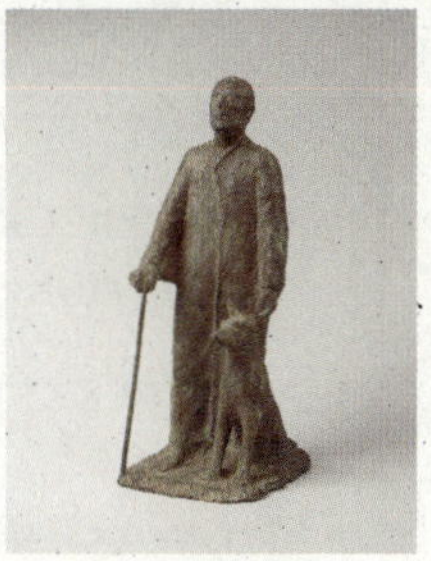

*Blind Man with Dog
(Blinder mit Hund)*
1933
Bronze
H.: 39 cm
ML 76/SK 101

Purchased by WRM from W.'s estate administrator Heinrich Kirchner, Munich, with funding from the Haubrich Fund, 1951.

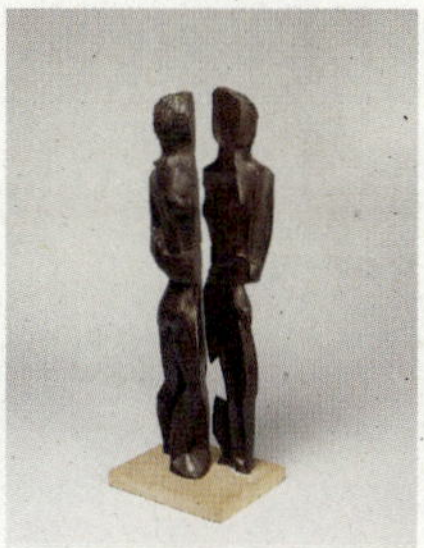

Zadkine, Ossip

**1890 Smolensk–
1967 Neuilly-sur-Seine**

*Intimacy or Narcissus
(Intimité ou le Narcisse)*
1950
Ebony
H.: 75 cm
ML 76/SK 169
Lecombre 426

Galerie Christoph Czwiklitzer. Acquired by WRM in exchange for Wilhelm Lehmbruck's *Kopf eines Mädchens* (*Head of a Girl*, formerly WRM SK 58) and with funding from the Haubrich Fund, 1958.

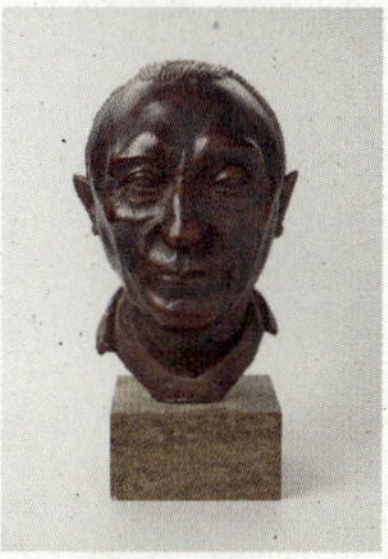

Zschokke, Alexander

1894 Basel–1981 Basel

Konrad Adenauer
1932 (cast after 1945)
Bronze
H.: 34.5 cm
ML 76/SK 75

Autohaus Fleischhauer, Cologne. Given to Haubrich for the Haubrich Collection, 1951.

Brief Lexicon

People, Institutions and Terms

Compiled by
Charlotte Neußer

AUTOHAUS FLEISCHHAUER

Business / Cologne

In 1924, when he founded his Cologne-Raderberg car dealership, Jacob Fleischhauer employed seven people. By 1950, he employed 570 people. In the 1950s and 1960s, the firm enabled the Wallraf-Richartz Museum to purchase major works of classical Modernism.

ADOLPHE **BASLER**
(1878–1949)

Art critic, art dealer / Berlin, Paris

Adolphe Basler was a Jewish art critic and a member of the Paris Café du Dôme circle. In addition to writing reviews, he also wrote monographs on artists such as Leonardo da Vinci, Henri Matisse and Moise Kisling, and began dealing in artworks at an early stage. B. was Paris correspondent for *Die Aktion*, the publication that gave Expressionism its breakthrough. He was a contact of → PAUL **CASSIRER**, faced stiff competition from → ALFRED **FLECHTHEIM** in Düsseldorf and was for a time a member of the Berlin Secession committee.

ANDREAS **BECKER**

→ **GALERIE DR. ANDREAS BECKER**

HANNA **BEKKER VOM RATH**
(1893–1983)

Gallery owner / Frankfurt am Main

Hanna Bekker vom Rath began as a painter and collector, later supporting the activities of artists known to her personally and trading as an art dealer. She turned the building known as the Blaues Haus (Blue House) in Hofheim into a place for artists to get together and to work. In 1929, B. founded the Society for Friends of the Art of Alexej von Jawlensky, which provided him with financial support. Artists such as Karl Schmidt-Rottluff and Ernst Wilhelm Nay were frequent guests at the Blaues Haus. B.'s paintings featured in exhibitions held by Ludwig Schames in Frankfurt am Main and by Fritz Gurlitt (→ WOLFGANG **GURLITT**) in Berlin. After 1933, B. began dealing privately in proscribed art. From 1940 onwards, she held secret exhibitions in her Berlin studio apartment. In 1945, the Blaues Haus was occupied by American troops. It survived the war intact, as did B.'s collection. In 1947, B. opened the Frankfurter Kunstkabinett in a ruined building. It featured artworks by formerly denounced artists. Two years later, the Kabinett moved to the building on the Börsenplatz that had formerly housed the Ludwig Schames Kunstsalon. Today, this gallery is run by Margarete Wegner.

IRMGARD **BENDER**

Collector / Bonn

Irmgard Bender is one of the three daughters of collector → CARL **STEINBART** who took over his art collection after his death.

IDA and FRIEDRICH **BIENERT**

Business owners, collectors / Dresden

In 1888, Ida Suckert (1870–1965) married the mill owner Erwin Bienert (1859–1931). Her salons at the family's villa in Dresden brought together the city's avant-garde. Guests included Otto Dix, Conrad Felixmüller, Walter Gropius, Paul Klee, Oskar Kokoschka, Emil Nolde and Mary Wigman. The dance instructor Gret Palucca – a frequent subject of Expressionist pictures – married the couple's son, Friedrich Bienert (1891–1961). Their collection survived the war and was transported from the Soviet Zone of Occupation to Munich. The family were forced to sell off their collection piece by piece in order to survive.

MORITZ **BING**
(1875–1947)

Lawyer / Cologne, Bern

Moritz Bing completed his legal clerkship in Cologne. In 1902, he was admitted to the legal profession at the Regional and District Court of Cologne. He entered into a partnership with Dr. Sauer, which was dissolved in 1933 due to discrimination against Jewish lawyers. He was finally barred from practicing law in 1938. B. was taken to Dachau concentration camp in November 1938 but was released ten days later. After this, he emigrated to Switzerland at the first opportunity and died in Bern in 1947. B. was able to bring a large number of his household effects to Switzerland by declaring them as an endowment for his daughter, who married in Switzerland in 1937.

After the war, his heirs sought reparations on a number of occasions for the property, assets, treasures and silver he was forced to leave behind in Germany and received a certain amount of compensation. In 1929, B. was a member of the → **KÖLNISCHER KUNSTVEREIN**.

BERNHARD A. **BÖHMER**

(1892–1945)

Sculptor, art dealer / Bielefeld, Güstrow, Berlin

In 1907, Bernhard Aloysius Böhmer began to study painting and sculpture at the School for Craftsmen and the Applied Arts. There, he met Marga Graeber, who later became his wife. After living in a number of places, the couple moved to Güstrow and settled close to Ernst Barlach's home. The friendship between Barlach and B. led to a close working relationship. After the death of → PAUL **CASSIRER** in 1926, B. worked as Barlach's assistant and secretary, and also oversaw the sale and exhibition of his artworks. B.'s commitment to his friend's work remained even after Marga B. left him in 1927 and embarked on an affair with Barlach. In 1931, B. married Hella Otte, the daughter of an industrialist. → PETER **BÖHMER** was the child of this marriage. From 1933 onwards, B. was in contact with the Protestant Art Service, which was later to be subordinated to the Reich Ministry of Public Enlightenment and Propaganda. B. was a friend of Rolf Hetsch (→ **VALUATION COMMISSION**), and knew Joseph Goebbels personally. As one of the four dealers authorized to deal in → **'DEGENERATE ART'**, B. was able to secure a large number of artworks to sell thanks to his good contacts. He appears to have passed works on to → THEODOR **FISCHER** in 1941. After the 'degenerate art' campaign came to an end, the Valuation Commission transferred the remaining confiscated art to B. in Güstrow (through the offices of Hetsch). Peter Böhmer inherited the collection when B. and his wife committed suicide in 1945, after the arrival of the Red Army. In spite of it being unclear whose property the artwork was, his aunt and guardian → WILMA **ZELCK** and her partner → ALBERT **DABERKOW** sold artworks from the collection after the war.

PETER **BÖHMER**

(1932–2007)

Wholesaler / Güstrow, Berlin, Hamburg

The son and heir of → BERNHARD A. **BÖHMER** survived the suicide of his parents in 1945. His aunt → WILMA **ZELCK** became his guardian, according to his parents' wishes. In May 1945, she began to relocate the artworks stored at Güstrow. B. moved with her to Rostock (where they became acquainted with → ALBERT **DABERKOW**), to Berlin, and, finally, to Hamburg, where B. trained as a wholesaler. In 1953, when he came of age, he took over administering his inheritance. B. did business with a variety of people in the course of selling the artworks, including Wolfgang and → ROMAN NORBERT **KETTERER**, → ALEX **VÖMEL**, the Commeter gallery, → **HAUSWEDELL & CO.** and the → KUNSTHAUS **LEMPERTZ**. Legal proceedings decided the question of ownership largely in favour of the Böhmers.

JOHANNES **BREDT**

(1888–1950)

Publisher, printer, collector / Münster

In 1912, Johannes Bredt took over the publishing house of his father (who had the same name), and became the proprietor of the Münster university printing press. His passion for collecting modernist art brought him into contact with the gallery owner → KARL **NIERENDORF**, resulting in a lifelong friendship. B. apparently got into financial difficulties and was forced to part with artworks in his collection.

BRITISH COUNCIL

The British Council was founded in 1934 with the mission of promoting relationships between Great Britain and other countries in the fields of culture, education and science. After 1949 it contributed to cultural and political 're-education' in Germany, for example through exhibition tours by British artists such as Henry Moore, under the direction of the → **BRITISH MILITARY GOVERNMENT**. From 1959 until the 1990s, the B.C. ran the Die Brücke British Centre in Cologne. This was its first branch in Germany, established by the Military Government (headquarters of the → **KÖLNISCHER KUNSTVEREIN** from 2002).

BRITISH MILITARY GOVERNMENT

After the Second World War the British Military Government tried to introduce a cultural policy modelled on British practice (the 'Projection of Britain') in its occupation zone (which consisted of the present federal Länder of Lower Saxony, Schleswig-Holstein and North Rhine-Westphalia). The British Centres in Germany became promotion centres, one of which was created in Cologne and was operated from 1959 until the 1990s by the → **BRITISH COUNCIL**. Here, small exhibitions by British artists such as Henry Moore were mounted.

BÜCHERSTUBE AM DOM

Bookstore, art dealership / Cologne

The Bücherstube am Dom ('bookshop near the cathedral') was founded in June 1931 by the businessman and collector Rudolf Metzger and his wife, the photographer Ilse Metzger-Salberg (1901–1947). In addition to offering an impressive selection of books, they held exhibitions of art and photography from the very beginning. The art historian → HANS **MELCHERS** (1902–1969) joined the business as a specialist and as a partner. He ran the business until 1950. After a year, the Metzgers sold their share of the business to Albert Schulze-Vellinghaus (1905–1967). As they were of Jewish ancestry, they chose to go into exile to escape persecution. Ilse left the country with her new partner, the artist Anton Räderscheidt. Hanns Meyer (1903–1968) began working for the business in 1932. Melchers and Meyer ran B.'s dealership in books and graphic arts (founded in association with Gottfried Becker in 1939) while Schulze-Vellinghaus was called up for military service in 1940. After the war, he remained a sleeping partner, but continued with his career as a journalist. The collection had been transferred to Maubach before the bombing of 1943. The bookstore and the graphic arts dealership were able to reopen in February 1946. The exhibitions were relocated to the Schwerthof and the Zeppelinstrasse. B.'s Moderne Galerie opened in new premises in 1966.

WALTHER **BUCHLER**

(1926–2005)

Businessman / Braunschweig

Dr. Walther H. Buchler was the great-grandson of the founder of the Braunschweig-based quinine factory Buchler & Co. His father, Walther P. Buchler, ran the business until 1978. He developed a process for synthesizing quinine and a technique for using radioactivity in medicine. B. acted as company secretary for this branch of the business. B. was brought into contact with art and architecture by his father. → LEOPOLD **REIDEMEISTER** was his brother-in-law.

HERMANN **BURG**

Art historian, art dealer / Cologne, Berlin

In 1919, Dr. Hermann Burg was a member of the advisory committee of the Düsseldorf art group Junges Rheinland, which also included → ALFRED **FLECHTHEIM** and → KARL ERNST **OSTHAUS**. A short time later, he opened a business dealing in old and contemporary art, first in the Salomonsgasse and later in the Hohestrasse in Cologne. In 1925, his gallery and the → **KUNSTHANDLUNG DR. BECKER & NEWMAN**, → **GALERIE SIGMUND SALZ** and → **GALERIE JAFFÉ-GUTTMANN** moved into the first Cologne gallery house, Unter Fettenhennen 11. In 1929, B. moved his art dealing business to Berlin. As an author, he wrote for publications such as the magazine *Kunst und Künstler*, produced by the → **CASSIRER** press.

JOSEPH **BURTHOUL**

Hat manufacturer, collector / Brussels

Joseph Burthoul's art collection was sold in 1926 via the Georges Giroux gallery.

PAUL **CASSIRER**
(1871–1926)

Gallery owner, publisher, auctioneer / Munich, Berlin

Paul Cassirer studied art history and other subjects in Munich, became acquainted with the Munich bohemian scene and was a co-founder of *Simplicissimus*. In 1889, he and his cousin Bruno opened a publishing house and art dealing business in Berlin's Victoriastrasse. C. moved in the Paris circles that centred on the Café du Dôme and Wilhelm Lehmbruck's studio, and his acquaintances included → ALFRED **FLECHTHEIM**. After parting company with his cousin in 1901, C. took over the art salon. In the face of the reactionary art politics of the Reich under the Kaiser, he became a pioneer of Impressionism, French modernism and the budding Expressionism movement in Germany. The → **DEUTSCHER KÜNSTLERBUND** was founded by a number of people, including Graf → LEOPOLD VON **KALCKREUTH**, to support the new trends; C. took over as business manager in 1904. From 1908 onwards, he resumed his publishing activities. His publications included *Pan-Presse*. In 1912, C., like → KARL ERNST **OSTHAUS** and Flechtheim, was a member of the working committee of the → **SONDERBUND EXHIBITION**. In 1913, he took over the directorship of the → **KÖLNISCHER KUNSTVEREIN** for a year. C. initially enlisted voluntarily, but later became a bitter opponent of the war, for which he was persecuted. He was forced to close his publishing company. From 1916, he ran an auction house jointly with Hans Helbing. Lots included artwork from Flechtheim's gallery collection and parts of the Osthaus collection. From 1917 onwards, C. lived in Switzerland. → VICTOR **WALLERSTEIN** worked at his gallery, and Walter Feilchenfeldt (1894–1953) and → FRITZ **GOLDSCHMIDT** worked at the auction house. Karl Haberstock and → THEODOR **FISCHER** trained with C. C.'s second wife was the actress Tilla Durieux. When their relationship failed, he committed suicide. His business partners Grete Ring and Walter Feilchenfeldt took over the gallery, which they were forced to close in 1933 along with the publishing house. In 1935, Ring and Feilchenfeldt opened a branch in Amsterdam. Before the occupation of the Netherlands in 1940, Feilchenfeldt moved to Ascona, then to Zürich. Ring moved to London in 1938.

HERBERT **CRAMER**
(died 1925)

Gallery owner / Frankfurt am Main

What little information we have on Herbert Cramer's gallery confirms that it opened in 1919 at Kaiserstrasse 21 in Frankfurt. It exhibited old art as well as contemporary works, primarily art by the Junges Rheinland and the Junges Westfalen groups. C.'s gallery modeled itself on the gallery run by → ALFRED **FLECHTHEIM**, with which it also had business ties. The gallery was allied to a graphic arts publishing company. It seems to have remained in operation until the year 1923.

CHRISTOPH **CZWIKLITZER**
(1914–1992)

Gallery owner / Cologne, Paris

Christoph Czwiklitzer was born in Breslau. He studied political and business economics, art history, psychology and philosophy in Berlin and Heidelberg. He worked as a journalist, antiquarian, auctioneer, art dealer and publisher. In the 1950s, he ran a gallery in Cologne. His business connections included Jean Arp, Henry Moore, Giorgio de Chirico and Ossip Zadkine. He left his collection of Picasso posters to the Kunstmuseum Heidenheim. From 1965, he lived in Paris.

ALBERT **DABERKOW**
(1912–1969)

Painter, art dealer / Düsseldorf, Berlin, Bad Homburg

Born in Düsseldorf, Albert Daberkow trained as a sign painter with the local business Leonhardt Tietz AG, with occasional attendance at the School of Fine and Applied Arts in Essen (→ ALFRED **FISCHER**). In 1937, he married Erika Fischer, who ran a small art dealing business in Rostock. She put him in touch with → WILMA **ZELCK** and → PETER **BÖHMER**. He and Zelck sold artworks formerly belonging to the deceased → BERNHARD A. **BÖHMER**. He left his family to live with Zelck in Berlin. The two fell out in 1950 due to embezzlements and secret sales by D., and D. went to live with his family in Bad Homburg. He continued to do business with Zelck, but only on commission.

DAS BELGISCHE HAUS

Culture institute / Cologne

In 1948, the 'Belgian house' association was founded to promote economic and cultural links. The association's building on Cologne's Cäcilienstrasse was constructed in 1950. Four years later the Belgian embassy took charge of the association, and the building provided extensive facilities for concerts, exhibitions and other events. The association gave Belgian artists the opportunity to present and sell art in the building's gallery. On a number of occasions, galleries or other institutions took up an exhibition first hosted by the B. H.

'DEGENERATE ART'

The term 'degenerate art' ('entartete Kunst') describes a defamation of modern art founded on racial theories and the programme of confiscation intended to 'cleanse' all German museums of modern art.

The German term *entartet* (degenerate) is derived from biology. In the late nineteenth century, it was applied to art in a pseudo-scientific manner. When the National Socialists came to power, aesthetic issues became politicized, and modern art, whose principles were opposed to the prevailing ideology, was described as 'degenerate'. It referred to supposedly inferior, 'rassisch' ('ethnic'), sexual, moral and artistic forms that offended against a German national sensibility, destroyed natural forms or were supposed to indicate a lack of ability. Headed by Joseph Goebbels's ministry of propaganda, two waves of confiscations aimed at securing the 'Verfallskunst' ('art of decay', or 'of decline') contained in German museums were staged, one in July and one in August 1937. In the first stage, artworks were obtained from museums with notable modern art sections for the 'Degenerate Art' exhibition. Only with the second wave of confiscations did the focus shift to liquidating the whole stock of modern art in German museums. Goebbels obtained a special order from Adolf Hitler that allowed the confiscation committees to confiscate any artwork they deemed to be 'degenerate'. Privately loaned works were officially exempt, and, should they nonetheless fall within the scope of the action, were to be returned. Under the leadership of Werner Hoffmann, executive director of the Reich Chamber of Fine Arts, the confiscated artworks were stored at Köpenicker Strasse in Berlin and were inventoried by Rolf Hetsch. Their fate was determined by the specially convened → **VALUATION COMMISSION**.

The 'Degenerate Art' exhibition opened on 19 July 1937, a day after the 'Great German Art Exhibition'. It denigrated modern art, particularly Expressionism. This defamatory show toured until 1941 and visited at least thirteen cities. It was intended to make people distrustful of avant-garde art and was also a statement of political aims. In 1938, the appropriation of the 'degenerate' artworks was legitimized retrospectively by the Act on Confiscations of Degenerate Art law. In the course of time, some of the museums received meagre reparations for the loss of a total of approximately 20,000 artworks.

DEUTSCHER KÜNSTLERBUND

Founded in 1903 in Weimar by the patron Harry Graf Kessler and the artists Lovis Corinth, Max Liebermann, Alfred Lichtwark and Max Slevogt and run by → LEOPOLD VON **KALCKREUTH**, the Deutscher Künstlerbund (Association of German Artists) was an independent body whose aim was to promote fine art and, in particular, to support young artists by means of annual exhibitions and by selling the work of its members. In the face of the repressive attitude of the imperial arts scene, it worked to achieve freedom and equality for a plurality of artistic trends and to support young artists. The D. K. was instrumental in the rise of modernist art, and ultimately outlasted imperial Germany. Its agenda for promoting modernism put the D. K. close to notable people connected with museums, patrons and art dealers, such as Bruno and → PAUL **CASSIRER**, who was appointed as executive director in 1904. After the Nazis came to power, the association's advocacy of modernist art was subject to increasing criticism, and in 1936 the D. K. was banned by the Reich Art Ministry. After the war, the artists Willi Baumeister, Karl Hartung, Karl Hofer, Ewald Mataré and Karl Schmidt-Rottluff revived the D. K., pursuing the same aims. → EBERHARD **SEEL** was appointed as executive director. Private collectors and institutions were once again able to acquire artworks for their collections at exhibitions held by the D. K.

DOM-GALERIE

Art and antiques dealer / Cologne

Founded in 1912 by Eduard Arthur Schmidt, the Dom-Galerie presented contemporary Cologne art – by artists such as the Junges Rheinland group and Arno Breker – alongside older art and selected antiques. For a time, the gallery's business premises were located at the Domhof. In 1934, it moved into the second story of the art building on the Schildergasse, together with the art dealers Fahrbach, Malmedé, and Hill, the picture frame and art dealers Alfred Otto Müller (Schmidt's son), and the → KUNSTHAUS **LEMPERTZ**. After Hitler came to power, D. presented work by German and French artists of the nineteenth century and by Rhenish artists of the twentieth century. We know that the gallery continued dealing in art into the 1940s.

FARBENFABRIKEN BAYER AG

Factory / Leverkusen

Founded in 1863 in Barmen by Friedrich Bayer and Johann Friedrich Weskott, Farbenfabriken Bayer was converted into an AG (a public limited company) and relocated to the Rhineland in 1881. In 1904, it amalgamated with BASF and subsequently with Agfa to form IG Farben. The F. B. was significantly involved in war production in both world wars. After 1945, it was placed under the control of the military authorities. In 1953, it resumed trading as an AG. In the 1950s, the F. B. assisted the Wallraf-Richartz Museum in making some purchases.

ALOYS **FAUST**

(died 1997)

Art and antiques dealer / Cologne

When exactly Aloys Faust began to be active as an art dealer is unknown. He worked for → ALFRED **FLECHTHEIM** at his Cologne branch and subsequently for → ANDREAS **BECKER**, after Becker took over the business in 1924. He travelled to Belgium, Paris and other locations to conduct business on his behalf. F. also occasionally worked for the magazine of the Cologne Progressives, *a bis z*. In 1933, F. went into business on his own account. From September 1936 onwards, he ran a gallery of modern art and antiques in Cologne. → JOSEF **HAUBRICH** was a regular business contact from 1933 onwards. After the war, F. supported Cologne artists who were friends of his, including → JOSEPH **JAEKEL** and Hans Schmidt, whom he allowed to exhibit in two rooms next to the antiques business on Rathenauplatz. His programme of modern art continued to include the Expressionists, the Cologne Progressives, Neue Sachlichkeit and the Cologne-based Rheinisch-Bergischer artists' circle.

HEINZ J. **FIRLE**

Art dealer / Cologne

Heinz J. Firle's art dealing business at Ebertplatz 11 existed until 1956. F. subsequently turned the premises into the modern cinema known as 'Bambi am Ring'.

ALFRED **FISCHER**

(1881–1950)

Director of a fine and applied arts school, collector / Essen

From 1911 to 1933, Dr. Alfred Fischer was director of the School for Craftsmen and the Applied Arts in Essen (later the Folkwang School). This institution was originally conceived by → KARL ERNST **OSTHAUS**. He espoused a modern construction style and novel forms of instruction. In 1914, F. and → EDMUND **KÖRNER** founded groups for interior decoration and 'reform' architecture in Essen. He was also a founding member of the → **SOCIETY FOR THE PROMOTION OF TWENTIETH-CENTURY GERMAN ART** in Neuss. After the Nazis came to power, F. was dismissed from his post as director. F. withdrew to Murnau and died having been able to work as an architect on only a handful of further occasions.

THEODOR **FISCHER**
(1878–1957)

Art dealer, auction house / Lucerne

After training as a teacher, Theodor Fischer began a career as an art dealer at the Bossard gallery in Lucerne, and subsequently worked in Berlin with → PAUL **CASSIRER**, along with Karl Haberstock. In 1907, he opened his own art dealing business in Lucerne, maintaining a branch in Berlin. Through Haberstock, F. had good contacts in National Socialist Germany. He was awarded the contract for the → **'DEGENERATE ART'** auction, which took place in Lucerne on 30 June 1939. Approximately 125 significant artworks from the 'degenerate art' initiative were auctioned, with the auction attracting international attention. We know that F. was involved in transactions at so-called *Judenauktionen* ('Jew auctions') and in dealing in stolen property. Many of the artworks came from the collection of → PAUL **ROSENBERG**. After the war, various actions were brought against F., who was forced to return a number of artworks. In spite of criticism of his business actions, he was deemed to have acted 'gullibly' in his dealings. F.'s art dealing business continued to operate after the war and was taken over by his sons.

ALFRED **FLECHTHEIM**
(1878–1937)

Gallery owner, publisher / Düsseldorf, Cologne, Berlin, London et al.

Alfred Flechtheim was the son of the biggest corn merchant in West Germany and began pursuing his passion for collecting modern art at an early stage. Artworks from his collection were first exhibited in 1906. He belonged to the circle of → KARL ERNST **OSTHAUS** from Hagen. In 1909, F. was one of the organizers of the seminal → **SONDERBUND EXHIBITION**. Through his contacts with Paris gallery owner → DANIEL-HENRY **KAHNWEILER**, he brought works of modern French art to Germany. In 1913, F. was supported by → PAUL **CASSIRER** in opening a gallery in Düsseldorf – very much in opposition to his father's business values. A year later, he entered the army and had to auction his gallery stock at Cassirer and Hans Helbing's auction house. It was the first auction of modernist art in which Fritz Gurlitt (→ WOLFGANG **GURLITT)** made a purchase. The gallery reopened in 1919. In 1921, F. was forced to leave the Rhineland due to the occupation of the Ruhr. He began by exhibiting in Cassirer's Berlin exhibition premises before opening a gallery in the neighbourhood in partnership with → GUSTAV **KAHNWEILER**, which he turned into the social centre of the Berlin art scene. He edited the magazine *Der Querschnitt*. Kahnweiler was briefly in charge of the gallery in Düsseldorf, before opening a branch in Frankfurt am Main jointly with F. in 1922. → ALEX **VÖMEL** worked for F. in Düsseldorf. F. founded a further branch in Cologne. Headed by → ERICH OTTO **JAFFÉ**, it closed in 1922. After the gallery's reopening in 1924, → ANDREAS **BECKER** took over as executive director. → ALOYS **FAUST** also worked there. → CURT **VALENTIN** worked for F. at the gallery in Berlin from 1928 onwards, if not earlier. The Kahnweiler brothers and F. tried to become Pablo Picasso's sole representation and to edge the → **ROSENBERG** brothers out. F. was financially affected by the global financial crisis. The anti-Semitic hostility of the incoming National Socialists also increasingly caused difficulties for F., who was Jewish. As a prominent apologist of modern art, he became the target of Nazi persecution campaigns, exemplified by the article 'Abgetakeltes Mäzenatentum. Wie Flechtheim und → **KAESBACH** deutsche Kunst machten' ('Jaded Patronage: How Flechtheim and Kaesbach Produced German Art', *Volksparole*, 1 April 1933). A planned auction in Düsseldorf was broken up by NSDAP adherents in 1933. In March of the same year, Alex Vömel opened a gallery at the Düsseldorf premises. Andreas Becker had taken over the Cologne gallery in 1924. F.'s other businesses had to be closed. F. emigrated via Switzerland to Paris and, finally, to London. He tried to continue his activities as an art dealer through his contacts with the Kahnweiler brothers and with Rosenberg. He had to sell some of the artworks in his collection to survive, and others were stolen, confiscated or lost. Until 1936, F. was able to travel to Germany to visit his wife Betti. He died in London in 1937. Betti F. committed suicide in 1941, shortly before she was to have been deported.

OTTO H. **FÖRSTER**
(1894–1975)

Museum director / Cologne

Otto H. Förster studied art history in Munich and Bonn, completing his doctorate under Heinrich Wölfflin in Munich. In 1921, he was working at the Wallraf-Richartz Museum in Cologne in a voluntary capacity and was involved in the cataloguing of the collection in 1922 as an academic assistant. After earning his habilitation in 1925, F. became curator of the Alte Galerie, whilst continuing to work as a lecturer at the Düsseldorf Academy of Art. In 1927, he decided to embark on a career in the City of Cologne's culture department, whilst also editing a number of publications and lecturing at the university. When Hitler came to power in 1933 and the leadership of all public institutions was purged, F. was made director of the Wallraf-Richartz Museum. A year later, F. joined the NSDAP and ostentatiously removed three paintings by Max Liebermann – who was regarded as 'too Jewish' – from the collection. These paintings were acquired by → JOSEF **HAUBRICH** for his collection via → ALOYS **FAUST** or by means of an exchange. Under F., the French art department was expanded. The new acquisitions, some of them from occupied territories, were financed by magazine sales. Under F., the museum acquired 650 such works – a proportionately large number, especially given the political climate.

The museum resisted confiscation drives by Nazi cultural agencies, continuing to exhibit works by denounced artists until 1937. F. frequently worked with Josef Haubrich on cultural-political and collection-related museum business. Both men were also involved in representing the museum to the outside world. F. was dismissed from his post as director in 1945 but was reinstated in 1957 after a vote by the Civic Council. By 1960, he also had overall responsibility for Cologne's museums.

GÜNTHER **FRANKE**
(1900–1976)

Gallery owner, publisher / Munich

Günther Franke began working at the famous Berlin graphic arts dealership

(Graphisches Kabinett → J. B. **NEUMANN**) at the age of eighteen. He took over as head of the Munich branch in 1923, after Neumann emigrated to New York. In 1930/31, the art dealing business was run under the names of both men. By 1937 if not before, F. was in sole charge of the gallery and running it under his own name. The political upheavals of National Socialism made it increasingly difficult to continue Neumann's programme of Impressionism, French modernism and Expressionism. F. provided financial support to artists, especially to Max Beckmann and Ernst Wilhelm Nay. This was achieved partly by purchasing their artworks for his own collection. Publicly, F. exhibited non-controversial Romantic artists, but he continued to deal in artists denounced by the Nazis in a number of locations, including Seeshaupt on the Starnberger See. His house became a place of concealment for his collection and a meet-ing point for proponents of modern art, including → JOSEF **HAUBRICH**. He appears to have made contact with the → **LE TANNEAUX DE SAINT PAUL** family during this period. From 1946 to 1963, F. reintroduced the German public to denounced art at the Villa Stuck, and exhibited contemporary abstract art. In 1969, F.'s Beckmann collection was exhibited at the → **KÖLNISCHER KUNSTVEREIN**.

GALERIE ÄNNE ABELS

Cologne

In 1946, Änne Abels (1900–1975) founded her Rhineland-based art salon at her parents' house. Before the war, she had worked in the family business, which was run by her brother, → HERMANN **ABELS**. A. sold diverse fifteenth- to nineteenth-century art from a small business space in the former Opernhaus-Kolonnaden. With the participation of Siegfried Adler (from 1949 onwards), the Galerie Änne Abels began specializing in more commercially popular Expressionist works, appealing to a broad cross-section of the public. From 1957 onwards, new gallery spaces were added dedicated to contemporary art (Abstract Expressionism, Nouveau Réalisme). The gallery lost a driving, innovative force when Adler left in 1966. In 1972, A. sold the gallery to Rainer Horstmann from Düsseldorf, although she continued to be active as an art dealer.

GALERIE HERMANN ABELS

Cologne

In 1919, after training as an art dealer, Hermann Abels (1892–1956) took over as director of the picture frame manufactory and art dealing business of his father, Wilhelm Abels (1867–1948). In 1935, after a number of changes of location, the family business (which also employed his sister → ÄNNE **ABELS**) moved to Wallrafplatz 6, close to the museum. The firm traded mainly in seventeenth- to nineteenth-century art, including the work of the Impressionists and the sculptor → JOSEPH **JAEKEL**. The business later expanded into Brücke and Blauer Reiter artworks and – following the shifts in taste of the 1950s – into French classical Modernism. A. handled artworks that German museums were forced to sell or exchange following denunciation by the Nazis. After the war, his son, Günther Abels, joined the gallery business, and ran it after his father's death.

GALERIE D'ART MODERNE

Basel

Marie-Suzanne Feigel (1945–1993) first established contacts and friendships with figures such as Gruppe 33, Walter Bodmer and Meret Oppenheim while she was studying at the applied arts school in Basel and the Academie Ranson in Paris. Feigel opened a gallery of modern art in 1945. She had the support of Bodmer and, significantly, of Georg Schmidt, director of the Kunstmuseum Basel and mentor of Gruppe 33. Jean Arp and Robert Delaunay featured prominently in her gallery's programme. Her Paris connections and her business links with gallery owners such as Maurice Lefebvre-Foinet, → CURT **VALENTIN** and → KARL **NIERENDORF** allowed her to expand her programme of artists to include classic Modernism and contemporary artists such as Marino Marini, Alexander Calder, Eduard Bargheer and certain members of Art Informel. Feigel brought artworks back from Central and South America and introduced them to a European audience. In spite of a number of interruptions, she was able to continue running the gallery, with the help of friends and relatives, until the year 1993, whilst also pursuing her own painting and poetry.

GALERIE ERNST ARNOLD

Dresden, Munich

The gallery's name goes back to its earliest days under the businessman Ernst Sigismund Arnold (1792–1840), who ran a business selling reproductions in Dresden in 1818. Under his successor Adolf Ludwig Gutbier (1841–1902), it became (in 1897) one of the first galleries in Germany to be declared a 'Königliche Hofkunsthandlung' (Royal Court art dealership). His son Ludwig (1873–1951), who studied art history, literature and history, took over the business in 1902, introducing more modern business practices. In 1906, he founded a gallery with extensive exhibition space. Gutbier exhibited modernist art. His exhibitions included works by the Brücke artist group. → FERDINAND **MÖLLER** began working at this gallery in 1912. A year later, he became director of the Breslau branch (1913–1923), before founding his own Breslau business. Ludwig Gutbier kept up contacts with a number of individuals, including his fellow art dealers at the Galerie Gerstenberg and, subsequently, → WILHELM **GROSSHENNIG**, → ALEX **VÖMEL**, the → **NIERENDORF** brothers and → GÜNTHER **FRANKE**.

In 1927, the economic situation forced Gutbier to close the gallery's branches. He retained the original gallery, where he exhibited Expressionist art until 1933. The gallery adapted to the political changes, but was forced to close by financial circumstances in 1937. He made a new start in Munich, where his business was aided by connections to prominent figures in the Nazi regime (achieved with the help of Gerdy Troost, the widow of an artist). Circa 1941, he handled some transactions for the Kunsthandlung Dabner art dealers in Paris and was able to continue running his business during the war. The Munich gallery was destroyed in 1944. Gutbier withdrew to Rottach am Tegernsee. After the war, the American military authorities confiscated his entire collection due to his connections with the upper ranks of the NSDAP, and he was forbidden from trading. After this, Gutbier acted as an art dealer on only a handful of occasions prior to his death. In 1958, his widow donated 600 prints to the Staatliche Graphische Sammlung in Munich.

GALERIE DR. ANDREAS BECKER

Cologne

The → **SONDERBUND EXHIBITION** made a strong impression on Andreas Becker (1894–1972). Then a law student, he decided to study art history as an additional subject. Moving in "Lunisten" circles, he met Max Ernst and Heinrich Hoerle. From 1922 onwards, B. was in contact with → ALFRED **FLECHTHEIM**. B. initially worked in a legal capacity at Flechtheim's Frankfurt branch, and took on the Cologne business after the occupation of the Ruhr region forced Flechtheim to move to Berlin. B. was interested in Rhineland artists and particularly in the Rhineland avant-garde. He also exhibited work by artists from other regions and, subsequently, work by East Asian artists. → LUISE **STRAUS-ERNST** worked with him for a time after parting company with Max Ernst. → ALOYS **FAUST** began his career working at this gallery and travelled to Paris and Belgium on B.'s behalf. B. entered into a business agreement with → ALFRED **NEWMAN** that led to the gallery being renamed 'Kunsthandlung Dr. Becker & Newman', a name it retained until 1934. After a number of relocations, B. moved into Cologne's first gallery house together with the galleries of → HERMANN **BURG**, → **JAFFÉ-GUTTMANN** and → **SIGMUND SALZ**, before ultimately returning to the Wallrafplatz. In 1937, Hans Heinrich Leumer became his business partner. The gallery was forced to close in the same year. B. went into exile in Paris. According to B.'s own version of events, he was arrested by the Gestapo during the German occupation and sent to Saarbrücken concentration camp before being detained in Cologne, both in the Gestapo prison and in Klingelpütz. He was released on 22 December 1943 through the intervention of his wife and was kept under police surveillance. After the war, B. became director of the Freie Volksbühne, and, in 1961, director of the → **KÖLNISCHER KUNSTVEREIN** in Cologne, replacing → JOSEF **HAUBRICH**, with the latter's approval. Between 1961 and 1969, he sat on Cologne's Civic Council as a Social Democrat, supporting a number of cultural and political projects. His subsequent art dealing activities were largely confined to the East Asia region.

GALERIE DER SPIEGEL

Cologne

Hein (1913–1994) and Dr. Eva Stünke (née Kahl, 1913–1988) founded their Cologne-Deutz gallery in the winter of 1945. They avoided including the name Stünke in their business title because Hein Stünke had been an officer – an Oberbannführer – in the Reich Youth Leadership. Instead, they called it the 'Galerie der Spiegel' ('gallery of the mirror'). Aiming to concentrate on contemporary art, the couple exhibited and supported artists from the Cologne region such as Jacob Berwanger, Peter Herkenrath, → JOSEPH **JAEKEL**, Ludwig Ronig and Friedrich Vordemberge, subsequently followed by new trends from the Art Informel, Surrealism, Op-Art, Nouveau Réalisme and Pop Art stylistic schools. Promoting and selling art by young German artists proved to be difficult, so the couple safeguarded their financial position by selling the works of classical Modernism that formed the backbone of the collection they had assembled prior to the Second World War. Their business branched out to include a workshop, a printing press and bookbinding workshop and the Galerie der Spiegel publishing house. The Stünkes were particularly close to Max Ernst, whom they popularized within Germany. In 1959, Hein Stünke organised a special graphic arts exhibition at documenta II in Kassel. He was a member of the documenta council in the following year. Together with his former employee Rudolf Zwirner (later a successful gallery owner), he founded the Association of Progressive German Art Dealers, which, in 1967, created the Kölner Kunstmarkt – the first modern art fair in the world and the forerunner of Art Cologne. From 1949 to the 1980s, this gallery was based in the Richartzstrasse. After a brief sojourn at Bonner Strasse 328, Werner Hillmann – former assistant, now director – brought it back to its original home in 1996.

GALERIE JACQUES DUBOURG

Paris

In 1922, Jacques Dubourg (1897–1981) began work at the Paris gallery belonging to Georges Petit, which closed in 1933. In spite of being called up for military service, he remained active as an art dealer, working in tandem with his wife. On the basis of transport information, it is known that he sold artworks to German buyers; D. is also supposed to have provided information on Jewish collections in Paris. By 1946 if not before, D. was holding exhibitions at 126, boulevard Haussmann. The gallery closed in 1972.

GALERIE FRICKER

Paris

In 1954, Jacques and Micheline Fricker opened a gallery of modern art at 177, boulevard Haussmann, which remained *in situ* until the 1970s. Jacques F. was a native of Alsace and grew up bilingual. As a gallery owner, he maintained both German and French contacts. From early on, he became interested in German Expressionist art and in Russian artists associated with the same movement, such as Wassily Kandinsky and Alexej von Jawlensky. He organized a large-scale solo exhibition for the latter artist in Paris in 1956 – the first of its kind in France. In 2007, works from the gallery's collection were auctioned at Paris's Yann Le Mouel.

GALERIE GOLDSCHMIDT & WALLERSTEIN

Berlin

Fritz Goldschmidt and Victor Wallerstein (1879–1944), both doctors of art history, went into art dealing after working at the Kaiser-Wilhelm Museum in Berlin. In 1917, Wallerstein began working at the gallery owned by → PAUL **CASSIRER**, who also owned the auction house that employed Goldschmidt. In 1919, Goldschmidt became independent, opening his own art dealing business which Wallerstein joined as an associate. A year later, they opened a business together. Wallerstein's contacts with artists such as Erich Heckel and Oskar Kokoschka led to the gallery opening a new 'modern department', where artworks by contemporary artists and sculptors were exhibited. In 1928, the gallery moved to premises at Victoriastrasse 21, where it continued to operate until 1933. Both men were Jewish, and whether the business survived after 1933 is unknown. In 1935, Wallerstein emigrated to Italy, dying in Florence in 1944. The fate of Goldschmidt is unknown. There is a watercolour portrait of Wallerstein by Oskar Kokoschka in the collection of → JOSEF **HAUBRICH**.

GALERIE HELIOS ART

Brussels

Maurice d'Arquian (1908–1975) studied art history in Louvain, Belgium, before beginning his career in art dealing at the Galerie d'Art Latin in Stockholm. This gallery exhibited Impressionist and avant-garde art. In the early 1950s, he returned to Belgium and opened the Helios Art gallery in Brussels. A short time later, d'Arquian founded branches in Paris and Zürich under the name Galerie Internationale d'Art Contemporain. Artists discovered and promoted by his Paris gallery included Yves Klein. D'Arquian organized the exhibition 'Art Contemporain' in Paris in 1963 and was co-initiator of the FIAC art fair of 1973.

GALERIE RUDOLF HOFFMANN

Hamburg

In 1946, Rudolf Hoffmann (1906–1966) opened a gallery of Old Masters and new works. Beginning in 1947/48, the gallery collaborated with → MICHAEL **HERTZ**'s publishing company to produce slim volumes on individual artists. In 1953, the gallery and the haute couture salon of Wilhelmine Hoffmann, alias Heele Brün, moved into the Villa am Rondeel. The combination of art and fashion created a unique meeting place for the milieu.

GALERIE JAFFÉ-GUTTMANN

→ ERICH OTTO **JAFFÉ**

GALERIE RALFS (OTTO and KÄTE RALFS)

Braunschweig

The ironware dealer Otto Ralfs (1892–1955) and his wife Käte (1898–1995) discovered their interest in modernist art through the Bauhaus. Otto became a friend and supporter to artists such as Wassily Kandinsky, Paul Klee, Lyonel Feininger and Alexej von Jawlensky. He bought their artworks for his collection, held exhibitions of their work and, in 1924, founded the Society of Friends of Modern Art in Braunschweig. In addition to this, the Klee-Gesellschaft, set up by Otto R. in 1925, provided financial support for Paul Klee until his death. Members included Rudolf Ibach (→ **GALERIE OTTO UND ETTA STANGL**) and → IDA **BIENERT**. In 1926, Otto R. organized a touring exhibition for Klee that went on show in venues such as the → **GALERIE GOLDSCHMIDT & WALLERSTEIN** and → **GALERIE ERNST ARNOLD**. His activities were brought to an abrupt end in 1933, when Hitler came to power. He transferred part of his collection (which has since gone missing) to Katowice. The remainder was destroyed in the bombing of Braunschweig. After the war, in 1947, the R.s established a business that traded in modern art, which Käte R. took over after her husband's early death.

GALERIE SIGMUND SALZ

(1894–1981)

Art dealer / Vienna, Cologne, Paris, New York

After studying painting and art history at the Academy of Fine Arts in Vienna, Sigmund (Sam) Salz abandoned his own painting career around 1920 and went into art dealing. He founded a gallery in Cologne. For a time, it was based in the first Cologne gallery house (Unter Fettenhennen 11), where → HERMANN **BURG**, → ERICH OTTO **JAFFÉ** and → ANDREAS **BECKER** also had their business premises. He exhibited artwork by Jean Arp, Georges Braque, Marc Chagall and James Ensor. The photographer August Sander created a portrait of him standing in front of his gallery. He was put under observation after the National Socialists came to power due to the modernist orientation of his gallery programme and his representation of Jewish artists, causing him to move to Paris. Through his personal contacts, S. became an art dealer trading in the work of the Impressionists and in modernist French art. At the end of the 1930s, he moved to New York, augmenting collections including those of Paul Mellon, Henry Ford II and David Rockefeller. He became an art dealer to the rich and famous, running his business for a total of fifty years.

GALERIE OTTO UND ETTA STANGL

Munich

Artworks from the collection of Otto's father-in-law, Albert Rudolf Ibach, a Wuppertal piano manufacturer and art appreciator, provided the basis for the first gallery run by Otto (1915–1990) and Etta Stangl (1913–1990), which was founded in Munich in 1948. It became Munich's second avant-garde art gallery (alongside that of → GÜNTHER **FRANKE**) to champion the art denounced by the Nazis. It later became increasingly associated with abstract art and, for instance, the artists of the French Art Informel movement. In 1953, the S.s founded their Kunstkabinett as a branch of their Munich business. They moved to the Luitpoldblock in the early 1960s. After Otto suddenly lost his hearing, the two gallery owners ceased their art dealing activities. Until their deaths, they worked to make the Franz-Marc Museum in Kochel a reality. This museum opened in 1986.

GALERIE ZAK

Paris

This Paris gallery was opened by the painter Jadwiga Kon, wife of the painter Eugeniusz Zak, following his death. Zak had previously taken part in an exhibition at → ALFRED **FLECHTHEIM**'s gallery in 1926. This gallery first emerged on the scene in the late 1920s, on rue de l'Abbaye near St-Germain-des-Prés, and became a highly regarded modern art institution. It is known to have had connections to the → **VALUATION COMMISSION** dating from before 1939, which allowed it to acquire and sell → **'DEGENERATE ART'**.

GALLERIA IL MILIONE

Milan

In 1930, Peppino Ghiringhelli founded the Galleria Il Milione in Milan in premises belonging to Pier Maria Bardi. He and his brother Gino exhibited works by Italian avant-garde artists such as Giorgio Morandi, Giorgio de Chirico, Fausto Melotti and Lucio Fontana, along with French modernist artworks, which they acquired through → LÉONCE **ROSENBERG** in Paris. After the war and the destruction of their premises, the brothers continued to run their gallery and also founded a publishing press.

JOHANNES GELLER

(1873–1954)

Lawyer, collector / Neuss

Johannes Geller was co-founder of the → **SOCIETY FOR THE PROMOTION OF TWENTIETH-CENTURY GERMAN ART** and the husband of → ELSE **GELLER-ZAERTLING**. He belonged to Düsseldorf's → **SONDERBUND EXHIBITION** circle and worked to promote cultural activities in Neuss. In 1943, he deposited his collection in Cologne's Wallraf-Richartz Museum for safety. After his death, his widow continued his involvement in the city of Neuss and the collection.

ELSE **GELLER-ZAERTLING**
(1898–1980)

Lawyer, collector / Neuss

In 1927, Dr. Else Zaertling became the first female lawyer to be admitted in the Neuss administrative district. In 1932, she married the widowed lawyer → JOHANNES **GELLER**. Together, they accumulated a collection of modernist art and maintained contacts with artists such as Paul Klee, Ewald Mataré and Heinrich Nauen. After the death of her husband in 1954, she donated the collection to the Clemens-Sels Museum in Neuss. She supported modernist art at this institution until her death.

GERLING-KONZERN

Insurance company / Cologne

Robert Gerling's insurance group was founded in Cologne in 1904. Over the following decades, he built it up into a successful business. During the National Socialist period, G. profited from state commissions. In 1945, Hans Gerling, son of the company's founder, was the first German insurance broker to be authorized by the military authorities. He commissioned a number of architects, including Arno Breker, to build the company's monumental new headquarters in Cologne.

HANS **GOLTZ**
(1873–1927)

Book dealer, gallery owner / Munich

Hans Goltz took over the U. Putze art and book dealing business in 1910 and made it into an international company. His art dealing activities began in 1912, with exhibitions of artworks by Franz Marc and Wassily Kandinsky. Financial difficulties bound him as a seller to the Blauer Reiter group, until he regained his independence by means of his own art dealing company, Neue Kunst – Hans Goltz. His programme ranged from Vincent van Gogh to the Expressionists. He took on administrating the legacy of Wilhelm Lehmbruck and was, for a time, Paul Klee's general representative. In addition to his art and book dealing business, G. held his first auction in 1914. He also founded the Goltzverlag publishing house and ran it for a year. In 1915, he was forced to close his exhibition spaces. He united the art and book dealing businesses under one roof. Inflation increasingly caused problems for G., but his unexpected death forestalled a further relocation. His widow and his son Hans-Joachim took over the business under difficult conditions: the Great Depression forced them to scale down and relocate, and the Nazis became aware of a link between G. and the denounced artists by 1937 if not before. As a result, the decision was taken to change the company's name and to reopen as the Bücherstube am Dom at Munich's Kaufinger Strasse 23. The archive and the bookstore were destroyed in the war. The Bücherstube am Dom (with no connection to the Cologne bookstore of the same name) reopened in 1948.

WILHELM **GROSSHENNIG**
(1893–1983)

Gallery owner / Chemnitz, Düsseldorf

Wilhelm Grosshennig was director and (from 1930 onwards) co-proprietor of the Gerstenberger gallery in Chemnitz (1902–1951). This gallery specialized in German Expressionism. G.'s contacts included leading German art dealers such as → PAUL **CASSIRER** and → ALFRED **FLECHTHEIM**, and their then employee → CURT **VALENTIN**. After Hitler came to power, G. was involved in selling modernist artworks from the Chemnitzer Museum, in conjunction with the gallery of → ALEX **VÖMEL**. G. was employed by Hermann Voss and → HILDEBRAND **GURLITT** as a 'buyer-in' for the 'Führermuseum Linz', acquiring artworks from the Netherlands and France. In 1951, G. opened a gallery in Düsseldorf, exhibiting a wide-ranging programme of classical Modernism. After G.'s death in 1983, the art collection and the archive were transferred to the Margret Heuser gallery.

HILDEBRAND **GURLITT**
(1895–1956)

Art historian, art dealer / Zwickau, Hamburg, Dresden

Hildebrand Gurlitt came from a family of art historians. His father, Cornelius, was an historian of art and architecture, whilst his uncle Fritz Gurlitt (→ WOLFGANG **GURLITT**) founded an art dealing business in Berlin that was later taken over by his son Wolfgang. After completing his doctorate in art history and working as a journalist for a time, G., a native of Dresden, became director of the museum in Zwickau, where he embarked on a programme of modernization and new acquisitions. By 1928, his programme was under attack from right-wing groups, leading to his dismissal in 1930. In 1933, he was also forced to resign from his subsequent position as director of the Kunstverein (Art Society) in Hamburg. G. expanded his art dealing activities and opened a gallery of prints and drawings in Hamburg, which he ran until 1942. He was one of the art dealers permitted to trade in → **'DEGENERATE ART'** (→ **VALUATION COMMISSION**). His friend Hermann Voss, director of the Dresden Gemäldegalerie, commissioned him and → WILHELM **GROSSHENNIG** as buyers for the 'Führermuseum Linz'. From 1943 to 1945, he succeeded Karl Haberstock in handling special commissions to broker artworks from occupied areas, for clients who included party and government figures. G. was rehabilitated after the war because of his Jewish heritage and his early championing of the 'denounced' modernist art. His role during the National Socialist period remains controversial. In 1947, he became director of the Düsseldorf art society, the Kunstverein für die Rheinlande und Westfalen. G. died in a car accident in 1956.

WOLFGANG **GURLITT**
(1888–1965)

Gallery owner, publisher / Berlin, Linz, Munich

Wolfgang Gurlitt continued to run the gallery founded by his father, Fritz Gurlitt (1854–1893), in Berlin after the First World War. Just like his cousin → HILDEBRAND **GURLITT**, he managed to make a name for himself on the international art market during the National Socialist period. He was also involved in selling confiscated works of → **'DEGENERATE ART'** abroad, but without any official commission. After the war, he directed the Neue Galerie in Linz until 1956, in which elements of his collection were shown and bought.

WILHELM (WILLY) **HAHN**
(1896–1988)

Music director, collector, art dealer / Cologne, Berlin et al.

Willy Hahn began studying law in 1919 but broke off to study music in Cologne and Berlin. In early 1923, he completed his examinations to qualify as a pianist and a director of music at the Berlin Conservatory. After employments in Aachen, Stuttgart and Stettin, he began working for the Berliner Rundfunk radio service in 1933. During the war, he was involved in providing musical entertainment to the troops.

He became interested in Expressionist art at an early stage, having been brought into contact with it by → KARL **NIERENDORF**. While he was still a student, he began buying art from sellers including → J. B. **NEUMANN**, → PAUL **CASSIRER** and → FERDINAND **MÖLLER**. During the National Socialist period, H. continued to acquire modernist art, including → **'DEGENERATE ART'**, from the art dealer → BERNHARD A. **BÖHMER**. His collection was affected by his constantly changing tastes and his financial situation. In the late 1950s, he turned his passion into a profession and became an art dealer officially.

JOSEF **HAUBRICH**

(1889–1961)

Lawyer, collector / Cologne

Josef Haubrich's father was director of the local Ortskrankenkasse (a regional health insurance company), and he gained an understanding of art at an early age through travelling and visiting exhibitions. He began studying law in Munich in 1907 and later studied in Berlin and Bonn, taking an interest in the arts scenes of all three cities. After completing his legal clerkship in Cologne, H. became an industrial lawyer. In 1912, he visited the → **SONDERBUND EXHIBITION**, and, like many of his contemporaries, was lastingly influenced by it. Haubrich began collecting intensively, on a wide spectrum that included modernist art. He began to specialize in modernist art in the mid-1920s. H.'s membership in a number of societies dedicated to promoting art, such as → KARL **NIERENDORF**'s Gesellschaft der Künste, the Friends of the Wallraf-Richartz Museum and the → **KÖLNISCHER KUNSTVEREIN**, and his good contacts with artists and with the art market, provided him with a useful network within the art system. Despite the denunciation of many of the artists featured in his collection after the rise to power of the National Socialists, H. retained his passion for collecting – especially for Expressionist and Neue Sachlichkeit works. His championing of denounced art and marriage to a Jewish woman (Alice Gottschalk, his third wife, who committed suicide in 1944) made H. an object of suspicion to the National Socialists. His collection, part of which had been stored with the Kölnischer Kunstverein in Untermaubach, survived the war, escaped confiscation and was donated to the city of Cologne in 1946. H. thereby provided a nucleus around which the museum's modern department could be rebuilt, giving it its own acquisitions budget. The collection became a model for acquisition and exhibition policy in the post-war years.

HAUSWEDELL & CO.

Auction house / Hamburg

Ernst Ludwig A. Hauswedell (1901–1983), the son of a Hamburg banker, first followed his father into the banking industry and then co-founded the Deutscher Buch-Club in 1927, to which he added an antiques dealership and an auction house in 1930. This became a leading auction house after 1935, trading as Hauswedell & Co. From 1963 to 1974, H. also ran a contemporary art gallery in Baden-Baden. His former colleague Ernst Nolte became a partner in the auction house in 1969. H. handed the business over to Nolte in 1977.

MICHAEL **HERTZ**

(1912–1987)

Gallery owner / Cologne, Paris, Bremen

Michael Hertz underwent his first apprenticeship with Wilhelm Goyert in Cologne. He became a travelling picture frame salesman, until the war put a stop to his activities. After the war, wishing to establish himself in the art dealing world, he approached the influential museum director → LEOPOLD **REIDEMEISTER**, who was planning a presentation of the collection of → JOSEF **HAUBRICH**. H.'s persuasive skills, through which a publishing licence was secured from the American occupying forces, as well as a stock of hard-to-obtain art printing paper, opened the door for the publication of the first, very modest catalogue of Josef Haubrich's collection by the Verlag Michael Hertz. H. later published artist books for the → **GALERIE RUDOLF HOFFMANN**. The publishing company's lack of success led H. to go back to work for an Alsace-based art print publishing business. This took him mainly to Paris and brought him into contact with the gallery owners → DANIEL-HENRY **KAHNWEILER**, Maurice Lefebvre-Foinet and Aimé Maeght. H. became sole representative in Germany for prints of Pablo Picasso and, for a time, for the paintings and bronze sculptures of Max Ernst. He continued his activities as a publisher of art prints and organized exhibition tours for Alexander Calder, Alberto Giacometti, Henri Laurens, André Masson, Joan Miró, Ernst Wilhelm Nay and Hans Uhlmann. Around 1955, he moved into an office in Bremen, before opening his first gallery space in 1962, where he exhibited contemporary East German artists such as Werner Tübke, Bernhard Heisig and Willi Sitte. In 1981, he passed the business on to his son Cornelius.

PAULA **HESS**

(1909–1991)

Düsseldorf, Hemmenhofen

Paula (Margarete Pauline) Hess was the partner of → WALTER **KAESBACH**. She entered his employment as a housekeeper in 1930. He moved to Hemmenhofen with her in 1933, leaving his collection to her on his death.

JOSEPH **JAEKEL**

(1907–1985)

Sculptor in metal, college tutor / Cologne

Joseph Jaekel trained as a goldsmith and silversmith at the Cologne School of Applied Arts and Crafts (1923–1926) and as a sculptor and metalworker (1926–1930). He began operating independently in Cologne in 1930. In 1934, he became a member of the Reich Chamber of Fine Arts and started to exhibit regularly at the group exhibitions of the → **KÖLNISCHER KUNSTVEREIN**. He maintained contacts with a number of figures in the art scene such as → ANDREAS **BECKER**, → ALOYS **FAUST** and the → **GALERIE HERMANN ABELS**. He visited the gallery of the → **NIERENDORF** brothers as a collector and buyer. After the war, in 1949, he was given a solo exhibition at the → **GALERIE DER SPIEGEL**. From 1947 to 1974, J. was director of the department for metal sculpture at the Cologne vocational school, the Werkschule.

ERICH OTTO **JAFFÉ**

Art historian, art dealer / Cologne

The art historian Dr. Erich Otto Jaffé took over as director of → ALFRED **FLECHTHEIM**'s original business in Cologne. He worked with → ANDREAS **BECKER** and → ALOYS **FAUST**. By 1924, if not before, J. went into business with the artist and fashion designer Alice Guttmann in the Galerie Jaffé-Guttmann. A year later, he moved into Cologne's first specialized gallery building, along with → HERMANN **BURG**, → **KUNSTHANDLUNG DR. BECKER & NEWMAN** and → **GALERIE SIGMUND SALZ**. On occasion, he collaborated with Becker-Newman, resulting in a temporary change to his gallery's name. The gallery presumably continued operating until 1931, exhibiting old and new art.

CARL OSKAR **JATHO**

(1884–1971)

Art historian, author, publicist / Cologne

From 1916 onwards, Carl Oskar Jatho organized evening lectures and discussions in his apartment in Cologne. He was a fixture in the artistic life of Cologne and a long-term member of a number of local artist groups including the Gereonsclub and → KARL **NIERENDORF**'s art society, the Gesellschaft der Künste, as well as Der Strom, *Bulletin D* and Dada. He was a personal friend of the artist Franz W. Seiwert, with whom he lived at the Kalltalgemeinschaft from 1919 to 1921. Most of all, he wrote for and supported the Cologne Progressives group, with whom he had become acquainted at his father's house. Articles by J. appeared in publications including *a bis z* and *Der Sammler*. J.'s apartment was destroyed in the early 1940s, along with parts of his collection. After the war, he wrote several publications on the rebuilding of Cologne, as well as an autobiography.

WALTER CARL JOSEPH **KAESBACH**

(1879–1961)

Art historian, academy director / Mönchengladbach, Düsseldorf, Hemmenhofen

After studying economics and art history, Walter Kaesbach became an assistant at the Nationalgalerie under Hugo von Tschudi and Ludwig Justi. He belonged to the circle of → KARL ERNST **OSTHAUS** from Hagen, which also included → ALFRED **FLECHTHEIM** and → PAUL **CASSIRER**. K. was a friend of → PAUL **MULTHAUPT**. In 1912, he visited the → **SONDERBUND EXHIBITION** in Cologne. K. volunteered for service during the First World War and became director of an army medical corps. He was able to include a number of artist friends in his medical corps in order to save them from being sent to the front: Max Beckmann, Erich Heckel, Heinrich Nauen and Otto Herbig. In 1920, K. became director of the city museum of Erfurt. He pushed for the → **SOCIETY FOR THE PROMOTION OF TWENTIETH-CENTURY GERMAN ART** collection to be donated to the city of Neuss. In 1922, K. presented his collection of major Expressionist artworks to the local museum of his home town, Mönchengladbach. In 1924, K.'s reputation as a modernizer brought him an appointment at the Düsseldorf Academy of Art. K. reorganized the institution and gave teaching positions to modernist artists such as Heinrich Campendonk, Paul Klee and Ewald Mataré. In the 1930s, this made him the target of National Socialist propaganda, along with Alfred Flechtheim. In 1933, he was relieved of his duties and barred from the institution. This was followed by forced leave of absence in 1934. With his partner → PAULA **HESS**, K. moved to Hemmenhofen on the Swiss border, where others, including Otto Dix, later joined him. K. tried to create opportunities for the discredited artists to exhibit their work at institutions such as the Kunstverein Schaffhausen. In 1937, K.'s Mönchengladbach donation was confiscated. After the war, K. did not resume his involvement in the art world. He lived on the proceeds of sales of artworks from his collection, which he left to his partner Paula Hess.

DANIEL-HENRY **KAHNWEILER**

(1884–1979)

Gallery owner, art historian / Mannheim, Paris

German by birth, Daniel-Henry Kahnweiler opened his first gallery in Paris in 1907. K. was on friendly terms with a large number of artists, which allowed him to obtain exclusive contracts with French classical Modernist artists who later rose to prominence, such as Georges Braque, Henri Laurens, Fernand Léger and Pablo Picasso. K. was friendly with the collector → ALFRED **FLECHTHEIM**, and became his business partner after he moved into art dealing. During the First World War, the French state confiscated K.'s gallery stock as enemy property and auctioned the artworks off cheaply. Many artists transferred to K.'s competitors, the → **ROSENBERG** brothers, but returned to him (as Picasso did) at a later stage – generally by 1920, if not before, when he and his partner opened the Galerie Simon in Paris. → ALEX **VÖMEL** completed his training with K. In addition to classical Modernism, K. now exhibited artworks by the Surrealist school. In 1937 he became a French citizen. As a Jew, the German occupation put him in a perilous situation. K. hid in the Limoges area, while the gallery continued to operate through the efforts of his sister-in-law Louise Leiris (now under her name). → MICHAEL **HERTZ** was one of K.'s business contacts after the war, purchasing mainly Picasso prints from him. The prestigious Galerie Louise Leiris still exists today.

GUSTAV **KAHNWEILER**

(1895–1989)

Art dealer / Berlin, Düsseldorf, Frankfurt am Main, Cambridge, London

→ DANIEL-HENRY **KAHNWEILER**'s younger brother also went into art dealing. In 1921, Daniel-Henry arranged for Gustav Kahnweiler to become a shareholder in → ALFRED **FLECHTHEIM**'s business in Berlin. He later became director of the Düsseldorf branch and, in 1922, director of the joint branch in Frankfurt am Main. Flechtheim and K. acquired primarily French classical Modernist works from the gallery run by K.'s brother in Paris. After Flechtheim was forced to leave Germany in 1933 and his business was shut down, K. emigrated to Paris. In the winter of 1935/36, he left Paris and emigrated to Cambridge in Britain, where he hoped to be able to continue operating as an art dealer. However, he found only a limited market for artworks from continental Europe. K.'s business only became viable again after he came into contact with the Mayor Gallery. In 1940, he was detained in an internment camp. From 1940 to 1942, he served in the Auxiliary Pioneer Corps. After the war, he became a prominent dealer in the artwork of Henry Moore, Renato Guttuso and other artists. After the deaths of K. and his wife, their collection was left to the Tate Modern in London.

LEOPOLD VON **KALCKREUTH**
(1855–1928)

Painter, graphic artist / Weimar, Karlsruhe, Stuttgart, Eddelsen

Leopold Karl Walter Graf von Kalckreuth's art showed an affinity to Impressionism. In his official activities, he combined tradition and modernity. He lectured at the Weimar art school and was director of the Stuttgart academy. In 1903 he became president of the → **DEUTSCHER KÜNSTLERBUND**, a post later occupied by → PAUL **CASSIRER**. → ERNST **KÖNIG** was his son-in-law, married to his daughter Bertha.

KESTNERGESELLSCHAFT

Art association / Hannover

The Kestnergesellschaft (Kestner Society), named after August Kestner (1777–1853), was founded in 1916 during the First World War. The aim of this independent institution was to invigorate cultural life and to provide modernist Hannover artists of various artistic philosophies with a place to exhibit. Beginning in 1930 under Justus Bier, the association became a trailblazer for modernist art. Exhibited artwork included German Expressionism and Neue Sachlichkeit. Membership subscriptions, contributions and proceeds from sales exhibitions enabled the Kestnergesellschaft to host numerous events. Lots at two auctions held in 1926/27 included artworks from Herbert Garven's collection. In 1933, the association refused to dismiss director Justus Bier on the grounds of his Jewish heritage. It was decided that the museum should close temporarily in 1936 and be converted into a private museum association with autonomy from official authorities. Bier went into exile shortly afterwards. The association continued to operate until 1945, and reopened in the Warmbüchnerstrasse in 1948.

STUTTGARTER KUNSTKABINETT ROMAN NORBERT **KETTERER**

Auction house / Stuttgart

Roman Norbert Ketterer (1911–2002) founded his auction house in Stuttgart in 1947. K.'s interest was increasingly focused on Expressionism. The Kunstkabinett attracted connoisseurs, museum people and international collectors such as David Rockefeller, Stavros Niarchos and Hans Heinrich von Thyssen-Bornemisza. K. was also the executor of Ernst Ludwig Kirchner's estate from 1954. He moved to Campione d'Italia for personal and business reasons in 1961, and opened the Roman Norbert Ketterer gallery there in 1963. His family still run the gallery and administer the estate.

HEINRICH **KIRCHHOFF**
(1874–1934)

Art collector, patron / Essen, Wiesbaden

Heinrich Kirchhoff lived as a man of independent means from 1908 until he died. He collected first Jugendstil and Impressionism from 1914, and then exclusively Expressionism. After 1917 he handed parts of his collection over to the Wiesbaden Museum department of paintings on permanent loan. Of those on loan, works by artists such as Otto Dix, Conrad Felixmüller and Emil Nolde were pulled out of the museum in 1933 and returned to K. His wife and heir Toni Kirchhoff sold the collection after he died in 1944. The Wiesbaden Museum tried to buy back works from the Kirchhoff collection after the Second World War.

HEINRICH **KIRCHNER**
(1902–1984)

Sculptor / Erlangen, Munich, Pavolding

In 1924, Heinrich Kirchner moved to Munich and completed a course of study in sculpture at the Academy of Fine Arts. He was subsequently given a position in the institution's casting workshop. He shared a studio with fellow sculptor Fritz Wrampe – who was shot by his lover in 1934. Wrampe's widow authorized K. to administer his estate. In 1937, K. took part in the 'Great German Art Exhibition' in Munich and provided a bronze eagle and swastika for the German pavilion in Venice. He had little enthusiasm for these state commissions and, although he was supported by Arno Breker, he declined to have his or Wrampe's works feature in exhibitions after the Nazis had confiscated artworks by both of them as well as by Wilhelm Lehmbruck in 1937. From this point on, he was considered to be 'politically unreliable'. In 1939, he was conscripted into the military. After the end of the war, he fled from internment as a prisoner of war in the American occupation zone. In 1948, he took part in the Venice Biennale for a second time, and in 1959 he was included in documenta II. In 1952, K. was appointed as a professor at the Munich Academy of Fine Arts. In 1970, after retiring as a professor, he moved to Pavolding, where he devoted himself to his artistic projects.

HANS **KOCH**
(1881–1952)

Doctor, collector / Düsseldorf

A dermatologist and urologist who trained in Berlin, Dr. Hans Koch was also a passionate collector. In 1917, after the closing of → ALFRED **FLECHTHEIM**'s gallery, he and his future wife Martha (née Lindner) decided to bring new life into Düsseldorf's art scene by founding the Bergh & Co. art cabinet, which saw ambitious exhibitions of artworks by the Expressionists, the Junges Rheinland group and the Dresden Secession. In 1919, K. exhibited an artwork by Otto Dix in the Rhineland for the first time as part of a group exhibition. Dix fell in love with Martha Koch and the two were married in 1923. After his divorce from Martha, K. married her sister Maria. K. was on friendly terms with → KARL **NIERENDORF**, whom he introduced to Dix and who was also in love with Maria for a time. Nierendorf admired and supported Dix to a much greater extent than K., but also enjoyed enough influence with him that, in 1921, he was able to mediate a portrait commission for K. The portrait of K. by Dix was sold by Nierendorf to → JOSEF **HAUBRICH** in 1923. The Bergh art cabinet was taken over circa 1920 by → J. B. **NEUMANN**. K. was a member of the → **SOCIETY FOR THE PROMOTION OF TWENTIETH-CENTURY GERMAN ART**.

KÖLNISCHER KUNSTVEREIN

Cologne

Founded in 1839, the Kölnischer Kunstverein has become a confident and independent force in the cultural life of the city. In the past, it bridged the gap between the local institutions and the regional art market. In the 1930s and 1940s, it primarily organized sales exhibitions, the proceeds from which supplemented its membership subscriptions and allowed the association to acquire artworks and to support artists and exhibitions. A percentage of the sales price would go to the current director, to supplement his minimal stipend. Between 1913 and 1914, → PAUL **CASSIRER** took over as artistic director of the K. K.

→ RICHARD VON **SCHNITZLER** acted as chairman for an extended period. → JOSEF **HAUBRICH**, who had been a member of the art association since 1925 and a member of the advisory council since 1932, served as acting chair from 1933 to 1936. In 1938, it was Haubrich who recommended → HANS **PETERS** as director for the K. K. He also handled the association's legal affairs and, even before he became a member, created contacts with galleries, including that of → KARL AND JOSEF **NIERENDORF**, which allowed the art association to secure exhibitions such as 'Der Strom' (in 1919). A number of people were associated with both the K. K. and the Society of Friends of the Wallraf-Richartz Museum: Schnitzler and Haubrich were active in the two organizations for a considerable period of time. In 1944, then director Toni Feldenkirchen moved Haubrich's collection to Schloss Graf Spee in Untermaubach, together with the K. K. collection. Haubrich brought it back to Cologne in 1945, prior to the occupation.

ERNST **KÖNIG**

(1878–1945)

Professor of chemistry, collector / Cologne, Breslau (today Wrocław)

Born in Cologne, Ernst König was the son-in-law of → LEOPOLD VON **KALCKREUTH** through his marriage to von Kalckreuth's daughter Bertha.

EDMUND **KÖRNER**

(1874–1940)

Architect, collector / Essen

Following his tenure as an artist and professor at the Darmstadt Mathildenhöhe, Edmund Körner (like → ALFRED **FISCHER**), became one of the avant-garde architects associated with the new construction movement in the industrial metropolis of Essen. His buildings – the Old Synagogue, the Stock Exchange and the Museum Folkwang building (destroyed during the Second World War) – changed the cityscape. In 1914, he and Fischer founded groups for interior design and 'reform' architecture in Essen. He was forbidden from working in 1933, and carried out no more commissions until his death.

KUNSTHANDLUNG DR. BECKER & NEWMAN

→ **GALERIE DR. ANDREAS BECKER**

HERMANN **LANGE**

(1874–1942)

Textiles merchant, collector / Krefeld

A silk manufacturer, Hermann Lange became an enthusiastic collector of modernist art at an early stage. He rose to become a board member of the Imperial Association of German Industry and of the United Silk Mills Corporation of Krefeld. It was probably in 1927 through the gallery owner → KARL **NIERENDORF** that L. was introduced to Ludwig Mies van der Rohe, who built him a villa in Krefeld between 1928 and 1930. L. bought art not only from Nierendorf, but also from → ALFRED **FLECHTHEIM**, → FERDINAND **MÖLLER** and Karl Buchholz. L. is known to have been an external member of the → **KÖLNISCHER KUNSTVEREIN** in 1929. His collection survived the war virtually intact, and in 1947 L. was able to loan artworks to the Kölnischer Kunstverein for the exhibition 'Von Nolde bis Klee'.

LE TANNEAUX DE SAINT PAUL

Le Tanneaux de Saint Paul is a Prussian aristocratic family. Francine von Finck, née L. and the wife of August von Finck, is the owner of the Schloss Seeseiten bei Seeshaupt estate at Starnberger See. The villa had previously (since 1922) been the property of Rudolf Simolin (1885–1945), an enthusiastic collector and patron of modernist art. He was a close friend of Max Beckmann, acting as his best man in 1925 and collecting his artworks. He was presumably in contact with → GÜNTHER **FRANKE**, who also owned a house in Seeshaupt. He represented Beckmann as an art dealer and also bought his artworks for his own collection, which he moved to Seeshaupt during the war.

KUNSTHAUS **LEMPERTZ**

Auction house / Cologne

The origins of the Kunsthaus Lempertz stretch back to the auction house of Matthias Heberle (1777–1840), founded in 1802 in Cologne. The first auctions took place in 1811. After Heberle's death, his employee Heinrich Lempertz (1816–1898) took over the business. In 1845, he and his brother opened a branch in Bonn that also traded in books. In 1875, Peter Hanstein (1853–1925) bought the firm and expanded it to include a publishing house. It is still run as a family business today. After the Second World War, both the book dealing business in Bonn and the art house were rebuilt. The book dealership continued trading until 2005. Josef Hanstein (1885–1968), his son Rolf (1919–1970) and his grandson Henrik (born 1950) turned the auction house into an internationally successful business. The degree of the busines's involvement in enforced sales during the Nationalist Socialist period has never been determined, and cannot be established due to the destruction of the archives during the bombing of Cologne.

BERTHOLD **LEVY**

Businessman / Cologne

Nothing is known about the businessman Dr. Berthold Levy other than that he was a member of the → **KÖLNISCHER KUNSTVEREIN** in 1929 and that he auctioned off glass pieces from his collection at the → KUNSTHAUS **LEMPERTZ** in 1931.

HERBERT WILHELM GEORG **LEYENDECKER**

(1885–1958)

Philosopher, art expert, art dealer and psychotherapist / Munich, Cologne, Berlin, Wiesbaden

As a student of philosophy, Dr. Herbert Leyendecker was considered an adherent of the Munich Phenomenologist school. He lived in Cologne between 1919 and 1922 whilst studying for his habilitation under Max Scheler. There, he became co-founder of the Society for New Music and organized an exhibition of abstract art. Records show that in 1922 he was acting as an art dealer as well as director of the Galerie van Diemen in Berlin (a post he held from 1920 until approximately 1965). → LEOPOLD **REIDEMEISTER** was also working at the Galerie van Diemen during this period. Leyendecker reportedly began operating as an independent art dealer and art historian in 1935. In 1943, he was bombed out and moved to Wiesbaden, where he opened the Galerie für Moderne Kunst. From 1948 onwards, he also worked as a psychotherapist.

ISMAR **LITTMANN**
(1878–1934)

Lawyer, notary, collector / Breslau (today Wrocław)

Ismar Littmann collected more than 6,000 Berlin Secession and Expressionist artworks – primarily artworks by the Brücke group. The Great Depression forced him to sell artworks for the first time, and the political situation as of 1933 placed him, as a Jewish lawyer, under increased pressure. In 1934, faced with this desperate situation, he took poison to end his life. In order to finance their own emigration, his heirs were forced to sell parts of his collection. Two hundred artworks were sent to the Berlin auction house of → MAX **PERL**, who set the date of the auction (auction no. 188) for 26/27 February 1935. Two days before this date the Gestapo confiscated eighteen of L.'s artworks from the auction, four of which were taken to the Berlin Nationalgalerie. The remainder were burned in 1936. The pictures that had been taken to the Nationalgalerie were declared 'degenerate' in 1937, resulting in the painting *Zwei weibliche Halbakte* by Otto Mueller being absorbed into the collection of → JOSEF **HAUBRICH** after the → **'DEGENERATE ART'** auction. It was donated to the Wallraf-Richartz Museum in 1946. The museum was able to re-acquire the picture after it was returned to the heirs of the former owner.

WOLFGANG **MACKE**
(1913–1975)

Bonn

Dr. Wolfgang Macke was the son of the artist August Macke. In 1960, he took over his uncle Carl Gerhardt's business in the manufacture and storage of chemical apparatus in Bonn, which is still in the possession of the family today.

MARATIER DR. LANGE

Paris

Georges Maratier was a Paris-based art dealer and publisher whose friends included Gertrude Stein. No further information could be found about Dr. Lange and his connection with M.

HANS **MELCHERS**
(1902–1969)

Book and art dealer / Cologne

In 1931, the art historian Hans Melchers, who gained his doctorate in Cologne, became co-founder of the → **BÜCHERSTUBE AM DOM**. He was considered extremely knowledgeable in the field and ran the business until 1950. In 1946, M. worked jointly with → WERNER **RUSCHE** to organize the first six exhibitions held at his gallery. After leaving the Bücherstube, he 'began a new enterprise in South Germany'. According to Central Collecting Point documentation, M. sold artworks to Maria Almas-Dietrich, one of Hitler's major art dealer suppliers for the 'Führermuseum Linz'.

MATHILDE (TILLE) **MODERSOHN**
(1907–1998)

Mathilde Modersohn was the daughter of husband-and-wife artists Paula Modersohn-Becker and Otto Becker. Her mother died shortly after her birth. M. inaugurated the Paula Modersohn-Becker foundation and made over the majority of the artworks in her possession to it.

FERDINAND **MÖLLER**
(1882–1956)

Gallery owner / Berlin, Cologne

In 1912, Ferdinand Möller, who had trained as a book dealer, visited the → **SONDERBUND EXHIBITION** in Cologne. In the same year, he decided to break into the art trade, getting a job at the → **GALERIE ERNST ARNOLD**. In 1913, he was running the gallery's Breslau branch. In 1917, he opened his own business at Museumsplatz 13. In 1918, he became executive director of Berlin's Freie Secession and opened a Berlin branch in immediate proximity to the Der Sturm gallery. In 1919, he founded his own publishing house. In 1920, he closed the Breslau gallery, transferring the business to Potsdam in the interim. In 1929, he hosted the exhibition 'Die Blaue Vier'. In 1932, he moved to the Lützowufer in Berlin, where, in 1933, he made his premises available to the National Socialist student association for the exhibition '30 Deutsche Künstler', which, in spite of efforts to close it on the part of the National Socialist League for German Culture, remained open. After moving premises again, this time to the Gross-Admiral-von-Köster-Ufer (formerly the Schöneberger Ufer, a name which has since been reinstated) in 1935, M. confined his business activities to dealing in old and modernist art. In 1938, M. became one of the four art dealers authorized by the → **VALUATION COMMISSION** to deal in → **'DEGENERATE ART'**. The other authorized dealers were → HILDEBRAND **GURLITT**, Karl Buchholz and → BERNHARD A. **BÖHMER**. M. restricted himself to taking on artists already connected with his gallery. He violated regulations by bringing purchased artworks into Germany and stored some of his stock in his house at Zermützel in the district of Neuruppin. M. was a friend of → OTTO **RALFS**. After the war, the central authority of the Soviet Zone of Occupation became a threat to M.'s collection, causing him to move to Cologne. The Cologne city authorities supported the construction of Wilhelm Riphahn's gallery building at Hahnenstrasse 11, seeing it as a welcome new asset to Cologne's cultural scene. M. was now able to hold impressive exhibitions and offer artworks of impressive quality by formerly denounced artists to institutions and to collectors such as → JOSEF **HAUBRICH.**

MASCHKA **MUELLER**
(1882–1952)

Maschka Mueller was born Maria Mayerhofer. In 1905, she became the first wife of the artist Otto Mueller. She remained close to him and continued to act as a model for him after they divorced in 1921. She acted as trustee of a part of Mueller's estate after his death in 1930.

PAUL **MULTHAUPT**
(1884–1933)

Engineer, entrepreneur, collector / Düsseldorf

In 1909 Paul Multhaupt began work as an engineer for Eduard Schloemann, whose daughter he later married. After the industrialist's death, he took over as head of Schloemann AG, a company which planned and constructed rolling mills and continuous casting plants. M. was a major supporter of modernist art who sponsored the Museum Folkwang in Essen (→ KARL ERNST **OSTHAUS**) and, in particular, the artists Heinrich Campendonk and Anton Räderscheidt. He also founded the Folkwang-Auriga-Verlag publishing house in Friedrichssegen/

Lahn. In 1933, an exhibition of M.'s collection was announced – the final exhibition at the → ALFRED **FLECHTHEIM** gallery. Some weeks previously, M. had committed suicide, presumably due to financial problems. His collection was dispersed.

HELLA **NEBELUNG**
(1912–1985)

Dancer, art dealer / Düsseldorf

In late 1945, Hella Nebelung, who was a former dancer, opened an art gallery in a ruined villa on Düsseldorf's Hofgartenstrasse, with the aid of friends – including the artist Peter Janssen, for whom she had acted as a model and who made artworks available to her. The gallery became a meeting place for the recovering art scene, and quickly developed a variety of business links in classical Modernism and, later, in abstract art. Nebelung maintained contacts with a number of galleries, including → **ABELS**, → **D'ART MODERNE**, → **DER SPIEGEL**, → **OTTO UND ETTA STANGL**, and gallery owners → HANNA **BEKKER VOM RATH**, → RUDOLF **HOFFMANN**, → **NIERENDORF**, → JOHANNES **GELLER** and → ALBERT **DABERKOW**. This allowed her to consistently present fresh artworks to her customers. These included → JOSEF **HAUBRICH**, who was inspired by her exhibitions and purchased artworks for his collection. In 1955, the gallery moved to Ratinger Hof, where it remained until N.'s death.

ISRAEL BER **NEUMANN**
(1887–1961)

Gallery owner / Berlin, New York et al.

In 1911, after training as a book dealer, Israel Ber Neumann – known as 'J. B.' – founded his graphic arts dealership under the name 'Graphisches Kabinett J. B. Neumann' in Berlin. He later opened branches in Bremen, Munich and Düsseldorf, where he took over Bergh & Co., which belonged to the physician and collector → HANS **KOCH**. From the beginning, the gallery focused on modernist prints and graphic works. Neumann became Max Beckmann's most significant representative and supporter. In 1923, he decided to sell his German businesses and move to New York. His long-term employee → GÜNTHER **FRANKE** chose to run the Munich branch, while Neumann went into business with the → **NIERENDORF** brothers in Berlin. In 1924, N. opened a graphic arts gallery in New York. He expanded it to become the New Art Circle Gallery, which became a popular meeting place for artists and collectors. N. continued working until his death in 1961.

FRANZ **NIENHAUS**

Entrepreneur, agent, collector / Cologne

Franz Nienhaus was a shareholder in – and later company secretary of – the Cologne firm Kyll & Co., a water treatment company. He sold artworks from his collection to → JOSEF **HAUBRICH**.

KARL and JOSEF **NIERENDORF**

Gallery owners / Cologne, Berlin, New York

In 1920, the brothers Karl (1889–1947) and Josef (1898–1949) Nierendorf founded the Galerie Nierendorf Köln – Neue Kunst in Cologne and later moved to Berlin and New York. During his time as a bank employee in 1911/12, Karl N. became acquainted with → ALFRED **SALMONY**, who introduced him to the Cologne art scene. His friends included artists of the Cologne Progressives group, as well as Max Ernst, Erich Heckel and → ANDREAS **BECKER**, who later became a gallery owner himself. The → **SONDERBUND EXHIBITION** of 1912 was a key experience both for him and for Josef N., but the brothers' decision to get involved with art was frustrated by military service. In a military hospital, Karl N. met the physician and collector → HANS **KOCH**. Returning to Cologne in 1918 Karl founded the Kairos-Verlag publishing company. His first project was the book series *Der Strom*, a name that was also adopted by an artist group. Out of this grew his art society, Gesellschaft der Künste, whose activities included concerts organized by Otto Klemperer and an Expressionist exhibition (in 1919) organized by → JOSEF **HAUBRICH**, in which → CARL OSKAR **JATHO** was involved.

In 1920, the gallery named Nierendorf Köln – Neue Kunst opened at Gürzenichstrasse 16, with Josef N. also working there. The two brothers exhibited Expressionist art, and especially the work of Otto Dix, for whom Karl became sole representative in 1922. In 1923, the gallery owner → J. B. **NEUMANN** offered Karl N. a post as director of his graphic arts dealership in Berlin. Neumann and Karl N. were business partners for some years, albeit with a number of interruptions. Josef N. continued to run the business in Cologne for a time, before moving to Berlin to assist Karl N. in 1924. The Düsseldorf branch, founded in 1925, lasted only a short time. During this period, the Berlin business was renamed GmbH Galerie Neumann – Nierendorf. The brothers N. had business connections with well-known galleries such as → **GALERIE ERNST ARNOLD**, Commeter, → ALFRED **FLECHTHEIM**, Fritz and → WOLFGANG **GURLITT**, Probst, Tannenbaum and Thannhauser. In 1928, Karl Blossfeldt's *Urformen der Kunst* was published on the initiative of Karl N. Financial difficulties during the Great Depression forced the brothers to scale down and to relocate their business. In 1933, the partnership between Nierendorf and Neumann was dissolved due to the political situation, and the brothers opened a business at Schöneberger Ufer 38 (then Gross-Admiral-von-Koester-Ufer 71). A year later, Karl N. suffered a heart attack. In 1936, he travelled to the USA. He decided to stay there due to the political situation in Germany. Josef N. continued to run the gallery in Berlin, but by 1939 he was dealing in modernist art from the gallery programme only on an unofficial basis. In 1937, Karl opened the Nierendorf Gallery in New York. In 1944, he opened the International Art gallery in Los Angeles (with Estella Katzenellenbogen). He had now resumed his contacts with Neumann. He also traded with → CURT **VALENTIN**. Karl N. died in 1947. His possessions were confiscated due to a lack of heirs in the United States and the lack of a return authorization for Germany. Much of the collection passed into the possession of the Guggenheim Foundation. In 1949, Josef N. also died suddenly, shortly before the Galerie Nierendorf reopened. His widow Meta and stepson Florian Karsch continued running his gallery and administered his estate.

KARL ERNST **OSTHAUS**
(1874–1921)

Businessman, collector / Hagen

The son of a banker, Karl Ernst Osthaus, who initially trained as a businessman, studied philosophy and art history. Having received an inheritance, he decided to set up an encyclopaedic museum in Hagen for the wider public. Influenced by Henry van de Velde, he began to promote and collect modern art that ranged from Impressionist to Expressionist art. His circle included → PAUL **CASSIRER**, → ALFRED **FLECHTHEIM**, → WALTER **KAESBACH** and → PAUL **MULTHAUPT**. In 1909, he became chairman of the → **SONDERBUND EXHIBITION** in Düsseldorf. After his premature death, his heirs sold much of his collection to the city of Essen, which was just constructing the new Museum Folkwang built by → EDMUND **KÖRNER**. In 1937, the Osthaus collection was particularly badly affected by the → **'DEGENERATE ART'** campaign. Parts of the collection were exhibited at the 'Degenerate Art' exhibition, and were subsequently exchanged or auctioned at → THEODOR **FISCHER**'s auction, going to new owners inside and outside of Germany. After the war, the museum made efforts to recover the artworks from the collection.

INGE **PEIPERS**

Barmen (Wuppertal)

Inge Peipers was the daughter of Bonn-based professor of psychiatry Felix Peipers. She married Karl Glaser and moved in the same circles as the artist Hans Hoesch.

MAX **PERL**

(1868–1931)

Auction house / Berlin

Max Perl's auction house first began trading in Berlin, holding auctions of books. In 1905, he expanded the programme to include auctions of graphic arts and painting. In 1914, an oil picture by Pablo Picasso was among the auction lots. In 1931, after P.'s death, Dr. Siegmund Kaznelson (1893–1959), a Jewish editor and publisher, took over the business. The auctions he presided over included auction 188, at which the collection of → ISMAR **LITTMANN**, which included Expressionist artworks, was to be auctioned off. It was interrupted by the Gestapo, and a number of artworks were confiscated. Some of them were later burned. Before Kaznelson emigrated to Jerusalem in 1937, his former trainee, Horst A. Rittershofer, acquired the auction house. He ran it under his own name from 1941 to 1971. In 1949, Kaznelson applied for restitution.

HUGO **PERLS**

(1886–1977)

Lawyer, art dealer, philosopher / Berlin, Paris, New York

In 1919, Hugo Perls, a philosopher and lawyer for the German foreign ministry, opened an art dealing business in Berlin. When he decided to become an art dealer, he already possessed an extensive collection of artworks by Edvard Munch and had commissioned Ludwig Mies van der Rohe to build him a house in 1910. He dealt primarily in German and French art, including the work of Caspar David Friedrich, Edgar Degas, Paul Gaugin, Paul Cézanne and Pablo Picasso. From 1931 onwards, he lived in exile in Paris, engaging in philosophical activity. His wife Käte Perls ran the gallery under her name. In 1941, P. settled in the United States, where he married his second wife, Eugénie Söderberg (1903–1973). His sons later became successful gallery owners in Beverly Hills and New York.

HANS **PETERS**

(1906–1962)

Art historian, publisher / Düren, Cologne, Bad Honnef

Hans Peters studied art history in Tübingen, Bonn and Münster. After completing his training, he ran the Leopold-Hoesch-Museum in Düren (beginning in 1936). In 1938, after experiencing hostility from the Reich Chamber of Fine Arts and the NSDAP, he resigned from all official posts and moved to Cologne. In 1939, he became executive director of the → **KÖLNISCHER KUNSTVEREIN**, having been recommended for the office by → JOSEF **HAUBRICH**. Although he volunteered for Wehrmacht service, he remained in Cologne and ran the Kunstverein until 1942. In 1940, however, he was accused of violating regulations and was officially forbidden from acting as director, forcing him to work in secret. In 1942, he was finally dismissed due to his exhibiting policy in the 'Der deutsche Westen' exhibition. P. moved to Bad Honnef, where he worked as an assessor of damaged artworks. He also traded in the work of Otto Dix and other modernist artworks, in collaboration with → HILDEBRAND **GURLITT**. In 1952, he established a publishing business in Bad Honnef.

LEOPOLD **REIDEMEISTER**

(1900–1987)

Museum director / Cologne

In 1905, when he was still a child, Dr. Leopold Reidemeister, the grand-nephew of Wilhelm von Bode, met Karl Schmidt-Rottluff (1884–1976). This marked the beginning of a lifelong friendship. After studying architecture, art history and East Asian languages, he worked for the Galerie van Diemen in Berlin whilst studying for his doctorate. → HERBERT **LEYENDECKER** began working at the same gallery in 1922. In 1924, R. began working in the East Asian section of the Berlin State Museums, of which he was made director in 1938. From 1939 onwards, he served as a soldier in Italy and played a prominent role in the German Military Art Protection. In 1945, he was quickly appointed as director of the Wallraf-Richartz Museum. From 1954 onwards, he was general director of Cologne's municipal museums. His activities focused on rebuilding the modernist art section, which had been destroyed by the National Socialists' art policy. The donation of → JOSEF **HAUBRICH**'s collection in 1946, together with R.'s acquisition policy, turned it into an internationally significant collection. After the inauguration of the new Wallraf-Richartz Museum in 1957, R. accepted the invitation to oversee the process of reconstruction – first as general director of the State Museums and later as head of the Prussian Cultural Heritage Foundation, and also as director of the Nationalgalerie. Finally, R. joined forces with Karl Schmidt-Rottluff and Erich Heckel in 1967 to found the Brücke Museum in Berlin. He continued to organize exhibitions at this museum until his death.

H. **RICHTER**

(1888–1976)

Artist / Berlin, Minusio (Switzerland), New York City

The name is a possible reference to the avant-garde filmmaker and artist Hans Richter. Hans Richter was the son of a landowner. He studied art in Berlin and Weimar. He had contacts with the Der Sturm artists' union. He was closely associated with the Futurists and, subsequently, with the Dadaists. In 1916, he was invalided out of the army. In the same year, he held his first solo exhibition in → HANS **GOLTZ'S** gallery in Munich. In 1933, R. emigrated to Switzerland. He subsequently settled in the United States.

LÉONCE **ROSENBERG**

(1879–1947)

Gallery owner / Paris

Léonce Rosenberg began his career in art dealing in his father's antiques dealing business, together with his younger brother Paul (1891–1959). In 1910, he left the family business. He went into business with an antiques dealership named 'Haute Epoche'. In 1911, his brother Paul opened his own art gallery in Paris. In addition to dealing in antiques, R. began to trade in significant numbers of Cubist artworks. He first represented Pablo Picasso in 1914 (prior to his brother doing so). He also represented August Herbin and Juan Gris. After the confiscation of the artworks owned by → DANIEL-HENRY **KAHNWEILER**, R. was employed by the French state as an expert artwork assessor, making him unpopular in the arts scene. After a brief spell of military service during the First World War, he continued to pursue his art dealing activities and to build up his own collection. In 1924, he opened the L'Effort Moderne gallery. In their representation of Picasso, the brothers had to compete with Daniel-Henry Kahnweiler and → ALFRED **FLECHTHEIM**, who tried to force them out. In 1921, R. was increasingly in financial difficulties. Parts of his collection were auctioned off in Amsterdam. The gallery, however, continued to operate until 1941. Léonce R. survived the war and died in Paris in 1947. To escape persecution as a Jew, Paul R. emigrated to New York in 1940, where he opened a new gallery. He was forced to leave behind, in German-occupied France, those parts of his extensive collection of Impressionist and modernist art that he had not been able to get abroad. They were confiscated, sold, exchanged or sent to Germany, by → THEODOR **FISCHER** among others. To this day, many of these artworks are considered lost. Only a small proportion of them have been returned.

MICHAEL **ROSS**

Artist, art restitution officer / London, Düsseldorf

Himself an artist, Michael Ross was stationed in Düsseldorf as an 'art protection officer' of the Monuments Fine Arts & Archives body (MFA&A). He did not remain in Germany for long, returning to his home city of London shortly after the end of the war. However, R. maintained contacts in Germany and coordinated Britain's involvement in the international exhibition 'Christliche Kunst der Gegenwart' in Cologne in 1948.

WERNER **RUSCHE**

Gallery owner / Cologne

After the Second World War, Dr. Werner Rusche opened a gallery on one level of his own private house in Cologne-Braunsfeld. In 1946, he organized his first six exhibitions (jointly with → HANS **MELCHERS**). He represented Expressionist and Rhenish modernist artists, and later expanded his programme to include abstract art from the districts of Bornheim and Alfter. In the early 1950s, R. increased his business connections in Paris and traded in French classical Modernist art.

ALFRED **SALMONY**

(1890–1958)

Art historian / Cologne

Dr. Alfred Salmony studied art history and archaeology with → LUISE **STRAUSS-ERNST**. During this period, he brought the young → KARL **NIERENDORF** into contact with the Cologne art scene. After gaining his doctorate, S. began work at the recently founded Museum for East Asian Art in Cologne as Adolf Fischer's assistant. In 1924, he was made deputy director. Immediately after Hitler came to power, he emigrated to the United States to escape the discrimination against Jewish citizens. He began a career in academia, teaching at New York University in 1942. He died in 1958 as he was crossing to Europe on board the Île-de-France.

RICHARD VON **SCHNITZLER**

(1855–1938)

Banker, collector / Cologne

Richard von Schnitzler began assembling his collection while he was still studying law and expanded it while working for his father's bank, J. H. Stein. He became a prominent figure in the artistic life of Cologne. Among other things, he was a board member and honorary chairman of the → **KÖLNISCHER KUNSTVEREIN** and belonged to the Society of Friends of the Wallraf-Richartz Museum, whose members also included → JOSEF **HAUBRICH**. In 1934, his collection was exhibited at the Kölnischer Kunstverein. When he died, a memorial service was held there in his honour. Lilly von Schnitzler, his nephew's wife, was an enthusiastic patron of Max Beckmann. She left artworks from her collection to Cologne's Wallraf-Richartz Museum.

EBERHARD **SEEL**

(1900–1978)

After the → **DEUTSCHER KÜNSTLERBUND** was re-founded in 1950, Eberhard Seel served as executive director until 1972. He organized a number of exhibitions for the association, including one, in 1953, that was a collaboration with → JOSEF **HAUBRICH** held in Cologne. S. acquired many of the artworks featured in this sales exhibition – by artists such as Jean Arp, Eduard Bargheer, Werner Heldt, Ernst W. Nay and Emil Schumacher – for his own collection. Works from this collection have since appeared at auctions on a regular basis.

SOCIETY FOR THE PROMOTION OF TWENTIETH-CENTURY GERMAN ART

Art association / Neuss

The Society for the Promotion of Twentieth-Century German Art was founded in 1915. Its purpose was to use subscriptions to buy modern art and to build up a collection that would be accessible to members. An emphasis was placed on the artists Ernst Ludwig Kirchner, Paul Klee, August Macke, Emil Nolde, Christian Rohlfs and Paul A. Seehaus. In addition to its executive director → JOHANNES **GELLER**, its founders included Rudolf Bosselt, Walter Cohen, Fritz Helmuth Ehmke and → ALFRED **FISCHER**. Members attracted by the society included collectors such as Josef Feinhals from Cologne, Alfred Hess from Erfurt, Albert Rudolf Ibach from Barmen (→ **GALERIE OTTO UND ETTA STANGL**), → HANS **KOCH** from Düsseldorf, Edwin Suermont of Burg Drove and Carl Georg Heise of the Hamburg Kunsthalle. Financial circumstances forced the society to disband in 1922, after seven years. Its collection – 250 artworks – was sold off to members at a private auction in Essen on 8 December 1924. Efforts had previously been made to keep the collection together, and → WALTER **KAESBACH** advocated donating it to the city of Neuss. A restricted auction was agreed upon, ensuring that all artworks were sold to members. These included the painting *Der barmherzige Samariter* by Heinrich Nauen, which eventually reached the collection of → JOSEF **HAUBRICH** via Fischer.

SONDERBUND EXHIBITION

Düsseldorf, Cologne

The Sonderbund Westdeutscher Kunstfreunde und Künstler (Special League of West German Art Patrons and Artists) was founded in 1905, with → KARL ERNST **OSTHAUS** as chairman. Its aim was to make modernist art accessible to a wider art-viewing public. It was a coalition of artists, art historians, museum professionals and art patrons, and it evolved a novel exhibition concept. After three exhibitions in Düsseldorf, its most significant exhibition took place in Cologne, and was co-organized by → PAUL **CASSIRER** and → ALFRED **FLECHTHEIM.** This exhibition represented the beginning of modernism in the Rhineland, and inspired figures such as → ANDREAS **BECKER**, → JOSEF **HAUBRICH**, → WALTER **KAESBACH**, → PAUL **MULTHAUPT**, → FERDINAND **MÖLLER** and → KARL AND JOSEF **NIERENDORF**, all of whom became involved in modernist art. It became a model for large-scale exhibitions such as the Armory Show (held a year later in New York) and the Kassel documenta exhibition. The Sonderbund broke up in 1912 due to internal disputes

RODOLPHE **STADLER**

(1927–2009)

Gallery owner / Paris

In 1955, Rudolf (Rodolphe) Stadler opened a gallery at 51, rue de Seine, which remained *in situ* until the 1990s. His programme consisted of work by abstract artists, including Lucio Fontana, Georges Mathieu and Antonio Saura.

CARL **STEINBART**

(1852–1923)

Banker, collector / Berlin

Carl Steinbart, a banker for the Berlin private bank Mendelssohn & Co, is considered a major collector of Impressionist art – and particularly of the artwork of Max Slevogt. He also supported younger artists such as Emil Nolde, Max Pechstein and Oskar Kokoschka. He associated with gallerists such as → PAUL **CASSIRER** and Fritz Gurlitt (→ WOLFGANG **GURLITT**), becoming a shareholder in their businesses. After Gurlitt's sudden death, S. maintained the gallery financially until Gurlitt's son Wolfgang took it over in 1907.

LUISE **STRAUS-ERNST**

(1893–1944)

Art historian, journalist / Cologne

Dr. Luise Straus studied art history in Bonn at the same time as → ALFRED **SALMONY.** In 1913, she met Max Ernst, who later became her husband. They settled at Kaiser-Wilhelm-Ring 14, which was also the home of → KARL **NIERENDORF**'s 'Gesellschaft der Künste'. In 1918, she began working at the Wallraf-Richartz Museum as a research assistant. In 1919, she ran this institution on a temporary basis until the election of Karl Schaefer. The Ernst home became a meeting place for the new Dada art movement in Cologne. A *ménage à trois* between Max Ernst, Paul Eluard and Eluard's wife, Gala, meant the end for S.'s marriage to Ernst, and they divorced in 1926. S. worked at a number of jobs to support herself and her son Jimmy: she worked for the → **KUNSTHANDLUNG DR. BECKER & NEWMAN** gallery as a secretary, was procured a job by Salmony cataloguing a porcelain collection and wrote articles for publications such as → ALFRED **FLECHTHEIM**'s *Querschnitt.* In 1933, facing persecution as a Jew, she emigrated to Paris, where she continued to work as an art journalist. In 1939, she fled to Cannes and wrote her memoirs at Manosque. She was arrested in 1944 and was deported on one of the last trains to Auschwitz

CURT **VALENTIN**

(1902–1954)

Book and art dealer / Berlin, New York

After starting out as a publisher in Hamburg, Curt Valentin went into art dealing – in 1928 at the latest, as this was the year in which he began working at → ALFRED **FLECHTHEIM**'s gallery in Berlin. In 1934 (anti-Semitic persecution had forced Flechtheim to leave Germany in 1933), V. transferred to Karl Buchholz's gallery. As the situation in Germany became increasingly precarious, the two decided to found a branch in New York. The Buchholz Gallery – Curt Valentin opened on 18 March 1937, with → KARL **NIERENDORF** among those in attendance. V. is believed to have brokered sales of → **'DEGENERATE ART'** between the Buchholz gallery and foreign buyers. He is also listed as one of the buyers at the 'degenerate art' auction hosted by → THEODOR **FISCHER** in Lucerne. In addition to this, a certificate issued by the Reich Chamber of Fine Arts is still in existence confirming that V. was permitted to sell German artworks to foreign buyers. From 1951 onwards, he ran the New York business under his own name, until his death of a heart attack. A year later, the Curt Valentin Gallery was dissolved.

VALUATION COMMISSION

In 1938, after the expropriation of → **'DEGENERATE ART'** from German museum collections, Joseph Goebbels set up the Commission for the Valuation of Products of Degenerate Art (known as the 'Verwertungskommission', or 'Valuation Commission', for short), with Franz Hofmann as director and Rolf Hetsch as advisor.
It oversaw the process of assessment, valuation, and disposal of the confiscated artworks. Artworks were divided into three categories: objects with an international value, worthless artworks, and artworks that could be used for propaganda purposes (for instance, in the 'Degenerate Art' exhibition). Artworks considered to have international value were stored at Schloss Schönhausen. The strategy of the V. C. (as of May 1938) was to offer these artworks to dealers and interested parties abroad in exchange for Old Masters or foreign currency. Some businesses, such as the → **GALERIE ZAK**, specifically asked for artworks in the V. C.'s possession, in order to be able to take part in the sales. Four gallery owners – → BERNHARD A. **BÖHMER**, Karl Buchholz, → HILDEBRAND **GURLITT** and → FERDINAND **MÖLLER** – were authorized by the V. C. to trade in these artworks. They could sell the artworks on commission, exchange them for other artworks or acquire them for foreign currency. It was explicitly forbidden to sell them to German buyers. However, all four art dealers are known to have broken this regulation. In 1939, it was also decided to sell approximately 125 major artworks on the international market at an auction hosted

by → THEODOR **FISCHER** in Lucerne. The most spectacular exchange was made by the German-Austrian husband-and-wife collectors Sofie and Emanuel Fohn, who were able to acquire 450 'degenerate' artworks in exchange for about twenty-five Germano-Roman artworks. The series of auctions officially ended on 30 June 1941. However, individual deals continued to be transacted. Part of the collection was transferred to Böhmer at Güstrow to protect it from war damage, while a smaller percentage was destroyed. The location of the remainder is unknown.

ALEX **VÖMEL**

(1898–1985)

Gallery owner / Düsseldorf

Book dealer Alex Vömel began his training at the renowned Paris gallery belonging to → DANIEL-HENRY **KAHNWEILER**, transferring to → ALFRED **FLECHTHEIM**'s Düsseldorf-based business in 1922. In 1923, he was appointed as company secretary. In 1927, he was promoted to the post of second managing director. In the period after the National Socialist propaganda campaign against Flechtheim but prior to Flechtheim's emigration in the autumn of 1933, V. ran the gallery under his own name. The circumstances of the takeover have never been established, but we do know that V. was a member of the SA and later of the NSDAP. Despite the devaluing and defamation of Expressionist and modernist art, Vömel was still able to make sales through business acquaintances such as Ludwig Gutbier (→ **GALERIE ERNST ARNOLD**). The artworks disposed of included modernist works sold by institutions after Hitler came to power, such as those from the Chemnitz Museum that V. sold with → WILHELM **GROSSHENNIG**. He also acted for uncontroversial artists such as Arno Breker. V. was able to continue running the gallery – under certain restrictions – until its destruction by bombing. In 1946, the gallery premises were completely destroyed, and V. had to rebuild his business. He expanded his programme to include contemporary artists. In 1953, his son Edwin started work at the gallery. In 1996, the gallery relocated to Orangeriestrasse 6.

WILMA **ZELCK**

(1910–1962)

Art dealer / Rostock, Berlin, Hamburg

Wilma Zelck, née Otte, was the sister-in-law of → BERNHARD A. **BÖHMER**. After Böhmer and his wife Hella committed suicide in 1945, she became the guardian of their son → PETER **BÖHMER**. Bernhard Böhmer's possessions included artworks from the → **'DEGENERATE ART'** campaign that had been purchased for foreign currency or exchanged (these were presumably remnants of the campaign offloaded by the → **VALUATION COMMISSION**), in addition to Protestant Art Service works and artworks formerly belonging to Ernst Barlach. In May 1945, Z. began transferring artworks from this disparate accumulation. Around 1946, she became acquainted with → ALBERT **DABERKOW** in Rostock through the art dealing activities of his wife. They became a couple, moved to Berlin along with Peter Böhmer and began to sell the artworks left by his father. In 1947, the [East] German Administration of Culture and Education in the Soviet Zone of Occupation discovered around one thousand 'degenerate' artworks in Z.'s possession, which were moved to the City Museum of Rostock. This represented only part of the missing art stock, as Z. and Daberkow succeeded in getting some artworks to West Berlin. In 1950, business disagreements led to the couple separating. Z. and Peter Böhmer moved to Hamburg. When Peter Böhmer came of age, he took over administration of his inheritance. Z. tried to set up as an art dealer in Salt Lake City, Utah, but failed and returned to Hamburg. She made no further efforts in the art business.

Timeline Josef Haubrich

Compiled by Ilona Ciesielski

1889
15 June. Ludwig Josef Haubrich is born in Cologne as the son of Nikolaus Wilhelm Haubrich and Maria Christine Hubertine Wilhelmine Haubrich née Ritzefeld.

1907
Passes his *Abitur* at the Gymnasium Kreuzgasse.
Starts to study law in the summer term at Munich University.

1907/1909
Continues his studies at Berlin University.

1910
Articled clerk examination at the Higher Regional Court in Cologne.
Then dissertation on *Die Diskontierung von Buchforderungen* (Discounting unsecured credits).

1915
Passes his bar examination and joins Heinrich Bodenheim's law office.

1916
Called up into the 1st Replacement Regiment of the 1st Regiment of Infantry Guards in Berlin-Weißensee, but not accepted because of a heart defect.
Becomes interested in modern art after encountering pictures by Franz Marc in Herwarth Walden's Berlin gallery.
25 May. Marries Johanna (Hanna) Bernhardine Clara Auguste Kux. Home in Cologne-Klettenberg, Siebengebirgsallee 17.

1917
5 November. Birth of son Karl-Klaus.

1918
The Haubrich family moves to Cologne-Marienburg, Eugen-Langen-Straße 29.

1919
20 January. Birth of daughter Ruth Luise.

1919/1920
Starts to collect Expressionist pictures systematically.

1922
Wife Johanna dies.

1923
4 May. Marries Dora Anna Amalie Antonie Timmermanns née Skirl. The marriage is short-lived.
Active member of the Kölnischer Kunstverein.

1929
25 July. Marries Alice Gottschalk née Grabowski, whose daughter Anneli also joins the family.

1932
Member of the Kölnischer Kunstverein board.

1936
Compelled to resign from the Kölnischer Kunstverein.

1939
State orders force him to give up his joint law practice with Dr. Bodenheim.
Moves his practice to his own home.

1943
Alice's daughter Anneli flees from the Gestapo. She is hidden in Switzerland with Haubrich's assistance.

1944
February. Wife Alice commits suicide in order to escape racial persecution by the Gestapo.
September. Marries Paula Anna Berta Wegelin née Sieb.
October. Compulsory service labour as a builder. Declared unfit to work because of a heart valve defect.

1945
February. Son Karl-Klaus killed in action.

1946
17 January. First meeting of the second city council summoned by the occupying power, which Haubrich joins as an independent. (Haubrich later joins the Social Democrat group and is a member of all the city councils elected from 17 October 1948 until his death.)
2 May. The Cologne city council unanimously accepts Haubrich's collection as a gift.

1951
Moves with Paula Wegelin into 1 Kämpchensweg in Cologne-Müngersdorf, a house built by Wilhelm Riphahn.

1954
16 June. Haubrich is awarded the Commander's Cross of the Order of Merit of the Federal Republic of Germany, at the suggestion of Chancellor Konrad Adenauer.

1956
Elected third deputy mayor of Cologne.

1959
17 September. Wife Paula dies.

1960
17 April. Marries Lucy Millowitsch in Argentina.

1961
5 September. Dies in Bad Münstereifel.
8 September. Funeral service by Cologne city council. Quiet burial at the West Cemetery in Cologne.

1987
Reburied in the Melaten Cemetery in Cologne.

List of Illustrations

Photo Credits
All photographs © Rheinisches Bildarchiv Köln für Museum Ludwig, Michael Albers except Die Photographische Sammlung/SK Stiftung Kultur - August Sander Archiv, Köln; VG Bild-Kunst Bonn, 2012 (p. 12), Erich Lambertin (p. 14 f.), Walter-Dick Archiv/Dietrich Maghun (pp. 16, 17, 28, 29, 31, 34 f.,37), Peter Fischer/Historisches Archiv der Stadt Köln (Best. 1401, pp. 20 l., 32), Hannes Maria Flach-Archiv (pp. 20 r.,22 f.), Staatliche Museen zu Berlin-Zentralarchiv (p. 24 f.),Hermann Claasen/LVR-LandesMuseum Bonn (p. 30 l.), Stadtkonservator Köln (p. 30 r.)

Colophon

This catalogue is published on the occasion of the new presentation of the Haubrich Collection at Museum Ludwig, on 3 August 2012.

Editor
Julia Friedrich

Assistance
Dorothee Grafahrend-Gohmert, Astrid Bardenheuer, Ulrich Tillmann, Ilona Ciesielski, Erec Gellautz

Translation
Brian Currid (List of Works and pp. 79, 80, 114, 129, 138, 148, 186, 204), Sylee Gore (Preface, Foreword and pp. 58, 64, 84, 102, 116, 164, 170, 176, 194), Malcolm Green (Josef Haubrich and pp. 45, 46, 48, 53, 54, 57, 71, 72, 100, 130, 152, 156, 163, 190, 201, 202), Michael Robinson (Lexicon and Timeline)

Copy-editing
Jennifer Taylor (Preface, Foreword, Masterpieces, Timeline), Sylee Gore (Haubrich), Anne O'Connor (List of Works and Lexicon)

Graphic Design
Carmen Strzelecki

Print
DZA Druckerei zu Altenburg GmbH, Altenburg

Printed in Germany

Cover
Marc Chagall, *Sabbath*, 1910

Published by
Verlag der Buchhandlung Walther König Köln
Ehrenstr. 4, 50672 Köln
Tel. +49 (0) 221 / 20 59 6-53
Fax +49 (0) 221 / 20 59 6-60
verlag@buchhandlung-walther-koenig.de

Bibliographic information published by the Deutsche Nationalbibliothek
The Deutsche Nationalbibliothek lists this publication in the Deutsche Nationalbibliografie; detailed bibliographic data are available in the Internet at http://dnb.d-nb.de.

ISBN 978-3-86335-174-8

This publication was made possible through the kind assistance of

EvS ERNST VON SIEMENS KUNSTSTIFTUNG
FREUNDE WALLRAF-RICHARTZ-MUSEUM MUSEUM LUDWIG

Distribution UK & Eire
Cornerhouse Publications
70 Oxford Street GB-Manchester M1 5NH
Tel +44 (0) 161 200 15 03
Fax +44 (0) 161 200 15 04
publications@cornerhouse.org

Outside Europe
D.A.P. / Distributed Art Publishers, Inc.
155 6th Avenue, 2nd Floor
USA-New York, NY 10013
Tel +1 (0) 212 627 1999
Fax +1 (0) 212 627 9484
eleshowitz@dapinc.com

With special thanks to
Hanna Schmandin, Verlag der Buchhandlung Walther König, Köln and Jörg Streichert, Freunde des Wallraf-Richartz-Museums und des Museums Ludwig.

Team Museum Ludwig

Director
Kasper König

Public Relations
Anne Niermann, Judith Schlereth, Leonie Pfennig

Education
Angelika von Tomaszewski

Facility manager
Ralf Feckler

Conservation
Petra Mandt, Kathrin Keßler, Astrid Schubert

Joinery
Armin Lüttgen, Michael Bangert, Leif Lenzner, Sebastian Orlitz, Daniel Schmidt, Sebastian Kahnt, Tom Fröhlich

Art Handling
Paul Esser, Jürgen Koll

Fundraising
Lisa Nadig, Dagmar von der Burg

Administration
Elke Reiff, Susanne Brentano, Karsten Zinner, Stephanie Lenhart, Armin Raupach